# The Law Relating to International Banking and Capital Markets

Third Edition

# The Law Relating to International Banking and Capital Markets

Third Edition

Professor Andrew Haynes

BA (Hons) Law, PhD, Hon LLD, Cert Ed, FRSA, FSALS, FHEA

Emeritus Professor of Law, University of Wolverhampton

Visiting Professor of Law, BPP University

Former visiting Professor of Law, University of Tyumen, Russia

Former visiting Professor of Law, University of Macau, People's Republic of China

Former Senior Visiting Research Fellow, Institute of Advanced Legal Studies, University of London

Bloomsbury Professional

LONDON • DUBLIN • EDINBURGH • NEW YORK • NEW DELHI • SYDNEY

# Dedication

For Bronwyn and James

# Contents

# Table of Statutes

*[All references are to paragraph number]*

# Table of Statutory Instruments

*[All references are to paragraph number]*

# Table of Cases

*[All references are to paragraph number]*

## C

**D**

## H



## I

## N

**O**



**P**

## V



## W

# Table of European Legislation

*[All references are to paragraph number]*

# Table of Treaties and Conventions

[*All references are to paragraph number*]

# Chapter 1 International Term Loan Agreements, Security and Guarantees

## Introduction

**1.1** The aim of this chapter is to provide a general overview of international term loan agreements. Many of the aspects commonly associated with such loans are dealt with elsewhere in this work and the remaining topics, many of which are of considerable importance in both a legal and practical sense, will be considered here.

**1.2** A number of different considerations affect the parties' decision to lend or borrow under a medium term loan agreement. Some of these considerations give rise to common interests and others to legitimate differences which pre-contract negotiations must resolve. Those drafting the loan documentation must, therefore, fully appreciate the nature and purpose of each particular loan agreement and the interests of the parties who contract under it.

**1.3** In practice many firms use or adapt the Loan Markets Association Primary Documents (LMA).[1] Of particular relevance in this context is the Multicurrency Term and Revolving Facilities Agreement (referred to in this chapter as 'the LMA agreement') created by a working party of the LMA themselves, the British Bankers' Association and the Association of Corporate Treasurers. It provides a very useful guideline but the circumstances of term loans vary so widely that significant changes will normally be made. It can be found as an appendix to this book. Where the LMA Agreement differs from or adds to the information below the fact is highlighted.[2]

**1.4** The first formal stage of the negotiation in practice is often for the bank and the borrower to draft a term sheet[3] setting out a summary outline of what is proposed in the term agreement. It is important that the term sheet is stated not to be legally binding as otherwise the

---

1 The Loan Markets Association was established in 1996 to standardise loan market documentation and primarily to help develop the secondary market in loan sales. Its members are market participants but it also works with governments regulators and tax authorities.

2 See, eg K Clowry, 'LMA Credit Documentation: a continuing evolution in a challenging environment.', (2020) 27(3) BJIB FL 157–159; C Dawson, 'The LMA's Primary Documents', IHL 2002/3 (Dec/Jan) Supp (Finance 2003) 2–3, and R Gray, S Mehta and D East 'Easier with the LMA.'(2010) 29(3) IFL Rev 68–70.

3 Sometimes referred to as 'heads of agreement' or 'heads of terms'.

language used could result in a binding contract coming into existence before either party intends it.[4]

## The nature and mechanics of medium-term loan agreements

**1.5** This chapter will concentrate upon medium-term loan agreements, that is to say, loans which have a term of between 1 and 15 years. Banks occasionally make corporate loans for more than 15 years but only in very special circumstances such as certain types of large scale project finance.

**1.6** Governments as well as corporate entities borrow substantially and many favour the medium-term loan facility. One of the main reasons for the continuing popularity of this instrument lies in its inherent flexibility as a lending medium. Medium-term loan agreements can be advanced in all shapes and sizes, providing for drawdown to be made immediately, (the 'bullet' drawdown), or within a short period of the loan being executed, or in accordance with a fixed amortisation schedule. Alternatively, the loan agreement may provide the borrower with a longer period in which to drawdown the facility and may afford considerable flexibility as to both timing and number of drawdowns which may be made. The most flexible form is the revolving facility which allows the borrower repeatedly to drawdown the loan or a portion thereof and to repay any drawn amount either at the borrower's discretion or in accordance with a pre-determined schedule.

**1.7** The flexibility of these instruments extends to the interest rate mechanisms under which they may operate. The interest rate may be fixed for the entire term of the loan, or occasionally for a shorter period in excess of one year. It is common, however, for loans to incorporate a floating interest rate mechanism, such a rate being tied to a short term market indicator. The market indicator used in most loans is the displayed screen rate on a system such as Reuters for sterling (SONIA)[5] or the euro (€STR)[6] as the case may be, being the rate at which the lending bank is able, in accordance with its normal practices, to acquire the relevant currency from the markets in order to fund the loan with a margin included for overheads and default risk.

4 In *New Media Holding Co LLC v Kuznetsov* [2016] UKHC (360) QB it was held that a term sheet which failed to state that it was not legally binding did bind the parties as the key issues were all clearly spelt out in legal terminology.

5 Sterling Overnight Interest Average. It is the average rate at which banks have loaned money to each other on the overnight inter-bank market the previous night. It is based on the central 50 per cent of the volume weighted distribution rounded to four decimal places. It is published each morning by the Bank of England at 9.00am.

6 Euro Short Term Interest Rate. This is published by the European Central Bank on each TARGET 2 business day based on unsecured loan transactions conducted and settled on the previous TARGET 2 business day. It is based on the central 50 per cent of the volume weighted distribution rounded to the third decimal place. It is published at 8.00am Central European Time.

**1.8** The rate at which banks in the market offer to lend the currency in question will obviously vary and some loan agreements specify the names of banks from which interest rate quotations must be obtained. SONIA therefore reflects the cost of funding the loan from the lender's standpoint, this being a fundamental feature of lending. A margin is added to SONIA and it this margin which compensates the lending bank for the risks and costs incurred. The margin also provides the bank with its operating profit on the loan facility. Another common example is 'x% above the base rate of ...... Bank plc for the time being'. The interest rate charged is the aggregate of the margin plus SONIA (or if a euro loan €STR) plus mandatory cost. Where the figure for the relevant one of these two rates is not available from a reference bank on the quotation day, the applicable rate is calculated on the basis of the quotations from the remaining reference banks. This is payable on the interest period date or six monthly if the interest rate period date is longer. Default interest on late payments is calculated at a higher rate and is also compounded with the overdue amount unpaid at the end of each interest rate period.

**1.9** The interest rate period for a loan can be selected by the borrower from those available either in the utilisation request or in a selection notice. Once made the choice is irrevocable. If no selection notice is given the contract sets out the relevant periods.

**1.10** If a market disruption event occurs then the LMA Agreement adopts the approach that the rate of interest for that interest period is the margin plus the rate notified by the lender as soon as practicable and in any event prior to the interest being due (the rate being that at which the lender can raise the funds to finance the loan from any source it might reasonably choose) plus the mandatory cost. A 'market disruption event' is defined in the agreement as one where at 9:00am on the quotation day the screen rate is not available and none or only one of the reference banks provides a rate to calculate SONIA or €STR for the relevant currency and interest period. Alternatively, it could occur because the lender gives notice prior to the close of business on the quotation day for the relevant interest period that the cost of obtaining matching deposits exceeds SONIA or €STR as the case may be.[7] If there is a market disruption event the borrower has a 30 day period to try and negotiate a substitute rate of interest.

**1.11** If the borrower does not pay any sum due under the LMA Agreement by the last date of the interest period for the loan or any unpaid sum, then the standard approach is that they must pay the lender break costs resulting from the late payment within three

7 This is less likely to be an issue today unless there is significant market disruption given that SONIA is calculated by the Bank of England from 7:00 am by the reporting institutions and calculated from the relevant transactions occurring between 00:00 and 18:00 UK time on the previous day. It is released at 9:00 am the following business day.

business. 'Break costs' are designed cover the interest which the lender would have received for the period ending in the late payment and can be substantial.

**1.12** There are limits to the lender's capacity to maintain freedom to reset interest rates during the term of the loan. *Paragon Finance PLC v Staunton*[8] determined that this could only be done where:

- the capacity to increase the rate is not utilised for an improper purpose, capriciously or arbitrarily;
- the rate is not increased on the basis of matters extraneous to the transaction and the surrounding events; and
- the capacity to increase the rate must not be carried out in a manner that no reasonable lender would do.

**1.13** The interest period will be stated and is normally monthly, quarterly or six-monthly. The interest calculation has one oddity. Sterling is calculated on a 365-day year and all other currencies on a 360-day year.[9] There is usually also an interest rate default sub-clause inserted here stating the interest rate payable if the borrower goes into arrears. Interest will also be chargeable on overdue interest. In the case of an Islamic borrower interest may not be acceptable to them and if the case should end up requiring enforcement in a court in an Islamic jurisdiction it may prove unenforceable if interest is being charged. Alternative arrangements to calculate a return in relation to the money loaned do however exist, in which case appropriate clauses will need to be inserted explaining what sums will be repaid and how they will be calculated.

**1.14** Due to the fact that the markets are unregulated they are considered vulnerable to external events and it is, therefore, common to incorporate specific clauses within the loan documentation to protect the banks against possible funding difficulties. The clause used is often referred to as the disaster clause and provides that if the markets are disturbed so as to affect the availability of funds or the determination of SONIA the parties shall negotiate in good faith to agree new terms upon which the loan will operate. This is discussed below under force majeure clauses. If the parties fail to incorporate an alternative interest rate it is unlikely that an English court would imply one in the event of future market disturbance. In such a case, the court would most probably find an implied term that the original interest rate, applicable before the market disturbance would continue to apply. This may have serious consequences for the lending bank depending upon how the prevailing market rates have moved since the last occasion when the interest rate was determined.

---

8 [2002] 1 WLR 685, 2 All ER 248.

9 This was adopted as a convenient way of enabling interest to be calculated on the basis of 12 notional 30-day long months each year. It applies even in a leap year.

**1.15** Additional flexibility is provided by the multicurrency options which can be incorporated within the terms of the agreement. Lenders in the loan markets are able to offer borrowers a multicurrency option under which the borrower is permitted, subject to certain qualifications, to draw down in any currency[10] and in some cases convert at a later date to a different currency. The SONIA rate attaching to such loans will obviously be the equivalent rate applicable to the currency chosen by the borrower.

**1.16** The currency of payment by the borrower will be specified. Payment will be specified to be in immediately available funds paid unconditionally[11] to a specified bank account. Once it has been paid the bank has no power to revoke the transfer,[12] not that it is normally likely to want to. The payment will be required to be in the currency of the country of that currency except in the case of loans in other currencies. London is a major US dollar lending centre and euro loans are also common. Clarification on this is important as otherwise payment might be made in a jurisdiction where there are exchange control problems or some other obstacle or cost involved in the transfer.

**1.17** In some instances there will also be a multi-currency clause where the borrower requires it. If the borrower requires to change the currency then he has to repay the loan and draw down the new currency. The exchange rate is normally the spot rate two business days before drawdown. This way no currency risk falls on the bank.

**1.18** The alternative structures, interest rate mechanisms and currency options outlined above can be combined is a variety of ways, and most lenders are willing to consider any practical combination to meet a specific need. In addition, the loan may be secured or unsecured, guaranteed or not, or be syndicated (see **Chapter 2**). Whatever form the final loan takes, there are certain fundamental legal issues which will undoubtedly arise, many of which have yet to be fully worked out.

## Some problems caused by the flexible structures

**1.19** Where the loan is advanced in the form of a revolving facility there is always a risk that a borrower may later exceed its own borrowing limits as it continues to repay and drawdown under the terms of the agreement. Similarly, the lending bank may experience

---

10 This is for obvious practical reasons going to be limited to convertible currencies.

11 *The Chikuma; Awilco of Oslo A./SV v Fulvia Spa di Navagazione of Cagliari* (1981) 1 AER 652, (1981) 1 WLR 314. See *Byles on Bills of Exchange and Cheques*, 30th edn (Sweet & Maxwell, 2019), Ch 13, Pt 1 and Chitty on Contracts, 36th edn (Sweet & Maxwell, 2025), Ch 8.

12 *Libyan Arab Foreign Bank v Manufacturers Hanover Trust Co (No 2)* [1989] 1 Lloyd's Rep 608. See Dicey, Morris and Collins on Conflict of Laws, 16th edn (Sweet & Maxwell, 2025), Ch 32 and Ch 33.

difficulties with future funding because of lending limits which are imposed in respect of individual borrowers or for all borrowers within a geographical area. These lending limits are normally the result of capital requirements imposed by the banking regulator[13] and the impact of other credit contracts. Furthermore, banks which provide a facility imposing future obligations upon the bank, for example, the obligation to make funds available under a revolving loan or to convert currency under a multicurrency option, may find that their ability to assign the loan at some later date is prohibited since many jurisdictions, including England, prohibit the assignment of continuing obligations,[14] though as will be seen this can be resolved by novating the loan agreement. (See **Chapter 3**)

**1.20** One final problem posed by the revolving facility is that any security taken over such loans may be discharged as the loan 'revolves', under the rule in *Clayton's case*.[15] This case is an application of the old equitable maxim that equity imputes an intention to fulfil an obligation. Therefore, the first payment into an account is taken to clear the first payment out. The impact of this is that a secured overdraft facility will lose the security once an amount equal to the original loan and any associated charges and interest have been paid into the account, even though sums have been paid out in the mean time. Fortunately, this problem can be avoided by appropriate drafting of a clause in the loan agreement.[16] However, this will cease to have effect on the insolvency of the borrower and in this instance the bank will have to freeze the secured account and open a second account into which to pay any further monies received.

## The structure of a loan agreement

**1.21** The structure of a loan agreement is based upon a very simple contract whereby the lender promises to advance a certain sum over a certain period of time to the borrower and the borrower promises to pay the loan with interest. Unfortunately, the legal difficulties and problems which are likely to arise if anything goes wrong in this simple contract are many and complex, and, therefore, a large number of additional provisions are normally included in order to protect the parties' respective interests.

**1.22** As we have already seen the very fact that many transactions are cross-border will bring into play principles of private international law with all its associated legal complications, and where the borrower

---

13 In the UK's case the Prudential Regulation Authority, applying the BIS's Basel III regulations.

14 Law of Property Act 1925, s 136.

15 *Clayton's Case* or *Devaynes v Noble* (1916) 1 Mer 259. See Head P, 'Clayton's Case and Connected Matters.' (2013) Jur Rev 501.

16 *Russell-Cook & Trust Co v Prentis* [2002] EWHC 227.

is a sovereign state or state entity, additional legal complications must be addressed.

**1.23** Negotiations between lender and borrower may take many weeks, especially in the case of very large loans, and the loan documentation must correctly reflect provisions which have been agreed. In addition to setting out the terms of the loan, the documentation should also provide an agreed basis for the performance of the various terms in the contract and in so doing anticipate and deal with the typical problems that might arise.

**1.24** We will now consider how the loan documentation may be structured to achieve its desired purpose.

## The 'drawdown' period

*What if the lender fails to lend or the borrower fails to borrow within the 'drawdown' period?*

**1.25** There are a number of reasons why the lending bank may, after executing the contract, decide not to make the funds available. The bank may erroneously believe that the borrower has failed to satisfy certain conditions precedent to the loan. Whatever the reason an English court is unlikely to compel the bank to lend even though it is contractually bound to do so, since specific performance is not normally available to enforce a lender's commitment to provide funds. However, an action is likely to be available in damages unless the bank has valid contractual reasons for not performing.[17] The borrower could also treat the failure to advance the loan as repudiatory breach of contract.[18] This would not however repudiate any rights the borrower had acquired prior to termination.[19] This is also important for the lender who is therefore able to enforce repayment of any sums already advanced.[20] There remains the possibility in such cases that the borrower would have an action in damages against the lender for any loss it might suffer as a result of any loss incurred in a transaction that was funded by the arrangement concerned.[21] It would seem reasonable to suppose that such potential loss would be in contemplation of the parties at the time the contract was entered into. This has proved to be a topical problem in recent years, as banks have in some cases tried to avoid fulfilling lending commitments because of their weakened capital position and increased caution as to the amounts they are prepared to lend and to whom.

---

17 *South African Territories Ltd v Wallington* [1898] AC 309. See also, Rawlings, P 'Avoiding the Obligation to Lend.' [2012] JBL 89–110.

18 *Moschi v Lep Air Services Ltd* [1973] AC 331.

19 *McDonald v Denny Lascelles Ltd* [1933] 48 CLR 457.

20 *Bank of Boston Conneticut v European Grain & Shipping Ltd* [1989] AC 1056.

21 *Hadley v Baxendale* (1854) 9 Exch 341; *Kpohraror v Woolwich Building Society* [1996] 4 All ER 119 and *Jackson v Royal Bank of Scotland plc* [2005] UKHL 3.

**1.26** The borrower's remedy in such a case would, therefore, lie in an action for damages. Damages for breach of contract are designed to give the borrower, as nearly as possible, the profit that he would have received had the lending bank performed its obligations under the loan agreement. However, not all loss suffered by the borrower is recoverable, for there must be a sufficient connection between the bank's breach and the borrower's loss. In other words the loss must not be too remote. The loss must arise naturally from the breach itself or have been reasonably foreseeable by the parties at the time they entered into the contract, as the probable result of the breach.

**1.27** The possible heads of damage would include:

(a) general damages, particularly where the borrower can only obtain a replacement facility upon more onerous terms; or

(b) damages for consequential or incidental loss, including expenses incurred by the borrower in procuring an identical loan elsewhere and any increase in the interest rate applied to the new loan.[22]

*Failure by the borrower to drawdown the facility*

**1.28** Foreign currency lending agreements in London do not normally commit the borrower to drawdown the facility but instead confer an option to borrow. The borrower is normally required to give notice of its intention to borrow and is only bound once such notice has been given. If the borrower fails to draw down the loan after irrevocably committing itself, it is unlikely that specific performance will be available as a remedy to the lender. However, damages may be available in certain circumstances, although it is unlikely that the lender would be able to claim pre-contractual expenses, including administrative costs and legal fees, unless a clause has been included in the agreement providing that such expenses became payable upon execution of the loan. Such clauses are relatively common in loan agreements, as are those which cover the payment of certain fees, notwithstanding the fact that the loan is never drawn down. Insofar as damages for breach of contract are concerned it is likely, bearing in mind the funding mechanism employed in the markets, that the lender will be able to recover general damages, provided the conditions outlined above in relation to the lender's breach are satisfied. The lender will obviously be under a duty to mitigate its loss. In other words, it must take all reasonable steps to minimise its loss, for example, employing the undrawn funds elsewhere.

---

[22] *Hadley v Baxendale* (above, n 21).

## Restrictions on the use or purpose of the loan

**1.29** Generally speaking, loan agreements do not impose restrictions on the manner in which the funds are to be used, although restrictions are common in rescheduling and project finance agreements. Sovereign borrowers would, no doubt, consider such restrictions an unwelcome interference in domestic affairs, and in practical terms it will obviously be extremely difficult for a lender to police effectively any restriction which is imposed on the use of funds. This difficulty is reflected in the wording of clauses which do attempt to impose restrictions, eg:

> '... without prejudice to the foregoing [restriction] none of the Agents, the Managers and the banks shall be bound to enquire as to the applications by the Borrower of the proceeds of the loan, nor shall any of them be, responsible for, or for the consequences of, such application.'

**1.30** Notwithstanding the enormous practical difficulty in restricting the use of funds, there are a number of legal considerations which may be of fundamental importance to the lender. In the most extreme case the borrower may utilise the loan proceeds for an illegal purpose, thus rendering the loan contract void under English law if both lender and borrower are aware of all the circumstances.

**1.31** Even if the lender is unaware of the illegal purpose at the time the loan is executed, it must prevent any further drawdown once it becomes aware of the illegal purpose, lest it be implicated in the illegality and lose its right to enforce the loan. The lender may also be at risk where the loan has been advanced to a sovereign state or state entity and the loan is not commercial in nature. In such a situation the borrower will prime facie be entitled to immunity under English law, thereby preventing the bank from enforcing the loan unless appropriate measures have been included within the terms of the loan documentation. (This issue and methods of resolving the problem are considered in **Chapter 11**.)

**1.32** Where the loan is granted in favour of a corporate borrower it may be important to determine whether the borrower intends to use the proceeds for an ultra vires purpose. Under English law the ultra vires law is almost dead.[23] In the case of limited companies the normal rule is that contracts ultra vires the directors' powers may be prohibited by court order brought at the behest of a shareholder provided the contract has not yet been entered into,[24] but that beyond that such contracts are normally enforceable.[25] However, in the case of companies created by Royal Charter, by Act of Parliament, and in the case of certain collective investment schemes, ultra vires contracts

23 Companies Act 2006, s 39.
24 Companies Act 2006, s 40(4).
25 Companies Act 2006, s 40.

may still prove unenforceable.[26] (This is discussed in Chapter **6** at **6.40** to **6.53**).

**1.33** Other restrictions may be imposed by the local laws of the borrower's own jurisdiction. Some, for example, place restrictions on loans which finance acquisitions and mergers. In every case, therefore, it will be important to obtain the advice of local counsel on issues similar to those highlighted above, and also to incorporate protective provisions within the loan documentation which enable the lender to bring effective enforcement proceedings should this prove necessary.

## Restrictions imposed upon the borrower within the terms of the loan documentation

**1.34** The lender taking the credit analysis decision in a term loan agreement usually bases his decision upon a series of assumptions and caveats. At the heart of these is the assumption by the bank that the borrower can repay, but that if they cannot the bank can enforce payment or rely on security. Should the need arise they would also want to be able to get out of the contract.

**1.35** These assumptions and caveats are effectively given contractual force by the incorporation of certain restrictive clauses within the terms of the loan agreement known as conditions precedent, representations and warranties, covenants and events of default. The restrictive clauses, when taken together, fulfil three specific functions: first, they help to provide the lender with detailed information concerning the borrower; secondly, they provide for certain contractual remedies within the framework of the loan agreement; and thirdly, they give the lender the benefit of certain remedies available under the general law.

### *Financial terms*

**1.36** This will state the date by which the loan must be drawn down and the structure, ie, is it a bullet loan, revolving, etc, and there will also be a clause setting out the currency and the type and length of notice that the borrower must give. It will normally also state the place of repayment of the loan. In some instances the bank will also insist on the use of the funds. However, if the borrower is well known to the bank and has a good credit rating the clause may just say that the loan is for 'working capital purposes'.

**1.37** The first part of the agreement will deal with the loan facilities themselves. In some cases there will be a facility for syndicated lending (see **Chapter 2**) and/or the loan being made in more than one currency.

[26] In the case of a contract entered into by an overseas company, subject to English law, it is the law of the home State of that company that will determine whether it is enforceable. *Merrill Lynch v Municipality of Piraeus* [1997] CLC 1214.

This is normally followed by details such as the date when the loan will be drawn down, the applicable currency and the proposed interest period. In the case of a revolving facility there may be a minimum drawdown amount on each occasion. It is possible that the lender(s) may not be able to make the required amount available in the currency required on that date or cannot be made available for legal reasons (usually resulting from the imposition of exchange controls), in which case the borrower must be notified. In that case an equal amount must still be made available in the base currency of the loan. There is also sometimes a facility included for the loan currency to be changed between optional currencies denominated in the original agreement. There are requirements determining how the exchange rate will be calculated by making that calculation against the base currency spot rate at the relevant time.

**1.38** Prepayments take place where the borrower decides to pay back some or all of the loan before it is due. A common reason for this is that the borrower has discovered a cheaper source of funds. This is normally allowed by the agreement but only at the end of an interest period. The reason for this is that the lending bank will have normally arranged its own funds on a parallel time basis.

**1.39** The agreement then deals with issues resulting from repayment, prepayment and cancellation. Once a repayment has been made, no part of that repayment can be re-borrowed unless it is a revolving credit. In the event that the loan becomes illegal the lender has to immediately notify the borrower, the commitment is cancelled and the borrower must then either make repayments by the last day of the relevant interest period, or earlier if the lender so notifies the borrower, but this cannot be earlier than the last date of any grace period permitted by law.

### The legal and practical significance of conditions precedent

**1.40** The agreement will go on to include conditions precedent, which, as their name implies, are elements that must be in place before the loan can be drawn down. Where a large arrangement consists of a series of loans they fall into two groups: those that are conditions precedent to all the loans in an arrangement and those which are conditions precedent to each loan. Even after the loan has become operative the borrower is normally required to satisfy further conditions prior to any subsequent drawdown. These conditions are known respectively as conditions precedent and conditions subsequent.

**1.41** The purpose of the conditions precedent is to suspend the lender's commitment until their security, if any, is perfected and satisfactory evidence has been received that all pertinent legal matters concerning both the borrower and guarantor, if any, are in order. They also seek to permit the lender(s) to withdraw from the agreement at any time before the conditions have been met. Insofar as English law is concerned, whether the conditions precedent manage to achieve this purpose will depend upon whether they are conditions precedent to the actual formation of the loan contract. If they are, the lender will be free to withdraw from the agreement at any time before the borrower meets the conditions.[27]

**1.42** The precise working of the clause will obviously be crucial in determining whether or not the lender is free to withdraw. As Gabriel points out, the wording of the conditions precedent in many agreements places the emphasis upon the borrower's right to borrow, and the conditions precedent operate only upon the lender's obligation to lend once the agreement has been executed. This means that:

> '...any withdrawal from its commitment to lend, even before the borrower has begun to satisfy any condition, would result in the lender breaching the contract and thus exposing itself to a suit at the instance of the borrower'.[28]

The danger in such a situation is that difficulties may arise after the loan has been executed if this were to occur before the conditions precedent have been satisfied, and these difficulties are not caught by other restrictive clauses. In such a case the lender would be unable to withdraw without breaching the contract as the agreement comes into place straight away but the loans are conditional on the conditions precedent. There is English authority which suggests that in such a case the lender cannot withdraw whilst the event can still be met.[29] It is, therefore, important for the lender to protect themselves by making sure the agreement expressly provides that a formally binding contract will not exist until the conditions precedent have been satisfied by the borrower, otherwise it will not be clear whether failure by the borrower to bring about the conditions precedent permits the lender to withdraw from the agreement, or merely suspends that agreement.[30] Following the banking crisis of 2008 a large number of banks withdrew loan facilities at an advanced stage of negotiations, and such a clause proved crucial to protecting their position.

### Conditions precedent normally found in term loan agreements

**1.43** The conditions precedent drafted into the loan agreement will vary accordingly to the particular circumstances of all parties who

---

27 *Pym v Campbell* (1856) 6 E & B 370; *Wood Preservation v Prior* [1969] 1 WLR 1077, [1969] 1 All ER 364; *North Sea Holdings NV v Petroleum Authority of Thailand* [1997] 2 Lloyd's Rep 418.

28 Gabriel, *Legal Aspects of Syndicated Loans* (Butterworths. London, 1986), p 44.

29 *Smith v Butler* [1900] 1 QB 694; *Felixstowe Dock and Railway Co v British Transport Docks Board* [1976] 2 Lloyd's Rep 656; *Alan Estates Ltd v W G Stores Ltd* [1981] 3 WLR 892; *Bentray Investments v Venner Time Switches* [1985] 1 EGLR 39.

30 *MacKay v Dick* (1881) 6 App Cas 251; *Re Anglo-Russian Merchant Traders* [1917] 2KB 679.

contract under the agreement but will often follow market standards, primarily those of the Loan Markets Association. First, any guarantees will have to be in place. These will usually be intra-group guarantees which may have associated security provisions and set off arrangements. Secondly, any authorisations by the board must be in place authorising named directors and/or the company secretary to sign the loan agreement and copies of this authority must be provided.[31] Thirdly, where relevant official consents such as exchange control consents are needed because of the location of the borrower or guarantor, they must be in place prior to the loan agreement becoming binding. Fourthly, there will be an undertaking that the representations and warranties (see below) remain accurate at the time of signing. Fifthly, that there are no events of default pending and sixthly that there has been no significant adverse change in the borrower's financial position since matters were agreed.

**1.44** In addition, where the borrower is incorporated it is usual for the lender to require copies of all relevant constitutional documentation. If the company was incorporated in England such documents would include the Memorandum and Articles of Association. In addition, copies of corporate authorisations such as board resolutions and, where required shareholders' sanctions would also be required. Where the borrower is a sovereign state or state controlled entity a variety of declarations and authorisations from both the state's government and its central bank will also be required.

**1.45** An additional, and very important, condition precedent is the requirement to furnish legal opinions, addressed to the lender, and drawn up by lawyers in the jurisdiction of the borrower and of the guarantor, where relevant. The legal opinions should address the legal implications of the loan documentation by examining the impact of the representations and warranties made by the borrower and any guarantor. However, it must be appreciated that legal opinions do not amount to a guarantee that the transaction is valid and binding, since this opinion will only relate to the laws of its own jurisdiction and will not cover any legal system which has an impact on the loan agreement.

### Conditions subsequent

**1.46** It is common practice when drafting loans to specify certain 'standard' conditions which must be satisfied at or before each subsequent drawdown. These include the condition that the representations and warranties made by the borrower at the time the loan was executed continue to be true, and that no event of default has occurred and is continuing or will result from the drawdown.

---

31 *British and Commonwealth Holdings plc v Barclays Bank plc* [1996] 1 WLR 1; *Credit Suisse International v Stichting Vestia Groep* [2014] EWHC 3103 (Comm).

**1.47** The aim of the conditions subsequent is to suspend any subsequent drawdown, unless the borrower's position, both financially and otherwise, is consistent with that as 'represented' in the agreement when the loan was originally executed.

**1.48** It can be clearly seen that the conditions, both precedent and subsequent, described above are included for the benefit of the lending bank(s), and therefore can be waived by such bank(s) as if they were never included in the first place.

### *Representations and warranties*

**1.49** A golden rule in every form of bank lending, be it purely domestic or international, is 'know your borrower'.[32] This rule is obviously difficult to satisfy in some types of lending, eg, foreign currency loans, since the close relationship which normally exists between bank and borrower, in domestic lending, is rarely evident. Nevertheless, there are certain fundamental facts about the borrower of which a lending bank must always assure itself, before granting any loan facility. It is principally in order to ascertain these fundamental facts that representations and warranties are incorporated within the loan documentation. In strict legal parlance representations are statements made, and warranties are undertakings given, by the borrower on the basis of which the lender makes the credit available.

**1.50** Representations and warranties commonly fall into two categories: (1) Those clauses giving various assurances as to the legal validity of the obligations into which the borrower is entering; (2) clauses relating to the financial condition of the borrower.

#### Representations and warranties commonly found in term loans

**1.51** The representations and warranties clause usually commences with a number of statements concerning the valid existence and authorisation of the borrower, and include that the borrower is validly existing under the relevant foreign law (if it is a foreign company) and has power to borrow or enter into other obligations, such as the giving of a guarantee, required under the agreement. When considering the capacity of the borrower it is usual to incorporate a statement that the borrower's legal status is as stated, ie, that it is a registered limited company. There have been problems with organisations based in some jurisdictions which appear to be companies but are not in the sense that English law understands it. There will also be a statement that the borrower's powers allow the loan. This is an issue because some companies' articles only allow them to borrow up to a certain multiple

[32] Indeed, due to the anti-money laundering laws this is now obligatory in the UK as it is in virtually all overseas states.

of fully paid up share capital. In such a case a vote by the shareholders would be needed to change the articles.[33] The borrower's authorisations must also be satisfactory. Thus, the director(s) or company secretary who signed the loan agreement must have been authorised by the board to so act. Also, the company must not be in contravention of any relevant laws or regulations, such as exchange controls or capital controls. There may also be statements to the effect that:

- any necessary government or regulatory approvals have been obtained;
- the loan is legally valid and enforceable and constitutes a binding obligation upon the borrower, enforceable in accordance with its terms and not in breach of any sanctions law;
- no litigation, arbitration or other proceedings are, to the best of the borrower's knowledge, threatened against the borrower which might adversely affect the ability of the borrower to perform its obligations under the loan agreement or any security provided there under;
- the borrower is not in breach of any of its other obligations which might materially affect its ability to perform its obligations under the loan agreement;
- no default has occurred; and
- the recent audited accounts of the borrower reflect a true and fair view of the borrower's financial condition and the borrower has no other material liabilities which are not disclosed in the accounts.

It is also common to incorporate an all-embracing material adverse clause which may read as follows:

> 'There has been no material adverse change since …in the financial condition of the Borrower or in the Borrower's ability to perform its obligations under this Agreement.'

The difficulty with this clause is that it begs the question: what is material? It could be argued that this question is answered by applying an objective test, and English authority certainly appears to support such a notion,[34] in which case the clause will operate in a most unpredictable manner. The lender should try to avoid such unpredictability, whenever possible, by incorporating either a materiality test or by making the test subjective, eg: 'material in the opinion of the lender.'

**1.52** Where the borrower is a sovereign state or state-controlled entity it is also common to include a statement that the borrower

---

33 Companies Act 2006, s 21(1).
34 *Docker v Hyams* [1969] 1 Lloyd's Rep 333, [1969] 3 All ER 808.

is subject to civil and commercial law with regard to its obligations under the agreement, a statement that the borrowing constitutes a commercial, rather than a governmental act and that the borrower does not enjoy immunity from set-off, suit or execution in respect of its obligations under the agreement, and finally, a statement that the borrower is a member of the International Monetary Fund.

### Evergreen representations and warranties

**1.53** In many cases, the representations and warranties given by the borrower are isolated statements reflecting the circumstances at the time the loan agreement is executed. This, to a certain extent, contradicts the position as perceived by the lending bank, which normally assumes that the matters represented will remain so throughout the full term of the loan agreement. This particular problem can be resolved in a number of ways. First, the borrower may covenant to maintain the status quo as reflected by the representations and warranties, although in practical terms such a covenant will be virtually impossible to satisfy, since many of the matters covered by the representations and warranties are likely to be beyond the borrower's control. An alternative approach to the problem is to include an appropriate event of default clause linked to the representations and warranties. Such a clause is commonly adopted, notwithstanding that most borrowers, particularly sovereign states, resent the imputation inherent in its inclusion. An additional solution is obtained by including a rather artificial clause within the loan agreement, which provides that the representations and warranties shall survive the execution of the agreement and remain true throughout the full term of the loan. Many loans also provide that the representations and warranties shall be deemed to be repeated at various times, usually before any subsequent drawdown during the life of the loan.

### The purpose and significance of representations and warranties

**1.54** There are several purposes which representations and warranties seek to address: they endeavour to provide remedies for misrepresentation in the event of an inaccuracy; they may operate as an estoppel against the borrower; and they may enable the lender to cancel the commitment and accelerate the loan if they are linked to an event of default. On a more practical note, they provide a checklist which serves an investigative function for the lender.

**1.55** Whether they achieve their desired purpose will depend to a large extent on how they are legally construed. There is a significant difference under English law between a representation and a warranty. A representation is a statement of fact, not of opinion or law, which is made before the loan agreement has been executed, and in reliance upon the truth of which the lender enters into the loan agreement. It is not, however, an integral part of the contract. A warranty on the other hand is a term of the contract itself. This distinction is of the utmost importance, since the availability of various common law remedies will be determined, to a large extent, by ascertaining whether the statement is a term of the contract. The key to discovering whether a statement is such a term lies in the intention of the parties and such intention is ascertained by applying an objective test.[35]

**1.56** Appropriate drafting techniques can, however, avoid problems which arise out of the distinction between representations and warranties by expressly making all statements warranties and, therefore, terms of the contract. Such an approach is common in loan agreements where the borrower 'represents and warrants' in respect of every clause in the appropriate section of the documentation. The fact that all statements are made warranties is unfortunately, not the end of the matter, since under English law there is an important distinction between warranties and conditions in so far as the available remedies are concerned. Strictly speaking, a warranty is a contractual term which affects some relatively minor aspect of the contract and therefore breach only entitles the innocent party to sue for damages. In general, there is no right to terminate the agreement for breach of warranty. A condition, however, is a term which affects an important aspect of the contract, and breach entitles the innocent party not only to claim damages but also to terminate the contract for the future. Cases also recognise an important group of intermediate terms which are neither conditions or warranties, breach of which justifies discharge if it amounts to a serious failure in performance.[36]

**1.57** The distinction between conditions and warranties was historically based on the intention of the parties as expressed in the contract, but cases suggest that the use of the words 'condition' or 'warranty' will not be conclusive. Where no intention is expressed, the distinction may be based upon the seriousness of the failure to perform the contractual term at issue. In other words, where the term broken is so important that it would be unreasonable to expect the innocent party to fulfil its obligations under the contract, it is likely that the term will be construed as a condition.[37]

---

35 *Oscar Chess v Williams* [1957] 1 WLR 370; *Dick Bentley Productions Ltd v Howard Smith (Motors) Ltd* [1965] 1 WLR 623. 'What a reasonable person having all the background knowledge which would have been available to the parties would have understood them to be using the language in the contract to mean.' Lord Hoffman in *Chartbrook v Persimmon Homes Ltd* [2009] UKHL 38, para 14. Courts will take a purposive and commercial approach in doing this. *Investors Compensation Scheme v West Bromwich Building Society* [1998] 1 WLR 896 (ICS).

36 *Hong Kong Shipping v Kawasaki Kisen Kaisha* [1962] 2 QB 26. Followed by *Maredelanto Companio Naviera SA v Bergbau-Handel GmbH, (The Mihalis Angelos)* [1971] 1 QB 174. See also P Todd, 'Contract damages following discharge for repudiation – revisiting later events.' LQR 2016, 132 (Jan) 122–149.

37 *Ibid.*

**1.58** The distinction between conditions and warranties under English law has become overlaid with technicalities, and their classification is at the very least unpredictable; it will, therefore, be most important for the lender to avoid any future classification problems by expressly incorporating various remedies within the terms of the loan agreement which cover the eventuality of the representations and warranties being untrue. This is achieved in most loans by linking the representations and warranties to an event of default, ie:

> 'It shall be an event of default in the event that any representation and warranty of the Borrower or the Guarantor in this Agreement or any other document delivered in connection with this Agreement proves to have been incorrect, incomplete or misleading ...'

Such a clause clearly indicates that the parties perceive the representations and warranties as fundamental to the contract, giving rise to the right to cancel the facility and accelerate in appropriate cases. In such a case the representations and warranties would be classified as conditions rather than warranties.

### *Covenants*

**1.59** Term loan agreements invariably contain certain undertakings with which the borrower is required to comply throughout the life of the loan. Such undertakings are generally referred to as covenants. The scope and purpose of the covenants which are used by those who draft the loan agreement tend to be as wide as the variety of lenders and borrowers who participate in the lending market. Their primary objective, when taken together, is to ensure the continued soundness of the credit facility being advanced and to give the lender(s) certain inside information on, and limited control over, the business of the borrower.

**1.60** The most important covenant made by the borrower is, of course, the borrower's promise to repay the loan either on a particular date or by a series of instalments. This promise to repay is reinforced by additional covenants, the scope of which will be a matter of detailed negotiation between the lender and the borrower. Negotiation of the covenants often proves a difficult exercise, since the parties often have sharply contrasting interests. The borrower will obviously endeavour to retain for itself the greatest possible freedom with regard to the management of its business, whereas the lender will endeavour to impose suitable restrictions over the borrower's operations in order to safeguard its lending. A balance must clearly be struck and much will depend upon the relative bargaining strengths of the parties. The covenants ultimately agreed upon, as with all clauses in the loan agreement, should be specifically tailored. It is, nevertheless, possible to consider certain 'fundamental' covenants which are commonly seen in term loans.

### THE FINANCIAL COVENANTS

**1.61** The financial covenants are designed to protect the lender's position should the borrower's credit worthiness begin to deteriorate.[38] They require a flow of financial information from the borrower to the lender which enables the lender to monitor the borrower's financial health, providing, of course, the lender is in a position to check compliance. Perhaps the most important covenant at the time of writing relates to a minimum level of earnings before interest, tax, depreciation and amortisation (EBITDA)[39] over the next 12 months. The purpose of this is to make sure that the borrower has sufficient available profitable income to service its debts.[40] 'Earnings' in this context means net operating income after deduction of capital gains and losses from non-current asset disposals and one off gains and losses, together with expenses. Pre-acquisition earnings from acquired companies should also be deducted. Sometimes the reference will be to EBIT and depreciation and amortisation will not then be taken into account.

**1.62** Ratio covenants, which define certain acceptable requirements in relation to the borrower's financial condition, are also commonly employed in this monitoring process. Such covenants may define the acceptable financial condition of the borrower with reference to the value of its net assets, after deduction of net liabilities, commonly defined as the minimum net worth threshold; the ratio between such assets and liabilities indicating the threshold above which the borrower 'covenants' to maintain its position. Similarly, the borrower may be required to maintain a certain 'ratio' as between current liabilities and current assets or to maintain working capital above a predetermined figure.

**1.63** The commonest financial covenants in declining order of popularity are:[41]

– Debt / EBITDA

– Debt / (EBITDA – capital expenditure)

– Interest coverage $\times \dfrac{\text{EBITDA}}{\text{Interest}}$

– Fixed charge coverage $\times \dfrac{\text{EBITDA}}{\text{Total debt + capital expenditure + tax}}$

---

[38] For a useful overview see J Day, P Omrod and P Taylor 'The determinants of financial covenants in bank-loan contracts.' (2004) 19(2) JIBL 33–39; P Taylor and JFS Day 'Evolution in the practices of UK bankers in contracting for medium term debt' [1995] JIBL 394 and P Taylor 'Loan documentation in the market for UK corporate debt: current practice and future prospects.' (1997) 12(1) JIBL 7.

[39] Income before the deduction of interest payments, taxation, depreciation of assets and amortisation of intangible assets and debt.

[40] For a more detailed discussion of this see P Wood, *International Loans, Bonds, Guarantees, Legal Opinions* (Sweet & Maxwell, London, 2007) pp 88–91.

[41] https://corporatefinanceinstitute.com/resources/knowledge/finance/debt-covenants/ [Accessed 31 January 2025].

- Debt / equity
- Debt / assets
- Total assets
- Net tangible worth
- Dividend payout ratio
- Limitations on mergers and acquisitions[42]

**1.64** A certificate can be required showing that the required covenants have been satisfied on the publication of each year's accounts. Compliance with the ratio covenants, provided they are appropriately drafted, should indicate that the borrower's business is being conducted in a prudent fashion, whilst breach of such covenants may be an indication of future financial difficulties, thereby operating as an early warning device. It must be appreciated, however, that financial covenants will only be as good as the raw financial information supplied by the borrower. Accounting standards vary enormously from one country to another and it should never be assumed that the high standards applied in the lender's home jurisdiction will be similar to those applied in the borrower's jurisdiction.

**1.65** Whatever form the ratio covenants take, the specific wording must always be clearly defined within the terms of the loan agreement. Most borrowers can easily arrange their financing and accounting procedures in such a way as to significantly change the value of 'working capital', 'liquid assets', 'minimum net worth', etc, as defined in everyday commercial life. The lender, therefore, must ensure that these and other key phrases are carefully defined in order to prevent accidental or deliberate avoidance of the financial covenants by the borrower. This is one area of the term loan agreement to which the lender is often prepared to negotiate. A set of ratio covenants that suit one type of business may not accurately reflect the finances of another. A more precise analysis of this is really an accounting rather than a legal issue and thus beyond the confines of this text.

**1.66** The financial covenants are given teeth by linking them to an event of default clause which is intended to enable the lender to demand repayment as early as possible whilst there is still some prospect of the borrower being able to meet the demand.

### How effective are ratio covenants?

**1.67** Where realistic parameters and clear definitions are selected for the ratio covenants there can be no doubt that a significant degree of

---

[42] Limitations on mergers and acquisitions are often dealt with elsewhere in the term loan document.

protection is afforded to the lender. However, their shortcomings must not be overlooked. The financial information required by the covenants will often take many months to prepare, and, therefore, it will be long after the event before any contravention is brought to the lender's notice. It has already been mentioned that accounting standards vary from country to country, and although the lender can partially overcome this by selecting appropriate auditors who will prepare the information, it must be appreciated that the ratio covenants will only be as good as the financial information supplied.[43]

**1.68** For the financial covenants to be of value the lender or any third party who has bought the loan repayments from them needs to keep a close eye on the annual accounts. If, as a consequence of this, the bank becomes closely involved in the financial operations of the borrower, there arises the possibility that the bank could become a 'shadow director' of that company. Unfortunately, the legal definition of this term is not quite as precise as might be hoped[44] and the relevant influence and control do not need to be over the whole of the business.[45] For this reason it is better for the lender to avoid become too prescriptive regarding how any issue arising should be dealt with.

### Material adverse change clause

**1.69** The main alternative to ratio covenants is a continuing material adverse change clause, which will typically provide that it shall be an event of default:

> '... if there is any material adverse change in the financial condition of the borrower which in the reasonable opinion of the bank may impair the ability of the borrower to perform its obligations under this Agreement.'

Even when the clause incorporates a materiality test its language will invariably pose difficulties of proof, due to its discretionary nature. However, some clarity was provided by Blair J in *Grupo Hotelero Urvasco SA v Carey Value Added SL*,[46] where he suggested that an adverse change would be material if it substantially or materially affected the borrower's capacity to repay.[47] The inclusion of the words 'in the reasonable opinion of the bank' appears to mean that an objective determination as to whether the material adverse change has occurred is unnecessary. It is sufficient that the bank honestly and

---

43 In some areas there is a trend to less all-embracing financial covenants. See K Clowry 'European Credit Documentation Trends: Covenant Lite or Covenant Empty?' (2014) 29(5) BJIBFL 296–298 and J Markland 'Coverlite – the new Cutting Edge in Acquisition.' (2007) 22(7) BJIBFL 379–381.

44 *Secretary of State for Trade and Industry v Deverell* [2001] Ch 340.

45 *Mckillen v Misland (Cyprus) Investments* [2012] EWHC 521 (Ch); *Smithton Ltd v Naggar* [2014] EWCA Civ 939.

46 [2013] EWHC 1039 (Comm).

47 See also *Decura IM Investments LLP v UBS AG* [2015] EWHC 171.

reasonably believes so.[48] Even so the potential for disagreement as a result of this subjectivity where the financial condition of the borrower is at issue means that well drafted financial covenants are far more suitable than an all embracing event of default clause. Well drafted covenants establish specific criteria, breach of which may be clearly identified by the lender, while at the same time guiding the borrower as to what must be done in order to avoid an event of default.

#### The negative pledge

**1.70** The majority of very large-scale term loan agreements are unsecured, and, therefore, most lenders feel it is vital, whenever possible, to fetter the borrower's ability to create or maintain secured indebtedness. In such cases the lender will tend to rely on the borrower's credit rating as an indication of their capacity to repay. In the event of the lender failing to control the borrower in this way, it may ultimately transpire that the borrower's unencumbered assets are unable to satisfy the lender's unsecured claim. In addition, it is common where security is taken to add a negative pledge clause to cover non-secured and future acquired assets.

**1.71** The mechanism adopted in most term loans to achieve this degree of control is the negative pledge clause, which typically provides that the borrower shall not create or permit to subsist any security, usually specified as:

> '... any mortgage, charge, pledge, lien or other encumbrance; over its assets or revenues unless the loan covered by the negative pledge is "equally and rateably" secured.'

### What does the negative pledge cover?

**1.72** It will be noticed that the wording in the example given is very broad and without more would probably place too heavy a restriction on the borrower's business. It is common therefore to word the negative pledge very restrictively and then list a number of exceptions to its operation.

**1.73** The most common relaxation relates to encumbrances granted to third party creditors which are 'equally and rateably secured.' The precise meaning of this phrase is not entirely clear, but it would appear to cover the situation where security is granted to a third party, the proviso being that such security must also be used to secure the original lender's position on the term loan equally and rateably with the third party creditors. An alternative view is that where security is granted to a third party an equivalent security is to be granted in favour of the

---

[48] *Çukurova Finance International Ltd v Alfa Telecom Turkey Ltd* [2013] UKPC 2.

original lender. Much will obviously depend upon the precise wording of the clause, a typical example of which might read as follows:

> 'The Borrower will not create or permit to subsist any mortgage, charge, lien, pledge or other security interest on or over any of its present or future assets unless all the Borrower's obligations under this Agreement either:
>
> (a) share (to the satisfaction of the lender) the security afforded by such mortgage, charge, lien, pledge, or other security interest, equally and rateably with the loan, debt, guarantee or other obligation secured thereby, or
>
> (b) receive (to the satisfaction of the lender) the benefit of either a mortgage, charge, lien, pledge or other security interest, on other assets or revenues of the Borrower which the lender judges to be equivalent to that granted to such loan, debt, guarantee or other obligation.
>
> Notwithstanding the above, there shall be disregarded for the purpose of this clause:
>
> (i) liens which arose or may arise by operation of law;
>
> (ii) any mortgage, charge, lien, pledge or other security interest not exceeding £...... or ...... per cent of [the] Borrower's tangible net worth;
>
> (iii) any mortgage, charge, lien, pledge or other security granted with the written consent of the lender.'

**1.74** The exemptions outlined in the above clause are only examples and their precise scope will be a matter for detailed negotiation between the parties – the Loan Markets Association for example has quite a brief clause.[49] The clause must not be too restrictive so as to effectively preclude the borrower from entering into normal commercial arrangements, and an ill-considered clause may actually force the borrower into taking undesirable financial measures to raise funds, such as selling valuable assets which might otherwise be pledged. It is obviously in the lender's interest to keep the borrower's financial condition as healthy as possible, and this should be borne in mind when the wording of the negative pledge is being negotiated.

### To whom should the negative pledge extend?

**1.75** Another important issue is whether the negative pledge should only cover security created by the borrower or whether it should encompass security created by related entities of the borrower.

---

[49] Multicurrency Term and Revolving Facilities Agreement, cl 22.3 under 'General Undertakings'. (See **Appendix**).

Where the borrower is a sovereign state, the clause may be drafted so as to extend over governmental agencies and instrumentalities, although most states would strongly resist any attempt to bring either central banks or state owned enterprises within its parameters. Similarly, in the case of a corporate borrower the clause may extend over its subsidiaries, even though the lender will not, at least under English law, have a direct right of recourse against the assets of such subsidiaries, but only against the value of the borrower's interest in them.

## The legal nature of the negative pledge

**1.76** It has already been stressed that the primary purpose of the negative pledge is to prevent third party creditors being preferred to the original lender who has advanced the term loan. The intention in the majority of loan agreements is to provide a mechanism whereby the borrower is required to consult the lender should it wish to create any secured indebtedness to third party creditors. In the event of the borrower falling to consult, the creation of such indebtedness will trigger an event of default in the original loan. If it can be shown that the third party creditor took his security with notice of the negative pledge clause, it may be possible for the lender to bring a claim against the creditor in tort for interference with the term loan contract. However, this would depend to a large extent on the precise wording of the negative pledge and the manner in which it was breached. The key point is that it would be necessary to prove that the later secured lender knew of the negative pledge in the earlier loan document. Under the Companies Act 2006, s 859 D (as amended) the particulars that require registration at the Charges Registry, Companies House include at CA2006, s 859 D(2)(c) 'whether any of the terms of the charge prohibit or restrict the company from creating further security that will rank equally with or ahead of the charge.' This means that negative pledge clauses now fall into two categories.

## Negative pledges which have been registered

**1.77** In these cases, constructive notice is given to the world at large provided registration of the charge takes place in the appropriate form and within the required 21-day time limit. Thus, such a negative pledge is very useful as a secured lender who finds the borrower has in some way damaged their financial interest by a later security granted elsewhere will have the capacity to sue the second secured lender by way of an action for the tort of interference with contractual relations. The threat of this means that other banks will be cautious about making secured loans in such a situation and will check for such negative pledge provisions at Companies House. This is now the normal procedure.

### Negative pledge clauses with no registration

**1.78** These appear unaffected by the changes to the charging provisions in the Companies Act 2006 and the situation thus remains as set out in the notes above. They will be very infrequent because the absence of registration will effectively render the clause worthless beyond it amounting to an event of default should the borrower breach it.

**1.79** In the event of the borrower breaking the negative pledge clause the lender can accelerate payment or bring court proceedings against the borrower for breach of contract. Should the lender win, they would still be an unsecured creditor for the amount of the judgment. It may be possible for the creditor to appoint a receiver.[50] This would seem to be an option where the lender also has taken security, but an unsecured negative pledge lender could also apply using the court's inherent power to appoint receivers. However, it seems that a court would not do this unless a normal debt action or injunction was inadequate.[51] It may also be possible to apply for an injunction against the third party who had taken security to stop them taking the benefit of it on the basis of there being a breach of the tort of interference with contractual relations.[52] There is also the possibility of an action in equity but this would be dependent on being able to prove that the third party had knowledge of the negative pledge clause.[53]

## THE PARI PASSU COVENANT

**1.80** The pari passu covenant is a companion of the negative pledge clause which covers only unsecured indebtedness. The pari passu covenant is normally worded in such a way that the borrower warrants that its obligations under the loan will not be subordinated to any unsecured creditor. In other words, that the rights of the term lender will always rank at least pari passu with the rights of the borrower's other unsecured creditors.

**1.81** The pari passu covenant is normally expressed as a continuing covenant, hence the words, '... will at all times'. Furthermore, the obligations owed to the lender are expressed to rank 'at least' pari passu in order to provide for the possibility of the borrower incurring

---

50 *Bond Brewing Holdings v National Australia Bank* [1990] 1 ASCR 445.

51 J Stone, 'Will the Court appoint a Receiver at the request of a Negative Pledge Lender?' (1991) 6(10) JIBL 405 and D Allan 'Negative Pledge Lending – Dead or Alive? How to reinvent the mortgage' (1990) 5(8) JIBL 330.

52 See McNight and Zakrewski, *The Law of Loan Agreements and Syndicated Lending*, 2nd edn (Oxford University Press. 2019). Also *Swiss Bank Corp v Lloyds Bank Ltd* [1979] Ch 548

53 *de Mattos v Gibson* (1858) De G&J 276, 45 ER 108; *OBG Ltd v Allan; Mainstream Properties Ltd v Young* [2007] UKHL 21DBS; *Bank Ltd v Tam Chee Chong* [2011] SGCA 47 where the Singaporean Court of Appeal indicated that the tort could be applied in the context of a negative pledge.

unsecured indebtedness which is subordinated to the lender's claim. Clearly, the lender would not wish to elevate such subordinated debt to the same position as its own.

**1.82** Many jurisdictions provide that certain classes of unsecured creditors will rank in priority to others, and since the clause has no effect on third parties, it is common to qualify the scope of the clause in favour of those creditors who are thus afforded priority. The efficacy of the clause once again lies in the fact that it is invariably linked to an event of default which permits acceleration and the right to demand repayment, preferably before the borrower becomes insolvent. Whether the clause, therefore, achieves its desired purpose will depend upon how effectively it can be policed, and this should be borne in mind by those drafting the agreement.

### *Additional covenants commonly found in term loans*

#### Use of proceeds

**1.83** We have already seen that in certain circumstances it may be necessary to impose restrictions on the use or purpose of the loan. Whenever this is deemed necessary it is common to reinforce the purpose clause with a specific covenant linked to an event of default permitting acceleration in the event of any breach. Once again, however, it may be very difficult to police such a covenant.

#### Anti-merger covenants

**1.84** Anti-merger covenants are relatively common where the borrower is a corporate entity and the primary purpose of such a covenant is to maintain the identity of the borrower. In rare cases the scope of the covenant may go much further than maintaining the identity of the borrower and may require key management figures to remain in office or to be replaced by persons approved by the lender.

#### Anti-disposal covenants

**1.85** Just as it may be important to maintain the identity of the borrower, it is likely that the lender will want to preserve the borrower's assets, which will be available for any future distribution. The clause may be drafted very widely to prevent any creeping disposals of all assets or may relate only to a small number of assets which the lender perceives as fundamental to the borrower's credit worthiness. Where the covenant is very restrictive it is common to incorporate numerous exceptions which permit the borrower to carry on its day-to-day business. The clause may be reinforced by a covenant requiring the borrower to maintain a certain level of insurance over specified assets and against such risks as prescribed by the lender.

The anti-disposal covenant obviously operates hand in hand with both the financial covenants and the negative pledge, the general purpose being to prevent the depletion of funds to which the lender must look for eventual repayment.

### *Events of default*

**1.86** Certain clauses will give the lender the right to terminate the contract. Whether they would wish to utilise this right is another matter as were the contract to be terminated it might well force the borrower into insolvency. This would not normally be in the lender's best interests. However, it is useful in that it puts the lender into a position of power in being able to threaten termination and thus negotiate from a position of strength. Key examples of such clauses are as follows.

#### NON-PAYMENT

**1.87** In the event that the borrower does not pay the due amount on the agreed place in the stated location in freely available funds and the agreed currency, it will normally be an event of default. It is common to include exceptions for failure to pay being the result of a purely administrative error, or a disruption event and provided it is paid within a certain number of business days of the payment date. Indeed, the LMA terms take this approach.[54]

#### FINANCIAL COVENANTS

**1.88** Failure to satisfy the financial covenants discussed above will also be an event of default.

#### MISREPRESENTATION

**1.89** Misrepresentation, which is discussed elsewhere in this chapter, and also in detail in **Chapter 2** (see **2.21** – **2.39**), will be an event of default if made by a borrower or guarantor prior to the lending agreement, guarantee or any connected document where it is material and misleading.

#### CROSS DEFAULT

**1.90** This refers to the failure by the borrower to make a payment under another lending arrangement, an event of default or termination

---

[54] Clause 23(1)(a).

event arising in relation to another lending agreement, any creditor becoming entitled to seize property under another lending agreement will be typical examples of this. It is normal to include a minimum sum in this clause so that trivial breaches of other agreements do not trigger the activation of this clause.

#### Attachment of assets

**1.91** Any attachment of the borrower's assets by creditors will be an event of default, although this clause is sometimes added to the insolvency clause in 'termination events' discussed below.

#### Obligor default

**1.92** If a subsidiary of the borrower providing a guarantee or security ceases to be a subsidiary it will normally be an event of default.

### *Termination events*

**1.93** Whereas an event of default gives the lender the option to terminate the contract, a termination event is one that results in the contract coming to an end regardless of choice by the lender.

*Insolvency*

**1.94** It will normally be stated to be a termination event where the borrower becomes insolvent or where steps are taken against them by a creditor in relation to failure to pay or where there is a winding up case brought or one involving dissolutions, reorganisation, winding up or administration of the borrower or a guarantor or provider of security. The clause will also be activated by the borrower entering into a scheme of arrangement with their creditors or by any security provided by the borrower being enforced. In practice, this is far and away the most common termination event.

#### Illegality

**1.95** This is the most extreme example as were there not to be a clause rendering the contract terminated there is the danger that in certain circumstances the contract could be void. The issue could arise because the contract becomes illegal under the law chosen in the choice of law clause in the contract or that of the jurisdiction in the unlikely event that this is different. It could be an issue if the contract becomes illegal in another state connected with the loan, though here it will depend on the exact circumstances. Prima facie the English courts will not enforce a contract where it is against the law of a friendly state affected by that contract[55] but if it is a case of a loan agreement that is effective under English law being unacceptable elsewhere purely for what English law would see as technical reasons,[56] eg interest payments being prohibited under Sharia'h law where the borrower is located in an Islamic state but the loan agreement is covered by English law and the jurisdiction of the English courts, illegality would not be an issue.

#### Force majeure

**1.96** This is a clause which results in the parties' obligations under the contract being terminated or adjusted in the light of an unexpected event. It is a civil law concept and must, therefore, be contractually incorporated in common law jurisdictions should its benefits be wanted. Current market practice in London seems to be to not have a general force majeure cause. If, however, the parties do wish to have one, they must determine which events they will wish to have this effect, short of those events that would frustrate the contract anyway. In that instance the Law Reform (Frustrated Contracts) Act 1943 would lead to the contract being frustrated and moneys paid prior to that could be recovered. In the LMA document that clause crops up as a market disruption sub-clause.[57] It applies when the bank determines that further deposits are not readily available on the deposit market specified. It allows the bank and borrower to negotiate for 30 days and if they cannot agree by then the bank can determine the interest rate on the basis of its funding costs from whatever source it might reasonably select.

**1.97** Other common versions are war, terrorist attacks, blockades, embargoes, breakdown of civil order and Acts of God. The burden of evidence rests on the party seeking to rely on the clause.[58] Notice provisions are also commonly included.

### *Payment mechanics*[59]

**1.98** Obviously a key element of any loan agreement is the obligation to make payments of interest and repayments of capital on time and

---

55 *Ralli Bros v Compania Naviera Sota, Sota v Aznar* [1920] 2 KB 287; *Foster v Driscoll* [1929] 1 KB 470.

56 *Tekron Resources Ltd v Guinea Investment Co Ltd* [2003] EWHC 2577 (QB), [2004] 2 Lloyd's Rep 26; *Mahonia Ltd v JP Morgan Chase Bank (No 1)* [2003] EWHC 1927 (Comm), [2003] 2 Lloyd's Rep 911; *Mahonia Ltd v JP Morgan Chase Bank (No 2), Mahonia v West AG* [2004] EWHC 1938 (Comm); *Baros Mattos Junior v MacDaniels Ltd, Mattos Junior v General Securities & Finance Co Ltd* [2004] EWHC 1188 (Ch), [2004] 3 All ER 299 & 2 All ER (Comm) 501; *Marlwood Commercial Inc v Kozeny* [2006] EWHC 872 (Comm).

57 Clause 11.2.

58 *Mamidoil-Jetfoil Greek Petroleum Co SA v Okta Crude Oil Refinery AD* [2003] 1 Lloyd's Rep 1.

59 Clause 29.

in both cases in the contracted currency. This should be done without set off or counterclaim. Should payment for costs, expenses or taxes be necessary then they should be paid in the currency in which they are incurred. This is the line adopted in the LMA Agreement.

**1.99** In the event of a change of control at the borrower's company the lender, or where appropriate their agent must be promptly informed and after that date the lender(s) are not required to continue to provide funds except in the case of a rollover facility. A notice terminating the loan can then be given and a notice period for this purpose can be inserted at this point. Of particular concern to a lender will be a change of control resulting in a lower credit rating for the borrower. Had this been the case at the outset the lender(s) may not have been willing to make the loan, or if so, on such favourable terms.

**1.100** The borrower also has the capacity to cancel the loan or any remaining part thereof. Prepayment is also possible although there is usually a minimum amount that can be prepaid and interest up until that point must be included. In addition, it can only be made after the end of the current availability period. This gives time for the lending bank(s) to make other arrangements to lend the money. Compulsory prepayment on change of control is sometimes phrased as an event of default which means the lender can cancel the commitments to lend and accelerate the loan. Alternately it can be inserted as a mandatory prepayment so as to avoid a reputation for default, should it occur.

### *Tax gross up*

**1.101** This clause is added on the assumption that any withholding tax that may be payable is paid under UK law. Essentially it states that the borrower must make any payments to the lender without any deductions for withholding tax. In the event of a withholding tax being introduced outside the United Kingdom the borrower must make the full payment to the lender regardless. There are certain exclusions and the notes to the LMA agreement state that:

> 'This is a complex area and in each case relevant treaties should be reviewed and, if appropriate, additional wording inserted to apportion risk as agreed by the Parties.'

### *Tax indemnities and credits*

**1.102** The following clause requires the borrower to indemnify the lender against any loss caused by taxation being paid in respect of a finance document, a tax credit or stamp duty. The LMA Agreement requires that in the case of VAT an appropriate VAT invoice must be provided.[60] There are also provisions determining that where the borrower pays VAT on a supply goods or services pursuant to the loan agreement, the lender will be indemnified against any cost.

### *Provisional Treaty Relief Schemes*

**1.103** There are provisions dealing with syndicated loans (see **Chapter 2**) that determine the borrower must indemnify the agent of a syndicate where they have incurred costs managing the syndicate.[61] They must also make provision to provide promptly any information that the Agent asks for and act in accordance with any notices from HM Revenue and Customs.

### *Increased costs*

**1.104** The LMA Agreement requires the borrower to pay within three business days any increased costs incurred by the lender arising as a result of a change in the law or relevant regulations made after the date of the lending agreement.[62] This does not extend to tax deductions or indemnities, which as seen above have certain specific arrangements attributable to the borrower wilfully breaching a law or regulation.[63]

### *Other indemnities*

**1.105** The LMA Agreement requires the borrower to agree that within three business days of it being demanded they will pay to the lender any costs arising from an event of default, failure to pay any amount due or not prepaid when required. They are also obliged to pay any costs necessarily incurred in investigating a default, entering into a necessary change of currency (see below) or where an agent has acted on an instruction. They must also pay promptly any costs incurred in preparing or amending the lending agreement.[64]

**1.106** As a counterbalance there is a requirement that the lender mitigates any costs that arise as a result of the illegality, tax gross up, increased costs and mandatory cost formula clauses. If this involves any costs the borrower must indemnify them.

---

60 LMA Multicurrency Term and Revolving Facilities Agreement, July 2017 version. Clause 13.7 (e) 'In relation to any supply made by a Finance Party to any Party under a Finance Document, if reasonably requested by such Finance Party, that Party must promptly provide such Finance Party with details of that Party's VAT registration and such other information as is reasonably requested in connection with such Finance Party's VAT reporting requirements in relation to such supply.'

61 Clause 12.3. The same applies with regard to the arranging bank in clause 12.2.

62 Clause 14.1.

63 Clause 14.3.

64 Clause 17.

**1.107** There is a fairly standard guarantee/indemnity clause for any guarantor(s) of the loan together with a release provision in the event of a guarantor stepping down as a result of the terms of the lending documentation.[65]

**1.108** The LMA representations, undertakings and events of default contain no great surprises. The borrower confirms that it is validly incorporated in its jurisdiction and both it and its subsidiaries have power to carry on their business and to own their assets. It also confirms that the lending agreement does not put it in breach of any law, regulation, constitutional document or agreement applying to either itself or a subsidiary or any of their assets and that any necessary authorisations are in force. There are also representations stating that it is not necessary for the borrower to make any deduction from repayments for tax or for stamp duty or similar tax to be payable on the document or for the documents to be filed with any authority in the borrower's jurisdiction.

**1.109** There are also the standard type of clauses stating that the borrower has not committed an event of default nor that one might reasonably be expected. If it has notification should take place. Any factual information provided remains accurate as do the financial projections which are undertaken to have been carried out on the basis of recent historical information and on the basis of reasonable assumptions. The borrower undertakes that its financial statements have been prepared in accordance with UK GAAP and fairly represent its financial condition or if not this must be expressly disclosed. Any material adverse change since the date of the financial statements must also be disclosed as must any change in the accounting practices, financial reference periods or the auditors. The financial statements must be in sufficient detail to enable the lenders to determine whether the financial covenants have been complied with. In addition, a compliance statement must be added, signed by two directors, stating in reasonable details what the computations are in the financial statements.

**1.110** There is provision, as long as the lender agrees, for all information that must be provided to be done electronically together with provisions as to how this should be done.

## Remedies for breach of covenant

**1.111** A conclusive evidence clause is needed in the lending agreement to determine the exact amount owed without lengthy disagreements with the borrower and these are enforceable provided there is no

[65] Clause 18. The form of the letter of resignation of the guarantor is at Sch 8.

demonstrable error.[66] The proof of any objection to this must be prompt and conclusive.[67]

**1.112** As we have already indicated the loan agreement will normally provide specific remedies for any breach of covenant by linking the covenants to an event of default. The wording of such an event of default will typically cover events such as non-payment, breach of the financial covenants, breach of any other obligation, misrepresentations having been found to take place, cross default, insolvency or insolvency proceedings, creditors' process, change in the ownership of the borrower, illegality, repudiation and material adverse change.[68]

**1.113** Breach of the covenants will, therefore, normally permit the lender to suspend and/or cancel the facility and accelerate the borrower's obligation to repay. However, this may prove to be of little practical effect if the borrower's financial condition has deteriorated so badly that it is unable to repay. The lender's only hope is that the covenants will act as an early warning system which may enable the lender to recover its funds before the situation is completely lost.

## Internal remedies

### *Set Off*

**1.114** As Philip Wood points out:

> 'Potentially one of the most useful remedies available to a bank lender on a default by the borrower is the ability to use deposits of the borrower placed with the bank to pay out the defaulted loan by a set off.'[69]

**1.115** Set off is a remedy which bridges the gap between the internal and external remedies since a clause covering the lender's right to set off may be incorporated within the terms of a term loan agreement.[70] Rights of set off also exist in equity, but only where given conditions are fulfilled.[71]

**1.116** Here the focus will be on the set off clause, which usually seeks to confer broader rights of set off than would be given in equity to strengthen the lender's position.

**1.117** The relevant LMA clause reads as follows:

---

66 *Van der Merwe v IIG Capital LLC* [2008] EWCA Civ 542

67 *North Shore Ventures Ltd v Anstead Holdings Inc* [2011] EWCA Civ 230; *Amey Birmingham Highways Ltd v Birmingham City Council* [2018] EWCA Civ 264.

68 Clause 23.

69 P Wood *The Law and Practice of International Finance,* 1st edn (Sweet & Maxwell,1980), p 173.

70 Clause 30.

71 *Geldof Metaalcontsructee NV v Simon Carves Ltd* [2010] EWCA Civ 667.

'A Finance Party may set off any matured obligation due from the Obligor under the Finance Documents (to the extent beneficially owned by that Finance Party) against any matured obligation owed by that Finance Part to that Obligor, regardless of the place of payment, booking branch or currency of either obligation. If the obligations are in different currencies, the Finance Party may convert either obligation at a market rate of exchange in its usual course of business for the purpose of the set-off.'

**1.118** It is debatable whether the courts in England would permit set off where the funds to be set off are in another jurisdiction other than that specified in the agreement. Set off in such cases would certainly not be allowed in equity and the specimen clause serves to illustrate how the loan agreement may attempt to extend the lender's rights. The problem with such a clause is that, under English law, if not carefully worded it may constitute the creation of a charge over the borrower's deposits, and if so construed will be void under s 869 of the Companies Act 2006 unless it is registered.[72]

### *Fees*

**1.119** There are a number of different fees which may be payable by the borrower in a loan agreement, although most of these are only levied if the loan is being syndicated.[73] Single lender medium term loans often do not always involve fees because of the competitiveness of the market and other potential sources of funds. Some borrowers, however, may be prepared to pay more in undisclosed front end fees rather than higher spreads as that may imply a poorer credit rating. As we have already seen, some of these fees may be payable even though the borrower does not drawdown the facility, and may, therefore, operate as a significant disincentive against the borrower seeking alternative funding once it has become committed under the original facility. The following are examples of the fees which may be payable.

#### Commitment fees

**1.120** In most loan agreements the lender will be committed to make the funds available as soon as the loan is executed, even though the borrower may not drawdown the facility immediately. In such cases the burden of risk rests heavily on the lender which may, as a consequence, require the borrower to pay a commitment fee on the undrawn portion of the committed facility, to compensate the bank for the risk it bears. The fee payable is usually expressed as a percentage

---

72 *Morris and others v Rayners Enterprises; Morris and others v Agrichemicals Ltd* also known as *Re Bank of Credit and Commerce International SA (in liquidation) No 8* [1998] AC 214, [1997] 3 WLR 909.

73 LMA Multicurrency Term and Revolving Credit Agreement, 18 July 2017, clause 12.

of the undrawn facility on a day-to-day basis. Fees of less than 1% are normally expressed in terms of basis points, and market practice recognises each basis point as referring to one hundredth of 1% as 'basis points'.

### Front end fees

**1.121** A variety of front end fees may be payable by the borrower depending upon the type of facility being advanced. These fees are normally payable once and for all shortly after the loan has been executed, and relate to the entire facility, regardless of whether it is fully drawn, cancelled or pre-paid. Front end fees are particularly valuable to the lender where there is a risk of early cancellation or prepayment, and they are commonly found in syndicated loan agreements where they are normally paid to each participating bank in proportion to the exposure being taken.

**1.122** Front end fees compensate the lending bank in three ways. First, the proportionate value of the fee levied will be greater if the loan is cancelled or prepaid by the borrower and will, therefore, to a certain extent, offset such cancellation. Secondly, the fact that such fees are levied, notwithstanding drawdown, may dissuade some borrowers from exploiting the market advantages of prepayment and may thus strengthen the negotiating position of the original lenders. Finally, the fact that in the current marketplace banks will often sell on the loan repayments to another party means that the front-end fees are a significant part of their profit on the transaction.

### Legal fees

**1.123** Medium term loan agreements obviously vary in complexity, and this is reflected in the level of legal fees. While legal fees are rarely large in percentage terms, they nevertheless tend to be a significant expense, and the lender should always provide for an express clause within the loan agreement whereby the borrower agrees to indemnify the lender in respect of such fees. That said, the emergence of standardised LMA complaint documentation has shown the capacity to greatly reduce costs unless there are drawn out negotiations over terms more prone to causing disagreement, such as financial covenants. Rather than make specific reference to legal fees, some loans incorporate an all embracing expenses clause, which requires the borrower to reimburse the lender for all expenses incurred in connection with the loan.

### Stamp duty

**1.124** In ascertaining which country's stamp laws will apply to the loan agreement much will depend on the nationality of the borrower and the law of the place where the loan is executed. The amount, if any, of stamp tax or duty payable will vary widely from one jurisdiction to another, and it is sometimes possible to avoid these taxes by executing the agreement in a jurisdiction which does not apply stamp taxes. Insofar as English law is concerned, loan agreements are not subject to stamp duty. Because different jurisdictions adopt a variety of stamp duty requirements, it is common for the lender(s) to insist that the loan documentation include a provision whereby the borrower agrees to indemnify the lender(s) against every eventuality as found at LMA clause 17 (see **Appendix**).

*The importance of controlling the jurisdiction in which the loan is executed*

**1.125** The importance of ascertaining and controlling the jurisdiction in which the loan is executed is highlighted **Chapter 10**. In some cases the place of execution will be self evident as the loan will be signed by all relevant parties in one place. Other cases, however, may be less clear, particularly where the agreement is signed by one party, say the borrower in one jurisdiction and then posted for signature by the lender in another jurisdiction. Under English law, such an agreement would be deemed executed in the jurisdiction where it is accepted, and where a postal method of acceptance is adopted this would be the place where acceptance is posted by the offeree.[74] If the communication is electronic then it will be the place of signature in the place of receipt of the party accepting.[75] Under English rules of private international law, if there is a conflict on the question of execution, the issue would fall to be determined by the proper law of the contract.

## External remedies

*Specific performance*

**1.126** An English court will not normally grant an order for specific performance where damages would be an adequate remedy. Nor will the court normally grant specific performance where the loan agreement makes provision for a more suitable remedy, for example, termination and acceleration.

*Prohibitory injunction*

**1.127** Although an English court would be reluctant to grant an order for specific performance which would require a positive act on

[74] *Henthorn v Fraser* [1892] 2 Ch 27.

[75] *Entores v Miles Far East Corp* [1955] 2 QB 327;*Tenax Steamship Co v Owners of the Motor Vessel Brimnes* [1974] EWCA Civ 15 and *Brinkibon Ltd v Stahag Stahl* [1983] 2 AC 34.

the part of the borrower, it would be much more favourably disposed towards the grant of an injunction which restrains the borrower from performing acts which are in breach of its obligations under the loan agreement. Thus, the borrower may be restrained from breaching an undertaking or covenant, providing the lender can act quickly, before the breach occurs. This once again highlights the importance of incorporating undertakings/covenants within the loan agreement which can be effectively policed by the lender.

*Other external remedies*

**1.128** There are a number of other remedies which may be available to the lender in the event that the borrower breaches the loan agreement, and most of these are considered elsewhere in this work. They include: the right to repudiate the contract and accelerate the sum outstanding; the right to sue the borrower for damages; the right to sue for outstanding amounts of interest and/or principal; the right to rescind the loan agreement and claim damages.

**1.129** As we have seen, the availability of such remedies will depend upon the circumstances surrounding the borrower's breach, and although they may provide the lender with a number of important safeguards, their availability will normally be subject to significant limitations. They should never be relied upon as a substitute for express remedies, which must always be incorporated into the loan agreement in order to bring a degree of certainty and predictability to the rights of the lender in the event that the borrower subsequently breaches the agreement.

## Restructuring

### Introduction

**1.130** Where the borrower encounters difficulties so that it is no longer able to meet its liabilities as they fall due, the lender may agree to open restructuring negotiations in the hope that the borrower will pull through its present financial difficulties. Such a course of action may be perceived as being more attractive than winding up proceedings which, as has already been seen, will realise for the lender only a small proportion of the sums owed. Insofar as sovereign borrowers are concerned, restructuring agreements tend to be even more complex than corporate restructurings.

**1.131** Insofar as the lenders are concerned, the most important components of the restructuring process will be:

- the rescheduling of the borrower's existing debt;
- the provision of new money; and

- the need to conclude formal arrangements for the maintenance of inter-bank lines of credit.

**1.132** One of the main advantages of restructuring is that control stays with the lenders, but there are a number of major problems which such a course of action pose for the lenders, not least the need to provide new money. It is hardly surprising that many lenders resent the need to provide new money, seeing it as a case of throwing good money after bad. As a consequence, the documentation evidencing restructuring agreements tends to be drafted heavily in favour of the lenders.

**1.133** Before considering some specific aspects of the restructuring process it must be pointed out that no two restructurings are ever the same and corporate and sovereign debt restructurings tend to be very different. There are no international guidelines governing the process of restructuring and discussion of this topic will, therefore, concentrate on general principles rather than specific examples. Many of the inherent difficulties in a restructuring exercise arise out of the sheer complexity of the negotiations which are necessary. A typical sovereign restructuring will involve tens, if not hundreds, of individual borrowers in both the public and private sector, with a corresponding number of separate credit instruments. The credits themselves will have been advanced in a multitude of different currencies at varying maturities, interest rates and margins. The documentation evidencing such credits will be equally diverse, ranging from one paragraph promissory notes to voluminous syndicated loan agreements. It is hardly surprising that the most difficult question is often the first: 'which of the borrowers' debts will be rescheduled?'

## The restructuring process

### *Declaration of a moratorium*

**1.134** Insofar as sovereign restructurings are concerned the restructuring process has generally commenced following an announcement by the state of a specific cut-off date upon which it proposes to suspend payment of its obligations, accompanied by an announcement of the opening of negotiations to reschedule. The major problem facing a corporate borrower, should it decide to commence restructuring negotiations by the declaration of a so-called moratorium, is that individual creditors, with minimal exposure may feel that their interests are best served by taking independent legal action against the borrower to enforce the debts they are owed. Such a course of action may have serious implications for the borrower's prospects, since its major creditors may be disinclined to restructure in a case where many minor creditors are actively seeking to enforce their rights by means of attachment or otherwise. Nevertheless, many corporate borrowers do survive this vulnerable stage, and the insolvency laws of both England

and many other states provide various procedures which may help to achieve a workable situation.

**1.135** Rather than declare a moratorium the borrower, and likewise the lender(s), may prefer the restructuring to be conducted privately, as between an individual debtor and an individual lender, or syndicate of lenders. Such a procedure will be unrealistic, however, when the borrower has many different creditors with whom it must negotiate.

### *Organisation of the restructuring*

**1.136** In most of the major restructurings the negotiations from the lending bank's side have been led by a so called 'steering committee'. The members of this committee are normally drawn from the leading bank creditors of the borrower and each committee is the product of the specific restructuring in question. No two steering committees have ever comprised the same banks, but although their members are appointed on an ad hoc basis, the manner in which these committees are formed and work on the restructuring has, to some extent, been formalised. In many of the sovereign restructurings, for example, the steering committee has comprised between 10 to 14 banks with a permanent chairman. A number of sub-committees have usually been appointed to deal with particular aspects of the rescheduling and these sub-committees have tended to work with the steering committee in supervising the drafting of the documentation for the rescheduling and new-money agreements, and generally, in implementing the restructuring itself.

### *Is there a duty upon any of the bank's creditors to take a role in the restructuring?*

**1.137** It has been suggested by at least one learned commentator[76] that certain banks may be under a contractual duty to assume a leading role in the restructuring negotiations. Those principally cited are the arranging banks and/or the agent banks in syndicated loan agreements.

**1.138** Professor Horn contends[77] that since both the arranging and agent banks have acted for and on behalf of the other syndicate members in both the formation of the syndicate and thereafter during the life of the loan, one may conclude that in a crisis, for example in a restructuring exercise, such banks will be obliged to take leading roles on behalf of the syndicate. Horn accepts, however, that such a duty is

[76] Clark, K 'Problems and Solutions to Sovereign debt Restructuring' (1984) IFLR (October) 4–8 and Horn 'The Restructuring of International Loans and the Debt Crisis' (1984) IBL 404–409.

[77] Horn (above, n 76).

remote, and would, in any event, be restricted to giving information about the crisis to the other syndicate members.

**1.139** This conclusion is very probably correct, since if one closely examines the contractual relationships which exist between the parties to a syndicated loan agreement it is clear that no such duty can be found to exist. The duties of the arranging bank, for example, will be confined to forming the syndicate and drafting the loan documentation. Such banks will cease to occupy any special position in the syndicate unless they also act as agent bank once the loan agreement has been executed. Insofar as the agent bank is concerned, its duties will only commence once the loan has been executed and, as we have seen, the loan documentation will usually restrict its duties, largely to administrative matters. The agent bank will normally be bound to inform the syndicate members of the events which give rise to the need for a restructuring operation. Few loan agreements, however, will give the agent bank power to conclude restructuring negotiations on behalf of the syndicate and even if the agent bank is prepared to participate in such negotiations it may, before so participating, require the express approval of each syndicate member.

**1.140** It will be most important for the members of the steering committee to ensure that they do not become agents of the banks on whose behalf they are acting in the restructuring negotiations.

**1.141** A further problem for the steering committee is that it may come to acquire certain confidential or inside information concerning the borrower. If such information is material, the members of the steering committee should insist upon the borrower disclosing it to the other bank creditors. English law would also take a stern view towards any secret deals which may be agreed between the members of the steering committee and the borrower.[78]

### *Identifying the debts which are to be rescheduled*

**1.142** As we indicated earlier, the first, and perhaps the most difficult issue to resolve in a sovereign restructuring is precisely which of the borrower's debts are to be included in the negotiations. In most cases it will only be necessary to restructure part of a country's debt, the problem is: which part? The category of debt ultimately selected must be sufficiently broad to enable the sovereign debtor to re-establish itself, yet not so broad as to prejudice the cooperation of the banks which are to participate in the rescheduling. The state debtor will have additional motives for keeping the rescheduled package as small as possible, since margins and fees will generally be higher than those found in the credits originally advanced.

---

[78] *Hirachand Punamchand v Temple* [1911] 2 KB 330; *Barrett v United-Island Records Ltd* [2006] EWHC 1009 (Ch).

**1.143** The restructuring negotiations will normally be restricted to the state's external debt; few sovereigns would countenance external interference over local currency obligations. External debt is generally recognised as debt payable in a currency other than the debtor's local currency, to creditors who operate outside the jurisdiction of the debtor.

**1.144** Identifying the external debt will give a basis upon which the rescheduling negotiations can commence, although, as has already been indicated, no two restructurings are ever the same. Furthermore, although the external debt will provide a starting point, it will still be necessary to distinguish, amongst the external debts identified, those that will be rescheduled and those that will not.

**1.145** A further criterion commonly applied is that of rescheduled maturity. In other words, the rescheduling is often limited to those credits originally scheduled to mature within a given period of time.

**1.146** In many sovereign reschedulings a critical division has been made between those debts having a term of more than 12 months to run and those with less than 12 months remaining.

### *The new money agreement*

**1.147** An essential component of most large restructuring arrangements is the need to supply the borrower with new medium-term credits or, as it is often called, fresh money. The amount so required is often expressed as a percentage of the lending banks' current exposure to the borrower, although it should be emphasised that there is no legal obligation upon any of the creditors to provide funds for the new money agreement. Most banks recognise, however, that they will have to carry rescheduled debt for several years, particularly in the case of sovereign debt. In addition, they recognise the need to provide fresh credits to various state and corporate borrowers, until more stable repayment positions can be achieved. Without the new money agreements it is difficult to see how many of the recent rescheduling agreements could have been reached.

**1.148** The fresh money is normally provided in predetermined stages and, for obvious reasons, a considerable degree of control is exercised over the borrower's ability to draw down the fresh money. For this reason the new money agreement is normally kept as an independent obligation, entirely separate from the old money documents.

### *Key provisions of the restructuring process*

**1.149** The documentation evidencing both the rescheduling and new money agreements will contain many of the clauses commonly found in international loan agreements, although the precise wording of the various clauses may differ to reflect the bargaining position of the respective parties. In most cases, therefore, the documentation will be drafted heavily in favour of the lenders.

**1.150** A fundamental principle exposed by these agreements is that the lenders which acquiesce in the restructuring arrangement will, in return, be repaid on a fair and reasonable basis. In other words, they will be given parity of treatment vis-à-vis those creditors with comparable indebtedness whose debts have not been included within the rescheduling. Comparable indebtedness, therefore, encompasses any other debt which satisfies the criteria used to identify the debt being rescheduled, but which, for some reason, is not so rescheduled on similar terms. In addition, the borrower will be expected to meet its non-rescheduled obligations in the terms outlined during the restructuring negotiations. Preferential payment of such debt will obviously be disadvantageous to those lenders which agree to reschedule their own credits.

**1.151** In order to promote parity of treatment, certain contractual provisions have become a common feature of the restructuring documentation. The precise wording of these clauses will obviously be tailor made for each particular restructuring and, for present purposes, some general principles will be highlighted.

### Comparable indebtedness covenants

**1.152** One method of achieving parity of treatment for different categories of comparable indebtedness is to ensure that the debtor expressly undertakes, within the restructuring agreements, not to pay comparable indebtedness' without the consent of the lenders whose credits are rescheduled.

**1.153** A major practical problem with this type of clause is that it will be difficult to monitor. Additionally, it may not be feasible for the debtor to comply with such a clause, since it may have the effect of disrupting its trading activities and thus be counterproductive insofar as the rescheduling lenders are concerned.

**1.154** The clause may also pose legal problems in that any attempt to enforce such a covenant may, under English law, lay the lenders open to an action in tort for inducing the debtor to breach contractual obligations owed to third party creditors.

### Mandatory prepayment provisions

**1.155** Another method by which the lenders may attempt to impose parity of treatment is by incorporating mandatory prepayment provisions within the restructuring documentation. Such provisions are similar to the sharing clauses which are commonly found in syndicated loan agreements and require that a reduction in the exposure of third-party creditors must be accompanied by a pro rata reduction in the exposure of those lenders whose credits have been rescheduled. The precise wording of the pro rata clause may vary and in some cases a mandatory prepayment will only be required if so requested by the lenders, or at least the majority of them.[79]

**1.156** Alternatively, a letter of priority could be drafted between the lenders whereby one party is given priority in repayment, normally in return for advancing further moneys. As there can be doubts as to whether the other banks will be receiving consideration for this a deed of priority may be used instead to guarantee enforceability.

#### Other clauses which seek to maintain parity of treatment

**1.157** In addition to the clauses already identified most restructuring agreements will contain, negative pledge clauses, pari passu sharing clauses and cross default clauses, the purpose of which will be to prevent discrimination and preserve equality as between creditors of the debtor. All of these clauses have been considered in detail elsewhere in this work and will not be dealt with any further here.

### *Availability of foreign exchange*

**1.158** In the case of most sovereign restructurings the crisis which led to the need to restructure will usually have been precipitated by an insufficient supply of foreign exchange to service the country's external debt. The immediate response of most governments when faced with a major debt crisis is to impose exchange control regimes with varying degrees of stringency. A sovereign state will obviously control the movement of foreign exchange following the introduction of such a regime and it will, therefore, be open to the sovereign to manipulate the allocation of foreign exchange to various state entity borrowers, for example, public corporations. It will be crucial in such a case for the lenders to inhibit the sovereign's power of discrimination with regard to foreign exchange, although in practical terms few sovereigns will be prepared to guarantee the availability of foreign exchange.

---

79 *Re Kaupthung, Singer and Frieldander* [2011] UKSC 48, *Manning v AIG Europe Ltd, Robinson v AIG Europe Ltd.* Also known as *Re SSSL Realisations* [2006] EWCA Civ 7, [2006] Ch 610, [2006] 2 WLR 1369. See also *Mills v HSBC Trustees (CI) Ltd* [2009] EWHC 3377 (Ch) and *Cattles Plc v Welcome Financial Services Ltd* [2009] EWHC 3027 (Ch). Discussed at J M Phillips, 'The Rule Against Double Proof Trumps Cherry v Boultbee' (2012) 27(2) BJIBFL 75–77 and D Marks, 'Double Proof Positive: a Return to the Proper Order of Things – the Rule Against Double Proof Trumps Set Off and the rule in Cherry v Boultbee.' (2012) 25(3) Insolv Int 33–37.

*Importance of supra-national organisations*

**1.159** There are at least three supra-national organisations which play an important role in sovereign restructuring negotiations. The Bank for International Settlements is often called upon to provide bridging finance whilst the recovery plan is being worked out and the World Bank has over the years developed a high level of expertise in supervising sovereign restructurings. It is without doubt, however, the International Monetary Fund (IMF) which plays the most important role.

**1.160** IMF membership will be vital to enhance a sovereign debtor's credit standing, and it is common for IMF membership to be a condition precedent in restructuring arrangements. Acceptance of any IMF recovery plan will also normally be a condition precedent and compliance with its terms a condition subsequent. The IMF will also play an important role in the dissemination of information concerning the debtor's financial condition, and its recovery scheme often becomes the cornerstone of the restructuring negotiations, with events of default in the new agreements commonly linked to the debtor's performance under its terms.

**1.161** Despite all the criticisms which have been levelled at the IMF's role in the international debt crisis its importance within the restructuring process cannot be over emphasised, and in many cases official creditors and commercial banks will simply refuse to commence restructuring negotiations until a recovery programme has been agreed between the IMF and the debtor country.

### Conclusion

**1.162** There can be little doubt that restructuring arrangements pose innumerable problems for those conducting negotiations on behalf of commercial bank creditors. This chapter has considered just a few of these difficulties, an extensive treatise being impossible owing to the ad hoc manner in which the arrangements are usually conducted. Each particular debtor, be it a corporate or a sovereign state, will have its own idiosyncratic problems, and it will be the job of the bankers, together with their lawyers, to address these problems in the restructuring agreements which are finally worked out.

## Other relevant agreements

### 'Floor/ceiling' agreements

**1.163** Floor agreements, ceiling, or cap agreements and floor ceiling or collar agreements are commonly used. A floor agreement is one entered into by a bank and a customer under which, in return for an up front and one time only fee, the bank provides the customer with protection against a fall in interest rates. The essential elements of the agreement are:

(a) a notional principal amount, for example, £10 million;

(b) a 'floor' rate below which the customer does not wish to see market interest rates fall, for example, 5% per annum;

(c) the market base interest rate to be used, for example, SONIA; and

(d) the tenor of the agreement, for example, × years and the reference periods to be used, for example, six months.

**1.164** On each agreed reference date, there are compared (a) the 'floor' rate, and (b) the base rate quoted in the market for deposits in the currency of the notional principal amount for delivery on the reference date and for a period equal to the reference period in question. If the market rate is lower than the 'floor' rate, then the bank pays the customer a sum calculated at an annual rate equal to the shortfall (expressed as a percentage rate) for the relevant reference period on the agreed notional principal amount. For example, SONIA for a notional principal amount is 0.5% on a given reference date for a six month (183 days) reference period. Using a 1.5% floor rate, the bank pays to the customer an amount calculated as follows:

$$\pounds 10\text{m} \times 1\%^{*} \times \frac{183}{365} = \pounds 50{,}136.98$$

* The difference between SONIA (0.5 %) and the 1.5% floor rate.

If, in fact, on a given reference date, SONIA is equal to, or more than, the floor rate, no payment is made by either party.[80]

**1.165** A customer might use a floor agreement in order to protect himself against a situation where he owned a floating rate investment, but had funded that investment on a long term, fixed rate basis. A ceiling agreement provides inverse protection, ie, against the risk of a rise in interest rates. The structure of a ceiling agreement is identical to that of a floor agreement, save that the bank pays the customer in the event that market rates of interest are higher than the chosen reference rate. A ceiling agreement might be used to enable the customer to hedge a fixed rate investment which has been funded by means of floating rate funds.

**1.166** Both floor and ceiling agreements involve the payment to the bank by the customer of up front fees. These fees are not cheap and the

[80] D Brigo and F Mercurio, *Interest Rate Models – Theory and Practice*, 2nd edn (Springer Verlag, 2006).

collar agreement has been designed to reduce the fees and to tailor the product more precisely to the customer's requirements. Under a collar the bank could sell to the customer a ceiling, ie the bank would grant ceiling protection in return for an upfront fee, and simultaneously the customer would sell to the bank a floor for an upfront fee on terms involving potential payments by the customer using a notional principal amount, reference dates and periods and a base market rate identical to those applicable to the ceiling it had purchased from the bank. The net effect would be that: (i) the two fees are netted out, normally producing one fee payable to the bank of an appropriately low figure; and (ii) payments would move from the bank if the market rate exceeded the chosen ceiling and from the customer if the market rate fell below the chosen floor. If the market rates were somewhere between the two, then no payments would be made. The customer has thus effectively collared his interest costs between the floor and the ceiling: he does not suffer if market rates rise above the ceiling but nor can he benefit if they fall below the floor.

## Insurance law considerations

**1.167** To the non-lawyer, the three instruments, namely, floors, ceilings, and collars might well be viewed as contracts of insurance. After all, in return for an up-front fee (the premium), the bank (the insurer) is undertaking with the customer (the insured) that, upon the happening of a specified contingency (market rates of interest moving above or below an identified fixed rate), the bank (insurer) will indemnify the customer (insured) against loss by paying the customer an amount sufficient to cover the customer against the excess or shortfall rate calculated on a pre-agreed principal amount.

**1.168** Are the three instruments to be regarded by the lawyer as contracts of insurance? The area of doubt seems to concern the question of whether the payment being made by the bank on each reference date is truly an indemnity against loss. It seems likely that the mere fact that the calculation of the amount of that payment is by reference to external market factors (current interest rates), rather than to the customer's specific individual circumstances, is not sufficient to prevent the transaction being regarded as an indemnity.

**1.169** The argument, in insurance's favour, would be that, since the protection is being purchased to hedge against the contingency of adverse rate movements, if the protection were not there, loss would follow if that contingency occurred, eg, the customer might be obliged to pay to the person funding it on a SONIA basis an amount of interest exceeding the yield on its fixed rate investment.

**1.170** On this basis, the three instruments could be viewed as contracts of insurance. The matter is far from clear, however, as many of the normal business characteristics of an insurance arrangement are absent and the court will take such absence into account. This can be seen from a dictum of Romer J in *Seaton v Heath*,[81] where he said:

> '... contracts of insurance are generally matters of speculation where the person desiring to be insured has the means of knowledge as to the risk, and the insurer has not the means or not the same means. The insured generally puts the risk before the insurer as a business transaction and the insurer on the risk stated fixes a proper price to remunerate him for the risk being undertaken.'

It is debateable how useful this definition is in the current commercial environment. One could scarcely argue that a bank selling a floor understands less well than the customer the nature of the risk of SONIA falling below a particular rate during a specific period. Equally, the idea of the customer putting these risks before the bank as a business transaction does not really ring true as a description of the three instruments. There are also definitions in the Regulated Activities Order[82] and of non-consumer insurance contracts in the Insurance Act 2015 and the prudential definition in GIM1030.

**1.171** As a result, the position has to be regarded as unclear. If, however, the three instruments were to be regarded as insurance contracts, what are the consequences? The first is that the contract would be one of the utmost good faith, requiring the 'insured' to disclose to the 'insurer' all material facts which would influence a prudent insurer. Frankly, where the insurer is a bank active in the interest rate risk management market, the idea of such a duty to disclose being imposed on a corporate customer seeking to control its interest costs is unrealistic. The area of worry would be in the context of a floor/ceiling or collar, where one might argue that there are two insurance contracts; the floor (where the customer is the insurer) and the 'ceiling' (where the bank is the insurer).The risk would be that the customer's obligations under the floor could be prejudiced by the absence of full disclosure by the bank of all material facts, eg, historical frequency of interest rates falling below the chosen 'floor.' The other area of risk concerns the statutory requirements governing insurance business. Essentially, if a person 'carries on' any 'insurance business' in the UK, an offence is committed by that person,[83] unless he is authorised to do so by the Prudential Regulation Authority and the Financial Conduct Authority.

**1.172** Clearly, 'business' denotes some element of continuity although there is some authority for the argument that an isolated transaction may, in some circumstances, amount to 'business'. If the sale by a

81 [1889] 1 QB 782.

82 Financial Services and Markets Act 2000 (Regulated Activities) Order, SI 2001/544 as amended, Arts 10–13.

83 Financial Services and Markets Act 2000 (FSMA 2000), s 23.

bank of a 'floor' or a 'ceiling' is a contract of insurance, then if that bank sells such protection sufficiently frequently for it to become a 'business', then unless the terms of their FCA license permitted it an offence would be committed. However, the relevant legislation[84] does not provide an exhaustive definition of 'contracts of insurance' in the context of regulation, and it would appear that the FCA's Handbook[85] does not bring such an arrangement within their interpretation of the definition.

**1.173** However, were this to be determined not to be the case an enforceability issue would arise because of the Financial Services and Markets Act 2000, ss 26-29. These deal with the enforceability of regulated activities being carried on in breach of the general prohibition on acting without FCA authorisation or where there is FCA authorisation but something has been done by a third party on contravention of the general prohibition.[86] The party who has so acted is deemed in possession of an unenforceable contract.[87] However, the other party can claim back any money or property paid plus compensation for any loss caused by having had to part with it.[88] The court does have the discretion to allow the contract to be enforced where it is deemed just and equitable.[89] The same principle applies to deposit taking in breach of the general prohibition.[90]

**1.174** Perhaps the common sense solution is to fall back on the argument that current market practice is to treat such contracts as not being insurance agreements. On the basis of the principle in *Goodwin v Robarts*[91] the courts would, therefore, follow the commercial practice. (This is discussed in **Chapter 4**).

## Documentation for 'collar' agreements

**1.175** The documentation for a collar agreement tends to follow the documentation applicable to derivatives (see **Chapter 6**). The rationale behind this is clear: although, on a given date, the nature of the obligations of the parties is such that a payment can only move from one of them, and not the other, each of them have a contingent future claim, or series of contingent future claims, on the other which has a business value and with respect to which the usual range of protections would be appropriate, eg, grossing up and compensation on termination.

---

84 SI 2001/544 as amended.
85 At FCA PERG 5.3.
86 Unless the party is exempt.
87 FSMA 2000, ss 26(1) and 27(1).
88 FSMA 2000, s 26(2).
89 FSMA 2000, s 28(3).
90 FSMA 2000, s 29.
91 (1876) 1 App Cas 476.

**1.176** For floor or ceiling agreements, one might take the view that the position is rather different. After all, only one of the parties (the customer) has the benefit of a series of future and contingent claims on the other (the bank): the bank received on inception of the transaction all the money that it is going to receive (the fee) and has accordingly no further interest in the inclusion in the document of any extra protections beyond the bald statement of its obligations to pay money to the customer in the event that interest rates move in the appropriate direction.

**1.177** In practice these days the ISDA standard form contracts are used by most market participants and relevant support documentation is also available.[92]

## Security

**1.178** In domestic transactions the taking of security is straightforward. In international transactions it is less common, in part because of the tendency for lenders to rely more on credit ratings, as discussed above, and in part because of the cost and inconvenience of enforcing cross-border security in many instances. In addition, the borrower may have provided negative pledge obligations to a previous lender (see above). Security may be taken in specialised areas such as project finance, and ship or aircraft finance but the specifics of this are beyond the scope of this book. In the case of syndicated lending and bond issues (see **Chapters 2** and **4**) security may be taken and will in these instances be held by a trustee holding the security for the benefits of the lenders as the parties for whom it will be held will tend to change and priorities could be lost if the security has to be periodically retaken.

**1.179** The reason for taking security is of course so that the lender can take priority over other lenders in the event of the borrower's insolvency and attach the assets that have been secured to take back the money owed to them. In the event of a Sovereign borrower (see **Chapter 11**) the lender may find a greater degree of reluctance to provide security to provide against the borrower's insolvency or a decision being taken not to repay the debt. In this event the lender will be able to enforce the debt against assets owned by the borrower provided an appropriate waiver of immunity clause was included. Typically, these might be bullion, investments or trade receivables due to the borrower which are outside the borrower's state. Alternatively, security might be held simply to enable the lender to take control of and manage the property or even the business of the borrower. This could arise where real property is concerned through the appointment

92 See, eg the ISDA Disclosure Annex for Interest Rate Transaction, 2024 edition.

of a Law of Property Act receiver.[93] Another reason for taking security may simply be to stop other lenders coming later and acquiring it. As seen this would be considerably safer than relying on a negative pledge clause.

## Conflict of laws issues and security

**1.180** If security is taken, the issue of which country's law shall apply may arise. This is a particular problem with movable assets such as ships and aircraft. With immovable assets such as land the problem is less common but may still arise where the security is provided in one jurisdiction for a loan in another.

**1.181** Tangible movables are governed by the law of the place where the assets are at the time of the transfer[94] and the following key principles apply.

- The validity of an expropriation or transfer of title – which would include the granting of a security interest – is governed by the law of the state in which the asset is situated at the time of the expropriation or other transaction, even if the asset is otherwise taken out of that state. The rule is subject to some exceptions such as where the foreign law is penal, oppressive or morally repugnant.
- An English court will not recognise the validity of any expropriation, disposition or transaction affecting a proprietary interest in movables according to the law of one state if the asset is outside that state at the time of disposition unless that disposition also conforms with the law of the state in which the asset is at the time of the transaction.

**1.182** In the case of ambulatory movables such as ships and aircraft the UK approach is to apply the law of the flag to issues relating to transfer and security. A problem however arises. If the *lex situs* of an asset originally determines its transfer and the validity of any security, and the asset then moves to another state, the state in which the asset is now located may treat its own law as having an overriding effect. Some states do this in relation to any creditor in their own jurisdiction while others only do so in the case of a bona fide purchaser of an asset there. In some states jurisdiction will be held to apply only in the case of further dispositions of the property. In many states the host state will not recognise charges over ambulatory assets unless the lender has taken possession subsequent to the charge. In some states the

---

93 Law of Property Act 1925, s 109.

94 *Cammell v Sewell* (1860) 5 H&N 728; *Inglis v Robertson* [1898] AC 616. See also D Osborne, 'Lex Situs and Aircraft' (2004) 3(Aug) LMCLQ 303–312 and I Fletcher, 'Law of Insolvency' 5th edn (Sweet & Maxwell, 2017), Ch 29, s 2. 'International Effects of English Bankruptcy'.

doctrine of constructive possession applies where the mortgage controls the indicia of possession such as the key to a building. It may also be recognised where a third party controls the movable and promises to hold it for the benefit of the mortgagee. Sometimes possession of documents of title is regarded as equivalent to possession, eg, by possessing bills of lading.

**1.183** In the case of intangible assets matters are more complex as in the UK security is usually taken by a floating charge or occasionally a bill of sale.[95] The latter requires the assets to be specifically described and the details must be registered at the High Court within seven days of the bill's creation[96] or in the normal way at Companies House if taken over a company's intangible assets. Attempts were made over a number of years by many lenders to take a fixed charge over intangible assets, primarily books debts owed to the borrower. This cause of this is that on the borrower's insolvency a lender holding a fixed charge is in a much stronger position than one holding a floating charge because they move to the top of the queue of those paid on insolvency. However, in *National Westminster Bank plc v Spectrum Plus Ltd*[97] the House of Lords (with seven judges sitting) determined that this could not be done. This was because the charger had not been deprived of access to the proceeds of the debts when they were paid. It required a full denial of access to satisfy the final requirement in *Re Yorkshire Woolcombers Association.*[98] The requirements there were that for a floating charge to be successfully taken it had to be over a class of assets, which changed from time to time and which the borrower could not access. It was insufficient to impose a partial restriction[99] and also insufficient to divide them into debts and their collected state.[100] The account must effectively be blocked, with the option by the chargee to release them at their own discretion. Alternately a fixed charge could be taken by the charger assigning the proceeds to the chargee.

**1.184** Floating charges remain, therefore, as the main source of security over book debts and future acquired property. They exist as an equitable interest and require registration at Companies House in the same manner as a fixed charge. However, a fixed charge created after the floating charge will still take precedence as will the liquidator's costs and the preferential debts. Problems arise in the case of overseas assets as many civil law jurisdictions do not recognise floating charges.

---

[95] The government were going to abolish this and modernise the law with the Goods Mortgages Bill 2017, but it was withdrawn and there are no current plans to change the law.
[96] Bills of Sale Act 1878, s 10.
[97] [2005] UKHL 41, [2005] 4 All ER 209.
[98] [1903] 2 Ch 284.
[99] *Re Cosslett (Contractors) Ltd* [1998] Ch 495.
[100] *Re New Bullas Trading Ltd* [1994] 1 BCLC 485.

**1.185** A detailed analysis of charges is beyond the scope of the book; however, it is possible to isolate key problems that arise in the taking of security on an international basis.

- Does the borrower have unencumbered title to the asset concerned? In the case of land, the relevant registers should be checked. In the case of aircraft, the Civil Aviation Authority register, or overseas equivalent, should be checked and in the case of ships the UK shipping register. This is in addition to a search being done of the company which owns the asset at Companies House (or the overseas equivalent).
- Has the borrower the power to grant security? Ultra vires is no longer generally an issue with UK companies or a considerable number of foreign ones, but even in the United Kingdom such issues can arise with companies created by Act of Parliament, companies created by Royal Charter and companies where a statute may impinge on their contractual powers. In addition, it should be considered whether the security been properly authorised by the directors.
- Does the security contradict any negative pledge provided to a third party? There may be evidence registered against the borrower at Companies House. Breach of this could put the borrower in default of that agreement and potentially in cross default of other term loans and derivative contracts.
- Is it property that can only be covered by a floating charge? Some countries do not recognise floating charges, and some do not recognise charges over future acquired property. Others may recognise such a state of affairs as a contractual obligation but not as a property right conferring priority.
- What are the registration procedures and what is the legal position if registration does not take place? Is the charge void or if not, how does it affect priorities?
- Should the security be held by a trustee? This may be necessary in the case of a bond issue or where there is a syndicated loan. If there is a trustee will all jurisdictions involved recognise his existence and if not will they view him as either the owner of the property or see it is an agent and principal relationship, and in either case how will this work legally?
- If there is a clause in the secured agreement prohibiting prepayments or limiting how they may be applied there may be problems in some jurisdictions where the borrower will still be able to pay the loan off as they wish. The choice of law and jurisdiction clause should however retain the contract within a known jurisdiction where possible.
- Is stamp duty payable and if so by whom?

- Will the court concerned have jurisdiction to enforce security? In the United Kingdom that is not likely to be a problem even with sovereign borrowers provided they have signed a contract with a suitably worded waiver of immunity and enforcement clause (see **Chapter 11**).
- What remedies are available on default? Can the asset be sold and if so is there a limitation on how? In some states it must be sold by auction. Are any duties imposed on the party enforcing the charge when selling? Does the lender become the owner or do they just take possession and in the latter case do they keep any income or do they have to account for it? Are exchange controls going to be an issue when it comes to repatriating the money?
- Maintenance of value clauses are sometimes inserted so that additional property must be secured if the value of the collateral falls below a certain figure. Some states do not recognise these; some do but only if the class of assets concerned are defined. If an attempt is made to take the additional security too close in time to the borrower's insolvency there can also be problems with enforcement.[101]
- Must the mortgage debt be expressed in the currency of the state local to the asset even if that is not the currency of the loan? If that is the case some type of indexation arrangement will be necessarily associated with a maintenance of charged assets clause. There may also be issues with both in some states, though this is less common than in the past.

The obvious solution is to take legal advice from a firm of solicitors in the state where the assets are situated. Where large international legal practices are concerned such arrangements can be made internally.

## Whole of business and synthetic securitisation

**1.186** Whole of business securitisation arises where the whole cash flow from a business or a segregated part of it is used to raise finance via a company created for that one purpose (a Special Purpose Vehicle or SPV). The originator (borrower) contracts to ringfence the assets and income concerned and to provide a fixed and floating charge over them to that SPV. It should be added that this has no connection with securitised bond issues (see **Chapter 5**). The similar name is used simply because both use an SPV.

**1.187** Vink defines the arrangement as '... a form of asset backed financing in which operating assets are financed in the bond market via a bankruptcy remote vehicle (SPV) and in which the operating

101 Insolvency Act 1986, ss 238, 239 and 240.

company keeps complete control over the assets securitised. In cases of default, control is handed over to the security trustee for the benefit of the note lenders for the remaining term of financing.'[102] It may also be financed by a bank.

**1.188** In practice what is achieved is that the bank or bond holders lending the money obtain the maximum security protection and in the event of the borrower's insolvency they can to some extent take control of the insolvency process. They also have the ability to sell the SPV to a third party who may wish to take over the financing, provided the documentation gives them the power. Thus:

FIGURE 1: WHOLE OF BUSINESS SECURITISATION

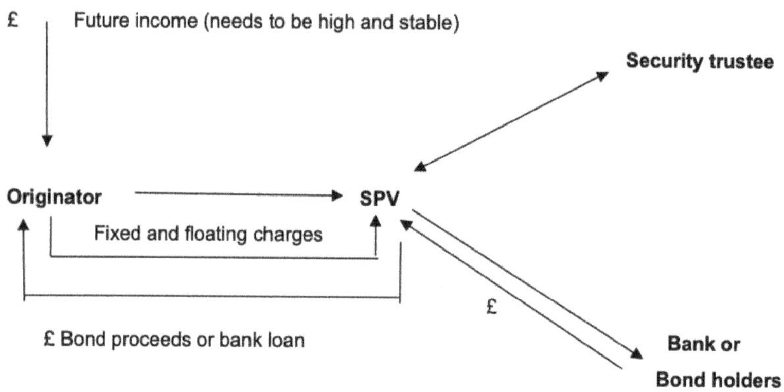


**1.189** Unlike an asset backed securitisation there is no transfer of the legal title to the future cash flow. The financing is not 'off balance sheet' for the originator. Thus, the use of the name 'securitisation' in this context is something of a misnomer. Indeed, the whole basis of the arrangement in the UK is that the SPV can take control of the originator on its insolvency by appointing a qualifying out of court administrator.[103] This is possible[104] by having substantially the whole of the originator's property covered by a number of qualifying floating charges which together relate to the whole or substantially the whole of the company's property. Alternatively, it can be achieved by charges or other forms of security covering the whole or substantially the whole of the originator's property, at least one of which is a qualifying floating charge.

**1.190** To work the arrangement requires an originator whose cash flows and earnings are high and predictable, that the business is one where it is not impossible to replace the originator with a third party,

---

[102] D Vink, 'A Primer on Whole Business Securitization' (2007) 1 Fiduciae at 7.

[103] Enterprise Act 2002, s 14(1), (2) and (3), inserted into the Insolvency Act 1986 at Sch B1.

[104] Under Enterprise Act 2006, s 14(3)(b) and (c), inserted into the Insolvency Act 1986 at Sch B1.

and where the speed of change in the originator's business is slow enough to permit monitoring and possible future control by the SPV.[105] Such arrangements should perhaps be seen as a category of secured lending which enables the originator to access large scale borrowing at a low rate of interest. Indeed, its attraction is that it tends to enable the originator to borrow larger sums over a longer period than would otherwise be possible.

**1.191** It is also possible to structure the arrangement with a credit default swap (see **6.17** and **6.18**) between the originator and the SPV with the credit default agreement requiring the SPV to make good any losses on the arrangement suffered by the originator.

FIGURE 2 SYNTHETIC WHOLE OF BUSINESS SECURITISATION WITH A CREDIT DEFAULT SWAP (CDS)

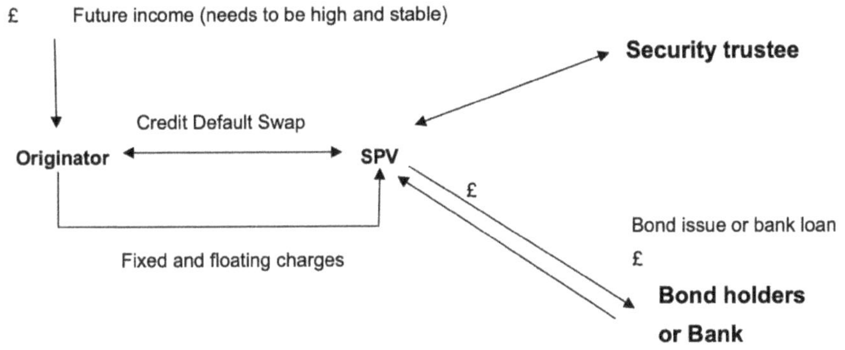


**1.192** McKnight is more precise in defining the arrangement as:

> '... intended to replicate much of the economic effect of a true sale securitisation but through the use of derivatives such as credit default swaps ... Instead of the originator transferring the underlying portfolio to the SPV at the outset of the transaction, the originator remains the owner of the portfolio but transfers the risk of default for some part of the portfolio to the SPV. This is done by ... entering into a credit default swap.'[106] (see **Chapter 6**)[107]

**1.193** This leaves the SPV carrying the risk of default of the assets covered by the swap and in return receives payment from the originator in proportion to the income they have earned from that portfolio of

---

105 Japan Credit Rating Agency Ltd, 'Whole Business Securitisation' (1 June 2012).

106 A McKnight, S Paterson and R Zakrewski, *Law Relating to International Finance*, 2nd edn (Oxford University Press, 2017), p 693.

107 See also the definition of synthetic securitisation in Regulation (EU) No 575/2013 of the European Parliament and of the Council of 26 June 2013 on prudential requirements for credit institutions and investment firms and amending Regulation (EU) No 648/2012 [2013] OJ L176/1 ('the Capital Requirement Regulation'), Art 242 (11): 'the transfer of risk is achieved by the use of credit derivatives or guarantees, and the exposures being securitised remain exposures of the original institution.'

assets. In the event of the SPV not wishing to carry the risk it faces under the contract it can enter into other swaps with third parties to cover the risk. It does not have to be a credit default swap as such but credit spread swaps or credit linked notes could be used.[108]

## Quasi security

### Hypothetication[109]

**1.194** This consists of the borrower providing the lender with the right to seize and sell an asset if a loan is not repaid. Technically the arrangement is normally structured as a sale of the assets with an obligation to buy them back at a slightly later date and a slightly higher price. In England and Wales, it is commonly used in the repo markets (repurchase agreements). Here the borrower transfers the possession of assets, usually a portfolio of shares, to the lender for a fixed time period. If at the end of that period the loan and interest is not repaid then the lender can sell the shares to cover the debt. It is also commonly used in brokerage where an investor asks the broker to buy investments at a margin. If the investor does not make a payment the broker can cover the amount by selling some of the shares. They can also be sold if the shares have dropped in value and the borrower does not meet a margin call.

### Rehypothetication

**1.195** This is an arrangement whereby a borrower will provide security to a lender, often in the form of a portfolio of shares for what is usually a short-term loan. Essentially the investments are sold in return for a commitment to buy them back at a slightly higher price at a slightly later date. Where this differs from a normal secured loan and hypothetication is that the borrower gives written consent for the lender to utilise the security in other deals. In return the lender quotes a lower interest rate as it can profit from use of the security. The borrower contractually abandons the equity of redemption and accepts that if it pays off the loan the lender may need to transfer back other securities of the same value as those used as security because the lender still has the tied up in another deal. Thus:

---

108 See I Bell and P Dawson, 'Synthetic Securitization: Use of Derivative Technology for Credit Transfer' 12 Duke Journal of Comparative and International Law (2002) 541 at 559 and DR Muńoz, *The Law of Transnational Securitization* (Oxford University Press, 2010), p 9.

109 *Hypotheca* is a non-possessory security interest originally found in Roman Law.

FIGURE 3 REHYPOTHETICATION

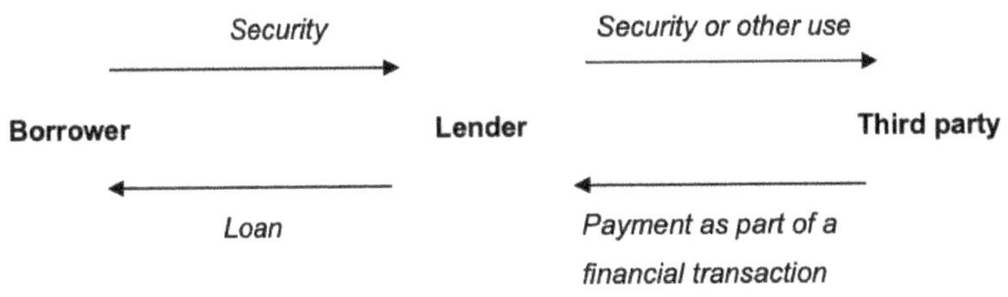


There are two methods of creating this arrangement:

- a security arrangement with a contractual right for the lender to re-use; or
- by transfer of the legal ownership of the collateral.

There is a great deal of this activity in what is called the 'prime brokerage' market, though it did develop a bad reputation for a while after the collapse of Lehman Bros in 2008, when a lot of security could not be returned.[110]

## Guarantees in international term loans

**1.196** The matter of guarantees as a general issue is beyond the scope of a text on international banking law. However, certain matters arise. The obvious purpose is to cover the scenario where the primary debtor cannot repay and, therefore, a secondary one is sought to commit themselves to do so by the lender. This might be sought from another company in the group or more commonly an omnibus guarantee from all the companies in the group.[111] A second reason is to make sure that a parent company exercises close control over a subsidiary because they have given a guarantee on their behalf or that the directors do because they have given personal guarantees. In some cases a guarantee may be sought from a central bank to secure non-interference in the event of exchange controls being brought back in or to stop a change in that state's law to the detriment of the lender. In any of these events the guarantee is also needed to give the lender a right over any security that is taken from another company in the group or a director as otherwise there is no legal basis for claiming against it.[112]

**1.197** Although the term 'guarantee' is widely used in practice many banks use a form of words that renders the so called guarantor a

---

110 It also developed one after the 1929 Wall Street crash.

111 Often in the form of an omnibus guarantee and set off which will often have security attached.

112 *Birkmyr v Darnell* (1704) 1 Salk 27; *Moschi v Lep Air Services Ltd* [1973] AC 331; *Argo Caribbean Group Ltd v Lewis* [1976] 2 Lloyd's Rep 286; *General Produce Co v United Bank Ltd* [1979] 2 Lloyd's Rep 255.

primary obligor to settle the debt.[113] Such an arrangement is called an indemnity.[114] The third possibility is a letter of comfort where a non-legally binding quasi-guarantee is given. The attraction of this to the 'guarantor' is that the arrangement will not appear on their balance sheet as a contingent liability. Normally large companies will stand by such obligations due to the damage to their reputations if they do not. This is not always the case however.[115]

**1.198** In some cases, the guarantee may be a more complex document including some of the terms normally found in the term loan agreement itself. This would occur where the lender wished to keep a close eye on the guarantor. Typical clauses would be covenants, a negative pledge, an undertaking to provide financial and other information, representations, warranties and grossing up clauses. If it is a syndicated loan the guarantee should have pari passu and sharing causes. Normally the guarantee will be made subject to the same law and jurisdiction as the loan agreement so that a single action could be brought against the borrower and the guarantor.

**1.199** If the guarantor is independent of the borrower and has not got the capacity to control him, additional terms will be included. A grace period is often provided so that the guarantor only has to pay a claim a set number of days after the maturity of any claim. This is to give the guarantor the opportunity to cure the borrower's default and thus the guarantor can be sure there is a genuine default before they pay. It is also not uncommon for the guarantor to object to being made liable for costs such as commissions, fees, liability under indemnities and grossing up clauses and in such cases the lender may agree to make the guarantee cover only the loan and interest. One possibility could be to get the guarantor to agree to adopt the loan in the event of it not being paid on schedule by the debtor. It is also a good idea to include a clause that prohibits the guarantor from applying sums received from the debtor to sums that the guarantor has not guaranteed. This can be extended to sums received by set off or from other security.

**1.200** In addition, the lender may not be able to accelerate on the debtor's default without calling on the guarantor first and this may be coupled with the period of default referred to above. If there is a default it may be provided that the lender shall take all steps to minimise his losses and that he should first proceed against the debtor perhaps

---

113 *Davys v Buswell* [1913] 2 KB 47.

114 In practice bank documents are usually hybridised in that the guarantor both agrees to guarantee the borrower's debt and also to be primarily responsible for payment. For a recent case on the issue see *NatWest Market NV and another v CMIS Nederland BV and another* [2025] EWHC 37 (Comm).

115 *Kleinwort Benson v Malaysia Mining Corporation* [1989] 1 All ER 785 and *Atlantic Computers Plc (in Administration)*, also known as *National Australia Bank Ltd v Soden* [1995] BCC 696. It depends on the exact words used *Bowerman v Association of British Travel Agents* [1996] CLC 451. For background see M Elland-Goldsmith 'Comfort Letters in English Law and Practice' IBLJ 1994, 5, 527–541 and H Ramsay 'Comfort Letters' (1995) 14 (7) IBFL 74–75.

on the guarantor's direction and only then against the guarantor. The guarantor may reserve the right to substitute himself as the creditor by purchasing the debt from the lender at any time, so that if there is evidence of a likelihood of the debtor defaulting, the guarantor can proceed against the debtor's assets immediately. An assignment of the debt by the debtor may also be prohibited as the identity of the debtor and their credit rating may be the very reasons the debt is being guaranteed.

**1.201** A guarantor, and especially one with no control over the debtor may wish to have a greater degree of control by requiring that the lender keep them informed concerning any matter that may affect his liability. This clause will of course require the debtor's consent because of the doctrine of banker-customer confidentiality.[116]

### Legal problems

**1.202** The formalities need to be observed, namely that a guarantee must be in writing. This is not the case with an indemnity but given the realities of international banking it always will be reduced to a written contract.

**1.203** Capacity is also an issue. In some states this is more likely to emerge as an issue than in others and it should be remembered that capacity will be governed by the law of the state in which the company is domiciled not that of the loan agreement when this is different.[117] Where the primary debt cannot be enforced, someone accepting a secondary liability will not be liable either. This is another reason for having the 'guarantor' accept primary liability as an indemnifier.

### Other considerations with guarantees

**1.204** Key issues to be considered are as follows:

- The governing law and jurisdiction should both preferably be the same as that governing the loan itself.
- The consideration should be stated to avoid running foul of the rule against past consideration.[118]
- The guarantee should be expressed to be a continuing obligation covering all liabilities of the principal debtor. This avoids the rule in

116 *Tournier v National Provincial and Union Bank of England* [1924] 1 KB 461.

117 *Merrill Lynch v Municipality of Piraeus, (No 2)* [1997] CLC 1214, 6 Bank LR 247. *Rimpacific Navigation Inc v Daehan Shipbuilding Co Ltd* [2009] EWHC 2941 (Comm); [2010] 2 All ER (Comm) 814.

118 *Roscorla v Thomas* (1842) 3 QB 234 subject to the limitations in *Pao On v La Yiu Long* [1980] AC 614.

*Clayton's case*[119] by preventing the guarantor's liability becoming fixed when the debtor becomes liable for a particular sum.

- There should be protective clauses to allow the lender to modify the obligations of the debtor without discharging the guarantor. Without this any modification would discharge the guarantor.[120]
- There should, when appropriate, be a clause enabling the lender to release a co-guarantor without discharging the other(s).
- There should be clauses enabling the lender to release security or deal with it without releasing the guarantor, and so that the security continues to be security for non-guaranteed debts even though the guarantor may have paid the non-guaranteed debts off. In effect the guarantor's rights of subrogation are excluded.
- There should be a clause enabling the lender to pay sums received from the guarantor into a suspense account.
- There may be a 'conclusive evidence' clause enabling the lender to state what the guaranteed debt is so that the guarantor cannot then challenge this.
- The guarantee may be for a limited sum or the 'whole debt' or for the whole debt with a provision limiting liability.
- The guarantee can be for a limited duration or for or a specific transaction, or it may be continuing.

## Comfort letters

**1.205** As already discussed, these are given by a party who does not wish to become legally bound and it is often provided by a parent for a subsidiary or one company in a group to another. Generally speaking, they begin with a statement that the comforter is aware of and approves the proposed loan or transaction and then states that the parent agrees to maintain an interest in the borrower's share capital, and will give some financial support. They may promise to maintain good management and not to take assets or money from the subsidiary. Clearly such a state of affairs is not desirable from the lender's point of view.

**1.206** In the UK, such letters are not normally binding but those drafting such an agreement for a firm providing the letter must be careful with the wording. Essentially in England and Wales a document

---

119 *Devaynes v Noble, (Clayton's Case)* (1816) 1 Mes 572. See 'Drafting Security Documentation to Rebut the Presumption in Clayton's Case: Continuing Security and Ruling Off Provision.' (2014) 29(1) BJIBFL 74.

120 *Marubeni Hong Kong & South China Ltd v Mongolian Government* [2004] EWHC 472, 2 Lloyd's Rep 198, QBD.

clearly stated not to be legally binding will be treated in this way by the courts.[121]

**1.207** It is wise to use terms such as 'this agreement is binding in honour only and does not constitute a legally binding contract'. A common wording is, 'It is our intention (or policy) to do …', but this seems less safe. It should not however be assumed that if the term 'letter of comfort' is used in the heading or the document that this will stop it becoming legally enforceable. The content and the wording of any related documents could have the opposite effect.[122]

**1.208** There are additional legal issues that may help protect a party providing a letter of comfort, for example the English law requirement that the terms of a contract must be sufficiently certain for a court to enforce it. The vagueness of many letters of comfort could well result in this rule determining that they are not enforceable.

**1.209** With overseas jurisdictions it is a more complex problem and local advice will be needed by the comforter's solicitors to make sure it is not legally binding there.

---

121 *Jones v Vernon's Pools* [1938] 2 All ER 626; *Rose & Frank Co v Crompton & Bros Ltd* [1923] 2 KB 657.

122 It depends on the precise wording. *Bowerman v Association of British Travel Agents* [1996] CLC 451.

# Chapter 2 Primary Syndication

## Introduction

**2.1** The business of syndicating loans developed principally because many loans became so large that no single financial institution had either the capacity or the desire to lend the entire sum on its own.[1] The amount of money involved may exceed the limits that the bank can lend because of the impact of the relevant legislation and bank regulations relating to capital adequacy.[2] Even if it does not do so the sum involved may exceed limits imposed by the bank's management for lending to a single borrower or put the bank above the limit that can be loaned to a particular market sector. There are a number of potential types of borrower in such situations. They are often large, multi-national public companies. They may also be sovereign borrowers, joint ventures, state owned institutions, or financial institutions such as lease hire companies buying and leasing aircraft or other expensive items to lease out. The form of the company will itself raise a number of issues, capacity and enforcement being critical ones. The term of the loan can be anything from six months, though it is not usually so short, or up to 25 years in the case of some project finance loans. Over recent years the size of syndicated deals has varied from US $20 million to US $55 billion[3] with a global syndicated loan market of US $782.79 billion in 2025.[4] Interest rates are normally variable, but this is effectively done by having a series of set terms with fixed rates which are reset according to a simple formula. The reset can be monthly or as far apart as six monthly.

**2.2** Current practice is that many syndicates are created by banks which plan on selling on their involvement in the syndicate (see **Chapter 3**) straight away. The banks themselves do not currently hold sufficient funds to provide the market with all the loans it requires. Thus a 'shadow market' has developed whereby other parties

---

1 The first was put in place in London in 1968.

2 Regulation (EU) No 575/2013 of the European Parliament and of the Council of 26 June 2013 on prudential requirements for credit institutions and investment firms and amending Regulation (EU) No 648/2012 [2013] OJ L176/1 ('the Capital Requirement Regulation'). The departure of the UK from the EU will not significantly affect this as the UK is a member of the Basel Committee where the relevant current regulations, Basel III were created. The EU Regulation enforces this subject to some significant additions.

3 T Rhodes, *Syndicated Lending,* 5th edn (Euromoney, 2009), p 20.

4 www.thebusinessresearchcompany.com/report/syndicated-loans-global-market-report [Accessed 1 January 2026].

holding large amounts such as pension funds, investment vehicles, hedge funds, insurance companies and some large corporations enter the market and buy the repayments of loans which have been made. In such a situation the bank will look to make a profit from a front-end fee for entering into the loan.

**2.3** The process of syndication is the process by which a group of banks lends directly to the borrower under a single loan agreement. The lending banks have always perceived syndication as nothing more than a collection of individual loan contracts conveniently documented in one single agreement.[5] This should not be confused with a funded sub-participation agreement which is examined in **Chapter 3**. That is the technique employed for a single bank to lend directly to the borrower and then cover all or part of its interest in that loan by borrowing from other lenders.

**2.4** As in the case of a single lender international term loan agreement, there is no such thing as a standard syndicated loan. The number of participating banks can vary enormously (from 2 to over 200), as can the amount being advanced. Some syndicated loans may be underwritten[6] though most are put together on a 'best efforts' basis, some are 'club' loans[7], some may be secured loans, some evidenced by notes and some guaranteed. All these factors will have a major impact on the documentation which evidences the transaction and the cost, but the basic underlying legal issues remain constant. The documentation itself tends to be lengthy.[8]

**2.5** A number of banks will, therefore, agree to each of them lending part of the money. There are two main ways of structuring such arrangements. The money might be loaned directly by the arranging

---

5 For a general overview see P Wood, *International Loans, Bonds, Guarantees and Legal Opinions*, 3rd edn (Sweet & Maxwell, 2019), Chs 1–3.

6 This occurs where the arranging bank(s) guarantee the entire loan, thus acting as an underwriter, and then puts together the syndicate. If the syndicate cannot be fully formed the arranger will be obliged to loan the balance and then sell that part of the loan on the secondary debt market.

7 Here the arranging bank has pre-arranged the loan with a group of banks that are already in place.

8 The arrangement does not amount to a partnership under the Partnership Act 1890 because the parties are not carrying on a business in common but simply engaging in a lending arrangement. In particular the Partnership Act 1890, s (2(2) states that the sharing of gross returns between parties does not in itself indicate that the parties are partners. For a further discussion see Bucheit 'Is Syndicated Lending a Joint Venture?' [1985] IFLR 12–14. See McKnight and Zakrzewski. *The Law of Loan Agreements and Syndicated Lending* (Oxford University Press, 2019) 3.26 – 3.29. Nor will it amount to a collective investment scheme. See the Financial Services and Markets Act 2000 (Collective Investment Schemes) Order 2001, SI 2001/1062 Art 3 and Sch 6. The recent case of *Kirschner v JPMorgan Chase Bank, N A* No 21-2726 (2nd Cir 2023) illustrates that they are not a security under New York state law.

bank[9] to the borrower, but the arranging bank then syndicates a major part of the loan. This has the advantage that the fact that the loan is being syndicated it can be hidden from the borrower. This may be important for the bank arranging the deal to maintain its relationship with an existing customer where the arranging bank does not want to risk a direct relationship developing between the borrower and any of the other banks, in case one of those banks steals the client from them.

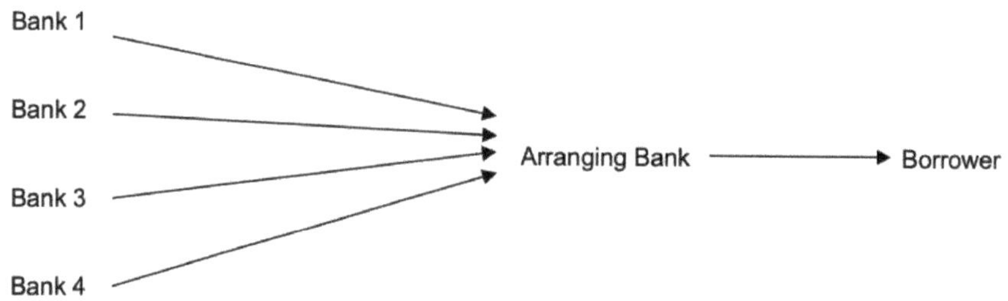


**2.6** Alternately one bank may arrange putting the deal together and the syndicate members may lend directly to the borrower (see diagram below). It may then continue as the agent bank, though on occasion another bank will end up doing this. Agency is discussed below at **2.63**.

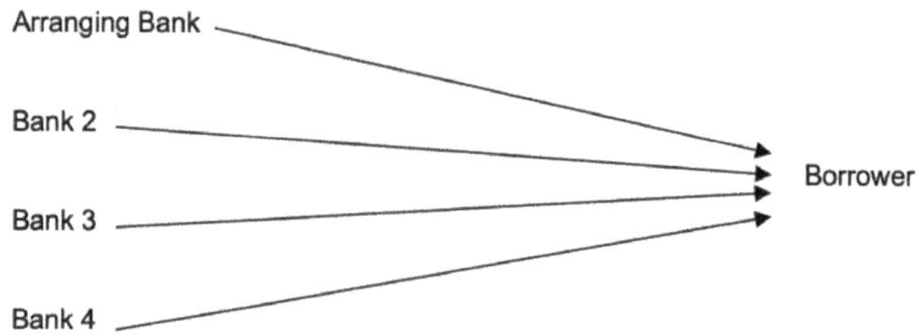


**2.7** In more recent times parties other than banks may join the syndicate or act as arranger due to banks having insufficient funds to satisfy the demands of the market place. Such parties, in what is termed the 'shadow market' have become more common. There is evidence that their initial involvement is more prone to occurring when the borrowers have lower credit ratings.[10] They are also more prone to making straightforward 'bullet' term loans rather than revolving credits or staged loans. This is discussed below.

---

9 Sometimes called an 'underwriter', 'mandated lead arranger' or 'book runner'. Sometimes the book runner may put the syndicate together whilst the arranger merely arranges the loan facility.

10 Iňaki Aldosoro, Sebastian Doerr and Haonan Zhou. 'Non-bank lenders in the syndicated loan market.' BIS Quarterly Review, March 2022, p 21

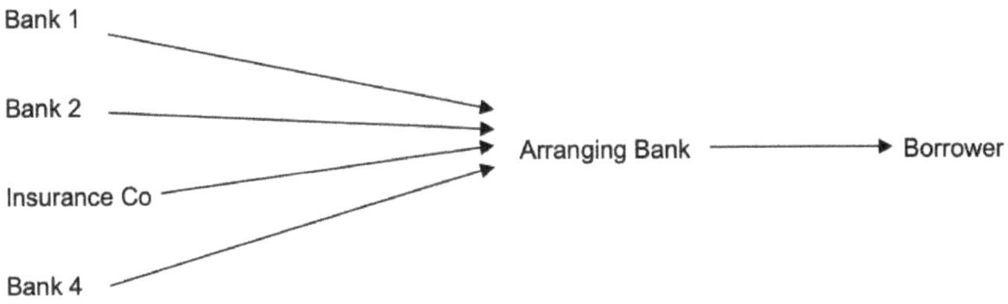


**2.8** The arranging bank has a range of functions of which the main one is, as its name suggests arranging the loan facility. It will be the main contact point and conduit of information between the borrower and the syndicate, and it must keep copies of all records and any information received from the borrower for onward distribution to the syndicate (see below). With a large syndication there may be more than one arranging bank.

## Arranging a syndicated loan

**2.9** There are a number of ways in which a borrower wishing to raise finance or engage in refinance can arrange to syndicate a loan. They may put the loan out to bid from banks or a number of groups of banks, though the process of engaging in attracting open tenders seems to be less common than in the past. Once the banks are chosen they will then settle in outline with the borrower the basic terms upon which the loan is to be promoted to potential participants. They will often use an open agreement along the lines of 'the agreement will contain clauses customary for this type of facility'. This will often mean that the Loan Markets Association (LMA) terms will be used, possibly in a modified form. (See **1.3**). There seems no reason why the initial agreement should not be worded to refer to the relevant LMA terms as they exist at a certain date.

**2.10** The arranging bank must be careful about the extent of the commitment it enters into in creating the syndicate. If a bank states that it will use 'reasonable endeavours' this only involves taking a single reasonable course of action. However, it is clear from *Rhodia International Holdings Ltd and Rhodia UK Ltd v Huntsman International LLC*[11] that 'all reasonable endeavours' equates to 'best endeavours' and involves near absolute commitment.[12] From the vantage point of the arranging bank a less extreme commitment is wise, though entering into such an obligation remains common.

---

11 [2007] 2 Lloyd's Rep 325.

12 Petkovic, D 'Arranger Liability in the Euro Markets.' Banking Law Journal. January 2008, 49–65.

**2.11** It is normal where the arranging bank still needs to put the syndicate together for that bank to promote the loan by approaching other banks in the market or otherwise generally soliciting interest from participants in the 'shadow market', ie non-bank parties who engage in commercial lending. There may already be a tender panel in existence which the arranging bank can approach. It is then common practice for them to provide detailed information relating to both the loan agreement and the borrower, as part of the promotion exercise. The final and most risky obligation which is normally placed upon them is for it to negotiate the terms of the syndication agreement, which will ultimately evidence the contract upon which the funds are to be advanced. A recent innovation is the utilisation of blockchain to create the syndicate. At the time of writing this is a rapidly developing area and should offer the opportunity for banks to put the syndicate together more quickly, thus leaving the funds in the banks' possession and thus not generating a profit for a shorter period of time. It also improves transparency and security. Other issues may arise once the syndication agreement is in operation. We will consider each of these steps in turn.

## Arranging the loan mandate

**2.12** As we have already seen the syndication process effectively starts when a bank obtains a mandate from a prospective borrower. The commitment placed upon the arranging bank within the terms of the mandate can vary, although they do not normally secure the mandate on a fully underwritten basis. Most mandates simply require the arranging bank to use its best efforts to arrange a suitable syndicate. As there is a rebuttable presumption that a commercial agreement is intended to give rise to legal relations between the parties it is a good idea for the arranging bank to limit any obligations which the mandate may imply. This must be achieved by express wording within the terms of the mandate itself.

**2.13** It is preferable for the arranging bank to state, quite specifically, that the parties do not intend to enter into any legal relations. If such a course of action were adopted the court would treat the mandate as binding in honour only. The words 'this does not constitute a legally binding offer' would achieve this desired purpose under English law.

## Arranging the syndicate

**2.14** Once the basic terms and conditions of the loan have been agreed with the borrower, the arranging bank will start to solicit interest from potential participants. Rather than send out details indiscriminately, they will normally target possible participants and then send out a package including a 'commitment letter' setting out the terms on which the bank will lend and 'term sheets' to the banks selected under cover of an enclosing letter which should deal with key relevant issues, such as the extent to which the loan is underwritten. These 'term sheets' are basically a synopsis of the borrower, the actual proposal and the fee structure applicable to different levels of the syndicate. These days they tend to be reasonably lengthy and detailed. Typical of the contents would be:

- details of the borrower and whether any intra-group guarantees are being provided. This may also include associated security and a requirement that necessary financial information will be provided by the borrower;
- details of the arranging bank;
- details of the agent bank[13] who will handle the loan once made and make sure the funds are available as and when contracted by the loan agreement. This could be the same party as the arranging bank who may continue in the role once the funds have been drawn down;
- details of the amount of the loan and the facility itself, for example, a bullet facility or revolving credit facility, or a multi-currency revolving credit facility as the case may be. Where it is not a simple bullet facility it will be necessary to detail the amounts to be drawn down at stated time periods unless the borrower is left with choice on this. The clause will go on to cover the purpose(s) of the loan. This may be very general and be stated for 'general commercial purposes' or it might be more specific and refer to a commercial activity, or in the case of refinancing the financing arrangement being replaced. The maturity period and interest rate (or method of calculating this) will also be detailed;
- repayment details and prepayment rights and terms;
- the borrower's obligation to reimburse any necessary start-up costs such as legal fees up to an agreed maximum figure;
- a summary of the terms of the loan which will tend to be along the lines discussed in **Chapter 1**;
- any methodology for changing the facility;
- transfer certificate details to facilitate any of the lending banks selling on their share of the loan (see **Chapter 3**);
- governing law and jurisdiction choice;
- that payments made under the agreement will be free of taxes;
- other clauses covering issues such as when this offer lapses, which will usually only be in only a few business days' time. There will also be details of the syndication arrangements; and

---

13 Sometimes called the 'administrative agent.'

- a fee letter detailing fees relating to commitment, utilisation, arrangement and agency.

**2.15** Those participants which indicate an interest to the arranging bank's original communication are then circulated with an information memorandum. Normally this is preceded by the intended recipient banks all signing confidentiality agreements regarding the contents. This is done for a number of reasons; the material is commercially sensitive and in some cases its becoming public knowledge could damage the borrower. In some instances, for example where the finance is to fund a takeover, the information might amount to unpublished price sensitive information and its release to a wider circle of people could give rise to accusations of insider dealing or market abuse.[14]

### *Contents of the information memorandum*

**2.16** The information memorandum is essentially a selling document, and its legal status and the obligations to which it gives rise will depend upon the nature of the information which it contains, and the circumstances surrounding its distribution. The information that will be supplied will vary; the precise nature of which will depend on whether it is a standard commercial loan, part of a project finance arrangement or a sovereign loan. In all situations the memorandum will be accompanied by a copy letter from the borrower giving them authority to release the information enclosed and the terms and conditions of the proposed loan. If the borrower has an extremely good credit rating the information memorandum will be made up of publicly available information and material from credit rating agencies.[15] On the other hand a borrower with a poorer credit rating will have meetings with the arranging bank and put together a bundle of material prepared by the borrower for dissemination to potential syndicate members. Not surprisingly it contains all the information they will need to make the decision, ie, annual financial statements for the previous three or more years, management accounts for the period since the last audited accounts, business plans and details of senior management and directors. There will be a statement covering the fees receivable by the arranging bank. It may also include additional material such as reports on the borrower and on that sector generally. Thus, there is an inverse proportionality between the creditworthiness of the borrower and the amount of information provided. The arranging bank will normally avoid being put in the position of having to provide information itself for the other potential syndicate members but act as a conduit for that provided by the borrower. This is to reduce their legal risk and is discussed further below.

---

14 Criminal Justice Act 1993, s 63 and Financial Services and Markets Act 2000, s 118.

15 T Rhodes *Syndicated Lending: Practice and Documentation* (Euromoney, 2009), p 247.

**2.17** In the case of a sovereign borrower the information memorandum will need different material. Typically, this tends to include the sovereign credit rating, economic details on the current and projected state of the economy, balance of payments figures, the economic growth rate, public and private sector debt and current economic plans for the future.

**2.18** The concern for the bank issuing this memorandum is of course the risk that it may be held legally responsible for any inaccuracies. The main risk insofar as English law is concerned arises in the law of misrepresentation, which is an untrue statement of fact that successfully induces the other party to enter a contract. In practice matters are rather more complicated than this as there are three relevant areas of law within the doctrine of misrepresentation that can be brought into play. Such potential liability only extends to those approached to join the syndicate, not to third parties who may later acquire a syndicate member's share of the loan on the secondary market. *Caparo Industries plc v Dickman and Others*[16] made clear that liability in negligence only extends to those where it is reasonably foreseeable, where there is a relationship of proximity between the parties and also where it is just and reasonable to impose liability. There is no proximity between the arranging bank and the secondary market. Likewise, normally any contractual liability would be limited to the other original members of the syndicated loan. Thus, we should examine any potential direct liability to the other syndicate members.

### *Flex provisions and fee letter*

**2.19** It is common for the mandate to include a power for the arranging bank to vary the terms of the loan to the advantage of the lenders, should the opportunity arise. This will normally occur because of a change in market conditions meaning that the loan cannot be made on its original proposed terms. This may permit the arranging bank to alter the loan amount, the interest rate, the structure, for example by moving portions of the loan between different parts of the loan and debt securities and possibly change the financial covenants to successfully complete the deal. An open-ended version of this clause is sometimes used which permits the arranging bank to amend any of the terms of the loan agreement if necessary.

**2.20** In addition, a fee letter is sent to the other lenders by the arranging bank setting out the relevant fees. These will normally be the arrangement fees, the agent bank's fees and potentially also contain a 'flex note' unless this is in a sperate letter (see immediately above).

[16] [1990] 2 AC 605; All ER 568.

## Misrepresentation

**2.21** Misrepresentation is an untrue statement of fact which successfully induces the other party to enter into a contract. It arises in three forms: fraudulent misrepresentation, negligent misrepresentation and statements covered by the Misrepresentation Act 1967. The misrepresentation takes place where it is received.[17]

### Fraudulent misrepresentation

**2.22** Where the arranging bank has been party to the preparation of an information memorandum which contains a statement which it knows to be false or is reckless as to whether or not a statement is true, then civil and criminal liability may attach. Any civil action would normally need to be brought in the tort of deceit.[18] As it would be necessary for the claimant to prove that the representor was dishonest or reckless, succeeding in such an action is normally going to be difficult but cases can succeed where there is clear evidence of an untrue statement.[19] Indeed, recent litigation states that the representor does not need to have engaged in conscious awareness that it is a misrepresentation.[20] Matters are also exacerbated by the fact that the civil action will be alleging behaviour that in many instances will amount to a criminal offence. Matters then become more difficult for a plaintiff because although it will be a civil action there are burden of proof issues.

> 'A civil court, when considering a charge of fraud, will naturally require a higher degree of probability that that which it would require if considering whether negligence were established. It does not adopt so high a degree as a criminal court, even when it is considering a charge of a criminal nature, but still it does require a degree of probability which is commensurate with the occasion.'[21]

> 'The case, like any civil case, may be proved by a preponderance of probability, but the degree of probability depends on the subject-matter. In proportion as the offence is grave, so ought the proof be clear.'[22]

---

17 *Alfred Dunhill Ltd v Diffusion Internationale de Maroquinerie de Prestige SARL*[2002] 1 All ER (Comm) 950.

18 *Derry v Peek* (1889) 14 App Ca 377.

19 *Smith New Court Securities v Scrimgeour Vickers (Asset Management) (2) Citibank NA* [1996] 4 All ER 769 where a fictional representation was made that there were other bidders for a shareholding where there were none and the claimant consequently lost around £11 million as a result.

20 *Credit Suisse Life (Bermuda) Ltd v Ivanishvili* [2025] UKPC 53.

21 Denning LJ in *Bater v Bater* [1951] AC 35.

22 Lord Denning in *Blyth v Blyth* [1966] AC 643.

In theory this means that the burden of proof remains the balance of probabilities but the more serious the allegation, the stronger must be the evidence. In practice this tends to mean that the standard of proof becomes more onerous.[23]

**2.23** It is not surprising therefore that very few actions are brought under this head. As will be seen the alternatives are more straightforward for a potential claimant.[24]

## Negligent misrepresentation

**2.24** The lead manager may, in appropriate circumstances, be liable for damages for negligent misstatements contained in the information memorandum on the basis of a line of cases commencing with *Hedley Byrne & Co Ltd v Heller & Partners Ltd,*[25] that is, on the basis that negligent advice/information is given by the arranging bank to a participating bank in a situation where a special relationship of trust or confidence exists between the parties, and that person, a participating bank, suffers foreseeable loss in consequence of that reliance.

**2.25** There are clearly a number of important caveats which must be satisfied before the *Hedley Byrne* doctrine can expose the arranging bank to liability for negligent misrepresentation, not least the need to establish a 'special relationship' between the lead bank and the participating banks. In *Hedley Byrne* itself, none of their Lordships were willing to lay down precise criteria for the existence of the 'special relationship,' preferring to rely on broad statements of general principle capable of being applied to a wide range of factual situations.

**2.26** It must also be established that the participating banks actually relied on the misrepresentation, and that their loss was caused by the misstatements contained within the information memorandum.

**2.27** An important aspect of the *Hedley Byrne* decision is that the statement containing the misrepresentation need not be one of fact but can be one of opinion or advice and, therefore, a potential claimant could rely on negligent misrepresentation in circumstances where an action for misrepresentation may otherwise not lie because the statement in question is one of opinion. Whether the arranging bank will be so liable for negligent misrepresentation will depend on all the circumstances. Factors of particular importance will be the extent to which the arranging bank was involved in the preparation and distribution of the memorandum and the manner in which it was used as a seller to solicit interest from potential participants. The complexity of the

---

23 *Re H (Minors) Sexual Abuse: Standard of Proof* [1996] AC 563 at 586 and *Re CD Northern Ireland* UKHL 33 (11 June 2008).

24 For a rare case of a bank having been deemed to make a fraudulent misrepresentation see *Royal Bank of Scotland plc v Highland Partners LP* [2013] EWCA Civ 328.

25 (1964) AC 465.

overall transaction will also be important, as will the access which syndicate members had to the source of information contained in the memorandum. These latter two factors will be particularly important where an unsophisticated participant is endeavouring to show that in a complex agreement, and with little or no access to the information, it relied almost exclusively on the skill and expertise of the lead bank.[26] However, in the large scale lending markets, banks entering into a syndicate are very unlikely indeed to satisfy the requirement of being unsophisticated. In addition, the arranging bank is normally merely acting as a post box for the borrower in terms of sending on information to the other banks.

**2.28** The key issue as to whether there is a duty of care owed by an arranging bank to the syndicate members was dealt with in *IFE Fund SA v Goldman Sachs International*.[27] Goldman's arranged a syndicated facility to finance a takeover. Some months after the takeover the corporate group that had borrowed the money collapsed as a result of the company that had been purchased having falsified its accounts to hide its true financial position. As a result of this the information memorandum had also contained this misleading information. The information memorandum contained, as is usual market practice, an exclusion clause stating that Goldman's were not liable for the information contained therein. It was held by the Court of Appeal that: (i) there was no claim available against Goldman's for negligent misstatement because of the exclusion clause; and (ii) an arranging bank does not owe a duty of care to participants, but could be liable if they did not act in good faith as there is an implied term to that effect. The information was contained in audited accounts and Goldman Sachs had not realised they were misleading the syndicate:

> '... it is only if Goldman Sachs actually knew that it had in its possession information which made the information in the syndication information memorandum misleading that it could be liable for breach of the representation of good faith, provided the necessary intention was proved.' (Collins LJ)[28]

**2.29** An example of where such information might arise occurred in an Australian case, *Natwest Australia Bank v Tricontinental Corporation Ltd*.[29] Here Tricontinental had been given a mandate by Pro-Image to put together a syndicate of banks to provide a syndicated loan of AUS $50 million to Pro-Image. Following the award of the mandate Tricontinental contacted several banks, one of which was Natwest and provided them with an information memorandum relating

---

26 A useful case in this context is *St Alban's City and District Council v International Computers Ltd* [1994] EWCA Civ 1296.
27 [2007] EWCA Civ 811.
28 *Ibid*, para 78.
29 (1993) ATPR (Digest) 46–109.

to the proposed facility that had been compiled by Tricontinental. This included the following disclaimer:

> 'The information herein has been obtained from the borrower and other sources considered reliable. No representation or warranty expressed or implied is made with respect to this information.'

The information memorandum also included information about contingent liabilities but did not mention two guarantees provided by Pro-Image amounting to AUS$ 45 million which Tricontinental knew about. Before signing the syndicated loan agreement an employee of Natwest had several telephone conversations with an employee of Tricontinental regarding the financial status of Pro-Image. Specific enquiries were made as to the existence of any contingent liabilities not mentioned in the information memorandum and Tricontinental's employee answered that there were only nominal ones. This was untrue.

**2.30** Natwest proceeded and the loan agreement included the following clause:

> 'Each of the Lenders severally represents and warrants to the Syndicate Manager that it has made its own independent investigation and assessment of the financial conditions and affairs of the Borrower in connection with its participation in the Facility and has not relied on any representation or information provided to it by the Syndicate Manager to induce it to enter into the Syndicated Facility Agreement. Each Lender warrants and undertakes to the Syndicate Manager that it shall continue to make its own independent appraisal of the creditworthiness of the Borrower while the Facility continues or the commitment is in force.'

**2.31** Shortly afterwards the guarantee was called upon and Pro-Image experienced financial problems and defaulted. Natwest then sued Tricontinental and their solicitor for AUS $11.5 million which was the amount of its participation in the syndicated facility.

**2.32** The Court held that Tricontinental was in breach of its common law duty because Tricontinental owed to Natwest a duty to use all reasonable care to ensure that the information conveyed by it was accurate and to give to Natwest all information which was known to it and was relevant to a decision whether or not Natwest would participate in the syndicated transaction proposed by Tricontinental.

**2.33** In *Sumitomo Bank Ltd v Banque Bruxelles Lambert SA,*[30] two syndicated loans were put together by Banque Bruxelles Lambert (the arranging bank) to make a loan to a special purpose vehicle to buy commercial properties. The borrower had no assets other than the

[30] (1997) 1 Lloyd's Rep 487.

properties being purchased and so insurance cover was to be taken out to cover any shortfall on the loan that might arise should the lenders have to foreclose on the loan and sell the properties. Here a statement was made by the arranging bank to the other lenders to the effect that credit insurance was being put in place to cover any shortfall between the security that was being taken and any outstanding debt at the date of enforcement. They also said that full disclosure had been made to the insurance company. On the collapse of the borrower the security was enforced and a shortfall arose. The insurer challenged that full disclosure had not been made to them by Banque Bruxelles Lambert, which was also the agent bank, and they refused to fully pay out. The arranging bank was then sued by the other banks in the syndicate for the outstanding amount. The ruling only dealt with preliminary issues but the court held that the arranging bank did owe the others a duty of care when making any disclosures and had to do so in a skilled and competent way.[31]

**2.34** This approach has since been followed in *J P Morgan v Springwell Navigation Corp*[32] and *Titan Steel Wheels Ltd v Royal Bank of Scotland plc.*[33]

**2.35** A more general duty to the other lenders also exists regarding executing the documentation. The case of *Golden Belt 1 Sukuk Co BSC(c) v BNP Paribas*[34] concerned an Islamic bond issue rather than a syndicated loan, but the same principle arises. In this instance, when executing the contract the bank used a signature that was laser printed rather than signing by hand. This was not a valid signature under Saudi law and the bonds were not enforceable. As the bank had taken on responsibility for executing the contract they had a duty of care to the other lenders not to be negligent in so doing and so were liable to them.

## Statutory misrepresentation

**2.36** The main factor here is the Misrepresentation Act 1967, specifically s 2(1) which states that:

> 'Where a person has entered into a contract after a misrepresentation has been made to him by another party thereto, and as a result thereof he has suffered loss, then, the person making the misrepresentation would be liable in damages in respect thereof

---

31 See, eg, G Skene, 'Syndicated Loans: arranger and participating bank fiduciary theory' (2005) 20(6) JIBLR 269, Shalini Sequeira, 'Syndicated Loans, let the Arranger Beware.' (1997) 12(3) JIBFL 117, and D Halliday and R Davies, 'Risks and responsibilities of the agent bank and the arranging bank in syndicated credit facilities.' (1997) 12(5) JIBL 182.

32 [2008] EWHC 1186 (Comm).

33 [2010] EWHC 211 (Comm). See also 'Sub-prime and Credit Crunch Claims: How Deep is Your Loss? (2008) 19(6) PLC 35–40.

34 [2017] EWHC 3182 (Comm)

had the misrepresentation been made fraudulently, that person shall be liable notwithstanding that the misrepresentation was not made fraudulently, unless he proves that he had reasonable grounds to believe and did believe up to the time the contract was made that the facts represented were true.'

The effective consequence of s 2(1) of this Act is that an arranging bank may be liable for misrepresentation if it can be shown that the arranging bank has made an incorrect statement or failed to state a material fact which makes a statement in the information memorandum misleading, unless such a statement were made reasonably and the arranging bank continued to reasonably believe in its truth until the time the contract was signed. Further, s 3 of the Act states that:

'If a contract contains a term which would exclude or restrict—

(a) any liability to which a party to a contract may be subject by reason of any misrepresentation made by him before the contract was made; or

(b) any remedy available to another party to the contract by reason of such a misrepresentation, that term shall be of no effect except in so far as it satisfies the requirement of reasonableness as stated in section 11(1) of the Unfair Contract Terms Act 1977; and it is for those claiming that the term satisfies that requirement to show that it does.'

This requirement is discussed below.

**2.37** The essential purpose of this Act is twofold. The first is to facilitate actions for negligent misstatement where there is no duty of care between the representor and representee with the result that no action would lie under *Hedley Byrne v Heller*. This is important given that the *IFE Fund* case discussed above made clear there is no duty of care in this situation. The second is to permit civil actions where the representor made an honest but inaccurate statement which did not amount to negligence, but which he was in a position to correct prior to the contract being signed, but did not do so.

**2.38** In addition, the syndicate member who claims that a misrepresentation has been given must have relied on the material misstatement when making its decision to participate and it must have played a 'real and substantial' part in making the decision to enter into the loan.[35] In *Peekay Intermark Ltd v Australia and New Zealand Banking Group Ltd* [36] a customer of the bank claimed under the Misrepresentation Act 1967, s 2(1) on the basis that they entered into risky investments in emerging markets and lost money due to advice given by the bank. The customer had signed a contract stating

---

[35] *Taberna Europe CDO II plc v Selskabet (Formerly Roskilde Bank A/S) (In Bankruptcy)* [2015] EWHC 871 (Comm).

[36] [2006] EWCA Civ 386; [2006] 2 Lloyd's Rep 511.

that it had not relied on advice from the bank and another containing a warning about the risks of emerging market investments. The Court of Appeal decided in favour of the bank, holding that the investment has not been misrepresented as the statements made by the bank were only preliminary informal statements. The Court added as an obiter that the customer was estopped from denying that it knew the nature of the transaction, having signed a risk disclosure statement that explained it, and also having had the relevant information provided to them in the final contract which they did to bother to read.

**2.39** The decision is rooted in the long standing traditional common law on this subject. To quote Jessel MR in *Redgrave v Hurd*:[37]

> 'If a man is induced to enter into a contract by false representation it is not a sufficient answer for him (the representor) to say, "If you had used due diligence you would have found out that the statement was untrue".'

However, whereas in the *Peekay* case the information has been communicated to the other party, or where it is reasonable to do so, to their agent, the representee cannot claim Jessel's logic covers them if the only reason they did not acquire the information is that they did not make a reasonable effort to read it.

**2.40** This offers some comfort to an arranging bank putting together a lending syndicate where the parties will later sign a syndicate agreement, but as the other cases discussed show, the comfort is limited and depends on the precise facts, representations and exclusions used. This principle has since been followed in *Foodco UK LLP (t/a Muffin Break) v Henry Boot Developments Ltd.*[38]

## Exclusion clauses

**2.41** The Unfair Contract Terms Act 1977 (UCTA 1977) states that liability for negligence cannot be excluded except 'in so far as the term … satisfies the test of reasonableness' (UCTA 1977, s 2(1)). Further, UCTA 1977, s 2(3) goes on to state:

> 'Where a contract term …purports to exclude or restrict liability for negligence a person's consent to or awareness of it is not of itself to be taken as indicating his voluntary acceptance of any such risk.'

**2.42** The test of reasonableness referred to in s 2(1) is clarified by UCTA 1977, s 11(1) which states:

---

37 (1881) 20 Ch 1.

38 [2010] EWHC 358 (Ch). See also A Trukhtanov, 'Misrepresentation: acknowledgement of non-reliance as defence' (2009) 125(Oct) LQR 648–670 and W Gooding, 'Selling Investment Products to Sophisticated Investors: Reflections on Peekay v ANZ' (2006) 21(11) JIBLR 628–633.

> '... the term shall have been a fair and reasonable one to be included having regard to the circumstances which were, or ought reasonably to have been, known to or in contemplation of the parties when the contract was made.'

Key issues here will be factors such as:

- the gravity of the misrepresentation;
- the bargaining position of the parties;
- their comparative sophistication;
- the access which the injured bank had to the information; and
- its ability to ascertain the facts for itself.

The potential obligations arising out of the relationship between the arranging bank and the participating banks may appear considerable, but in practice such obligations, or at least those outlined above, are either qualified or completely negated within the terms of the loan agreement.

**2.43** The fact that an arranging bank will normally be a conduit for the relevant information rather than its source and that the remainder of the lending syndicate will tend to be sophisticated financial institutions themselves means that they will face an uphill struggle to try and evade an exclusion clause after they have signed it. The fact that the signing process that will normally have been preceded by those banks taking legal advice from a major law firm or in-house counsel and that the loan agreements tend to be based on the market standard makes it even more difficult for them to avoid the consequences of signing.

**2.44** Of particular importance will be the strength of the bargaining positions as between the arranging bank and the participating banks. Where all parties are relatively sophisticated it will be easier to satisfy the test of reasonableness. The arranging bank should be wary of potential participants which are unsophisticated, in the sense of having had little exposure to syndicated lending. In practice major banks tend to be very experienced in this area. This is more of an issue than in the past with the emergence of the shadow market and parties such as pension funds, fund managers, hedge funds, insurance companies and large corporates entering the market. However, the court will tend to uphold exclusion clauses in such cases as the disadvantaged party may have received some corresponding benefit for agreeing to the clause.[39] These are also sophisticated financial institutions with access to top quality legal advice and in any event they are less likely to enter the market as original members of the syndicate but to enter by way of

[39] *Raiffeisen Zentralbank Österreich AG v The Royal Bank of Scotland plc* [2010] EWHC 1392 (Comm).

the secondary market (see **Chapter 3**), in some cases immediately after the loan has been put into effect. Thus, they will often not be recipients of the information memorandum and the key issue will be any information they receive from the seller of the debt.

## Fiduciary duties

**2.45** It appears that this can arise as an issue in the context of the promotion stage as became apparent in the case of *UBAF Ltd v European American Banking Corporation.*[40] Here it was claimed by the plaintiffs (UBAF) that they had been misled by the second bank (EABC) which had invited them to take part in a loan. EABC had a long history of dealing with a group of borrowers, the Colocotronis Shipping Group. They proceeded to send out term sheets and background material relating to a loan to two of Colocotronis's members. One statement included was that the loans were 'attractive financing to two companies in a sound a profitable group'. UBAF then participated in the loan, but the borrowers later defaulted. In the course of an interlocutory appeal Ackner LJ stated that EABC could be said to have acted in a fiduciary capacity for the other syndicate members. They had both solicited participation, held security for the loan and acted as security trustees. In this instance the courts were considering the issue of fiduciary duty partly as a claim in negligence was time barred but that it would not block a claim on these grounds. The general view is that this conclusion rested on the particular facts of the case and that the normal position is that arranging banks are not fiduciaries. (See Lord Browne-Wilkinson in *Henderson v Merret Syndicates Ltd*).[41]

**2.46** However, matters may not be this clear cut. In *NatWest Australia Bank v Tricontinental Corporation Ltd*[42] (see **2.25** above) there was held to be a breach of the fiduciary duty to disclose all facts as to the affairs of Pro-Image known to Tricontinental. The disclaimer clause in the information memorandum did not affect the question as to whether a sufficient relationship of proximity existed to give rise to the duty of care contended by NatWest. The information memorandum related specifically to information provided and did not seek to effect, release or discharge Tricontinental from any duty or obligation to provide information which it may have been under a duty to provide. A commercial banker in the position of Tricontinental and with its knowledge of Pro-Image ought to have known that if the guarantees were disclosed to NatWest it would not in all probability have entered into the syndicated loan agreement; thus NatWest succeeded. This case does suggest that fiduciary duties may have a significant role to play in relevant litigation in the future.

---

[40] [1984] QB 713.
[41] [1994] 3 WLR 761 at p 799
[42] (1993) ATPR (Digest) 46–109.

**2.47** To what extent then can the arranging bank be a fiduciary? This is not easily answered; however, it would seem that fiduciary obligations can arise not only in the traditional relationships, but also in any case where one party, the arranging bank, undertakes to perform some task on behalf of another, the participants. Case law indicates that courts are prepared to extend the traditional principles to cover relationships which previously might not have been thought to give rise to a fiduciary relationship.[43] In the light of these decisions it now seems more likely, although it should be emphasised that there has never been an English case directly on this point, that an arranging bank would in appropriate circumstances be held to be in a fiduciary relationship with the participating banks. The argument in favour of such a relationship would, however, be more credible if it could be shown that the arranging bank acted on behalf of the participants during the negotiation process in a specific way, for example, in cases where only the arranging bank had access to the borrower and its relevant financial information at the relevant time, or where the arranging bank was in a position of advantage, due to its close relationship with the borrower, which effectively forced the participants to rely on the arranging bank's expertise.

**2.48** The following extract from the judgment of Dawson J in *Hospital Products International Pty Ltd v United States Surgical Corporation* [44] conveniently summarises some of the relevant factors which the court may take into account in deciding whether a fiduciary relationship exists:

> 'It is usual – perhaps necessary – that in such a [fiduciary] relationship one party should repose substantial confidence in another in acting on his behalf or in his interest in some respect. But it is not in every case where that happens that there is a fiduciary relationship … There is, however, the notion underlying all the cases of fiduciary obligation that inherent in the nature of the relationship itself is a position of disadvantage or vulnerability on the part of one of the parties which cause him to place reliance upon the other and requires the protection of equity acting upon the conscience of that other.'[45]

In other words it will be rare that a participant bank will be able to claim the arranging bank owed them a fiduciary duty but as the above analysis shows it is not impossible.

## Negotiating the loan documentation

**2.49** Another matter of concern to the arranging bank will be the extent to which it may owe duties and liabilities to the participants

---

43 *Brian Pty Ltd v UDC* [1983] NSWLR 490; *United States Surgical Corporation v Hospital Products International Pty Ltd* [1983] NSWLR 157 and *Coleman v Myers* [1977] 2 NZLR 255.

44 [1984] HCA 64; 58 ALJR 587.

45 *Ibid* at p 628.

during the negotiation and drafting of the syndicated loan documentation. Insofar as market practice is concerned, it is clear that during the negotiation process the arranging bank acts on behalf of the borrower in terms of putting the loan together but, as has been seen, can owe duties to participating banks.

**2.50** A typical exclusion clause to clarify the situation might read as follows:

> 'Neither the Arranging Bank, Agent Bank nor any manager, nor any director, officer, employee or agent of any of them shall be responsible to any Bank for:
>
> (i) any failure by the Borrower or the Guarantor (if relevant) to fulfil any obligation under this Agreement: or
>
> (ii) any recitals, statements, representations or warranties contained in this Agreement or in any certificate or other document referred to, or provided for, or received, under this Agreement: or
>
> (iii) for the value, validity, effectiveness, genuineness, enforceability or sufficiency of this Agreement.'

As the above example indicates, the clause will be drafted very widely, but without more, such a clause would not be enough to protect the arranging bank against all potential liability and a number of additional precautions may be necessary, in appropriate circumstances.

## The arranging bank

**2.51** However, in the minority of cases where the arranging bank is in a fiduciary relationship with the participating banks, it will determine the nature of the obligations between them.[46] This is subject to anything that may have been placed in the information memorandum by way of an exclusion clause (see above). This is important as the arranging bank will wish to control the range of obligations which the law would otherwise place on it. These are set out below.

### No conflict

**2.52** The arranging bank will not be allowed to enter into engagements in which it has, or can have, a personal interest conflicting, or which possibly may conflict, with the interest of those it is bound to protect.[47]

---

46 See, eg, R Davies and D Halliday 'Risks and Responsibilities of the Agent Bank and the Arranging Bank in Syndicated Credit Facilities' (1997) 12(5) JIBL 182.

47 *Aberdeen Railway Co v Blaikie Bros* [1854] 1 Macq 461, 471 per Lord Cranworth LJ. See also *Phipps v Boardman* [1967] AC 46; *Kelly v Cooper* [1993] AC 205, [1994] 1 BCLC 395.

This principle may cause particular difficulty for an arranging bank which holds participations in some of the borrowers' other credits which conflict with the provisions in the loan agreement in which it is acting as arranging bank. It could also cause problems where the arranging bank is in a pre-existing banker-customer relationship with the borrower and is in possession of confidential information as a result.

### No profit rule

**2.53** The arranging bank will not be allowed to use its position for the purpose of gaining personal profit.[48] Without more, this would cause grave difficulties for the arranging bank, since the compensation it receives, by means of the arranger's fee, is one of the main reasons why many banks desire to act in the capacity of arranging bank

### Duty to disclose

**2.54** The arranging bank will be under a duty to disclose information which is relevant to a potential participating bank's decision as to whether it should join the syndicate.[49] A participating bank seeking to rely on this duty would need to establish that a reasonably prudent arranging bank would have disclosed the information in question. Expert evidence will often be required to show what a reasonably prudent arranging bank would have disclosed.

**2.55** In addition to the fiduciary obligations outlined above, the arranging bank in its capacity as the participant's agent, will be under a duty to exercise due care and skill in negotiating the loan agreement with the borrower. It is clear that no action will lie against the arranging bank unless its failure to exercise reasonable care is the effective cause of loss suffered by the participant(s). Whenever possible the participants should be given time to consider the documents themselves and be encouraged to take independent legal advice on their sufficiency. One final precaution which the arranging bank may wish to take is to obtain a specific warranty from the participants, normally within the terms of the agreement, that they will be responsible for making their own independent investigation into the sufficiency of the loan documentation and that they will continue to be so responsible.

**2.56** Providing the arranging bank takes the precautions which have been outlined above, it is reasonable to assume that an English court would find that banks which participate in syndicated lending are capable of looking after their own interests, and therefore would

---

[48] *Imageview Management Ltd v Jack* [2009] EWCA Civ 63, [2009] 1 WLR (D) 56.
[49] *Brian Property v UDC* [1983] NSWLR 490.

not be allowed to obtain redress in the courts against the arranging bank should events not turn out as the participants would have wished.

### Execution of the agreement

**2.57** The final responsibility of the arranging bank is to arrange for the execution of the loan agreement itself. This may take place at a ceremony at which all the parties to the agreement attend and sign. In some instances the arranging bank will have powers of attorney signed by the participant banks and then sign on their behalf. As is seen in **Chapters 9** and **10** of this work the precise location of execution can have an impact on the legal obligations to which the agreement may give rise. Once the loan agreement has been executed the arranging bank can drop out of the picture, since its obligations have been met and the responsibility of administering the loan falls upon the agent bank, which will now be considered. In some cases, however, the arranging bank and agent bank are the same party, so the role will simply develop.

## The agent bank

### The duties of the agent

**2.58** The distinction between the arranging bank and the agent bank is clear since the adoption of the standard LMA syndicated lending agreement[50] in the market, despite the fact that the same bank often fulfils both functions. Most loan agreements make a clear distinction between the two roles, and in practice the responsibilities of the agent only come into operation after those of the arranger have ceased, namely, upon execution of the agreement. The agent bank is in a somewhat idiosyncratic position, being normally appointed by the borrower but being an agent of the participating banks. Syndicated lending agreements normally include a clause which states the responsibilities and obligations of the agent.

**2.59** The functions of the agent are basically administrative and it is normally paid an appropriate fee by the borrower for carrying out its obligations. Its obligations should be clearly spelt out within the agreement in the hope of limiting any potential liability. Of particular concern will be the fact that the laws of certain jurisdictions impose obligations upon agents which may bear little resemblance to those to which the agent assumed it would be subject. To clarify matters the LMA Syndicated Loan Agreement defines the powers of an agent for

---

[50] See section 10 of the LMA Multicurrency Term and Revolving Facilities Agreement, April 2020 version, as amended.

the purposes of the syndication.[51] In *Torre Asset Funding and another v The Royal Bank of Scotland plc*[52] the role and duties of the agent were examined. Here the syndicated loan was based on the LMA standard form contract which, inter alia, sets out the powers of the agent and states that they are 'solely mechanical and administrative in nature.' The Court was asked to declare that there was an obligation on the agent to pass on information regarding the borrower which exceeded the requirements set out in the loan agreement. The Court determined that the obligations imposed on the agent were those set out in the loan agreement and that additional obligations should not be imposed and upheld the LMA wording excluding liability. The judge did however add an obiter to the effect that a lender cannot simply assume that their role is always purely administrative. Lenders must therefore consider whether to ask for wider powers to be placed on the agent than the standard LMA agreement sets out. If this is not done the common law obligations set out below following **2.62** will apply unless excluded.

**2.60** The contractual duties in the LMA Agreement at **26.3** are listed as being:

'(a) The Agent's duties under the Finance Documents are solely mechanical and administrative in nature.

(b) Subject to paragraph (c) below, the Agent shall promptly forward to a Party the original or a copy of any document which is delivered to the Agent for that Party by any other Party.

(c) Without prejudice to Clause 24.8 (*Copy of Transfer Certificate, Assignment Agreement or Increase Confirmation to Company*), paragraph (b) above shall not apply to any Transfer Certificate, any Assignment Agreement or any Increase Confirmation.

(d) Except where a Finance Document specifically provides otherwise, the Agent is not obliged to review or check the adequacy, accuracy or completeness of any document it forwards to another party.

(e) If the Agent receives notice from a Party referring to this Agreement, describing a Default and stating that the circumstances described is a Default, it shall promptly notify the other Finance Parties.

(f) If the Agent is aware of the non-payment of any principal, interest, commitment fee or other fee payable to a Finance Party (other than the Agent or the Arranger) under this

51 See clauses 26.2 and 26.3 LMA Multicurrency Term and Revolving Facilities Agreement, April 2020 version, as amended.

52 [2013] EWHC 2670 (Ch).

Agreement, it shall promptly notify the other Finance Parties.

(g) The Agent shall have only those duties, obligations and responsibilities expressly Specified in the Finance Documents to which it is expressed to be a party (and no others shall be implied).'

**2.61** Insofar as English law is concerned, an agent owes a number of implied duties or obligations to his principal, some of which are particularly relevant in the context of international syndicated loan agreements. Unless these are limited or excluded by the syndicated lending agreement the common law duties set out below will apply.

### *Duty to exercise reasonable care and skill*

**2.62** This aspect of an agent's obligations has already been considered with regard to the obligations imposed upon the arranging bank. There can be little doubt, however, that it poses a much more significant threat to the agent bank, because of the nature of the agent's obligations under the loan agreement. The agent may find itself in a particularly difficult position when the borrower is approaching insolvency or where an event of default has occurred. In addition, where a loan agreement gives the agent a discretion with regard to the performance of its obligations, such discretion must be exercised with due care and skill.

### *Duty to act personally*

**2.63** Unless the agent bank has been expressly or impliedly authorised to delegate some or all of its obligations to a third party, it owes the participants a duty to act personally.[53] This prohibition on sub-delegation is normally covered by a clause in the loan agreement, which permits the agent bank to perform its duties by or through its agents or employees.

### *Duty not to permit a conflict of interest*

**2.64** The agent bank will be under a strict duty not to allow its own interests to come into conflict with those of the participating banks, unless those banks, with full knowledge of the material circumstances, consent. Since many agent banks also hold a participation in the credit facility being syndicated, or may have separate facilities outstanding in favour of the borrower, it is not difficult to envisage how such a conflict of interest could arise.

---

[53] *John McCann & Co v Pow* [1975] 1 All WR 129.

*Duty not to make a secret profit*

**2.65** The agent bank is in a similar position to the arranging bank with regard to the fees which are normally paid for the agent's services. It is common practice, therefore, to include an appropriate clause within the terms of the agreement, or some accompanying document, whereby the participants are made aware of any fees which are so payable. In addition, the clause should be worded so as to permit the agent to engage in banking business with the borrower. Such business would technically be in breach of the secret profit duty unless relaxed by the agreement.

### Protecting the agent bank within the loan agreement

**2.66** Because of the onerous implied obligations which may be imposed upon the agent bank, it is common practice for banks appointed as agents to insist upon protective clauses being incorporated within the loan agreement.

## The functioning of the syndicate

### Agent's responsibilities under the terms of the agreement

**2.67** The loan agreement will normally seek to define, as closely as possible, the agent's duties. Some may go further and provide that the agent shall not be under any duties except for those expressly set out in the agreement. The duties commonly include: the duty to administer payments and receipts as between the borrower and the syndicate; the duty to examine any relevant documentation which is required from the borrower; and the duty to inform the syndicate members if it becomes aware of a default. Most loan agreements also place the agent bank under a duty to determine the prevailing interest rate on the appropriate interest dates, normally by consultation with the reference banks.

**2.68** Some of these duties might be exercised at the discretion of the agent bank, but when a discretion is allowed it should be clearly defined in order to avoid any future disagreement between the agent and the participants as to its precise scope and purpose. The extent of any discretion varies enormously, both in respect of the loans in which discretion may be granted, and also specific clauses over which the discretion may operate. The discretion may be limited by a typical provision which reads:

> 'In the exercise of all its rights powers and obligations under this Agreement the Agent shall act in accordance with the instructions of the Majority Banks, but, in the absence of any such instructions, such Agent may (but shall not be obliged to)

act as it shall deem fit in the best interests of the Banks and any such instructions and any such action taken by the Agent in accordance therewith shall be binding upon all the Banks.'

**2.69** Some loans limit the discretion even further by requiring the agent to consult with the participants before taking any action. The problem with a discretion which is so limited is that it may operate against the interests of the participants in the event that the agent needs to act quickly to protect the participants' interests. This problem may be particularly acute on the occasion of a default, where, as we shall see, it may be crucial for the loan to be terminated and accelerated as quickly as possible to maximise the syndicate's chance of recovering monies owed by the borrower.

### Claw back provisions

**2.70** In the event that the agent bank makes a repayment of either interest or principal to a participant before it has obtained the relevant funds from the borrower, normally because of time differences between different countries, it is commonly given authority, within the terms of the loan agreement, to claw back such moneys in the event the borrower fails to make the relevant payment. The clause is normally also worded to permit claw back of payments made in the opposite direction. In other words, where payments have been made to the borrower, for example, on a drawdown date, before the appropriate funds have been obtained from the participant banks.

### Replacement of the agent

**2.71** The agreement will normally make provision for the replacement of the agent bank should this prove necessary. If a replacement is required because of the agent's insolvency any moneys paid to the agent, but not distributed before its insolvency, will be traceable in equity under English law. A syndicate may, however, insist on greater protection against the agent's insolvency and require it to hold all moneys received under the syndicated loan in a separate trust account until such moneys are distributed to the participants in accordance with the agreement.

### Exclusion of liability

**2.72** In addition to the various provisions outlined above, most syndicated loan agreements will also contain elaborate and extensive exculpation clauses. A typical example might read as follows:

'Neither the Agent nor any of its directors, officers, employees or agents shall be under any liability or responsibility of whatsoever kind to any of the Banks:

(i) arising out of or in relation to any failure or delay in performance or breach by the Borrower of any of its obligations hereunder or by any party under any of the documents referred to hereunder; or

(ii) for any statements representations or warranties in this agreement or under any document referred to herein or for the validity effectiveness enforceability or sufficiency of this agreement or any of the other documents referred to herein or be obliged to enquire as to the performance by the borrower or any other party hereto or thereto of any of the terms or conditions hereof or thereof, but the Agent shall promptly notify each Bank of any event of default of which the personnel of the Agent having the conduct of the matter the subject of this agreement have actual knowledge; or

(iii) for any inaccuracy or deficiency in or omission from any information furnished to any Bank by any Agent and without prejudice to the generality of the foregoing any inaccuracy deficiency or omission which renders any information so furnished misleading; or

(iv) for any action taken or omitted to be taken hereunder or in connection herewith unless caused by its own gross negligence or wilful misconduct.'[54]

As has already been seen in this chapter, exclusion clauses will be subject to strict interpretation and an English court would construe such a clause according to the laws relating to misrepresentation and unfair contract terms. Whether such a clause would effectively protect the agent will depend on the precise circumstances.

### General indemnity for the agent bank

**2.73** In addition to the all-embracing exculpation clause previously mentioned, most syndicated loan agreements will include a clause whereby the participants agree to indemnify the agent, rateably in accordance with their respective participations, for any losses incurred by the agent in the performance of its duties. The right to an indemnity will obviously be lost if the agent acts outside the scope of its authority or performs its duties negligently.

---

54 See also clause 26.10 LMA Multicurrency Term and Revolving Facilities Agreement, April 2020, as amended.

### Are the duties extended in default?

**2.74** One final issue worthy of mention relates to the obligations of both the arranging bank and the agent bank in a default. It is probable that under English law it would be restricted to giving information, concerning the default, to the participating banks.

## The relationship between the syndicate members

**2.75** It was identified at the commencement of this chapter that the traditional perception is that a syndicated loan is nothing more than a number of quite separate credits advanced to the borrower under one single loan agreement. Bankers and their lawyers have viewed the loan documentation as a convenient means of pulling together the various credits which comprise the entire loan. Few have ever doubted that each individual lending bank has a quite separate and independent contractual relationship with the borrower.

**2.76** It is also well recognised that as well as having contractual relationships with the borrower, the syndicate members have contractual relations as between themselves. Such relations are governed exclusively by the clauses contained within the agreement, and provisions such as the sharing clause and the set off clause are examples of how the loan documentation is structured in such a way as to bind the banks together.

**2.77** Notwithstanding the various binding clauses contained within the agreement, banks have always perceived their obligations with the borrower as being several, and this view is normally reinforced within the terms of the documentations along the following lines:

> 'The rights and obligations of each Bank under this Agreement are several to the intent that
>
> (i) failure of a Bank to carry out its obligations under this Agreement shall not relieve any other party hereto of any of its obligations hereunder,
>
> (ii) no Bank shall be responsible for the obligations of any other Banks or Agent hereunder, and
>
> (iii) each bank may, subject as expressly stated herein, exercise its rights and pursue its remedies hereunder independently of the Agent and the other Banks.'

### Could the relationship be construed as a partnership or a joint venture?

**2.78** As discussed above, a syndicate will not constitute a partnership by reason of the fact that the banks share gross, not net, returns. As the wording of the specimen clause above covers the precautions which the participants should take in order to avoid the syndicate being construed as a partnership/joint venture the question should not arise. However, this factor should be borne in mind when drafting a syndicated loan agreement or amending the LMA terms.

### The impact of the sharing clause

**2.79** One of the most effective binding clauses found within a syndicated loan agreement is the sharing or redistribution of payments clause which reinforces the underlying philosophy of syndication, namely, that each lender should receive pro rata payments and that the borrower should not be permitted to discriminate in making such payments. The precise wording of the clause will, however, be crucial in order to determine whether this basic philosophy is in fact upheld.

### Disagreements

**2.80** Once the syndicate is in operation the arrangements determining any issues arising will be set out in the syndicate agreement. The main two issues arising here are a syndicate member wishing to sell their share of the loan and disagreements between the parties. The first of these two issues is dealt with in **Chapter 3**. In the case of disagreements arising between the syndicate members the methodology for resolving this will be found in the syndicate agreement, which normally includes a voting system to resolve any matters that cannot be resolved by negotiation. In *Redwood Master Fund Ltd v TD Bank Europe Ltd* [55] the syndicate agreement empowered syndicate members to vary some of the terms by a majority of two thirds by value, a common arrangement on non-core issues.[56] There were three separate syndicate facilities made available to the borrower and some of the lenders in the initial facility novated their share of the facility to other banks. (See **Chapter 3** for novation.) Thus, the initial facility no longer had the same make up of banks as the second. The borrower then ran into financial difficulties and suggested a restructuring which, amongst other things, would have involved the borrower drawing down some of the first facility to pay off the second. There was a vote covering the banks in all three facilities and just under 82% agreed with the borrower's proposals. The members of the first facility who were disadvantaged by this challenged the vote under the principle in *British American Nickel Corpn v M J O'Brien Ltd* [57] which stated

---

[55] [2002] EWHC 2703; (2003) *The Times,* 30 January (Ch D).

[56] Core issues such as debt reduction, changes in interest rates etc often require a unanimous vote.

[57] [1927] AC 369. See also *Peters American Delicacy Co v Heath* [1938–39] 61 CLR 457; *Howard Smith v Ampol Petroleum* [1974] AC 821; *Greenhalgh v Arderne Cinemas* [1951] Ch 286; *Shuttleworth v Cox* [1927] 2 KB and *Sidebottom v Kershaw, Leese & Co Ltd* [1920] 1 Ch 154.

that a majority must exercise a vote for the benefit of those entitled to vote as a whole and not for the benefit of some. They also complained that the majority had acted in bad faith. The Court determined that the claim must fail on both counts. There was no evidence of bad faith. The syndicate arrangement did not treat the lenders in each of the three facilities as separate categories. It was designed to permit an overall majority vote to resolve problems. The fact that a vote ended up disadvantaging a minority did not necessarily mean that the majority had abused its power.

**2.81** The relationship between the syndicate members is a balance between independent and collective rights and obligations. A balance clearly has to be struck by those drafting the agreement in order to satisfy the needs of both the syndicate as a whole and the individual participants thereto. In the final analysis the banks or their lawyers will need to be satisfied at the voting arrangements and the wording of the contract before they commit themselves. Once the agreement is signed they will be caught by its contents. Any dispute will be judged in the light of Lord Hoffman's four principles in *Chartbrook v Persimmon Homes*,[58] namely that:

(1) interpretation involves ascertaining the meaning which the document would convey to a reasonable person having the background information which would reasonably have been available to the parties at the time they negotiated the contract;

(2) 'background information' is taken to mean anything that would have affected the manner in which the terms in the document would have been understood by a reasonable man;

(3) 'background information' does not include the parties' previous negotiations and any subject declarations of intent. These would only be admissible in an action for rectification; and

(4) the meaning of a document has to be disaggregated from the meaning of its words. 'Background information' would assist a reasonable man in determining what the words mean.[59]

**2.82** This area can be a particular problem when there are disputes over whether or not to enforce the debt or any security in relation to it because the lenders are not all in agreement. The syndicate management clauses in the syndicated loan agreement will determine the relationship between the lenders and also between the lenders and the agent in this regard. The key issue will be the exact wording in the relevant clause(s), but the commonest in the current market is for an agreement to be binding if supported by two thirds of the lenders; the value of each share of the vote normally being determined

---

58 [2009] UKHL 38.

59 See also *Mannai Investment Co Ltd v Eagle Star Life Assurance Co Ltd* [1997] 2 WLR 945.

by the amount of the outstanding loan being held by each bank. Many agreements require that certain steps require the unanimous agreement of the lenders. Commonly the relevant terms are those relating to: extension of the payment dates, release of security and also a unanimous agreement including the agent where the change affects their rights or obligations.[60]

**2.83** A recent case in Hong Kong has muddied the waters somewhat. In *Charmway Hong Kong Investment v Fortunesea (Cayman) Ltd and others*[61] a dispute arose over enforcement. The case involved a syndicated loan of over $600 million by a group of 16 lenders to a group of construction companies in China on LMA based terms. Following the borrower's default two thirds of the lenders by outstanding amount started enforcement proceedings against the borrowing group's assets. Following a number of trades in the secondary market of segments of the syndicated loan there was a change in composition of the lenders, the majority of whom then gave notice to terminate proceedings. A minority group of the lenders then challenged this change of approach and they sought the right to enforce their rights by way of insolvency proceedings against the borrower's group; a course of action which was opposed by the majority lending group.

**2.84** The majority relied on clauses 2.2 (b) and (c) of the LMA Multicurrency Term and Revolving Facilities Agreement, which states:

'– the rights of a Finance Party under the Finance Documents are separate and independent rights;

– a Finance Party may, except as otherwise stated in the Finance Documents, separately enforce those rights; and

– a debt arising under the Finance Documents to a Finance Party is a separate and independent debt.'

They argued that this meant that a lender can sue for a debt owed to it independently.

Harris J determined that where a borrower is in default the enforcement of the whole debt is the issue. He stated that the agreement[62] required the lenders to make available 'term loan facility in aggregate amount equal to the Total Commitments' which thus created a single aggregate loan from the syndicate members and thus the debt was owed to the syndicate as a whole, not to its component members separately. Secondly, the loan agreement[63] had provided the agent with the

---

60 P Rawlings 'The Management of Loan Syndicates and the Rights of Individual Lenders' (2009) 24(4) JIBLR 179.

61 [2015] HKCU 1717.

62 In this regard replicating clause 2.1 of the LMA Multicurrency Term and Revolving Facilities Agreement, April 2020, as amended.

63 Clauses replicating clauses 23.13 (Acceleration) and 29 (Payment mechanics) of the LMA Multicurrency Term and Revolving Facilities Agreement, April 2020, as amended.

administrative power to act on the instructions of the majority lenders and thus no single lender could take proceedings. Finally, he added that syndicated loans are in market practice normally only enforced by a majority, or if the lending agreement so specifies, by a super majority. Thus, the majority took precedence and the minority could not take proceedings.

**2.85** However, following this case the LMA issued guidance that they did not believe that an English court would adopt the same approach as it was not in line with market practice and they believed that the standard LMA loan documentation gave individual lenders an independent right to enforce. Further, they issued an amended version of their standard loan agreement[64] granting separate and independent rights to each lender in a syndicate. However, there must remain some doubt as to the position on syndicated loans which use an earlier version of the text.

**2.86** Even where a majority decision is allowed a court may strike it down if the decision conflicts with other parts of the agreement. A complex structure was at issue in *Redwood Master Fund Ltd TD v Bank Europe Ltd* [65] where the loan was in three separate facilities. The borrower requested the lenders' consent to breaches of some of the financial covenants in the loan agreement and access to part of loan facility A and at the same time to repay facility B. Facilities A and B were made available by different lenders. The relevant clause in the loan agreement required that two thirds of the lenders had to consent to any change. This was an overall figure and did not require the majority in any of the three facilities that made up the loan arrangement. The majority was 82% but a small minority lender challenged on the basis that the majority had to use their vote for the benefit of all the lenders. This argument was rejected by the court on the basis that the loan agreement contained no such provision and was carefully drafted. Even where the drafting is not precise the majority principle will still be difficult to challenge:

> 'Powers given to majorities to bind minorities are always liable to abuse; and, whilst full effect ought to be given to them in cases clearly falling within them, ambiguities of language ought not to be taken advantage of to strengthen them and make them applicable to cases not included in those which they were apparently intended to meet.'[66]

The traditional English view goes at least this far. In *Goodfellow v Nelson Line (Liverpool) Ltd*[67] Parker J stated that:

---

64 5 November 2015.
65 [2002] EWHC 2703 (Ch).
66 *First National Bank of Louisville v Illinois Bank and Trust Co of Chicago* 933 F 2d 466 (1991, 7th Cir) at 489.
67 [1912] 2 Ch 324 at 333.

> 'The powers conferred ... on a majority must of course be exercised bona fide, and the court can no doubt interfere to prevent unfairness or oppression, but subject to this each ... may vote with regard to his individual interests.'

This could only really be challenged where the vote was motivated by dishonest considerations exercised for an improper purpose.[68]

**2.87** With regard to enforcement of the debt the same principle applies unless the wording of the relevant clause(s) appears to permit an individual or a minority to do so,[69] though this is not standard market practice.[70] This is important in the context of the secondary debt market where banks and other parties not involved in the original syndicated loan may purchase the involvement of one of the lenders in the transaction. If the borrower is in financial difficulties they may have been able to buy this involvement at less than full value. It would clearly pose a threat to syndicated loans containing the right of a lender to sell their involvement if such a third party could then enforce the debt without the agreement of the other lenders. The process of transferring a loan is considered in the next chapter.

---

68 See *Redwood Master Fund Ltd v TD Bank Europe Ltd* [2002] EWHC 2703 (Ch) at 105.

69 *A I Credit Corp v The Government of Jamaica* 666 F Supp. 629 (SDNY 1987); *The Commercial Bank of Kuwait v Radfidain* Bank 15 F 3rd 238 (2nd Cir 1994).

70 It is worth adding that this is not a unanimous view. See Smith J's minority judgment in *Beal Savings Bank v Sommer* 8 NY 3d 318, 300 (2007) at 332, but it is the majority view and most would disagree with Smith J's position.

# Chapter 3 Secondary Syndication – Loan Transfer

## Introduction

**3.1** Asset sales on the secondary loan markets, have become a more important part of the financial system over recent decades. The big rise in activity initially arose as a result of the 1980s sovereign debt crisis where banks sought to reduce their exposure to certain sovereign debts by selling on some of the loans. Then banks and certain other financial institutions then began through the 1990s and 2000s to utilise the secondary market more extensively to maximise the available profits.[1] Then again after the financial crisis of 2008 many banks had to sell loans on to reduce the size of their balance sheet. Indeed, as of 2026 many banks will make loans or partake of syndicated loans with the intention of immediately selling them on as they can book a profit by doing so, primarily from front end fees.

**3.2** In parallel to these events the market was further developed by the development of securitisation (see **Chapter 5**), the entry into the market of non-banking institutions, funds investing in loan products and the expansion of the leveraged buyout market in the corporate sector. Finally, in various parts of the world organisations were set up to facilitate standard form documentation and operational procedures to make it easier to use the secondary debt market. In the UK, the Loan Markets Association (LMA),[2] in the US the Loan Syndication and Trading Association (LSTA)[3] and in Asia the Asia Pacific Loan Markets Association (APLMA)[4] all helped facilitate market activity in this way.

**3.3** The increasing use of asset sales by banks in the UK was further facilitated by a number of factors. Some banks wished to remove some of the assets from their balance sheet for capital adequacy reasons following the development of the Basel rules,[5] some wished to use re-use funds already loaned by utilising the funds elsewhere for a higher profit margin, some wished to reduce their exposure to a particular market sector or particular client, some wished to quasi-syndicate by making the initial loan itself and then sell part of it on, some to trade

1 T Rhodes *Syndicated Lending: Practice and Documentation* (Euromoney, 2009), p 581.
2 See www.lma.eu.com [Accessed 12 February 2026].
3 See www.lsta.org [Accessed 12 February 2026].
4 See www.aplma.com [Accessed 12 February 2026].
5 These are recommendations on banking supervision issued by the Basel Committee.

a loan on and profit from a margin differential and some to get rid of a risky debt or one that was is in default.

**3.4** In recent years the continued stimulus for the asset sales market has derived from the need for banks to continue to satisfy their customer's needs for new credits, whilst staying within externally and internally imposed ratios imposed on the use of capital and the return on assets and equity. Unfortunately, an excessive focus on the short term and greed by many at various levels in the banking system led to the over expansion of the secondary debt market, with many banks and other financial institutions holding debt paper acquired on the secondary market originally issued through securitised techniques (see **Chapter 5**) without fully assessing the risks associated with it.

**3.5** An asset sale is the process by which a bank disposes of a loan to another bank in a manner which will allow the selling bank to remove the loan from its balance sheet as an asset. Central to achieving this objective is the ability of the selling bank to demonstrate that it has successfully transferred the credit risk of the borrower to the buying bank. Throughout this chapter this simple model will be used as the basis for legal analysis, although it is misleading to assume that this is by any means the only type of activity which properly comes under the broad umbrella of the term 'asset sales'. Commitments to lend and contingencies, such as the risk under swap contracts or the risk of non-reimbursement under letters of credit or bankers' acceptances, can be, and often are, sold by banks. However, to simply explain, the expression 'seller' or 'selling bank' will be used to describe the person disposing of the risk in question, the expression 'buyer' or 'buying bank' to describe the person assuming the risk and the expression 'sale' or 'disposal' (and cognate expressions) to refer to the method of passing risk whether by novation, assignment financed participation, or otherwise.

## Methods of sale

**3.6** What, then, are the legal techniques that may be employed by a bank to achieve the sale of a loan?[6] The following principal techniques are commonly employed under English law. In practice the declining order according to how frequently they are used are: novation, funded participation, legal assignment, equitable assignment, non-funded participation and trusts. However, in terms of the activity it is more helpful to first deal with those methods where the debt is actually sold on, ie, novation, legal assignment and equitable assignment and

6 For useful background see Allen, M 'Asset sales – an analysis of risk for buyers and sellers' (1987) 2(1) JIBL 13–21, Barratt J 'Distressed debt – the sale of loan assets' (1998) 13(2) JIBL 50, Oldnall J 'The Age of Consent' (2010) 25(2) JIBLR 89–93 and Dewulf-Verstraeten S 'Removing loans from banks' balance sheets – an overview of the techniques, the markets and the regulatory issues.' (1992) 7(8) JIBL 300–314.

then the methods where the bank retains the loan but covers the balance sheet effect by utilising sub participation, risk participation and synthetic securitisation. Finally, we will briefly consider the use of trusts in this situation.

## Novation

**3.7** In the context of the sale of a loan, 'novation' is the name given to an arrangement whereby the mutual rights and obligations of the selling bank, and the other parties to the underlying loan documentation, are relinquished and discharged in consideration of the establishment of new rights and obligations, on identical terms, between the buying bank and such other parties. In other words, the novation gives rise to an entirely new contract between the original parties to the loan (other than the seller) and the buyer. Currently it seems to be the most commonly used method of debt transfer between banks in the London markets and also in Europe.

**3.8** It could be argued that novation produces the ideal result from the perspective of both buyer and seller. The seller relieves himself of his obligations to the borrower and this may be particularly important when a bank is selling commitments to lend, which is something it will be unable to achieve by an assignment or the granting of a participation agreement (see below). The buyer, on the other hand, puts itself in the same position as the original lender. It will have a direct contractual relationship with the borrower and will have all the rights and benefits which it would have had if it had been a party to the original facility. As it is a new contract consideration will be required but in the context of international banking this is unlikely to prove a problem as the bank or other institution acquiring the loan will be paying to acquire it.

**3.9** A major difficulty with a novation, however, is the fact that it can be a cumbersome method of selling a loan asset since it requires the agreement of all the original parties to the loan. Such agreement may be particularly difficult to obtain in a conventionally structured syndicated loan agreement. As Collins MR pointed out:

> 'A debtor cannot relieve himself of his liability to his creditor by assigning the burden of the obligation to somebody else; this can only be brought about by the consent of all three, and involves the release of the original debtor'.[7]

**3.10** There are also problems where the debt is secured, as the process of novation will release any security and it will need to be retaken. The procedure for retaking mortgages or charges and re-registering them is straightforward enough and, apart from Land Registry fees, inexpensive. However, as the charges are to now be

---

7 *Tolhurst v Associated Portland Cement Manufacturers (*1900) 2 KB 660 at p 668.

taken at a later date, prioritisation will be lost if a third party has taken charges over the property in the meantime. For this reason it is common in the context of syndicated lending (see **Chapter 2**) and bond issues (see **Chapter 4**) to hold security on trust to avoid problems of this sort.[8] This is discussed further in **Chapter 4**.

**3.11** Notwithstanding the practical problems which it may pose, novation is the most commonly used means of disposing of assets especially where the asset takes the form of a contingent liability such as that under a backstop loan facility or a revolving credit. This is largely facilitated by the practice of including in the loan document transfer language setting out procedures for the future novation by lenders of their respective rights and obligations under the loan document. A modified example of such language is contained in Clause 24 of the LMA's Multicurrency Revolving Credit Facility.

> 'Subject to this clause 24, a lender (the 'Existing Lender') may … transfer by novation any of its rights and obligations to another bank or financial institution or to a trust fund or other entity which is regularly engaged in or established for the purpose of making, purchasing or investing in loans, securities or other financial assets ('the New Lender')'

**3.12** Various conditions follow in 24.2:

'(a) The consent of the Company is required for a … transfer by an existing Lender, unless the … transfer is to another Lender or an affiliate of a Lender….or made at a time when an Event of Default is continuing.

(b) The consent of the Company to a … transfer must not be unreasonably withheld or delayed. The Company will be deemed to have given its consent five business days after the Existing Lender has requested it unless consent is expressly refused by the Company within that time.

(c) The consent of the Company to a … transfer must not be withheld solely because the … transfer may result in an increase in the Mandatory Cost ………'

This continues at 24.3 which adds amongst other things

'(b) A transfer will only be effective if the procedures set out in Clause 24.6 (*Procedure for transfer*) is complied with.'

8 *British Energy Power & Energy Trading Ltd v Credit Suisse* [2008] EWCA Civ 53. See also 'Syndicated Loans' (2008) 23(4) BJIBFL 211; Freshfields Bruckhaus Deringer, 'Agency' (2008) 19 (3) PLC 54. Also *Fiona Trust & Holding Corp v Privalou* [2007] UKHL 40, [2007] 4 All ER 951; *Argo Fund Ltd v Essar Steel Ltd* [2006] EWCA Civ 241, [2006] 2 All ER (Comm) 104 and *Robinson v Bird* [2003] EWCA Civ 1820, [2003] WTLR 257.

**3.13** The transfer language of this clause simplifies the process of novation by obtaining the agreement in advance of all parties to the loan document to any future novation. In doing so it takes advantage of the principle of English law that an offer may be made 'to the public at large' which was established in the well-known case of *Carlill v Carbolic Smoke Ball Co*.[9] Such an offer may be accepted by anyone who satisfies the conditions specified in the offer. Thus, the novation itself can be facilitated by the scheduling to the loan document a short form of transfer certificate. The execution of the certificate by the selling and buying bank and the delivery to the borrower or the agent bank of the executed certificate will complete the novation. The transfer method has, therefore, borrowed the old established principle of English law that an offer may be made to the public at large without it being necessary for the offeror to know the identity of the other party to the contract. This approach was confirmed by the High Court in *Argo Fund Ltd v Essar Steel Ltd*[10] where it was also suggested obiter by Aikens J that a novation which failed because the transferee did not fall within the category of permitted transferees required by a term in the original loan agreement (banks or other financial institutions in this case) could not take effect as an assignment. The exact outcome in any case will use depend on the precise terms used in the loan agreement.

**3.14** Loan agreements typically take the approach to novation and assignments that there is a requirement for the consent of the borrower not to be unreasonably withheld or delayed, for novation, or assignments or other transfers of rights and/or obligations outside the selling bank's own group. Where obligations are novated it is invariably the case that the borrower's consent will be required as the borrower will be taking a credit risk on the transferee. An international novation (or for that matter an assignment) may also have disastrous consequences for the buyer if full regard is not had to the position under local law.

**3.15** Notwithstanding these difficulties there are an increasing number of situations where novation will be the preferred route. It gives the buyer a beneficial interest in a debt, the new debt arising from the novation. This may be vital where the buyer is seeking to take advantage of an available tax credit in its own jurisdiction. With weaker credits, and certainly where rescheduled or potentially reschedulable debt is involved, the buyer will often wish to have a directly enforceable claim against the borrower. Indeed, the wishes of seller and buyer will usually coincide in such a situation since the seller will want the consequences of, and the responsibility for, handling any default or restructuring which may occur to fall upon the buyer.

---

9 [1893] 1 QB 256; see also *New Zealand Shipping Co Ltd v AM Satterthwaite & Co Ltd (The Eurymedon)* [1975] AC 154.

10 [2005] EWHC 600 (Comm), 2 Lloyd's Rep 203.

**3.16** The attractiveness of novation to the original lender is that it is effective to transfer all the existing rights and obligations on an identical basis to the buyer of the debt. This makes it ideal to transfer debts where there is an ongoing obligation on the lender to make further payments, as is the case in revolving credit facilities. So where a need arises to transfer the seller's obligations under a loan facility to the buyer, as with a revolving or back stop facility, then novation provides the only solution. It is normal both in assignments and funded participations to impose an obligation on the assignee or sub participant to fund future payment obligations of the seller. Such undertakings will, however, only normally operate contractually between seller and buyer. If the buyer defaults, the borrower can still insist on the seller performing its contractual obligations to the borrower under the terms of the loan facility. Under a novation the borrower agrees to discharge the legal obligations owed by the seller in consideration of the buyer assuming identical obligations. The rights and obligations of a participant or a transferee under a novation are capable of straightforward analysis. Under a novation the transferee will normally assume obligations identical to those which remain to be performed by the original lender. The rights of the transferee under a novation will in most cases be identical in content to those of the original lender.

## Legal assignment

**3.17** The starting point for a consideration of this is the Law of Property Act 1925 (LPA 1925), s 136, which states in subs (1) that:

> 'Any absolute assignment by writing under the hand of the assignor (not purporting to be by way of charge only) of any debt or other legal thing in action, of which express notice in writing has been given to the debtor, trustee or other person from whom the assignor would have been entitled to claim such debt or thing in action, is effectual in law (subject to equities having priority over the right of the assignee) to pass and transfer from the date of such notice:—
>
> (a) the legal right to such debt or thing in action;
>
> (b) all legal and other remedies for the same; and
>
> (c) the power to give a good discharge for the same without the concurrence of the assignor …'

Therefore, in essence, a legal assignment consists of a written agreement, signed by the assignor transferring the debt involved, with notice of the fact having been given to the debtor. If all these elements cannot be satisfied a legal assignment cannot validly take place. This will usually tend to occur in practice because the debtor has not been notified, normally because the assignor does not wish to prejudice their future relationship with them. There is also a problem if only part of the debt is to be assigned to the buyer. An assignment of part of a debt is not 'absolute' as it was regarded as unfair for a debtor to be put in a position where he could not dispute the debt if the assignee could sue in their own right. If the assignment were absolute the assignee would be able to sue for the debt alone.[11] Also, the assignor of part of a debt cannot sue for the retained part of the debt without joining the assignee as a party to the action. Finally, the assignment will not be valid under s.136 if is not perfected because it is not in writing. However, as can be seen below an equitable assignment may still be a possibility to resolve such problems.

**3.18** A legal assignment is operative to give the assignee the full legal and beneficial interest in the debt with the result that the assignee will be able to sue the borrower directly without any need to rely upon the assignor to assist in the enforcement of the debt. However, unless the other parties to the loan contract agree otherwise, an assignment will only operate to transfer rights and benefits, it will not operate to transfer obligations.[12] The selling bank will, accordingly, remain obliged even after the assignment to perform any obligations owed to the borrower which remain to be performed. These obligations may be significant with, say: a staged project finance loan, a revolving loan or even with a fully drawn term loan where, say, a multicurrency option exists which may require top up payments on interest payment dates or, sometimes, the repayment and re-advance of the loan where currencies are switched.

**3.19** It is important when drafting an assignment agreement to deal with the question of set off as otherwise the debt held by the assignee may be reduced by set offs applying to it. This is especially an issue where the assignor is the main banker to the debtor and operates a number of accounts on their behalf and is maintaining them, apart from the debt being assigned. Such set offs may arise as a result of the contractual relationship between the assignor and the borrower or they may arise at equity. Alternately, where the debt relates to a contract for the sale of goods, services, land or another debt there remains the potential for a cross claim arising from the contractual relationship between the debtor and the other party to that contract. This could result in a set off reducing the size of the debt in the hands of the assignee. The contractual approach adopted is to require the debtor to confirm that:

- the contract being assigned has no contractual rights of set off;[13]

---

11 *Forster v Baker* [1910] 2 KB 636

12 *Trendtex Corporation v Credit Suisse* [1980] QB 629, *Tolhurst v Associated Portland Cement* [1902] 2 KB 660 and *United Dominions Trust v Parkway Motors* [1955] 2 All ER 557.

13 '...[T]he right to set off can be excluded by agreement...' Neill LJ in *Coca Cola v Finsat International Ltd* [1996] EWCA Civ J0425-9 at p 52 B-D

- no rights of set off exist at the time of assignment; and
- no rights of set off have been asserted at the time of assignment.

However, this is not fool proof under English law and in some jurisdictions may be of limited effect.

**3.20** Another problem is that if assignment is debarred by the original loan agreement, or more commonly is only permissible at the borrower's consent, and this is not forthcoming, the assignment will not be valid against the debtor.[14] That said, this would be an unusual situation as the granting of consent is the normal approach.

**3.21** It is a basic principle of assignment that it takes place subject to equities and, amongst other things, this means that the debtor whose obligation has been assigned should not then be in a worse position than if there had been no assignment.[15] Thus, the assignee is not in a position to recover a greater amount from the debtor than the assignor could have done had no assignment been created.[16]

**3.22** A useful starting point for a discussion on the rights and obligations of the buyer is an examination of the basic principle that an assignee acquires the rights but not the obligations of the assignor. Thus, in the absence of the consent of all parties to the original loan agreement the assignor will remain obliged to perform all the obligations which it originally contracted to perform vis-à-vis the borrower, although it is invariably the case that any assignee will be required in the assignment to agree to fund the assignor's payment obligations.

**3.23** On a more practical level, however, circumstances will arise when it will be desirable, or even critical, that the assignee performs the obligations of the assignor. Most obviously this will be the case where the assignor defaults in the performance of an obligation which is a condition to the assignor obtaining some benefit under the loan agreement. Similarly, where defaults by the assignor under the loan facility will potentially give rise to a consequence adverse to the interests of the assignee, such as a termination of the loan contract or action for breach of contract with the attendant possibility of set offs and counterclaims. In such a case the assignee may find that performance of the contract is a small price to pay to protect his interests.

**3.24** Nor is it true that the assignee of a loan will necessarily acquire all the rights of the seller under the loan facility being sold. Two overriding principles may come into play which may make any assignment ineffective or restrict the rights transferred by such

---

[14] *Linden Gardens Trust Ltd v Lenesta Sludge Disposals Ltd* [1994] 1 AC 85.

[15] *Dawson v Great Northern & City Railways Co* [1905] 1 KB 260.

[16] However, *Technotrade Ltd v Larkstore Ltd* [2006] EWCA Civ 1079, [2006] 1 WLR 2926 may threaten this in cases where the debtor breaches the contract. The assignment cannot be used by the debtor to escape obligations.

assignment. These are the principles that a debt is not assignable if the debtor is put in a worse position than he would have been but for the assignment, and the principle that personal contracts are not assignable. Taking the first of these it is doubtful whether an assignee would, unless the loan agreement otherwise provides, acquire the benefit of such protective provisions as grossing up provisions in tax clauses or indemnities under increased cost clauses or, indeed, the benefit of any indemnity under the loan agreement.

**3.25** The borrower should make it clear within the terms of the loan documentation that it is not liable to gross up for taxes or indemnify against increased costs where no such liability would have arisen but for the assignment.

**3.26** To return to the original point of this analysis, the reason why a borrower may find its position prejudiced by an assignment is that it is often the case that the loan documentation will make it clear that the benefit of all rights under the loan facility extends to assignees or transferees. If so, the principle that the debtor cannot be put in a worse position by an assignment will clearly be displaced. It is important, therefore, for an assignee to check the loan documentation closely to establish what rights it will actually acquire irrespective of what the assignment agreement may purport to say on the subject. Conversely assignors should beware writing assignments which assign 'all the assignor's rights, benefits and title in, to and under' the relevant loan agreement, as to do so may make the assignor potentially liable to the assignee in contract or in an action for misrepresentation.

**3.27** The principle that personal contracts are not assignable is a related but different principle from that just discussed. Here, the focus is not so much on an increase in the debtor's burden under the loan contract, but the degree to which the contractual relationship between the parties involves personal skill or confidence. The question is whether 'it can make no difference to the person on whom the obligation lies to which of the persons he is to discharge it.' As the courts appear to apply an objective test in answering this question and do not examine, for example, whether one creditor is more likely to pursue his rights and remedies more vigorously than another,[17] it is a principle which will be of limited application in the context of the assignability of loan agreements.

**3.28** One can, nonetheless, imagine circumstances where the continued involvement in a loan of a particular bank might give rise to the implied non-assignability of the loan. This might be the case, for example, in a complicated project financing where a particular bank might have an important monitoring or administrative function. It is more likely, however, that this role would be carried out by a bank in

---

17 *Fitzroy v Cave* [1905] 2 KB 364.

a capacity other than as lender and in such a case there should be no reason why its rights as a lender could not be assigned.

**3.29** From what has been said earlier in this chapter it is hardly surprising that the assignee will normally take the contract assigned as he finds it. In other words he will not, by virtue of the assignment be put in a better position than the assignor. If a debt is mistakenly or fraudulently assigned at a time when it has already been paid or if such debt is void or unenforceable, then the assignee will have no choice but to look to the assignor for his remedy.

## Equitable assignment and charge

**3.30** In simple terms, a legal assignment is an assignment which satisfies the conditions in the Law of Property Act 1925, s 136, an equitable assignment is one which does not. This section is effectively a reproduction of s 25(6) of the Judicature Act 1873[18] which came into force to deal with the consequences of removing the separate courts for equity and common law and which created a statutory assignment in addition to the arrangements that had previously been available.[19]

**3.31** In current commercial practice the key factor is that the assignor may not wish the debtor to know that the repayments are being assigned and thus a common law assignment cannot take place. It is this issue of giving notice to the debtor which today is more significant than technical distinctions between legal and equitable assignments. This is because:

(a) until notice is given, the borrower may continue to discharge the debt by making payments to the assignor with all the practical problems of tracing which this may present on liquidation of the assignor;

(b) priorities as between competing equitable assignees may turn on the order in which notice has been given. Essentially this is the position but the rule in *Dearle v Hall*[20] states that although interests normally rank in the order of their creation, where there is more than one equitable assignee who has taken without notice

---

18 For useful background articles see Bridge M 'The nature of assignment and non-assignment clauses' (2016) 132(Jan) LQR 47–67, Edelman J and Elliott S 'Two conceptions of equitable assignment' (2016) 131(Apr) LQR 228–250 and Tolhurst CJ 'Equitable assignment of legal rights: a resolution to a conundrum.' (2002) 118 (Jan) LQR 98–123.

19 A summary of the pre-existing law can be found in Peel (Ed), *Treitel on The Law of Contract*.16th edn (Sweet & Maxwell, 2025), pp 764–768.

20 (1823) 3 Russ 1. In *Ward v Duncome* [1893] AC 369 the House of Lords determined that the priority of dealings applies regardless of the conduct of competing assignees which could be argued to undermine the whole original purpose of *Dearle v Hall*. The Law Commission did recommend the abolition of the rule in Consultation Paper No 164 but this did not make it through with the recommendations adopted in the Companies Act 2006 (Amendment of Pt 25) Regulations 2013.

of a previous equitable assignment, priority arises in the order in which they give notice to the debtor; and

(c) notice prevents the debtor from setting up any new rights of set off, counterclaim or equities which it may have against the assignor.

**3.32** In broad terms it may be said that, provided notice of assignment is given later to the underlying obligor, as far as English law is concerned the differences between a legal and an equitable assignment are more apparent than real. Indeed, providing notice to the ultimate obligor will normally convert the equitable charge to a legal one provided insolvency proceedings have not commenced, after which it will be too late.[21] An equitable assignment gives the assignee the powers of a beneficial owner. He will not have unfettered powers of legal action, but in practice all that means is that he must join the assignor as party to the action. If the assignor will not co-operate they can be joined to the action by being made a co-defendant. However, if insolvency proceedings have commenced against the assignor, the assignee's interest would appear to be an unregistered charge which would be unenforceable. If an unsecured assignee could take proceedings, they would be an unsecured creditor with implications for the amount that would finally be received.[22]

**3.33** However, suppose that the assignor has become insolvent. This is a low risk with banks as, on the rare occasion that they fail, the government tends to rescue them due to the financial and political damage that would result from a bank failure. However, the original assignment could well have been to a corporation or a hedge fund and with such parties the risk of failure is much higher. This is a problem with an equitable assignment as it really creates an equitable charge in the form of a lien or trust.[23] Originally, prior to the Judicature Act 1873, an equitable assignment was the only type of assignment available and the view following that Act was that only a legal assignment created a transfer of the legal title. Clearly, as stated above if the debtor is notified then, if failure to notify is the sole reason for the assignment being equitable (and it usually is) then it is too late if an attempt is made to do so after the debtor has fallen into insolvency because it would be void under Insolvency Act 1986, s 127. Therefore, the safe route is to register equitable assignments as charges at Companies House. This would have to be done within 21 days of the charge being created or it would be void as a charge as against any subsequent liquidator, administrator or creditor.[24]

---

21 Insolvency Act 1986, s 127 and Sch B1, paras 42 and 43.

22 For a general discussion see Walton P 'Assignments of Book Debts – outright transfers of rights or unregistered securities?' (2018) 1(1) Wolverhampton Law Journal 1–19.

23 *Diplock v Hammond* (1854) 2 Sm & Giff 141, *Collyer v Fallon* (1823) Turn & R 459 and *Gorringe v Irwell India Rubber and Gutta Percha Works* (1886) 34 Ch D 128.

24 Companies Act 2006, ss 859A and 859H.

**3.34** It has been suggested that a significant defect of the notified equitable assignment as compared to a legal assignment is that a bona fide legal purchaser of the debt without notice of the prior equitable interest may rank ahead of the equitable assignment in terms of priority. However, it seems[25] that the bona fide purchaser is displaced by LPA 1925, s 136, which subjects legal assignment to 'equities having priority over the right of the assignee'. Of course, the granting of a legal assignment after an equitable assignment has previously been granted by the selling bank assumes fraud on the part of the selling bank. The risk of such a fraud is normally discounted by buying banks in the asset sales market.

**3.35** The question of notice is an issue that will often be more in the interests of the assignee, and therefore it is often the assignee who will give notice of the assignment to the debtor, and the agent bank in a syndicated credit. It is surprising that the right to give or the responsibility for giving notice is not expressly given to or imposed by English law on the assignor or assignee. It would appear that either can give notice and that notice need not be given formally or in writing, unless s 136 applies, in which case it must be in writing. Indeed, it is sufficient that the debtor is aware of the assignment although his awareness may be derived from sources other than the assignor or the assignee.[26]

## Funded participation (sub-participation)

**3.36** The second most popular legal technique used in the off balance sheet disposal of assets is funded participation, often known as sub-participation. The term has now been recognised by the Privy Council in *Lloyds TSB Bank PLC v Clarke (Liquidator of Socimer International Bank Ltd) and Chase Manhattan Bank Luxembourg SA*.[27] It is normally used to describe a funding arrangement between the seller and the participant under which the participant places funds with the original lender on terms that those funds will only be repaid to the participant together with interest thereon as and when corresponding amounts of principal and interest are received from the borrower under the loan to which the participation relates.[28] The participation is thus non-recourse to the selling bank in the sense that the seller is not liable to make payments to the participant if corresponding amounts are not received from the borrower. The participant has no proprietary

---

25 *Dearle v Hall* (1828) 3 Russ 1.

26 *Lloyd v Banks* [1868] Ch App 488. Here the notice was acquired by the debtor reading a newspaper.

27 [2002] UKPC 27; [2002] 2 All ER 992. See also *Street v Mountford* [1985] AC 809 where the same issue arose in relation to a lease, *Agnew v Commissioner for Inland Revenue* [2001] 2 AC 710 where the issue arose in relation to a floating charge and *Cotton v Heyl* [1930] 1 Ch 510.

28 One advantage of this is that the original lender will be able to offset one loan against the other for capital adequacy purposes.

rights in the facility and is an unsecured creditor for the funds should the seller become insolvent.[29] The legal validity of the arrangement is based on the fact that loans repayable on a contingency are recognised by the common law.[30]

FIGURE 1: PARTICIPATION BY AN INCOMING BANK FOR A BANK IN A SYNDICATED LOAN

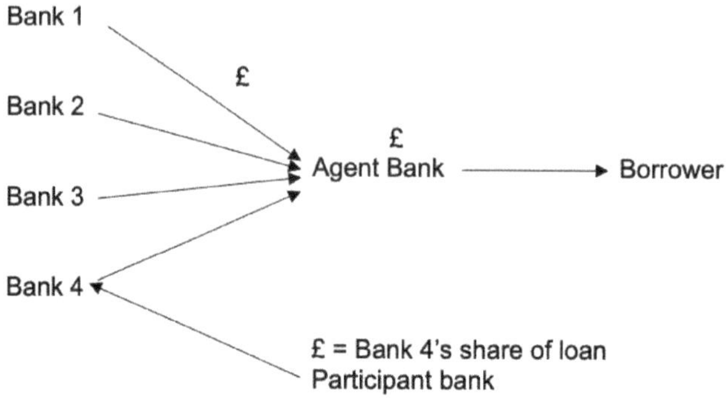


**3.37** The important distinction between a participation on one hand and an assignment or a novation on the other is that the participation is an entirely separate contractual arrangement from the underlying loan agreement and there is, accordingly, no contractual nexus between the participant and the borrower. In basic legal terms this means that the participant will not be able to sue the borrower in the event of default by the borrower in performing its obligations under the loan agreement. It will have to rely on the original lender to take recovery action, although, as will be seen later in this chapter, it may be able to exercise some influence over the actions taken by the lender following a default.

**3.38** From this legal distinction between participations, novation and assignments flows an equally significant commercial distinction. The party taking a loan participation acquires a double credit risk: that of the borrower and of the original lender. If the original lender goes into liquidation, the participant will find that monies subsequently recovered from the borrower will not be applied in satisfying the original lender's liabilities under the participation, but rather towards the liabilities of the original lender owed to its general body of creditors. The participant will thus be an unsecured creditor.

**3.39** The popularity of the loan participation will, double credit risks notwithstanding, appear less surprising due to the impact of non-UK legal aspects of asset sales, in addition to any contractual restrictions in loan documentation which can impede the disposal of loan assets. This is much less common than was the case in the past as market

---

29 *Lloyds TSB* case, above.
30 *Waite Hill Holdings v Marsha* [1983] 133 NLJ 745.

participants are realistic about the possible future need of a lender to sell the loan.

**3.40** Mention has already been made of the attraction and popularity of funded participation as a method of disposing of assets. This derives essentially from the legal nature of the funded participation, which establishes a distinct and separate legal relationship between seller and buyer. Accordingly, participation does not involve a transfer of the beneficial ownership in the underlying loan debt or indeed any of the rights of the seller in respect of the underlying loan facility.

**3.41** For these reasons it is unusual to find in a loan document any express attempt to restrict the granting of such participations. Further, and equally importantly, it is rare for the law of the borrower or any guarantor, where they are non-UK entities, to seek to impose conditions on or otherwise seek to regulate the granting of a funded participation. Nor will a participation normally attract adverse tax consequences in the borrower's or the guarantor's jurisdiction.

**3.42** A buyer which is interested in establishing a banker-customer relationship with the borrower may refuse to accept a funded participation as it prevents them from having a contractual nexus with the borrower. Indeed, it is often the desire to maintain a legal and contractual relationship with the borrower which drives sellers towards the use of this arrangement as a sale instrument. For example they may wish to appear to the borrower to be the lender to maintain a successful ongoing relationship. Where relationship factors are less relevant a seller may defer to the buyer's wishes for a novation or an assignment.

**3.43** There is an additional form of participation called risk participation which is non-funded and used much less frequently. It is discussed below.

**3.44** Typically, the participation will contain protective language along the following lines:

> 'It is further agreed that the Original Lender is and shall remain entitled to:
>
> (i) exercise or refrain from exercising any or all of its rights and powers arising under or in connection with the Loan Agreement or any document relating thereto; and
>
> (ii) agree to any amendment or waiver of the terms of the Loan Agreement or any other such document. Provided that, in exercising or refraining from exercising such rights and powers or agreeing to such amendment or waiver, the Original Lender shall have regard to all relevant circumstances including the interests of the Participant and the Original Lender shall not be entitled under this Clause to agree to any such amendment or waiver which would directly result in the reduction of the Loan otherwise than by repayment.'

The limits of the protection which this language may afford the original lender can be seen if we take the example of a refinancing of the old loan. In such a case the existing lenders will be required to make a new loan to the borrower on the revised terms and this new loan will be applied in or towards repayment of the old loan. The irony here is that repayment of the old loan will trigger an obligation on the part of the original lender to pay out his participant under the participation. Thus, it may be that, just at the point at which the borrower's credit deteriorates, the participant finds that his participation is paid out. It is no consolation to the original lender to say that he is not legally obliged to enter into any rescheduling arrangements. The rescheduling may represent his only realistic hope of recovering his money and the pressures to cooperate may in any event prove difficult to resist.

**3.45** It is to counter the possibility of the borrower's credit risk returning to the original lender in this way that banks selling participations have sought to protect their position on rescheduling. A typical clause may read as follows:

> 'If the persons to whom is owed at least fifty per cent, of the Borrower's indebtedness, or any class of the Borrower's indebtedness of which the Advances outstanding under the Participated Facility form part, agree to any readjustment or rescheduling (howsoever described) of such, or such class of such, indebtedness, then the Original Lender may agree to, or participate in, such readjustment or rescheduling on such terms as the Original Lender thinks fit and, for these purposes, the Original Lender shall be entitled, inter alia, to:
>
> (i) agree to any release, novation or payment of any of the Borrower's indebtedness under the Participated Facility;
>
> (ii) undertake on its own behalf any obligations in connection with such readjustment or rescheduling;
>
> (iii) treat any principal amounts advanced to it by the Participant hereunder as if the same had been advanced to it by the Participant in respect of the Original Lender's obligations in relation to such readjustment or rescheduling and, to the extent that the Original Lender so treats such amounts, retain for its own account any principal amounts which would otherwise have been payable to the Participant pursuant to [refer to relevant clause];
>
> (iv) treat any amounts (other than amounts of principal) which would otherwise have been payable to the Participant pursuant to [refer to relevant clause] as if the same had been principal amounts advanced to it by the Participant in respect of its obligations in relation to such readjustment or rescheduling; and

(v) convert, at such rates as may be determined by it, any amount treated by it as having been advanced to it by the Participant in respect of its obligations in relation to such readjustment or rescheduling into such currencies as such obligations may from time to time be denominated.

Provided that in agreeing to, or participating in, such readjustment or rescheduling the Bank shall have regard to all relevant circumstances including the interests of the Participant.'

**3.46** Having established that the rescheduling will not entitle the participant to be paid out under the terms of the participation, the clause will normally continue by providing that the original lender's sole obligation thereafter is to pay to the participant amounts corresponding to monies received under the rescheduling which are attributable to the amounts paid by the participant to the seller under the original terms of the participation. A participant will owe no obligations to the debtor but will normally contractually undertake with the original lender to fund any payment which the original lender has to make to the borrower under the terms of the loan facility.

**3.47** A participant will not be able to claim the direct benefit of any of the lender's rights under the loan contract. Any protections required by the participant against such matters as taxes, increased costs, illegality, reserve asset costs and so forth will have to be separately negotiated with the selling bank. It is unlikely that the seller will be prepared to accord the participant the same protections which the borrower will give to the seller. At best a seller may agree to pass on amounts corresponding to those recovered from the borrower under the loan agreement. Without careful contractual drafting it will be far from certain precisely what the original lender will be entitled to claim under these provisions, following the granting of a participation.

## Risk participation (non-funded participation)

**3.48** Where the underlying risk which the bank is seeking to lay off takes the form of a non-funded asset then the document used to dispose of the risk is sometimes described as a risk participation. This type of instrument would commonly be used where the bank has a contingent liability, such as under a guarantee, or where it is contemplated that its legal liability will effectively be funded by its customer, as with liabilities under letters of credit or accepted bills of exchange. Under the risk participation the participant receives a fee for compensating the bank in the event of default in the performance by the bank's customer of its obligations. As such, the risk participation might well be viewed under English law as a contract of insurance.

FIGURE 2: RISK PARTICIPATION BY A PARTICIPANT BANK FOR A BANK GUARANTEEING PART OF A SYNDICATED LOAN

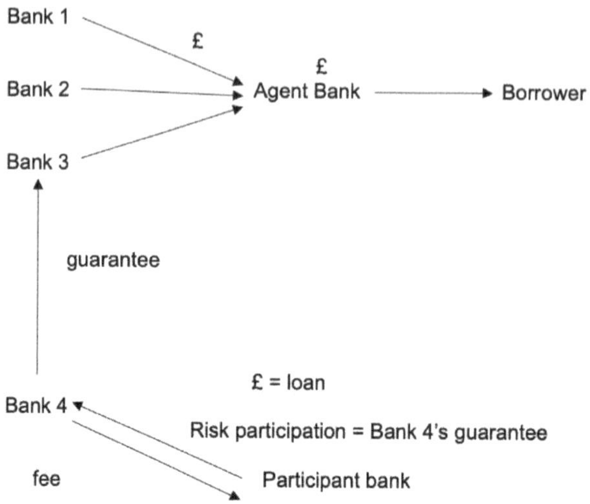


These arrangements have similar characteristics to the more commonly used credit default swaps which are discussed in **Chapter 6**.

## Synthetic securitisation

**3.49** Synthetic securitisation[31] exists where some of the risk associated with a pool of loans the bank has made is transferred to an investor, usually via a derivative, typically a credit default swap (see **6.15** and **6.16**). The originator, normally a bank, will buy from a third party (the 'investor') credit protection against a pool of loans and the credit will pay up if there is any shortfall from the underlying loan portfolio being paid to the bank. The bank retains ownership of the relevant assets and the investor takes on the risk of default in relation to the stated portfolio of obligations which are retained by the originator. Alternately a guarantee might be issued by the investor. It is called 'synthetic' because the loans are not transferred to a third party but remain on the bank's balance sheet. At first glance this looks similar to risk participation but there are differences in how the bank's capital requirements are affected and in practice synthetic securitisation structures can become more complex. This is discussed in more detail at **5.26** to **5.29**.

## Trusts

**3.50** Although of little relevance in the specific context of banks selling a loan or a part of a loan to others, trusts do have a role to play

31 Sometimes called 'significant risk transfer'.

in two main circumstances. One is where a trust vehicle is used to hold money for the benefit of a beneficiary or a group of them. This can exist in the form of a trust vehicle which is utilised as a holding vehicle for a pool of funds for the benefit of the settlor or a third party to whom the beneficial interest may have been transferred. These arrangements are also sometimes used in the distressed debt market. Trusts are also used by US originators as part of a securitisation structure as the US IRS do not recognise limited companies as being outside the corporate group of the originator. (See **Chapter 5**).

**3.51** The case of *Barbados Trust Co Ltd v Bank of Zambia and another*[32] held that if a loan agreement debars a transfer or only permits it subject to a contingency that has not occurred, then the party who has sold the debt cannot agree to then hold it on trust for the benefit of the supposed assignee. This effectively over rules what was thought to be a precedent to the contrary in *Don King Production Inc v Warren (No 1).*[33] In any event there is no evidence that in the years since the *Don King* case the markets have tried to adopt this approach as a regular method of debt transfer. It is not surprising that it is not more popular; a bank rendering itself a trustee to pass a share in a syndicated loan to another bank would be subject to the very strict rules applying to trustees and may become a fiduciary in relation to the debt concerned. This is an unappealing arrangement from their point of view and thus the trust is not likely to be used as a method of debt transfer.[34]

## English law considerations

**3.52** Having described the legal nature of the various sale techniques it might be helpful at this juncture to isolate a number of specific English law issues which a prudent seller or buyer should consider before concluding any asset sale. These issues will be considered under the following headings:

(a) credit risk;

(b) contractual restrictions;

(c) confidentiality; and

(d) liability of seller to buyer.

---

32 [2007] EWCA Civ 148

33 [2000] Ch 291; [1999] 2 All ER 218 See also *Re Turcan* [1888] 40 Ch D 5 and *Linden Gardens Trust Ltd v Sludge Disposals Ltd* [1994] 1 AC 85

34 See, eg *Barbados Trust Co Ltd v Bank of Zambia* [2007] EWCA Civ 148, [2007] 2 All ER (Comm) 445, and for a discussion of some of the issues M Smith, 'Locus standi and the enforcement of legal claims by cestui que trust and assignees' (2008) 22(3) TLI 140, and M Smith 'Equitable Owners Enforcing Legal Rights' (2008) 124 LQR 517.

## Credit risk

**3.53** Consideration of credit risk might conveniently be looked at both from the viewpoint of the credit risk of the borrower and the credit risk of the selling bank. The principal objective of the selling bank is to transfer the borrower's credit risk to the buying bank. As we have seen, this is generally achieved either by novating or assigning the debt to the buyer or by passing the risk to the buyer by means of a non-recourse, funded participation.

**3.54** One must consider, however, the situation where the borrower seeks to restructure or refinance the original loan facility either because he has run into financial difficulties and needs time to pay or, conversely, because he is now able to obtain better terms from other lenders. In such a situation the distinction between a funded participation on one hand and an assignment or novation on the other is seen at a practical level. As the seller of a funded participation remains the legal lender of record and beneficially entitled to receive repayment of the underlying debt, it will be to the original lender that the borrower and, where they are involved, central banks and other regulatory authorities, will look to agree the restructuring or refinancing of the loan.

## Contractual restrictions

**3.55** As assignment involves the transfer of rights arising as against the borrower under the relevant loan facility, it is not surprising that a borrower will seek to regulate when and upon what conditions assignments may occur. The borrower's case will be even stronger where the transfer of obligations owing to the borrower is contemplated. As an example of the type of restrictions which will commonly be negotiated, clauses 24 and 25 the LMA's Multicurrency Revolving Credit Agreement present a fairly standard set of provisions, consent of the borrower (not to be unreasonably withheld) being required unless the assignment or transfer of the lender is intra group.

**3.56** The consequences of failing to observe such contractual restrictions are clear. The novation or assignment will be invalid as against the borrower and may involve the seller in a claim for breach of contract. Indeed, the failure by the seller to deliver to the buyer what had been bargained for might mean that the novation or assignment would not even survive as a contractual arrangement binding seller and buyer alone.

**3.57** Although it is relatively common to find contractual restrictions on assignment within the terms of a loan document, effective restraints on the granting of participations are rare. This has been due to the fact that the participation does not involve any transfer of rights or obligations arising under the loan facility and, therefore, the general view seems to be that the granting of participations is a private matter between lender and participant and of no concern to the borrower. Whilst this may be correct from a strict legal point of view, the extent to which participants may influence the way in which the lender exercises its rights under the loan facility occasionally leads to a requirement that the borrower's consent be obtained or at least that notice of the participant's name be given. Of greater concern in this context is the question of confidentiality.

## Confidentiality

**3.58** Whatever the express contractual restrictions set out in the loan documentation, the ability of a lender to novate, participate or assign may be effectively restricted by considerations of confidentiality. A relationship of banker and customer exists between borrower and lender, and under English law, as well as in most other jurisdictions, a bank owes a duty of confidentiality to its customers.[35] Consequently, any disclosure by the lender to third parties of the terms of or, indeed, even the existence of any loan facility may well constitute a breach of this duty. Disclosure of information provided to the lender pursuant to or in connection with the facility would also clearly give rise to a claim for breach of this duty. Since the sale of a loan asset will normally necessitate the disclosure, at the very least, of the terms of the underlying loan, a seller could potentially find the path to such a sale blocked even where the loan documentation does not expressly prohibit sale in the manner proposed.

**3.59** The duty of confidentiality under English law is, thankfully for sellers of assets, not an absolute one.[36] The most relevant qualification of the duty for our purposes is where disclosure is made with the express or implied consent of the borrower.[37] A glance at clause 24.2, 24.6 and 24.7 of the Loan Markets Association Agreement discussed above will reveal the type of express disclosure language that a well drafted loan agreement typically contains. Implied consent is a concept which is a little more difficult. Is there implied consent where the loan agreement expressly allows assignments and participations without consent? Very probably it is, especially given that the participants in the original loan are experienced bankers who know full well that here is a real possibility that at some stage the loan may be novated or assigned. The case of holding that there is implied consent is strengthened where the salient terms of the facility are revealed publicly in the press with the consent of the borrower or where the borrower is made aware of the possibility of sales occurring and assents thereto. Indeed, in some instances of the last two examples the situation may amount to express consent. It will depend on the exact circumstances. Arguably in such circumstances

---

35 *Tournier v National Provincial and Union Bank of England* [1924] 1 KB 461, *Lipkin Gorman v Karpnale* [1989] 1 WLR 1341 at 1357 per May LJ.

36 *Tournier*, above.

37 *Turner v Royal Bank of Scotland plc* [1999] Lloyd's Rep Bank 231 at 235 suggests that the possibility of implied consent should be treated cautiously.

once the information disclosed is already in the public domain the issue ceases to be an element, at least as far as the facts in the public domain are concerned. There may also be data protection issues.[38]

**3.60** Breach of the duty of confidentiality will give rise to an action for damages in respect of loss arising from the breach. In the majority of cases, however, it will be difficult to discern precisely what loss has been suffered, if any. However, in a situation where, for example, defaults under the loan agreement or other facilities are revealed to third parties or where details of more favourable terms are disclosed to competitor banks, it will be much easier to identify the potential loss which may be claimed.

### Potential liability of seller to buyer

**3.61** The absence of any substantial case law on this subject makes analysis of the potential liability of a seller to the buyer most difficult. Insofar as the assignment or participation agreement is concerned, the responsibility of the seller to the buyer in relation to the borrower's financial condition and the adequacy and legalities of the underlying loan documentation will largely be disclaimed.

**3.62** The scope of disclaimer provisions in most agreements should leave the buyer in no doubt that the principle of caveat emptor is alive and well. The language of a typical disclaimer clause might read as follows:

> 'The Original Lender makes no representation or warranty and assumes no responsibility with respect to:
>
> (i) the due execution, legality, validity, adequacy or enforceability of the Loan Agreement or any document relating thereto, or
>
> (ii) the financial condition of the Borrower or any other party to the Loan Agreement or any document relating thereto; or
>
> (iii) the performance by the Borrower or any other such person of its obligations under the Loan Agreement or any other such document; in particular but without limitation, if the Borrower or any other person shall fail to perform any of its obligations under the Loan Agreement or any document relating thereto, the Participant shall have no recourse to the Original Lender in respect of such failure; or
>
> (iv) the accuracy of any representation or warranty made by the Borrower or any other party in the Principal Documents or any document relating thereto or contemplated thereby; or

---

[38] The Privacy and Electronic Communication Regulations 2003, the Data Protection Act 2018, the UK General Data Protection Regulation and the Data (Use and Access) Act 2025.

(v) the accuracy of any opinions or certificates delivered or to be delivered under or in connection with the Principal Documents or any document relating thereto or contemplated thereby.'

**3.63** Whether all these provisions would be upheld where the seller suspected or had reason to believe that all was not well so far as the loan documentation or the financial condition of the obligor was concerned is another matter. Further, such provisions will not necessarily assist where the seller has made contrary oral or written representations or warranties at or prior to the time of sale. Where the seller was subsequently discovered to have no title to the underlying debt there must also be a real risk that the sale would be set aside on the ground that there is a total failure of consideration.[39]

**3.64** Less clear, however, would be the situation where the debt sold is, for example, subject to equities such as set off claims, or where prior defaults had occurred or, indeed, were subsisting at the time of sale. In the absence of express provisions a court would have to find some representation or warranty made by the seller outside the terms of the sale agreement or read some implied term into the contract by reference, perhaps, to an established market practice[40] of only selling loans free of such claims or defaults. Much would turn on the state of the seller's knowledge of such circumstances at the time of sale.

**3.65** An assignor will also be under a duty, on a continuing basis, not to do any act in derogation of its grant.[41] If the assignment is equitable, the assignor as holder of the legal interest in the debt for the assignee may also be subject to the duties of a fiduciary. In the case of a participation arrangement the original lender does not have a relationship of trust or agency with the participant. Any claim which a participant might bring for actions of the original lender which effectively deprive him of what he had bargained for would most likely have to be founded in contract.

## Local law

**3.66** Our consideration of the legal aspects of asset sales has so far centred on the English law aspects of such transactions. Where the asset being sold is a loan made by an English incorporated bank to an English borrower, the buyer is an English incorporated bank also and the sale takes place in London, there is generally from a legal perspective no reason to look outside the realms of English law to conclude a sale to the satisfaction of both seller and buyer.

---

39 *Marnham v Weaver [*1899] LT 412.

40 There is a tendency for courts to recognise prevailing market practice. This is illustrated by a string of cases running from *Martin v David Boure* (1601) Croke Jac 99 ER to *Godwin v Robarts* (1876) 1 App Cas 476.

41 *Gerard v Lewis* [1867] LR 2 CP 305.

**3.67** Unfortunately, few asset sales are as simple as this and cross-border elements abound, and this is primarily the case with novation and assignment.[42] At one level the issue is one of governing law: what is the proper governing law of the particular aspect of the asset sale at issue? At another level the issue is how tax authorities, central banks and other regulatory authorities in other countries will view the changed circumstances brought about by the sale of the asset.

**3.68** Aside from English law the other jurisdictions which are chiefly relevant to any consideration of the legal, tax and regulatory aspects of a sale include:

(a) the jurisdiction of the borrower and any guarantor;

(b) the jurisdiction of the place of sale; and

(c) the jurisdiction of the buyer.

**3.69** The jurisdiction of the borrower or any guarantor will be relevant in a number of respects, the most obvious being in relation to questions of enforceability. Irrespective of compliance with the requirements of the loan documentation, it may not be possible for an assignee or transferee to enforce his claim against the borrower in the borrower's or the guarantor's own courts unless any consents have been obtained or notices given which are required to be obtained or given as a matter of the borrower's or guarantor's own law.

**3.70** Whether an English court would take cognisance of dissimilar overseas law requirements is another matter. An English court might well apply choice of law rules and take the view that the assignment of a loan governed by English law would be valid notwithstanding failure to comply with an overseas procedural formality. On a practical level overseas courts may not take the same view when asked to give or enforce an English judgment if notice of assignment had not been duly served.

**3.71** If there is a failure to observe local rules which require the buyer to obtain exchange control or other consents from their regulatory authorities, it may effectively prevent a borrower from meeting its obligations to the buyer of the debt. Priorities as against the borrower may turn on the technical requirements of the borrower's law as to such matters as formalities or the nature of the instrument of sale.

**3.72** The attitude of the tax authorities to the sale of a loan made to a borrower in their jurisdiction is the issue which most emphasises the importance to seller and buyer of considering the wider implications of the sale. In many jurisdictions the method of sale used and the location of the buyer will be critical in determining such questions as whether any withholding tax which exists in relation to the original loan will increase as a result of the sale, whether any withholding tax

---

[42] Rhodes (above, n 1), p 591.

which previously did not exist will arise and whether any exemption from withholding tax which has been given will continue to run for the benefit of the buyer.

**3.73** Aside from the strict legalities, many central banks and in those states that still have them, exchange control authorities, require certain information relating to the transfer of assets for which they regard themselves as being responsible. Whether it is the borrower, the seller or the buyer who should give the requisite information is sometimes open to interpretation, as are the consequences of failing to notify. It is most important, however, for both the seller and the buyer to appreciate the implications of displeasing such authorities.

**3.74** The place of sale and the jurisdiction of the buyer will be particularly relevant when considering tax issues such as stamp duty or withholding taxes. The concern here is more in relation to stamp duties attracting to the sale instrument or taxes arising on payments to be made by the seller to the buyer.

**3.75** Two examples may be considered in this context. First, the seller of a loan outside some states will find that the sale is potentially liable to stamp duty in that state on the sale irrespective, it seems, of whether the method of sale adopted is assignment or participation. The tax attracts because the asset is being sold out of the home state, not because a home borrower is involved or because the currency of the asset is in its currency. Secondly, the seller of a loan made to a borrower in some states may find himself liable as a paying agent to deduct withholding tax on payments of interest made by the borrower through the seller, as with a non-notified assignment, or by the seller to the buyer under a back to back arrangement, such as a participation. Whether the tax is deductible will in the main depend on the location of the buyer and whether he is able to book the asset in a jurisdiction where he is able to claim the benefit of any applicable double taxation treaty.

**3.76** Although it is not possible to generalise, as the preceding two examples demonstrate, it would be fair to state that it is unusual for a participation to have implications outside the country of both the selling bank and that of the governing law of the underlying loan facility and the sale contract. The opposite might be said of novation and assignments and this is another important reason for the enduring popularity of the funded participation as a means of 'sale'. The distinction is perhaps understandable when one considers the nature of the various sale methods. Novation and assignment involve a transfer of rights and give the buyer beneficial ownership of a debt directly enforceable against the borrower. A funded participation agreement does not involve any dealing in the underlying rights and simply establishes a separate contractual relationship between buyer and seller. The participation is clearly, therefore, less significant in relation to matters of enforceability and the payment obligations of the borrower. Revenue authorities may however be look through the strict legal relationship and accord assignments and participations similar treatment.

## Taxation

**3.77** The tax aspects of an asset sale are critical from the point of view of both buyer and seller as any adverse tax consequences will usually result in a tax liability in excess of the profit that either party can expect to make on the asset sale. The UK tax aspects of any asset sale can conveniently be considered under three headings:

(a) stamp duty;

(b) withholding tax; and

(c) distributions.

### Stamp duty

**3.78** An assignment of a debt is chargeable with stamp duty because for this particular purpose 'loan capital' is covered by the definition of 'stock' on which, inter alia, stamp duty is charged. There are exceptions in Finance Act 1986, s 79 for specific categories of loan capital provided they are not equity related. The definition of 'loan capital'[43] covers most loans. There is also an exception for loans with an excessive return. Premiums are not common but loans often include limits on redemption and prepayment such as notice periods and a requirement that any prepayment must be made from the end of the loan period to shorten the loan. There may also be an administrative fee in such cases. Such arrangements should not bring a loan within the exception. The other exceptions are less relevant in this context.

**3.79** Neither novation nor participations involve the transfer or assignment of a debt which is one of the reasons for their popularity. Both simply involve the establishment of contractual relations between borrower and transferee and seller and buyer respectively and, for this reason, neither should attract any liability to pay stamp duty.

**3.80** The current rate of assessment is 0.5%, on the amount or value of the consideration for the transfer. Stamp duty must be paid within 30 days of the relevant transfer. Failure to stamp on or prior to the due date gives rise to a liability to pay interest on the unpaid duty in addition to certain specified penalties.

**3.81** The principal consequence of not paying stamp duty is not that the instrument effecting the assignment is invalid but that it cannot be

[43] Finance Act 1986, s 78.

produced in evidence in an English court. Where a suitable alternative venue can be found English stamp duty may not be relevant as a foreign court may disregard the requirement to pay the duty.

**3.82** Before proceeding further it should be mentioned that the duty does not apply to all assignments of debts. The ambit of the duty is established in the Stamp Act 1891, s 14(4), which limits the applicability of the duty to:

> '... an instrument executed in any part of the United Kingdom, or relating wheresoever executed, to any property situate, or to any matter or thing done or to be done, in any part of the United Kingdom ...'

**3.83** The difficulty for any person relying on this wording is in showing that the applicable assignment does not relate to any property situated in the UK or to any matter or thing to be done there. These expressions have been given a broad interpretation by the courts and it may be fatal, even if the only connection with the UK is that the borrower is in the UK or that the agency function under a syndicated credit is carried out here. Certainly, the connection would almost certainly be established if obligations under the loan facility have to be performed in the UK, with a loan denominated in sterling.

**3.84** Some attempts to bring an assignment outside the charge to stamp duty have focused on the fact that stamp duty is a tax on instruments. If the assignment is effected otherwise than by use of an instrument of transfer then no stamp duty will arise. One method of achieving this is for the seller to make an offer to assign to the buyer which is accepted by the buyer making payment of the requisite purchase price. Even if one ignores, as it is probably correct to do, concerns of an extension of the *Furniss v Dawson*[44] principle to this type of scheme there may be practical difficulties in the way of its success. This is because any subsequent written record of the transaction would tend to attract stamp duty. Within this category may come subsequent written acceptances of the offer made by the seller and even the giving of notice of assignment to the debtor.

## Withholding tax

**3.85** The withholding tax position in the UK is governed by a requirement for a 20 per cent[45] deduction to be made from any payment of interest. The relevant exceptions in the context of term and syndicated loans arise where a loan is made by a UK bank or a

---

44 [1984] AC 474, 2 WLR 226, STC 153. This case extended the *Ramsay* principle in *Ramsay v IRC* [1982] AC 300 and *IRC v Burmah Oil Co Ltd* [1982] STC 30, HL (Sc) which essentially states that entirely artificial arrangements created to avoid tax which have no real underlying commercial purpose will not avoid tax assessment.

45 There are proposals to increase this to 22 per cent from 2027.

bank in the UK.[46] There is another where the borrower is a UK bank.[47] Finally the existence of a network of double taxation treaties between the UK and overseas governments also assists in many cases because the relevant treaty often removes the need to for withholding tax to be deducted, or alternately may reduce it. The commonest situation where this would be an issue will be where some of the banks which took part in the syndicate from which part of the loan is being sold, did so from outside the UK.

**3.86** If payments are not made direct to the assignee but routed through the assignor, then both the borrower and the assignor may in the Revenue's view have a liability to deduct tax should they be non-UK banks. The same issue arises on a funded participation. Again, each of the two contracts will have to be looked at separately.

**3.87** Novation, involving as it does, the creation of new contractual rights and obligations, does not give rise to a tax treatment of interest payments which is different from that applicable to interest payments made by the borrower to the original lenders.

### Expense or distribution?

**3.88** There do not appear to be any problems arising here. A payment of interest to a participant is regarded as an expense in making profits, not a distribution of profits for the purposes of calculating liability to tax.

## Regulation of asset sales

**3.89** Perhaps one of the most significant factors contributing to the continued growth and innovation in the asset sales market in the UK has been the refusal of regulatory authorities to impose any significant restrictions on the activities of banks involved in this market. Clearly the debt held by a bank is a factor in calculating its requirements for the purposes of prudential supervision by the Prudential Regulation Authority. An analysis of the content of this is, however, beyond the scope of this book.

**3.90** Turning briefly to UK securities law we will find that asset sales make little impact. The prospectus requirements of the Companies Act 2006[48] will not normally apply as the sale document will not constitute a debenture. This is so even if the sale is by way of novation using a transferable loan certificate or transfer certificate, as the certificate of transfer does not contain any acknowledgement of

---

[46] Income Tax Act 2007, s 879.
[47] *Ibid*, s 878.
[48] See also the FCA's new Public Offers and Admissions to Trading Regulations which replaced the UK Prospectus Regulation from January 2026.

indebtedness or covenant to pay but is merely the means of effecting the novation.

## Development of the market

**3.91** By way of conclusion some current developments in the asset sales market will be considered and the legal and regulatory issues surrounding these developments identified.

### Secondary market

**3.92** The introduction of concepts of transferability into loan documentation was principally designed to encourage the completion of the process of securitisation for loan assets by simplifying secondary market trading of the loan. (See **Chapter 5**) This was achieved by the same method which enabled the initial sale of the loan. The first, and indeed any subsequent, buyer of the loan was issued with a transfer certificate or transferable loan certificate which facilitated subsequent novation of the loan.

**3.93** In some cases this method of sale will not be attractive or desirable. Novation or assignment of the loan will involve the cooperation of the borrower both in accepting the principle of transferability in the original loan documentation and, often, in approving individual transfers. Furthermore, novation may have unfortunate legal consequences because it involves the creation of a new contract:

- priorities may be lost;
- exchange control consents may have to be renewed in cases where they are relevant. This may be an issue with loans involving borrowers in developing states or a party acquiring the debt being located in such a state; and
- problems could arise with withholding taxes where a party acquiring the debt is not a UK bank or from a state covered by a suitable double taxation treaty.

In other words the insertion of a transfer mechanism simplifies the process of transfer but does not avoid those disadvantages which a novation has compared with, say a funded participation. That said however, novation and assignment remain common method of debts transfer, perhaps in part because the last two of these disadvantages are no longer a common issue.

**3.94** It is hardly surprising, therefore, that some institutions have seen an alternative or additional path to securitisation in the transferable participation. Making a participation transferable simply involves applying to a participation the same techniques as are applied to a loan to make it transferable. Similarly, subsequent sales can be facilitated by delivering to each new buyer a form of transfer certificate which can be used for any resale. The original lender has thus securitised the loan without the need for any involvement or, indeed, knowledge on the part of the borrower. From a regulatory and securities perspective the transferable participation should not be treated any differently from a transfer certificate or a transferable loan certificate. The tax treatment of the transferable participation is similarly straightforward. Stamp duty will not attach to transfers as they operate by way of novation. No withholding tax will arise in the UK merely because of a change in participant. Although the selling bank will have assisted secondary market trading of the underlying loan it will be at a cost, namely, that the seller remains lender of record and will continue to have a contractual relationship with the participant originally holding the participation. A subsequent sale does not allow him to drop out of the picture.

**3.95** The transferable participation will still be a useful tool for any seller or buyer even in the absence of a genuine secondary market in assets. The purchase of assets for re-sale, the trading of sovereign debt in the debt swap market and the booking of assets sold or bought to satisfy short term needs and requirements or under evergreen or renewable facilities are all examples of transactions where the element of transferability will greatly assist the subsequent management of the asset sold.

## Corporate investors

**3.96** Traditionally, the asset sales market has been a bank to bank market. The increasing sophistication of corporate investors and the attraction of the relative size of yields on loan assets as compared to those available to such investors in the bond or commercial paper market at certain points in the economic cycle has led to the corporate sector becoming involved. The development of the shadow market with participants such as pension funds, insurance companies and hedge funds, amongst others, has also widened the market further.

# Chapter 4 Primary Securitisation – Bond Issues

## Introduction

**4.1** Essentially a bond is a piece of paper issued by a borrower to lenders stating the terms of the loan and, if applicable any associated security. They evidence the loan, the interest charged and the terms of issue. It is not a new concept: the earliest known bond issues were made by the Mesopotamian army around 2500 BC.[1] In practice bond issues are normally unsecured as the major issuers are able to rely on their own credit ratings to attract investors. The issue is normally for a large number of bonds, each representing a very small proportion of the total amount being raised by the borrower. Often they are straightforward with no other complicating factors. These are termed 'vanilla issues'. They may be issued by companies, public corporations and central, local and national governments, in which case they are called 'gilts'.[2] Some issues are made on stock exchanges and others are made publicly, but off-exchange private sales of bonds can also occur.

**4.2** A key element of this piece of paper is that it is negotiable,[3] ie, its ownership is transferable and can be sold on by the lender to a third party. There are thus two markets: the primary market where the initial bond issue is made, and the secondary market where trading in the bonds takes place. The lenders themselves tend to be banks, insurance companies, pension funds, investment funds and well-off private investors.

**4.3** A simultaneous, connected issue of two or more bonds on different terms, and therefore different interest rates is called a 'structured issue'. For example: secured issue of three years at 2% pa, and unsecured issue of three years at say 3% pa and, less commonly, a deferred issue of three years at say 5% pa. The actual interest rate offered will depend on two factors: the prevailing interest rates in the economy at that time and the credit rating which the bond attracts from the rating agencies. Put simply, the higher the credit rating of the

---

1 E Swan, *Building the Global Market* (Kluwer, 2000), p 28.

2 In one recent year 48% were issued by banks and other financial institutions, 22% by governments and public-sector bodies, 20% by industrial and commercial companies and the balance by supra-national bodies such as the World Bank. G Roberts, *Law Relating to International Banking* (Gresham Books, 1997), p 98.

3 See, eg, *Bechuanaland Exploration Co v London Trading Bank* [1898] 2 QB 658 and *Edelstein v Schuler* [1902] 2 KB 144.

bond the lower the interest rate that the borrower can get away with offering. The bond will not automatically be given the same rating as the issuing company, though this will be an influencing factor.[4] Other elements that will affect it will be the availability of bank or intra-group guarantees, the term of the bond and any security supporting the bond.

**4.4** Whilst bonds have normally been issued in paper form, the recent emergence of blockchain-based contracts has raised the possibility of issuing bonds in this way. Blockchain[5] [6] based bonds are sometimes referred to as Initial Coin Offerings or ICOs and are often used to invest in cryptocurrencies. Any debt raising arrangement of this type will need to be carefully examined to see if it falls within the definition of a bond. If it does, then the same laws and regulations will apply to it as if it were issued on paper.

## Negotiability

**4.5** Historically bonds have always been 'negotiable' which means that the ownership of the bond can be transferred to another person without any involvement by the issuer. The party to whom the bill has been negotiated then has an enforceable debt against the issuer and a right to any remaining interest payments. Without this element the issuer would find it difficult to find a large enough market to issue the bonds into and those who take up the bond issue would then need to hold them until maturity.[7]

**4.6** Whether a bond, note or commercial paper will be regarded under English law as negotiable will depend on whether they are so regarded by the custom of the market. Ultimately, the question as to the custom of the market will need to be decided by a court based on evidence provided by experts particularly as to the existence of an active secondary market. There is a long standing tradition within the common law of recognising mercantile practice, ie, if it is the tradition of those in a commercial market place to recognise an arrangement, the common law will render the arrangement enforceable. This appears to be the underlying logic behind cases such as *Martin v David Boure*[8]

4 Normally a minimum rating of BBB from Standard & Poors or Fitch or Baa from Moody's and upwards is necessary for a company to be able to raise funds from the bond and equity markets.

5 Sometimes referred to as 'digital ledger technology' though some have argued the two terms do not have an identical meaning.

6 For a fuller explanation of blockchain see A Haynes and P Yeoh, *Law and Regulation of Cryptocurrencies and Cryptoassets*, 2nd edn (Routledge, Taylor & Francis, 2026). Ch 2.

7 See W Blair, 'Negotiability and Estoppel' (1988) 3(1) JIBL 8–10. There is evidence of this lack of a large secondary market where Islamic bonds are concerned as there are religious objections to trading debt at a discount.

8 (1601) Croke, Jac, 99 ER 6.

and *Shelden v Hentley*.[9] In the latter case Justice Jones remarked: 'it was the custom of merchants that made it good'. In *Williams v Williams*[10] the judge ruled that: 'this custom of merchants … is part of the common law which the judges will take notice of ex officio'. *Gorgier v Mieville*[11] specifically recognised that bearer bonds were negotiable, and the well-known case of *Goodwin v Robarts*[12] saw the House of Lords effectively accept the recognition of mercantile practice principle.[13] It would now seem inconceivable that bonds, notes or commercial paper would not be regarded by the courts as negotiable or that a court would hold them not to be negotiable instruments.[14] This is of fundamental importance.

**4.7** It also facilitates the existence of bond clearing systems, the main ones being Clearstream,[15] CREST[16] and the Depository Trust Corporation.[17] Custodians and holders of securities can open accounts at these institutions and enter the bonds into them. From that point on, any trading in those bonds is carried out electronically by the clearing house whilst the bonds themselves remain there. This does raise interesting legal questions as to whether a bond that is traded in such a manner is being negotiated. From the point of view of enforceability it does not matter as there is a clear contractual nexus which appears to be enforceable under the laws of the jurisdictions in which the clearing systems are based.

**4.8** A number of other elements, however, need to be considered when deciding whether or not a particular form of bond, note or commercial paper is likely to be negotiable. These include the following:

(a) A number contain legends restricting the right of the holder to offer, sell or deliver them in the US, subject to limited exceptions. The view is generally held, however, that even with a restrictive legend, if the custom of the market is to treat the note or commercial paper as negotiable then that is what it is.

(b) Cash payments – it has been suggested that negotiability requires that the holder be able to obtain cash, but that, given the constraints which have been placed on such a provision, by reason of foreign laws and settlement procedures which may preclude or obviate the necessity for cash payments, it is no

9 (1692) 2 Shower KB 160, 89 ER 860.
10 (1693) Carthew 269, 90 ER 759.
11 (1824) 3 B & C 45, 107 ER 651.
12 (1876) 1 App Cas 476.
13 See also *Crouch v Foncier of England Ltd* (1872–3) LR 8 QB 374 and *Edelstein v Schuler* [1902] 2 KB 144.
14 Under the Bills of Exchange Act 1882, s 72 the question of negotiability would be dealt with by the law of the place where the instrument was when the apparent negotiation took place.
15 An international central securities system based in Luxembourg and Frankfurt.
16 A UK-based central securities depository handling equities and other securities including bonds.
17 Based in the US.

longer common to give a cash payment option and this does not destroy negotiability.

(c) The laws of the jurisdiction of the issuer of the note or commercial paper may in some way conflict with the laws governing the note or commercial paper themselves.

**4.9** The bond, note and commercial paper come closest in their format to a 'promissory note'. Under English law, a promissory note is defined in the Bills of Exchange Act 1882, s 83(1) as follows:

> '... a promissory note is an unconditional promise in writing made by one person to another, signed by the maker, engaging to pay, on demand or at a fixed or determinable future time, a sum certain in money, to, or to the order of, a specified person or to bearer.'

The question which falls to be determined, therefore, is whether a bond, note or commercial paper is a promissory note under the Bills of Exchange Act. The form of bond, note and commercial paper which we will consider throughout this chapter has most of the characteristics required. Unfortunately, the example, by reason of the obligation to gross up in respect of taxes required to be deducted and, in particular, the exceptions to that obligation, means that the common note or commercial paper are not 'a ... promise ... to pay ... a sum certain ...'. Indeed any provision which qualifies in any respect either the time for payment or the amount payable, or which imposes any condition on payment, will prevent a note from being a promissory note for the purposes of the Bills of Exchange Act. As Wood put it:[18]

> '... the requirements set out in the Act as to certainty of amount and unconditionality will almost never be satisfied by bearer bonds in the form found in international bond issues. Thus an instrument with a floating rate of interest or a currency indemnity is uncertain. If it has events of default, it is conditional.'

**4.10** Many bonds however are issued at a fixed rate of interest and not all bonds contain such contingencies and will therefore satisfy the definition. More contentious is the suggestion that an events of default clause will cause a bond to be contingent.[19] Any contract can face termination through the Law Reform (Frustrated Contracts) Act 1943 and the contractual situations in a typical bond issue simply extend this to situations where a bond holder will wish to accelerate payment. It is distinctly possible that such bonds are promissory notes.

**4.11** There are seven main different categories of bonds issued by corporations:

---

18 P Wood, *International Loans, Bonds, Guarantees, Legal Opinions* (Sweet & Maxwell, 2007), p 210.

19 Wood, ibid.

(1) **domestic bonds** issued in the issuer's home country denominated in the domestic currency of that country. Companies with poorer credit ratings sometimes make such issues subject to support from a bank in the form of a letter of credit (see **Chapter 7**). These tend to be reasonably high denomination bonds. Certain types of bond, however, involve banks and some are issued pursuant to a facility under which banks or other financial institutions have a commitment to purchase them.

(2) **Foreign bonds**, where an overseas corporation or body issues bonds in another state in the currency of the issuing state.

(3) **International bonds**, which are bonds issued in Europe, very often the United Kingdom in US$ or other non-domestic currencies. This is driven by the holdings of those currencies in London. They used to be called 'eurobonds' and sometimes still are but as they have nothing to do with the euro, the similarity of name after the introduction of the European currency led to confusion and so the name has tended to be dropped. Each such bond tends to have a relatively low value and they are fixed term, bearer documents containing a description of the applicable terms.[20]

(4) **Note Issuance Facilities (RUFs, also known as Note Purchase Facilities, Note Issuance Facilities or Grantor Underwritten Notes)** are notes issued on the basis that the underwriters will lend any shortfall to the issuer on the bond issue.

(5) **Commercial paper** is a short-term unsecured debt paper issued by companies with a high credit rating. They are used by large companies with good credit ratings as an alternative to a credit line at their bank.[21] It normally runs for up to a year (270 days in the US) and is replaced on a rolling basis. It is often issued at a slight discount and has a lower interest rate to compensate. They do not involve an arrangement for a bank or financial institution to commit themselves to buy them.

(6) **Sukuk** bonds which are those created to satisfy the requirements of one of the schools of Islamic law. This has been a rapidly growing part of the market in recent years. As it is a specialised area it will only be examined briefly.

(7) **Convertible bonds**. These are bonds which can be converted to another form of investment, typically shares on or after a certain date or on the happening of a contingency.

---

20 The first such issue took place in 1963, was lead managed by S G Warburg Co and guaranteed by Istituto per la Recostruzione for the benefit of Finsider. See I M Kerr, *A History of the Eurobond Market, The First 21 Years* (Euromoney, 1984), p 11.

21 The first was issued by Marcus Goldman in 1869.

**4.12** Arguably numbers 1 to 5 on this list are different types of the same legal arrangement. Sukuk, as will be seen below have an essential legal difference in that the bond holder has to have an exposure to the underlying business of the bond issuer, thus making the arrangement have certain similarities to a non-voting preference share. Convertible bonds are fundamentally different because of their convertible nature resulting in them having the capacity to change into a different type of security.

**4.13** This chapter will examine the main types of bond and then go on to consider the method of sale, the relevant documentation, the functioning of the secondary market, regulatory issues and ends with a comparison with syndicated lending.

## Types of bond

### Domestic, Foreign and International bonds

**4.14** These categories of bonds contain terms describing the corporation borrowing the funds, the amount of the bond denomination, the rate of interest and the intervals for its payment. Also included are the terms for repayment of the principal, the issuer's covenants and events of default. The terms and covenants involved are similar to those seen in term loan agreements (see **Chapter 1**), but because in a bond issue they are drafted by the borrower the clauses are much briefer and less all embracing. In addition, there may be incorporation by reference of the terms of any guarantee or bondholder trust deed. As the bond is a bearer instrument transfer may take place by simple delivery and the identities of the parties do not have to be revealed either by endorsement or registration at the company who issued the bonds. Consequently, taxes, exchange control restrictions and securities regulation that ban the holding of foreign bonds can be circumvented

**4.15** The biggest bond issues are usually carried out by well-known multinational companies or government bodies. The crucial factor will be the cost of borrowing. Over the last 40 years there have been changes in the respective costs of borrowing by syndicated lending, securitisation and bond issues, and the scale on which these methods of borrowing are used inevitably reflects this. Their respective profit margins tend to vary over time. At times investment banks acting as underwriters have discovered that their capacity to market and distribute any bonds they had contracted to underwrite and/or sell was so great that they rarely needed to allocate capital against the bonds they had underwritten. This had advantages from the point of view of the profitability of the arrangement, the risk involved and the liabilities shown on the underwriter's end of year accounts.

**4.16** Those who invest in such bonds are a disparate group. They range from institutional investors such as pension funds, investment vehicles, hedge funds, insurance companies and banks to individuals seeking a return higher than can be obtained from bank deposit accounts and mutual deposits. Banks have tended to be most attracted to floating rate bonds because of their obvious need to protect themselves against the risk on their floating rate obligations on the inter-bank market and on many of their loans. Perpetual subordinated floating rate notes issued by high credit rated companies can be held as a portion of bank capital in satisfaction of capital adequacy requirement in many states.

**4.17** A large-scale bond issue involves three groups of financial intermediaries. Such an intermediary may belong to more than one group simultaneously. The first group is that of between two and three managers responsible for managing the issue and its stabilisation. They usually delegate the negotiation and preparation of documents to a lead manager. The underwriters are a larger group, and they agree to take up any bonds not sold by the selling group and thus assume the legal liability for the economic success of raising the funds for the issuer. The third group, the selling group, comprises several hundred intermediaries who sell the bonds to investors, using their well-developed list of customers. Occasionally this standard approach is varied: in a private placement a manager or group of managers subscribe for the whole issue and place it with private clients or even a single investor. In the United States the structure is slightly different with there usually being a combined group of managers and underwriters, usually called 'underwriters', and the selling group.

**4.18** How are the bonds issued? A key factor here is to determine whether or not the bonds are going to be listed. A second factor is whether or not security is attached to the bond. These issues will be considered in turn.

## Unlisted bonds

**4.19** If a bond issue is not to be listed on a stock exchange the issuer will have to decide whether to issue the bonds itself or to pay a financial body to issue them on its behalf. If the latter then a manager, or in a large issue, a group of managers will draft the bond and arrange to sell the issue. There will then be the underwriters who take on the financial risk of the issue by agreeing to cover any shortfall in the bond issue. Finally, there are the selling agents who as their name suggests are responsible for arranging to sell the bonds. On occasion this will not be necessary as the existing bondholders may agree to roll over to the new bond issue or the managers may be able to place all the bonds with their clients. In the US the underwriting role is carried out by the same people as the managers and the joint function is termed underwriting.

### Listed bonds

**4.20** If an issue of bonds is to be listed on a stock exchange then the rules of that exchange will have to be followed. The details of this are beyond the contents of the book but it is an area that needs to be dealt with carefully. The exchange rules not only require the preparation of all the relevant documentation but also imposes time limits relating to when each document must be ready in relation to the issue itself.

### Secured bonds

**4.21** If a bond is secured a practical problem arises. As the bonds may change hands, how is the security to be maintained? If each time a bond is sold the security is retaken then priorities will be lost with regard to anyone who has taken security over the same asset in the meantime. In addition, it would be costly to keep retaking security, especially if is in the form of land as the Land Registry fees are quite high. Also, with a large bond issue the security would need retaking almost every day. The solution is for the security to be held by a trustee who holds it for the benefit of whoever the bondholders are at any moment in the future. If there is no security a fiscal agent is appointed instead. Stock exchange listings of secured bond issues normally require this arrangement. We must therefore consider their respective functions.

### Bond issue by trust deed

**4.22** Sometimes a bond issue is made subject to a trust deed. This is normal if the bond issue is subject to security as the trustee holds the security and normally has powers of sale and distribution. The common practice of placing bonds in a depositary with ownership changing hands without the bonds being moved[22] tends to be best facilitated by a trustee who is able to act on behalf of the bondholders at any moment in time. The trustee operates in a more independent way than a fiscal agent (see below), but his position is more subtle than merely being 'an independent party playing a crucial bridging role between the parties'[23] not least because of the potentially disparate interests of the various parties to the bond issue, and indeed between the bond holders themselves. The trustee's presence tends to reduce the risk of a rogue bond holder starting intemperate legal proceedings, but, on the other hand, if there is a solid basis for dispute the trustee's presence can facilitate bond holder action as the trustee can facilitate the necessary steps being taken and the overall costs will be split between all the bond holders.

---

22 This is now the standard form of holding bonds.

23 A Herbert, 'Why have a trustee for a Eurobond issue?' (1987) 2(1) JIBL 48 at 49. P Rawlings 'The Changing Role of the Trustee in International Bond Issues.' [2007] JBL 43–46.

**4.23** A security holding trustee in a bond issue holds a rather unusual position. In some respects he will function as agent for the bond holders and in others the role is independent and determined by the contents of the trust deed, which is discussed below. The trustee is the party who has the capacity to commence proceedings on behalf of the bond holders and as a result of this any disgruntled bondholders have to act through them rather than directly. To stop unrepresentative individuals or small groups from so acting the trust deed will set out the precise basis on which a trustee can be required to act, ie, a requirement that x% of the bond holders by value can require the trustee to act. In so doing the trust deed will normally require the bond holders to indemnify the trustee against any legal costs incurred during proceedings. If the trustee does not act then the bond holders can either try bringing an action themselves or seek a court order that the trustee is acting in breach of the trust deed by failing to bring proceedings. The case would then come down to a judicial assessment of whether there was a breach of the bond issue which rendered legal action appropriate.

**4.24** The trustee can also help avoid disputes by the trust deed granting the power to them to waive minor breaches of the issuing documentation, provided they are convinced it is not going to materially prejudice the bond holders if they do so. This state of affairs was the basis of the dispute in *Concord Trust v Law Debenture Trust Corp Plc.*[24] Here the trust deed stated:

> 'The Bond Trustee at its discretion may, and if so requested [or directed] by [the relevant number of bondholders] shall (subject ... to being indemnified to its satisfaction), give notice to the Issuer and the Guarantor that the Bonds are, and they shall immediately become due and repayable at their relevant redemption value, together with the accrued Interest Amount as provided in the Bond Trust Deed, upon the occurrence of any of the following events (Events of Default)'.

The House of Lords held that once the trustee was validly instructed by the requisite number of bond holders he was obliged to take enforcement action and had no discretion in the matter. The fact that an event of default had occurred had been accepted by the court.

**4.25** A second issue arose, namely whether the trustee was entitled to an indemnity when this enforcement action was taken. Lord Scott stated that the trustee was entitled to an indemnity for legal costs where the claim had a reasonable chance of success. As there was no express or implied term to the effect that the trustee would not give an invalid notice to the issuer, he was entitled to an indemnity for wrongly bringing an action for breach of contract. In the case of an

---

[24] [2005] UKHL 27, [2005] 1 WLR 1591. See also *In the Matter of Colt Telecom group plc* [2002] EWHC 2815 (Ch), [2003] BPIR 324. For a useful discussion see A McKnight, S Paterson and R Zakrewski, *Law Relating to International Finance*. 2nd edn (Oxford University Press, 2017), p 541.

indemnity for tort[25] it was determined that as there was a contractual relationship between the issuer and trustee and as this contained no implied term there could not be a tortuous obligation either.[26] He added that as the trustee was obliged to take action by the bondholders he could not, therefore, be negligent towards the issuer by doing so.[27]

**4.26** If a trustee is appointed a number of legal issues arise, not least the relevant rules of equity. Indeed:

> '… judges have often warned against the wholesale importation of equitable principles inconsistent with the certainty and speed which are essential requirements for the orderly conduct of business affairs.'[28]

However, hopefully the wording of a trust deed will be designed to clarify any problems in this regard.[29] What duties then do the trustees have to satisfy? They must act in good faith when dealing on behalf of the beneficiary and must act on their behalf with the degree of care, skill, prudence and diligence and act honestly and in good faith.[30] They must also show the level of skill as is reasonable given the expertise the trustee claims to have,[31] though the trust deed can reduce this obligation and often does. If the trust deed has given them a discretion as to when to act they will not be in breach of trust in failing to exercise it if that discretion is absolute. If it is qualified it will depend on the exact wording of the relevant terms and the precise behaviour of the trustee. Usefully the wording of the trust deed will qualify any fiduciary duties that are owed by the trustees:[32]

> 'In these situations it is the contractual foundation which is all important because it is the contract that regulates the basic rights and liabilities of the parties. The fiduciary relationship … must accommodate itself to the terms of the contract so that it is consistent with, and conforms to them. The fiduciary relationship cannot be superimposed upon the contract in such a way as to

---

25 In this instance, negligence – a claim that the trustee had conspired with the bondholders to cause injury by unlawful means to the issuer and a claim that the trustee had unlawfully interfered with the issuer's business.

26 This seems inconsistent with the obiter in the Privy Council decision in *Tai Hing Cotton Mill Ltd v Liu Chong Hing Bank Ltd* [1986] AC 80.

27 See M Kokkinoftas 'Relief of Forfeiture: Equity's Anomolous Intervention Following an Event of Default.' UCL JL and J 2016, 5(2), 266–284; D Whitehead 'Pride or Prejudice' (2011) 30(5) IFL Rev 32–33 and E Cuvett and J Walker 'New Issues for Trustees in the Credit Crunch' (2009) 24(4) BJIB & FL 215–218.

28 Lord Browne-Wilkinson in Westdeutsche Landesbank Girozentrale v Islington LBC [1996] AC 669 at 704.

29 For a useful discussion see P Rawlings, 'The changing role of the trustee in international bond issues' [2007] JBL 43.

30 Millett LJ in *Armitage v Nurse* [1998] Ch 241 at 253–254.

31 Trustee Act 2000, s 1.

32 This is crucial because of the onerous nature of the obligations that equity will otherwise impose, eg *Keech v Sandford* (1726); *Caffrey v Darby* (1801) 6 Ves 488; *Re Second East Dulwich etc Building Society* (1889) 68 LJ Ch 196; *Bray v Ford* [1896] AC 44, Sel Cas Ch 61 and *Boardman v Phipps* [1967] AC 46; *Target Holdings v Redfern* [1996] AC 421 and *Bristol & West Building Society v Mothew* [1998] Ch 1.

alter the operation which the contract was intended to have according to its true construction.'[33]

**4.27** A potential complicating factor is Companies Act 2006, s 750(1), which states that:

(a) in a trust deed for securing an issue of debentures; or

(b) in any contract with the holders of debentures secured by a trust deed,

is void in so far as it would have the effect of exempting a trustee of the deed from, or indemnifying him against, liability for breach of trust where he fails to show the degree of care and diligence required of him as trustee, having regard to the provisions of the trust deed conferring on him any powers, authorities or discretions.[34]

This is an element which needs to be taken into account, at least where a bond issue is made by a company registered in England or Wales.[35] That said there does not seem to have been much litigation in this field, largely because disputes tend to have focused on disputes over whether the trustee should start proceedings against the bond issuer.

FIGURE 1: PARTIES TO A BOND ISSUE BY TRUST DEED

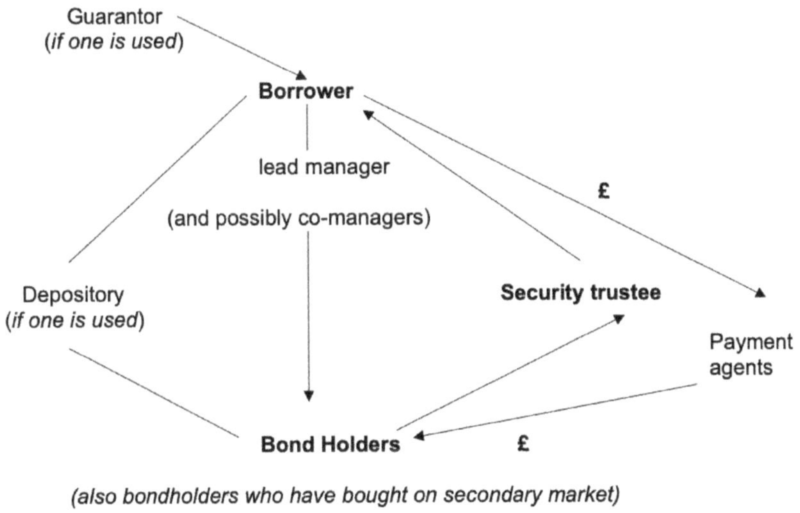


[33] Mason J in *Hospital Products Ltd v United States Surgical Corp* (1984) 156 CLR 41 at 97. See also *Kelly v Cooper* [1993] AC 205 and *Lorenz v CSK Corp* 736 F Supp 650 (W D Pa 1990).

[34] This subsection does not invalidate (a) a release otherwise validly given in respect of anything done or omitted to be done by a trustee before the giving of the release; (b) any provision enabling such a release to be given:
(i) on being agreed to by a majority of not less than 75% in value of the debenture holders present and voting in person or, where proxies are permitted, by proxy at a meeting summoned for the purpose, and
(ii) either with respect to specific acts or omissions or on the trustee dying or ceasing to act. Companies Act 2006, s 759(2).

[35] Companies Act 2006, s 1(1) limits this statute to companies registered in England and Wales.

**4.28** Until recent times this area did not provide a fertile basis for legal disputes because of the tendency of parties to such arrangements to settle such disputes, but the market place has changed. The increasing numbers of 'junk' bonds, ie, distressed debt bonds being traded has increased, and such bonds being of low credit rating often have a security interest attached. Rawlings makes the point that when a dispute arises the holders of such debt are less interested in reaching a settlement because the borrower is by definition in or bordering on financial difficulty. They therefore have an interest in the borrower's underlying financial position and their assets. Such parties are more prone to litigation and therefore in the coming years we could well see a significant rise in the number of actions in this area.[36]

## Bond issue by fiscal agency arrangement

**4.29** Sometimes, however, a fiscal agency arrangement will be entered into instead of using a trustee.[37] By their nature agents act on behalf of their principal and lack the independence of a trustee. As their principal is the issuer of the bonds, it is the issuer on whose behalf they act rather than acting on behalf of those buying the bonds as is the case with a trustee. In England and Wales this also means that a separate paying agent will be needed as is the case when a trustee is utilised, as the trustee is limited to acting in a fiduciary role. However, the role of trustee is commensurate with adopting a general monitoring rather better than this can be done by an agent. Should the bond go into default an issue covered by a trust deed will be determined by the trustee stating that the issue is in default, whereupon it becomes repayable. In the case of a defaulting issue covered by an agency agreement the bondholders must each accelerate their own bonds. There are advantages with a trustee from the operational point of view as where there is an agent, a bondholder, or group of bondholders cannot act unless the trustee has failed to do so. In the event of there being appropriate grounds for acting a trustee would normally act, taking the responsibility, cost and inconvenience away from the bondholders. If there is no trustee, the right of action falls to the bondholders which has the dual risk of multiple actions and rogue bondholders bringing inappropriate actions. Minor changes can also be agreed to by the trustee which can be useful from an administrative point of view. In the minority of cases where the bond issue is secured a trustee has to be used as they hold the security and are responsible for any dealings in it. There are cost disadvantages with a trustee however, as not only will they have to be paid, but the paying agent as well.

---

36 Rawlings (above, n 29).

37 See S Häseks, 'Trustees Versus Fiscal Agents and Default Risk in International Sovereign Bonds.' (2012) 34(3) Eur J Law Econ 425–448.

FIGURE 2: PARTIES TO A BOND ISSUE BY FISCAL AGENCY AGREEMENT

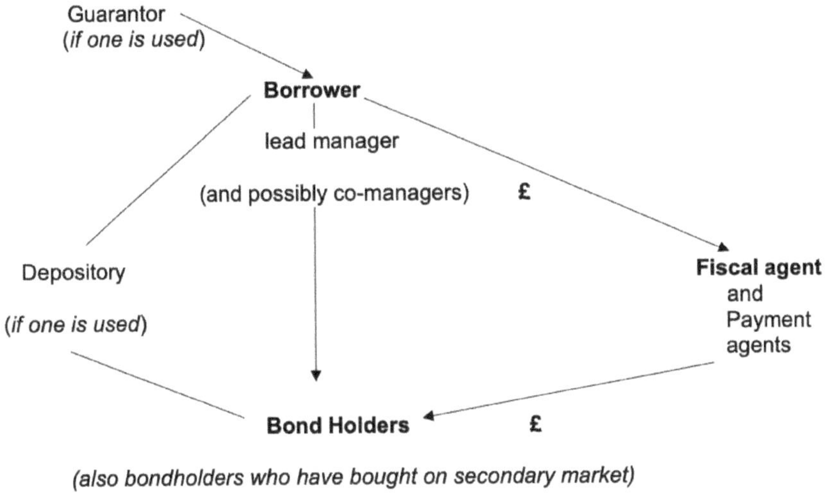


## Documentation

**4.30** The documents that pull all these parties together to perform the functions associated with the issue of the bonds, and may also include a bondholder trustee or alternatively a fiscal agent, are as follows:

(a) The prospectus or information circular providing information about the issue and given to the selling group.

(b) A subscription agreement between the managers and the issuer setting out the terms upon which the managers agree to purchase or procure purchasers for the bonds. This is entered into immediately after agreement has been reached on the coupon and issue price and after the issue has been underwritten. As seen below, in this document the issuer agrees to issue and the managers jointly and severally agree to offer the bonds to the selling group on the terms of the selling group agreement. In addition, they agree to purchase bonds not subscribed and paid for by the selling group or underwriters on the specified closing date. In English practice the managers offer the bonds on behalf of the issuer, to the selling group. In the United States, the underwriters purchase the bonds from the issuer as principal and sell them on to the selling group.

(c) An underwriting agreement between the managers and the underwriters setting out the terms on which the underwriters agree to underwrite the issue. Here the underwriters agree to underwrite a specified principal quantity of bonds. Any underwritten commitments are taken up on the terms of the selling group agreement. The managers can allot bonds not taken up or paid for to any underwriter up to its underwriting commitment. The underwriters obtain an underwriting commission for this function. The underwriters authorise the managers to stabilise the price of the issue, in order to maintain an orderly distribution of bonds. If the managers exercise their right under the subscription agreement to terminate the subscription agreement under the conditions precedent or the market disruption clause, the underwriting agreement is simultaneously cancelled except for the stabilisation liability.

(d) Selling agreements between the managers and the selling group members, setting out the terms upon which members of the selling group agree to deal in the bonds. The main purpose of this agreement is to throw the onus upon selling group members to comply with securities regulation and it therefore contains elaborate selling restrictions. In addition, the selling group agreement prohibits the selling group members from making representations other than those contained in the prospectus and from selling as agent of the issuers or managers and provides that sales are to be made on the basis of the final offering circular. The selling group members indemnify the managers and the issuer against breaches of the selling restrictions. The selling group agreement then sets out the rights of the managers to terminate the selling group agreement if the subscription agreement is terminated, as described above for the underwriting agreement. The agreement also sets out the timetable, payment arrangements and delivery arrangements for closing the issue of the bonds.

(e) The agreement between the managers delegating the organisation of the issue to the lead manager and providing for the division of the management commission and the underwriting shares.

(f) If there is a trustee there needs to be a trust deed between a financial institution as trustee and the issuer whereby the trustee is appointed trustee for the bondholders to protect their interests.

(g) A fiscal agency agreement, or where there is a trustee, a paying agency agreement, between the issuer and a bank, whereby the issuer appoints a fiscal or paying agent and sub-paying agents, which are always banks, in various international centres to make payments to the bondholders.

(h) A global bond pending printing of the definitive bonds.[38]

(i) The bonds themselves issued by the issuer and containing the terms of the loan.

---

[38] There is often a temporary global bond printed at the outset stating the key basic facts. This will be replaced by a definitive bond in due course containing more detailed particulars. Given the tendency for bonds to be held by centralised computer based systems, the definitive bond is not always issued.

Five key documents will be looked at in more detail. These are the prospectus or offering circular, the subscription agreement, the trust deed, the paying agency agreement and the agent bank agreement.

### The prospectus or offering circular

**4.31** The exact format and content of this will be determined by whether it is an offer for an exchange traded bond or not. If it is then the comments made below under 'regulatory issues' will apply. If not, then the denomination of the bond will determine whether or not a full prospectus has to be issued. The smaller denominated bonds tend to be caught by this.

**4.32** The key information that will need to be included in either document will be:

- The details of the bond issue, the issuer and the managers (normally investment banks) who are responsible for issuing the bonds.
- The terms and conditions of the issue determining the form, denomination and title of the issue, the legal status of the issuer and the details of any guarantor. It is traditional to include a negative pledge on behalf of the issuer and any guarantor though in a shorter form than found in term loan documentation. Full details of how, where and when the interest payments will be made are set out along with details of how the principal will be repaid.
- There will also be terms covering redemption and purchase of the bonds. This will cover redemption at maturity, at the option of any note holder together with any formalities that must be satisfied in such an instance, redemption by the issuer and any cancellation interest requirements. This would typically be 50 or 60 days' notice. The facility for redemption by the issuer for tax reasons is normally included to cover the eventuality of additional costs being incurred by the issuer or guarantor as a result of changes in the tax laws.
- The appointments of the paying agents will be determinable at the behest of the issuer or guarantor subject to them undertaking to maintain a principal paying agent at all times.
- Taxation payment obligations are imposed on the issuer and guarantor to make any payments to the bond holders so that the amount received by them is not reduced by any changes in the tax laws. It is common to add qualifications, for example where the bond holder has some other reason beyond holding the bonds for attracting the tax liability.
- A maximum time limit for payment will also be made.

- The events of default are stated to be a basis for the trustee (where one has been appointed) acting at their discretion and if so directed by a proportion of the bond holders; this is usually 20%. The trustee has to certify that in their opinion the event is materially prejudicial to the interests of the bond holders. The one exception where this is not needed is a failure to repay principal by the issuer. Here the materiality is obvious. If the arrangement only has a paying agent the bond holders have to act themselves. Key events of default will be failure by the issuer or guarantor to satisfy any obligations under the trust deed, notes, coupons, paying agency agreement for more than a set period, usually 30 days. Alternately where there is a trustee he can certify before the expiration of that time period that the breach is not capable of remedy. The bankruptcy of the issuer, guarantor or any of their subsidiaries or the filing for bankruptcy against them or a determination that they are unable to pay their debts are all events of default. Likewise, the failure by any such party to make a payment or an indication that they will not do so, or their failing to carry on a substantial part of their business will amount to an event. Also, the appointment of an administrator or receiver or the taking into possession of a substantial part of the assets of the issuer, guarantor or one of their subsidiaries or the exercise of enforcement, distress or execution against any of their chattels. It is also usually an event of default for the issuer to cease to be owned by a particular parent company and where the issuer needs a particular license to carry on business, eg an FCA license in the United Kingdom, the loss of that license will be an event of default.

**4.33** In the event of bonds becoming lost or being destroyed, an arrangement for replacing them is normally included. Another key issue that will be referred to will be bond holders' meetings. (In the event of there being a trustee this will also be referred to in the trust deed, see below). Key issues will be the quorum, the right of the trustee to amend the terms and conditions under which the bonds are issued and/or the trust deed, provided he is convinced this will not be materially prejudicial to the bond holders and which is of a formal, minor or technical nature, or which is necessary to correct an error. There will be a requirement that the trustee notify the bond holders accordingly. A provision is normally included permitting the trustee to substitute the guarantor in place of the issuer as principal debtor. However, the wording of many bank guarantees effectively makes them an indemnity, so this clause may not then be needed. There is usually also the provision for the trustee to agree to replace the guarantor by a subsidiary in the same corporate group.

**4.34** The prospectus or offering circular will include notice provisions. As the bond holders are often a numerous and widely spread group, it is normal to permit notification to them to take place by notice. In the United Kingdom, this may be by notice in the *Financial Times* or, if the bond issue is on the London Stock Exchange, then an online Regulatory Information Service will be used with the bond holders then regarded as having been notified. If the bonds are issues through a clearing system they will arrange notification. The issuer will often also make an announcement on its own website.

**4.35** The issuer will normally take the opportunity to add a clause retaining the right to engage in further bond issues in the future. Such issues to rank pari passu with the existing one. As seen in the discussion of the *Concord Trust* case above, the trustee will be given an indemnity. Governing law and jurisdiction clauses will be added. Finally, there may be a clause determining the use of the proceeds of the bond issue. Sometimes this will be for a specific purpose, but commonly it is for 'normal commercial purposes' or 'to enhance the medium-term funding capabilities of the issuer'.

**4.36** Full details of the issuer's business activities and current financial situation will be set out along with details of the directors and senior management. General information about the issue will be set out and also the details of the various parties to the bond issue, such as the issuer, guarantor, auditors, trustee, principal paying agent, other paying agents, listing agent and the legal advisers.

## Subscription agreement

**4.37** This agreement between the issuer, guarantor, lead manager and the managers will detail the bond issue and the agreements entered into between the parties to this agreement to facilitate the bond issue. If the bond issue is going to be listed on an exchange, details of the application will be set out of the obligations on the issuer and guarantor to provide all necessary documents and take all necessary steps to obtain the listing. The lead manager will be authorised to arrange the advertising of the issue at the lender's expense. Sometimes there is an addition to the effect that should it not prove possible to arrange a listing on the exchange of choice then the issuer will take steps to try and arrange a listing elsewhere.

**4.38** The issuer and guarantor will engage in a number of representations and warranties to the managers. Typically, these will cover both parties being legally incorporated in a stated jurisdiction, that the bond issue is within the laws of that state and the memorandum and articles of association of both companies and that the contract is legal, valid, binding and enforceable under the laws of the same jurisdiction. It will normally state that the bonds will constitute unconditional obligations of the issuer and that they will rank pari passu amongst themselves and at least pari passu with all other present and future unsecured obligations of the issuer, except where the law may otherwise require. The issuer warrants that they have obtained all necessary authorisations, consents and approvals for the bond issue and the execution and delivery of this contract, the issue documents and any performance required by the issuer under this agreement and for the offering circular (or other relevant document according to the nature of the issue). They also undertake to make all payments under the bonds free of any tax that might be applicable. In addition, there will be an undertaking that the offering circular (or other relevant document) contains all the relevant information, is not misleading and that there are no material omissions, and also that it contains all the information that investors and their advisers would reasonably expect to facilitate a reasonable assessment of the issuer and their finances. Additional undertakings will be that no material litigation is taking place, that there has been no material adverse change since the last audited accounts and that those accounts were prepared in accordance with the law and accountancy provisions applying in the jurisdiction concerned. Likewise, there will be undertakings that no event of default has occurred and that the issue is in line with any relevant legal requirements in the jurisdiction concerned.

**4.39** The guarantor will also normally represent solely to the managers that they also have been appropriately incorporated and have the necessary capacity, that the agreement does not breach any domestic legal requirement or their memorandum or articles of association, that the agreement is legal, valid, binding and enforceable and the same status, approvals, taxation and content of the offering circular requirements that the issuer represented. Likewise, they will warrant that there is no material litigation, material adverse change in their financial position and no event of default.

**4.40** The issuer and guarantor will undertake to the managers that they will indemnify them against costs incurred as a result of any misrepresentation or breach of any warranties. They will undertake to notify them of any material change affecting the representations and warranties prior to payment being made to the issuer on the closing date and in the event of this occurring the managers have the right to be discharged. They will also undertake they have not and will not engage in any directed selling efforts or solicitation with regard to the bonds.

**4.41** All the rights that the managers obtain under this agreement should be expressed to continue in force despite the completion of the bond issue.

**4.42** The issuer will agree to pay a stated commission and a selling commission to the lead manager for the account of the managers and this in turn can be deducted from the subscription moneys. The issuer will also agree to reimburse the lead manager for any necessary costs for professional advice, documentation, printing, listing and advertising relating to the issue or its management. Lastly, the issuer will pay any necessary stamp duty, registration fees and other taxes required by the bond issue.

**4.43** A closing date will need to be stated on which the managers need to obtain the subscription moneys. There may be provision for postponing this. On the closing of the issue the managers' obligations will be conditional upon the delivery of the global note to a depositary (if the issue is going to be so held) designated for the purpose by Clearstream, CREST or the Depository Trust Custodian. In addition, it will be dependent on the receipt of legal opinions, a tax opinion, letters of comfort from the auditors, a closing certificate from the issuer, an incumbency certificate signed by the issuer and an acceptance by the process agent that they have agreed to receive any legal or other process. The closing of the issue will also be dependent upon the execution and delivery of the issue documents, confirmation of listing (where it is a listed bond issue), confirmation that there has been no material adverse change in the financial condition of the issuer and any guarantor, that any representations remain accurate as at the closing date and that there have been no acts of force majeure. The lead manager will normally be given the power to waive any of these on behalf of the managers at its discretion. Alternately, they can decide to notify the issuer and guarantor that the parties are released from their obligations. Some obligations might well be stated to survive, eg, indemnities, the survival of legal obligations under the agreement and costs indemnities. The managers will normally continue to be bound by any selling restrictions.

**4.44** There will be standard choice of law and jurisdiction clauses, details of any process agents and consent to enforcement and waiver of immunity (where necessary).

## The trust deed

**4.45** Clearly this will only be created if a trustee is to be used. It tends to be a substantial document covering covenants regarding repayment and interest in relation to the bonds, the form of the bonds, covenants by the issuer and guarantor, the procedure for cancelling the notes, the details of the guarantee (assuming there is a guarantor), negative pledge provisions, details regarding enforcement proceedings, and the application of any funds the trustee receives. Further, it normally includes notice provisions for payments to bondholders, the trustee's powers to invest any moneys being held, procedures if only part payment is made on a bond, the issuer's and guarantor's covenants and of course the details of how the trustee will be remunerated. Provisions may be made supplemental to the Trustee Act 2000 but also it will normally be made clear that despite the agreement, the trustee will be liable if they fail to maintain the necessary levels of care and diligence that are appropriate under the arrangement. The trustee will also have powers of delegation and to appoint agents but this is usually stated to be subject to prior consultation with the issuer and any guarantor.

**4.46** It will normally also be added that other agreements can be entered into between the issuer, guarantor and trustee without infringing on any fiduciary duties on the trustee. As has been seen above, the courts interpret fiduciary duties according to any contracts creating them,[39] so this may be of limited necessity. The trustee will normally have a power to waive the agreement provided the trustee is satisfied that the bondholders will not be materially prejudiced as a result.

**4.47** If there is a guarantor, the trustee will be given the power to substitute them for the issuer where appropriate. There will be provisions for both the retirement and the removal of the trustee. Their powers will be determined to be those granted by the trust deed in addition to those provided by the law and equity.

**4.48** Finally, there will be the normal clauses determining governing law and jurisdiction. Further the schedules to the trust deed will normally include the form of the bond and provisions for bond holders' meetings.

## Paying agency agreement

**4.49** This will set out the names of the issuer, guarantor, principal paying agent, other paying agents and any trustee (should there be one). The paying agents will be appointed by the document and brief details of the bond issue set out. As with a prospectus or offering circular, there will be the capacity to replace lost, damaged or destroyed bonds, together with the paying agent's obligation to cancel any replaced bond and to notify the issuer, guarantor and any other paying agents of the fact that the replacement has taken place.

**4.50** The basis for paying the principal paying agent the amounts needed to make the interest payments, and in due course repayment of the principal to the bond holders will need to be set out. This needs to include precise details of the manner and time, eg, freely transferable sums in a stated currency by 10 am in the local time on the due date in a stated city by electronic transfer of funds, normally by SWIFT. The principal paying agent will be debarred from exercising any lien, right of set off or similar arrangement against the issuer or guarantor. There is a requirement that the agent repay any funds that are not used because any claim has become void. Again, details of how and when this must be done will be set out. Notification requirements requiring the agent to notify the issuer, guarantor, other paying agents and any trustee will be set out requiring notification of the failure of the funds to arrive in time for payment. A typical deadline would be 12 noon on the next to last local banking day before the due date of any payment.

---

39 *Concord Trust v Law Debenture Trust Corp plc* [2005] UKHL 27, [2005] 1 WLR 1591.

Should the money arrive later, correcting notification will then be needed.

**4.51** A crucial element will be the details of payments to bond holders and a requirement that the paying agents do not pay out on cancelled or replaced bonds. Once full payment of principal is made back to a bond holder that bond must be cancelled by the paying agent. Where payment is to be made against presentation of a temporary global note, the paying agent must make sure a note of the amount of interest or principal is made, and in the case of part payment of principal that the amount left is noted in the schedule to the temporary global note with signature and notation to that effect. Paying agents are debarred by the agreement from exercising any right of lien, set off or similar claim against anyone to whom it may be required to make a payment under the agreement.

**4.52** Where a paying agent other than the principal makes a payment in relation to the bonds they must notify the principal paying agent, who in turn must repay them. Details need to be set out determining the currency, date and time, the bank and city concerned and that it must be in freely available funds. The principal paying agent has an equivalent right, once it has made a payment under the agreement, to take funds for its own account out of the fund received for the purposes of the agreement. Where a paying agent pays funds under the agreement prior to the principal paying agent being in receipt of funds to cover the payment, and the principal paying agent is not in a position to reimburse them, the issuer will contract to indemnify the paying agent for the amount and any costs, loss or other expense to satisfy the issuer's obligations.

**4.53** If there has been an actual or potential event of default, the trustee will be empowered to notify the issuer, guarantor, principal paying agent and other paying agents in writing that they will require the principal and other paying agents to act in line with the paying agency agreement on behalf of the trustee.

**4.54** The paying agents' duties will be set out and the key ones will be to keep records of all bonds and coupons delivered pursuant to the agreement and of their redemption, cancellation or destruction. In addition, they will be required to maintain a record of all certifications they have received in accordance with any temporary global note. Finally, it will agree to make records available to the issuer, guarantor, other paying agents and the trustee. The paying agents will also be required to make available such information as is necessary to maintain these records and shall copy to the other parties any certification it receives in accordance with the terms of a temporary global note. Other duties of the paying agents will be: delivering bonds and coupons for cancellation to the principal paying agent; and notifying the issuer, guarantor, other paying agents and any trustee after each payment date of the number of any bonds or coupons which have been paid against surrender. The principal paying agents will also be required to cancel bonds and coupons sent to them by the issuer for the purpose, to notify the other parties of bonds and coupons which have not been surrendered, be responsible for the publication of relevant notices to the bondholders and confirmation thereof to the other parties and shall destroy surrendered bonds and coupons. The issuer will also contract to let the principal paying agent know when bonds have been redeemed.

**4.55** All paying agents must issue voting certificates when asked to by the bondholders in line with the relevant agreements and keep a record of the same. They will do the same with notices to redeem to the bond holders, such notices being released on the dates in the agreement to facilitate the payment of interest and the repayment of principal. At the end of the due period the paying agents must all notify the principal paying agent of the amount and numbers of the bonds deposited with them and they in turn are required to notify the issuer and guarantor.

**4.56** Provisions will be made for the payment of fees and expenses to the paying agents and their terms of appointment. They are stated to be permitted to presume that the holder of any bond is its legal owner except where notified to the contrary or where the law deems they cannot be, they are also permitted to instruct solicitors and other experts where appropriate. The paying agents are stated to owe no duties other than those set out in the agreement and their fiduciary duties will be limited to the issuer, guarantor, and where there is one, the trustee. Even then, as seen above, fiduciary duties will be circumscribed by the agreement. They also obtain an indemnity from the issuer and if they become involved the guarantor, against losses, liabilities, costs and claims arising from the exercise of their powers.

**4.57** The basis on which the paying agency agreements will terminate will be included. The agent can normally resign on one month's notice. The issuer and guarantor can terminate on the same basis. Termination is automatic when a secured party takes possession of security, or a receiver, liquidator or administrator is appointed over the paying agent. Likewise, if the paying agent becomes insolvent, enters into an arrangement concerning its debts, or is wound up.

**4.58** Replacement paying agents can be appointed by the issuer or guarantor. They can also be appointed by the resigning paying agent with the agreement of the issuer, guarantor and any trustee, subject to the replacement being a suitable, experienced financial institution. Once resignation or revocation occurs the paying agent is released from their obligations under the agreement but must deliver to whoever replaces them any money and papers and provide reasonable assistance. Where the principal paying agent ceases to act they are required to deliver to the issuer up to date copies of its records. There will normally be a merger clause stating that if the paying agent merges with another entity, that entity must become the legal successor to the paying agent, to the extent permitted by law.

**4.59** There will be standard notice provisions and choice of law and jurisdiction clauses which will normally be non-exclusive. Finally, there will usually be a statement that the agreement can be modified by agreement between the parties without the consent of the bond holders.

## Agent bank agreement

**4.60** This is a shorter and simpler document than the two preceding ones, stating that the agent bank is appointed and accepts the position. Their key role will be to determine the rate of interest, coupon amount and interest payment dates applicable to the bonds. They must notify this to the issuer, guarantor, any trustee and the paying agents. If there is an event of default the agreement will state that the trustee will then notify the agent bank to act as their agent.

**4.61** The agent bank will be contracted to be entitled to fees and expenses incurred in executing the agreement and beyond this with the agreement of the issuer. The issuer will also contract to be liable for all stamp duty, taxes and registration fees which are necessary as a consequence of this agreement and to indemnify the agent bank with regard to any damages, costs or expenses arising as a result of any claim against it arising in relation to the agreement.

**4.62** The agent bank is allowed to resign, usually at 30 days' notice to the issuer and guarantor. The same notice period normally applies if the issuer wishes the agent bank to step down and in either event the trustee and principal paying agent should also be informed. In either instance it is subject to a successor being appointed and the bond holders being notified. Power for the issuer to appoint a successor agent is standard. Termination of the agency is automatic if the agent bank becomes insolvent or steps suggesting serious financial problems occur, eg, a secured creditor taking possession of property, a receiver, liquidator or administrator being appointed or the agent bank entering into an arrangement with its creditors. Whatever the cause of the agent bank's departure they contract to provide the issuer and the successor with up-to-date copies of all records and provide reasonable assistance to their successor. In return they are released from their obligations.

**4.63** If the agent bank merges with another or is taken over the new entity should accept the same obligations and rights as the agent bank and the issuer and guarantor contract to accept them on the same basis. The agreement will also have standard notice and process clauses together with others determining forum and jurisdiction. Where appropriate a waiver of immunity clause will also be inserted.

## Note issuance facilities

**4.64** A useful starting point is to compare the note with some of the common characteristics found in an international bond. The principal distinctions, some of which we will consider in greater detail later in this chapter, are that bonds are generally listed instruments whereas notes are generally not; bonds are generally issued in small denominations of between US$1,000 and US$10,000 each, whereas notes are generally issued in large denominations, often of US$250,000 or more; bonds generally have maturities of between 3 and 15 years, depending on current market conditions, notes generally have maturities of up to one year; and, in view of their longer maturities, bonds almost universally have extensive terms and conditions relating to their repayment and constitution.

## The note market

**4.65** These originally emerged[40] from the Certificate of Deposit market in London. Definitions, or rather the lack of legal definitions, and the use of different names to distinguish one bank's product from another's has often caused confusion to those who participate in the note market. A plethora of names have been used: Note Purchase Facility; Note Issue Facility ('NIF'); Revolving Underwriting Facility ('RUF'); Grantor Underwritten Notes ('GUN') and so on. To the extent that these facilities involve the issue of notes, the definition used at the beginning of this chapter will continue to apply. For ease of reading, however, the term notes will be used.

**4.66** Some of the key documentary issues will now be analysed.

### Revolving underwriting facilities

**4.67** The facilities syndicated in the note market have taken many forms. However, underlying each of them is an obligation on the part of certain banks and financial institutions to subscribe for notes at a price which will give the issuer funds at a fixed margin over say, SONIA. This obligation only arises in circumstances where the notes cannot initially be sold to others.

**4.68** The greatest variations in documentation arose because of the methods adopted by different banks for initial sales. Some have involved a tender panel, ie, a group of banks, brokers and dealers assembled to bid for the issuer's notes; others have permitted only the arranger of the facility to place the notes at a fixed price, known as sole placing agency.

---

40 Specifically the 1978 arrangement by Citicorp for the New Zealand Shipping Corporation.

**4.69** Because of the basic legal obligation, notes borrowed heavily for their legal structure from the syndicated loan agreement and, therefore, many of the legal and commercial issues which present themselves in a syndicated loan agreement also fall to be considered when a note is being documented.

**4.70** As with the syndicated loan agreement, the conditions precedent to each issue of notes are particularly important to those undertaking the underwriting commitment. On the one hand the issuer will want to be assured that it will receive the funds, particularly when it may be more difficult to place a public issue. On the other, as with banks in a syndicated loan agreement, the underwriters will not want to take an unqualified risk. In particular, they will be reluctant to take the risk of external factors which might make the issuer's paper less attractive to investors who, in normal circumstances, would be relied upon to purchase notes which the underwriters would otherwise be obliged to purchase.

## External risk factors

**4.71** The usual risks which are dealt with in note documentation are the same as those for a syndicated loan, namely illegality, increased costs and withholding tax provisions. Insofar as illegality is concerned, it is commonly provided that the underwriters' commitment to purchase notes will be subject to cancellation in the event of such illegality.

**4.72** A clause will be added covering increased costs, such as the cost of maintaining additional capital to cover the off balance sheet risk weighting given by the Prudential Regulation Authority and referred to earlier.

**4.73** As a result of the potential imposition of withholding tax it will be necessary to include a clause obliging the issuer to gross up for any amounts which it is required to deduct either under the facility, whether in respect of fees payable thereunder or otherwise, or, on occasions, in respect of the notes themselves as a separate obligation from any grossing up obligation which may appear on the form of note itself. Each of these circumstances would increase the cost to the banks of purchasing the paper and make that paper less attractive in the market, thereby reducing the bank's potential earnings.

**4.74** In addition to the factors which have been outlined, which principally affect the banks, there may be others which prejudice the ability of the banks to sell the notes to potential investors. These would include conditions relating to a change in the issuer, such as its creditworthiness or the validity of its obligations, and these are normally dealt with in the documentation by way of cross reference to the representations and warranties. Perhaps the most important warranty will relate to the information memorandum which in the context of a note, as opposed to a syndicated loan agreement, takes on greater significance and a slightly different form. It is important to take a slightly closer look at information memoranda generally and the additional liabilities that this may incur for underwriters.

## Information memoranda and other offering material

**4.75** The basic intention of underwriters in a note facility is to on sell to investors the notes which they are obliged to purchase under the facility. Consequently, they will normally wish to have at their disposal an information memorandum and, or at the very least, the issuer's latest financial statements to distribute to potential purchasers. Unlike a bond, which as stated earlier is generally a listed instrument, information memoranda prepared for prospective purchasers of notes are not always subject to any statutory or regulatory requirements as to their contents. This is because their denomination is higher than the figure, below which the laws or financial regulations of the country concerned would require a full prospectus. The distribution of any such information may well give the implication that the information may be relied on by the potential purchaser and this may incur liability on the distributor of the information. It is common to include on the inside cover of all such memoranda specific language displacing any implications as to the reliability of the information.

**4.76** The relationship between the issuer and a bank that undertakes to purchase the notes is straightforward. The bank's status reduces the risk of the FCA[41] and other rules applying. However, the bank(s) concerned will need to communicate with their customers to try and place the notes. In the case of corporate clients, again there is no problem. However, where private clients are concerned the Financial Promotions Order 2005[42] becomes relevant. This lays down the requirements where financial promotions are made with regard to investments as defined therein.[43] This definition included debt paper such as bonds and notes. Essentially the statutory instrument has a very wide definition of promotional communications that are covered, including unsolicited real time communications, solicited real time communications and non real time communications. 'Real time' covers the spoken word whether spoken in someone's presence or over the phone or conference link, and 'non real time' covers other methods such as letters and e-mail. A detailed examination of financial services regulation is beyond the scope of this book, but banks in such situations should check to see whether they fit within the exceptions

41 In particular COCON the Code of Conduct and BCOBS the Banking Conduct of Business Sourcebook.

42 SI 2005/1529 as amended.

43 The relevant list of 'controlled investments' in the Financial Promotions Order is not identical to those in the Regulated Activities Order, SI 2001/544 (as amended), but both include bonds.

listed in the statutory instrument, or if not make sure they satisfy the communication requirements set out therein when dealing with private clients in this context. It is also necessary to make sure that someone authorised by the Financial Conduct Authority specifically for the purpose of issuing financial promotions takes responsibility for issuing it.[44]

## Misrepresentation and negligence

**4.77** Under English law, if a person makes an untrue representation as to a matter of fact to another person who, in reliance on it, is induced to enter into a contract with the former, the former is liable to compensate the latter for any damage suffered by him as a result. (This is discussed in detail in **Chapter 8**). Alternatively, the liability would be in damages for breach of warranty if the person who suffered the damage could show that there was an express or implied term of the contract between them that the matter of fact represented was true, when in fact it was not. In these circumstances the claimant does not have to prove reliance on the fact represented as a factor inducing him to enter into a contract.

**4.78** It follows that it is generally safer, from a legal point of view, for no representation whatsoever to be made and no information be distributed. If some information is given, however innocently and however helpful the provider of that information is trying to be, if it subsequently turns out to be incomplete while appearing to be complete or is inaccurate, the law will normally treat the omission or inaccuracy as misrepresentation. This is clearly of importance to intermediaries which, in the case of notes, would include the banks who are underwriting and also the members of any tender panel who themselves will wish to on sell notes for which they successfully tender. It is advisable, therefore, in addition to the specific disclaimers that are included on the inside cover of information memoranda to incorporate further protective provisions within the note documentation which would oblige the issuer to confirm on each occasion that notes are to be issued, the accuracy and completeness of the information memorandum and, if necessary, the latest financial statements, and oblige the issuer to indemnify each of the intermediaries for any damages, etc suffered by them as a result of distributing the information memorandum containing inaccuracies or misrepresentations.

**4.79** In addition, any arranger who distributes such information to members of the tender panel or other banks will normally want to include a specific provision within the documentation which limits the extent of his responsibilities.

---

44 Financial Services and Markets Act 2000, s 21 as amended by the Financial Services and Markets Act 2023, s 20.

**4.80** To add to these concerns, consideration must also be given to the Financial Services and Markets Act 2000. Before addressing this statute (or at least the relevant statutory instruments issued pursuant to it), which forms part of the overall regulatory environment in which notes and commercial paper are issued, it is important to examine the nature of commercial paper documentation and to consider the structure of the instruments themselves.

## Commercial paper

**4.81** The nature of these is discussed in the introductory part of the chapter. We will now turn to consider some of the issues to which these documents give rise.

### The dealer agreement

**4.82** The common form of dealer agreement originally borrowed heavily from the form and content of the revolving underwriting note facility and simply omitted those sections which attempted to protect the banks against the various underwriting risks which have already been discussed. As a result the documentation is much shorter than that found in a typical revolving underwriting facility.

**4.83** The principal parties to the dealer agreement are the issuer itself and the dealers. Some agreements also include a guarantor, if so required, and an issue agent. Insofar as the issuing agent is concerned it is not uncommon for him to be party only to the agency agreement and not the dealer agreement.

**4.84** It is common for agreements to fail to set out any specific mechanics for reaching agreement to issue notes but rather leave it to the parties to decide on what terms and by what means such an agreement is reached. The only limitations placed on the parties tend to be as follows:

- that no issue can take place until the conditions precedent are satisfied;
- that the aggregate amount outstanding under the programme shall not exceed a specified amount;
- that the minimum denomination of notes, at least initially, is not less than say US$500,000;
- that the dealer must take delivery of notes either in global form or in definitive form but cannot split his allocation between the two. This provision is included so as to avoid any problems arising in the European clearing systems of identifying the owners of the global and definitive notes in relation to a particular series of notes, by virtue of the fact that the European clearing systems

treat all notes of a particular series as fungible with each other whether they are represented in one form or two;

- the method by which the subscription price will be calculated. It is also possible to issue commercial paper on an interest bearing basis although it is often issued at a discount instead.[45] This leads to the purchase price formula being calculated on a different basis and the form of the note varying slightly to incorporate a reference to the payment of interest;
- the dealers will not offer, sell or deliver the notes except in accordance with the detailed restrictions contained in the agreement; and
- perhaps most importantly, the basis on which each agreement to issue and purchase notes is entered into under the agreement.

**4.85** Generally speaking, very little negotiation need take place over the terms of this agreement and the only areas in which the dealers generally feel the need to be protected are, first, those in relation to funding costs, should agreement be reached to purchase notes and the representations and warranties subsequently not turn out to be true, and, secondly, those in relation to any liabilities that may incur as a result of distributing the information memorandum on behalf of the issuer and the guarantor to third parties arising out of some statement in that information memorandum being untrue, etc.

## Forms of commercial paper

**4.86** The principal considerations, aside from those mentioned elsewhere in this chapter, are whether or not to give the option to the issuer of issuing global notes, which is now the predominant method, whether or not to make any global note exchangeable for definitive notes, and, if the global note is to be exchangeable, when it is to be exchangeable.

**4.87** The form of the global note will be lodged with one or other of the clearing systems or a common depositary on behalf of both. In order to give those persons who have entries in their accounts in the clearing systems direct rights against the Issuer, it is necessary for the issuer and, if there is a guarantor, the guarantor to enter into a deed of covenant upon which they can sue directly without involving the clearing systems, as holders of the global note in having to sue on behalf of their account holders.

45 Sometimes they are issued at a discount.

## Sukuk (Islamic bonds)

**4.88** Islamic bonds are discussed at length in the context of Islamic secondary securitisation in **Chapter 5** and that being the case this chapter will just provide a brief overview. Essentially Islamic bonds must satisfy two key elements. One is that the bond holder cannot be paid interest but must instead be sharing in the risk of the business issuing the bonds. Any return must be calculated by reference to that firm's performance. In addition, the activities carried out by the bond issuing firm must not be un-Islamic so that the bond holder is not financing something that their religion is opposed to. These matters must be certified as compliant by the relevant Islamic Board of Supervision. These added complexities tend to result in the process of forming an Islamic bond being significantly more time consuming and expensive when compared with a traditional western bond issue.

**4.89** Problems arise however because in many jurisdictions there are disparate interpretations of how Islamic law should operate. This leaves a bond issue created subject to Islamic law open to challenge if a jurisdiction in which it comes before a court that does not take the same view as those who drafted the arrangement in another. In part this is a consequence of different standards of interpretation of the Islamic religion rather than just how it should be applied to finance law. In practice this problem is normally solved by making sure the choice of law and jurisdiction clause in the relevant certificates is made subject to the law of a state where the Islamic Board of Banking Supervision have approved the precise nature of the arrangement being utilised. However, even this is not foolproof. In 2017 Dana Gas, a UAE company found a US$ 700 million Islamic bond issue could not be repaid because it was held to have been illegally constructed under the UAE legal system.

**4.90** This may be one of the reasons for the failure of a significant secondary market to develop in Islamic bonds through a reduction in the number of potential buyers for religious reasons as there is a religious objection to buying debt at a discount. Exacerbating this is the failure of many of the relevant accountancy regulators to develop a precise methodology for determining exactly what an investor has purchased as an interest where such investments are concerned.[46] Despite these problems Islamic bond finance is growing rapidly and currently stands at in excess of US $5.79 billion in the UK alone as of 2025.

---

[46] FE Vogel and SL Hayes III *Islamic Law and Finance: Religion, Risk and Return* (Martinus Nijhoff,1998) p.13.

## Convertible bonds

**4.91** Essentially these are bonds which at a future date or contingency can be traded for shares in the company which issued the bonds. This date may be at the behest of the company, in which case the bond holder is taking a significant risk. The company that issues these can normally offer a lower interest rate than they would otherwise have to issue and still sell the bonds. They also face the avoidance of repaying the debt as this will be covered by the shares that replace them. These may be issued at a later date than the bond issue by the company or bought on the open market. In the former case the company may save a significant amount of money, though at the cost of diluting the value of existing shares. Such arrangements are sometimes found when investment banks provide finance to companies to carry out a corporate takeover. Part of the loan may be in the form of a convertible bond with the option to convert to shares in the new combined company.

**4.92** The attraction for the convertible bond holder is that the value of the shares which replace it may end up having a significantly higher value than the bonds. The converse may of course also be the case.

**4.93** The issuing documentation's main difference when compared with ordinary bonds is that the prospectus or offering memorandum is going to have to set out full details of the nature of the convertible bond issue and the basis on which the conversion may take place.

## Deed of covenant

**4.94** As stated above the purpose of the deed of covenant is to give account holders in the European clearing systems direct rights against the issuer. The deed operates as a unilateral declaration by the issuer to pay 'relevant account holders' should the global note not be paid and it becomes void pursuant to its terms, ie, it is not exchanged for definitive notes subsequent to a failure to pay thereon.

**4.95** The use of a deed poll is an ancient method under English law for conferring benefits on third parties provided it is, of course, executed by deed. The same principles apply to the giving of a deed of guarantee which is the commonly adopted method for giving guarantees whether the notes are issued either in global or definitive form and obviates the necessity to print and execute a full-blown guarantee on the back of each definitive note.The purpose behind the adoption of these methods is twofold: to reduce the costs of issuing paper under a commercial paper programme; and to acknowledge the reality of the market in which this paper is issued, sold and traded, namely through clearing systems by sophisticated financial institutions who have accounts in clearing systems.

**4.96** It is against this background that a variety of issuing and paying agency agreements have been drafted to accommodate the particular procedures adopted by these agents, and it is for this reason no specimen is included, as each agent tends to have its own particular style of wishing to enter into the documentation and conforming changes between that agreement and the dealer agreement will need to be made where necessary.

**4.97** In summary, therefore, the documentation is comparatively simple, not in need of significant negotiation and capable of being produced and signed in a short timeframe. Having said this, however, the dealers will want to be able to solicit interest for these notes by being able to distribute an information memorandum. The effects of such an information memorandum and potential liabilities incurred in distributing the same have already been considered.

### Discount/interest bearing

**4.98** Whether or not bonds, notes or commercial paper are issued at a discount from their face value giving them a yield to maturity, or in interest bearing form, will depend upon the particular nature of the investors to whom the banks or dealers which purchase them are directing their sales effort. It is common in today's markets to provide for all types of notes and there is no intrinsic legal difference between the types of instrument beyond those mentioned above.

### Currencies

**4.99** Bonds, notes and commercial paper are only freely capable of issue in major currencies. It is possible to issue bonds, notes and commercial paper denominated in other currencies.

### Guarantees

**4.100** It is common also to find that issuers are mere finance vehicles and that, therefore, for credit purposes a guarantee is necessary. These can be given in one of two ways, namely, to set out the form of guarantee duly signed by the guarantor, on the form of the note, normally on its reverse, or to have the guarantor execute a deed poll, which is a unilateral declaration in favour of holders of all notes, that it guarantees all payments due by the issuer under the notes.

## The regulatory and legal framework

**4.101** Much of the regulatory and legal framework with which bankers, issuers and lawyers are concerned is directed towards the protection of investors. No clear definition exists as to whom the investors in bonds, notes or commercial papers are, but primarily it seems to be banks, building societies, central government agencies, the treasury departments of large corporations and wealthy individuals. The regulatory and legal framework is not drafted with these types of investors in mind, rather they are directed towards ordinary retail investors. In practice, therefore, the consumer protection psychology of these rules is primarily relevant to low denomination bonds.

**4.102** This then takes us to the financial regulatory issues. A detailed examination of financial services regulation is outside the scope of the book but it is useful to touch on the key issues. Where listed debt is to be issued the firm's solicitors will need to carry out due diligence of the information memorandum, listing particulars and supporting documentation. If they are going to be listed, the bonds themselves have to be submitted in line with the UK Listing Authority rules and, in the case of bonds submitted for listing on the Professional Securities Market, the relevant listing rules for the market and in either case comply with the exchange's admission and disclosure standards. The launch will take place with the lead manager inviting the syndicate involved to place the bonds and the issuer will sign and execute all the relevant documents. The bond issue will then be made and the issuer will continue to be bound by the exchange's disclosure and transparency rules covering matters such as inside information, annual accounts, dissemination of key information and the treatment of investors. The degree of protection for investors in bonds, not surprisingly relates to their vulnerability. Thus, a bond issue of low denomination bonds to retail investors will attract greater disclosure obligations than one aimed at wholesale investors or when listing is on the Professional Securities Market.

**4.103** Any advertising or other promotion of the bond issue, whether listed or not is caught by Financial Services and Markets Act 2000, s 21, as amended by the Financial Services and Markets Act 2023, s 20 which states that such promotions can only be issued by a body with an FCA licence and specific approval to issue promotions. Thus, the issuer will normally need to arrange for their investment bankers to arrange this. Matters become more complicated if the promotion is aimed at retail investors as the Financial Promotions Order 2005[47] then potentially applies. As discussed above this provides certain requirements in relation to the manner and content of promotions.

## Negotiable/debenture

**4.104** The precise meaning of 'debenture' is a subtle one. It is clearly caught by art 77 of the Regulated Activities Order 2001, as amended.[48]

[47] SI 2005/1529.
[48] The Financial Services and Markets Act 2000 (Regulated Activities) Order 2001, SI 2001/544, as amended.

Nevertheless, though it may be difficult to determine what is and what is not a debenture, as Gower points out, 'the juristic nature of the underlying transaction is never in doubt'. The description which has received most favour was given by Chitty J in *Edmonds v Blaina Furnaces Co*, where he described it as a term which imports or acknowledges a debt. This definition was given wider interpretation the following year in *the Levy* where Chitty J remarked that it:

> '... means a document which either creates a debt or acknowledges it, and any document which fulfils either of these conditions is a debenture'.

Applying these, and more recent interpretations, to bonds, notes and commercial paper, it is difficult to argue that such instrument is not a debenture. Certainly, it is clear that the regulatory authorities have assumed this to be the case and seem to expect those in the market to treat sterling commercial paper as if it were a debenture.

## Taxation issues

**4.105** Tax will always be a factor in determining how a company should raise funds. However, where bond issues are concerned matters become more complicated because many bond issues are made on secondary basis through offshore special purpose entities to raise money more cheaply (see **Chapter 5**). A detailed analysis of taxation is however beyond the scope of this book.

## Bonds and syndicated lending – a comparison

**4.106** The most important distinction is that a syndicated loan (see **Chapter 2**) normally interposes a bank between the ultimate lenders of the funds and the borrower, resulting in two distinct contracts. In the case of bond issues the enduring contract is a single one between the investors and the issuer, the terms of which are set out in the bond itself, sometimes supplemented by the terms of a trust deed. Another distinction is that the investor is not involved in the negotiation of the terms of the bond issue. This is done by the arranging bank on behalf of the managers and underwriters. Other methods are used to protect the bondholder. These methods are adopted because the bondholders are such a diffuse and anonymous group. The first method is the statutory regulation of the issuing of securities, requiring a prospectus, a proper level of disclosure, remedies and sanctions, including criminal liability for failing to satisfy the relevant laws. A complex network of exceptions and exemptions allows the bond market to operate with minimum compliance with such securities regulation so the level of protection is not as high as for domestic investors. The other method adopted is the bondholder trust deed.

**4.107** The process of offering the loan is dissimilar with a syndication involving an information memorandum, whereas a bond issue, especially one involving bonds, will tend to involve a prospectus or offering circular according to jurisdiction. The latter is a much more complex, structured document which is considerably more expensive and time consuming to produce. However, where the bonds are for large denominations a prospectus is not normally required and a simpler document can be produced.

**4.108** The loan document itself is more complex in the case of a syndicated loan. The bond issue will contain similar terms but in shorter, simpler language. This is because, in the case of a syndicated loan, the lenders have traditionally negotiated detailed protections for themselves. Although the Loan Markets Association standard terms are now often used or adapted, they reflect the traditional approach. In the case of bond issues, a simpler, shorter set of clauses is offered by the borrower and tends to be sufficient for the market place. Also, a syndicated loan will contain all the terms of the arrangement, whereas with a bond issue the arrangements will be spread between a range of documents, which, as seen above include subscription agreements, agency agreements and trust deeds, etc. The clauses that will not be found in a bond issue are a set off clause and material adverse change of control clause for the obvious reason that they would not be relevant, but these are standard in syndicated loans.

**4.109** The loan facility itself is also different with a syndicated loan being available in a number of forms, either bullet loans, multicurrency loans, revolving credit facilities and so on. A bond issue on the other hand will normally be arranged as a one off loan, normally for a set term, by the bondholders. It is sometimes the case that bonds may be issued by a borrower on a rolling, periodic basis, but each bond issue remains a one off loan. In addition, a syndicated loan will normally be at a floating rate of interest, whereas bonds are usually fixed but longer term ones may be floating. Prepayment is also normally permissible in syndicated loans, subject to the limitations described in **Chapter 2**. In bond issues prepayment is not normally available in shorter term bond issues.

**4.110** Another major distinction is the transferability of the loan asset in a bond issue. As stated above bonds are negotiable by delivery, whereas as seen in **Chapter 3**, the legal devices necessary to transfer participations in a syndicated loan are more complex and cumbersome. Another distinction is that bonds, floating rate notes excepted, are fixed interest securities. Finally, in bond issue documentation there are rarely pro rata sharing clauses, set off clauses and 'increased costs' protection as are found in syndicated loans, and the events of default tend to be more limited in a syndicated loan.

**4.111** In the event of the borrower getting into financial difficulties it is potentially easier to arrange a restructuring with a group of banks than a very large and disparate collection of bondholders in different parts of the world and speaking different languages. Many of them are also not financial experts. Additionally, it is unrealistic to expect bondholders to make new funds available in the event of the borrower getting into difficulties, whereas banks are likely to view such requests more sympathetically, provided they are satisfied that there is a realistic plan in place to repay the funds in due course.

# Chapter 5 Secondary Securitisation

## Introduction

**5.1** Securitisation exists in two forms. In its simplest form it consists of raising finance by issuing bonds or commercial paper. This is discussed in **Chapter 4**. There is a second, more complex form known as known as secondary securitisation, and in the United States it is often referred to as structured finance,[1] though technically this is a wider term. This consists of issuing bonds from a second company, the interest on which and repayment of which are paid by the income stream of the original company. Perhaps the best definition is Feeny's:[2]

> '... the process by which debt is made marketable. On a wider interpretation securitization[3] .... involves the unbundling and repackaging of already existing loan portfolios into securities. These securities are then sold, thereby removing the asset from the originator's balance sheet..'

This is sometimes referred to as 'asset backed securitisation'

Reis Roy[4] defines secondary securitisation as consisting of 'utilising balance sheet assets as security and financial support to raise off balance sheet finance from the capital markets'. This has the benefit of clarity and brevity, but it is worth adding that the balance sheet assets used by the originating company raising the funds are part of its future income. This money is not just used as financial support but is normally transferred to the second organisation, the special purpose vehicle or entity, to provide funds for payment of interest to the bond holders and in due course to repay their capital.

Thus, the core elements of asset backed securitisation look like this:

---

1 J Kravitt, *Securitisation of Financial Assets* (Aspen Law & Business, 1996), p 11 and also SL Schwarcz, *Structured Finance: a Guide to the Principles of Asset Securitization* (Aspen Law & Business, 1993), p 41. Technically, the expression 'structured finance' ought to be reserved for layered bond issues.

2 PW Feeney, *Securitization – Redefining the Bank* (St Martin's Press, New York, 1995).

3 The spelling 'securitization' is American.

4 C Reis Roy, 'An Analysis of the Law and Practice of Securitisation', (PhD thesis, University of Wolverhampton, 2008), p 1.

FIGURE 1

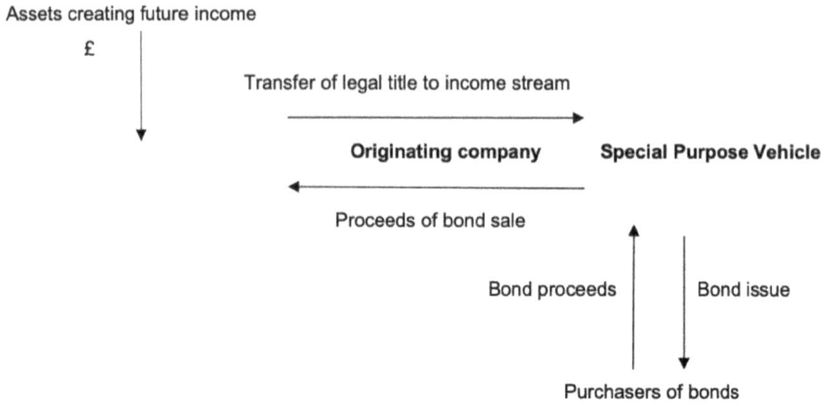


For the purposes of convenience such structures will be referred to throughout this chapter as 'securitisation'.[5]

## History

**5.2** As a concept, securitisation has a reasonably long history.[6] The post-Second World War years saw rapid economic development in the so-called 'sunbelt'[7] states in the southern United States, but a disproportionate amount of the available investment capital resided in the north-eastern states. The US federal structure combined with the banking regulations of the time obstructed direct inter-state banking activity. As a result, finance was raised in the north-eastern states, and in some cases bonds were issued there to lend the money for development and construction in the 'sunbelt' states.

**5.3** Mortgage securitisation developed in its current form in the United States in the 1970s when banks lending money on residential mortgages found that the appetite of the market place for such loans exceeded their capacity to provide them from their own balance sheet. The modern US market for such arrangements expanded rapidly when

---

5 The key regulatory factors are: The Prudential Sourcebook for Banks, Building Societies and Investment firms (BIPRU) at Ch 9, the Prudential Sourcebook for Investment Firms (IFPRU) at Ch 4.12, if mortgages, regulated contracts or consumer credit income is involved MCOB and CONC and lastly the prospectus and disclosure rules in the FCA Handbook.

6 The essential construct of raising finance in one jurisdiction to lend it in another arguably originated with the knights templar in the 12th century. This developed further in England in the reign of Edward 1 (1272–1307). Two Italian banks raised money in Italy to finance Edward's military activity. In turn the repayment of the funds raised in Italy was made by a tax on wool exports from England to the low countries. In the late 19th century, railroad companies in the United States had considerable difficulty raising sufficient finance due to the underdeveloped nature of the US capital markets at the time. Some of it was provided by European banks, and they in turn placed securities with their clients in Europe to raise the money.

7 In particular Florida, Texas, New Mexico, Nevada and California.

the US government helped facilitate the further expansion of the market by creating funding institutions like the Federal Home Loan Mortgage Corporation,[8] the Federal National Mortgage Association[9] and finally the Government National Mortgage Association.[10] These organisations used their financial power and the benefit of their government guarantee, (albeit at the time an implicit one in the case of the first two institutions) to raise money on the US domestic bond markets to fund the acquisition of loans from the mortgage banks.

**5.4** From that time on a US bank could make a loan subject to a mortgage to a purchaser of real property and then sell the mortgage loan and the mortgage to one of these three federal agencies and thus remove the loan from its own balance sheet. The federal agencies, in turn, raised cash through the bond markets by issuing bonds, the principal source of repayment for which would be the mortgage loans purchased from the mortgage banks. The mortgagor was able to obtain relatively cheap funds because the interest rate payable on agency securities was, generally, lower than the cost of funds of the original mortgage bank. The result of this was a major expansion of the market as the banks could then lend again to the property market. Consequently, the need for legal and administrative documentation developed and became standardised. Most mortgage loans that conformed to certain key requirements eventually became funded by one of the three agencies, and they all had similar standard documentary and credit requirements. The more standardised the origination process became, the easier it became to securitise loans. By the late 1980s originators started to pool receivables such as credit card receivables and issue securitised bonds against their future income and the securitisation market expanded further.

**5.5** By 1985 the first mortgage-backed issue in London was made by the Bank of America. The issue was made through their SPV, the Mortgage Intermediary Note Issuer (No 1) Amsterdam BV.[11] By 1991 this market had grown to £840.5 million in the third quarter alone.[12] From then on the market continued to grow until the financial crisis of 2008 led to a temporary falling off. Since then it has grown to £209 billion in 2024.[13]

**5.6** The next stage in the development of the US market saw private corporations enter the market to fulfil the role of funding institutions. The debt issued by these issuers did not carry a US federal guarantee but was still likely to yield a lower interest rate than the debt paper

8 Otherwise known as FHLMC or more commonly 'Freddie Mac.'

9 Otherwise known as FNMA or more commonly 'Fannie Mae.'

10 Otherwise known as GNMA or 'Ginnie Mae.'

11 E Ferran, *Mortgage Securitisation – Legal Aspects* (Butterworths, London, 1991), p 2.

12 *Financial Times* Survey 'Asset Backed Finance' 1991, and 'Housing Finance', August and November 1991.

13 J. Suarez 'Securitisation Data Report Q4 2024 and 2024 Full Year.' www.afme.eu [Accessed 16 February 2026].

issued by the mortgage banks themselves because of the high credit rating the securitised bond issue could attract. The reasons for this are examined later in the chapter. As with the three federal agencies mentioned above, these companies also purchased mortgage loans and mortgages from the originating mortgage banks and financed the arrangement by issuing bonds or trust certificates in the US debt markets. However, over time the newer private issuers of mortgage backed securities tended to migrate to include loans that did not conform to the agencies' underwriting standards, primarily because the amount advanced to the borrower was higher than the agencies' maximum advance relative to the value of the respective properties being purchased or because of the borrower's poor credit history. This was exacerbated by a federal requirement dating back to the period of President Carter in the late 1970s to the effect that banks should lend a certain proportion of their residential mortgage lending to disadvantaged social groups. During President Clinton's term of office it was made a requirement of bank audits that the auditor's check on this. Thus, the banks greatly extended their lending to those with a poor credit history.

**5.7** Then in 2002 the Sarbanes Oxley Act[14] was passed to protect the public in the aftermath of the Enron fiasco. Section 302 resulted in the chief financial and chief executive officers having to sign statements declaring that everything had been truthfully disclosed and they also had to personally guarantee the financial statements. There were also obligations imposed generally on directors and senior officers. Major corporations thus found the prospect of raising funds through direct bond or equity issues less attractive than before.[15] As a result, raising funds through secondary securitisation involving offshore bond issues became more attractive as such personal guarantees were not needed from the directors of the originating company in relation to the accounts of the SPV.[16] (Technically for US securitisations a trust has to be used, called a special purpose entity or SPE.)

**5.8** The market then developed further as independent corporations found ways of skilfully structuring portfolios of mortgage loans so that they could obtain higher credit ratings. In some cases this resulted in portfolios of mortgage loans to those with very poor credit histories obtaining AAA ratings for the first 28% of the loans repaid from that portfolio. Thus, the reality of the financial risk of the mortgage loan itself started to diverge from the apparent safety of the related securitised bonds on offer. This was crucial as buyers of bonds tend to rely on the ratings given by rating agencies as the primary basis for determining the safety of the bond issue.

---

14 Pub L 107–204, 116 Stat 745.

15 L McDonald, *A Colossal Failure of Common Sense* (Ebury Press, 2009), p 73.

16 Though the liability under this Act would remain as far as the originating company (or group) is concerned.

**5.9** The securitising of residential property loans was a major source of news in the 2007/08 banking crisis. Many banks over extended themselves by excessive residential mortgage lending, bonds were then issued by the SPV against the future flow of receivables from these loans. As residential property prices continued to rise, in large measure because of governmental economic policy in the US and the UK amongst others, this process continued and accelerated. Eventually the market became over inflated and once residential property prices began to fall the market would no longer accept the bond issues. The banks concerned then found themselves in a situation where the borrowers were in many cases incapable of maintaining the payments on their loans, the security for those loans, the residential property, was rapidly declining in value and the bond markets would no longer accept the bonds issued by the banks' SPVs.

**5.10** Meanwhile the technique had extended its range elsewhere in the developed world from the start of the 1990s, to assets other than residential mortgages. The implementation of the Basel Accord, which lays down minimum capital and solvency ratio requirements for banks incorporated in the G10 countries,[17] resulted in further pressure on banks to improve their solvency ratios and securitisation was one of the techniques employed by banks to remove assets from their balance sheets and so achieve this. Securitisation could, therefore, be used as a device to reduce capital requirements on banks. The net effect was that the process proved on the one hand a more profitable way for banks to raise finance and a cheaper method of borrowing for other originating companies than going to the banks. Recently in the UK the Securitisation Regulations 2024[18] have made the market place more attractive to issuers and investors in the UK.

## Originating assets

**5.11** It is worth asking what type of future income an originating company might find the markets willing to accept as a source of funds for a bond issue. Those that seem to be accepted most often in the market place are residential and commercial mortgages, financing and operating leases usually for cars, ships and aircraft, credit card receivables, project finance loans, other loans, whether consumer or corporate, trade receivables, conditional sale and hire purchase agreements and any other income stream whose amount is reasonable easy to predict.[19]

---

17 Belgium, Canada, France, Germany, Italy, Japan, the Netherlands, Sweden, Switzerland, the UK and the US who cooperate through the G10 through their ministers of finance and central bank governors, normally meeting once a year in connection with the annual IMF meeting.

18 SI 2024/102.

19 Where the assets backing the bond issue are themselves bonds the arrangement is called a collateralised debt obligation or CDO. Where it is predominantly made up of corporate loans it is often referred to as a collateralised loan obligation or CLO.

**5.12** The list is limited only by the imagination of the originator, or their advisors, and what the market can be persuaded to accept. Market experience suggests that commercial and industrial loans are more difficult to securitise. When the bonds themselves are issued those buying them have a number of concerns: the quality of the loan assets concerned; the security which is available in association with the assets; guarantees; maturity periods; the size and regularity of instalments; consumer credit termination issues; substitution rights; the potential for the loans being restructured; and above all else the credit rating. This last issue is examined below.

## The special purpose vehicle or entity

**5.13** The structure has to be created so that the funds receivable from the originator are 'purchased' by the special purpose vehicle or entity. The primary purpose of this vehicle is to receive the originator's receivables which have been purchased and also to issue the bonds. The origination income will then be utilised to pay interest to the bond holders, and in due course, the debt owed to them. For this to operate effectively the SPV or other entity must be independent from the originator. If not, the whole arrangement would fail as the SPV would be a subsidiary rather than an independent entity and the finances of the SPV would need to appear in the originating group's consolidated accounts. Thus, an SPV must not have the same directors as the originator, nor should the originator itself be one of the directors. Indeed, in the UK under the rules of the Prudential Regulation Authority (PRA), if a bank supervised by the PRA wishes to remove assets from its balance sheet by means of a securitisation, it cannot hold any equity interest in the SPV at all. The relationship will be governed by contracts between the originator and the SPV and its directors. Such vehicles exist in different forms.

### Special Purpose Vehicles (SPVs)

**5.14** This SPV will have a low level of capital relative to the quantities of money it is handling.[20] It exists purely for the purpose of obtaining the receivables, issuing the bonds which may be backed by those receivables, transferring the proceeds of the bond issue to the originator and in due course paying interest and in turn capital repayment to the bond holders.[21] For this reason its legal powers will be restricted. As already discussed, it is necessary for the originator

[20] Slaughter and May 'Model Guide to Securitisation Techniques' (2010), pp 9 and 10
[21] There have been instances of SPVs engaging in other financial activities beyond this, but it is unwise for this to be allowed outside certain specific areas, eg, reinvestment of surplus funds, as it raises the possibility of the SPV having an insolvency risk which could reduce its credit rating.

not to have any of its directors as directors of the SPV. They must be separate and will often be local accountants who specialise in this type of work. It is sometimes located in an off shore tax haven and in other cases in the same host state as the originating company. The key factors that will determine this are: the cost of setting up and establishing the SPV, the minimum capitalisation requirements in the jurisdiction concerned, disclosure requirements, the rate of taxation on interest payments, assets and VAT, any licensing or authorisation process that might be entailed and the applicable insolvency law.

### Special Purpose Entities (SPEs)

**5.15** Whilst the legal position in the United States is outside the scope of this book, it is worth mentioning very briefly the different approach adopted there for tax reasons. This consists of not utilising a company but a trust[22] (an SPE).[23] Under US tax law there are three types of trust: grantor trusts; owner trusts; and master trusts. The first of these can be created to have tax-exempt status,[24] but must not participate in profitable business, not vary the terms of the investment and only pay interest on a single class of securities. This debars them from being used if reinvestment of new receivables is to be carried out. Their main use is for receivables such as mortgages and other instalment loans where the receivables pass through the trust to the investors and no reinvestment is needed. When reinvestment is required an owner trust will be appropriate as the trustees can engage in business activities which is necessary when the income from the originator accrues from short term obligations such as credit card receivables. It is also useful where over collateralisation is used (see below) as some of the income will need to be invested. Finally, master trusts are used when the vehicle requires access to multiple markets at the same time.

### Multi-seller structures

**5.16** Regardless of whether a company or trust is used, it is possible to have a multi-seller securitisation conduit set up. These receive a number of originators' assets and make bond issues on their behalf. Such issues are often managed by a bank and tend to be most attractive to originators whose bond issues were not attracting credit ratings of sufficient standing to facilitate issuing bonds at low enough rates of

22 For a discussion of this see C Reis-Roy, 'Securitisation Structures in the US' (1997) 13(1) JIBL 19.
23 This is when the US refers to such arrangements as a 'pass through' structure.
24 See US Department of Treasury Regulations, s 301.7701–4.

interest to be attractive to the originator.[25] They can also be attractive where the originator wishes to make a bond issue insufficient in size to justify the costs of an independent SPV or SPE. The benefits of the multi-seller approach tend to be savings in cost and time. On the other hand, there can be significant upfront costs for the party creating the vehicle which may not be recouped until a few transactions have been undertaken.

**5.17** For the purposes of convenience all such independent vehicles will be referred to as SPVs for the remainder of the chapter.

### Structured Investment Vehicles (SIVs)

**5.18** These are US based vehicles, usually bank sponsored, which work along similar lines to SPVs (see above). They issue Commercial Paper (see Chapter 4 at **4.11** and **4.81-4.95**) on a rolling basis and use the funds to buy assets which create a higher but longer term return such as a pool of mortgage assets. Thus, the activity is financially driven from the SIV whereas with an SPV the activity is sourced by the originator which uses the SPV to raise funds by issuing bonds. They tend to be more heavily capitalised than SPVs. Since the 2008 financial crisis they have been less heavily used. The arrangement thus looks like this.

FIGURE 2

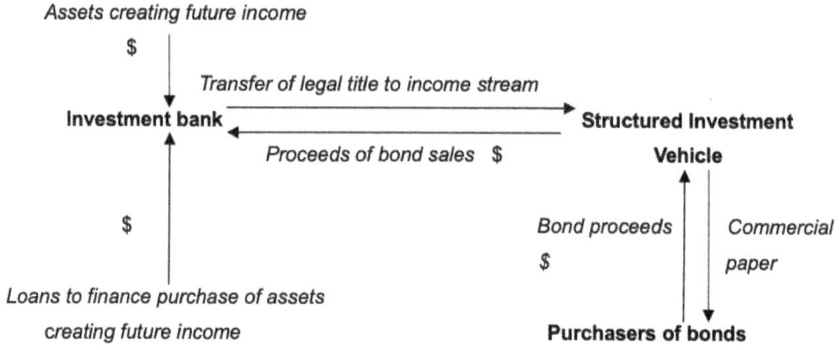


## Credit aspects

**5.19** Credit enhancement may be facilitated by arranging for the issue to be backed by a financial institution with a sufficiently high credit rating, should the assets involved be unlikely to provide this. Here a fee will have to be paid in return for the service provided. In cases where the bond issue consists of more than one level of

[25] SL Schwartz, 'The Global Alchemy of Asset Securitisation' (1995) International Financial Law Review, May, p 30.

debt, only the higher level of debt might be guaranteed rather than all of them. Only a small number of banks, all of them with high credit ratings, carry out such work. Alternately, a letter of credit (see Chapter 10) could be provided through a bank or an insurance policy be taken out to guarantee payment if there is a shortfall. Another possibility is to carry out enhancement internally to the structure. This can be done in a number of ways. First, it could be done by overcollateralising by paying additional amounts to cover the eventuality of some of the receivables not being paid, eg, **103%** of value to be paid instead of 100%. Secondly, it could be done by creating a split structure of senior and subordinated levels. This can be arranged so that the senior levels are overcollateralised. The lower level(s) will attract investors by offering higher interest rates. It could be done by having a degree of interest rate spread in the cash flow or by utilising derivative contracts to hedge against any risks inherent in the financial structure, eg, currency risk or a mismatch between fixed or floating rate interest on the originator's income against the bonds being issued by the SPV. There is no legal limit on what can be provided – it is simply a case of providing for the eventuality that the originator's income stream may not cover the financial costs being incurred. The arrangement then looks like this.

FIGURE 3: SECURITISATION WITH EXTERNAL CREDIT PROVIDER

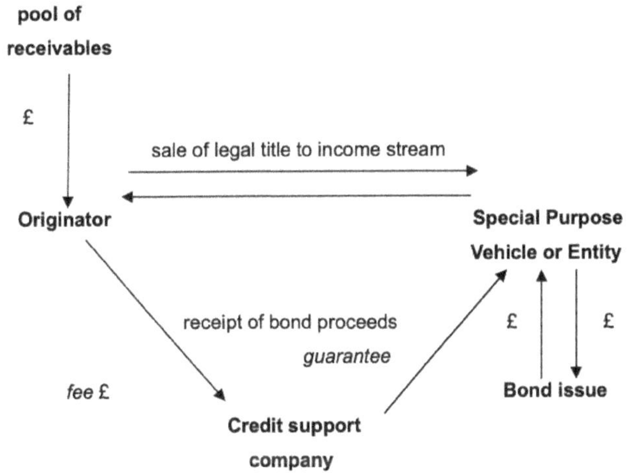


## Liquidity aspects

**5.20** Another issue that needs to be addressed is that of the liquidity of the structure. That is, whether the funds received from the SPV's bond issue raises sums of the required amount at the appropriate time to transfer the needed amount to the originator. This is a particular issue with a rolling programme with regular bond issues from the SPV and regular transfers from the originator in the opposite direction. In such a case it is possible to pay a financial institution to act as liquidity provider and make up any shortfall or hold any surplus, so that the correct amounts are provided on the required dates.

**5.21** This may be achieved by the provision of liquidity facilities by a third party, letters of credit, insurance cover, debt structures designed to facilitate liquidity, guaranteed investment arrangements or substitution programmes. The arrangement looks like this.

FIGURE 4: SECURITISATION WITH LIQUIDITY SUPPORT PROVIDER

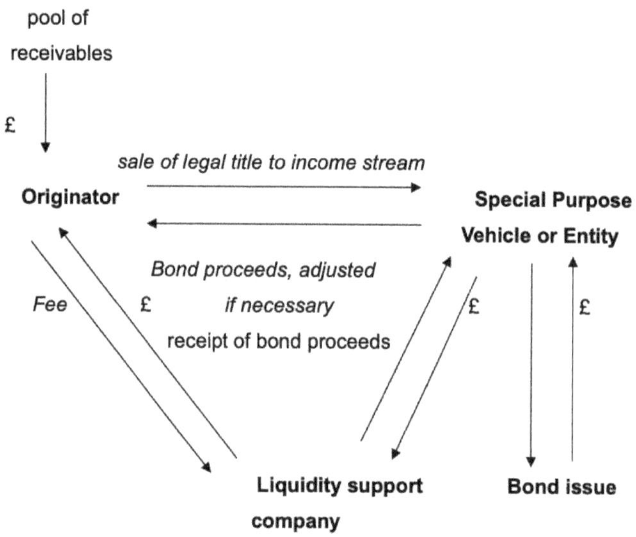


**5.22** In some instances it may be difficult to get such a structure to operate effectively because the bonds need to be issued from a jurisdiction with a currency other than the currency used in the jurisdiction where the SPV is based. The originator however will normally want the bond proceeds to be in the same currency that it generates its income in. Here a contract for differences (see **6.9**) may be used between the SPV's bankers and the issuer. In this instance a contract is signed whereby the SPV's banker and the bank or other financial institution issuing the bonds sign a contract whereby the net difference between the proceeds of the bond sales on one hand, and the amount needed to settle the interest on the bonds, the capital repayment on the bonds and any associated overheads on the other, are netted off against each other in the respective currencies, and any balancing sum paid. This can also be an advantage if the jurisdiction in which the relevant parties are located would impose stamp duty on a transfer of funds. Contracts for differences are normally immune from this. Thus:

FIGURE 5: SECURITISATION USING A CONTRACT FOR DIFFERENCES TO HEDGE CURRENCY RISK

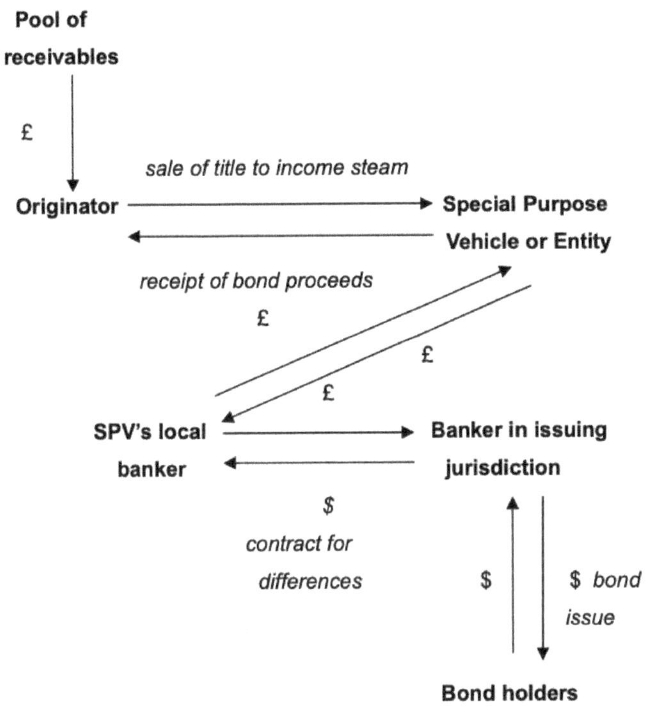


**5.23** It is sometimes the case that a double special purpose vehicle will be adopted in cases where over collateralisation is being used to assist in obtaining a good credit rating. In such cases the initial transfer of the receivables will be from the originator to SPV 1. This will be a true sale for the purposes of insolvency risk.[26] The receivables are then transferred to SPV 2 on a true sale basis for the accounting rules. SPV 2 will then issue the bonds. When the arrangement is eventually terminated SPV 2 will re-transfer any outstanding receivables to SPV 1 which can then be hived up into the originator.[27]

**5.24** Finally, it is often the case that a professional trustee will be used for the purposes of managing the bond issue. This adds another element to the final structure, which often resembles this:

[26] See FRS 5.
[27] See Schwartz (above n 24).

FIGURE 6 SIMPLIFIED OVERALL SECURITISATION DIAGRAM

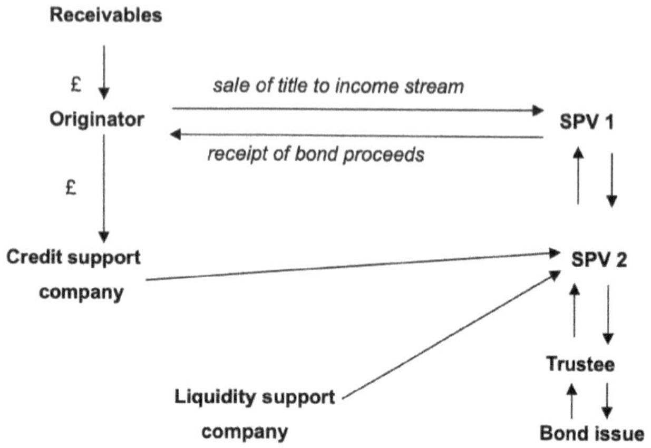


**5.25** Again, a contract for differences could be used rather than a true sale between the originator and the SPV. This is called synthetic securitisation. It should be borne in mind that in practice the group structure can become more complex than this. In particular, if the bond issue is carried out on a public basis, it would involve the parties discussed in **Chapter 4**.

## Synthetic securitisation

**5.26** Synthetic securitisation[28] exists where the underlying assets are not transferred to an SPV but some of their risk is transferred to an investor via a derivative, typically a credit default swap (see **6.15** and **6.16**). The originator, normally a bank, will buy from a third party (the 'investor') credit protection against a pool of loans and the credit will pay up if there is any shortfall from the underlying loan portfolio being paid to the bank. This is usually done by a credit default swap being entered into between the bank and the investor at the start of the transaction with the bank retaining ownership of the relevant assets and the investor taking on the risk of default in relation to a stated portfolio of obligations which match those retained by the originator. Alternately a guarantee might be issued by the investor. It is called 'synthetic' because the loans are not transferred to a third party but remain on the bank's balance sheet.

FIGURE 7 SIMPLIFIED DIAGRAM OF SYNTHETIC SECURITISATION

[28] Sometimes called 'significant risk transfer'.

**5.27** The arrangements can be funded or unfunded. If funded the bank retains the protected funds from the investor. If unfunded the bank takes credit protection payment from the investor if a credit event occurs. The precise structures that are used to achieve these arrangements can vary. The arrangement may involve the bank issuing collateral for the arrangement.

**5.28** Such arrangements do not always use an SPV. Those that do see the SPV placed between the bank and the investor as a mere conduit. If there is collateral it can be held by either the SPV or the bank. The following diagram provides a typical arrangement, but it should be noted that there are variations in how these are structured.

FIGURE 8 SYNTHETIC SECURITISATION

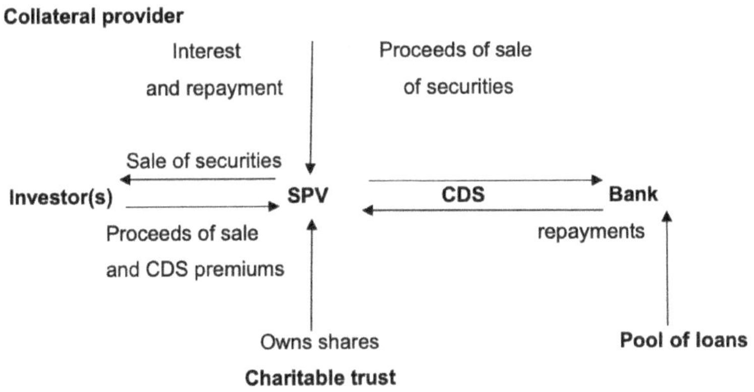


The proceeds of sale deposited with the collateral provider are used to finance the payments owed by the SPV to the bank (originator) under the CDS and any remaining collateral returned on repayment of the securities.

**5.29** The primary reason for such arrangements is that banks can use them to reduce the amount of capital they have to hold under the Basel III banking regulations. A detailed analysis of this is outside the scope of the text.

## Islamic securitisation

**5.30** Whilst an analysis of Islamic law generally is beyond the scope of this book Islamic bonds were mentioned in **Chapter 4** and so it is worth considering the position where Islamic bonds are issued through a securitised structure as such arrangements are found in the jurisdiction of England and Wales.

**5.31** Islamic law itself is a generic term covering five main schools of Islamic thought[29]: the Shafi, Hanboli, Hanafi, Maliki and the Ibadi[30] and each has a slightly dissimilar approach to interpreting Islamic law. On some of the key issues in modern finance there are different positions found between them. In addition to this, Islamic financial law involves two main methods of analytical thought; the critical and the constructionist. In essence, the former adopts a revisionistic approach to interpreting Islamic law and the latter recognises western style financial products which can operate within Islamic law. Critical theoreticians see the constructionist approach as an artificial method that distorts the role of Islamic law and interpret it as essentially nihilistic.[31] Here we consider securitisation primarily from the vantage point of Islamic Shafi law as it is the main utiliser of Islamic securitisation.

**5.32** All Islamic law forbids a return, reward or compensation charged in a transaction for the provision of a loan or in the rescheduling of a debt,[32] and any positive, fixed, predetermined rate of return that are guaranteed regardless of the performance of an investment.[33] The relevant term for this is riba, which when translated, means an 'increase' or 'an addition' and denotes any increase or advantage obtained by the lender as a condition of the loan, or a fixed and guaranteed rate of return under a profit sharing agreement. In its best known form, this prohibition disallows the earning or paying of any benefit, monetary or otherwise, on a loan of money, and is based on the principle that a loan should be characterised as a shared risk enterprise or charitable activity and not as a profit-making venture.

**5.33** Notwithstanding that Islamic securitisation does not have a definition that is uniformly accepted or consistent amongst Islamic scholars, the concept underlying it is an adaptation of conventional asset backed securitisation in accordance with shariah law. In essence, Islamic securitisation involves using the cashflow, creditworthiness and collateral of tangible halal assets to support an offering of Islamic bonds (sukuk) which are discussed in the next paragraph, all in accordance with generally accepted principles of shariah law. Clearly this raises serious issues as the lenders (the buyers of the

---

29 Four sunni and one shia, though if smaller Islamic sects are included there are a large number of sub groups. An exact number is a subjective issue as there are disagreements as to whether some sects are technically Moslem.

30 D El-Hawary, W Grais and Z Iqbal, 'Regulating Islamic Financial Institutions: the Nature of the Regulated.' World Bank Policy Research Paper 3227 (25 February 2004)

31 HA Hamoudi, 'Muhammad's Social Justice or Islam Cant. Langdellianism and the Failure of Islamic Finance.' (2006) 40 Cornell International Law Journal, p 3

32 JM Taylor, Islamic Banking – The Feasibility of Establishing an Islamic Bank in the United States, 40 Am Bus L J 385, 416 (2003). See also Seniawski BL, Riba Today: Social Equity, The Economy, and Doing Business Under Islamic Law, (2001) 39 Colum J Transnational L 701, 707.

33 Iqbal, Munawar and Abbas Mirakhor, *An Introduction to Islamic Finance – Theory and Practice* (Wiley Finance Editions, John Wiley & Sons, Inc, 2006).

securitised sukuk) would not normally have a direct exposure to the underlying assets of the originating company but receive a return in lieu of interest and repayment by the SPV which in turn owns the income stream transferred to them by the originator, which in turn still owns the underlying assets. Thus, the possibility of an adapted form of securitisation to satisfy Islamic law has to be considered. In practice though matters are not so straightforward. The return on Islamic bonds, though described in many cases as a dividend return is normally expressed as a fixed percentage.[34] Such bonds are referred to as 'sukuk' which translates as an 'Islamic investment certificate' and this term is used throughout the rest of the chapter.[35]

**5.34** There is a general agreement between the various Islamic schools on seven key issues[36] that are banned: interest, excessive uncertainty, gaming, transactions in an unauthorised subject matter, restructuring debts on a compensatory basis, trading discounted debt, and forward rate agreements in currencies. The first two of these obviously raise key issues in the context of securitisation and are considered below. In addition, two more (gaming and forward rate agreements) are relevant in the context of utilising derivatives to hedge currency risk. How Islamic securitisation can be structured in the light of this will now be considered.

**5.35** In the context of securitisation the value of the assets should equal the value of the sukuk. However, such a structure would not satisfy the requirements of a traditional asset backed securitisation structure, as an Islamic lease or Ijarah structure would involve the originator selling the assets to an SPV and then having to lease them back. The SPV would use the leasing funds to finance the payments on the sukuk. In the event of default they will have contracted to buy the assets at a stated price. In reality such an arrangement is more akin to a leasing agreement under which a party pays rental payments to the other with the cash flow forming the basis upon which the sukuk are issued.

**5.36** The relevant AAOIFI Standard[37] categorises ijarah bonds as either certificates in leased assets, or certificates in usufructs of existing assets. They are defined as:[38]

34 MH Kamali and AK Abdullah 'Islamic Finance: Issues in Sukuk and Proposals for Reform' (International Institute of Advanced Islamic Studies, Kuala Lumpur, 2014), p 2.

35 A Thomas, S Cox and B Kraty 'Structuring Islamic Finance Transactions' (Euromoney, 2005), p 154. See also MS Lablou and J Tanega 'Islamic Securitisation Part II – A proposal for International Standards, Legal Guidelines and Structures.' (2007) 22(7) JIBLR 359 at 366.

36 AA Tariq 'Managing Financial Risks of Sukuk Structures' available at www.Islamicfinance.de [Accessed 17 February 2026].

37 AAOIFI Issued Standard 17.

38 AAOIFI Shariah Standard at No 17 Sections 3/2/1 and 3/2/2 respectively.

> 'certificates that carry equal value and are issued either by the owner of a leased asset or an asset to be leased by promise, or by his financial agent, the aim of which is to sell the asset and recover its value from subscription, in which case the holders of the certificates become owners of the assets....(and)....documents of equal value that are issued either by the owner of usufruct[39] of an existing asset or a financial intermediary acting on the owner's behalf, with the aim of leasing or subleasing this asset and receive rental from the revenue of subscription. In this case, the holders of the certificates become owners of the usufruct of the asset.'

**5.37** The process is that a party sells an asset, ie, the income stream from the lease (see Figure 9 below). In practice, this type of transaction is typically structured in one of three ways. First, the owner agrees to sell an asset (the income stream) which is leased to a third party directly to investors with or without a repurchase option; the owner issues sukuk to investors, each investor acquires all legal and beneficial rights to the income from the lease; the sukuk proceeds represent the purchase price; investors receive the return under the lease during a specified period; the investors exercise the repurchase option and the original owner repurchases the asset, including any residual lease, for an amount equal to the outstanding principal amount under the sukuk on the on the repurchase date. Where there is no repurchase option, the investors may continue to own the asset or may sell it to a third party. The securitisation can also be created in this way but with an Islamic bank substituted for the SPV.

**5.38** In addition, the owner of an existing asset can assign a beneficial interest in it to investors and/or a SPV acting as a financial intermediary. This type of transaction is typically structured in one of two ways, either an owner of an asset that is subject to a lease with a third party assigns a beneficial interest in the lease to the SPV; then the SPV issues the sukuk, the proceeds of which represent the purchase price of the beneficial interest; investors and the SPV receive the receivables under the lease during a specified period. Alternately, the owner of an asset that is not subject to a lease 'head leases' the asset to the SPV which then issues sukuks, the proceeds of which represent the purchase price of the interest under the 'head lease'; the owner sub-leases the asset from the SPV; then the investors receive the return under the sub-lease.

---

39 This is a legal right *in rem* found primarily in civil law jurisdictions that unites the right to use something with the right to derive profit from it.

FIGURE 9 ISLAMIC SECURITISATION

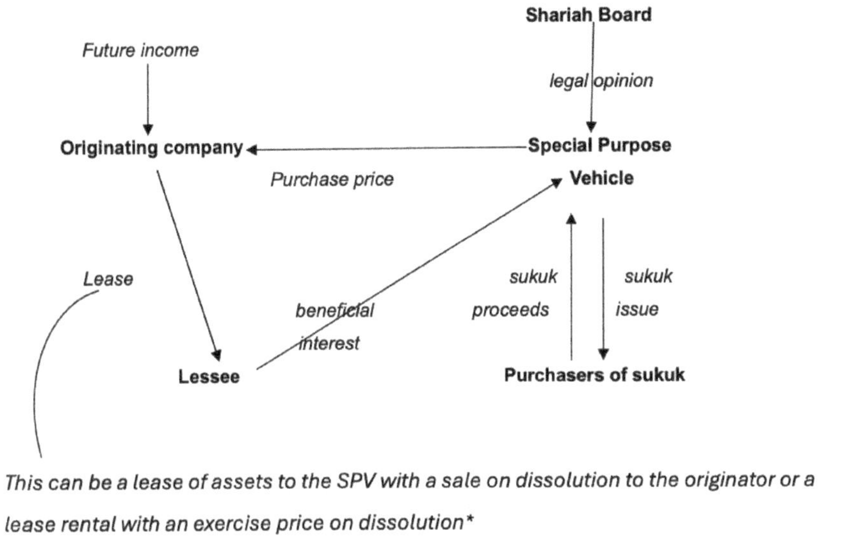


** See IMF Working Paper, 'The Economics of Islamic Finance and Securitization' (May 2007).*

**5.39** The sukuk are issued under a shariah-compliant prospectus or a similar offering document which sets out the details of the mudarabah agreement, profit and loss distribution, the nature of the assets, payment terms and details regarding maturity of the sukuk and the termination of the agreement. The sukuk offering should not be supported by, nor should the prospectus or the offering document make reference to, any guarantee provided by the issuer unless it has been certified as shariah compliant by the relevant shariah board. Nor should the offering be made on the basis that investors will receive a guaranteed return. An Islamic bank typically acts as the arranger and underwriter of the sukuk, and its shariah board will approve by issuing a written fatwa before investors are permitted to purchase the sukuk. AAOIFI Shariah Standard provides some assistance here: 'It is permissible in contracts of exchange such as contracts of sale or intellectual property but not in fiduciary contracts.' Thus, the availability of a guarantee will depend on the nature of the underlying contract.[40]

**5.40** The relevant Islamic Board standard is the AAOIFI Standard[41] which categorises ijarah bonds as either certificates in leased assets, or certificates in usufructs of existing assets. They are defined as:[42]

---

40 AAOIFI Shariah Standard No 5 at 2/1/1.
41 AAOIFI Issued Standard 17.
42 AAOIFI Shariah Standard at No 17 Sections 3/2/1 and 3/2/2 respectively.

'certificates that carry equal value and are issued either by the owner of a leased asset or an asset to be leased by promise, or by his financial agent, the aim of which is to sell the asset and recover its value from subscription, in which case the holders of the certificates become owners of the assets....(and)....documents of equal value that are issued either by the owner of usufruct[43] of an existing asset or a financial intermediary acting on the owner's behalf, with the aim of leasing or subleasing this asset and receive rental from the revenue of subscription. In this case, the holders of the certificates become owners of the usufruct of the asset'.

**5.41** Structures used to issue mudarabah bonds differ according to the nature of, and complexities involved in, the project that is being financed. In its simplest form, for example, to finance the construction of a building, the originator will issue an offering document to investors together with a mudarabah agreement. Once investors have accepted the investment opportunity and executed a copy of the agreement, a mudarabah partnership is established. This partnership then incorporates a project company and enters into a construction/project agreement with a developer. The sukuk proceeds fund the construction of the building either as lump sum paid upon its completion, or periodically in installments during the construction phase. Upon completion of the building the developer delivers the building to the project company. In western legal terms this more closely replicates a secured loan than a traditional securitisation, so its usefulness in the context of the latter is limited.

**5.42** This can be taken a step further[44] by creating lease pools. This could be done by the originator creating a pool of leases of items leased by that company and effectively engaging in a sale and leaseback of them, thus providing the originator with liquidity. However, in this instance the other members of the pool, who have thus effectively provided finance, are part owners. Ijarah[45] tend to be most common in complex, multi-jurisdictional securitisations.[46]

---

43 This is a legal right *in rem* found primarily in civil law jurisdictions that unites the right to use something with the right to derive profit from it.

44 FE Vogel and SE Haynes III, *Islamic Law and Finance: Religion, Risk and Return.* (Kluwer Law International, 2015), p 264..

45 An Ijarah is a fixed term lease and is traditionally used in one of two contexts. The relevant one is that in which ijarah is used relates to the owners of assets and properties, and means, literally, to transfer the ownership of a particular property to another person in exchange for rent and in due course the residual value of the asset. It is generally used as a form of investment, and as a method to acquire finance.

46 MJT McMillen, *Islamic Law in Practice* (River Stone Publishing, 2015).

## Salam structure

**5.43** A salaam is a purchase and sale transaction whereby on the date of the agreement the purchaser pays the seller for an asset that is delivered by the seller on a future specified date to satisfy a current need. They are defined by the AAOIFI as 'certificates of equal value issued for the purpose of mobilising salam capital so that goods can be delivered on the basis of salam to be owned by the certificate holders'.[47] The two fundamental requirements of a salaam transaction are that the purchase price must be paid in full on the date of the agreement and the purchased assets must be ascertainable in terms of its nature, quality or quantity and place of delivery. The payment must be for the full amount of the price, otherwise there will be a debt for the balance. The legal position would then be a partial or whole debt balanced against a debt, which is prohibited. Delivery must also be certain so the asset may not be one that might not be available to be delivered.[48] It is widely accepted across various schools of Islamic law. This has the potential to be used as part of a simple securitisation structure but does not seem to be heavily used in practice.

## Wakalah structure

**5.44** This is a type of agency arrangement where the agent is appointed for a specific task.[49] In the participatory mode this involves the party providing the finance (in the context of securitisation, the sukuk holders) providing equity investment and sharing in the profits and losses. If carried out on a non-participatory basis the lenders provide finance for a specific purpose, eg, purchasing an asset and selling it on, hopefully for a profit. It can also be constructed in an accessory form where the agent acts on behalf of the buyer. It is not possible for the arrangement to guarantee a particular return as this will breach the tenets of many schools of Islamic law.

**5.45** In the context of a securitised sukuk issue the originator sells the beneficial interest in assets to the sukuk holders and then manages the assets on their behalf, and in so doing has an obligation to the sukuk holders to maintain them. The arrangement is regarded as shariah complaint provided a minimum of one third of the portfolio is in the form of fixed tangible assets or interests in land.[50]

---

47 AAOIFI Shariah Standard at No 17, 3/3.

48 AAOIFI Shariah Standard 2004, 5a 171. See also W al-Zahayli, *Usul al-Riqh al-Islami* ('The Roots of Islamic Jurisprudence') (Dar al-Fikr al_Mouaser, Beiruit, Lebanon, 2003), Vol 1, p 263.

49 AAOIFI Shariah Standard at No 46.

50 Ali MI 'Sukuk: Perception, Innovation and Challenges' p 59, in MH Kamali and AK Abdullah (above n 34).

## Murabahah structure

**5.46** A murabahah[51] contract is a convenient method of financing the acquisition of an asset. In its simplest form, it is a transaction made possible by a series of contemporaneous agreements between an Islamic bank, the purchaser and seller of an asset pursuant to which the bank will contemporaneously purchase the asset from the seller and re-sell it to the client at a purchase price that includes a fixed amount of profit. This profit element of the purchase price is a fixed amount determined at the outset of the transaction by a top up being added on top of the purchase price by the seller. It thus operates as a type of deferred sale. The AAOIFI[52] define them as: 'certificates of equal value issued for the purposes of financing the purchase of goods through murabahah so that the certificate holders become the owners of the murabahah commodity.' It is an acceptable arrangement in Shafi based systems.[53] Examples of receivables that have been so used include marketing rights,[54] bonds exchangeable for shares,[55] rights derived from distribution licenses,[56] and a mixture of lease income and the proceeds of selling air time.[57] To give validity to a murabahah agreement, the risk associated with ownership must lie with the Islamic bank during the period, however brief. The arrangement is widely used in corporate securitisation.

**5.47** Given that, as discussed, there is inconsistency amongst Islamic jurisdictions and scholars with respect to the interpretation and application of shariah law in this area, 'generally accepted principles' are those rules and interpretations expressly or by implication chosen by the parties to govern their agreements. Usually, this would be the version and interpretation of shariah law utilised in the jurisdiction most connected to the transaction. That in practice is usually the state of the originator, which is where any insolvency risk relating to the originator is likely to lie. Thus, it will be acceptance by the legal system of that country as to whether or not there has been a 'true sale' of the assets concerned to the SPV that is crucial. It will also have been in that state that an Islamic scholar and the local Islamic Board of Banking Supervision will also have validated the scheme if it was to be put into effect. If this was done it is extremely difficult for a third party to challenge the validity of an arrangement.

**5.48** Structuring a securitisation transaction in accordance with shariah law is a two-stage process. Firstly, the pool of assets that will potentially support the bond offering are scrutinised to determine

---

51 Derived from the Arabic word for 'profit'.
52 AAOIFI Shariah Standard at No 17 at 3/5/.
53 Ali MI 'Sukuk: Perception, Innovation and Challenges' p 60 in MH Kamali and AK Abdullah (above n 34).
54 SABIC 2006.
55 Telekom Malaysia 2006.
56 Saudi Electricity Co 2007.
57 Etisalat of the UAE 2010.

whether they offend the Islamic prohibition by involving assets that are connected with what Islam considers as sinful activities; such as gambling, alcohol, lewd entertainment, or the sale of pork products amongst others. In strict Islamic jurisdictions,[58] particularly, the more conservative ones, this is relatively easy given that activities such as gambling and alcohol are banned completely. However, in other jurisdictions this may not be as clear cut in cases where the issuer of the sukuk has subsidiaries involved in, for example, cable television services, casinos, or fast food restaurants that sell and serve pork products where the banned element is a minor part of the operation as a whole. Alternatively, an issuer with excessive debt, or one who directly or indirectly provides conventional financial services and charges interest would technically be barred from issuing interest bearing sukuk because of the prohibition.[59] However, in such cases payments to charity can be made of an amount equal to the profit on the part of the loan whose purposes are deemed un-Islamic and this is taken as cleansing the prohibited element.

**5.49** Similarly, the prohibition on uncertainty would prevent issuing bonds in connection with projects that are considered under shariah law to be overly speculative or risky, which technically would potentially bar issuers from engaging in certain types of hedges, forward contracts, and contracts for differences; products which are commonly used in structured finance transactions in non-Islamic jurisdictions.[60] This would appear to debar a securitisation with an added derivative structure to hedge currency risk which would be useful where the sukuk are issued in a different currency from the originator's income. However, there is a way around this and it is discussed below.

**5.50** Since shariah law forbids engaging in activities involving excessive risk, the offering document provided to investors must clearly set out the material terms of the lease so that investors can make an informed decision as to the creditworthiness of the bonds.

**5.51** Once a pool of assets has been isolated and approved as halal, the second stage involves ensuring the sukuk offering itself is halal, including the underwriting, standards, issue placement and the

---

58 Eg, jurisdictions which are, at least, members of the Organization of Islamic States (OIS) or the Islamic Development Bank (IDB). Most Islamic jurisdictions that are members of the OIS or IDB have legal systems at least partially influenced by shariah law (often combined, in the case of Egypt or Pakistan, with colonial European common contributions), or, in the case of conservative theocratic monarchies like Saudi Arabia, almost entirely guided by Islamic law.

59 A Berschadsky, 'Innovative Financial Services in the Middle East: Surmounting the Ban on Interest in Islamic Law' 9 U Miami Bus L Rev 107, 108 (2001).

60 B Sabahi, 'Islamic Financial Structures as Alternatives to International Loan Agreements: Challenges for American Financial Institutions' (Boston Univ. Sch. of L., Working Paper No. 385, 2004).

procurement of ratings.[61] Sukuk offerings marketed at non-Islamic investors or in non-Islamic jurisdictions also need to comply with local laws of the relevant jurisdiction. Local laws dealing with bankruptcy, trusts (if relevant), corporations, prospectuses, securities, secured transactions, perfection of security and tax will all have an impact on the sukuk offering.

**5.52** Under an Islamic securitisation transaction, investors share an exposure to the business risk associated with the asset pool, and each investor is compensated for such exposure with a share of the profits commensurate to the amount of exposure in lieu of a pre-determined interest payment. This significant disparity, when compared to conventional securitisation where investors invariably hold secured contingent claims to pre-determined interest and principal payments, is based on the notion that business relationships are formed to share the business risk and return in assets and transactions that are considered halal. A determinative factor of halal is the funding or production of real assets rather than investment in financial securities to create a cashflow, which according to shariah law amounts to speculative activity and is offensive to the prohibition on riba, particularly where the securities are interest bearing debt or issued by an issuer or in a manner that offends the halal requirements.

### Asset backed or asset based?

**5.53** If one of the above is used as part of a securitisation structure there results an argument as to whether such an arrangement should be an asset backed or asset based structure.[62] The asset in the context of a traditional securitisation will be the income transferred from the originator to the SPV. If it can be structured on this basis then an Islamic securitisation can function in all other aspects as a non-Islamic one. However, if ownership of the underlying asset must be transferred then it would no longer be a traditional asset backed securitisation.[63] In either case it is vital that there is insulation between the originator and the SPV for insolvency purposes. If not, then the advantages potentially available for a higher credit rating for the SPV and its sukuk issue than the originator disappears. Thus, if the securitisation is asset based the rating of the originator and its future income become affected by

61 R Wilson, 'Overview of the Sukuk Market', in NJ Adam, and A Thomas (eds.) *Islamic Bonds: Your Guide to Issuing, Structuring and Investing in Sukuk* (Euromoney Books, London, 2004).

62 See, eg, the Accounting and Auditing Organisation for Islamic Financial Institutions (AAOIFI) 2008 pronouncement that Islamic securitisation can be asset backed and the Islamic Financial Services Board's edict that it should not be, (Standard 7, 2009). For a useful discussion see FA Manjou 'The Ping-Pong of the Asset-Backed/ Asset-Based Sukuk Debate and the Way Forward.' In MH Kamal and AK Abdullah (above n 34).

63 In the UK this requires rending the transfer immune to a claim by any future liquidator of the Originator under any of Insolvency Act 1986, ss 178(1), 186(1), 238, 239 or 423 or the equivalent if it is another jurisdiction.

exposure to those underlying risks. The AAOIFI's view is that sukuk certificates must give '...a common title to shares and rights in tangible assets, usufructs and services or equity of a given project of a specified investment activity.'[64] They also[65] permit allowing the repurchase of assets at market price or at an agreed price at the time of repurchase. Such arrangements are also utilised by the ISDA/ IIFM Master Agreement which is discussed below. The history of such arrangements is relatively short with the first being issued in 1990 by Shell MDS and by 2025 total issues for the year exceeded US $3,963.75 billion.[66]

## Asset types

**5.54** As explained, the assets financing the sukuk issue must be shariah complaint. This has led to a degree of inventiveness in parts of the market place to maximise those available. This can be done by blending assets, some of which can be non-compliant by the use of non-physical (non-cash) assets[67] for up to 70% of the finance.[68] These 'asset light' and blended structures have been banned by the AAOIFI[69] but still seem evident in the market place. The key factor arising is the percentage a particular Islamic school will permit. The Malaysian government have sought to resolve any problems by developing the structure further as the following example of a sukuk issue they created shows.[70]

FIGURE 10 SECURITISED ISLAMIC SUKUK ISSUE

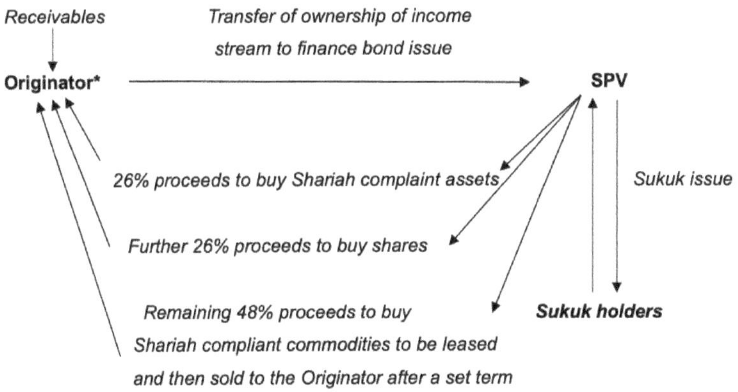


* *In this case the Originator is the government of Malaysia.*

---

64 See, eg, Moody's credit rating of First Gulf Bank. Moody's Investors Services.
65 At AAOIFI Standard 12.
66 Islamic Financial Services Industry Stability Report 2025. Islamic Financial Services Board.
67 Known as wakālah sukuk.
68 R Haneef 'The case for Receivables-Based Sukuk: A Conveyancce between the Malaysian and the Global Shariah Standards or Buy al-Dayn?' MH Kamail and AK Abdullah, (above n 35), p 144.
69 AAOIFI Shariah Board Ruling of February 2008.
70 Haneef (above n 68), pp145–6.

**5.55** Thus, an adapted securitisation structure can be used to satisfy the requirements of Islamic Shafi law.

## Types of sukuk

**5.56** Today Islamic sukuk have similar characteristics to conventional asset backed securities issued by an SPV under a securitisation transaction. Akin to 'pass through' certificates, the sukuk represent an ownership interest in the underlying asset(s) or its usufruct. More elaborately, they are:[71] '[c]ertificates of equal value representing after closing subscription, receipt of the value of the certificates and putting it to use as planned, common title to shares and rights in tangible assets, usufructs and services, or equity of a given project or equity of a special investment activity.'

**5.57** They are generally categorised as either asset-backed sukuk, which offer fairly predictable returns to their holders based on the underlying asset; or asset-based bonds, which offers less predictable returns due to the profit and loss sharing in the underlying investment.[72] They fall into their respective category based on the type of agreement that is used to structure the sukuk.

**5.58** Notwithstanding the similarities many Islamic sukuk differ from conventional asset backed securities in two respects. Firstly, they are not viewed as contractual debt obligations of an issuer obliged to pay holders interest and principal on specified dates, rather they are claims to an undivided beneficial ownership in the underlying assets. Thus, the sukuk holders are entitled to share in the cashflow generated by the underlying assets in addition to being entitled to share in the proceeds of the realisation of the underlying assets. The second disparity is that not all sukuk are tradeable on the secondary market. This is discussed below.

**5.59** Also, the issuing of sukuk as part of the securitisation structure raises other Islamic law issues. Asset backed securities are permissible under Shariah law provided they represent claims against individual assets and securitisations normally represent a claim against individual assets which have been pooled which should be acceptable. In addition, bonds are normally issued at a rate of interest whilst on a shariah issue the sukuk will need to be performance linked. An Islamic securitisation structure can be used under which the holders possess an 'undisclosed beneficial ownership in the underlying assets and a

---

[71] Shari'ah Standard No (18), 'Investment Sukuk', published by the Accounting and Auditing Organisation for Islamic Financial Institutions (AAOIFI) in November 2002 (the 'Standard').

[72] Islamic Financial Services Board, Exposure Draft No 2, Capital Adequacy Standard for Institutions (Other Than Insurance Institutions) Offering Only Islamic Financial Services (2005), at p 52.

share in the revenues generated by the sukuk as well as a share in the proceeds upon realization.'[73] Usami defines them as:[74]

> '...certificates issued in the name of the owner or bearer in order to establish the claim of the certificate owner over the financial rights and obligations represented by the certificate. Sukuk represents a common share in the ownership of the assets made available for investment, whether these are non monetary assets, usufructs, services or a mixture of all these plus intangible rights, debts and monetary assets. These sukuk do not represent a debt owed to the issuer by the certificate holder.'

**5.60** It should be added that some of the critical scholars[75] regard this as essentially un-Islamic because the issues often base themselves on common interest rates, eg, SONIA. Certainly, such sukuk have in some cases defaulted precisely because they were structured as debt instruments.[76] Islamic sukuk are structured in many ways depending on how the parties' relationship with each other is structured, and the nature and intended ownership of the underlying assets.

## Choice of law and jurisdiction

**5.61** Islamic sukuk are often traded in major financial centers such as London, but the assets that are used to finance the issues are usually in an Islamic state. That being the case there is a potential jurisdictional matter with the key issue being the location of the originator and the assets which have been assigned, which may not be in the same place. Even if the sukuk have been issued subject to English law and English jurisdiction,[77] any dispute arising over payment arising on the insolvency of the originator is likely to end up being heard in the court in which the originator was incorporated. Thus, the issue will arise of having to satisfy that state's law if the issue is to be held valid and the 'true sale' held to be valid[78].

## Secondary Islamic bond markets

**5.62** Illiquidity however remains a key problem with Islamic sukuk as there is no effective second hand market. This is because a sukuk that represents a debt to the holder cannot be traded under shariah law, for a debt cannot normally be traded for an amount other than its

---

[73] Lablou and Tanega, (above n 16).

[74] MI Usami, 'Fixed Income Securities, Shari'a Perspective' [2006] p 4, www.sbp.org.pk (Accessed 17 February 2026].

[75] S Anjum 'Islamic Finance: Structuring of Shariah Compliant Securitisation for a Global Market.' LLM Corporate Finance Law, International Corporate Law and Governance, University of Westminster, School of Law, (2006),

[76] MH Kamali and AK Abdullah 'Islamic Finance: Issues in Sukuk' (above n 34), p 2.

[77] See ISDA/ IIFA Master Agreement Schedule.

[78] MH Kamali and AK Abdullah (above n 34).

face value. Thus, the holder is often effectively obligated to hold the sukuk until maturity or sell them at par, which is not always practical. This is a corollary of the fact that shariah law only permits the holding of sukuk that reflect a direct interest in an underlying asset as well as the fact that a debt can normally only be sold on at its full value. That said, the latter point would not be an issue for many of those buying sukuk in a jurisdiction that does not apply Islamic law such as England and Wales. Unlike shares, which some Islamic scholars accept as undivided ownership of a company's real assets, sukuk tend to reflect a generic interest in underlying assets. Some Islamic scholars[79] are adopting a constructive approach regarding this issue, but for the time being a significant secondary market does not exist in the way it does for western style corporate bonds. There are however steps being taken to develop one. To the extent that there is a secondary market it tends to operate largely at country and regional levels because of the lack of cross border infrastructure that would facilitate trading.[80] At present liquidity platforms are being expanded, but the problem remains and fears of a lack of capacity to sell sukuk in the secondary market inevitably depresses the price at which the sukuk issue can be launched.[81] To be tradeable there needs to be the capacity to transfer ownership of the right to the underlying asset or the proceeds thereof. Sukuk satisfying the AAOFII definition[82] ought to be able to achieve this. It requires that the '...manager issuing sukuk must certify the transfer of ownership of such assets...and not keep them as his own assets.'

**5.63** As mentioned, sukuk can normally only be traded on a secondary market at par value. At this price in normal market conditions there would be no economic incentive for anyone to buy. However, there is an exception where the sukuk issue is financed by physical assets. As such assets can be sold as a discount so can any sukuk that represent them.

**5.64** There was a particular problem a few years ago when the US$ declined in value and some of the Arab states decoupled their exchange rate from the US$, and as shariah sukuk issues were often denominated in US$ there was a consequential currency risk for the sukuk holders. The normal hedging arrangements that non-Islamic bodies use to hedge currency risk: (futures, options and contracts for differences), are not normally available to them. So, in Islamic securitised sukuk issues the sukuk has to be denominated in the same

---

79 NZ Dato and Y Zaky (SG Abod ed), *An Islamic Perspective of Stock Markets – an Introduction* (1992) and MA Mannan, 'Understanding Islamic Finance: A Study of the Securities Market in an Islamic Framework' (Islamic Development Bank, 1988).

80 NS Shah, The Financial Ambassador of the Malaysian International Islamic Financial Centre. Speech, Kuala Lumpur, 12 November 2013.

81 N Almaskati, 'Revisiting the question of liquidity: are sukuk less liquid than conventional bonds?' (2023) 14(7) Journal of Islamic Accounting and Business Research. Emerald Insight, 1121–1132.

82 2008, Standard 17, Arts (2)1 and (5/1/2)2.

currency as the originator's or either the originator or bond holder would have to carry a currency risk. In many cases both would end up doing so as the originator of an Islamic securitisation will often not be earning its income in US$ and the sukuk holder is risking a decline in the value of the originator's currency which would reduce the value of any assets used by the originator to back the sukuk issue. This would be a particular problem in the event of the originator's insolvency with an asset-based securitisation. At a time of currency unpredictability, it is insufficient to hedge in a currency that is pegged to the currency concerned as the peg may be broken. In any event there is a method of hedging currency risk that is acceptable to Islamic Shafi law and this is discussed below.

**5.65** Thus, securitisation provides a safer investment than a traditional sukuk in the event of solvency problems.[83] To quote Ghani[84] 'People have to remember that most sukuk are unsecured investment instruments....those assets are there to facilitate a financial obligation of the issuers. They are not there to provide security to the investors'. However, the point with traditional securitisation is in the event of non-payment the bondholders would be looking to the assets that had been transferred to the SPV to provide the payment.

## Credit enhancement

**5.66** As Islamic law does not allow contracts which involve excessive risk, issues can arise with regard to credit enhancement arrangements which most commonly takes the form of over collateralisation in the calculation of the debt to be transferred to the SPV relative to the sum raised by the bond issue. It can also take the form of risk participation (see **Chapter 3**) where a surety is paid a fee in return for an undertaking to cover any shortfall if the income being underwritten does not materialise or does not do so in full.

**5.67** It has also been suggested that the requirement that the seller should have possession at the time the contract for sale is entered into can be settled by reference to prevailing custom. It has been argued that in a modern capital market that this can be satisfied by actual or constructive possession.[85] Some Islamic schools adopt a more liberal approach and thus the Shariah Board will have the last word on

83 MH Kamali and AK Abdullah 'Islamic Finance: Issues in Sukuk.' (above n 35), p 5.

84 BA Ghani in J Ferry 'Scuppered by Sukuk' (17 February 2010) available at www.risk.net/derivatives/structured-products/1591029/scuppered-sukuk [Accessed 17 February 2026].

85 Sharia'h Standards AAOIFI, 2003. Ch 1. For a general discussion see P Uberoi and AR Khadem 'Islamic Derivatives: Past, Present and Future' in MK Hassan and M Malknecht *Islamic Capital Markets* (Wiley, Chichester, 2011), p 149.

whether a particular credit enhancement arrangement is permissible.[86] This leaves over collateralisation as the safest arrangement to satisfy this requirement. Thus, the originator will provide more than 100% of the amount anticipated as the sum required to service the costs of the sukuk issue, interest payments and repayment. Other steps that have been taken to make the potential sukuk purchasers feel secure are for the originator to agree to maintain gearing ratios, to maintain a stated debt service coverage ratio and not to declare a dividend in a year when the debt service coverage ratio falls below a certain figure. This all tends to assist with the credit rating given to the sukuk issue.

## The rating process

### Introduction

**5.68** The rating agencies, the primary ones being Standard & Poors, Moody's and Fitch Investors,[87] rate, amongst other things, states, companies and bond issues and between them account for around 95% of ratings. These ratings are a convenient tool for those in the market to quickly determine the credit risk associated with a party or a bond issue.[88] However, in the case of securitised bond issues the normal approach for assessing bonds does not work. With a primary bond issue (see **Chapter 4**) the rating will be determined by an analysis of the balance sheet and profit and loss account, coupled with an analysis of the issuer's business position and prospects with a view of determining the likelihood of them repaying their debts, or in the case of a bond issue, the debt concerned. In the case of a secondary or securitised issue the rating is determined by an analysis of two factors. First, the originator's assets that are the source of the income stream that will be transferred to the SPV. Secondly, the extent to which this income stream and any monies transferred to the SPV are bankruptcy remote, ie, immune from actions by creditors other than those engaged in the securitisation process itself. Thus, if the originator became insolvent it should not affect the income stream to the SPV from the originator's assets. For this to be the case the legal structure involved must be watertight and in turn a liquidator of the originator must not be able to challenge the securitisation arrangement on the grounds that it is

---

86 This does not just invoke signing off the original documentation but also an ongoing review of the documentation and contracts and their implementation. AAOIFI Shariah Standard No. 17.

87 These agencies were originally established to provide ratings of the US railroad companies and their share and bond issues in the late 1800s. Ratings were provided to investors for a fee. In the early 1900s the arrangement was changed so that the main source of finance for the rating agencies became the firms they were rating.

88 F Partnoy, 'How and Why Rating Agencies are not like other Gatekeepers', (Legal Studies Research Paper Series No 07–46, University of San Diego School of Law), p 59 and F Partnoy, 'The Siskel and Ebert of Financial Markets: Two Thumbs Down for the Rating Agencies' 77 Wash U L Q (1999) 621.

not a true sale, ie, absolute transfer by way of sale of the originator's future income to the SPV, otherwise the structure will not work. In the event of an originator's insolvency it is vital that a liquidator cannot have the payments to the SPV set aside on the grounds that they represent onerous property,[89] seek rescission,[90] a transaction at an undervalue,[91] a preference[92] or a transaction defrauding creditors.[93] Fortunately the legal requirements for a true sale are fairly clear[94] and it is also clear that the courts take the view that a transaction should be interpreted according to the legal intent of the parties.[95] Provided the legal documentation creates a sale or assignment of the debts concerned the courts will recognise it as such. These concepts are now examined in turn.

### Disclaimer of onerous property

**5.69** Under s 178(1) of the Insolvency Act 1986, the liquidator of a company may, by the giving of notice, 'disclaim any onerous property ... notwithstanding that he has taken possession of it ... or otherwise exercised rights of ownership in relation to it.' 'Onerous property' is defined as including any 'unprofitable contract' and 'any other property of the company which is unsaleable or not readily saleable or is such that it may give rise to a liability to pay money or perform any other onerous act'. A disclaimer operates to determine, as of the date it is made, the rights, interests and liabilities of the company in or in respect of the property disclaimed. A liquidator would have a difficult job convincing a judge that the cheapest method of raising finance in terms of the interest rates being offered is 'onerous'.

**5.70** This has the potential to be a problem in securitisation arrangements if the documents are not properly drafted as, in the event of the originator failing, its liquidator could seek to have the contract under which it has to provide a portion of its future income to the SPV set aside on the basis that it is more attractive from the liquidator's point of view to access the receivables to be assigned to the SPV than the bond proceeds. This may be to avoid the costs associated with the bond issue. The SPV would in such a case become a creditor of the originator 'to the extent of any loss or damage' but any such claim would leave the SPV in the position of an unsecured creditor. This would be disastrous for the arrangement, a key purpose of which is to keep the income stream from the originator to the SPV immune from the originator's financial position.

---

89 Insolvency Act 1986, s 178.
90 *Ibid* s 186.
91 *Ibid* s 238.
92 *Ibid* s 239.
93 *Ibid* s 423.
94 *Re George Inglefield* [1933] 1 Ch 327.
95 *Welsh Development Agency v Exfinco* [1992] BCC 270, BCLC 148.

## Rescission of contracts

**5.71** Under s 186(1) of the Insolvency Act 1986:

> 'The court may, on the application of a person who is, as against the liquidator, entitled to the benefit, or subject to the burden of a contract made with the company, make an order rescinding the contract on such terms as to payment by or to either party of damages for the non performance of the contract, or otherwise as the court thinks fit.'

Under s 186(2) any such damages can be proved as a debt on winding up. Again, such a claim would leave the claimant as an ordinary unsecured creditor. That the right under s 186 may be pursued needs to be borne in mind and, therefore, the contractual documentation should remove the risk of this as far as possible.

## Transactions at an undervalue

**5.72** On the application of either a liquidator or administrator under s 238 of the Insolvency Act, a court may set aside a transaction entered into by the company in relation to whom they have been appointed where within the preceding two years[96] they 'entered into a transaction with any person at an undervalue'.[97] An 'undervalue' is defined by s 238(4) as occurring where:

> '(a) the company makes a gift … or otherwise enters into a transaction … on terms that provide for the company to receive no consideration; or
>
> (b) … enters into a transaction … for consideration the value of which, in money or money's worth, is significantly less than the value … of the consideration provided by the company.'

**5.73** There is a however a key caveat in s 238(5) which states that a court:

> '… will not make an order … if it is satisfied —
>
> (a) that the company which entered into the transaction did so in good faith and for the purpose of carrying on its business; and
>
> (b) that at the time it did so there were reasonable grounds for believing the transaction would benefit the company.'

In the context of a securitisation structure being created the originating company will by definition be doing so for the good of the business and it would be an unusual state of affairs indeed if they

---

[96] Insolvency Act 1986, s 240(1)(a).
[97] *Ibid* s 238(2).

were doing so other than in good faith. This is made simpler by the fact the test is a question of fact not law. Key factors to be considered are: the originator's financial position at the time the securitisation was established; the planned use of the borrowed funds and the relative costs of alternative sources of finance. If the originator is solvent at the time of creating the securitisation and the arrangement appears to be in the normal course of business, it would be surprising if a court were willing to use s 238 to overturn it. Nonetheless, when drafting the relevant documentation, lawyers must bear in mind the potential risk of this section and should include a statement of solvency from the originator's directors and auditors and should also make clear in the documentation that the transaction is entered into in good faith, for the purposes of carrying on the originator's business and that there are grounds for believing that it will benefit the originator.[98]

## Preferences

**5.74** On the application of either a liquidator or administrator under s 238 of the Insolvency Act, a court can make such order as it thinks fit or restore the parties to their prior position where a contract has been entered into as a preference in the preceding six months, or two years in the case of a connected person. A preference is determined to have been given by a company if:

'(a) that person is one of the company's creditors …; and

(b) the company does anything or suffers anything to be done which … has the effect of putting that person into a position which, in the event of the company going into insolvent liquidation, will be better than the position he would have been in if that thing had not been done.'

There must also have been an intention to so benefit the other person.[99] If the other person is a connected person the desire to so benefit will be presumed unless the contrary can be shown.[100] For an order to be made under s 239, as with s 238 above, the company must have been unable to pay its debts within the meaning of s 123 of the Insolvency Act at the time of the preference or must become unable to pay its debts within the meaning of such section as a consequence of the preference.

**5.75** In the context of a securitisation the lawyers drafting the documentation should again be sure to include a declaration of solvency from both the originator's directors and the auditors. It should be made clear that the part of the originator's future income being contracted

98 For a useful recent decision see *Hill v Spread Trustee Ltd* [2006] EWCA Civ 542, [2006] BCC 646. The principle also arose in *re Yates (a bankrupt)* [2004] EWHC 3668 (Ch), [2005] 5 BRIR 476.

99 Insolvency Act 1986, s 239(5).

100 *Ibid*, s 239(6).

to the SPV is a fair and reasonable price for the proceeds of the bond issue(s) and that therefore no preference exists. In addition, it should be made clear that the SPV is not a connected person as its directors are independent from the originator and its directors.

## Defrauding creditors

**5.76** Section 423 of the Insolvency Act 1986 applies where a transaction has been entered into at an undervalue. In such a situation a court may, on the application of the liquidator or administrator of a company, or with the leave of the court, on the application of a victim of the transaction, set aside a transaction if the company has made:

> '… a gift to the other person or he otherwise enters into a transaction with the other on terms that provide for him to receive no consideration; … or he enters into a transaction with the other for a consideration the value of which … is significantly less than the value … of the consideration provided by himself.'[101]

Such an order can be to restore the parties to their prior position. The court must however be satisfied that the person entering into the transaction did so for the purpose of:

> '… putting assets beyond the reach of a person who is making, or may at some time make a claim against him, or … of otherwise prejudicing the interests of such a person in relation to the claim which he is making or may make.'[102]

**5.77** In the case of the creation of a securitisation structure this should not normally be a problem. As has already been stated with regard to IA 1986, ss 238 and 239, the lawyers drafting the documentation should state therein that it is believed that the part of the originator's future income being contracted to the SPV is a fair and reasonable price for the proceeds of the bond issue(s) and that, therefore, no transaction is taking place that could defraud a creditor and neither should there be any question of putting assets beyond the reach of those who may make a claim, provided it is a bona fide transaction.

## The credit rating itself

**5.78** This assesses the risk attached to non-payment of interest on the bond and the risk of non-repayment of capital on maturity. It will cover both best case and worst case scenarios during the lifetime of the bond. The idiosyncratic nature of securitisation issues adds a degree of complexity to the process. There are five essential elements

---

101 *Ibid* s 423(1).
102 *Ibid* s 423(3).

to evaluating the risk: collateral risk; cash flow risk; legal risk; third party risk and structural risk.

### Collateral and cash flow risk

**5.79** The key element here is the risk relating to the underlying assets which are used as the basis for the securitisation issue and the cash flow that emanates from them. The risk is reduced by the fact that in the event of the assets not producing sufficient income to meet the bond payments, the assets can be sold and the proceeds used to clear the debt. In addition, as has been discussed above, there is the possibility of a collateral support arrangement, perhaps with a bank or insurance company.

**5.80** Cash flow and market value analyses can be used, though which of these is most appropriate will depend on the structure that has been adopted. The former assesses the cash flows which the bond purchasers will eventually receive and also the timing of them. This last point is particularly important with long term bonds. The risk element may be mitigated where the arrangements allow unpaid interest to accrue. The latter focuses on the capacity of the collateral to pay off the bond on maturity if this is not done by the issuer.

**5.81** The likelihood of the obligor paying is clearly a key issue and there are two key elements to this. The potential benefit to the obligor of defaulting on the debts and the credit quality of the obligors need to be considered. The likely loss and potential variability will need to be calculated and then measured against the security support. It is also necessary to consider each of the main categories of collateral in turn.

**5.82** The risk factors in relation to corporate loans are the credit quality of the assets themselves and the diversity and quantity of firms in the pool of receivables. The risk of default on the asset concerned will be calculated on a historic basis. It will cover both the risk of default and how widespread the default is likely to be. Other factors which will be considered are, as is appropriate, industry concentration and concentration of elements of production such as inputs, sales markets and location.

**5.83** There is, despite the inherent risk, a large potential market for trade receivables as a class of assets. If the structure is a single seller programme the credit rating will involve an assessment of the collateral. If the structure is a multi-seller conduit programme, the record of the programme manager will be analysed. Key elements will be the concentration risk, the extent to which the sellers can keep financing their receivables, and the manager's capacity to tell which companies have declining credit quality in good time to stop buying assets from them. Trade receivables are potentially riskier than many of the other areas because many commercial parties will be purchasing on credit without security and in some cases with a high risk element over their capacity to meet the invoice.

**5.84** Private hospitals are in receipt of income from a variety of sources, the commonest in the UK being private health insurance programmes such as BUPA, PPP and similar policies. In the US much of it will also be coming from federal programmes such as Medicare and Medicaid.[103] Clearly not all these providers will have the same degree of risk attaching to them. Another key element will be the extent to which the insured programmes run by the hospital are entirely met by insurance and the extent to which the individuals concerned are being charged for part of the cost as the insurance is often for less than 100% of the cost.

**5.85** Motor vehicle leases are also commonly used. There are two main categories. One is hire purchase arrangements where the lessee has an obligation to pay in full and convert himself into a purchaser. The other is a lease hire arrangement or contract hire arrangement where the vehicle is leased for a finite period with no requirement that the hirer then purchase. (In the United States these arrangements are called 'closed end' and 'open end' respectively.) As well as the usual analyses of the risk of the loans there is the security element, ie, how much of the debt is covered by the potential resale value of the vehicles concerned.

**5.86** Aircraft leases can also be used as a basis for securitisation. In addition to the points made in relation to vehicle leasing, a particular problem with aircraft is that they are hugely diverse in terms of their resale value and the likelihood of resale being speedy. Some aircraft types in good condition can be immediately resold at a premium. Others are very difficult to sell at all. It is, therefore, necessary to check on the type of aircraft and, particularly in the case of older aircraft, their condition, eg, when were the engines last replaced?

**5.87** Car dealer loans are short term loans to car dealers to finance the inventory of cars they are buying for resale. In the US they are called 'floor plan' loans. The loans have to be repaid within a given period of the cars being sold. They generally have good credit ratings but can be risky in an economic downturn as at present, when a large number of car dealers may be unable to sell on the cars they have bought. In this event it is normal for credit quality triggers to be used to run down the scheme. Should this happen there is usually a promise to pay the investors within a stated period.

**5.88** Commercial insurance premium loans usually require that the premium be paid at the outset, though in the event of the policy being cancelled, partial repayment is possible. Companies will often borrow

[103] There are other US schemes as well, including the Federal Employees Health Benefits Program, the State Children's Health Insurance Program and the Veterans Health Administration.

the money for the premium. Such loans can be pooled and used to back bond issues, though they will tend to be short term as the insurance payment will often be for a year and the bond will need to have a slightly shorter maturity date. The credit analysis will involve the financial status of the borrowers, the differential between the outstanding loans and the repayable amount under the insurance policies and the credit quality of the insurers concerned.

**5.89** Commercial mortgages are also often securitised and come in two main types: transactions which consist of one large property, or a small group of them. These are common in the US. Present and future cash flows and the current and future value of the properties will be considered.

**5.90** Residential mortgages are, as we saw earlier, where the modern securitisation market was born. They are fairly straightforward. The value of the underlying property is assessed as is any guarantee, usually from an insurance company to cover any shortfall in the event of non-payment by the borrower and resale of the property not covering the loan. A crucial element is the proportion which the mortgages concerned represent of the resale value of the respective properties. In the UK it is normal to take out insurance cover where the mortgage represents over 80% of the purchase price of the property. Certain types of mortgage have higher risk ratings than others. The relevant region's economic condition and environmental factors will also be relevant.

**5.91** There is a distinct US market in manufactured housing. These are mass produced housing units which are shipped to development sites. They constitute low cost housing and are regarded as fairly risky as they tend to be bought by people on low incomes who are statistically more likely to default. The houses tend to be located in certain regions, which makes them susceptible to economic downturns. They also tend to have low levels of equity.

**5.92** Credit card receivables are also often used. The repayment profiles of the card holders will be examined as will the relationship between the income of the portfolio and the percentage of outstanding debt. This may leave some surplus for credit support. The quality of the original credit screening for credit card owners and the recovery capacity are also vital.

**5.93** Unsecured personal loans will be looked at on the basis of the same essential principles as credit card receivables. There are, however, two key differences. The loans tend to be for a fixed period and amortise, both of which reduce the potential risk. Car loans tend to be characterised by 100% loans which rapidly cease to cover the economic value of the vehicle should they be heavily used, though lease hire contracts will require the user to pay for excess mileage and damage to the vehicle. Key factors to consider will be the type of car, geographical region, owner profile, the proportion of second-hand vehicles and the mix of vehicles in the pool.

### Legal and third-party risks

**5.94** This is the risk that the structure may not work, whether because the originator cannot remove the assets from their balance sheet, third parties using insolvency laws threatening the viability of the arrangement or legal or regulatory issues raising the cost of obtaining funds through a securitised bond issue. The structure can be created to cope with these issues and the matters involved are discussed at various points in the chapter.

### Structural risks

**5.95** These will cover the elements in the structure itself. Key elements will be: credit support arrangements; commingling; reinvestment; loss allocation; cash flow allocation; interest rate spread; changes in credit enhancement; winding down revolving structures; repurchase provisions; liquidity facilities; prepayment; and advancing guarantees.

## The ratings

**5.96** Once the above has been carried out, the agency concerned will provide its rating opinion. The different agencies have slightly different grading systems but they are all broadly similar. By example, the Moody's system offers two ratings.

### Short-term debt ratings

**5.97**

- Prime 1 – superior ability for repayment of senior short-term debt.
- Prime 2 – strong ability for repayment of senior short-term debt.
- Prime 3 – acceptable ability for repayment of senior short-term debt.
- Not Prime – outside the rating.

### Long-term debt ratings used by all major agencies

**5.98**

- Aaa – The best quality with well protected interest margins, secure principal and good security.

- Aa – High quality in all respects. Tend to be smaller arrangements than Aaa or may have less protection.
- A – Favourable bonds with upper grade qualities. Adequate current security but some long-term risk.

In the case of the ratings below, where two different alternatives are stated the first is that provided by Standard & Poors and Fitch, the latter by Moody's. The list is slightly simplified. Some rating agencies will add further detail.

- Bbb or Baa – Medium grade debt. Adequate protection for interest rates and principal security are currently available but some long term potential threat to either. Tend to have some speculative element.
- Bb or Ba – speculative and with only moderate protection.
- B – Not desirable investments. Little future assurance of payment.
- Ccc or Caa – Poor. May be currently in default or a present risk in operation threatening payment of interest or repayment of capital.
- Cc or Ca – Highly speculative. Usually in default.
- C – Lowest rating. Means there is no real investment potential.

Below this level the different agencies have different categories of companies in or nearing default.

**5.99** There are also national ratings which become an issue where the party buying the bonds is in a different jurisdiction from the parties involved in the securitisation. Parties whose location could be an issue in this context are: the originator; the SPV; liquidity providers guarantors and swap counterparties. This is crucial as: 'This sovereign rating acts as a "ceiling" for foreign currency denominated securities of any entity that falls under the country's political control.'[104] Thus, if the state has a sovereign rating of AA, this is the maximum that can be awarded to the issue. Thus, relevant parties are normally located in AAA rated states.

**5.100** Ratings can be qualified by following them with a + or – showing where the rating agency anticipates where the next movement will be or indicating by the addition of another smaller letter to indicate whether the rating is at the top or bottom end of that category.

---

[104] C Reis Roy, above p 30.

## Why securitise?

**5.101** The commonest reason is that funds raised by this method should involve lower interest rates than bank borrowing, as securitised debt is potentially accorded a higher credit rating than the originator's own debt, and also allows sub-investment grade originators to access the international capital markets. It provides the originator with access to a new source of funds, particularly over the medium and long term. In addition, it potentially frees existing capital reserves to finance the business, provides a quick increase on assets and improves liquidity, especially in the case of ongoing multi-seller bond issues. Another is that it is possible for the originator to remove the assets involved from their balance sheet, thus reducing gearing. Another advantage is that the arrangement may also be confidential. It provides access to the international capital markets which may not otherwise have been available for the originator. As a result it may also be possible to arbitrage and access cheaper funds in other markets. It may also be used where bank loans would not have been available. Only the assets concerned with the securitisation are affected, which is more attractive from the borrower's point of view than secured lending which tends to involve a fixed, and in jurisdictions where they exist, a floating charge over the borrower's assets up to the level of the debt, interest and costs. There may also be liquidity advantages particularly in a revolving issue. The arrangement will not normally fall foul of negative pledge clauses[105] in the favour of the originator's lending bank covering the assets that have been transferred from the balance sheet. It also diversifies the originator's funding sources and provided there are no financial problems the originator will find the arrangement should not have an impact on their relations with other lenders. Securitisation affects only the assets securitised whereas in a secured financing security is frequently taken over all the assets of the borrower, present and future. Securitisation leaves other assets free to be financed using different methods. In addition, the registration procedures that are needed in the case of charges and mortgages are not an issue here.

**5.102** As a result of handling the structure there will also be potential indirect benefits for the originator, such as having improved management information relating to the firm's finances and improved systems and controls in the origination, management and realisation of assets. It also allows originators to benefit from arbitrage opportunities in the market, eg, to take advantage of foreign exchange arbitrage opportunities in the case of repackaging assets, inefficiencies in the market pricing of the underlying instruments; and it offers the ability to recover 'extra value' held within the structure by the use of various profit extraction techniques.

---

[105] See **Chapter 1**.

**5.103** Finally, for banks engaging in securitisation with their own assets, it will assist in meeting their capital adequacy requirements because provided that local accounting treatment is amenable to such an approach, the transfer of assets will reduce balance sheet assets and, therefore gearing, and, in the case of banks, will improve capital adequacy ratios. In particular banks have found the process attractive because the removal of assets from their balance sheet and the emergence of the proceeds of the securitised bond sale on their profit and loss account as 'cash in hand' means that the moneys they hold on their banking book reduces and the sum on their trading book increases. Changes to capital regulations have however limited the extent to which banks can do this.

**5.104** The downside is primarily the costs involved, particularly: legal fees, accountancy fees, software and bond issue costs. Between them these can mean that in the initial stages it is not a cheap option. The reduction in gearing may also make it more difficult for the originator to raise funds in future. In some jurisdictions stamp duty will also have to be paid on the transfer of receivables to the SPV. There may also be something of a time lag whilst the bond proceeds go through. Finally, it may be necessary for the originator to negotiate with its bankers if the receivables concerned are subject to a charge.

**5.105** As far as the SPV is concerned, key issues are going to be the tax position in the host jurisdiction and their inter-relationship with the tax system in the jurisdictions of the originator and the bond holders. The prospectus requirements in jurisdictions into which the bonds are to be sold are also vital. The cost of a bond issue can be extremely high. Some jurisdictions, however, have a more restricted requirement for issues which are aimed entirely at expert investors who are seen as being capable of looking after themselves. In some jurisdictions this state of affairs is presumed where the bond denomination is above a certain size.

**5.106** In the case of banks or financial institutions securitising, there are clearly capital adequacy/financial resources implications. However, regulators in the more developed jurisdictions have not been slow to impose regulations dealing with the problem. Another issue for regulators is going to be the capacity originators have to transfer the moneys owed to them by third parties. In this country assignment, novation and participation all offer potential routes (see **Chapter 3**).[106] However, if a legal system does not offer a safe method of doing this, a securitisation will not be possible unless there is the facility of utilising non-domestic law and this being recognised by the domestic courts. Likewise, the insolvency laws must not be a threat

---

[106] See the Securitisation part of the PRA Rule book, particularly Chapter 2, arts 6–9 and Chapters 4–6 of the PRA Rule book, the Securitisation Regulations 2024, the Securitisation (Amendment) Regulations 2024 and the FCA Securitisation Sourcebook (SECN).

to a properly structured 'true sale' of receivables. If the structure is not fireproof it will not be possible to get a credit rating for the bond issue.[107]

**5.107** As far as the bond investors are concerned the main advantage is that they have the opportunity to purchase investment grade asset backed securities of varying maturities, interest rate bases and currencies. Such paper is normally extremely liquid, although there were interruptions to the secondary market in the financial crisis of 2008–9. The credit rating agencies have already done the hard work determining the investment quality of the bonds to make the investment decision easier, though there are now concerns in the market that there may be occasions on which rating agency assessments are over optimistic. There are always risks associated with any investment and particular ones may arise in this context are prepayment of the bonds and some bonds may be less liquid than more straightforward vanilla bonds, so in these cases investors should be prepared to hold them to maturity. However, the buyers of the bonds will be investing in a separate pool of assets rather than in a corporate entity generally, so risk is limited to the non-performance of assets, rather than general corporate risk. It also allows investors to have access to assets and markets previously unavailable to them and so, as a result, allows them to diversify their currency and risk profiles.

## Accounting issues

**5.108** The transfer of a portion of the originator's future income to the SPV results in that capital sum being removed from the originator's balance sheet. The funds received from the offshore bond issue appear in due course on the originator's profit and loss account as cash in hand. Thus the arrangement is referred to as 'off balance sheet'. The willingness of the market to take up the bond issue is determined by the credit rating the bond issue receives, and as has been seen, provided the transaction is done on an arm's length basis the key issue will be the future income's safety as a source of the income and capital repayment for the bonds.

**5.109** The challenge in all this falls into a number of areas. Perhaps the key element is the position under the accountancy provisions. The position in the UK, the US and states applying the IASB rules is that such structures may be used to provide off balance sheet finance, but that suitable disclosure must be made in the notes to the accounts so that the accounts represent a true and fair view.[108] In some less developed

---

[107] For a useful summary of this see C Reis Roy, 'Rating Securitisation Structures.' (1998) 13(9) JIBL 298.

[108] In the UK Financial Reporting Standards, in the US the Statement of Financial Accounting Standards adopts a similar approach. The International Accounting Standards deal with the issue. See in particular IFRS 9.

parts of the world the national regulations do not deal with the issue, leaving the risk of an originator removing receivables, which were formerly listed as assets on its balance sheet, and having securitised, holding those moneys as cash without this background being apparent to those who deal with them later. However, the increasing acceptance of the IASB principles in such states is reducing this as a problem. Companies in such states can still tend to find it difficult to raise funds through securitisation, not least because they tend to be in locations where accounting procedures are not well policed and third parties are wary of trusting figures in the originator's accounts. This is a more intractable problem.

## Transfers from the originator to the SPV

### Transfers of equitable title

**5.110** In most securitisations the sale by the originator of the receivables to the SPV will transfer only the equitable interest and not the legal interest in the relevant receivables. As already seen in **Chapter 3**, under s 136 of the Law of Property Act 1925 transfers will only ever take effect in equity unless and until certain conditions are fulfilled. One of those conditions requires that notice in writing of the assignment be given to the debtor. In most securitisations notice may only be given to the debtor in limited circumstances, for example upon the occurrence of a default. Until notice is given to the debtor and all the other requirements of s 136 are fulfilled, the debtors will be entitled to continue to make payments under the relevant contracts to the originator, and obtain good discharge in respect of such payments, and, accordingly, payments made by a debtor to the originator may be set off by the debtor against a subsequent claim by the SPV for those amounts. A debtor may set off against the SPV claims against the originator arising prior to receipt by the debtor of notice of the assignment, although the giving of notice to the debtor will not preclude a subsequent claim by that debtor to be entitled to set off against the SPV.

**5.111** A later assignee of, or fixed chargee in respect of, an underlying contract in respect of which notice had been given to the debtor prior to notice being given in respect of the transfer from the originator to the SPV, would take priority over the SPV's claim. The SPV cannot preclude the modification of the terms of the underlying contract, although it will protect itself through a number of contractual undertakings in the sale agreement; and the SPV would have to join the originator as party to any action which the SPV may wish to take against a debtor. If the originator did not consent to being joined as a plaintiff in such proceedings it would be necessary to join them as co-defendant. If the originator were to go into administration or liquidation before the SPV's legal title had been perfected, there would be statutory prohibitions on joining the originator as co-defendant without leave of court, or, in certain circumstances the consent of the administrator or liquidator.

**5.112** Note that interests in loans are normally transferred for stamp duty reasons by way of offer and acceptance ie, the originator offers to sell the relevant loan to the SPV and the SPV accepts such offer by payment whereupon equitable title is transferred. In such circumstances even if notice of assignment is given to the debtor, legal title will not be transferred until a written assignment is executed.

**5.113** In some cases transfer is by novation, sub-participation or by the title to the future income being transferred to a trust (**see Chapter 3**)

## Mortgage-backed securities

**5.114** Mortgages forming the backing for an issue of mortgage-backed securities are typically legal mortgages. The transfer of a legal mortgage can be complete or incomplete. If it is complete, this means that the legal title to the mortgage is vested in the transferee absolutely. If it is incomplete, the transferee acquires an equitable title to the mortgage but the transferor remains its legal owner and holds the legal title on trust for the transferee. In a mortgage securitisation the mortgages are usually sold to the SPV by means of an incomplete transfer only but with provision made for the transfer to be completed in certain specified circumstances eg, default. The main reason why securitisations proceed on the basis of incomplete transfers of legal mortgages are the Land Registry fees. To be complete a transfer of a registered charge must be registered at HM Land Registry. This is not only time consuming but expensive. The equitable interest in the mortgage is transferred by the originator agreeing to sell and the SPV agreeing to purchase the pool of debts and related securities. Under English law a sale and purchase agreement is effective to transfer the equitable title to the assets which are the subject matter of the agreement provided that the agreement is one in respect of which an order for specific performance would be granted. Specific performance is a remedy which is granted at the discretion of the courts but the discretion is exercised on well settled principles and the court will usually grant specific performance of a contract relating to an interest in land.

**5.115** Risks associated with an incomplete transfer include the following. Where the land is registered the SPV will take subject to a disposition of the mortgages by the originator to a purchaser in good faith and without notice of the SPV's rights, provided that such purchaser itself registers its disposition at HM Land Registry. Note that in securitisations this risk is effectively minimised by requiring the charge certificates for the relevant mortgages to be kept in the custody of the SPV or its agent. This effectively prevents any registered disposition of a mortgage because the Land Registry rules require that the charge certificate must be placed on deposit at the Land Registry before any dealing can be registered. In addition, until execution of the deed of transfer and, in the case of registered land, registration at HM Land Registry, the SPV will not itself have a power of sale. Note however that pending such transfer and/or registration the SPV will, through operation of a power of attorney, be given the right to exercise the power of sale of the originator as attorney for the originator.

### Powers of attorney

**5.116** The SPV will rely on a power of attorney in a number of circumstances, for example, to exercise the power of sale as described above, or to execute transfers of receivables as attorney to enable the originator to obtain legal title. The security power of attorney is expressed to be irrevocable and is given to secure either a proprietary interest of the donee, or the performance of an obligation owed to the donee, so long as the donee has that interest or the obligation remains undischarged. It also provides the ability to achieve flexibility within the financing structure so that, for example, short term assets such as trade receivables can fund medium term debt, and vice versa. This can reduce overall funding costs.

## How will the SPV sell bonds?

**5.117** The issuing of debt to securitise existing incoming cash flow can take a number of forms.[109] The most common are publicly issuing debt instruments, privately placing debt instruments, commercial paper issues, medium term notes and mezzanine issues. The issuance of debt paper has already been covered in **Chapter 4**. Essentially, any type of bond issue can be made by the SPV subject to satisfying the necessary legal and where appropriate regulatory formalities. The key issues for the originator will be the cost of the arrangement as against the amount of money that can be raised by the bond issue and the interest rate involved.

**5.118** In a relatively small issue the private placement of bonds may be sufficient. In other cases a public issue will be necessary with the additional overheads that such a process entails. Alternatively, the issuance of debt through a general issuing vehicle, often provided by a bank can be used. This is useful in cases where the issue may be too large for a private placement but not so large that a full-scale public issue with a purpose created SPV would be cost effective.

---

[109] S Smith, 'Structuring Securitisation Transactions' at the Conference on Structured Lending, (IBC), held in London on 13 November 1995.

Alternatively, asset backed commercial paper or medium-term notes could be issued.

**5.119** The type of security eventually issued will depend on a number of legal and commercial factors, including in particular whether the asset types concerned are capable of being transferred or whether a secured debt approach is more appropriate. Is the asset acceptable to the market, does the originator want to be identified with a securitised debt issue or does it prefer to maintain anonymity? What are the applicable securities laws that a public issue of debt would entail. Normally full compliance with securities laws in all jurisdictions in which the debt is being offered will be needed and usually will be accompanied by the requirement to satisfy stock exchange listing rules if listing on a securities exchange is required.

## Other risk issues in the transfer of assets from the originator to the SPV

**5.120** Under s 859A of the Companies Act 2006 charges created by companies registered in England and Wales are void against a liquidator, administrator and any creditor of that company, unless prescribed particulars of the charge together with the instrument by which the charge is created or evidenced, are delivered to or received by the Registrar of Companies for registration within 21 days after the date of the creation of the charge. When a charge becomes void because of a failure to register within the 21 day period it will mean that the charge becomes void on the 22nd day. Under CA 2006, s 859H the money secured by it immediately becomes repayable. Accordingly, recharacterisation of a sale as a secured loan will have the consequence that the money secured by it will technically become repayable by the originator to the SPV. In a securitisation, if the sale were recharacterised as a secured loan the charge arising from such recharacterisation would be one to which CA 2006, ss 859A and 859H apply because the parties will have intended the sale to take effect as a sale the parties will not have effected any registration under s 859A.

## Charge or sale?

**5.121** This raises the key issue of whether the arrangement is a sale or a secured loan. The essential differences between them were analysed in *re George Inglefield Limited*[110] and identified as being as follows. In a transaction of sale the vendor is not entitled to get back the subject matter of the sale by returning the purchase price. In a case of a secured loan the mortgagor is entitled until foreclosure to get

[110] (1933) Ch 1.

back the subject matter of the mortgage or charge by returning and/or repaying to the mortgagee/chargee the loan secured by the mortgage or charge. If a mortgagee realises the subject matter of the mortgage for a sum which exceeds the amount owing to the mortgagee under the relevant loan, the mortgagee has to account to the mortgagor for the surplus. If a purchaser sells the subject matter of the purchase and realises a profit, he does not have to account to the vendor for the profit; and if a mortgagee realises the mortgaged property for a sum that is insufficient to repay the amounts owing to him under the relevant loan, the mortgagee is entitled to recover the balance from the mortgagor by way of an unsecured debt claim. If a purchaser were to resell the purchased property at a price which was less than the price paid by the purchaser to the vendor for the property on the original transfer the purchaser would not be entitled to recover the balance from the vendor.

**5.122** The logic was upheld in the later case of *Chase Manhattan Asia Ltd v Official Receiver of First Bangkok City Finance Ltd*[111] and *Curtain Dream plc v Churchill Merchanty Ltd*[112] where it was held that the state of affairs agreed between the parties should be determined by ascertaining their real intention from the documents and the factual matrix. A case that utilised this approach was *Welsh Development Agency v Export Finance Co.*[113] In outline Parrot Corp Ltd (P) carried on the business as a manufacturer and seller of computer discs. To help facilitate this, the Welsh Development Agency (WDA) provided a guarantee in return for an indemnity and the WDA took a charge over P under what is now s 860 of the Companies Act 2006. P sold most of its goods overseas though the arrangement involved was slightly complex. P negotiated to sell the goods overseas and then sold them to Exfinco (E), an associated company, who in turn sold them on as undisclosed principal with ECGD support. There was a master agreement between P and E under which goods were invoiced to the customer in P's name with payment to be made to a bank account in P's name, controlled exclusively by E. Under the master agreement, title was not to pass to the buyer until payment of the purchase price had been made. Under the agreement E was also entitled to deduct payments according to the extent to which payment was received late and it also received indemnities against liabilities on the sales by P. Thus:

---

111 [1990] 1 WLR 1181 (PC).

112 [1990] BCC 341.

113 [1990] BCC 393. See also *Re Cimex Tissues Ltd* [1994] BCC 626, [1995] 1 BCLC 409. J Vella, 'Sham Transactions' (2008) 4(Nov) LMCLQ. 488, and S Henderson, 'Mahonia; purchase contract or loan, and what does it matter?' (2003) 18(2) BJIB & FL 47.

FIGURE 11

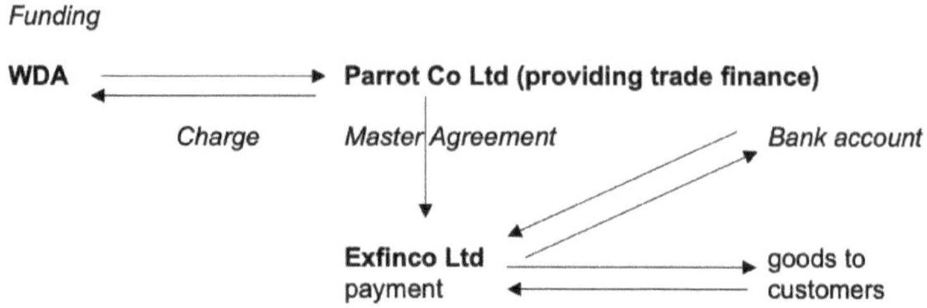


**5.123** As a result of this arrangement E had, at all times, a fund to meet the future obligations of P and could discharge liabilities out of this fund relating to the whole of its dealings with P. The termination provisions in the agreement between P and E provided that upon termination of the agreement P would be obliged to satisfy all claims owing to E by the buyers and when this payment had been made E would transfer all interests that E had in the goods to P.

**5.124** In due course P went into receivership and the WDA claimed that the monies owed to P by the buyers in respect of goods sold through E were subject to its charge. E claimed to be entitled to the monies as payment for the goods which it owned pursuant to its purchase arrangements described above. The Court of Appeal held that the agreement was one of sale and not a secured loan on the basis that a transaction should be given the commercial effect intended by the parties to the transaction as evidenced by the documentation, assuming the documents are not a sham, ie, a transaction designed to give the appearance of creating legal rights and obligations different from the actual legal rights and obligations which the parties intended to create. Moreover, there was no one clear touchstone by which it was possible to say that a transaction was not a sale of goods but a charge or mortgage on the goods and what the court had to do was to examine the agreement as a whole to examine the nature of the legal relationship created by the parties. The presence of provisions in the documentation which were similar to provisions found in a secured financing, for example, the discount provisions and the right of retention on termination were not inconsistent with the agreement being an agreement for sale.

**5.125** Thus, it is important to look at the documentation taken as a whole. It would be unwise to interpret this case as meaning that documentation which purports to create a sale can contain any number of provisions which would also be contained in loan documentation and still constitute a sale. It is essential that any legal opinion obtained in relation to a securitisation covers the true sale issue and that the provider of that opinion specifically addresses the question of recharacterisation.[114] Key issues in the documentation include: the

---

[114] See V Selvam, 'Recharacterisation in "True Sale" Securitisations: the "Substance over Form" Delusion' [2006] JBL 637.

profit extraction mechanic and the way in which it is drafted; the degree of recourse to the originator and the circumstances in which recourse may be had, such as breaches of warranty, insolvency of the debtor; and any right of the originator to repurchase the assets sold, as distinct from an obligation to repurchase in the circumstances following breach of warranty.

## Conclusions

**5.126** There has been no case law successfully challenging the specific structures discussed in this chapter and that which there has been has tended to be in the context of disputes over the interpretation of clauses in the contracts involved in the arrangement. For example, *Canary Wharf Finance II Plc v Deutsche Trustee Co and others*[115] saw an interpretation of the 'spens' or 'make whole' clause which protects fixed rate investors on the early termination or redemption by providing stated compensation. *Hayfin Opal Luxco 3 SARL and another v Windemere VII CMBS plc and others*[116] explored whether an interest rate provision was a penalty. *Credit Suisse Asset Management LLC v Titan Europe and Others*[117] interpreted whether a class of bond holders should receive additional interest due on the underlying loans following a default. Finally, *UBS AG, London Branch v Glass Trust Corp Ltd, Fairhold Securitisation Ltd*[118] analysed whether a bond trustee was required to pay legal and financial expenses incurred by a group of bond holders. *Banca Generali SPA v Sovereign Credit Opportunities SPA*[119] held that bondholders in a trade finance securitisation could dismiss the fiscal agent without the issuer's consent following an event of default. Finally, *NatWest Market NV v CMIS Nederland BV*[120] determined that lenders could claim against an indemnifier from the original payment date as the wording of the contract indicated that they had entered into an indemnity not a guarantee.

**5.127** Securitisation has clearly had an enormous impact on world finance over the last 35 years. It has caused a large scale increase in the capacity of larger companies to access debt on a cost effective basis from the world capital markets. It has facilitated banks in restructuring their balance sheets to lend on a more profitable footing and it has offered investors in the bond markets the opportunity to invest in a wide range of products with high credit ratings. Its flexibility is apparent from the wide range of uses to which money raised through securitisation has been used. On one hand it has proved useful in developing countries, for example, China utilising it to raise money for

115 [2016] EWHC 100 (Comm).
116 [2016] EWHC 782 (Ch).
117 [2016] EWCA Cv 1293.
118 [2017] EWHC 1788 (Comm).
119 [2024] EWCA Civ 886.
120 [2025] EWHC 37 (Comm).

project finance to build motorways and infrastructure. On the other, troubled institutions in developed nations have been able to use it to clear up their balance sheets. For example, in the past some Japanese banks have issued heavily over collateralised paper to clear excess debt from their balance sheets.

**5.128** Its impact by 2008 had been a key element in engendering a world financial crisis largely caused by short-sighted policies by bank directors and political leaders and an insufficient understanding of the financial products involved in world banking by both. It is important to remember however that this is not a result of any inherent flaw in the nature of securitisation that these problems have arisen, but their inappropriate use. Properly utilised, securitisation can continue to be a key ingredient in world finance. In 2025 in the UK alone £4.1 billion was raised by asset backed securitisation, €315 billion in Europe overall, and US$ 1.5 trillion in the United States.

# Chapter 6 Derivatives

## Introduction

**6.1** A derivative contract is a financial instrument whose value is determined by the value of an underlying commodity, currency, interest rate, index or other variable of measurable financial value. Thus, their name – the value of the contract 'derives' from the value of the underlying subject matter. For example, a contract to buy a certain amount of US dollars at a future date and at a pre-agreed price in sterling, would be a contract to derive a profit or loss according to the value of the US dollar against that of sterling. Derivatives contracts can normally be traded.

**6.2** There has been a judicial interpretation provided in *Lomas v JFB Firth Rixson Inc*:[1]

> '...a transaction under which the future obligations of one or more of the parties are linked in some specified way to another asset or index, whether involving the delivery of the asset or the payment of an amount calculated by reference to its value or the value of the index. The transaction is therefore treated as having a value which is separate (although derived) from the values of the underlying asset or index. As a result, the parties' rights and obligations under the transaction can be treated as if they constituted a separate asset and are typically traded accordingly.'

**6.3** More complex derivatives go further than this and are priced using differential mathematical calculations to suggest that the value of the derivative is based on an underlying item of value but the link may be hypothetical, eg, fixed floating rate interest swaps (see below) are sometimes calculated from a swap yield curve[2] rather than an interest rate.

**6.4** Derivatives are also seen as contingent claims[3] and this term is occasionally used as an alternative. Such arrangements fall into three main categories: futures, options and contracts for differences.[4]

---

1 [2012] EWCA Civ 419 at para 2 per Longmore LJ, following *Firth on Derivatives Law and Practice* (Sweet & Maxwell).

2 Ie, a graph illustrating the level of interest rates as a function of time.

3 John C Hull, *Options, Futures and other Derivative Securities* (Prentice-Hall International, 1993), p 1.

4 This is a slight over-simplification as there are different views on how caps, floors and OTC options are classified; see, eg, S Henderson, 'Credit Derivatives' in Hudson (ed), *Modern Financial techniques, Derivatives and Law* (Kluwer Law International, 1999) and S Henderson, 'Credit Derivatives' in Hudson (ed), *Credit Derivatives: Law, Regulation and Accounting Issues* (Sweet & Maxwell, 1999).

These will be discussed in turn below. Many such contracts are traded on specialist exchanges, these are called 'exchange traded contracts'. The remainder are traded privately between the parties to the arrangement. These called 'over the counter' or 'OTC' contracts. Futures and options contracts are found in both forms. Contracts for differences are by their very nature a private contract and thus they normally only exist in OTC form, although some are exchange traded, for example in the US on execution facilities.[5] Derivatives fall into the category of 'off balance sheet items' for the purposes of accounting and have a value which is separate from that of the underlying asset.[6]

**6.5** These arrangements have an extremely long history, with futures contracts being traded as long ago as 1700 BC in Mesopotamia.[7] Other, more complex types of derivative did not appear until later, with contracts for differences first appearing in Flanders in the 1530s[8] and options being traded in Antwerp by the early 1600s.[9] As will be seen below, in the current period they are heavily used by banks, both on their own behalf and when dealing for clients. The different types of contract will now be considered.

## Futures

**6.6** A futures contract has been defined as 'an agreement between two parties to buy or sell an asset at a certain time in the future for a certain price'.[10] The critical factor is that it will not normally be performed as a contract for the delivery of the asset as, were this to be the case, it would be a commercial contract for future delivery. The critical issue with a derivative contract is that in the case of a futures or options contract the arrangement will be closed out before the delivery date and the parties (known as counterparties[11] ) will settle up. The party who has benefited from the price movement in the underlying asset (known as being 'in the money') will receive that amount from the counterparty (who will be 'out of the money').[12] No payment is

---

5 These are regulated by the Securities and Exchange Commission (SEC) regulating security based swaps and the Commodity Futures Trading Commission (CFTC) regulating other swaps.

6 *Lomas v JFB Firth Rixson Inc* [2012] 2 All ER (Comm) 1076. See also Firth,on Derivatives Law and Practice. (Sweet & Maxwell, 2017). pp 1–3.

7 E Swan, *Building the Global Market* (Kluwer, 2000), p 28 and British Museum tablet WA 90349.

8 C de Vallalon, 'Provechoso tartado de cambios y contractions de mercaderes,' cap XV, Valladoid, 1542 and Swan, above, n 8, at pp 143–144.

9 There is some evidence that that options may have emerged slightly earlier in Japan, see L Lu-Jen Li and P Lejot (eds), *Financial Markets in Hong Kong* 1st Edn,(Oxford University Press, 2006), p 209.

10 Hull, above, n 3 at p 3.

11 The term came into use because in many contracts, especially contracts for differences, either party could be seen as both a buyer and a seller.

12 In the case of exchange traded futures payment will be from the party who is 'out of the money' to the exchange and from the exchange to the party who is 'in the money'. This is discussed below.

needed by either party prior to that time. Such arrangements are most commonly carried out with regard to the future price of currencies, equities, commodities and bonds.

## Options

**6.7** An option contract is an arrangement whereby one counterparty contracts to buy, and the other to sell an asset at a future date, at a price agreed now. The holder of the contract has to pay a deposit to enter into the contract and then has the right, but not the obligation, to perform. The deposit will be calculated in proportion to the risk to the other party. The holder may forfeit the contract and walk away, though the counterparty would then keep the deposit. The party who has received the deposit is however bound by the arrangement and is obliged to perform. This will involve making the payment to the holder or receiving it from them, the precise amount of which will be determined by the price movement in the underlying asset (or other matter). An option to buy is called a call option, whilst an option to sell is called a put option. The price is known as the strike price or exercise price. The date is known as the maturity date, exercise date or expiration date. The commonest type of option is an 'American style' which can be exercised at any time before the determination date; slightly less common are 'European style' options which can only be closed out on the termination date. This is often interpreted to mean during the last month. A 'swaption' is an option to enter into a swap contract at a date in the future. This option would be exercised should movements in the price of the debt, asset or interest rate concerned render such a step desirable.[13]

**6.8** The widespread popularity of these contracts is partly based on the existence of a safe way of trading the underlying asset if it is a 'vanilla' European style option, ie, one with no complexity such as a mathematical formula being added. This is the Black-Scholes formula which enables a party to calculate the appropriate time and manner of trading the underlying asset to create a financial hedge and eliminate risk.[14]

## Contracts for differences

**6.9** These have been defined as:

> '... an exchange of cash flows. Where one party has an obligation which it does not want, it exchanges that obligation with another party for an obligation which it does want.'[15]

---

13 A Hudson, *The Law on Financial Derivatives* 2nd edn, (Sweet & Maxwell, 1998), p 54.

14 Known as 'continuously revised delta hedging'.

15 A Hudson, *The Law on Financial Derivatives* 4th edn, (Sweet & Maxwell, 2006), p 47.

In the United Kingdom they are defined by statutory instrument[16] as agreements, the aim of which is to secure a profit or avoid a loss, by either or both of the parties, by reference to fluctuations in the value of property or an index or other factor. A key exclusion arises in the context of financial services regulation where one of the parties is to take delivery of property to which the contract relates and where money is received as a deposit on the basis that interest will be paid on it, calculated by reference to fluctuations in the value of an index. There are two types of agreement: swaps and forward rate agreements. The relevant sub-categories of contracts for differences will be looked at in turn. Common specific types of such contracts are as follows.

### Currency swaps

**6.10** The basic structure of a currency swap was for a party to borrow funds in their own currency and then arrange with another party who was borrowing in their respective currency to pay the difference between themselves in proportion to changes in the exchange rate between the two currencies. This was useful when major economies still had exchange controls[17] as a party could effectively access exposure to a currency they were not at liberty to borrow. At periodic intervals fees corresponding to interest payments on the relevant currency amounts are exchanged. The currency swap has the further advantages of not constituting borrowing and thus operating as an 'off balance sheet' activity and of stamp duty not being payable as it would be if the capital sum had literally been swapped.

**6.11** At the time of its modern inception the principal economic justification for a currency swap was that it enabled an investor to acquire a foreign currency denominated investment, whilst at the same time entitling it to re-acquire the amount of its investment in its domestic or other currency of account at a specific future date, thereby eliminating any exchange risk which might otherwise have been incurred on such foreign currency investment. Although the abolition of exchange controls in the world's developed economies removed one of the original justifications for currency swaps, the volume of currency swaps transacted continued to increase rapidly as corporate treasurers saw the arbitrage opportunities which currency swaps offered. Accordingly, it is usually the case that at least one party has access to a particular capital market or source of funds to which the counterparty either does not have access or can only gain access to on less attractive terms the respective requirements of both entities can be met by a swap.

---

[16] The Financial Services and Markets Act 2000 (Regulated Activities) Order 2001, SI 2001/544 at art 85.

[17] They were suspended in the UK in 1979 and later abolished in 1987.

**6.12** Swaps in relation to currencies are now often found as cross currency interest rate swaps. These use the same essential structure to access the interest rate on another currency. The parties agree to exchange equivalent amounts at the then current spot rate of exchange in two different currencies. This initial exchange is effected on the commencement date of the swap. Additionally, the parties agree to effect re-exchange of the same principal amounts on a specified future date. During the term of the swap the parties make periodic payments to each other, the amounts of which are calculated by reference to the principal amounts exchanged and to fixed and/or floating rates of interest. In other words, the payments made represent the difference between the two respective financial positions – thus the name 'contracts for differences'. It will not necessarily be the case that the respective payments are made on the same periodic basis, for example, the fixed rate payer may make annual payments whilst the floating rate payer makes payments on a semi-annual basis. It is common, however, for both payments to be made on a six monthly basis.

### Interest rate swaps

**6.13** It is from arbitrage that the interest rate swap evolved. One entity can borrow fixed rate funds more cheaply than another entity but wishes to raise floating rate funds. The other is able to raise floating rate funds at a lower margin than the margin which it pays when raising fixed rate funds.[18] The counterparties can independently borrow identical principal amounts in the same currency for the same period from different markets and/or funding sources, one paying a floating rate of interest and the other a fixed rate. Through a rate swap, which may either be a direct contractual arrangement or be through intermediaries, the counterparties 'swap' interest obligations. The first agrees to pay to the second periodic payments calculated by reference to the principal amount and to a fixed rate of interest whilst the second agrees to pay to the first amounts calculated by reference to the principal amount and a floating rate of interest. Alternately, the net difference between the two payments could be made.

### Commodity swaps

**6.14** The usefulness of swaps has resulted in there having been a considerable increase in the number of types created. Commodity swaps fix the price of a defined commodity over an agreed period of time. For example, one party may wish to guarantee the price it has to pay for a commodity and be concerned at the prospect of it going up in price. The other party may be exposed to that commodity going down

---

[18] For an interesting discussion, see Woolf LJ in *Hazell v Hammersmith and Fulham LBC* [1991] 1 All ER 33 at 63.

in price. For example, they may produce that commodity or be a bank which has loaned a large amount of money to companies that have. One party may sign a swap contract requiring it to pay the amount below £x per tonne for the quantity needed over the period required and the counterparty to pay them if the price is higher. The first party will then enter into the open market and contract to buy the necessary amount of that commodity at the current market price as and when needed. If the market price of the commodity concerned goes up the company will have to pay the higher price in the market place, but the difference between the current market price and the price under the swap contract will then be received from the swap counterparty, normally by settlement at six monthly stages. If the market price drops it will be possible to buy the commodity more cheaply, but the amount saved relative to the swap price will have to be paid to the counterparty under the swap contract. Thus, for one counterparty the price of the commodity concerned is guaranteed for the length of the swap contract. For the other counterparty a hedge is created against the price of that commodity dropping at the cost of having to pay out should the price rise. In this way for example, airlines can hedge against rises in the price of aviation fuel by buying such contracts and oil companies hedge against its decline in value. A manufacturer could hedge against an increase in the price of electricity whilst an electricity provider could hedge against its decline, to take but two examples.

## Credit swaps

**6.15** A credit swap exists when a party who is exposed to a credit risk, ie, the risk that a counterparty will fail to settle, uses a swap transaction to move that risk to another party. There will remain a credit risk, namely that of the counterparty with which the swap is being entered into not performing, but this is presumably going to be considerably less likely or the arrangement will not be entered into. The counterparty risk on the swap deal can be measured by looking at the credit rating of the proposed counterparty provided by the rating agencies.

**6.16** Credit swap arrangements can be found in a number of forms.

### *Credit default swaps*

**6.17** These provide that on the occurrence of a defined credit event a payment will be made in return.[19] It is the commonest type of credit swap and they are traded on an enormous scale. In essence one party to such an arrangement contracts that in the event of default they will provide a stated sum to the counterparty. This sum normally covers

[19] This could be failure to pay, entering insolvency or a credit rating downgrade below a particular level to name but three.

the value of a bond holding or loan. Thus, that party has de facto insurance cover for its debt not being paid, though the arrangement does not satisfy legal definitions of insurance. Thus:

FIGURE 1

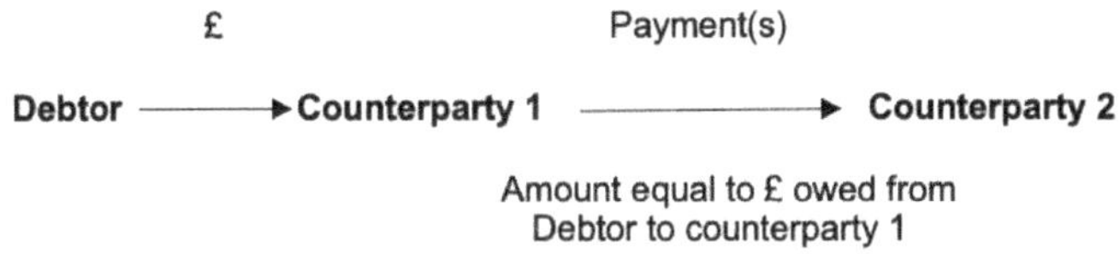


Banks have founded such arrangements attractive as they can obtain cover for certain debts and thus reduce their exposure to a particular client, or sector and in turn reduce the capital they have to hold.

**6.18** Counterparty 1 may decide in due course to swap out of this transaction with another party – counterparty 3. In the event of the debtor having its credit rating reduced or getting into financial difficulties the value of the swap will increase in value in the hands of counterparty 3 as counterparty 2 is now more likely to have to pay up. Counterparty 3 could then await any payment due under the contract or sell to another party and cash in the profit straight away. This potential attracted a large number of financial speculators into the market and by 2007 at the start of the global financial crisis US $62.2 trillion of them were traded, though this reduced to US $38.6 trillion the following year when the financial crisis occurred.[20] When traded in this way the arrangement looks like this.

FIGURE 2

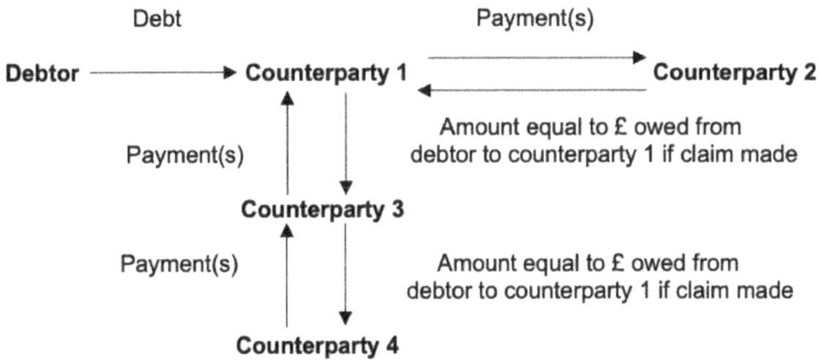


*Total return swaps*

**6.19** Here one counterparty will pay all the income from, and any capital appreciation in the value of a debt instrument to the other.

[20] ISDA Market Survey 'Notional Amounts Outstanding at Year End; all surveyed contracts 1987 – present.'

In return they will be entitled to a stated interest payment and an indemnity against capital depreciation.

*Credit spread swaps*

**6.20** Such arrangements consist of payment being linked to a defined credit spread over a benchmark yield.

**6.21** Credit derivatives do not always exist as swaps, they also appear as options or embedded securities.[21]

**6.22** The respective extent to which such derivatives are used varies enormously. In the OTC market 80.21% of the derivatives relate to interest rates, 12.04% to foreign exchange, 2.6% are credit default swaps, 1.26% equities and 0.3% commodities, with a range of assets making up the rest.[22]

**6.23** To approach this from a different angle the use of derivatives by large companies pans out as follows.

ISDA SURVEY RESULTS:

DERIVATIVES USAGE BY THE WORLD'S LARGEST COMPANIES

Usage by Sector

| Sector Name | Total | % Using Derivatives | % Using Interest Rate | % Using Forex | % Using Commodity | % Using Credit | % Using Equity |
|---|---|---|---|---|---|---|---|
| Basic materials | 86 | 97% | 70% | 85% | 79% | 0% | 6% |
| Consumer goods | 88 | 91% | 81% | 84% | 39% | 1% | 9% |
| Financial | 123 | 98% | 94% | 96% | 63% | 76% | 80% |
| Health care | 25 | 92% | 80% | 72% | 8% | 4% | 20% |
| Industrial goods | 49 | 92% | 86% | 86% | 37% | 2% | 20% |
| Services | 40 | 88% | 75% | 85% | 35% | 3% | 13% |
| Technology | 65 | 95% | 86% | 92% | 15% | 6% | 15% |
| Utilities | 24 | 92% | 92% | 88% | 83% | 0% | 8% |
| Total | 500 | 94% | 83% | 88% | 49% | 20% | 29% |

## Swapping out

**6.24** When a swap contract is sold it cannot simply have its benefits and obligations passed on in the way that can be done with exchange

[21] E Swan in A Hudson (ed), *Credit Derivatives* (Sweet & Maxwell, 1999), p 3.
[22] BIS Quarterly Review (July 2015), p A 14.

traded and OTC futures and options. In the case of a swap the parties have an ongoing contractual relationship. Thus, if Co A and Co B enter into a swap contract and Co B then wishes to reverse the position they have contracted into two possibilities arise. The first is that Co A is prepared to cancel the contract. This possibility may not be available and so it will be necessary to find a new counterparty, Co C, who wishes to swap in on the same terms currently enjoyed by Co B. Thus, the final position will be: Co A swaps with Co B, Co B reverses the swap with Co C. As a consequence Co B remains a counterparty of both Co A and Co C. The net effect is that Co B has now escaped from the consequences of the swap contract but has ongoing obligations which must be performed and this will cause them problems if one of its counterparties fails to do so. By such an arrangement, the party will inevitably increase its exposure as it then carries the risk of default by both the original swap counterparty and the new swap counterparty. In practice Co B will not usually be able to find a counterparty who will 'swap in' on exactly the same terms as Co B originally had, most probably because of a change in the value of the underlying subject matter. They may thus end up still swapped into Co A and then swapped out on slightly different financial terms with Co C.

### Forward rate agreements (FRAs)

**6.25** A 'forward rate agreement,' is an essentially simple concept enabling banks and other large companies to hedge interest rate risk. The buyer is hedging against interest rates going up and the seller against them going down. Two parties are involved and the following elements are agreed: a notional principal amount; a future settlement date; a maturity date; which will typically be a specific number of months after the settlement date; a fixed rate of interest; for the payment of which one party is responsible; and a floating rate of interest, for example SONIA or €STR, for the payment of which the other party is responsible.

**6.26** Having agreed these items, the parties await the arrival of the settlement date. On that date, the agreed fixed rate of interest is compared with SONIA or €STR (as the case may be) quoted by prime banks in the London Interbank Market for deposits in the currency of the agreed notional principal amount, for delivery on the settlement date and for a period equal to the period between the settlement date and the maturity date.

**6.27** If the relevant SONIA/€STR proves to be lower than the agreed fixed rate, then the percentage shortfall is multiplied by the agreed notional principal amount and by a fraction, the numerator of which is the number of days between the settlement date and the maturity date and the denominator of which is 360 if the currency of the transaction is not domestic sterling, or 365 if it is. The result of that multiplication then falls due as a debt owed by the first counterparty to the second.

**6.28** Of course, it is possible that market rates of interest will have moved in a different direction: the relevant SONIA/€STR might have proved to be higher than the agreed fixed rate of interest – in this case, the excess if multiplied as described above and the result falls due as a debt from the second counterparty to the first.[23]

## Forward foreign exchange contracts (Fx forwards)

**6.29** Here a party may face an exchange rate risk which typically occurs because they wish to import goods from overseas at a future date. The exporter will usually wish to be paid in their own currency or sometimes US$ and in the interim the exchange rate could move against the importer making the purchase more expensive. Thus, a forward foreign exchange contract is entered into with a bank whereby the importer agrees a rate of exchange now to purchase that currency on the future date when it is needed and thus moves the currency risk to the bank who will provide the requisite amount of foreign currency on the agreed future date.

**6.30** Technically this is not a derivative as it is usually a financing vehicle for a trading contract, but it is so similar in nature that it warrants being mentioned.

## Caps, floors and collars

**6.31** Some lending arrangements are structured with a floating interest rate which will not rise above a certain level, in return for which the borrower normally pays a fee. This is called a cap. Alternately, the opposite can happen where the borrower may borrow on the basis that if interest rates drop, his interest rate will not drop below a certain floor. The bank may pay a fee for such an arrangement. A combination of these, called a collar can also be set up where the floating interest rate only oscillates between two levels. These arrangements sometimes use documentation similar to derivatives, but as they are essentially an aspect of lending they are dealt with in **Chapter 1**.

**6.32** The examples given above provide an overview of the basic derivative types. However, sometimes they may be combined in more complex structures. For example, swaptions are a right (but not an obligation) to enter into an interest rate contract for differences either as a fixed rate payer or receiver. The counterparties to a deal can construct whatever arrangement suits them and they are not constrained by the precise examples given here.

---

[23] It should be added that there is no uniformity of expression here. Hudson uses 'forwards' to cover all of exchange futures trading: A Hudson, *The Law on Derivative Contracts* (Sweet & Maxwell, 2006), p 44.

## Issues arising

**6.33** Four critical areas need to be examined. They are:

- utilisation;
- capacity;
- documentation; and
- the theoretical threat from the gambling laws.

### *Utilisation*

**6.34** There are a number of ways in which financial institutions may utilise derivatives. These are:

- hedging;
- speculation;
- arbitrage;
- reducing capital for regulatory purposes; and
- to reduce credit risk concentration.

#### Hedging

**6.35** A key purpose in utilising derivatives is hedging. Hudson[24] describes this as a 'matching of income and risk'. It is probably wider than this and encompasses the structuring of a financial arrangement to control the extent of the risk being undertaken in a wider series of transactions. At its simplest this may involve taking up a derivative position in relation to an underlying commodity so that any adverse price movement in that commodity or any direct or indirect financial impact it may have is partly covered by the derivative contract. A perfect hedge is occasionally created where the financial risk is entirely covered, but generally this is not cost effective. Thus, the hedging process is one of controlling the degree of risk, not removing it completely.

**6.36** For example, suppose a British company faces a potential loss because it has bought an asset in a foreign currency with a fixed maturity period. If the exchange rate moves against it the company could face a loss when it exchanges the proceeds into sterling on the maturity date. The company could, however, enter into a swap transaction with the same maturity date, swapping the same amount of the foreign currency concerned for sterling. On the maturity date it would then face no exchange rate risk.

---

24 Hudson, *ibid*, p 11.

**6.37** Likewise, a company may wish to hedge interest rate risk. Suppose a company has heavy floating rate liabilities but its income is tied to fixed interest rates. It would face losses if interest rates rose. Interest rate swaps could be used to bring its balance of fixed and floating rate borrowing into line with its other assets and liabilities

### SPECULATION

**6.38** Derivatives are often used to speculate, ie, to take up a financial position in the view that it will improve. Derivatives offer a particular advantage in that the party taking the speculative position is not encumbered by any incidental cost (apart from purchasing an option) and incidental formality. The underlying subject matter could be equities which are commonly subject to stamp duty and dealing costs. A futures contract in equities or an equity index would allow an equivalent financial position to be taken without such overheads. In the case of commodities such as oil an exposure to price changes can also be made without the costs and inconvenience of storage.

**6.39** It is a common misconception that speculation is a process whereby parties acquire excessive risk through derivatives with a danger to themselves, and potentially, systemically to the market. It is often the case that the speculative element consists of the transfer of risk from a party that cannot afford to carry it to one who can. Those institutions with surplus capital reserves may be in a position to utilise derivatives to take over risk from other organisations. Provided the scale of the risk being taken over is within the financial capability of the organisation concerned, the arrangement can increase the stability of the financial marketplace.

**6.40** Thus, the speculative element that may be present in some derivative transactions is not usually a sign of financial irresponsibility by one of the participants but is usually a sign of a risk migrating to the parties best capable of carrying it. In terms of the impact of derivatives this is one of their most important effects. Namely, the stabilising of markets through risk transference. As was seen above in the context of credit derivatives, the safety of this approach is dependent on the financial skills of the parties involved as well as their financial strength.

### ARBITRAGE

**6.41** This consists of the taking of a profit by purchasing on one market and selling on another where the price is higher or taking advantage of a time delay between the impact of an event and its consequential price movement. In the case of derivative contracts, the arbitrage opportunities are wider in that positions can be taken to cover price movements without having to enter into a contract in the underlying subject matter from which the profit is being sought.[25]

---

[25] Hudson *ibid*, p 12.

#### REDUCING CAPITAL FOR REGULATORY PURPOSES

**6.42** The Basel banking regulations[26] require banks to set aside a certain amount of capital in proportion to the financial risks involved in their activities. Derivatives are one of the methods that can be used to reduce this. For example, credit default swaps (see **6.17** and **6.18**) can be used to move the credit risk associated with a loan to a third party and thus the outstanding amount of the loan does not need to have money set aside against it.[27] A detailed analysis of banking capital requirements is outside the scope of the book.

#### REDUCING CREDIT RISK CONCENTRATION

**6.43** Banks are required by the capital requirements and their own internal risk controls to limit the amount they lend to a connected group of borrowers and also to any sector overall, for the obvious reason that this reduces the risk exposure to a collapse of a borrowing group or a rapid market decline in a particular sector. Again, credit default swaps can be used to move the credit risk from a borrower or group of them to a third party.

**6.44** These five categories are not mutually exclusive. Banks, fund managers, hedge funds, other financial institutions and the corporate treasury departments of large companies will all enter into a large number of derivative and other financial arrangements which are carefully structured to satisfy that institution's risks, needs and ambitions.

### *Capacity*

**6.45** The increasing range of parties involved in swap transactions has raised the question as to the potential impact of the ultra vires rule on the validity of such arrangements.' The key issue is whether they, or their counterparty has the necessary contractual capacity and whether the party signing on their behalf has.

#### LIMITED COMPANIES

**6.46** The ultra vires rule is determined by s 39(1) of the Companies Act 2006. Essentially there is no problem for companies as:

---

26 Basel 3 and 3.1.

27 Nicolò, A and Perlizzon, L, 'Credit Derivatives: Capital Requirements and Strategic Contracting' EFMA Basel Meetings (March 15 2006).

> 'The validity of an act done by a company shall not be called into question on the ground of lack of capacity by reason of anything in the company's constitution.'[28]

The only potential problem is that shareholders in the company concerned could get an injunction debarring the directors from proceeding with a contract which was ultra vires the company if legally binding obligations have not already been entered into,[29] though in practice, given the speed at which derivative contracts are normally entered into, this right is somewhat academic. Directors also have virtually unlimited power to bind their company as s 40(1) states that a director will bind the company in any contract entered into in good faith by a third party. Good faith is presumed and is not rebutted simply by the third party knowing that the act was outside the company's powers.

### Overseas companies

**6.47** Contractual capacity is normally governed by the law of the jurisdiction of the domicile of the corporation or other entity concerned[30] whilst the terms of the contract will be governed by the proper law, which will normally be chosen in the Schedule to the Master Agreement governing the transaction. The constitutional documents of the corporation, etc will need to be considered. Problems can arise as there are jurisdictions where relaxation of the ultra vires doctrines has not yet fully taken place. In particular, banks and financial institutions are in some cases established by the host state's equivalent of a statutory instrument. Even where the ultra vires doctrine has been abolished the courts of that jurisdiction may regard a breach of the instrument as contrary to public policy, leaving contracts in breach of it unenforceable.

**6.48** It is not unusual to find such instruments granting general powers to invest. These may be widely interpreted by a court, but the case of *Hazell v London Borough of Hammersmith and Fulham Borough Council* [31] is worth remembering. In that instance a statutory power to: '... do anything (whether involving expenditure, borrowing or lending of money or the acquisition or disposal of any property or rights) which is calculated to facilitate, or is conducive or incidental to,

---

28 This does not apply to charitable companies.:Companies Act 2006, s 39(2). In this instance it only applies where the third party does not know the company is a charity or gives full consideration and does not know that the transaction is ultra vires.

29 CA 2006, s 40(4).

30 This is so regardless of any choice of law and jurisdiction clause in the contract concerned.

31 (1992) AER 545. For a discussion of this see A Hudson above n 23, Chs 7 and 9. Also P Birks, 'Trusts raised to avoid unjust enrichment: the Westdeutsche case' [1996] RLR 3. 'Public Authorities, Ultra Vires and Restitution' in Burrows (ed), *Essays in the Law of Restitution* (Oxford University Press, 1991) and R Chambers, 'Banks, Swaps, Restitution, Trusts and Compound Interest' (1996) 20 Mel UL Rev 848.

the discharge of their functions ...'[32] was held not to cover derivative transactions. The wording of the relevant statute was later replaced but it does illustrate the danger that the ultra vires law is sometimes relevant. There are other instances of overseas jurisdictions where the capacity made available to certain types of institution is similarly vague. Enforceability could, in certain circumstances depend on how flexible the relevant court might be.

**6.49** In *Merrill Lynch v Municipality of Piraeus*[33] a derivatives contract entered into by the Municipality of Piraeus was claimed to be non-enforceable on the grounds that it was ultra vires and that the person who signed on their behalf did not have authority to do so. It was held by the English court that the law determining the party's capacity was that of Greece and that under Greek law the contracts were enforceable.

### Corporations created by Act of Parliament, Charters granted by Act of Parliament or Royal Charter

**6.50** The statute or Charter concerned would have to be examined to ascertain the powers granted as the organisation does not have the power to contract outside the scope allowed. The legal position with regard to the directors' powers is as for limited companies. It may be restrained by acting injunction being brought.[34] In practice such statutes and charters do not normally specifically deal with an organisation's power to utilise derivatives, but if any limitation is imposed on a power to invest *Hazel v Hammersmith and Fulham LBC*[35] suggests that the matter should be approached with caution. Certain other types of organisation have limitations imposed on their contractual capacity. In this context the most important are the following.

### Local authorities

**6.51** The case of *Hazel v Hammersmith and Fulham LBC*[36] made clear that local authorities were not enabled by the then s 111(2) of the Local Government Act 1972 to enter into contracts for differences. The case involved some rather strange reasoning by the House of Lords which arguably appeared to misunderstand the essential nature of derivative contacts by seeing them as essentially a type of gambling. A more charitable interpretation of the case could see the court's attitude

---

32 Local Government Act 1972, s 111(2).
33 [1997] CLC 1214.
34 *Att Gen v Manchester Corporation* [1906] 1 Ch 643; *Hazel v Hammersmith and Fulham LBC* [1992] 2 AC 1, at 43
35 [1992] 2 AC 1.
36 *Ibid.*

as being driven by the enormous scale of the derivatives activity that had been entered into exceeding an investment arrangement.

> '.... the council had entered into 592 swap transactions and 297 of these were still outstanding. The total notional principal sum involved in all the transactions entered into by the council amounted in aggregate to £6,052 million .... The council's actual borrowing on that date amounted to £390 million, its estimated expenditure for the year... was £85.7 million and its quoted budget for that year was £44.6 million.'[37]

**6.52** However, the section has since been replaced by the Local Government Act 2003, s 12 which gives local authorities a power to invest:

> '(a) for any purposes relevant to its functions under any enactment, or
>
> (b) for the purposes of the prudent management of its financial affairs.'

This still might not entirely solve the problem as Hammersmith and Fulham LBC's involvement with derivatives was so vast and rashly structured that they were arguably not entirely relevant to its functions and certainly were not prudent!

### Local authority pension schemes

**6.53** The capacity of local authority pension schemes to utilise derivatives incudes any 'investment'[38] for local authority assets. It can include 'a contract entered into in the course of dealing in financial futures, traded options or derivatives.'[39]

### Building societies

**6.54** Section 10 of the Building Societies Act 1997[40] states that:

> '... a building society shall not do, and shall secure that each of its subsidiary undertakings does not do, any of the following things, namely ...
>
> (c) enter into any transaction involving derivative instruments;
>
> but a contravention of this subsection shall not invalidate any transaction or other act.'

---

[37] *Hazel v Hammersmith and Fulham LBC* [1992] AC 1, per Lord Templeman.
[38] Reg 10 of the Local Government Pension Scheme (Management and Investment of Funds) Regulations 2016.
[39] Reg 3 (r)(a) of the Local Government Pension Scheme (Management and Investment of Funds) Regulations 2016.
[40] Inserting a new s 9 in the Building Societies Act 1986.

However, s10(4) of the Building Societies Act 1997 empowers building societies to utilise derivatives in their capacity as manager of a collective investment scheme, to limiting the impact on the building society of interest rates, exchange rates, an index of retail prices, residential property prices or security prices. They can also enter into contracts for differences to limit the impact on them of interest rate and exchange rate changes applicable to loans, shares or deposits.

Consequently, building societies would appear to be safe counterparties where the ultra vires rule is concerned. In addition, s 10 inserts into the Building Societies Act 1986, s 9A(1) which permits any third party to enforce such contracts.

### *Insurance companies*

**6.55** Many of these were created by Act of Parliament and some of the older ones by Royal Charter and a few were originally created as friendly societies.[41] The rules already discussed apply here. Also relevant are the Financial Services and Markets Act 2000, the FCA Handbook and the relevant body's constitutional documents which between them determine their powers.

### *Unit trusts*

**6.56** Again, the same two separate issues arise here, with regard to the special nature of the trust and the contractual capacity of trustees themselves. Unit trusts are allowed to utilise derivatives by the FCA's regulations governing collective investments. There are limitations, however, which vary according to the category of unit trust involved. The trustees' powers are also determined by the trust deed. These should be examined by the counterparty to make sure that the arrangement is not ultra vires the trustees. Likewise, the investment capacity of the trust will be set out in the deed.

**6.57** It is clear that monies paid pursuant to such an ultra vires contract are reclaimable along with costs and simple interest provided the payments were made in good faith[42] but financial institutions will not wish to place themselves in a position where legal proceedings may be necessary.

**6.58** Market practice often involves market participants being cavalier about the ultra vires rule. This may change if a significant party in the market place becomes insolvent and the liquidator successfully uses the doctrine to avoid contracts.

---

[41] S Firth, *Derivatives Law and Practice* (Sweet & Maxwell), para 2.28.

[42] *Westdeutsche Landesbank Girozentrale v Islington LBC; Kleinwort Benson Ltd v Sandwell District Council* [1996] AC 669, [1996] 2 All ER 961, [1996] 2 WLR 802.

## Netting

**6.59** Where two parties enter into a number of contracts with each other it is possible to contract on the basis that only the balance of the various sums is ever owed, with the various sums concerned being set off against each other. Traditionally this was called an account current.[43] This should be distinguished from set off as the latter operates during the operation of the contracts to which it relates but ceases to do so on the insolvency of one of the parties.[44] The vital point is that the netting arrangement is not stated to operate only on insolvency as if this were the case the agreement would be struck down under *British Eagle Ltd v Compagnie Nationale Air France*[45] as being intended to override the insolvency rules. Provided the netted off balance is stated in the contract to be the only sum owing at any time between the parties then the insolvency of one party will not override the arrangement. Today netting has developed into the growing range of arrangements that have been created to meet the ever more complex contractual situations which have arisen as a result of the increasing sophistication of the derivatives market. The issue of netting is crucial in derivative contracts as it fundamentally affects the degree of financial risk to the parties. Thus, suppose two parties enter into a range of derivative contracts between themselves, with A owing a total of £50 million to B, and with B owing a total of £49 million to A. Should B become insolvent, A would normally have to pay all monies they owed but might find a liquidator, administrative receiver or administrator refusing to honour the other contracts ('cherry picking') as is permitted by the relevant insolvency legislation. A would then be an unsecured creditor for the sums they were owed with little prospect of recovering most of the money. However, if there were a master agreement for all the derivatives which contained a netting arrangement, only £1 million would be at issue. Likewise, if only one debt is ever owed it cannot be claimed that the arrangement is a preference that the counterparty has an advantage over other creditors of the insolvent party.[46]

**6.60** Importantly, a liquidator cannot 'cherry pick' and avoid a derivative contract simply because it is 'out of the money' because of the Insolvency Act 1978, s 178 which states that a transaction is not an 'unprofitable contract' simply because it is financially disadvantageous or the party could have made a better bargain.[47] The question then arises as to when 'cherry picking' would be possible. There has been

---

[43] *The Mecca* (1897) AC 286.

[44] *British Eagle International Airlines Ltd v Compagnie National Air France* [1975] All ER 390.

[45] [1975] 1 WLR 758.

[46] *Re BCCI (No 8)* [1998] AC 214; *Re BCCI (No 11)* [1997] 2 WLR 172 and *Stein v Blake* [1996] 1 AC 243, but potential limitations imposed by *IRC v Scottish Provident Institutions* [2003] STC 1035.

[47] *Re SSSL Realisations (2002) Ltd* [2006] Ch 610. See also Goode R *Principles of Corporate Insolvency Law* 4th ed (Sweet & Maxwell, 2011), p 200 and Firth S *Derivatives Law and Practice* (Sweet & Maxwell), para 5-3.

extensive litigation relating to Lehman's collapse and it did not prove a major issue.

**6.61** Consequently, much legal effort has been expended in drafting such netting clauses. Indeed, the ISDA (see below) has put a great deal of work into analysing how effective netting provisions will be in a wide range of jurisdictions. This has in part been aided by the increasing willingness of the banking regulators to allow such arrangements to be used to reduce the amount of capital which a banking institution must retain to safeguard against financial risk. There are a number of types of netting of which the most important in this context are the following.

## Payment or settlement netting

**6.62** This is the simplest type of netting arrangement. It consists of a contractual agreement that the debt which exists at any one time is the net balance of the amounts mutually owed between the parties. It is utilised by the ISDA 2002 Master Agreement[48] (discussed below) which does this by acting, as its name suggests, and combines a number of contracts being traded between two parties so that there is a single governing contract which facilitates that all sums owed between the counterparties in the same currency are set off against each other for the purposes of settlement and that this is the only debt that exists at any time under the operation of the Master Agreement.

## Netting by novation

**6.63** Novation, which is discussed in **Chapter 3** is an arrangement where one contract between parties is replaced by another, later agreement. Once this is done the trading contracts concerned can have their gains and losses offset against each other under clause 2 (c) of the ISDA Master Agreement 2002. Such netting may be carried out because the Master Agreement is closed out or because one of the parties has become insolvent.

## Close out netting

**6.64** This is the type of netting utilised by the ISDA Master Agreements when contracts are closed out. Essentially it consists of providing that in the event of the contract being terminated a particular method of calculation will be used to determine what amount should be paid by one counterparty to the other. More than one option is available and the parties can also make amendments to the standard approach by adding appropriate wording to the schedule.

---

48 And for that matter the 1992 version which is still used by some parties.

Under clause 2 (a) (iii) ISDA Master Agreement 2002[49] an event of default or termination event will normally bring the contract to an end and the netting provisions will apply.

**6.65** Under clause 6 (a) the contract will close out automatically. This will not always be to the commercial advantage of the non-defaulting counterparty and thought should be given as to whether an amendment should be made to the Schedule (see below) to make an amendment giving a non-defaulting party the power to elect to continue. A party suffering loss due to close out is entitled to compensation. If this were not the case any party that was 'in the money' would have a vested interest in closing out.

**6.66** The contract will also have to specify how the close out amounts are to be calculated. Under ISDA two calculations are made provided no event of default has occurred. The first involves obtaining quotations for the replacement of each type of transaction terminated under the master agreement. The other calculation involves working out the value of any payments due before the termination date. The two figures are then aggregated. There must of course be a close out for this to apply[50] and it must be due to a breach of contract, ie, a party must have failed to perform a contractual obligation.

## Multilateral netting

**6.67** This has been brought into being because of the huge volumes of trading on the derivative exchanges, where the parties contract through the exchange itself. It is also utilised by clearing houses where the exchange does not have a clearing system. Essentially each sale will be made by the vendor to the exchange and then immediately from the exchange to the buyer and it thus it consists of all the parties contracting, including the exchange or clearing house. Thus, the exchange is a counterparty to each deal and the payments are netted off against each other reducing risk. The exchange rules will state that in the case of a party becoming insolvent or being unable to complete the contracts it has entered into all the contracts it is involved in will be netted. As well as hugely reducing financial risk it also massively reduces the administrative workload.[51]

**6.68** This approach has also been adopted in OTC derivatives by way of using a central counterparty and for this to work there needs to

---

49 See also clause 2(a)(iii) of the ISDA Master Agreement 1992.

50 *Edgeworth Capital (Luxembourg) SARL v Ramblas Investments* [2017] 1 All ER (Comm) 577; *Pioneer Freight Futures Co Ltd v TMT Asia Ltd* [2011] 2 Lloyd's Rep 96.

51 The relative ease with which LCH Clearnet was able to manage the aftermath of Lehman Brothers collapse is an illustrative example. There were some problems; namely identifying the clients to whom uncleared positions related and clients wishing to move their positions to another exchange member facing a delay in getting their margin payments back, but overall the situation was controlled.

be a critical mass of derivative contracts requiring to be cleared. There is an issue in that the derivative dealers will have to post collateral with the central counterparty which involves a front end cost.

### Cross product netting

**6.69** This consists of contracting that a disparate range of contracts in various currencies shall all be netted. It is possible to do this in many cases, subject to suitable drafting. Whether this will work effectively will depend on the applicable law in the state concerned.

**6.70** In all these cases, cherry picking[52] is not a risk as only one debt ever existed. Likewise, if only one debt is ever owed it cannot be claimed that the arrangement is a preference.[53]

## Documentation and master agreements

**6.71** Although on exchange transactions are sold on the standard terms of the market concerned the same is not true of OTC contracts which could contain such terms as the counterparties might agree. The increased volume of transactions in the 1990s gave rise to several important developments in the area of documentation. As the number of market participants and the level of competition increased, so transactions were concluded more quickly and control shifted from the transaction originators to the dealers. The terms are now agreed by dealers directly with the relevant paperwork being sent on to the respective parties' legal representatives. They will subsequently exchange the formal documentation governing the transaction.

### Confirmations and master agreements

**6.72** The first stage of a trading relationship between two parties will often be to create a confirmation between the parties, confirming the details of the deal which the traders have agreed between themselves either by telephone or electronic communication. The confirmation normally gets completed on the firm's software and is sent on to someone with the authority to check and clear its content before forwarding it to the counterparty. Alternately, in some cases they may refuse and return it to the trader.

**6.73** The confirmation will in due course be replaced by a master agreement (see below) which is a more complex document covering a wider range of issues and going into more detail. The confirmation itself will cross refer to this and make clear that the deal will proceed on the

---

52 Insolvency Act 1986, s 129.
53 *Ibid*, s 239.

basis that a master agreement will be put in place. It should be added that this approach, desirable as it is, does not always hold up in practice. Dealers in fast moving markets in some firms simply go ahead with deals and leave the contractual paperwork to be sorted out afterwards. Larger and better run firms have procedures to stop this happening.

## ISDA master agreements

**6.74** The master agreement is designed to cover all derivative transactions between the parties and includes the legal eventualities that require clarification and of which the key ones are termination events, events of default and netting arrangements. The schedule will contain any amendments the parties wish to make to the standard form master agreement and the credit support deed[54] will provide details of any security or guarantees provided. The confirmation will document a particular transfer and will be read subject to the master agreement to which it is effectively appended.[55] In practice, parties which have only just started dealing with each other often find a number of confirmations being put into place prior to the amendments to the master agreement in the schedule being agreed. In this event the respective legal departments need to give thought to the protection that needs adding to the wording of the confirmation.[56]

**6.75** Transactions are documented in reasonable detail in view of the desirability of dealing comprehensively with the events, both fault related and non-fault related, which might give rise to an early termination and with the determination of the compensation upon early termination. Participants became increasingly aware in the 1980s of the advantages of standardising documentation so as to minimise the exposure between the time when the terms of a particular transaction are agreed and the time when the formal documentation was signed. It also minimised the associated legal costs. The emergence and evolution of master agreements together with standard form documentation is a response to this awareness and the primary movers in this have been the International Securities and Derivatives Association ('ISDA').

**6.76** ISDA themselves are a private organisation who exist to encourage the prudent and efficient development of derivatives

---

54 There is an alternative Credit Support Annex that is designed to operate under New York State law.

55 It can assist in clarifying the relationship between the parties where this is not fully done by the Masters Agreement: *Caiola v Citibank NA* 295 F 2nd 312 (2nd Cir 2002).

56 *Lehman Brothers Commercial Corporation v China International Ltd* [1995 – 6 Transfer Binder] ED SEC L RED (CCH) 99.000; *Petroleum and Lehman Brothers Commercial Corporation International Ferrous Metal Trading Co* 179 F Supp 2nd 118 (SDNY, 2000) illustrate the importance of making sure the documentation clarifies everything in advance. The absence of a written advisory agreement where both parties are businesses will be a strong pointer against its existence. *JP Morgan v Springwell Navigation* [2008] EWHC 1186 (Comm) p 604.

business. They seek to do this by promoting an efficient market through developing effective documentation, promoting good risk management policies, encouraging high standards of conduct, advancing public understanding of derivatives, educating its members in relation to the legal, documentary, accounting, tax technological and practical issues and creating a forum to facilitate all of these. They also engage in political lobbying to facilitate laws and regulations being passed that improve the operation of the derivative markets. Since its creation in 1985 it has grown from an organisation with 10 members and one office in New York to over 1,000 members from 78 countries by 2026.[57]

**6.77** The ISDA has published and periodically updated a standard form master agreement, the most recent version of which was published in 2002, though some firms still use one of the earlier versions.[58] In addition there are two support contracts – the credit support deed and the credit support annexes. These will be considered in turn. The forms themselves are designed to be directly used by adding names, dates and details, rather than merely being a precedent from which a contract can be drawn up. The schedules on the forms are designed to facilitate a range of amendments to the basic text, indeed clause 1 (b) states that, 'in the event of any inconsistency between the provisions of the Schedule and the other provisions of the Master Agreement, the Schedule will prevail.'

**6.78** However, before the parties enter into the agreement it is necessary that they agree how they will confirm the contract pending the signing of the master agreement. The original agreement will normally be reached by electronic means or telephone. The crucial point is for the parties to agree on a procedure which will result in a provable agreement being reached in a manner which will be recognised by the legal system of the jurisdiction(s) governing the agreement. A problem which arises in this context is that the speed at which many trades are carried out pre-empts the completing of the contractual process in the considered way in which the application of suitable risk based compliance approaches would require. There is evidence[59] that in some firms this does not happen because the trades have been completed so quickly that no formal written contract has come into existence at all. The solution is for firms where this has been a problem to put in place electronic systems and to make sure that traders do not enter into binding contracts until certain steps have been taken in using the internal system so created. Once a derivative contract has been agreed between the counterparties' dealers the process should be that

---

57 As at 27 November 2025.

58 In particular the 1992 Agreement is still used by some parties with amendments made to the schedule according to their normal trading practices and negotiations with counterparties.

59 A Hudson, *The Law of Financial Derivatives* 4th edn (Sweet & Maxwell, 2006), pp 108–111.

a formal written contract (normally in the ISDA form explained below) is then entered into after the confirmations have been made.

## The ISDA 2002 Master Agreement – terms

**6.79** The agreement contains broadly common clauses, of which the most important are payment provisions, representations concerning the absence of litigation and the accuracy of specified information, agreements, events of default, termination events, provisions for early termination, methods of calculating payment and early termination, provisions dealing with withholding for tax, payer and payee tax representations, agreements to provide tax forms, tax agreement, payment of stamp duty, tax events, transfer to avoid termination event, contractual currency, offices for multi-branch parties, service of process and representations.

**6.80** Clause 1 deals with issues of interpretation. The definitions themselves are to be found in clause 14 but are referred to at this point. The determination that inconsistencies between the wording of the agreement and the schedules are to be decided in favour of the latter (discussed above) is set out as is the fact that the master agreement itself and all transactions entered into on reliance on it and all confirmations are part of a single contract. A key issue here is that netting can then be carried out across all relevant transactions (see above).

**6.81** Clause 2 sets out the obligations of the counterparties. These cover both parties being required to make the payment and deliveries described in the confirmation on the date and place of account specified in freely transferable funds. Failure to do this could of course cause financial loss to the recipient, so a failure to meet this requirement could give rise to a claim for damages. To facilitate the need of a counterparty to meet this requirement, any change of the account for payment or delivery must be notified by five business days prior to the settlement date.

**6.82** Clause 2(a)(iii) is particularly important in that it states that an out of the money party's obligation to pay is subject to the condition precedent that the other party is not in default. A non-defaulting party can decide to terminate the ISDA agreement and the valuation methodology is applied to determine what sum the out of the money party must pay to the other. There is no requirement to do this however and if a party calculates that it will be more profitable to wait because they believe the contract will move further into the money, they can elect to do so. In practice the evidence of the Lehman insolvency was that those in the money demanded payment and those out of the money sometimes elected to wait, hoping that matters would improve. Statistically most opted to close out by electing an early Termination Date.[60] Such arrangements do not amount to a breach of

[60] S Firth, *Derivatives Law and Practice* (Sweet & Maxwell), para 10.24.

the insolvency laws as was confirmed by the Court of Appeal in *Pioneer Freight Futures Co Ltd v TMT Asia Ltd.*[61] It was determined that on default the payment obligation was suspended, but remained a debt, payable in the indefinite future, if the default was ever remedied.[62]

**6.83** Any calculation made under the 2002 Master Agreement involves identifying the non-defaulting party's loss of bargain resulting from early termination – *Lomas v JFB Firth Rixson*[63] and *Lehman Brothers International (Europe) v Lehman Brothers Finance SA.*[64]

**6.84** Clause 2(c) deals with netting of payments (see above). In essence, it states that where more than one transaction is due to be settled on the same date and in the same currency, the matter can be settled by the party who owes the largest sum paying the net difference. In this clause the parties may also elect which transactions to net and extend the netting to other transactions – called multiple transaction payment netting. This election may be set out in the confirmation but will normally be found in the schedule.

**6.85** Clause 2(d) deals with withholding tax. Each party represents that no withholding tax will apply to the payments made under the agreement. In the event that withholding tax is imposed on one of the two parties they will agree on whom it will fall. If, however, it is imposed as a result of a connection between the payee and the taxing authorities as a result of the payee having become voluntarily resident in the jurisdiction, that party will normally have to pay the tax.

**6.86** Clause 3 sets out the representations that each counterparty makes. These are:

- proof of status, ie, that the counterparty validly exists under the laws of the jurisdiction of its home state. For example, in some states corporations must renew their certificate of incorporation every year. It should be noted that a choice of law clause in the schedule will not affect this sub-clause as the host state of a party will always determine its constitutional status;
- that each party has the power to sign the document and that the signing of the agreement does not put the party in conflict with any other agreement;
- that neither party is breaching the terms of any applicable law, any constitutional document applying to it or any court order by signing the agreement;

---

61 [2011] 2 Lloyd's Rep 96.

62 Thus overruling on this point *Marine Trade v Pioneer Freight Futures* [2009] EWHC 2656 (Comm) and *Lomas v JFB Firth Rixson* [2010] EWHC 3372 (Ch). For a useful analysis see Lord Justice Briggs 'How has English law coped with the Lehman collapse' in D Faber and N Vermunt (Eds), *Bank Failure: Lessons from Lehman Brothers* (Oxford University Press, 2017), pp 119–120.

63 [2012] EWCA Civ 419.

64 [2012] EWHC 1072.

- that all government consents that are necessary have been obtained and are in force;
- that the legal obligations entered into are enforceable;
- that there is no event of default occurring or about to occur (see below for events of default);
- that the parties undertake that there is no litigation pending against them that is likely to affect its ability to perform the agreement. It is common to insert a financial figure in the schedule and potential awards below this will not be considered relevant litigation;
- that information provided by each party is hereby confirmed to be accurate. Some of this will be material set out in the schedule;
- that all representations are to be considered material to the contract; and
- that each party represents that it is entering into the contract as principal and not as an agent.

**6.87** The parties may require that the relevant agreement only becomes effective upon delivery of specified documents and evidence as to the due authorisation and execution of, and the obtaining of all consents in connection with, the relevant agreement. Unlike a conventional loan agreement, the conditions precedent will frequently apply to both parties. Many agreements include delivery of documentation evidencing the authority of the person who executed the contract as a covenant which must be complied with within a specified period of the agreement being signed. Where both parties to a contract are banks it is less usual to find conditions precedent. Legal opinions are not normally required in connection with inter-bank derivatives although it is common practice for banks to take opinions in respect of corporate counterparties. Corporate counterparties may also be required to deliver a copy of their latest financial statements as a condition precedent.

**6.88** Clause 4 requires that certain information be furnished. The commonest ones (which need to be added to part 3 of the schedule) to be required are financial statements, authorising resolutions, legal opinions, and certificates confirming the current status of directors and officers. Where necessary, eg, government or agency consents, must be kept up to date. The parties also agree to provide upon reasonable demand any documents that might be needed to make a payment. The parties also agree to comply with any necessary laws. This is inserted to stop any other clause being void for illegality should a term transpire to be against the laws of a relevant state. Finally, where stamp duty is required in one jurisdiction as a result of one of the parties being based there, that party must pay the stamp duty and also indemnify the other party against any liability that may as a result fall on them.

**6.89** Clause 5 deals with events of default and termination events. The former includes failure to pay, breaches of the agreement itself if not remedied within 30 days after notice of the failure is given to them, and repudiation by either party. A cross default can also act as an event of default. Such an event may be defined in the schedule but in any event a failure to satisfy a payment above a threshold amount defined in the schedule in another contract will suffice. This may not necessarily be directly related to the contract in hand, but the failure on the other contract is a potential sign that there is a credit risk associated with the counterparty in the current contract.

**6.90** The events of default found in the standard ISDA Master Agreement documentation are usually relatively limited in scope when compared with those found in conventional loan documentation. Under a conventional loan agreement, once the facility has been drawn down by the borrower there are few, if any, remaining obligations to be performed by the lender. Accordingly, it is in the lender's interests to ensure that the events of default are drafted so as to enable it to accelerate the loan as soon as it becomes apparent that the borrower is in financial difficulties. By contrast, under an agreement covered by the ISDA Master Agreement 2002[65] the parties will both normally have continuing obligations (see above) and, accordingly, the events of default, or the majority thereto will be reciprocal, both parties having the benefit, and, if too strictly drafted the burden, thereof. The events of default customarily contained in swap agreements are non-payment of amounts due under the agreement, breach of a covenant which is not remedied within any agreed grace period, material breach of representation or warranty and insolvency. Such agreements may also include a cross default, although this is frequently limited either to default on other derivative transactions or to other transactions between the parties or their affiliates. Care should be taken to ensure that any cross default clause does not catch derivatives prematurely terminated as a result of the occurrence of a non-fault related event.

**6.91** In relation to default remedies, the agreement should entitle the non-defaulting party either to leave the agreement in place and sue the counterparty for breach of contract or to terminate the future payment obligations of both parties under the agreement, thereby giving rise to the right to receive compensation determined in accordance with the compensation provisions contained in the agreement.

**6.92** If a party or a credit support party becomes insolvent or is reduced to a state that normally precedes liquidation a default is regarded as occurring. Likewise, if another company takes over a counterparty or credit support provider and merges with them and then fails to adopt all the obligations of the party taken over or merged with, a default occurs.

---

65 And for that matter the 1992 version.

**6.93** The section also covers termination events, which cover it becoming illegal to perform some aspect of the agreement, force majeure which has an impact on a party's ability to pay or perform and the situation where a counterparty merges with another entity which is materially weaker from a financial point of view as a result. Tax events are included and cover situations where an increase in tax costs impact on one counterparty. In addition, other termination events can be added of which the most common are credit related, eg, if a counterparty's long term debt securities are downgraded below a certain level by a named rating agency. Additional events may be added to the schedule. If an event is illegal it is to be treated as an illegality not a force majeure event. If an illegal act or force majeure occurs and the office affected is not the head or home office of the party affected, the head or home office should then perform. If this is not done then s 10(a) applies (see below). If the other party wishes performance to take place and the head or home office does not perform because it would also give rise to illegality or force majeure it will amount to an event of default.

**6.94** Clause 6 covers early termination and the application of close out netting (see above). If an event of default occurs and the party in default receives 20 days' notice of an early termination date, the contract will terminate on that date, or if an automatic termination date is stated in the schedule, on the happening of the relevant event. If a termination event occurs, the party that becomes aware of it must provide all the information concerning it that the other party might reasonably require. Should a force majeure event occur, each party must make all reasonable effort to notify the other and each should try to provide the other with all the information that the other person might reasonably require. If a taxation event occurs affecting one party or a tax event on merger occurs and the burdened party is the affected party, that party must take all reasonable steps short of incurring other than incidental expenses, to transfer the agreement within 20 days to an office or affiliate where the termination event will not apply. If a tax event occurs with both parties affected, each party will take all reasonable efforts to reach agreement within 30 days of notice of the occurrence of the event. If there is a tax event upon merger the burdened party must be given 20 days' notice of termination.

**6.95** Since any reduction in the amount received by either party to a swap will adversely affect the economic viability of the transaction for the recipient it is customary to include in derivative documentation (particularly in relation to cross-border contracts) a grossing up provision requiring the parties to gross up payments in the event of any withholding tax being applicable so as to ensure that the payee receives the full amount which it would otherwise have received. However, a requirement to gross up will almost invariably result in the transaction becoming uneconomic from the point of view of the party required to pay the additional amounts. Accordingly, under a derivative agreement, it is customary to include a right whereby the party required to gross up can terminate. Such a right will usually require the parties to negotiate in good faith, initially in order to seek a substitute basis for making payments which will avoid the necessity for payments to be made subject to taxes and for the affected party to gross up. Only where the parties are unable to agree upon such an alternative basis will the affected party be entitled to terminate.

**6.96** Once an early termination occurs as a result of an event of default both parties must provide a calculation of the amount and details of the account to which it is to be paid. The amount will be the close out amount(s) for the non-defaulting party for each of the transactions that is terminated, plus the unpaid amounts owing to the non-defaulting party less the unpaid amounts owing the other way. If this is a positive number, the defaulting party pays it to the non-defaulting party and vice versa.

**6.97** If, however, the early termination results from a termination event the calculation is different. One approach will apply if there is one affected party and a different one if both are. In the former case the method in the previous paragraph is adopted. In the latter each party determines the close out amount(s) whether positive or negative for each terminated transaction. The early termination amount is then the sum of half of the difference between the higher amount so determined by one party and the lower by the other. To this is added the unpaid amounts owing by the second party to the first, less any amounts owing the other way. If this is a negative number the second party pays it to the first and if a positive sum, vice versa.

**6.98** If the termination event is an illegality or force majeure then the early termination amount is calculated in line with the previous two paragraphs except that in determining the close out amount the determining party will obtain mid-market quotations or values that do not take into account the current creditworthiness of the determining party.

**6.99** The necessities of the law may require amendments to be made in terms of how such calculations are made if one party has become insolvent. Also, a failure to pay an early termination amount will not amount to an event of default if the reason for the payment not being made is that it would be illegal or if the non-payment is caused by force majeure. The amount concerned is to be then treated as unpaid and accrues interest. The parties also contract that these calculations are reasonable pre–estimates of loss. This is to stop either party challenging them as penalty payments.[66] Such a state of affairs arises is defined as:

---

66 *Total El Makdessi v Cavendish Square Holding BV* [2015] 3 WLR 1373 significantly changing the law in *Dunlop Pneumatic Tyre Co v Selfridge* [1915] AC 847 and *Clydebank Engineering and Shipbuilding Co Ltd v Don Jose Ramos Yzquiero y Castaneda* [1905] AC 6. For a useful discussion see Nicholson A 'Too Entrenched to be Challenged? A Commentary on the Rule Against Contractual Penalties post Cavendish v Makdessi and Parking Eye v Beavis.' (2016) 22(3) European Journal of Current Legal Issues.

> '...the correct test for a penalty is whether the sum or remedy stipulated as a consequence of a breach of contract is exorbitant or unconscionable when regard is had to the innocent party's interest in the performance of the contract. Where the test is to be applied to a clause fixing the level of damages to be paid on a breach, an extravagant disproportion between the stipulated sum and the highest level of damages that could possibly arise from the breach would amount to a penalty and thus be unenforceable.' Per Lord Hodge in *Tolal El Makdessi v Cavendish Square Holding BV*.[67]

**6.100** The non-defaulting party, or non-affected party as the case may be, can elect to set off any payments owed between the parties. This is contracted to be available even if sums set off include amounts not arising under this master agreement, irrespective of currency or place of payment.

**6.101** Certain points should be borne in mind in the context of this indemnification arrangement. Under the principles laid down in *Hadley v Baxendale*[68] it was held that unless the party in breach of a particular contract was aware of another transaction or agreement to which the non-defaulting party was a party, the defaulting party would not be responsible for any loss of profit or other damages incurred by the non-defaulting party as a consequence of its inability to fulfil such other transaction or agreement. It was held in *Victoria Laundry (Windsor) Ltd v Newman Industries Ltd*[69] that if at the time of entering into the contract the parties were aware of other contracts the performance of which was dependent upon the fulfilment of the first contract, then in the event of a default under the first contract the defaulting party would be liable in respect of any losses or damages suffered by the non-defaulting party as a consequence of the non-defaulting party being unable to fulfil its obligations under the other contract. In the context of derivatives this is particularly relevant given that both parties will usually be entering into transactions under which their obligations are hedged by entering into the derivative or which are substantially the reverse of it. This will almost invariably be the case for intermediary banks which have 'matching' derivatives on either side. Accordingly, in the context of an indemnification approach, it is a good idea to make specific reference to matching transactions entered into by each party in order that any loss or damage incurred by such party in relation to such matching transactions may be brought into account in the event that the contract is prematurely terminated. Whilst such a provision entitles the parties to bring into account transactions entered into prior to the termination date, it is uncertain whether it would entitle the non-defaulting party to enter into a replacement contract at the

---

67 [2015] 3 WLR 1373 at para 255, heard in association with *Parking Eye Ltd v Beavis* [2016] AC 1172.

68 (1854) 9 Exch 341; *Kpohraror v Woolwich Building Society* [1996] 4 All ER 119 and *Jackson v Royal Bank of Scotland plc* [2005] UKHL 3.

69 [1949] 2 KB 528.

time of breach/termination. Accordingly, further provisions can be added to the schedule, entitling the non-defaulting party to attempt to enter into arrangements in order to cover its exposure by virtue of termination of the existing derivative and to mitigate losses which might otherwise be incurred.

**6.102** It is possible to determine damages by reference to the cost to the non-defaulting party of entering into a replacement contract with another counterparty on substantially the same terms as those applicable to the terminated derivative. The cost to the non-defaulting party of arranging such a replacement is usually determined by reference to quotes provided by leading dealers in the relevant OTC market. One advantage of an agreement value approach over a formula is that it is considerably simpler from a documentary viewpoint and the amount is considerably easier to calculate. It is also argued that an agreement value approach more accurately reflects the action which would be taken by a non-defaulting party in the event of termination of an OTC derivative and, accordingly, is more likely to produce a figure which corresponds to its actual losses or gains. However, this is clearly only likely to be the case in circumstances where there is a market of sufficient depth and there is an implicit assumption in the agreement value approach that the derivative market concerned will continue at the same level throughout the term of the relevant contract. However, in relation to any type of OTC derivative in respect of which quotations are not readily available, an alternative fall back approach is recommended. Whilst it is accepted that the non-defaulting party should obtain more than one quotation it is wise that if the non-defaulting party is to mitigate its losses, the agreement value should correspond to the lowest quotation obtained from the average of a pre-agreed number of quotes. The agreement value approach does not make any allowance for any differences in the credit standing of the original counterparty and the replacement counterparty. It must be a live quotation in the course of exchange traded derivatives. It is not possible to take the last available one if, for example the markets are closed for a public holiday – *Lehman Brothers Finance SA v Sal Oppenheim Jr & Cie KGAA.*[70]

**6.103** One risk which is common to the various approaches is that where the terms of the relevant agreement provide for one way compensation payments (ie, only the defaulting party is required to make payment upon premature termination) there is a greater likelihood of the provision being construed as a penalty and accordingly, not being enforceable.[71] The English courts will however seek to give effect to freely negotiated contractual terms and would probably give effect to a provision in a derivative agreement entitling the innocent

70 [2014] EWHC 2627 (Comm).

71 *Tolal El Makdessi v Cavendish Square Holding BV* 3 WLR 1373 and *Parking Eye v Beavis* [2016] AC 1172.

party to retain any windfall profit provided that retention of such profit did not of itself constitute a penalty. It is thought to be the case, however, that where compensation provisions may result in payment being made by either the defaulting or the non-defaulting party (two-way payments) the chances of such provisions being construed as a penalty are more remote.

**6.104** Clause 7 requires that the counterparty's prior written consent be obtained before the other party transfers its interest in the agreement or any obligation under it to a third party. There are two exceptions, the first is where the transfer results from merging with another entity and the second is where the transfer is of early termination money owing to the transferor by a defaulting party.

**6.105** Clause 8 states that payment must be made in the specified currency to validly discharge the debt. In the event of a court order requiring that money be paid in a currency other than the one contracted to be paid, and loss results to the party suing as a result of exchanging the currency over, the party who suffers loss is entitled to be recompensed. A judgment currency clause is normally included in order to protect the parties against foreign exchange losses which might be incurred as a result of payment being made by the counterparty otherwise than in the currency of obligation, whether pursuant to a court judgment or otherwise. Such a provision should always be included in currency agreements and in any cross border rate contract. Generally speaking, such provisions are in similar form to the currency indemnity provisions found in loan agreements and, accordingly, their enforceability is subject to the same uncertainty.

**6.106** Clause 9 covers a set of miscellaneous issues, most of which would be found in a term loan agreement. These relate to the agreement constituting the entire agreement between the parties, amendments only being effective in writing, obligations surviving the agreement, the remedies being cumulative, counterparties and confirmations being treated as originals and headings not being treated as part of the agreement. Of particular importance here are the interest and compensation terms.

**6.107** Clause 10 states that where a party has entered into a contract through a branch office it agrees that it will be committed as though its head office had signed.

**6.108** Clause 11 deals with indemnification expenses and clause 12 is a standard notices provision. The case of *Lehman Brothers International I (Europe) (in Administration) v Exxonmobil Financial Services BV*[72] suggests that default notices only need to state that an event is being treated as an act of default and does not have to specify

72 [2016] EWHC 2699 (Comm).

the particular event.[73] A requirement that it should could always be added to the Schedule (see below) if it was thought necessary.

**6.109** Clause 13 deals with the issue of governing law and jurisdiction. The usual choice is either English and/ or New York State law and the appropriate submission to the jurisdiction will usually be included including appointment of a process agent to receive service. Although there are stylistic differences between English law and New York law governed agreements, virtually all derivative contacts will be enforceable under the laws of either jurisdiction.[74] Where appropriate, a waiver of immunity clause should also be included.

**6.110** Whilst the chosen governing law will govern the contractual obligations of the parties, the laws of other jurisdictions will continue to be relevant; the effect of the insolvency of one of the parties will be determined by the law of the jurisdiction in which the insolvency proceedings are commenced. Questions of the corporate capacity of a party to enter into and perform a derivatives contract and of the authority of the person signing the agreement will be determined by the law of the jurisdiction of such a party.

**6.111** Clause 14 sets out the definitions. Where, as is often the case, a derivative is being entered into in connection with another transaction, a borrowing or an investment, for example, the definitions need to reflect the nature of the underlying transactions being hedged by the derivative and for this reason additions may be needed to the schedule. This may require additions to the schedule. Particular attention should be paid to drafting the definitions so as to ensure that the provisions of the derivative match those of the underlying obligations; for example, floating interest rates should be calculated by reference to the same underlying rates and in respect of identical calculation periods so as to ensure that the floating payments under the swap equal the relevant payments under the underlying obligation insofar as is possible. Care should also be taken to check that the various 'business day' definitions conform so as to ensure that the relevant amounts are received on the same dates as the underlying obligations that are to be discharged.

**6.112** The payments clause will contain the provisions for the making of the fixed and/or floating periodic payments in the case of both currency and rate swaps. In the case of a rate swap under which all payments are being made in the same currency, it is advantageous where the payment dates coincide, to provide for the payments to be netted off against each other with only an amount equal to the excess of the larger amount over the smaller amount being paid. Netting was

---

73 This case did not deal with the ISDA Master Agreement but with the Global Master Repurchase Agreement. Nevertheless, the logic of the case potentially applies.

74 The contract is capable of functioning under many common law jurisdictions and variants have been designed for other civil law states.

considered in more detail above but in essence there are principal advantages arising from payments being made on a net basis:

(a) it is safer from a credit exposure point of view and avoids the problem of the conditionality of payments, since the parties do not need to be concerned as to whether the other party has made its payment;

(b) in the case of a cross-border contract, netting of payments has the advantage of reducing or, in some cases, eliminating, payments which might otherwise be subject to withholding taxes; and

(c) it reduces the sum at risk of being caught by any re-imposition of exchange controls.

**6.113** Under a currency swap, payments may be made gross, and since they are denominated in different currencies netting can be achieved by converting one of the amounts due into the currency of the other amount at the then current spot rate of exchange and requiring only the excess of the larger amount over the smaller amount to be paid by the party owing the larger amount.

**6.114** This clause will also contain the payment mechanics, designating the time and place at which, and specifying the relevant bank accounts to which payment is to be made. Whether or not payments are being made on a net basis, it is customary to include a provision to the effect that the obligations of the parties to make each payment shall be conditional upon the other party having already made, or contemporaneously making, all payments then due, thereby at least attempting to reduce the risk of one party being required to pay in circumstances where the counterparty has failed to pay. Although it is the desire of both parties to a swap to ensure that neither one is required to make payment unless and until it receives the corresponding payment due from the counterparty, in certain circumstances this will not be possible. For example, in the case of a dollar/yen currency swap it is inevitably the case that the party making the yen payment on any particular payment date will be required to make such payment prior to the corresponding dollar payment being made by the counterparty. This will be the case in any currency swap where the time difference between the financial centres in the countries of issue of the relevant currencies in both financial centres is such that at no time are banks open for business in both centres at the same time.

**6.115** From a credit point of view the safest way of eliminating the exposure risk for the party making the first payment is for the parties to establish escrow arrangements with one or more banks. Such an arrangement would require each party to pay the amount due to be paid by it to the escrow bank and to give to the escrow bank instructions to pay that amount to the counterparty upon receipt by the escrow bank of the amount payable by the counterparty on the payment date. One difficulty with such an arrangement is that, where the parties are in different time zones, the party paying in the financial centre which opens later will be required to pay the relevant amount to the escrow bank on the previous business day in order to ensure that payment can be made at the specified time in the other financial centre. The current practice appears to be to avoid such cumbersome and expensive payment mechanisms, particularly where one of the parties is a bank. In currency swaps, where the exposure risk is increased as a result of the amounts of principal to be re-exchanged at maturity being considerably greater than the periodic payments, the parties may be given the right to request such an arrangement.

**6.116** An alternative method of dealing with the exposure risk is to provide that a party receiving any payment in advance of the time at which it is required to make the corresponding payment to the counterparty will be deemed to hold such amount in trust for the counterparty until such time as it makes its own payment to the counterparty. Due to the complications engendered by the law of equity parties should take legal advice before committing themselves to this.

**6.117** One further change in circumstances which may give rise to an early termination option exercisable by the affected party is a change in reserve, liquidity and risk/asset ratio requirements. The effect of such change may be to impose upon banks additional costs in connection with derivatives. An increased costs clause is normally included.

## The ISDA Master Agreement – completing the Schedule

**6.118** Part 1 offers the opportunity to add to the events of default clause. The most obvious addition to make would be to add clarification regarding the availability of credit support providers in addition to the statement incorporated into the main text. In addition to this it is a good idea to include all affiliates of the counterparty as credit support providers and a generic description of '*all affiliates*' is commonly applied and will cover parent companies, subsidiaries and other brother organisations. Alternately, all the relevant organisations could be listed in the Schedule but this has the disadvantage that another company coming into being or being acquired during the duration of the ISDA contract would not be covered. Perhaps adding a sentence to include such additional organisations on the end of the list would be the optimal approach. In some instances no other organisations are mentioned because one party is happy enough with the credit rating and reputation of the other.

**6.119** It is an issue that needs taking seriously as was illustrated by the collapse of Lehman Bros in 2008. Lehman Bros Holdings Inc filed for bankruptcy on 15 September 2008, but Lehman Brothers Special Financing Inc did not until 3 October 2008. A counterparty to the latter company could thus have regarded the earlier insolvency of Holdings as a termination event provided appropriate wording had been added.

If it was not included an event which was a termination event would have to be awaited, probably 3 October or some other relevant event occurring prior to that date.

**6.120** Failure by another party to provide security or a guarantee could also be added as an event of default or termination event as is wished. It could also be the case that the parent companies of the contracting parties have an ISDA agreement between them which may contain an addition of affiliates to this part of the Schedule, in which case failure of the parent agreement will have an impact on the agreements between the subsidiaries.

**6.121** The other issue is to consider specified transactions being included as an event of default. The ISDA definition in clause 14 is very wide[75] but does not include a threshold limit, so the counterparties may wish to include referring to one. However, even a minor default could be evidence of a larger issue but even so stating a minimum sum is common. It is also normal practice not to include a grace period as it may be necessary to move quickly in the case of the counterparty starting to develop performance problems or becoming insolvent. Any problems this could cause could be mitigated in part by adding a 'cure period'. A failure to deliver securities under a repo agreement to an affiliate of the counterparty or a guarantor of the repo should be stated to be an event of default on an ISDA agreement with the other counterparty.

**6.122** It is common for failure on any contracts between counterparties and third parties to be caught as events of default and in this instance threshold amounts are sometimes added. If this is to be done it is important that there is a clear methodology stated for calculating it.

**6.123** Part 1 (c) of the schedule relating to cross default is in practice the most heavily negotiated part of the schedule.[76] It is necessary to determine the threshold amount of any failure that will give rise to such default. This may not be the same for both parties but either way they need specifying in this part of the schedule. It is also necessary to consider whether to include 'Specified Entities' here and how widely it is wished to define them. It is common to expand the definition of 'Specified Indebtedness' to include derivatives and obligations resulting from trading and leasing obligations. It can also be reduced by excluding bank deposits which represent borrowed money.

**6.124** A further issue arising with cross default is whether it should be amended by wording being deleted so that ISDA clause 5 (a)(vi)(1) has the cross acceleration element removed. This is commonly done by the words 'or becoming capable at such time of being declared'

---

[75] Eg it includes 'any Credit Support Provider of such party or any applicable Specified Entity of such other party'.

[76] Denning M, 'ISDA Master Agreement and Credit Support Annex: Negotiation Strategies.' ISDA Conference, 12 July 2017, London.

being deleted. The 'Threshold Amount' referred to in the subclause is a defined term in clause 14, but this merely states 'means the amount, if any, specified as such in the Schedule.' The approaches commonly adopted include stating in the schedule that this is either a fixed sum, stating a percentage of a key figure such as a counterparty's net asset value or 3% of shareholders' equity or the lesser of any of the above. It is not unusual for the amount to be set at zero but then to include the notional amount or market value of a derivative.

**6.125** The Credit Event Upon Merger clause, 5 (b)(v), requires each party to have a clear understanding of its counterparty to understand what is likely to reduce its credit worthiness. This can be difficult in some cases, for example where the counterparty is a complex trust structure or pension fund. One approach is to use a credit rating decline to a certain level as the trigger. It also has to be determined whether the provision applies to just one of the counterparties, or both.

**6.126** At Schedule 1(e) the parties have the capacity to choose automatic early termination which will result in the contract being automatically terminated on the occurrence of an insolvency related event. A common provision that is inserted is:

> 'provided, however, that with respect to a party, where the Event of Default specified in Section 5 (a) (vii) (1), (2), (4), (5), (6) or to the extent analogous thereto, (8) is governed by a system of law which does not permit termination to take place after the occurrence of the relevant Event of Default, then the Automatic Early Termination provisions of Section 6 (a) will apply to such party.'[77]

Factors to be taken into account will include the counterparty's bankruptcy laws which will be determined by the host state of the state in which that company is located. It is not affected by any choice of law or jurisdiction clause in the ISDA schedule. Also, the losses that a party may occur if the counterparty becomes insolvent will potentially extend to additional loss caused by not having the ability to dismantle hedges or to create a new hedging structure in time. This can occur because the insolvency event occurs quickly and unexpectedly and this may be exacerbated by a delay in the party becoming aware of the insolvency event affecting the counterparty. The crucial case here was *Lehman Brothers International (Europe) Ltd v Lehman Brothers Finance SA*[78] which dealt with the calculation of the close out amounts under the 2002 ISDA Master Agreement. The Court of Appeal determined that when a transaction was terminated under the 2002 Agreement there is no requirement to assume that the replacement transaction would

[77] Denning, *ibid.*
[78] (2013) EWCA Civ 188.

continue until maturity[79] with the result that the economic impact of termination rights must be taken into account.[80] Any replacement contract needs to reflect the creditworthiness of the party obtaining quotes and option rights should also be factored in. The methodology for closing out payments is the single valuation measure found in clause 9[81] and is more flexible than that found under the earlier version of the ISDA Agreement. The Lehman Bros failure tested this fairly thoroughly.[82] In addition, *Fondaziane Enasarco v Lehman Brothers Finance SA*[83] made clear that a party seeking a replacement contract was not limited to those seeking them from parties with the same credit rating as the defaulting party.

**6.127** The currency that the calculations need to be made in must be chosen. If no choice is made the default choice under clause 14 in the definition of Termination Currency is the € where the Choice of Law is English and the US$ where it is New York. Thus, any potential costs to a counterparty resulting from the choice of currency needs to be considered when drafting the Close Out amount definition in the schedule.[84] It was determined by the Supreme Court in *Lehman Brothers (Europe) (In Administration)*[85] that it will not otherwise be a non-provable debt.[86]

---

79 It does however depend on the precise circumstances. See *Anthracite Rated Investments (Jersey) Ltd v Lehman Brothers Finance SA* [2011] EWHC 1822 (Ch) and *Lomas v Firth Rixson Inc* [2012] 2 All ER (Comm) 1076.

80 The case determined that the wording of the 2002 ISDA Master Agreement stopped the approach approved by *Peregrine Fixed Income Ltd v Robinson Department Store Plc* [2000] CLC 1328 and *Australia and New Zealand Banking Group Ltd v Société Généràle* [2000] CLC 833.

81 This was a development from the earlier 1992 ISDA Master Agreement which many thought caused problems in having a method of calculation based on market quotation which could be a problem in unusual market conditions where quotes may not be available as happened in 2008. The 2002 contract also provides more guidance and is clearer.

82 See, eg, Parker E and McGarry A, 'The ISDA Master Agreement and CSA: close out weaknesses exposed in the banking crisis and suggestions for change' (2009) 24(1) BJIB&FL 16–19. Charles G L, 'OTC Derivative Contracts in Bankruptcy: The Lehman Experience' New York Business Law Journal. ( 2009) 13(1). Fleming LJ and Sarkar A, 'The Failure Resolution of Lehman Bros.' *Economic Policy Review*, 31 March 2014. Also McNamara C and Metrick A. 'The Lehman Bros Bankruptcy F Introduction to the ISDA Master Agreement.' (2019) 1(1) Journal of Financial Crises 137 and Wiggins RZ and Metrick A, 'The Lehman Bros Bankruptcy G: The Special Case of Derivatives' 2019) 1(1) Journal of Financial Crises 151.

83 [2015] EWHC 1307 (Ch).

84 *Lehman Brothers International (Europe) v Lehman Brothers Finance SA* (2013) EWCA Civ 188.

85 *Re Lehman Brothers International (Europe) (In Administration), Re Lehman Brothers Ltd (In Administration), Re LB Holdings Intermediate 2 Ltd (In Administration),* also known as *Joint Administrators of LB Holdings Intermediate 2 Ltd (In Administration) v Lomas* [2017] UKSC 38; [2017] 2 WLR 1497; [2017] BCC 235.

86 The case related not to the ISDA Master Agreement but to subordinated loans but the logic seems applicable.

**6.128** Additional termination events may be added and this is another area that is often contested.[87] A critical factor will be the nature of the counterparty. Thus, in the case of a trust it may be that a trustee's resignation will be a factor, a decline below a certain level of net asset value in a fund or a credit rating downgrade below a certain level for a company. Here it is necessary to determine which credit rating agency will be referred to[88] and to decide which rating is being referred to. It is better to choose one than have an average or a split as this can confuse the event. Is it the company itself, its debt or a bond that is being hedged? If the event occurs one option is to permit the counterparty to mitigate the downgrade by providing more collateral. In the case of a fund, its nature may change the perceived appropriate net asset value; for example, it will tend to be higher in the case of a fund with a high proportion of funds under management.[89] These triggers should relate to a specific document such as interim accounts or end of the month statements. Delivery of that document by a certain time after the end of the month should be listed in Part 3 of the Schedule. Failure to deliver at all should be listed as a separate termination event.

**6.129** Where the counterparty is an investment manager, termination events should include: merger with another fund, the insolvency of the manager, any constraint on the manager's license or the replacement of the manager. These will not always be a problem but it is safer to have the option of terminating in such situations. Likewise, a material adverse change in the other party's financial position or a significant change in their investment guidelines should be included. Another possible termination event would be a key person ceasing to be an adviser. Any changes made should not be drafted to have an impact on clause 11 of the Agreement which provides an indemnity for costs for the non-defaulting party.

**6.130** Where derivatives relate to loans, eg, a contract for differences hedging a loan or securitisation a counterparty should not agree to allow a banking counterparty to terminate because the loan being hedged has been sold. The release of security by a counterparty is however more of a threat and consideration should be given to including it as a termination event where the counterparty's consent has not been given. Other factors that could be included are changes to the financing documentation, failure of the obligations under the contract for differences to be equally and rateably secured on a pari passu basis with the obligations that are owed to the lenders.[90] In addition, defaulting under the related loan needs adding unless it is sure that the cross default provision in clause 5 (vi) covers it.

---

87 G Wood, 'CLS Services Ltd at ISDA Master Agreement and Credit Support Annex: Negotiating Strategies', ISDA Conference, 12 July 2017, London.

88 Normally it will be either Standard & Poors, Moody's or Fitch.

89 A Yip, 'ISDA Master Agreement and Credit Support Annex: Negotiation Strategies' ISDA Conference, 12 July 2017, London.

90 Yip, *ibid.*

**6.131** Any termination event needs to be precise and not too open ended, otherwise there is too much scope for potential future disagreement and litigation. Consideration should also be given to whether any listed termination event should be shown to have a material adverse effect and what the mechanics should be. Another potential additional termination event would be to extend the Credit Event upon Merger to a party acquiring in excess of x% of the firm.

**6.132** Other possibilities are changing the grace period in clause 12 and the definition of Local Business Day in clause 14. Likewise, there may be an amendment to the allowance for 15 days in clause 5(vii) relating to the counterparty's bankruptcy.

**6.133** Once the additional credit events have been agreed the next step is to determine a time limit within which an event of default must be exercised: twenty days from a stated event being quite common. If this is not done there is the danger that a party might exercise the remedy later, perhaps because market conditions have changed and they now wish to escape from the contract.

**6.134** Part 2 of the Schedule deals with tax representations which is a specialised tax area. The counterparties may also have different ones according to their tax jurisdiction and what type of entity they are.

**6.135** The agreement to deliver documents in Part 3 requires documents to be specifically named and a time period be stated. It is preferable to state 'within × days' or 'x local business days'[91] rather than 'as soon as reasonably possible'. Any guarantees should be included as named documents[92] as should a copy of the certified board resolutions granting the power to certain people to sign documents, together with a copy of the company's or institution's constitutional documents and financial statements.[93] If there are any credit support documents copies should also be included. Finally, legal opinions (see **Chapter 13**) should be included and a conclusion needs to be reached as to whether the view of an internal counsel is acceptable or whether it should be required from a large law firm. Not only do the latter have the availability of a wider range of expertise, they will also have far greater insurance cover. The availability of a clean legal opinion is of greatest importance for those entities which have detailed regulation, such as insurance companies, utilities and municipalities.[94]

**6.136** In Part 4 the focus moves from the counterparty to both parties. It is partly a question of where you wish to receive notice and

---

91 This is a defined term in clause 14.

92 Failure to record these caused problems in the Lehman insolvency.

93 With the financial statements a view needs to be taken on whether they should be annual, quarterly or monthly and whether they should be audited accounts, which would normally be the case with annual ones. The cure period also needs considering as cl 5(a)(ii) provides a 30-day cure period after notice of failure which will apply unless overridden by amendment in the Schedule.

94 Denning above n 80.

partly where the other party does. However, it is worth focusing on the counterparty's structure to consider where you would prefer to serve notice on them. If a corporate group, where is the head office: if an international fund, where is the manager located? Also, which jurisdictions are the various parts of the organisation in, and where would you want to sue them? Clause 10 is relevant here in that if it is agreed that an office other than the head office has contracted, the counterparty will have a right of recourse against the head office as well.

**6.137** At Part 4(e) there is the option to add the identity of a calculation agent. Normally this is a neutral third party whose function is to determine the sum of money over which there may be a dispute. Sometimes both parties use different ones, sometimes the same one and sometimes they do not use one at all. It is necessary to agree which transactions the calculation agent will deal with and whether there is to be a predetermined dispute arrangement involving the calculation agent.[95] On some occasions though a firm may have the in-house expertise to carry out the necessary calculations and therefore not wish to farm the job out at all.

**6.138** Clause 4(f) facilitates adding details of credit support documents, however whilst any English Credit Support Deed should be inserted here an English Credit Support Annex need not as title has already been transferred. Credit support provisions should be included as should guarantors.[96] The choice of law should also be stated.

**6.139** Clause 4(i) gives parties the option to decide whether or not to include Multiple Transaction Payment Netting, which they normally will. This is defined in clause 2 (c) and covers the netting off of payments in the same currency and the same transaction to determine the outstanding debt. This should not be confused with close out netting under clause 6 which determines the calculation to be applied if there is an event of default. Multiple Transaction Payment Netting can be contractually applied to more than one transaction.

**6.140** At the end of the Schedule 5 there is the opportunity to add any extra provisions. One element that is often added where a counterparty is a bank arises because of the Bank Recovery and Resolution Regulations 2025 in the UK[97] and Article 55 of the Bank

95 This may involve specifying the time frame within which a calculation agent's conclusions can be challenged, how a substitute calculation agent can be structured, who has the power to appoint a substitute calculation agent and what time frame is involved, how long they have to report back and how should they determine the results, when any payment should be made if the dispute has not been resolved and what determinations will result from any ISDA Protocol which the parties may accept.

96 In this context 'guarantor' will extend to the provider of a letter of credit.

97 The Financial Services and Markets, The Bank Recovery and Resolution (Amendment) Regulations 2025, SI 2025/862 amending the Bank Recovery and Resolution (No 2) Order 2014, SI 2014/3348.

Recovery and Resolution Directive[98] in the EU which require banks to include in their contracts the requirement that in the event of their insolvency a bail in might occur and that this could result in money owed under the ISDA Agreement[99] being reduced or converted into shares.[100]

**6.141** Parties may agree here to record conversations and that they be used in any proceedings. There may be jurisdictional issues here affecting validity of the term according to where the case is held. Where the jurisdiction is New York, the parties can agree to waive the right to trial by jury which parties are normally happy to do as any litigation is likely to be too complicated for non-experts. There may also be amendments to clause 7 which limits the right to make a transfer without the counterparty's agreement. This can be important to stop the transfer of the contract to a counterparty that you could not contract with, to make sure any transferee has a satisfactory credit rating or to make sure the transfer is guaranteed by a suitable party if the transferee themselves is not acceptable.

**6.142** At this point it is normal to exclude the Contracts (Rights of Third Parties) Act 1999 to stop third parties seeking to enforce rights under the ISDA Agreement. Also common is to set out a requirement that notice to terminate must be in writing.

**6.143** Clause 2(a)(iii) is usually amended here to avoid payment to part of a structure where the other party may be about to default. Problems arose because of the decision of the court in *Lomas v JFB Firth Rixson*[101] where it was determined that a party could rely on clause 2(a)(iii) indefinitely.[102] ISDA has produced an amended version[103] stating that ninety local business days after notice the clause shall cease to apply. The number of days can also be amended in the Schedule.

**6.144** It may be appropriate to add here a requirement that the counterparty cannot terminate an outstanding option or cap, or at least has limitations imposed on the right to terminate, where the transaction is outstanding. Finally, it is common to add here that the parties are deemed to adhere to the ISDA 2002 Master Agreement Protocol and the ISDA UK 2020 EMIR Portfolio Reconciliation, Dispute Resolution and Disclosure Protocol.

---

98 Directive 2014/59/EU of the European Parliament and of the Council of 15 May 2014 establishing a framework for the recovery and resolution of credit institutions and investment firms [2014] OJ L173/190.

99 It does not extend to secured amounts or money caught by EU margin rules.

100 See also ISDA 2016 and 2017 Bail in Protocols under Art 55. These are limited to those EU States that have passed legislation implementing Art 55.

101 [2010] EWHC 3372 (Ch). This case was dealing with the 1992 ISDA Master Agreement but the reasoning effectively applies to the 2002 Agreement as well.

102 This is not the case in the US.

103 June 2014 amended version of 2002 ISDA Master Agreement.

## ISDA Credit Support Agreements

**6.145** In 1994 the ISDA produced a Credit Support Annex for use in providing financial security for derivatives transactions governed by master agreements governed by New York State law. In 1995 the ISDA also produced two further credit support documents for use with master agreements governed by English law. The Credit Support Annex (Transfer) conveys legal title to the counterparty whilst the Credit Support Deed (Security Interest) creates a charge over assets for use as security to the master agreement to which it relates. Unlike the previous two forms of credit support documentation, it does not operate as part of the schedule to the master agreement to which it relates but as a stand-alone arrangement. In England and Wales, the security interest also requires registration under s 859 of the Companies Act 2006. Further in 2016 they produced a Credit Support Annex for Variation Margin under English law. An analysis of the content of these goes beyond the scope of the book.

**6.146** The effect of these contracts being introduced was not initially what ISDA had in mind. It was anticipated that it would result in a wider range of parties becoming engaged in the OTC derivatives market as those with lower credit ratings would be able to involve themselves on the basis of the security they provided. In practice it has resulted in some of those previously using the markets utilising the credit support arrangements to enable them to contract on more favourable terms than would otherwise have been possible. More recently, however, the market place seems to have been entered by an increasing number of relatively smaller companies. Some of whom have utilised credit support arrangements.

## Derivatives trading

**6.147** As the volume of OTC derivatives business increased, greater attention has been focused on trading. As interest and/or exchange rates move, so the benefit which a party derives from a particular derivative contract will increase or decrease and such party may, prior to the expiry of the term of the derivative, wish to realise its gain or, alternatively, restrict its exposure. Furthermore, a party which has entered into a derivative in connection with a matching investment or borrowing may wish to terminate because it has decided to reduce its investment or has prepaid its borrowing. Optional termination rights can also be considered for inclusion in the agreement by the parties. A party's voluntarily right to terminate a swap will be subject to payment of an early termination payment calculated in accordance with a pre agreed formula. In the absence of such a right, a party may seek to realise its gain or terminate its exposure under a particular contract by way of assignment.[104] OTC derivative agreements usually

[104] Law of Property Act 1925, s 136.

contain contractual restrictions on the right of the party to assign and/or transfer its rights and obligations under the relevant swap and, therefore, the prior consent of the other party will usually be required.

**6.148** Some banks attempt to include a right to transfer both their rights and obligations to third parties or, where more restrictively drafted, to third parties which fulfil specified criteria, eg, the transferee is in the same group of companies or is a recognised bank. From an English law viewpoint, it is incorrect in the context of a swap to talk in terms of an assignment. In view of the mutual obligations of the parties to a swap to make future payments, transfer of a swap requires not only an assignment of rights but also an assumption of obligations, ie, a novation is required to which the other original counterparty must be a party. For a fuller discussion of this see **Chapter 3**. Accordingly, it will be necessary to obtain the concurrence of the original counterparty to such arrangement. The proposed transferee may have an inferior credit standing to the transferor or, even if the transferee has a similar credit standing, there may be other valid reasons why the original counterparty would wish to withhold its agreement to the transfer. Clearly, the counterparty would not be willing to consent if such transfer or assignment were to give rise to withholding taxes or other increased costs, eg, as a result of different treatment for the purposes of permitted exposure or adequacy requirements imposed by the Prudential Regulation Authority.

## Master agreements and insolvency issues

**6.149** As seen above, a master agreement creates a standard set of terms and conditions which can be incorporated into all derivative transactions between the parties to such agreement. Such an agreement enables the parties to document subsequent transactions by way of a short confirmation, which may be given by electronic transmission or written contract, the principal purpose of which is to set out the financial terms of the particular derivative and, to the extent required, modify or supplement the terms of the master agreement.

**6.150** One issue of particular interest in connection with master agreements is the relationship between the various contracts entered into pursuant to the agreement and, more particularly, whether they will be treated as part of a single transaction or as a series of related individual transactions having standard terms and conditions in common. One advantage of their being treated as wholly separate transactions is that, to the extent permitted by the terms of the master agreement, the parties will be able to dispose of individual contracts. The alternative approach, namely to regard the subsequent contracts as part of the same transaction, has obvious credit analysis advantages and may also ensure that all contracts under the master agreement are afforded the same treatment in the event of the insolvency of the relevant counterparty. Given the executory nature of most derivative contracts, ie, under which both parties have obligations remaining to be performed, treating the various contracts as a single transaction is of value in preventing a liquidator from adopting those derivative contracts under which the insolvent counterparty has gained a benefit as a consequence of movements in interest and/or exchange rates whilst repudiating those which have moved to the disadvantage of the insolvent party, and in respect of which the non-defaulting party would be required to claim in the liquidation of the insolvent party as an unsecured creditor. A master agreement under which the various contracts are regarded as a single transaction enables the solvent non-defaulting party to have all derivatives showing a benefit to the insolvent party netted out against those which show a benefit to the non-defaulting party.

**6.151** As discussed above, a master agreement has obvious attractions from a credit exposure point of view. Where the payment dates under different derivatives coincide it is usually the case that the master agreement will provide for netting of all payments due in the same currency on the same day and is only to the extent that the aggregate amount payable by one party exceeds the aggregate amount payable by the other party that payment will actually be made. It is customary under the terms of a master agreement to provide that an early termination will apply simultaneously to all contracts under the master agreement and for liquidated damages to be calculated on an aggregate net basis. Notwithstanding the credit exposure advantages, it is desirable to include a degree of flexibility. For example, in relation to cross border or currency swap master agreements, it should be borne in mind that circumstances may arise in which only some of the swaps are affected, eg, illegality in relation to specified, but not all, foreign currencies. Additionally, the likelihood of one of the parties wishing to transfer individual contracts should not be ignored.

**6.152** A recurrent concern in many banking transactions is what happens if the borrower becomes insolvent? In the case of a simple loan, the position is normally straightforward; the lender can prove in the insolvency for a liquidated sum equal to the outstanding amount of the loan. In the case of many derivatives, there will potentially be future flows of funds to both parties. As previously discussed, a rate swap under which all payments are being made the same currency may provide for payment on a net basis and for only the balance to be paid one way or the other. However, in the case of a currency swap, netting off, although possible, will not normally apply and there will be periodic payments both ways in addition to the final payments on maturity of the swap of the principal amounts exchanged. If one party to a swap becomes insolvent, the last thing that the solvent party will wish to do is to have to continue making payments to the insolvent party with no prospect of receiving corresponding payments from the other party.

**6.153** Under English insolvency law neither the making of an administration order or a winding up order nor the passing of a resolution by a company to be voluntarily wound up will, of itself, terminate contracts to which the insolvent company is a party. However, whilst an administrator has power to carry on the business of the company of which he is appointed administrator he is not bound to perform contracts to which the company is a party. Such a failure is, however, likely to result in a repudiation of the contract. Similarly, a liquidator can perform a contract to which the company of which he is appointed liquidator is a party but is not bound to do so and can repudiate the contract or application can be made to the court for the contract to be rescinded.

**6.154** Whilst on the basis of current interest or exchange rates it might appear to an administrator or liquidator that it would be to the benefit of the insolvent company for a derivative contract to be continued, there will be a risk that if rates subsequently move the other way, the liquidator or administrator will ultimately end up in a negative position. The liquidator or administrator may, therefore, decide not to perform the derivative and in the case of a liquidator repudiate it or seek its rescission.

**6.155** As has been described above, OTC derivative agreements normally contain events entitling either party to terminate the obligations of both parties to make future payments which would have been made in the ordinary course, on the occurrence of specified events of default which will invariably include insolvency proceedings in relation to the other party. Upon termination of the future payment obligations of the parties by the non-defaulting party, the relevant compensation provisions will apply. Where the operation of such provisions can only result in a payment to the non-defaulting party, the payment will be expressed to be by way of liquidated damages and to represent a pre-estimate of the losses which will be incurred by such party as a result of the early termination. If, however, the calculation could result in a payment either way, it will be more difficult to categorise it as anything other than a pure contractual obligation. In the former case, the liquidator or administrator might seek to avoid the payment on the basis that it represents a penalty (see **6.99** above) and not a genuine pre-estimate of the loss suffered by the non-defaulting party. If the argument succeeded, the solvent party would be left having to prove its actual loss. If the payment consists of no more than a bare contractual payment obligation, then the repudiation of the contract by the liquidator will result in a repudiation of the obligation to make the payment contracted for and the other party will then have to prove in the liquidation for its actual loss. The liquidator could, acting in this way, seek to have some other method of calculating the loss used.

**6.156** The making of an administration order will not of itself prevent the non-defaulting party from exercising its rights to terminate its obligation to make future payments under a derivative, but it may prevent such party from taking any action to recover any amounts expressed to be payable to it as a result of the early termination, since under s 11(3)(d) of the Insolvency Act 1986, during the period when the administration is in force:

> 'no … proceedings and no execution or other legal process may be commenced or continued … against the company or its property except with the consent of the administrator or the leave of the court.'

These restrictions would not, however, appear to restrict the exercise of rights of set off.

**6.157** Rule 14.24 of the Insolvency Rules 2016[105] provides that, where there are mutual debts between a company in administration and a solvent company, and rule 14.25 where one party is in liquidation, the smaller debt shall be set off against the larger debt and that only the balance shall be accounted for by the solvent company or shall be proved for by the solvent company in the insolvency of the other company. The effect of these provisions should be that, where two parties have entered into several derivative transactions some of which show a benefit to one party and others show a benefit to the other party, the solvent, non-defaulting party should be able to set off any amounts payable by it to the insolvent party against the amount payable to it by the insolvent party. The set off provisions not only apply to amounts immediately due and payable at the commencement of the winding up, namely, in the case of a voluntary winding up, at the time the resolution is passed or, in the case of a winding up by the court, when the petition for the winding up is presented, but also to other amounts payable, provided they could be ascertained when the account was taken. Where currencies other than sterling are involved they probably have to be converted into sterling at the time when the winding up commenced. The set off principle is extended to moratoria by Insolvency Rules 2016, rule 14.23A.

**6.158** The foregoing description of the effect of insolvency is based on English insolvency law. However, this will not always be applicable, even if the relevant derivative agreement or agreements are governed by English law. The law to be applied in any insolvency proceedings will be the law of the place where the proceedings are instituted. If, therefore, an English bank enters into a swap with an Italian company in respect of which insolvency proceedings are commenced in Spain, the effect of the insolvency on the contractual rights and obligations of the parties will generally be determined in accordance with Spanish law. The law of the relevant jurisdiction in which the insolvency

[105] SI 2016/1024.

proceedings are taking place may be substantially different from that of England.

## Gaming and potential unenforceability

**6.159** This is not really a legal problem anymore. The recent case of *Nextia v Royal Bank of Scotland*[106] seems to have finally resolved the complexities of this area of law. The facts of the case were that Nextia purchased a five-year interest rate contract for differences to hedge the interest rate on floating rate loans it had taken out. The loans however had a shorter maturity date than the contract for differences. When the loans required renewing the bank insisted on a higher rate of interest even though the market level for interest rates had fallen. As well as paying more for their loans this also had the effect of causing Nextia to lose out on the contract for differences which protected them if interest rates went up, and market rates were now going down. In the Court of Appeal, Voss LJ determined that:

> 'The fact that a contract for differences of the kind that is in issue in this case would have been regarded as a wagering contract at common law with all of the consequences that might flow from that must ... have been superseded by the modern legislation and in particular by ss 10 and 335 of the Gambling Act 2005.'[107]

**6.160** Section 10(1) of the Gambling Act 2005 states that betting does not include contracts for regulate activities under the Financial Services and Markets Act 2000. Section 335(1) of the Gambling Act 2005 states that: 'The fact that a contract relates to gambling shall not prevent its enforcement.' Added to this, s 412 (2) of the Financial Services and Markets Act 2000 states that:

> 'no contract will be void or unenforceable under the gaming laws provided:
>
> '(a) it is entered into by either or each party by way of business;
>
> '(b) the entering into or performance of it by either party constitutes an activity of a specified kind or one which falls within a specified class of activity; and
>
> '(c) it relates to an investment of a specified kind or one which falls within a specified class of investment.'

**6.161** The first element is that at least one of the parties must be entering into the agreement 'by way of business'. This was given a wide meaning in a case which determined the point in relation to the statutory term now replicated in s 412, *Morgan Grenfell & Co Ltd v*

---

106 [2014] EWCA Civ 740.

107 At para 22.

*Welwyn Hatfield District Council*[108] where Hobhouse J said that it was only necessary for one of the parties to the contract to be entering into it for business purposes to avoid falling foul of the gaming laws. He went on to say that 'business' in this context meant a transaction that was not personal or casual. Furthermore, the burden of proof was on the party seeking to have the contract set aside.

**6.162** The next question is whether the 'entering into or performance' of the agreement falls within a 'specified class of activity' and is a 'specified class of investment'. These are defined by The Financial Services Markets Act 2000 (Regulated Activities) Order 2001.[109] In effect they represent the entire range of investments and activities that are regulated under the post-2001 financial services regime. Thus, the wide effect of s 412 should stop the gaming laws representing a threat to the enforceability of any specified investment including all derivatives.

[108] [1995] 1 All ER 1.
[109] SI 2001/544, Pts II and III as heavily amended by subsequent statutory instruments.

# Chapter 7 Performance Bonds, Contract Guarantees and Standby Letters of Credit

## Introduction

**7.1** Performance bonds, contract guarantees and standby letters of credit are encountered primarily in international supply or construction contracts. They are used in construction contracts to ensure the financial standing of a contractor and his ability to fulfil an obligation into which he has entered. They are also commonly used in international contracts of sale where the buyer wishes to insure against the seller being unable to supply the goods sold, or where the seller wishes to insure against the failure of the buyer to pay the purchase price or meet his other obligations under the contract of sale. In more recent times they have also been used in securitisation structures (see **Chapter 5**) where a bank provides credit support for the scheme by a letter of credit being provided to the special purpose vehicle.

**7.2** The documents which are used to guarantee the obligations outlined above are described by a variety of names and there is little uniformity in the use of terms. The distinction between a contract guarantee and a contract bond would seem to be one of words and/or form rather than of substance, and for the purpose of this chapter the words guarantee and bond will be used synonymously.

**7.3** As a general rule bonds or guarantees are used by English bankers, whereas the standby letter of credit was originally a product of banking practice in the US. This chapter will initially examine the bond or guarantee under English law and conclude with a brief discussion of the standby letter of credit.[1] Commercial letters of credit are normally used in the import/export trade and are thus outside the scope of this book. A reader wishing to examine this area should use a text on the law of international trade.[2]

---

1 For a general overview see J Chuah, *Law of International Trade: Cross-Border Commercial Transactions* 7th edn (Sweet & Maxwell, 2023), Ch 11; P Todd, *Bills of Lading and Bankers' Documentary Credits* 4th edn (Routledge, 2007); F M Ventris *Bankers' Documentary Credits* 3rd edn (LLP, 1998).

2 From the vantage point of legal theory such contracts are abstract payment undertakings. See R Goode, 'Abstract Payment Undertakings' in P Cane and J Stapelton (Eds), Essays for Patrick Atiyah (Clarendon Press, 1991), p 209 and D Horowitz, *Letters of Credit and Demand Guarantees: Defences to Payment* (Oxford University Press, 2010), pp 1–3.

**7.4** The function of such arrangements is to compensate the beneficiary, nothing more. Thus, in *Cargill International SA v Bangladesh Sugar and Food Industries Corp*[3] it was held that a buyer who had made a claim following the seller's breach of contract must repay the seller as the buyer had suffered no loss requiring compensation. It is also an implied term of a performance bond that the beneficiary will account to an applicant for the amount by which a payment exceeds his true loss.[4] If the claim was made in good faith then the underlying contract will not have been broken. Effectively, the overpayment is treated as having been made by the issuer on behalf of the applicant.[5]

## The bonds or guarantees which may be given under English law

**7.5** There are a number of different bonds or guarantees which a bank's customer may be called upon to provide in favour of his overseas buyer or seller. The principal ones are bid or tender bonds, performance bonds, advance payment bonds and retention money bonds.[2] Each of these may be given in either first demand or conditional form.

### Bid or tender bonds

**7.6** Bid or tender bonds will be given in support of a customer's tender for a particular contract, as assurance of the customer's intention to sign the contract and comply with the terms of such contract in the event of his tender being accepted. If the tender is accepted and the customer fails to proceed as planned, the party to whom the bond has been advanced – the beneficiary – will simply make demand under the terms of the bond. The purpose of such a bond is to compensate the beneficiary for the additional costs he may bare in re-awarding the contract to another party in the event of the tendering party's default. These costs may be significant in circumstances where the beneficiary is forced to publish new tender conditions and commence the tender process afresh. Depending on the circumstances, a bid bond may be issued for a fixed sum of money or a fixed percentage of the submitted tender.

**7.7** Once the tender has been accepted, and assuming that the customer is willing to proceed, it will normally be necessary to replace the bid or tender bond with a suitable performance bond. Some bid bonds, however, are drafted in such a way that they automatically become performance bonds once the bid is accepted. If the customer

---

3 [1998] 1 WLR 461.

4 *Tradigrain SA v State Trading Corporation of India* [2005] EWHV (Comm) 2206.

5 See also *Cargill International SA v Bangladesh Sugar & Food Industries Corp* [1996] 2 Lloyd's Rep 524; *Comdel Commodities Ltd v Siporex Trade SA* [1997] 1 Lloyd's Rep 424; and *TTI Team Telecom International Ltd v Hutchinson 3G UK Ltd* [2003] EWHC 762, [2003] 1 All ER (Comm) 914.

fails to furnish an appropriate performance bond within the requisite time the beneficiary will be at liberty to cancel the contract and call on the bid or tender bond originally given. The bid bond should be returned once the contract has been signed and the appropriate performance bond issued and in addition, all bid bonds covering the unsuccessful bids should be returned to the appropriate parties.

**7.8** A common problem with bid or tender bonds is that they are often unilaterally extended. Such bonds tend to be issued for a period of 90 days in the first instance, but, especially in construction contracts, the overseas employer is hardly ever ready to award the contract after 90 days and accordingly seeks to have the bond extended. Further extensions are often necessary with major contracts and in many cases the employer is simply stalling for time until he secures the best possible deal for himself. Negotiations often proceed for many months, and this may well have serious cost implications for the bidder. For example, the effect of inflation in some countries during lengthy negotiations may make the final contract price commercially unattractive, as may currency exchange movements. Whenever possible, the bidder should negotiate suitable conditional wording within the terms of the bond to give some degree of protection against these problems.

### Performance bonds

**7.9** Performance bonds are the most common instruments issued and are given by a bank in support of a customer's obligation to fulfil a specified contractual commitment. In many situations, the overseas party will be uncertain whether, for example, the seller will be able to supply the goods sold, or to satisfy his other obligations under the contract. In such a case the performance bond will, especially when issued in first demand form, safeguard the buyer's position. Should the seller fail to meet his obligations, the buyer will simply make demand on the bond under whatever terms have been agreed between the parties.

**7.10** Performance bonds are normally required within a few weeks of the contract being awarded, although in some cases, particularly in negotiated contracts, the bond may be required at the moment the contract is executed. In the event of the bond being required before the contract is signed, the issuing bank should qualify its commitment in order that it will only become effective once the underlying contract has been executed.

**7.11** A common problem with performance bonds is that they are often issued for 10% of the full contract price and there is rarely any provision made within the terms to reduce liability under the bond in relation to the progress of work under the contract. This is because the overseas employer will generally view the bond as covering the complete contract and therefore the contractor will be at risk until total performance has been rendered. Experience has shown that unscrupulous beneficiaries are quite prepared to make demand on such bonds even though the underlying contract has been virtually completed. Whenever possible, the contractor should seek to protect himself by including suitable wording within the terms of the bond, whereby his liability is reduced in accordance with work carried out on the underlying contract. It is essential in such cases to provide for some independent party, for example, a building surveyor, who will conclusively certify the amount of work which has been carried out. The independent third party will play an important role in cases of dispute which frequently arise between the parties to the underlying contract.

**7.12** One case saw a party unsuccessfully attempt to get a court to treat a performance bond as a guarantee. In *Caterpillar Motoren GmbH & Co KG v Mutual Benefits Assurance Co*[6] a German company entered into contracts to deliver two power stations to Liberia and also entered into two subcontracts with ICE to provide construction services at the two relevant sites. Each of these subcontracts required ICE to enter into performance bonds and advance payment bonds in favour of Caterpillar to protect them in the event of ICE's non-performance. These bonds were issued by Mutual Benefits Assurance. When a dispute later arose Caterpillar claimed it was ending the contract and asked ICE to return the advance payments and further money as compensation. Caterpillar then claimed against Mutual Benefits against the bonds and they refused to pay, claiming that the arrangements were guarantees which could only be claimed against in the event of an arbitration award under the terms of the subcontracts. The question then arose as to the precise status of the bonds/guarantees. Teare J stated that the correct approach was to apply the normal terms of construction in the context of the knowledge the contracting parties would have at the time they entered into the contract. That being the case the documents were on demand bonds.

**7.13** Importantly, 'Paget's presumption', although considered, was rejected in this case. This is the argument set out in *Paget's Law of Banking*[7] and applied by Longmore LJ in *Wuhan Gouyu Logistics Group Ltd & anr v Emporiki Bank of Greece SA*[8] that:

> 'Where an instrument (i) relates to an underlying transaction between the parties in different jurisdictions, (ii) is issued by a bank, (iii) contains an undertaking to pay 'on demand' (with or without the words 'first' and/or 'written') and (iv) does not contain clauses excluding or limiting the defences available to a guarantor, it will almost always be construed as a demand guarantee.'[9]

6 [2015] EWHC 2304 (Comm).
7 11th edn (Butterworths, 1996), p xx.
8 [2012] EWCA Civ 1629.
9 Interestingly in this case the Mutual Benefits Assurance Co was not registered as a bank, but this was not treated as a relevant issue by the court, suggesting that 'Paget's presumption' may be treated more widely by the courts than its drafting suggests.

Critically he had added everything must in the end depend on the words actually used by the parties.'[10]

**7.14** The normal response when a party that has provided the other with the benefit of a performance bond then becoming insolvent is to trigger the bond. In *Ziggurat (Claremont Place) LLP v HCC International Insurance Co Plc*[11] the contractor who had been hired by Ziggurat to build a block of flats had provided such a bond. They later became insolvent leaving a large payment owing to Ziggurat to cover them hiring another party to complete the building work. The performance bond was thus triggered, and it made no difference that Ziggurat had served notice that they would have to hire others two days before the insolvency occurred because the contractors had already stopped work on the project. The debt was a consequence of the insolvency.

## Advance payment bonds

**7.15** Advance payment bonds are issued in circumstances where the overseas buyer makes advance payments to the seller of a given percentage (anything between 10% and 20%) of the full contract value. They are particularly common in construction contracts where an employer advances money to the contractor to enable him to commence work, order equipment and materials, engage personnel and subcontractors, begin drawings, etc.

**7.16** The taking of the bond will safeguard the position of the buyer/employer, enabling him to obtain repayment of the sum advanced in the event that the seller/contractor fails to carry out his obligations in the underlying contract. The bond so issued may provide for the liability of the issuing bank to be reduced, usually pro rata, in accordance with performance by the seller/contractor, and it is common in such a situation to insist on progress certificates, which not only give evidence that proper use is being made of the advance payment, but also indicate the work which has been carried out.

## Retention money bonds

**7.17** Retention money bonds are given in support of contracts which call for a percentage of each payment to be withheld until the contract has been completed and accepted by the overseas buyer/employer. The bond will enable the seller/contractor to receive the total amount of each 'work in progress' payment made by the buyer/employer, thus improving his cash flow position. The bond will obviously protect the

---

[10] At 25.
[11] [2017] EWHC 3286 (TCC)

overseas beneficiary, who will simply make demand should the seller/contractor fail to meet his contractual commitments.

**7.18** Retention money bonds are normally issued for either the full amount of expected retentions or a fixed percentage of the contract value. In either case the bank's actual liability should be limited to the progress payments actually released by the overseas buyer/employer.

### First demand or conditional?

**7.19** Bonds or guarantees can be given in either first demand or conditional form and it will be necessary to examine the precise wording in order to determine the nature of the commitment which is being made by the issuing bank to the overseas beneficiary. There is a presumption against a guarantee being a first demand guarantee unless it is a banking instrument.[12]

**7.20** If the bond is given in first demand form (known to many bankers as the 'suicide form') the obligation to make payment under its terms arises on first demand without proof or conditions. The advantage of such a bond is obvious, since it can be called on by the beneficiary without proof of loss caused by breach of the underlying contract, or any other form of breach.

**7.21** The documentation evidencing such bonds is usually unambiguous. For example, in the case of *Edward Owen Engineering Ltd v Barclays Bank International*[13] the relevant clause in the bond simply read, '... payable on demand without proof or conditions'. Lord Denning said that such a bond must be honoured, 'according to its terms ... The bank must pay ... on demand ... without proof or conditions. The only exception is where there is a clear fraud of which the bank has notice'. This last point is discussed later in the chapter.

**7.22** The exact wording used in the bond will, therefore, be crucial in determining exactly when a bank has to pay and also to determine whether it is a demand bond or guarantee. Thus, in *Trafalgar House Construction (Regions) Ltd v General Surety and Guarantee Co Ltd*[14] a performance bond was put in place to cover any losses resulting from a subcontractor's completion of a leisure complex. It stated specifically that 'on default by the Subcontractor the Surety shall satisfy and discharge the damages sustained'. The subcontractor became insolvent and the claimants then had to complete the contract. When they claimed on the bond the issue arose as to whether it amounted to a demand guarantee or a common law guarantee. If it amounted to a demand guarantee then the claimant could simply demand the money.

---

12 *Marubeni Hong Kong & South China Ltd v Mongolian Government* [2005] EWCA Civ 395, [2005] 1 WLR 2497.

13 [1978] QB 159.

14 [1995] 3 All ER 737.

If it was a common law guarantee actual proof of loss would have to be provided. The court held it was the latter, the key factor being the reference to 'damages sustained'.[15] For a bank, or a law firm acting for a bank, it is crucial to avoid the danger of legal proceedings involving the bank occurring prior to payment arising as a result of the wording, leaving it open for the court to interpret it as a common law guarantee. If it is a demand guarantee, then the bank can pay and leave any legal disputes to the two parties involved in the underlying contract.[16]

**7.23** In the event of litigation, the courts examine the content of the clauses rather than the titles or labels used in the contract. In *Vossloh Aktiengesellschaft v Alpha Trains (UK) Ltd*,[17] Vossloh (VA), had a subsidiary which manufactured railway engines and sold them to Alpha. VA agreed to provide a parent company guarantee/ bond to Alpha guaranteeing the performance of their subsidiary and indemnifying Alpha against loss resulting from default. Later Alpha complained that the trains provided were defective and demanded compensation under the guarantee equal to the cost of repairing the engines and compensating their own customers. Alpha claimed the guarantee/ bond was an on demand bond whereas VA argued that it was a conditional bond requiring proof of breach of contract. The court determined that on the wording of the guarantee it was a conditional bond and default had to be proved prior to a claim being made.[18]

**7.24** Thus, when drafting bonds it is wise to keep them as clear and simple as possible and to pay attention to the accuracy of any detail in the wording. Any minor element could potentially defeat a claim. In *Ermis Skai Radio and Television v Banque Indosuez Europe SRL*[19] a claim was made under a bond referring to a contract signed on 13 September 1995. The bond stated that payment was to be made under a contract to be concluded after issuing the bond on 14 September 1995. The inaccuracy and inconsistency defeated the claim. The court does not have the capacity to amend or import terms and can only enforce the terms as drafted, except in very limited circumstances which are discussed below.[20]

**7.25** In the case of a conditional bond or guarantee the obligation to make payment will be conditional upon the party to whom the bond is

---

15 See also *Frans Maas v Habib Bank* [2001] Lloyd's Rep Bank 14.

16 *TTI Team Telecom International Ltd v Hutchinson 3G UK Ltd* (23 January 2003, unreported).

17 [2010] EWHC 2443 (Ch).

18 In the course of their analysis the court referred, inter alia, to *Marubeni Hong Kong v the Government of Mongolia* [2005] EWCA Civ 395 which said that performance bonds were specialised legal instruments normally found in the banking industry, and that cases based on banking may not provide useful guidance in cases outside the banking system.

19 26 February 1997 (unreported).

20 *Odebrecht Oil & Gas Services Ltd v North Sea Production Ltd* [1999] 2 All ER (Comm) 405; *State Trading Corporation of India v E D & F Man (Sugar) Ltd* (22 July 1981, unreported); and *Uzinterimpex J S C v Standard Bank* [2008] EWCA Civ 819.

issued (the beneficiary), proving default by the party who is to perform the subject matter of the bond (the seller/contractor).

**7.26** First demand bonds are normally provided by banks on behalf of their customers, whereas insurance companies were originally the most important source of conditional bonds. Such companies are generally unwilling to issue first demand bonds, believing them to be commercially unsafe. The banks, on the other hand, traditionally preferred first demand commitments which enable the bank to stand clear of any contractual dispute which may arise between the parties to the underlying contract. However, banks also issue conditional bonds.

## Conditional bonds

**7.27** Conditional bonds afford considerable protection to the seller/contractor, as payment under its terms will normally be conditional upon the beneficiary proving:

(a) an unremedied breach of contract by the seller/contractor; and

(b) loss caused by such breach.

**7.28** Unlike the position in first demand bonds, it will be necessary for the bank issuing the conditional bond to become involved in the underlying contract in order to be satisfied that the conditions of payment have been met. This poses a number of significant problems for the bank, and in order to safeguard its position the bank will normally require appropriate provisions to be drafted within the bond documentation, relieving the bank of any need to involve itself in any contractual dispute between buyer and seller.

**7.29** The provisions commonly adopted require documentary evidence of breach before the payment obligation can be triggered. Bonds containing such provision cannot be described as truly conditional, nor first demand, and they will be considered in detail later in this chapter.

**7.30** The International Chamber of Commerce (ICC) publish the Uniform Rules for Contract Guarantees which provide a set of internationally acceptable rules which can be incorporated into performance bonds and letters of credit by cross reference. The rules seek to secure a uniformity of practice between the parties and endeavour to balance their respective interests without losing sight of the commercial purpose which underpins these instruments. The most significant areas covered by the rules include the definition of terms commonly used in bonds or guarantees, the liability of the guarantor to the beneficiary, the latest dates for claims under bonds, the documentation required in support of claims, the termination date of the instrument, and the settlement of disputes and arbitration procedures.

**7.31** However, the usefulness of the ICC rules is limited. For example, they are not expected to prevail over any foreign law which prescribes the text of any given bond or which stipulates the time period on which a claim can be made. The ICC also provides a code of practice to deal specifically with the problems arising from first demand bonds or guarantees. It does provide a useful starting point when bonds are being negotiated, and it is common for them to be drafted on the basis that 'the ICC terms apply except insofar as they are contradicted by the terms herein'.

## The documentary bond

**7.32** The party who originally requested the issue of the bond (the seller/contractor) has no protection against unilateral, unfair and/or capricious demand by the beneficiary when the bond is issued in first demand form. This has led to financial catastrophe for many contractors over the years, and in order to mitigate against the harsher implications of first demand bonds it is common to see protective clauses drafted within the terms of the documentation affording a degree of protection against an unscrupulous beneficiary.

**7.33** The first demand bond can be mitigated in a number of ways by linking the bond to performance of the underlying contract. Even the most absolute undertaking inevitably contains some reference to the underlying contract, even though it may only be a reference to the contract number. However, bankers who are prepared to mitigate must do so with caution lest they find themselves embroiled in any ensuing dispute which arises between their customer (the contractor) and the beneficiary with regard to the underlying contract. One way in which the contractor may attempt to soften a first demand bond is by incorporating a clause requiring documentary proof of the contractor's default before payment can be made to the beneficiary. Arbitral awards and surveyors' reports are examples of documents which may be required in such cases. Whenever such a clause is included, the bank must ensure that all parties will be bound by the documentary evidence. In other words, the findings of the surveyor or arbitrator must be conclusive and not subject to appeal, otherwise the bank will be placed in the invidious position of not knowing whether to pay when the beneficiary produces the documentary evidence required.

**7.34** As Goode pointed out,[21] bonds which are triggered solely by presentation of one or more documents to the issuing bank are in fact unconditional undertakings, because proof of default is not a condition of the bank's duty to pay, which must be fulfilled as soon as the stipulated documents are presented. The documentary requirement clearly prevents the bond from being triggered by a simple demand and, therefore, affords a considerable degree of protection for the contractor,

---

[21] Originally at H Lloyd (ed), *The Liability of Contractors*, (Longman, 1986), p 99.

who cannot complain when the bank makes payment following an independent report that the contractor is in default of the underlying contract. The documentary requirement will also enable the bank to stand clear of the underlying contract, providing, as we have already seen, that the document presented is deemed to be conclusive proof of default by the contractor.

**7.35** It would appear that such bonds are a half-way house, since they cannot be classified as 'first demand', nor are they truly 'conditional'. Perhaps it is more useful to classify bonds as either 'documentary', ie, triggered solely by the presentation of documents, or 'non-documentary', ie, dependent upon proof of actual default.

**7.36** Even in circumstances where no documentary evidence is required, it is common for the issuing bank to insist upon the beneficiary making a formal statement within his demand, that the contractor has breached some term of the underlying contract. It has been suggested by commentators in some jurisdictions that such an 'effective clause' entitles the bank, in cases of doubt, to request further information. This is unlikely to be the position under English law, provided that the beneficiary makes his demand on the terms provided for within the bond. The issuing bank may, of course, seek clarification where compliance has not been satisfied by the beneficiary.

**7.37** The legal position of banks issuing first demand bonds on behalf of their customers is that when issuing a first demand bond on behalf of its customer to an overseas beneficiary, the bank enters into an absolute undertaking, and must meet its obligations under the bond, even if its customer objects and contends that the beneficiary's demand is unjustified. The bank will not be concerned with the relations between its customer and the beneficiary, nor whether its customer is in default of contractual commitments. This is because under English law the first demand bond is a primary obligation on the part of the bank, comparable to an indemnity rather than to a true guarantee. A truly conditional bond, however, which requires proof of default in the underlying contract, will be a secondary obligation. This distinction is of the utmost importance, since in the case of a secondary obligation the bank will be under no liability at all in the event that the principal obligation does not come into being or if it has already been discharged. In the case of a primary obligation the bank could be liable, notwithstanding that the underlying contract never comes into being or is null and void.

**7.38** It will also be necessary for the sum of money being claimed to be 'ascertained and certain' under a conditional bond as well as any specific criteria required by the contract being met: *Yuanda (UK) Co Ltd v Multiplex Construction (Europe) Ltd*.[22] Merely making a statement to that effect is insufficient.

---

22 [2020] EWHC 468 (TCC)

## Remedies

**7.39** Normally any remedy for non-performance will be that of damages equal to the loss. An unusual case in this regard was that of *Simic v New South Wales Land and Housing Corporation*[23] in the Australian High Court.[24] Here two unconditional performance bonds were arranged with a bank by a constructor in favour of the party employing them, the New South Wales Land and Housing Corporation. However, by error the beneficiary of the bonds were referred to therein as 'the New South Wales Land & Housing Department Trading as Housing NSW', a non-existent entity. In due course they made a demand on the bonds but the bank refused to pay, arguing that they were not the party named on the bonds. The Court held that the autonomous nature of such bonds means that the bank must pay against documents and not concern themselves with the underlying contract and the parties. However, in this case they were right to refuse to pay. The Court went on to say that rectification could be used in this case with the name of the beneficiary of the bond being corrected. Once so corrected they could then claim on the bond.

**7.40** Another possibility is that specific performance could be appropriate. In *Liberty Mercian Ltd v Cuddy Civil Engineering Ltd and Cuddy Demolition and Dismantling Ltd,*[25] the second of two cases between these parties, Liberty entered into a contract with Cuddy Civil Engineering (CCE), but as they were a dormant company the work was carried out by Cuddy Demolition and Dismantling (CDD). It had been agreed between Liberty and CCE that a performance bond would be provided and it was accepted in evidence that the terms of this had been agreed between the parties. However, this was never put into effect and when Liberty Mercian wished to claim there was no bond in existence for them to claim against. In the resulting proceedings against both CCE and CDD it was determined that as CCE were a dormant company the normal approach of awarding damages would have been worthless as CCE had no assets. The Court was also influenced by the fact that as CCE had contracted but allowed CDD to carry out the contract, and as CDD had been financing the litigation in this case, there was clearly a financial relationship between the two parties. As a result CDD were required to provide CCE with the finance to arrange the performance bond that had been agreed and that Liberty Mercian could then claim against it.[26]

---

23 [2016] HCA 47.

24 Australia's highest court.

25 [2013] EWHL 2688 (TCC).

26 The Court also made a similar order for specific performance against CCE and CDD with regard to collateral warranties from a sub-contractor, Quantum GB Ltd in favour of Liberty, but this is not immediately relevant to performance bonds.

## Defences

**7.41** The international business community is always concerned about abusive calls on guarantees by overseas beneficiaries. This abuse has been particularly prevalent in the case of first demand bonds, and injunctions are regularly sought in the English courts to prevent the banks from making payment, when the demand is deemed unjustified. Banks, however, have long been aware that timid submission in the face of such an injunction will seriously devalue their own international paper. Bankers place their international reputation on the line when giving first demand bonds, and it has become a basic proposition in international trade that nothing, or very little should come between a bank and its obligation to make payment when demand is made. The English judiciary have taken a harsh approach to the enforcement of these instruments, and it is now well settled that the only exception to the general rule, that banks must honour first demand bonds 'without proof or condition,' is in cases where the bond is called on fraudulently, and the bank has knowledge of such fraud. The only other cases where a claim has been refused are where the demand is a forgery, is made illegally, is invalid and in very limited circumstances where it is a nullity.[27]

### Fraud

**7.42** The basis of the fraud defence is rooted in the well known US decision in *Sztejn v J Henry Schroder Banking Corp*[28] which was later followed in England by the House of Lords in *United City Merchants (Investments) Ltd v Royal Bank of Canada*[29] and more recently in *Power Projects Sanayi Insaat Ticaret Ltd Sirketi v Star Assurance Co Ltd.*[30] The essential point of these cases was that the autonomy principle was upheld.[31] In the *United City Merchants* case an overseas buyer arranged for a letter of credit to be issued in favour of the seller in London. This was to be paid against a full set of bills of lading that had to evidence that the goods had been shipped on or before 15 December 1976. The goods were loaded one day after that, but the bills were filled in with 15 December as the loading date. When the sellers, who had received the bills in return for payment, presented them the confirming bank they refused to pay because they had evidence that the goods had not be loaded by the date on the bill. The House of Lords determined that:

27 Horowitz goes further in *Letters of Credit and Demand Guarantees: Defences to Payment* (Oxford University Press, 2010) where she argues at Ch 3 that nullity is also a defence. However, whilst she argues a convincing case the relevant law does not clearly offer this.

28 31 NYS 2d 631 (1941).

29 [1983] 1 AC 168 (HL).

30 [2024] EWHC 2798 (Comm).

31 Ie, the letter of credit should be looked at autonomously from the underlying contract between the seller and the buyer.

> 'The whole commercial purpose for which the confirmed irrevocable documentary credits has been developed ... is to give the seller an assured right to be paid ... that does not permit of any dispute with the buyer as to the performance of the contract of sale being used as a ground for non-payment .... To this ... there is one established exception, that is where the seller, for the purpose of drawing on the credit, fraudulently presents to the confirming bank documents that contain, expressly or by implication, material representations of fact that to his knowledge are untrue.'[32]

However, the sellers in this case were not the cause of the fraud and they had honestly presented the bills believing them to be valid. They were thus able to succeed but in the process of the case the court had clearly accepted that where letters of credit are concerned the old maxim that 'fraud unravels all' can apply.

**7.43** Fraud is extremely difficult to establish under English law and it is worth considering the attitude of the English courts where fraud has been at issue. A key case to consider this with regard to first demand bonds was *RD Harbottle (Mercantile) Ltd v National Westminster Bank Ltd.*[33] The facts of this case were that the claimants had entered into three contracts of sale with Egyptian buyers. Each contract required the claimants to provide performance bonds, equal to 5 per cent, of the full contract price, in favour of the Egyptian buyers. The first demand type performance bonds were issued by an Egyptian bank, following the buyers' insistence that they be issued locally, and were supported by a counter indemnity issued by Harbottle's own bank, the National Westminster Bank. The claimants sought an injunction restraining the National Westminster Bank from making any payment under the terms of the counter indemnity, alleging that the demands made by the buyers were fraudulent and without justification. The claimants also claimed that the buyers had not performed their obligations under the contracts, as they had failed to open the necessary letters of credit for payment of the purchase price. The case came before Kerr J in the High Court, when the National Westminster Bank applied for the injunction to be set aside on the grounds that the bank had no option but to pay on demand. In his judgment, Kerr J stated that the courts will rarely interfere with such irrevocable obligations undertaken by banks and will not be concerned with disputes relating to the underlying contract of sale. This effectively ruled out as irrelevant the claimant's contention that the buyers had failed to open the necessary letters of credit. That, in other words, did not constitute fraud sufficient for any exception to be made. The judge drew an analogy with cases dealing with confirmed letters of credit,

---

32 *United City Merchants (Investments) Ltd v Royal Bank of Canada* (above n 29) at 182 following.

33 [1978] QB 146, [1977] 2 All ER 862.

suggesting that such cases applied equally to first demand performance bonds. The injunctions were consequently dismissed, thus permitting the bank to make payment under the counter indemnity. It was also made clear in the court's judgment that any claim by the seller for breach of the buyers' obligations on the underlying contract must be the subject of a separate action.

**7.44** Two Court of Appeal cases[34] quickly followed the *Harbottle* decision and both placed first demand bonds on a similar footing to irrevocable letters of credit, insofar as the position of the issuing bank is concerned. Lord Denning went even further by declaring them to be, 'virtually promissory notes payable on demand'.

**7.45** The second of these cases, *Edward Owen Engineering Ltd v Barclays Bank Ltd*[35] gave rise to the possibility that the fraud defence may be split. Lord Denning's judgment foresaw two possible problems: that the documents are forged or that the request for payment is fraudulent.[36] This also leads on to the interesting question: is a claim that has 'no honest belief' by the claimant the same as fraud?[37] Perhaps the simplest approach is to apply the fraud on the documents defence to letters of credit and that of 'no honest belief' to demand guarantees.[38] Unfortunately the cases have not been this straightforward.

**7.46** A later case which considered the question of fraud was *United Trading Corporation SA v Allied Arab Bank Ltd*[39] where the Court of Appeal held that interlocutory injunctions restraining a bank from honouring its obligations under the bond would only be granted where the only realistic inference to be drawn from the evidence is that the beneficiary called on the bond fraudulently, and the bank has actual knowledge of the fraud. The relevant date for establishing knowledge of fraud on the part of the bank is the date on which the bank makes payment. A bank could be liable in negligence if it complied with a demand which it knew to be fraudulent, but no liability would attach in cases falling short of 'actual knowledge.' A case where a demand was clearly fraudulent on the relevant date was that of *Kvaerner John Brown Ltd v Midland Bank plc.*[40] Here a performance guarantee

---

34 *Howe Richardson Scale Co Ltd v Polimex-Cecop and National Westminster Bank Ltd* [1978] Lloyd's Rep 161; *Edward Owen Engineering Ltd v Barclays Bank International Ltd* [1978] QB 159, [1978] 1 All ER 862.

35 [1978] QB 159.

36 Historically the law of forgery did include an intent to defraud but it is a distinct area of law from fraud, raising the possibility that forgery is a distinct defence if known to the paying bank.

37 *State Trading Corporation of India Ltd E D & F Man (Sugar) Ltd* [1981] Com LR 235 (CA); *United Trading Corporation SA and Murray Clayton Ltd v Allied Arab Bank Ltd* [1985] 2 Lloyd's Rep 554 (CA); and *Banque Saudi Fransi v Lear Seigler Services Ltd* [2007] 1 All ER (Comm) 67 (CA) can all be seen as supporting this approach.

38 See, eg, D Horowitz, *Letters of Credit and Demand Guarantees: Defemnces to Payment* (Oxford University Press, 2010), Ch 5, where this is discussed at length.

39 [1985] 2 Lloyd's Rep 554.

40 [1998] CLC 466.

was issued on terms that the beneficiary had to give 14 days' written notice of demand. When the demand was made it certified that the required notice had been given when it clearly had not been. The court determined that this was a fraudulent claim and issued an injunction debarring payment.[41]

**7.47** In *Banque Saudi Fransi v Lear Siegler Services Inc*[42] it was held that if a bank's customer wishes to stop a payment they must show that it is 'seriously arguable' on the material available that the only realistic inference was that the beneficiary could not honestly believe in the validity of the demand. To resist summary judgment in relation for a claim to return the funds in the case of a fraudulent claim the customer will face the 'high hurdle'[43] of proof in clearly demonstrating fraud by the beneficiary and that the bank knew of the fraud when they paid out.

**7.48** In *Montrod Ltd v Grundkotter Fleischvertreiber GmbH & Standard Chartered Bank plc*[44] the Court of Appeal held that an issuing or confirming bank must pay a letter of credit governed by UCP 500 where the documents that the beneficiary has presented under the credit were apparently conforming on their face and bona fide and presented by the beneficiary. It later transpired that the documents were a nullity on the basis of falsehood. The Court of Appeal stated that they would not extend the fraud exception to a situation where the beneficiary was unaware of the falsehood at the time of presentation.

**7.49** The judgment of Ackner LJ in the *United Trading* case crystallises the difficulty facing a party seeking to establish the fraud exception:

> '... The evidence of fraud must be clear, both as to the fact of fraud and as to the bank's knowledge. The mere assertion or allegation of fraud would not be sufficient. We would expect the court to require strong corroborative evidence of the allegation, usually in the form of contemporary documents, particularly those emanating from the buyer. In general, for the evidence of fraud to be clear, we would also expect the buyer to have been given the opportunity to answer the allegation and to have failed to provide any, or any adequate answer in circumstances where one could properly be expected.'

**7.50** Following the *United Trading* case it would now seem that the contractor, if he is to have any chance of success, would be well advised to institute proceedings against the beneficiary, thereby giving notice of the fraud allegation and providing an opportunity for the beneficiary to respond. However, this in itself will not be enough, and the contractor

---

41 See also *Tukiye IS Bankasi v Bank of China* (17 December 1997, unreported).

42 [2006] EWCA Civ 1130.

43 Arden LJ *ibid.*

44 [2002] 1 All ER (Comm) 257.

will also have to institute separate proceedings against the instructing bank in order to prevent payment from being made. A major problem presents itself here, since, as we have already seen, the instructing bank has no contractual relationship with the beneficiary, and in order to prevent the instructing bank from making payment to the issuing bank under their indemnity agreement, the contractor must adduce clear evidence that the issuing bank's claim upon the instructing bank is also fraudulent. In almost every conceivable case this will be impossible to prove. The contractor's only alternative would be to bring proceedings directly against the issuing bank. This would again be doomed to failure since, as has already been seen, no contractual relationship exists between these parties with regard to the guarantee itself and any attempt to bring an action in tort by claiming that the issuing bank owed the contractor some duty of care would undoubtedly fall on deaf ears in most foreign courts. The same situation arises should the contractor attempt to acquire an injunction preventing the beneficiary from claiming against the guarantee.[45] One possible step is that the claimant could apply for a freezing injunction preventing the claimant from parting company with the funds received under the bond pending the outcome of a case into the legal validity of the claim.

**7.51** Matters were taken further in *Balfour Beatty Civil Engineering Ltd v Technical & General Guarantee Co Ltd* [46] where the issue arose as to what the legal position would be if there was some evidence of fraud at the time the demand guarantee was called on but it only became clear at a later date. Waller LJ determined that there were three possible responses:

- if the evidence had become clear, no judgment could be given in favour of the beneficiary as the issuing bank would have a claim for the same sum;
- if the evidence was insufficient to enable summary judgment on the part of the issuing bank but was nonetheless very significant, then two possibilities emerge. Either judgment would be entered with a stay of execution, or it would not be until the counterclaim had been considered by the court; or
- if the evidence was less significant the beneficiary would be able to obtain judgment and the issuing bank would have to counterclaim or sue separately.

**7.52** Bankers should also be aware of the risk they run should they refuse to make payment once demand is made. It is an oft used saying that a banker's word is his bond, and a bank which is prepared to break its word will find few people prepared to accept its international paper.

---

45 *Czarnikow-Rionda Sugar Trading Inc v Standard Bank London Ltd* [1999] 1 All ER (Comm) 890.
46 [2000] 68 Con LR 108.

**7.53** The cases discussed above have rendered the fraud exception a very limited basis for obstructing payment. This must certainly be the case wherever a correspondent bank is used and those seeking bond support should be clearly informed of the potential risk they face. In order to prevent such difficulties arising, many banks will only advise their customer (the contractor) of the position after payment has been made. This will prevent him from bringing proceedings against the bank unless he becomes aware of a potential claim from an independent source. Insofar as English law is concerned the bank which adopts such an approach is safe, since there is no obligation to inform the customer either before or after payment has been made.

**7.54** The position would obviously be different if the bank had expressly agreed to inform its customer before making payment. This would place the bank in an invidious position since its customer, upon being informed by the bank, may take immediate steps to prevent payment from being made, whereas the primary obligation of the bank would be to make immediate payment under the terms of either its bond or counter indemnity. Consequently, the bank would be forced to resist any attempt by its customer to prevent payment. This is a position which few banks would wish to be left in.

**7.55** It is essential therefore that the customer seeking support in the form of a first demand bond should understand the obligations which arise upon its issue. To this end, the bank should make certain that the relevant information is given to its customer before issue. Well informed customers can have no cause for complaint should they insist upon bond support and ultimately find themselves paying a heavy price. The *United Trading* decision is also noteworthy for highlighting a problem which had previously troubled bankers for some time. In his judgment Ackner LJ said that a bank could arguably be liable in the tort of negligence if it complied with a demand by the beneficiary which it knew to be fraudulently made. It seems probable that in cases falling short of 'actual knowledge' the position of the paying bank should not be prejudiced in any way by the decision.

## Illegality of the underlying contract

**7.56** The courts will not enforce illegal transactions. In the case of conditional guarantees and demand guarantees this could arise through the illegality of the underlying contract. In Gr*oup Josi Re v Walbrook Insurance Co Ltd*[47] illegality in the underlying contract was held to amount to a defence. Unfortunately, matters are complicated by the judgment in *Mahonia Ltd v J P Morgan Chase Bank (No 1)*[48] and *Mahonia Ltd v West LB AG (No 2)*[49] which said that the factors that

[47] [1996] 1 WLR 1152.
[48] [2003] 2 Lloyd's Rep 911.
[49] [2004] All ER (D) (Aug).

should be considered in relation to illegality were the gravity of the offence and the degree of connection between the underlying contract and the payment instrument.[50] In practice it is only in conditional guarantees that illegality in the documents could realistically be an issue. It is unlikely to arise with demand guarantees. However, in practice there will be few instances where a conditional guarantee would be illegal in itself in English law. The issue is normally going to arise with regard to the underlying contract.

**7.57** First though, a key problem arising is that illegality is an elastic concept. It could be taken to mean contracts that are criminal,[51] contracts that may be carried out in a way that is illegal, eg, delivering cargo by an overloaded ship,[52] a lawful subject matter applied for an unlawful purpose,[53] a contract involving a minor criminal provision,[54] or a contract to carry out an act in breach of public policy.[55] The key question is, how many of these could lead to the successful raising of the illegality defence? There certainly needs to be a connection between the illegality and the contract and in this context a remote connection will not be sufficient. However, a loan knowingly made to repay a loan for an illegal purpose is unenforceable[56] which has an obvious parallel with letters of credit. In short if illegality is present the contract could well be void and a bank should refuse to involve itself with a related guarantee. In 2026, the UK Supreme Court determined that a letter of credit could not be enforced where the subject matter were leasing contracts that financed aircraft leasing that were illegal under sanctions laws, even though the contracts had been legal when entered into.[57]

**7.58** A guideline can be found in *Fisher v Bridges*[58] where it was stated:

> 'It is clear that the covenant was given for payment of the purchase money. It springs from, and is the creature of the illegal agreement; and, as the law would not enforce the original illegal contract, so neither will it allow the parties to enforce a security for the purchase money, which by the original bargain was tainted with illegality.'

---

50 Commentators have taken different views on how this should be interpreted, eg N Enonchong, 'The Autonomy Principle of Letters of Credit: an Illegality Exception?' [2006] 3(Aug) LMLCQ 404 and GT McLaughlan, 'Letters of Credit and Illegal Contracts: The Limits of the Independence Principle' (1989) 49 Ohio ST LJ 1197.

51 *Foster v Driscoll* [1929] 1 KB 470; *Regazzoni v K C Sethia Ltd* [1958] AC 301 (HL).

52 *St John Shipping Corporation v Joseph Rank Ltd* [1957] 1 QB 267.

53 *Langton v Hughes* (1813) 1 M & S 593.

54 *Sutton v Hutchinson* [2005] All ER (D) 127 (Nov) (CA).

55 *Pearce v Brookes* (1866) LR 1 EX 213.

56 *Spector v Agenda* [1973] Ch 30.

57 *Unicredit Bank GmbH, London branch v Constitution Aircraft Leasing (Ireland) 3 Ltd and another; Unicredit Bank GmbH, London branch v Celestial Aviation Services Ltd* [2026] UKSC 10 applying Russia (Sanctions) (EU Exit) Regulations 2019, SI 2019/855 in Chapter 2, Part 5, regulation 28(3)(c).

58 (1856) 3 E & B 642.

The same principle was accepted in the *Mahonia* cases mentioned above, though it transpired that there was no illegality in the underlying contracts in those cases.[59]

**7.59** Therefore, with the underlying contract, a bank involving itself in a letter of credit or demand guarantee should refuse to proceed if there is illegality in the underlying contract and if there is any doubt on the point, legal advice should be taken. Erring on the side of caution is the best step. As far as the guarantees are concerned the banks use their own standard wording largely based on ICC, and it is unlikely to prove an issue.

## Illegality of the bond or letter of credit

**7.60** The courts will not enforce illegal transactions. The likelihood of this happening with the bond or letter of credit itself is remote. As discussed above most transactions are carried out by reference to UCP 500 which provide an internationally agreed basis for operating. However, in very rare cases it could conceivably arise, for example because of a tightening in the law relating to the acceptability of interest payments in an Islamic state where the issuing bank is based. As far as English law is concerned this is a theoretical rather than a practical issue.

## Forgery

**7.61** It is debateable whether this is really an area distinct from that of fraudulent claim. However, were a claim to be submitted with a forged signature, and were the bank being asked for payment to become aware of this prior to making payment, they should not pay as a forged signature will render the document a nullity.[60] In the case of a documentary bond the contract between the issuing bank and the payor will require the presentation of certain documents. Knowledge of a forged signature on the part of the paying bank will mean they know that a valid presentation of such documents has not taken place.

**7.62** However, cases involving forged signatures have tended to involve banks that have paid out in good faith against forged signatures. In that situation the issuing bank is safe and can take the payment from the payor's account. The authority for this is the House of Lords decision in the House of Lords in *Gian Singh & Co Ltd v Banque de l'Indochine* where Lord Diplock said:

> 'The fact that a document presented by the beneficiary under a documentary credit, which otherwise conforms to the requirements of the credit, is in fact a forgery does not, of itself, prevent the issuing

---

[59] Another issue arising is that if the underlying contract is illegal the bank may need to consider making a suspicious transaction report to the National Crime Agency if the bank may potentially be handling the proceeds of crime by facilitating payment.

[60] Lord Diplock left this point open in *Gian Singh & Co Ltd v Banque de L'Indochine* [1974] 1 WLR 1234.

bank from recovering from its customer money paid under the credit. The duty of the issuing bank, which it may perform either by itself, or by its agent, the notifying bank, is to examine documents with reasonable care to ascertain that they appear on their face to be in accordance with the terms and conditions of the credit.'[61]

## Nullity

**7.63** One must be careful in referring to a general defence of nullity as such in English law.[62] For example in *Montrod v Grundkotter Fleischvertiebs GmbH*[63] the issuing bank paid out in response to the submission of a document provided to them by a third party on the reasonable assumption that the agent had Montrod's authority to act, which was not the case. It was held that the bank which paid out against the documents provided were acting within their contractual powers under the letter of credit and UCP 500 which was incorporated by cross reference, as there was no reason by them to believe that the documents tendered were either fraudulently presented or had forged signatures. The Court did not see there being a general defence of nullity which would assist the party whose funds had been paid out.

**7.64** However, a document could be so badly or incompletely drafted that it amounts to a nullity but from a realistic point of view banks are not going to issue such a paper except rarely and by error. A case which suggests that nullity may provide a slightly wider defence than this arose in Singapore in *Lambias (Importers and Exporters) Co Pte Ltd v Hong Kong and Shanghai Banking Corporation.*[64] Here the defendant bank had rejected documents tendered under a letter of credit which included a quality and weight inspection certificate required to be countersigned by a named individual. The Court held that the certificate contained discrepancies which entitled the bank to refuse the documents tendered and went on to find that the inspection certificate was in any event a nullity in that, not only did it fail to state the particulars of the goods and their quality and weight, but that, having been issued by the beneficiary instead of the applicant, it had been countersigned by an impostor.

Goh Phai Cheng JC observed:

> 'The law cannot condone actions which, although not amounting to fraud per se, are of such recklessness and haste that the documents produced as a result are clearly not in conformity with the requirements of the credit. The plaintiffs in the present case are not guilty of fraud, but they were unknowingly responsible for having aided in the perpetration of the fraud. In such a case

---

[61] The same principle appears in UCP 7.

[62] Hooley R. 'Fraud and Letters of Credit: Is There a Nullity Exception?' Cambridge Law Journal vol 6, No 2 (2002) p 279–281. See also Donnelly K 'Nothing for Nothing: a Nullity Exception for Letters of Credit?'. Journal of Business Law, 2008, 4, 316–343

[63] [2001] EWCA Civ 1954, [2002] 1 WLR 1975, [2002] 3 All ER 677.

[64] [1993] 2 SLR 751 at 765–766.

where the fraud was discovered even before all other documents were tendered, I think it is right and proper that the plaintiffs should not be permitted to claim under the letter of credit.'

## The relationships created by first demand bonds

**7.65** The legal relationships created by the issue of a first demand bond amount to three or four distinct contracts, depending upon whether a correspondent bank is used in the transaction. Overseas beneficiaries normally insist upon the bond being issued by a national bank based in their own country and, therefore, for the purpose of this discussion we shall consider the four-party scenario. The first contract is that between employer and employee in a construction contract, or buyer and seller in a sale of goods contract. This is the underlying contract pursuant to which the bond is issued. The second contract reflects the relationship between the employee and his own bank, the instructing bank. The employee will normally instruct his own bank to cause the correspondent bank to issue the first demand bond in favour of the beneficiary. The instructing bank, before effecting such instructions, will require a counter indemnity from the employee, the terms of which normally permit the bank to debit the employee's account for all claims received and paid to the correspondent. The third contract reflects the relationship between the instructing bank and the correspondent bank which ultimately issues the bond to the beneficiary. This relationship is frequently characterised as a counter guarantee or counter indemnity, given by the instructing bank in favour of the correspondent bank. The precise wording of the guarantee will be as crucial as that in the bond itself because of the knock-on effect which it has for both the instructing bank and the beneficiary. The fourth and final contract is the most fragile in the entire structure and relates to the bond itself which is issued by the correspondent bank to the beneficiary.

FIGURE 1: BOND ISSUED BY THE SELLER'S/CONTRACTOR'S OWN BAN

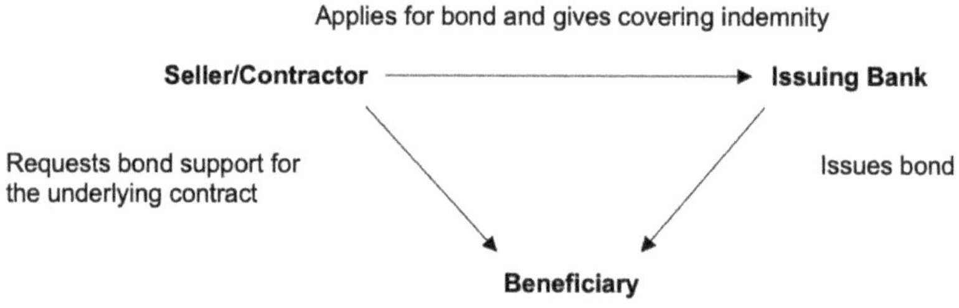


### Autonomy from the underlying transaction

**7.66** In *Sirius International Insurance Ltd v FAI General Insurance Ltd*[65] there was a subsidiary agreement between the applicant and the beneficiary. The banks were not parties to this transaction

[65] [2002] EWHC 1611, [2002] 2 All ER (Comm) 745.

which laid down conditions limiting the circumstances where the beneficiary could draw down the credit. The applicant attempted to rely on this agreement to prevent the beneficiary drawing down if this would infringe the subsidiary agreement. It was held that they could do so.

FIGURE 2: SITUATION CHANGES WHERE BOND IS ISSUED BY A CORRESPONDENT BANK

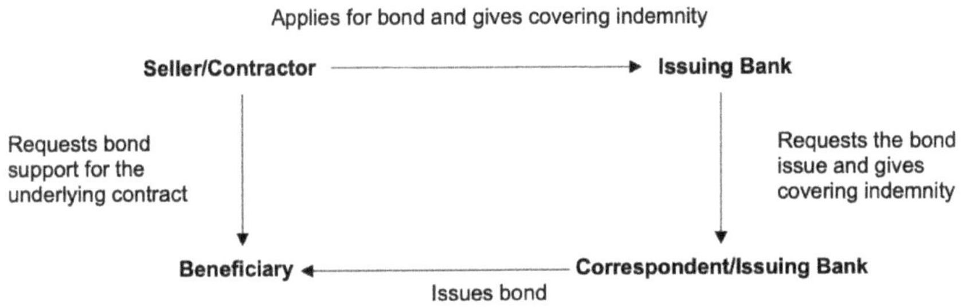


## The importance of private international law

**7.67** As in all international banking contracts, principles of private international law will play a crucial role in determining the rights and obligations of the various parties described in the above scenario. In order to highlight the importance of private international law only hypothetical jurisdictions need adding, for example, an English contractor/supplier instructs his own bank, which is based in London, to procure the issue of a first demand bond through a correspondent bank, based in a foreign state, in favour of a beneficiary in that state.

**7.68** Such a scenario will, of necessity, bring into play private international law principles should any dispute arise, and it is therefore surprising that choice of law and forum clauses are not always found in any of the four contracts outlined above. One reason for this may be due to the fact that the relevant documents are often nothing more than short letters or email attachments with few standard clauses. However, the significance of such clauses cannot be overemphasised, and if they are omitted or badly drafted a significant degree of uncertainty enters the picture.

**7.69** In determining the parties' obligations under a contract, English courts apply the proper law concept, under which the court will apply the law selected by the parties within the contract documentation, as the law governing their particular contract. Where no express choice is made, the courts will endeavour to find an implied choice and if there is none, they have come to accept that the proper law is that law with which the transaction has its closest and most real connection. (This is discussed in detail in **Chapter 9**).

**7.70** The proper law also appears to be the formula used by the courts in order to ascertain the law of first demand bonds. In the case of *Edward Owen Engineering Ltd v Barclays Bank International Ltd*,

Brown LJ stated that in the absence of express provision, the proper law of first demand bonds is that with which the transaction has its closest and most real connection. This approach has been favoured for some time in relation to letters of credit and it is hardly surprising that the courts should use identical criteria to ascertain the proper law for both instruments.

**7.71** If the proper law principle is applied to the four-party situation outlined above and it is assumed that no express or implied choice has been made in any of the contracts, the significance of such a clause, or lack of it, becomes readily apparent. The contract between the contractor/supplier and its own bank, the instructing bank, would be governed by English law, whereas the contract between the instructing bank and the issuing bank may be governed by either English or the law of another state, depending upon the significant contacts which that contract has with England and that state. The contract between the issuing bank and the beneficiary will obviously be governed by the overseas state's law, but the law governing the underlying contract will not be so easily identifiable.

**7.72** It is not inconceivable that of the four contracts outlined, three may be governed by different systems of law. Consequently, the parties may find themselves bound by terms quite different from those originally intended. The seriousness of such a situation can best be identified by considering a problem which regularly arises in practice.

**7.73** Each of the four contracts within the typical scenario outlined above should contain an expiration date on which the obligations of the various parties cease. It is not uncommon, however, to find the beneficiaries of on demand bonds insisting upon repeated extensions and threatening to make demand if such extensions are not granted. This has the effect of keeping the bond alive for many years and is further compounded by the fact that the laws of some countries do not recognise the expiration of the issuing banks' obligation until the beneficiary has surrendered the instrument or issued a declaration of release. Thus, even though the bond issued in our example may incorporate an expiry date, if both the contract between issuer and beneficiary, and that between instructing bank and issuing bank, are found to be governed by the overseas state's law, then the instructing bank may find itself obligated under its counter indemnity long after the supporting counter indemnity, which it took from the employee, has expired. The instructing bank should obviously try to avoid such problems by incorporating an English governing law clause within the terms of the counter indemnity which it gives to the issuing bank. A specific expiry date may afford little protection in the event of the indemnity being governed by an overseas state's law.

**7.74** Where the bond is actually issued by an English bank to an overseas beneficiary the problem remains the same and unless the bank takes appropriate precautions within the bond documentation it may find itself bound by completely inappropriate legal provisions.

**7.75** The terms of the bond should also incorporate a clause stipulating which courts will have jurisdiction to hear any dispute relating to the bond. The principal objective behind such a clause is to confer effective jurisdiction upon the desired courts by fulfilling all the necessary procedural requirements, thereby minimising the risk that the chosen forum might decline jurisdiction.

**7.76** Arbitration is an obvious alternative to litigation and has frequently been used in bond issues. Here again, however, it will be crucial to stipulate where arbitration will take place, and also that the arbitrator's findings will be binding on all parties. The bank which pays in accordance with an arbitral award will not want to be concerned about the prospect of an appeal being made by the losing party.

## Safeguarding the position of the issuing bank

### Obtaining counter indemnities

**7.77** The attitude of the English courts to first demand bonds clearly shows that in the absence of fraud, the issuing bank will be bound to make payment when demand is made by the beneficiary. Issuing banks should therefore obtain counter indemnities from either the instructing bank or the seller/ contractor, depending upon the circumstances. Where the bond is issued by a correspondent bank (see Figure 2 above), that bank will obtain an indemnity from the instructing bank which should cover all costs incurred as a result of the bond issuance. We have already seen how important it is to carefully word both the bond and counter indemnity to ensure that one does not expire before the other. The instructing bank will in turn obtain a counter indemnity from its own customer, the seller/contractor, the terms of which will normally permit the bank to debit its customer's account for all claims received and paid. See Figure 2 above.

### Syndication

**7.78** In recent years contractors have become involved in very large overseas contracts, often with foreign governments, which require the support of correspondingly large bonds. In many of these contracts individual banks have been unwilling to take the exposure on their own, preferring to syndicate the bond, thereby spreading the risk.

**7.79** The structure of the syndicated bond facility closely resembles a typical syndicated loan agreement, apart from the fact that it is usually built on a first demand bond, issued in favour of the employer/ beneficiary. See Figure 3 below.

## Two recourse obligations

**7.80** As we can see from Figure 3 below, the diagram is made up of two distinct recourse obligations under a syndicated bond facility. The first is between the issuing bank and the syndicate banks, (the participants) and this specifies the terms upon which the syndicate will severally reimburse the issuer for any loss it may suffer under the bond. The obligation of each participant will normally be pro rata its commitment under the syndicate facility.

**7.81** The reimbursement obligation of each participant may take the form of standby letters of credit issued by the participants to the issuer, rather than a simple clause in the facility agreement itself. Some bankers consider that standby letters of credit provide them with a greater degree of protection than would be the case under a contractual indemnity provision. This would not be the case under strict English legal principles. However, in a purely practical sense it may well be easier to obtain reimbursement when a standby letter of credit has been issued, particularly when the facility has become embroiled in a highly politicised environment.

## The recourse obligation imposed on the seller/contractor

**7.82** The second recourse obligation is that imposed upon the seller/contractor and may run either directly to the issuing bank or to the participants in reimbursement of payments they may have made to the issuer. The facility agreement commonly provides for the appointment of an agent bank which may collect payments made by the seller/contractor and apply them either to the issuing bank or the participants (pro rata), depending upon the terms of the agreement.

## Other provisions in the syndicated bond agreement

**7.83** The terms of the facility will also include many of the standard clauses found in a syndicated loan agreement, including representations and warranties given by the seller/contractor, covenants and events of default. The precise wording of these clauses will obviously depend upon the circumstances of each particular case and it will be vital to obtain the opinion of local counsel to ensure that they impose valid and binding obligations upon the seller/contractor.

**7.84** Documentation of syndicated bond issues is obviously a complex affair and will certainly add to the seller's/contractor's costs, probably making the proposed contract much less attractive. In addition, where the bond is required urgently, it may be impossible to arrange a syndicate quickly enough. Nevertheless, for banks wishing to spread the risk it is a most effective mechanism and may hold additional advantages for the seller/contractor whose name will be publicised to a large market, thereby broadening exposure to the most important financial institutions.

FIGURE 3: SYNDICATED ISSUE

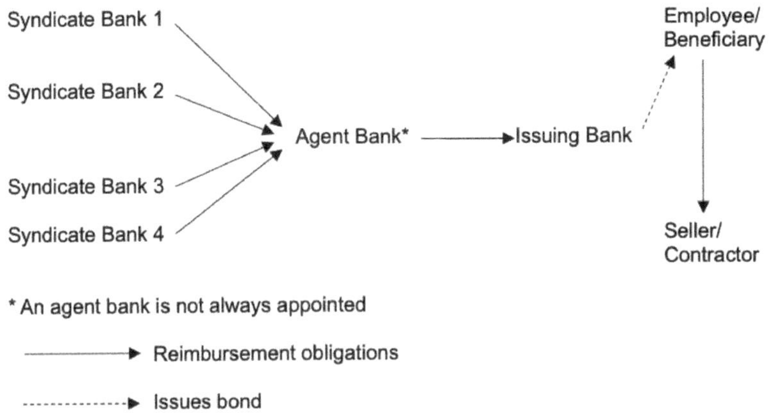


## Safeguarding the position of the seller/contractor

### Insurance support and the Export Credits Guarantee Department

*Private insurance*

**7.85** Insurance cover can be obtained by the seller/contractor from the private insurance market against the unreasonable or unjustified calling of first demand bonds. Such cover may protect the seller/contractor not only against unfair calling but also where he defaults on the underlying contract for specified political reasons beyond his control.

**7.86** Premium rates from the private market vary from country to country and from contract to contract, with higher rates in higher risk countries where inevitably cover will be most wanted. There can be little doubt that, once again, such cover will significantly add to the cost of the proposed contract.

*UK Export Finance (UKEF)*

**7.87** Additional support can be provided by UK Export Finance (UKEF) which operates a bond support scheme as well as providing for unfair calling of bonds. Support is given by means of an indemnity to the issuing bank[66] (see Figure 4 below) under which UKEF is unconditionally liable to reimburse the bank in full for sums called under the terms of the bond. Any payment made by UKEF becomes the subject of a separate claim against the seller/contractor under the related recourse agreement.

---

[66] Originally established in 1911, it is a department of the UK central government.

**7.88** Provision for unfair calling can be obtained from UKEF by means of an insurance policy fully covering any loss suffered by the seller/contractor, but in order to make a successful claim it must be shown that the seller/contractor was not in default on the underlying contract, or that failure was due to circumstances beyond his control.

**7.89** UKEF offers number of different types of policy designed to provide financial and insurance protection for those engaged in exports. The precise range of products available changes from time to time in line with perceived market need. The latest can be found at www.ukexportfinance.co.uk.[67]

### *Correspondent banks*

**7.90** Overseas buyers/employers often insist upon bond support being issued by a national bank based in their own country. The difficulties facing the seller/contractor in such a situation have already been highlighted, and it will be virtually impossible for him to prevent payment even where the demand is fraudulent. Bankers should, therefore, encourage their customers to negotiate with the beneficiary and attempt to persuade him to take the bond directly from the customer's own bank. UK banks have many branches based overseas and these may be used where an overseas beneficiary insists upon the bond being issued by a bank based in the local jurisdiction, and if this can be achieved, much of the additional cost, delay, and most important of all, risk will be avoided.

FIGURE 4: UKEF BOND SUPPORT SCHEMES

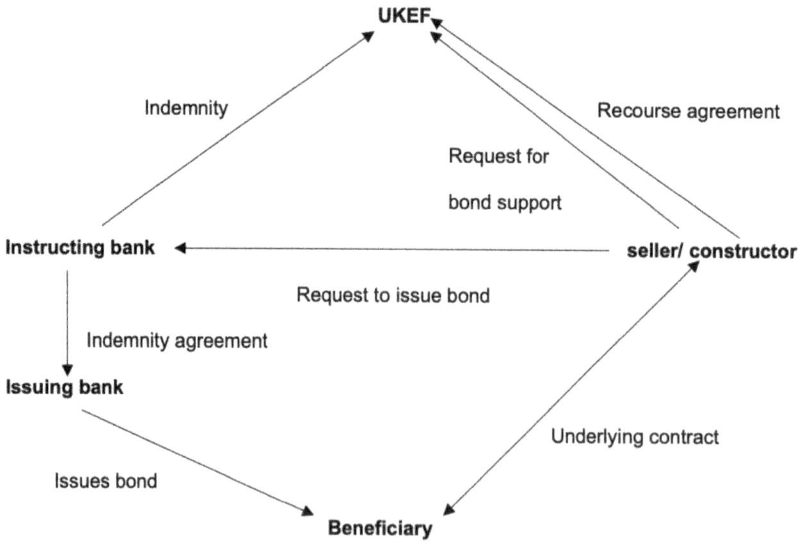


[67] For further details see www.gov.uk/government/organisations/uk-export-finance [Accessed 25 February 2026].

## Conclusions

**7.91** The requirement to provide bonds and standby facilities in support of contractual obligations will continue to be an important factor in international trade. These instruments enjoy enormous popularity with overseas buyers as well as bankers who are constantly refining the documentation used in order to satisfy market needs. Whether such instruments maintain this popularity will depend to a large extent upon the attitude of the courts, and in particular their willingness to enforce contractual undertakings according to their terms. This explains, to some extent, the harsh attitude which has been adopted by the English and courts to the fraud exception. If they had not done so the instruments would have lost their commercial efficacy.

**7.92** In practice, as seen above, the critical issue is the exact wording of the bond concerned and parties should take very precise care in determining their contents. Cases such as *Caterpillar Motoren GmbH & Co KG v Mutual Benefits Assurance Co,*[68] *Vossloh Aktiengesellschaft v Alpha Trains (UK) Ltd*[69] and *Simic v New South Wales Land and Housing Corporation*[70] all discussed above illustrate that it is vital to make sure the wording is precise and accurate in the context of the circumstances being covered. This is exacerbated by the ease with which a minor error can lead to a bond being unenforceable because of the very wide definition of fraud in this particular context.[71] Alternately, it can go to the heart of the legal status of the contract as in *Trafalgar House Construction (Regions) Ltd v General Surety and Guarantee Co Ltd.*[72]

---

68 [2015] EWHC 2304 (Comm).
69 [2010] EWHC 2443.
70 [2016] HCA 47.
71 See also *Lukoil Mid-East Ltd v Barclays Bank Plc* [2016] EWHC 166 (TCC), BLR 162 and *South Lanarkshire Council v Coface SA* [2016] CSIH 15, BLR 237.
72 [1995] 3 All ER 737.

# Chapter 8 Contractual Remedies and Issues Arising

## Introduction

8.1 In the event of a dispute arising between the borrower and the lender a number of possible options follow. Such disputes also arise from time to time in derivatives deals and bond issues. For these reasons the wording used in the original agreement will be critical in trying to resolve any dispute. If this cannot be done, perhaps because the borrower or counterparty has cash flow problems, a restructuring of the arrangement may be necessary. If all else fails, the lender or counterparty may need to commence litigation, or in extreme cases put the borrower or counterparty into administration or liquidation. In the case of sovereign borrower or counterparty the last option is not available and litigation may not be seen as practical. Thus, some type of restructuring may well be the only option available. These possibilities are all now considered.

## Clauses in the agreement

### Events of default clause

8.2 The events of default clause is perceived by most lenders and counterparties as being a key element in the contract, since it is the events of default which give the agreement teeth, by describing the circumstances in which the lender can demand repayment. As Ryan succinctly put it some years ago:

> 'A prudent bank lender, before committing to lend for a term to any borrower, sovereign or private, considers and determines those possible events which, if they occurred, would impair the prospect of repayment. Those events are typically specified in the loan agreement with the borrower as events of default.'[1]

The events of default clause is often one of the most contested clauses in drafting the entire loan agreement, and it is crucial for those negotiating the loan to appreciate both its scope and practical

[1] Ryan, 'Defaults and Remedies under International Bank Loan Agreements with Foreign Sovereign Borrowers – a New York Lawyer's Perspective'. [1982] 1 U Ill L Rev 89.

significance.[2] However, as already seen, the standard ISDA Master Agreement sets a market standard in derivatives deals and to some extent the LMA Agreement does the same for term loan agreements, although in loan agreements significant changes are often made.[3] In bond issues the clause tends to be shorter and less prone to being contested due to the nature of the structure.[4] In term loans, a very extensive clause covering many different events of default may be viewed as highly desirable insofar as the lender is concerned, but if such restrictions make it impossible for the borrower to use the funds for their intended purpose, the clause may very well operate against the lender's interests. Therefore, a fair balance should be struck between the interests of the lender and the borrower. This balance will vary enormously from one loan agreement to another, since it will depend upon the particular circumstances of negotiating power of the parties to the agreement. For this reason, the default clause, like many other clauses in a term loan, should always be tailor made. There is no such thing as a fully standard events of default clause.

### *The commercial and financial objectives of the clause*

**8.3** The principle objective behind the events of default clause has already been identified, namely, to describe those circumstances in which the lender or counterparty can terminate the agreement and demand immediate repayment. In practice, however, the problem is usually more subtle and lenders, particularly bank lenders, will normally only demand repayment in extreme cases. This is because banks are in business to lend money and if the borrower is able to repay most bankers would not wish to terminate the loan and demand repayment just because of a technical default. Such action would, at the very least, seriously prejudice relations between bank and borrower and may, in certain circumstances, have more far reaching consequences. The insolvency of a borrower is not in the bank's long term financial interests if the borrower could have survived and continued to deal with the bank.

**8.4** There are undoubtedly many different categories of default, some more serious than others, and not all of them necessarily bring about a termination of the loan. The default may be nothing more than a technical default, in which case the lender is unlikely to terminate the loan and demand repayment.[5] Alternatively, it may be the first sign

---

2 See Ch 1 above.
3 *Ibid.*
4 See Ch 4 above.
5 For a useful analysis see M Wolter and D Rösch, 'Cure Events in Default Prediction' European Journal of Operational Research. Nov 2014, vol 238, issue 3, pp 846–857, doi.org/10.1016/j.ejor.2014.04.046. Also RR Zabel, 'Credit Default Swaps: From Protection to Speculation' 4 Pratt's J Bankr L 546.

that the borrower is experiencing financial difficulties,[6] for example, a late payment of interest, thereby acting as an early warning device to the lender which may consequently decide to monitor the borrower's activities more closely, rather than terminate and demand repayment immediately. In an extreme case, default may be so serious that the borrower or counterparty is unlikely to fulfil its financial commitments. In such a situation it will be most important to be able to act quickly in order to recover as much as possible from the borrower or counterparty and/or any guarantor.

**8.5** It must be appreciated, therefore, that an event of default does not necessarily bring about a termination of the contract. Indeed, it can be said with some confidence that termination and acceleration of a loan or derivative contract, because of an event of default, is the exception rather than the rule. The principle reason for this is that lenders are rarely able to recover fully the total indebtedness owed by the borrower. Experience has shown that at best the existing loans of the borrower will be renegotiated, but this will be a time-consuming and expensive business and may involve writing off either unpaid interest and/or capital. It may also lead to irreparable damage in the relationship between the parties to the arrangement. At worst the default may precipitate the liquidation of the borrower/counterparty, in which case there may be little hope of the lender recovering anything more than a small proportion of the amount owing.[7] In the case of derivatives this will tend to be mitigated by the netting arrangements in the standard ISDA agreements.[8]

**8.6** Notwithstanding the fact that breach of an event of default rarely triggers acceleration, one cannot overemphasise the importance of drafting appropriate events of default within the terms of the agreement, which, on the one hand recognises a balance of interest between the parties, but on the other, enables the lender to speak from a position of strength should anything go wrong.[9] In such negotiations the lending bank in a term loan will often have quite a powerful position. The lender will, at the very least, be able to use the threat of acceleration as a leverage device during any restructuring negotiations, at which time it will be most important for the lender's rights to be on a par with those of other unsecured creditors, thereby preventing the borrower from preferring those creditors to the lender. In the case of OTC derivatives, the use of standardised contracts, primarily ISDA

---

6 The collapse of Carillion in 2018 was preceded by such warning signs. The company was reverse factoring its receipts by getting its bankers to provide finance for them in advance and then taking excessive amounts of time to pay its own debts. Thus, the scale of its indebtedness and cash flow problems were not immediately apparent.

7 In the case of an unsecured loan the lender will rank well down the list of people to be paid off on the borrower's insolvency. In the event of the loan being secured or there being a guarantor the situation is much safer.

8 See Ch 6 at **6.59–6.70**.

9 The LMA Multicurrency Term and Revolving Credit Agreement of 18 July 2017 lists the events of default at cl 23. Current term loans tend to be 'LMA compliant'.

leaves less room for manoeuvre, though the process of amending the Schedule gives some scope. On a bond issue on the other hand the issuer will not wish to over burden themselves with obligations and so the events of default will tend to be more restricted.

**8.7** As discussed in **Chapter 6** the willingness to accept a delay in payment may be significantly reduced in derivatives contracts as opposed to term loans. It is common for the standard ISDA agreement to have the Schedule amended regarding termination to be automatic on the occurrence of an insolvency related event except where the contract is governed by a system of law which will not permit this.[10,11]

## Actual breach and anticipatory breach

**8.8** Events of default fall into two basic categories, namely, actual default, such as non-payment of principal or interest, and anticipatory default. The fundamental difference between these two categories is that in the former, the contract will almost certainly have been breached, whereas in the latter, the clauses operate primarily as an early warning device putting the lender on notice that an actual default, ie, non-payment, is imminent. The anticipatory default clauses will, hopefully, enable the lender either to terminate the loan and obtain repayment before the borrower's financial position worsens, or to obtain some form of security to safeguard its position should this be possible.[12]

**8.9** We will now turn to consider some specific clauses which are commonly incorporated into term loan agreements, derivative master agreements and bonds.

### *Failure to pay*

**8.10** The most basic event of default is failure by the borrower to pay principal and/or interest on the loan as and when it falls due. Such failure is prima facie inconsistent with the continuation of the lender's commitment, and a clause covering such an event should obviously be incorporated into every loan agreement. The same applies to bonds and derivatives contracts with payments due from counterparties. It must be appreciated, however, that there are a variety of reasons which may lie behind the borrower's or counterparty's failure to pay, and the clause should be worded in such a way as to take account of this. Where the failure to pay arises because the borrower or counterparty does not possess the necessary funds it is a clear indication that the borrower/counterparty is experiencing serious financial difficulties,

10 At Sch 1(e).

11 M Denning, 'ISDA Master Agreement and Credit Support Annex: Negotiation Strategies.' ISDA Conference, (London, 12 July 2017).

12 In many states there are laws which will invalidate security if taken out within a given period of the borrower's insolvency and most states also have registration requirements.

and non-payment is likely to recur. In such a situation the lender or counterparty would not wish to qualify its ability to terminate the agreement and call for repayment before the other party becomes completely insolvent. Few cases, however, will be so clear cut. The borrower or counterparty may be experiencing a temporary cash flow problem or the failure may be due to an administrative error on the part of the lender or within the international banking system. In such cases immediate termination of the loan would be inappropriate and may have catastrophic consequences for an otherwise financially sound borrower or counterparty, amongst other things, due to the impact of cross default clauses.

**8.11** In order to safeguard the borrower against such harsh consequences some lenders/counterparties are prepared to incorporate grace periods within lending agreements. Where a grace period is included, the default will be deemed not to have occurred, in so far as the triggering of remedies is concerned, until a specified number of days have elapsed since the payment fell due. The period of grace given must be long enough to enable the borrower to remedy a technical default but not too long so as to prejudice the position of the lender. It follows that the parties may agree different grace periods for different types of payment, for example, principal, interest; fees and duties, etc, each period reflecting the importance attached to each type of payment. Grace periods for non-payment tend to be very short and they are rarely given for non-payment of principal.

*Breach of representations and warranties*

**8.12** Since the borrower's or counterparty's representations reflect the basic legal and factual assumptions upon which the lender extends the loan or financial facility, it is hardly surprising that breach of those assumptions would be deemed an event of default. Indeed, as indicated in **Chapter 1** the primary purpose of the representations and warranties are to trigger an event of default, not to provide a means of obtaining damages should they turn out to be untrue.

**8.13** An event of default linked to the breach of a representation or warranty will afford greater protection to the lender if the representations are deemed to be continuing, and in such a case the borrower will commonly seek to mitigate against the harsher implications of the clause. One way in which this and other clauses may be softened is by the incorporation of a materiality test, ie:

> 'Any representation or warranty made or deemed to be made by the Borrower under this Agreement or in any certificate, document or financial or other statement furnished at any time under or in connection with this Agreement shall prove to have been incorrect or misleading in any material respect when made or deemed to be made … then such an event shall be deemed to be an event of default.'

The problem with such a clause is that it begs the question of what is 'material?' This problem may be overcome by specifying a financial limit whereby materiality is to be gauged. Unfortunately, however, representations and warranties do not normally lend themselves to such a test. In practice, therefore, the ambiguity inherent in materiality tests will have a high risk of leading to uncertainty between the parties and at worst, litigation on its precise meaning.[13] For this reason most lawyers discourage the use of materiality tests and utilise in their place appropriate grace periods which should, of course, only operate in relation to those breaches of the loan agreement which can be remedied.

### *Breach of covenants*

**8.14** The importance of the covenants given by a borrower in a term loan agreement or a counterparty in the ISDA Master Agreement have both been considered earlier in this work, and it is common, as in the case of representations and warranties, to link their breach to an event of default.

**8.15** The LMA Multicurrency Term and Revolving Facilities Agreement provides that this occurs if:[14]

'(a) A member of the Group:

(i) is unable or admits inability to pay its debts as they fall due;

(ii) suspends making payments on any of its debts; or

(iii) by reason of actual or anticipated financial difficulties, commences negotiations with one or more of its creditors with a view to rescheduling any of its indebtedness.

(b) The value of the assets of any member of the Group is less than its liabilities (taking into account contingencies and prospective liabilities).

(c) A moratorium is declared in respect of any indebtedness of any member of the Group.'

As we have already seen, the covenants given by a borrower cover a wide variety of its activities, and it is likely that the lender will perceive some as being more important than others. Indeed, it is common practice in term loans for the lender to consider some covenants so fundamental or incurable that any breach would be deemed an automatic event of default. Precisely which covenants the lender considers fundamental will obviously depend upon the circumstances of each individual case.

---

13 *Docker v Hyams (No 1)* [1969] 1 WLR 1060; [1969] 1 Lloyd's Rep 487; [1969] 3 All ER 808; (1969) 113 SJ 381. See also Firth, *Derivatives Law and Practice* (Sweet & Maxwell), Ch 4, 'Liabilities Arising from Derivatives Trading'.

14 At cl 23.6 of the LMA Multicurrency Term and Revolving Credit Agreement of 18 July 2017.

**8.16** Most lenders recognise that any leeway given to the borrower, in the form of grace periods, must be considered very carefully. Breach of a single covenant may signify that the borrower or counterparty is on the verge of collapse, and in such a case it will be crucial for the lender or counterparty to act as quickly as possible in the hope of obtaining repayment before the borrower falls into liquidation. As an alternative to grace periods a materiality test may be included in respect of those covenants which the lender does not consider fundamental to the protection of its interests. The problem of uncertainty will once again apply to the operation of the materiality test, and it is probably the case that such a test is even less appropriate in the case of covenants than for breach of representations and warranties.

**8.17** In the case of the ISDA Master Agreement, derivative counterparties have very little time to conform to requirements for payment or delivery without being in breach of contract. Section 5(a)(i) states that there is a breach where there is:

> 'Failure by the party to make, when due, any payment under this Agreement or delivery ... required to be made by it, if such failure is not remedied on or before the Local Business Day or in the case of any such payment on the First Local delivery Day in the case of any such delivery, after, in each case, notice of such failure is given to the party.'[15]

Failure to perform on any other aspect of the contract however has considerably more leeway. Section 5(a)(ii)(1) continues:

> 'Failure by the party to comply with or perform any agreement or obligation (other than an obligation to make any payment ... delivery ... or to give notice of a Termination Event ...) if such failure is not remedied within 30 days.'

**8.18** The litigation following the insolvency of the Lehman Bros group tested this considerably. The fact that insolvency has occurred may become apparent very quickly and this issue was discussed in Chapter 6 in the context of *Lehman Brothers International (Europe) Ltd v Lehman Brothers Finance SA*[16] and a number of related cases.[17] Suffice to say that an understanding of the impact of the Lehman insolvency is crucial to anyone drafting such clauses.

---

15 ISDA 2002 Master Agreement.

16 (2013) EWCA Civ 188.

17 See, eg, E Parker and A McGarry, 'The ISDA Master Agreement and CSA: close out weaknesses exposed in the banking crisis and suggestions for change. (2009) 24(1) BJB&IFL J 16–19. GL Charles, 'OTC Derivative Contracts in Bankruptcy: The Lehman Experience' New York Business Law Journal. Spring 2009, vol 13 no 1. LJ Fleming and A Sarkar, 'The Failure Resolution of Lehman Bros.' Economic Policy Review, 31 March 2014 Also C McNamara and A Metrick, 'The Lehman Bros Bankruptcy F Introduction to the ISDA Master Agreement.' Yale School of Management 15 November 2014 and RZ Wiggins and A Metrick, 'The Lehman Bros Bankruptcy G: The Special Case of Derivatives.' Yale School of Management 1 October 2014.

*Cross default*

**8.19** The cross default clause is the principal anticipatory event of default and is an essential safeguard for the lender or derivative counterparty, since it provides a most effective early warning device providing it is appropriately drafted. Default on a payment elsewhere is often a warning sign of that party having cash flow problems. The LMA Multicurrency Term and Revolving Facilities Agreement provides[18] that it will amount to cross default when:

'(a) Any Financial Indebtedness of any member of the Group is not paid when due nor within any originally applicable grace period.

(b) Any Financial Indebtedness of any member of the Group is declared to be or otherwise becomes due and payable prior to its specified maturity as a result of an event of default (however described).

(c) Any commitment of any Financial Indebtedness of any member of the Group is cancelled or suspended by a creditor or any member of the Group as a result of an event of default (however described)

(d) Any creditor of any member of the Group becomes entitled to declare any Financial Indebtedness of any member of the Group due and payable prior to its specified maturity as a result of an event of default (however described).

(e) No Event of Default will occur under this clause 23.5 if the aggregate amount of Financial Indebtedness or commitment for Financial Indebtedness falling within paragraphs (a) to (d) above is less than (£.........) (or its equivalent in any other currency or currencies).'

**8.20** Such a clause is intended to prevent the bank from being placed at a disadvantage in the event of the borrower or counterparty defaulting under one of its other credit facilities. A lending bank will normally want to play an active part in any decision which is made concerning the fate of a borrower. The cross default clause should provide for this by enabling the lender to accelerate its own facility whenever this is necessary to obtain a seat at any subsequent creditors' meeting, which is convened to discuss the borrower's future. The clause also strengthens the pari passu principle that all creditors in the same class should be treated alike. Lenders in the term loan markets and derivative counterparties have always attached a great deal of importance to this principle and it is recognised as the primary purpose of the cross default clause.

---

18 At cl 23.5 of the LMA Multicurrency Term and Revolving Credit Agreement of 18 July 2017.

WHAT ARE THE IMPLICATIONS OF THE CLAUSE?

**8.21** The cross default clause is generally recognised as being the most important anticipatory event of default, but its consequences can be catastrophic for both parties to the contract due to the domino effect which the clause may set into motion. Those negotiating the clause must appreciate these consequences, and it is hardly surprising that the precise wording of the clause is often a contentious aspect of the negotiation process.

**8.22** Most creditworthy borrowers should, in the event of an emergency, be in a position to repay a small percentage of their outstanding indebtedness, but the domino effect brought about by the operation of the cross default clause, which will normally have been included in all of the borrower's international credits, is likely to ruin most borrowers. The effect which the clause is likely to have should significantly enhance the impact of the default sanction. However, its implications are so severe that they may operate against the lender's or derivative counterparty's interest in a potential default. The knowledge that the clause, if triggered, will almost certainly bring about the total collapse of the borrower/counterparty often prevents it from being employed.

**8.23** Notwithstanding the comments made above, the sanction of the cross default clause remains severe and the borrower or counterparty will normally seek to mitigate its effect. Grace periods and materiality tests are often requested, but the lender should be aware of the problems which such softening techniques pose. Lenders should resist grace periods which start to run, not when the default occurs or when the borrower becomes aware of the default, but when the lender informs the borrower. Delay in triggering any event of default may have serious consequences for the lender's position and, therefore, grace periods, if granted, should be for a very short period of time, should start to run at the earliest possible time, and should only cover technical defaults or administrative delays on the part of the borrower.

**8.24** Another way in which the borrower may seek to soften the clause is by requiring that it can only be triggered if the borrower's default on the third party credit is above a certain threshold figure or that the default is under a particular type of facility. This can be dangerous though. Even a small non-payment could be a symptom of a serious financial problem.

**8.25** Any restriction imposed upon the operation of the clause may put the lender at risk, particularly where third party creditors of the borrower are not subject to similar restrictions. In such a case the restrictions should be resisted by the lender, and in any event, many experienced negotiators would argue that in the event of a default it is crucial to keep one's options as flexible as possible.

THE WORDING OF THE CROSS DEFAULT CLAUSE

### What should the clause cover?

**8.26** Because of its importance, many lenders seek to word the clause in the widest possible terms. An example of how this can be achieved is seen in the specimen clause given above, which includes the phrase 'any Financial Indebtedness.' Without more, such wording would cover all financial obligations owed by the borrower, from the £20 bill for a book to £20 million owed on a syndicated loan agreement. Such a clause is clearly unrealistic insofar as both lender and borrower are concerned, since it would almost certainly change the term loan into a demand loan and may trigger an event of default in a number of the borrower's other credit obligations because of the domino effect of the clause. It is hardly surprising, therefore, that borrowers normally resist such widely drafted clauses and attempt to restrict their scope to well defined classes of indebtedness, such as borrowed money, unsecured credits or to commercial bank credits. In the case of the ISDA Master Agreement a counterparty can argue in pre-contract negotiations that the Schedule to the Agreement needs to have a qualification adding limiting the circumstances in which the cross default will apply in the same way.

**8.27** Sovereign borrowers will be particularly anxious to limit the scope of the clause, and it is relatively common in such cases to restrict its operation to the external indebtedness of the borrower. External indebtedness is normally defined as indebtedness owed to non-residents or indebtedness which is denominated in a currency other than that of the borrower's own country.

**8.28** Another important consideration with regard to corporate borrowers is whether the clause should cover subsidiaries. Where the lender takes such subsidiaries into account, when taking the credit analysis decision, they should be included, as should any guarantor where relevant. However, where the borrower is being analysed in isolation it may be totally inappropriate to widen the scope of the clause unnecessarily.

### When should the clause crystallise?

**8.29** Since it is in the lender's interest to negotiate as wide a cross default clause as possible, most clauses are drafted in such a way as to enable the lender to terminate and accelerate its own loan even though the borrower's other credits are not accelerated. This type of clause is sometimes referred to as the 'capable of cross default clause', since it permits the lender to accelerate its own loan in the event that any of the borrower's other credits are *capable of* being accelerated. Whether or not the other credits are in fact accelerated is irrelevant.

**8.30** The *'capable of'* formulation places the lender in the strongest possible position, since it enables the lender to be the master of its own destiny. A borrower which accedes to such a clause will consequently find itself in a perilous position, since the clause will nullify the effect of any grace periods operating over events of default in its other loan agreements. Such a clause may also prejudice the borrower's relations with its other creditors, who will undoubtedly be less than happy if they themselves have agreed upon cross default clauses which end up being triggered in the event of actual acceleration of a third-party credit.

**8.31** The obvious danger with any cross default clause that may be triggered prior to actual acceleration of other indebtedness, or which does not take into account grace periods, is that it may set the domino effect into motion whilst the borrower is making a bona fide attempt to remedy the breach. As indicated earlier, such a course of events is likely, without more, to drive almost any borrower into liquidation.

## Can the clause be effectively policed?

**8.32** One final problem posed by the cross default clause is that in practice its usefulness may be curtailed due to the standards of secrecy which term lenders, particularly banks, are expected to maintain.[19] As with many clauses in a term loan agreement, the clause must be capable of being effectively policed, in other words the lender must have fairly full information on the position with regard to the borrower's other indebtedness, and in particular, whether it has defaulted upon such indebtedness. Without such information the cross default clause is useless as an early warning device, and it will fail to maintain pari passu treatment if third party creditors are able to enforce against the borrower without the lender becoming aware.

**8.33** In conclusion, it can be said that although the cross default clause is perceived as crucial to protect the position of the lender in most term loan agreements and derivative contracts, its limitations should not be overlooked. Furthermore, those negotiating its precise wording must be aware of the serious consequences to which the clause may give rise. As we have already indicated, lenders will obviously want as wide a clause as possible, but this may place the borrower in default virtually from the moment the loan agreement is executed. Such a consequence can hardly be in the interests of either the borrower or the lender.

---

19 *Tournier v National Provincial and Union Bank of England* [1924] 1 KB 461; *Turner v Royal Bank of Scotland* [1999] 2 All ER 664; Lloyd's Rep Bank 231. Qualified by *Christofi v Barclays Bank Plc* [2000] 1 WLR 937; [1999] 4 All ER 437, also *Re Durrani (Entrepreneurs: Bank Letters: Evidential Flexibility)* [2014] UKUT 295 (IAC); [2014] Imm AR 1019.

### Liquidation or moratorium

**8.34** The laws of most countries recognise that bankruptcy or liquidation of the borrower will constitute an event of default regardless of what is stated in the loan agreement. However, such an eventuality should still be specifically covered within the events of default, since the relevant legal procedures in the country of the borrower's domicile may be disadvantageous to the lender, or at least not as advantageous as the lender would wish. The LMA Multicurrency Term and Revolving Facilities Agreement provides[20] that it will amount to insolvency where:

> 'Any corporate action, legal proceedings or other procedure or step is taken in relation to:
>
> (a) the suspension of payments, a moratorium of any indebtedness, winding up, dissolution, administration or reorganisation (by way of voluntary arrangement, scheme of arrangement or otherwise) of any member of the Group other than a solvent liquidation or reorganisation of any member of the Group which is not an Obligor.
>
> (b) a composition, compromise, assignment or arrangement with any creditor of an member of the Group;
>
> (c) the appointment of a liquidator (other than in respect of a solvent liquidation of a member of the Group which is not an Obligor) receiver, administrative receiver, manager or other similar officer in respect of any member of the Group or any of its assets; or
>
> (d) enforcement of any Security over any assets of any member of the Group, or any analogous procedure or step is taken in any jurisdiction,
>
> Or any analogous procedure or step is taken in any jurisdiction.'

**8.35** Once again, this particular clause tends to be drafted very widely, but unlike the cross default clause it will rarely be a contentious issue as between the parties. Where the borrower falls into liquidation or specifically states that it is unable to pay its debts, there can be no question of the loan being continued. Similarly, where subsidiaries or guarantors have been included as part of the credit, they also should be included within the ambit of the clause.

### Sovereign debt moratoria

**8.36** Sovereign states are not generally subject to bankruptcy or insolvency proceedings since there is no international regime

---

20 At cl 23.7 of the LMA Multicurrency Term and Revolving Credit Agreement of 18 July 2017.

governing states which are unable to pay their debts. However, quasi-government entities and government owned corporations do normally fall within the scope of such proceedings and, where relevant, it is common to incorporate such entities within the terms of the clause. This is discussed further at **Chapter 11**.

**8.37** The equivalent to bankruptcy insofar as a sovereign state is concerned is the declaration of a moratorium on the repayment of its debts, and although formal proceedings are rarely involved, the practical effect for the lender is, if anything, even more catastrophic, since under a moratorium all payments are frozen, whereas in a bankruptcy there is always a chance of receiving a percentage of the sums owed. Because the threat of moratorium is so serious it is common to include an appropriate event of default either when lending to a sovereign or where a sovereign is guaranteeing the loan. Such a clause might read:

> 'It will be an event of default if the Borrower declares any general moratorium on its indebtedness or upon any indebtedness assumed or guaranteed by it.'

In practical terms, the clause is unlikely to be of any assistance, since acceleration after the moratorium has been declared will rarely enable the lender to obtain repayment, and in most cases the declaration will be followed by lengthy rescheduling negotiations.

**8.38** Nevertheless, it will be important for the bank to retain the ability to accelerate upon such an occurrence, otherwise it may not have a voice during the rescheduling process.

### Changes in the control of the borrower

**8.39** The lender may have made its credit decision on the assumption that the borrower will continue to be controlled by some larger entity. This will commonly arise when the loan is being advanced to a government owned corporation or a subsidiary of a large company. In such a situation the lender will want to review its position in the event of control by the parent being severed. An appropriate event of default will permit the lender to make such a review, ie:

> 'the Borrower ceases to be a subsidiary of ........................ or ceases to be under the voting control of ........................'.

**8.40** Where the parent exercises a significant degree of control over the borrower it will be crucial for the lender to insist upon a guarantee from the parent. Some lenders prefer to take matters one stage further and require the parent or state to join the borrower as principal debtor, particularly where the lender is fearful that the borrower may be nationalised or expropriated, as can happen with companies engaged in the exploitation of natural resources. Although the term 'guarantee' is widely used in practice many banks use a form of words that renders the so called guarantor a primary obligor to settle the debt and such an arrangement is called an indemnity. Many bank guarantees thus end up with a hybridised arrangement that is part guarantee and part indemnity. This is discussed further at **Chapter 1** at **1.196**. There are similar but more complex provisions in the ISDA Master Agreement and Credit Support documents.

### Disposal of assets

**8.41** Disposal of all or part of the borrower's assets is a common event of default in corporate loans, although it is common to incorporate practical limitations which ensure that the borrower will be able to carry on with its normal trading activities. The lender will be particularly concerned to prevent the borrower from disposing of assets which form the underlying basis of the loan, or from disposing of assets which are essential for the continuing viability of the company's business. In order to safeguard the lender's position still further an event of default should also be linked to an anti-disposal covenant.

### Sovereign borrowers and IMF membership

**8.42** Where the borrower is a sovereign state, it is common to provide that it shall be an event of default if the borrower ceases to be a member of the International Monetary Fund (IMF) or is unable to use the IMF's resources.[21] It is well recognised that a healthy relationship between a state borrower and the IMF is a sign that the borrower is conducting its financial affairs in a prudent fashion. Continued membership is, therefore, a source of great comfort to many state lenders in the term loan markets. On the other hand, a breakdown in relations between the borrower and the IMF usually signifies that all is not well and will, at the very least, put the lender on enquiry.

**8.43** Of more practical significance is the fact that IMF membership may give the state borrower access to direct financial assistance which may help the borrower to overcome a short term liquidity crisis, though it should be remembered that the IMF will only assist its members during temporary difficulties. If the borrower's problems are deep rooted IMF membership may be of limited practical help.

**8.44** Additional protection may also be afforded to the lender by requiring the borrower to maintain a stand by arrangement with the IMF. Such an arrangement enables a member to make purchases of foreign currency from the IMF at regular intervals. Since lack of

---

[21] IMF membership is often a condition precedent and continued membership a condition subsequent. Sometimes failure to be a member is an event of default, sometimes it is put in the representations and warranties and a breach of this would be an event of default.

foreign currency is one of the main factors behind many sovereign loan defaults, the ability to obtain such currency may be perceived as crucial for the continuation of the loan.

### Material adverse change

**8.45** The 'material adverse change' clause is another contentious event of default which is commonly drafted into international loan agreements. The purpose of this clause, as its name suggests, is to permit the lender to accelerate the loan in the event that a material and adverse change occurs in the financial condition or operation of the borrower. A straightforward clause might determine that a material adverse change shall arise where:

> '... there shall occur any other event which in the judgment of the Lender would materially and adversely affect the ability or willingness of the Borrower to perform its obligations under this Agreement.'

**8.46** The clause operates as a safeguard of last resort, a sweeping up provision which it is hoped will give some protection to the lender if all else fails. Its inclusion should not, however, lure the lender into taking a soft approach to the more specific events of default, some of which have been outlined above. There is no substitute for appropriately drafted events of default, and it could be argued that where such events are included within the loan there should be no need to incorporate an all embracing material adverse change clause. Nevertheless, many lenders perceive the clause as crucial and, as the many documents in the market place indicate. That said the LMA Multicurrency Term and Revolving Facilities Agreement[22] has deleted the clause, which was previously at 23.12. However, it is typically drafted in the widest possible terms, the intention being to cover any conceivable circumstance which may affect the borrower's willingness or ability to perform its obligations under the loan. This intention is normally reinforced by giving the lender sole discretion in determining whether a material adverse change has in fact occurred. The problem with the clause lies in the generality of its language which poses obvious difficulties of proof, and this problem may not be solved simply by placing any discretion solely in the hands of the lender, particularly if the discretion is exercised unreasonably.

## Remedies on default

**8.47** The remedies available to a lender in the event of a borrower defaulting on its obligations can be conveniently divided between

[22] 18 July 2017 version.

those which are commonly included within the terms of the loan documentation – the internal remedies – and other remedies existing under general principles of law which may, or may not, be specifically referred to – the external remedies. Injunctions and specific performance are discussed briefly in **Chapter 1** at **1.126 – 1.127.** The remaining issues are discussed below.

## The internal remedies

### *Termination of the agreement and acceleration of the maturity*

**8.48** The most basic sanction available to the lender in the event of a borrower's default is the right to declare the outstanding portion of the loan immediately due and payable and to cancel any commitment to provide further loans.[23] The ability to exercise this right swiftly, in other words, with no grace period, will be fundamentally important in certain circumstances. In the case of the ISDA Master Agreement stated netting provisions will apply to determine the sum payable.

### *Other internal remedies*

**8.49** There are a number of other remedies which may be available to the lender in the event that the borrower breaches the loan agreement, and most of these are considered elsewhere in this work.[24] They include: the right to repudiate the contract and accelerate the sum outstanding; the right to sue the borrower for damages; the right to sue for outstanding amounts of interest and/or principal; and the right to rescind the loan agreement and claim damages. Where a third party takes security whilst knowing that it puts the borrower in breach of a negative pledge clause, an action in the tort of interference with contractual relations is potentially available against that third party.

**8.50** As we have seen, the availability of such remedies will depend upon the circumstances surrounding the borrower's breach, and although they may provide the lender with a number of important safeguards, their availability will normally be subject to significant limitations. They should never be relied upon as a substitute for express remedies, which must always be incorporated into the loan agreement in order to bring a degree of certainty and predictability to the rights of the lender in the event that the borrower subsequently breaches the agreement. In derivative contracts the ISDA Master Agreement covers the points but variation may be required by the counterparties in the Schedule.

---

[23] In the case of a syndicated loan the agent bank will often have the power granted to it to take this step for administrative convenience. In those cases where there has to be conferment with other syndicate banks the agent bank will still normally have the task of notifying the borrower.

[24] See Ch 1.

## Restructuring

**8.51** Where the borrower encounters difficulties so that it is no longer able to meet its liabilities as they fall due, the lender may agree to open restructuring negotiations in the hope that the borrower will pull through its present financial difficulties. Such a course of action may be perceived as being more attractive than winding up proceedings which, as we have already seen, will realise for the lender only a small proportion of the sums owed. Restructuring agreements are particularly common insofar as sovereign borrowers are concerned and, therefore, the precise wording of the clause should be carefully considered. A typical example might read as follows:

> 'Then in any such event and at any time thereafter if such event is continuing, the Bank may, by notice in writing to the Borrower cancel any undrawn amount of the facility and declare the loan forthwith due and payable, together with all interest accrued thereon and all other amounts payable hereunder.'

Such a clause should enable the lending bank to act quickly in the event that circumstances so require, subject to the proviso that the event of default must be continuing. In other words, the event of default which triggers the termination/acceleration clause must not only have been breached but must also be continuing at the time the right to terminate and accelerate is exercised. If the borrower cures the event of default before such right is exercised, the bank will have lost its right, at least in so far as that particular event of default is concerned, but once the right has been exercised by the bank, the borrower loses its ability to cure. Restructuring is discussed more fully in **Chapter 1**.

**8.52** Another possible limitation which may operate upon the lender's contractual right to terminate and accelerate the loan relates to the application of equitable principles. However, it would appear that appropriate cases to which equitable principles can be applied to prevent termination/acceleration will be rare. The most likely equitable principle which may operate against the interests of the lender is the equitable principle of good faith which has been applied to the enforcement of acceleration clauses. The courts have looked at the materiality of the event of default in order to establish whether the lender's acceleration is in such bad faith as to require equitable intervention by the courts. In the case of derivative contracts the parties normally contract at arm's length and so the issue does not arise.[25] *J P Morgan Chase v Springwell Navigation*[26] confirmed that the position as far as the courts are concerned is that where two businesses have contracted there is a strong inclination to regard them

[25] Indeed, the pervading logic behind the ISDA 2002 Master Agreement is that the parties are contracting on an arm's length basis. See *Proctor & Gamble v Banker's Trust* 925 F Supp 1270 (FD Ohio 1995).

[26] [2008] EWHC 1186 (Comm).

as contracting at arm's length where there is no term in the contract to indicate that one is relying on the other:

> 'The reluctance of the courts to interfere between commercial counterparties in relation to substantial transactions reflects the strong business need for commercial certainty.'[27]

**8.53** Insofar as English law is concerned, the courts have made it clear that certainty and predictability of clauses negotiated between commercial parties must be upheld and therefore, the application of equitable limitations upon the lender's right to terminate/accelerate is not particularly significant.[28] Where the lender's right to accelerate is discretionary all that seems to be required is that the discretion is exercised honestly, in good faith.[29]

## Waiver

**8.54** The lender's use of waivers may also place a significant limitation upon its ability to terminate/accelerate the loan. In practice, most lenders will explore every possible avenue before terminating the loan and enforcing its remedies and, notwithstanding an event of default, where the borrower is essentially creditworthy it is common for the lender to grant an appropriate waiver.

**8.55** Whenever such a waiver is granted it should be dealt with in writing in order to bring certainty both to the circumstances in which it was granted and to the manner in which it will operate.

**8.56** Waivers which are granted orally, or by conduct, for example where the lender permits the borrower to draw down the loan in full knowledge that breach of an event of default has occurred, pose particular problems. This is because it will be extremely difficult to ascertain the circumstances in which the waiver will operate.[30] The parties may ultimately find themselves in disagreement, the borrower arguing that its default is covered by the lender's oral or implied waiver, and the lender arguing that it is not so covered. A lender should never allow itself to fall into this position and in order to avoid any such possibility, it is common practice to send out a no waiver letter whenever there has been a breach of the loan agreement by the borrower. This practice should safeguard the lender against any future contention by the borrower that certain clauses in the loan have been continually waived. It will also encourage specific negotiation between

---

27 *Ibid* at 604.
28 *The Brimnes* [1974] 3 All ER 88; *The Laconia* [1977] 1 All ER 545 and *The Chikuma* [1981] 1 All ER 652, [1981] 1 WLR 314, also known as *Awilco of Oslo A/S v Fulvia SpA di Navagazione of Cagliari*.
29 *Docker v Hyams* [1969] 3 All ER 808.
30 *Birmingham and District Land Co v London and North Western Railway Co* (1888) 40 Ch D 268.

the parties on the question of whether, and in what circumstances, any waiver will operate.

## Acceleration

**8.57** One final, and very practical limitation on the lender's right to terminate/accelerate, is that by exercising such a right the lender may cause the borrower's other credits to be accelerated due to the impact of cross default clauses. As we have already indicated, it is most unlikely that the lender will recover anything more than a small percentage of the sums owing if the domino effect of the cross default clause is activated. In the majority of cases it is likely that such a course of events will culminate in lengthy and expensive rescheduling negotiations.

## Default interest

**8.58** Term loan agreements invariably make specific reference to default interest which the borrower must pay in the event that it fails to make payment of any amount on the due date. Default interest will normally be payable whenever there is delay in payment, regardless of whether or not the loan is terminated and/or accelerated.

**8.59** The rate of default interest can, in some cases, be significantly higher than the normal rate charged on the loan, thereby acting as a penal measure. In most loans, however, the figure will be a modest increase above the normal rate. Lenders should be particularly wary of default interest provisions which operate as a penal measure, since a number of jurisdictions, including England, refuse to admit penal rates of interest and permit only the recovery of costs. The question that arises in this context is: what is a penalty? *Cavendish Square Holdings BV v Tula El Makdessi; Parking Eye Ltd V Beavis*[31] moved on from the traditional view in *Dunlop Pneumatic Tyre Co v Selfridge.*[32] The Supreme court believed that 'the Dunlop test remains useful for a straightforward damages clause because interest will rarely extend beyond compensation for the breach but they do not lend themselves well to more complex cases.'[33] Where a small increase is made in respect of default interest, the lender could properly contend that the clause operates as a compensatory device against additional expenses which may be incurred.

**8.60** It was held that 'whether the impugned provision is a secondary obligation which imposes a deterrent on the contract breaker out

---

31 [2015] UKSC 67; [2016] AC 1172; [2015] 3 WLR 1373; [2016] 2 All ER 519.
32 [1915] AC 847.
33 N McMichael and C Arthurs, 'Penalty Clauses in Continuity: Changing the Rules of the Game?' Pennington Marks (22 January 2016).

of all proportion to any legitimate interest of the innocent party in the enforcement of the primary obligation'[34] is the critical factor in determining whether the clause should be struck down as a penalty. Lord Hodge added that the 'correct test for a penalty is whether the sum or remedy stipulated as a consequence of a breach of trust is exorbitant or unconscionable when regard is to be had as to the innocent part's interest in the performance of the contract.'[35] Crucially it was added 'in a negotiated contract between properly advised parties of comparable bargaining power, the strong initial presumption must be that the parties themselves are the best judges of what is legitimate in a provision dealing with the consequences of breach.'[36]

**8.61** Thus, in term loans and derivatives contracts the existing market provisions are not at risk for being struck down as penalties. The situation is not so clear cut in the case of bond issues because the respective negotiating power of the parties is not so balanced. However, in this instance it is the borrower that is responsible for drafting the contract and they are extremely unlikely to impose excessive obligations on themselves.

### General default indemnity

**8.62** In addition to the clause specifically covering default interest, most loan agreements also require the borrower to indemnify the lender against any loss which the lender sustains because of the borrower's default. Such a clause might read as follows:

> 'The Borrower shall indemnify the Lender against any loss or reasonable expenses which the Lender may sustain or incur as a consequence of any default in the payment of principal or interest on the loan, or any other amount due under the loan, or as a consequence of the occurrence of any event of default under the loan.'

As the wording of the specimen clause indicates, the lender will normally seek to draft the clause as widely as possible, in order to cover any loss associated with the default. This is equivalent to the LMA approach found in clauses 14 and 15.[37]

### Set off

**8.63** This is the facility for the bank to use deposits made by the borrower at the bank to pay out on a defaulted loan by the same party

34 At para [32].
35 At para [255].
36 For useful comment see Stamp M, 'The Penalties Rule in Corporate Contracts – is it Offside?'. (2016) 37(7) Comp Law 219–222. Peel E, 'Unjustified Penalties, or an Unjustified Rule Against Penalties?' (2014) 130 (Jul) LQR 365–370 and Day W, 'Penalty Clauses Revisited' [2014] JBL 512.
37 LMA Multicurrency Term and Revolving Facilities Agreement, 18 July 2017 version.

by setting the two sums against each other. Set off is a remedy which bridges the gap between the internal and external remedies since a clause covering the lender's right to set off may be incorporated within the terms of a term loan agreement. Rights of set off also exist in equity, but only where given conditions are fulfilled.

**8.64** The English law of set off has been dealt with elsewhere in this work[38] and here attention is focused upon the set off clause, which usually seeks to confer broader rights of set off than would be given in equity.

**8.65** The LMA Multicurrency Term and Revolving Facilities Agreement provides:[39]

> 'A Finance Party may set off any matured obligations due from an Obligor under the Finance Documents (to the extent beneficially owned by that Finance Party) against any unused obligation owed by that Finance Party to that Obligor, regardless of the place of payment, booking branch or currency of either obligation. If the obligations are in different currencies, the Finance Party may convert either obligation at a market rate of exchange in its usual course of business for the purpose of set off.'

It is debatable whether the courts in England would permit set off where the funds to be set off are in another jurisdiction or in a currency other than that specified in the agreement. Set off in such cases would certainly not be allowed in equity and the LMA clause serves to illustrate how the loan agreement may attempt to extend the lender's rights. In essence, it is normally possible to set off provided there is mutuality between the parties.[40]

## External remedies

**8.66** Specific performance and injunctions are potentially an issue, especially the latter. They are covered in **Chapter 1**.

### *Other external remedies*

**8.67** There are a number of other remedies which may be available to the lender in the event that the borrower breaches the loan agreement and most of these are considered elsewhere in this work. They include: the right to repudiate the contract and accelerate the sum outstanding; the right to sue the borrower for damages; the right

38 See Chapters 1 and 6.

39 At cl 30.

40 *Morris and others v Rayners Enterprises; Morris and others v Agrichemicals Ltd also known as Re Bank of Credit and Commerce International SA (in liquidation) No 8* [1998] AC 214 [1997] 3 WLR 909.

to sue for outstanding amounts of interest and/or principal; and the right to rescind the loan agreement and claim damages.

**8.68** As seen above, the availability of such remedies will depend upon the circumstances surrounding the borrower's breach, and although they may provide the lender with a number of important safeguards, their availability will normally be subject to significant limitations. They should never be relied upon as a substitute for express remedies, which must always be incorporated into the loan agreement in order to bring a degree of certainty and predictability to the rights of the lender in the event that the borrower subsequently breaches the agreement.

# Chapter 9 Governing Law

## Introduction

**9.1** Many of the legal problems associated with international banking transactions arise because such transactions inevitably impinge upon the laws of more than one state. At the very least two systems of law will be applicable, assuming the transaction is truly international, and in many transactions considerably more than two. For example, a syndicated loan agreement could potentially impinge upon the laws of as many states as the number of parties to the arrangement if they are based in different jurisdictions and if there were security that could be located in a different jurisdiction again. Even in a simple two party loan agreement a number of different legal systems may become involved, for example, because an independent currency is used, or the loan is guaranteed by a third party based in a third country.

**9.2** Whenever a court handles a case which contains a foreign element, principles of private international law, or conflict of laws as it used to be known, come into operation. Essentially the objects of private international law are: to ascertain whether a court has jurisdiction to determine the case before it; to identify which system of law the court will apply to the facts of the case before it; and to determine whether the court will recognise or enforce a judgment obtained in a foreign court. It is the purpose of this and the next chapter of this book to consider these objects and in particular their impact upon international banking transactions.

**9.3** It is vital that the legal aspects of any international banking transaction be made as predictable as possible. This question of predictability does not normally pose a significant problem in purely domestic banking transactions, since the rights and obligations of the various parties will normally be determined by the local system of law under which they contract. This will not necessarily be the case in international banking and it will therefore be crucial to structure the transaction documentation within a competent legal framework. The most effective way in which this can be achieved is by selecting both the system of law which governs the substantive aspects of the transaction by a suitable clause in the contract, and the courts which will have jurisdiction to resolve any disputes that may arise. In practice this is normally done in a short clause, typically found towards the end of the contract.

## Choice of law

**9.4** It has already been stressed that the parties entering into an international banking transaction will expect their rights and obligations to be as well defined and predictable as possible. The most effective means of achieving this goal is by incorporating an express choice of law clause within the terms of the contract documentation which, hopefully, will be recognised as the applicable law. (Prior to the Rome Convention it was normally referred to as the 'proper law.')

**9.5** North described the applicable law of the contract as:

> '... [a] convenient and succinct expression to describe the law that governs many of the matters affecting a contract. It has been defined as that law which the English or other court is to apply in determining the obligations under the contract.'[1]

The typical clause which is used to identify the proper law is normally the shortest in the contract and a common example would read:

> 'This agreement shall be governed, construed and interpreted in accordance with the laws of England.'

The law chosen should obviously relate to a specific legal system and where, as in the US, a federal system operates, the district, eg, the state of New York, should be referred to.

## Factors influencing choice of law

**9.6** There are many factors which might influence the parties in their selection of a governing law. In the context of international banking the main reasons are often tradition and convenience. The bank's solicitors will already have standard term documentation on their computer system and will as far as possible seek to utilise that. Others, such as patriotism, tradition, familiarity and convenience can be at least as important as legal considerations such as: the competence of the chosen legal system to adjudicate upon and enforce the contract; the stability of the legal system so chosen; and the perceived independence and sophistication of both the legal system itself and the personnel who adjudicate. It may also be important in some contracts to insulate the agreement, so far as possible, from both political interference and changes of law in the borrower's own jurisdiction. In order to achieve this insulation, the parties may be forced to select a completely independent system of law. Alternatively, the parties may prefer to select the system of law which is most closely connected with the contract.

---

1 Cheshire, North and Fawcett, *Private International Law*, 15th edn (Oxford University Press, 2017).

**9.7** Whatever factors the parties themselves perceive as significant, one cannot overemphasise the importance of both English and New York state law with regard to the choices which are ultimately made. Both London and New York enjoy pre-eminence as centres of international banking and both have a well-developed and extensive body of commercial jurisprudence which is well attuned to modern international banking business. The courts in both jurisdictions are widely regarded as impartial, are presided over by judges who are experienced in international commercial disputes and are capable of determining complex cases. All these are significant factors which often persuade parties to stipulate that either English or New York law shall govern their contractual relationships, even where the parties or the proposed banking transaction may not have a close link with either jurisdiction. However, there will be little point in selecting a system of law to govern an international banking contract if the choice fails to be recognised by the courts in the country where proceedings are ultimately brought.

## Will an express choice of law be recognised?

**9.8** It is obviously impossible to consider the attitudes of all courts throughout the world to this important question of party autonomy with regard to choice of law. The focus in this chapter is the position under both the old and the new English rules of private international law.

- Contracts entered into since 17 December 2009 are governed by the Rome I Regulation.[2] This applies throughout the EU, with the exception of Denmark[3] which decided to seek a derogation. In many respects the Rome I Regulation follows the same course as the earlier Rome Convention, but there are significant differences. The Rome I Regulation came into effect in England and Wales by the Law Applicable to Contractual Obligations (England and Wales and Northern Ireland) Regulations 2009[4] and continues to apply as UK assimilated law despite the UK's departure from the EU.[5]

- Those contracts entered into between April 1991 and 16 December 2009 with an English choice of law clause are still governed by the Rome Convention which was implemented into domestic law by the Contracts (Applicable Law) Act 1990. Following the case of *Hellenic Republic v Nikiforidis*[6] a contract entered into during that period could be covered by the later Rome I Regulation if the

---

2 Regulation No EC 593/2008.

3 Denmark is still governed by the old Rome Convention

4 SI 2009/3064.

5 Article 66 of the Agreement on the withdrawal of the United Kingdom of Great Britain and Northern Ireland from the European Union and the European Atomic Energy Community (OJ [2020] L29/7.)

6 (Case C-135/15) [2017] ICR 147.

relevant national court decides that the relationship between the parties has undergone such a fundamental change that a new contract has arisen as from a date later than 16 December 2009.

- Contracts entered into prior to this date and certain contracts entered into since (see **9.9** below) are still governed by English common law.
- Finally, the Rome II Regulation on non-contractual obligations can be of relevance to international banking. These four legal approaches will be examined in turn. It should be added that the Rome I Convention does not apply to certain areas of law and this is now discussed.

**9.9** The common law rules applicable to conflicts apply today only in certain circumstances, namely a number of contractual obligations, and personal and proprietary rights. Everything else is governed by the Rome I Regulation. Those matters potentially relevant to international banking which are still governed by the common law are:

- questions involving the capacity or status of natural persons;
- obligations arising under bills of exchange, cheques, promissory notes and other negotiable instruments to the extent that the obligations under such negotiable instruments arise out of their negotiable character;
- arbitration agreements and agreements on the choice of forum;
- questions governed by the law of companies and other bodies corporate or unincorporate, such as the creation, legal capacity, internal organisation and winding up of companies and other bodies corporate or unincorporate and the personal liability of officers and members as such for the obligations of the company or body;
- the question of whether an agent is able to bind a principal, or a party to bind a company or body incorporate or unincorporate third party;
- evidence and procedure; and
- the constitution of trusts and relationship between a settlor, trustee and beneficiary.

In all other circumstances the matter is determined by the Rome I Regulation.

**9.10** However, there is another category of cases, which until 10 January 2009 were governed by the Private International Law (Miscellaneous Provisions) Act 1995, Pt III. This governs actions in tort, (leaving aside defamation and renvoi) and essentially states that:

> '… the applicable law is the law of the country where the events constituting the tort …occur.'[7]

---

[7] Private International Law (Miscellaneous Provisions) Act 1995, s 11(1).

From 11 January 2009 the Rome II Convention applies to such cases and continues to do so since the UK's departure from the EU. This is examined further below at **9.40** following.

## Rome I Regulation

**9.11** The Regulation[8] is heavily based on the preceding Rome Convention as far as international banking is concerned, although a significant part of the developments between the two instruments arose in the field of consumer contracts which are outside the scope of this text. Article 3(1) states that:

> 'A contract shall be governed by the law chosen by the parties. The choice shall be made expressly or clearly demonstrated by the terms of the contract or the circumstances of the case. By their choice the parties can select the law applicable to the whole or to part only of their contract.'

It does not matter whether the law chosen is that of an EU Member State.[9] In this regard essentially the same approach as is found in the common law and the earlier Rome Convention. So, it does not only apply to contracts between nationals of EU Member States. For example, in a contract between an American bank and a Brazilian borrower which comes before an English court, the English court will determine the proper law of the contract by reference to the Rome 1 Regulation not any principles of common law, or New York or Brazilian law. Equally the application of those rules may result in the proper law being the law of a non-contracting state, such as New York law.

**9.12** Article 3 (3) adds that:

> 'Where all other elements relevant to the situation at the time of the choice are located in a country other than the country whose law has been chosen, the choice of the parties shall not prejudice the application of provisions of the law of that other country which cannot be derogated from by agreement.'

The critical words are the final ones as, if the law concerned can be derogated from, the choice of law will normally stand. A recent case illustrates its effect. In *Banco Santander SA v Campanhia Carris de Ferro de Lisboa* [10] the two institutions were resident in Portugal and entered into seven contracts for differences (see **6.7–6.22**) subject to the

---

8 For some useful background analysis see: R Fentiman, 'Methods and Approaches. Choice of Law in Europe: Uniformity and Integration' 82 Tulane Law Review 2021 (2007–2008), Michaels R, 'The New European Choice of Law Revolution' Tulane Law Review. May 2008, vol 82, No 5 and Tang Z, 'Law Applicable if the Absence of Choice – The New Article 4 of the Rome 1 Regulation.' Modern Law Review, Sept 2008, vol 75, issue 5, pp 785–800.

9 Art 2.

10 [2016] EWCA Civ 1267; [2017] 1 WLR 1323.

ISDA Master Agreement (see **6.79** et seq). The effect of these contracts was that Campanhia would have to make interest payments to the other party under a formula relating the amounts payable to standard interest rates. The effect of this formula was that when interest rates reached near zero by 2009 that party had to pay very large sums of money. Matters were complicated by the fact that Banco Santander had entered into a back-to-back contract with another company in its corporate group, resident in Spain. The choice of law clause in the contract stated that English law applied. Campanhia argued that they should not have to keep paying because:

- they lacked capacity to enter into the contracts;
- Portuguese law's mandatory provisions overrode the choice of English law; and
- the contracts breached Portuguese securities law.

It was held that Article 3(3) of the Rome 1 Regulation was a narrow exception to Article 3(1) and only applied when all the other relevant elements relevant to the situation at the time of choice only applied to one state. Here there were international elements such as the use of the standard ISDA Master Agreement, the international nature of the relevant financial market and the back-to-back contract with a Spanish company. It was also held that the relevant Portuguese laws were not mandatory.[11] The contracts were therefore enforceable.

**9.13** Much of the remainder of the Rome I Regulation deals with areas irrelevant to this book. However, Article 10 adds that:

> 'The existence and validity of a contract, or of any term of a contract, shall be determined by the law which would govern it under this regulation if the contract or term were valid.'

This is relevant where we discuss ultra vires in **Chapter 1**.

The Regulation[12] thus determines that the law once chosen to the satisfaction of the Regulation covers interpretation, performance, the consequences of breach, limitation periods and nullity. If, like the UK, a contracting state encompasses several legal jurisdictions, each separate jurisdiction is considered separately for the purposes of identifying the proper law: see Article 22.

## Determination of the proper law

### *Express choice of law*

**9.14** In practice, virtually all international banking law contracts will contain an express choice of law clause with the exception, on occasion

[11] Article 437 of the Portuguese Commerical Code
[12] Rome I Regulation, Art 12.

of letters of credit. These do not always have such a clause because the instructing bank will assume that if a legal dispute arises to which it is a party it will tend to be a dispute with their client as to whether a requested payment should be made to the issuing bank. In such a case the home law of the state in which the bank is operating will normally be the relevant law.

**9.15** Article 3 affirms the principle of party autonomy, already affirmed under English common law rules in *Vita Food Products Inc v Unus Shipping Co Ltd*.[13] There is no requirement under the Rome I Regulation that a choice of law has any connection with the underlying contract, as was said with regard to the Regulation's predecessor:

> 'We know that the law applicable to contracts and the obligations arising from them is not always that of the country where the problems of interpretation or enforcement is an issue.'[14]

**9.16** The combined effect of Articles 1 and 3 is that parties who are in the country and whose contract is connected with only that country may nonetheless, subject to the exceptions examined below, choose a different governing law from the law of that country.

**9.17** One case in which this arose was *NM Rothschild Ltd v Equitable Life Assurance Society*[15] where a Guernsey-domiciled bank made money available to a Greek borrower domiciled in Greece. The agreement stated that it was governed by the laws of Guernsey. Later the bank had to take enforcement proceedings which the Greek borrower sought to defend by claiming that all elements of the contract applied in Greece and that the contract was invalid because certain mandatory provisions of Greek law had not been included. The court disagreed, pointing out that the bank was domiciled in Guernsey and Guernsey law would be applied as had been contracted.

**9.18** A additional case was *Caterpillar Financial Services Corp v SNG Passion*,[16] a case involving a loan denominated in euros provided by an American bank to a French lender, the loan to be drawn down by a shipbuilder in Singapore pursuant to an agreement written in English. Repayments were to be made by the French borrower to a bank account in London for an account of the lender in Dublin. The French borrower later tried to argue that the loan agreement was solely connected with France, and that as certain mandatory requirements under French law had not been met, the agreement was invalid. It was held that this was not the case and that in any event Article 3(3) of the old Rome Convention refers to '... the other elements relevant to the situation at the time of the choice ...'. In the case in hand this would cover wider elements than the contract itself, eg, the fact that contract

---

[13] [1939] 1 All ER 513.
[14] Guiliano-Lagarde Report.
[15] [2002] EWHC 1022 (QB).
[16] [2004] EWHC 569 (Comm), [2004] Lloyd's Rep 99.

was in English, the lender American and drawdown in Singapore. Had the case been decided under the Rome I Regulation the court's decision would surely have been the same as Article 3 essentially permits the parties to make a choice of law and does not limit this except in the very limited situations discussed above.

**9.19** In practice, virtually all international banking law contracts will contain an express choice of law clause, with the occasional exception of standby and commercial letters of credit (see **Chapter 7**).

**9.20** So, in summary, the Rome I Regulation permits an express choice of law which involves the application of a law which:

(a) has the closest and most real connection;

(b) does not have the closest connection, but which has some apparent connection with the transaction;

(c) has no apparent or actual connection with the, contracts, but which has some underlying connection, eg, insurance;

(d) has no apparent or actual connection with the contract, but which is chosen as a neutral law in an international contract; and

(e) has no apparent or actual connection with a transaction, all of whose elements are connected with one other legal jurisdiction.

**9.21** Article 4 deals with the situation where the parties have not made a clear choice of law. The problems discussed above remain. Article 4(1)(b) states that if there has not been an express choice of law 'a contract for the provision of services shall be governed by the law of the country where the service provider has his habitual residence.' In the case of companies, the 'habitual residence' is determined to mean[17] the place of central administration. A complication is added to the effect that:

> 'Where the contract is concluded in the course of the operations of a branch, agency or any other establishment, or if under the contract, performance is the responsibility of such a branch, agency or establishment, the place where the branch, agency or other establishment is located shall be treated as the place of habitual residence.'

It is likely that many of the international banking facilities described in this book would amount to a service and so this is particularly relevant. It is also necessary to consider Article 4(2) which also states that the contract would be governed by 'the law of the country where the party required to effect the characteristic performance of the contract has his habitual residence.' However, Article 4(3) does potentially assist in that it states:

---

17 Article 19.

> 'Where it is clear from all the circumstances of the case that the contract is manifestly more closely connected with a country other than that indicated (above) the law of that other country shall apply.'

**9.22** Nothing in the Rome I Regulation restricts the application of the rules of the forum to a situation where they are mandatory, irrespective of the law otherwise applicable to the contract. The general principle in the UK is that statutes will not apply to a contract unless the governing law of that contract is a law of a part of the UK. However, this does not apply if a statute is an overriding statute, applicable regardless of an express choice of law, eg, statutes affecting the rights of consumers. Where an overriding or pre-emptory statute applies, the effect of an express choice of a foreign law will be limited to the extent required by the statute. For example, in Scotland it has been held that hire purchase legislation of the forum applied to all relevant contracts entered into in the forum, notwithstanding the express choice of a different law. Such mandatory local laws do not necessarily nullify a choice of law, their effect depends on the terms.

**9.23** In Article 21 there is a public policy exception. The choice of foreign law may be disregarded by English courts, if they are the court of the forum, if it would be manifestly incompatible with English public policy.

### *Implied choice of law*

**9.24** Article 3(1) provides that the choice of law by the parties must be 'made expressly or clearly demonstrated by the terms of the contract or the circumstances of the case'. The latter part of this is the Regulation's equivalent of the common law test of implied choice of law. That is, the circumstances of the case are reviewed to determine whether or not an inference can be drawn that the parties intended a particular legal system to govern the contractual relationship when an express choice has not been made. It is a matter of construction not a question of substantive rules.

**9.25** The Giuliano Lagarde Report[18] describes this aspect of Article 3(1) thus:

> '[the provision] recognises the possibility that the court may, in the light of all the facts, find that the parties have made a real choice of law although this is not expressly stated in the contract.'

The Report draws the same distinction as the common law between inferred intention and the closest and most real connection. The English

[18] This aide memoire to interpretation was drafted to be used in accordance with the Rome Convention, on which the Rome I Regulation is very heavily based. Such aids to interpretation are used in many EU Conventions and Regulations to help fill the gap left by the absence of relevant judicial precedent on the points at issue.

cases show the inability of the courts to maintain the separateness of these two tests. There may be a corresponding blurring between this aspect of Articles 3(1) and 4.

**9.26** The Report provides examples of inferred intention:

(1) The contract is in a standard form which is known to be governed by a particular system of law, even though there is no express statement to this effect, eg, the *Amin Rasheed* case[19] where the contract was underwritten by a Lloyd's style insurance policy.

(2) '...a previous course of dealing between the parties, under contracts containing an express choice of law, may leave the court in no doubt that the contract in question is to be governed by the law previously chosen where the choice of law clause has been omitted in circumstances which do not indicate a deliberate change of policy by the parties.'

(3) Choice of forum. Subject to the other terms of the contract and all other circumstances of the case, common law authority held that an agreement that litigation or arbitration should take place in a country usually permitted the inference that the law of that country was intended as the proper law of the contract. On the other hand, in *Compagnie Tunisienne de Navigation SA v Compagnie d'Armament Maritime SA*[20] the House of Lords held that an arbitration clause was merely one of the factors to take into account to determine whether an implied choice of law could be inferred, albeit a 'weighty indication' or a 'strong inference'.

(4) A reference to particular provisions of a system of law without an express choice of the whole of that law.

**9.27** Article 4 adds that the extent to which the applicable law has not been chosen in the context of a contract for services, (which according to the categorisation used in Art 4 is the most relevant to international banking transactions):

> '(1) (b) a contract for the provision of services shall be governed by the law of the country where the service provider has its habitual residence.'

'Habitual residence' is, in turn defined by Art 19 which adds:

> '(1) For the purposes of this Regulation, the habitual residence of companies and other bodies, corporate or unincorporated shall be the place of central administration....'; and
>
> '(2) Where the contract is concluded in the course of the operations of a branch, agency or other establishment, or if, under the contract, performance is the responsibility of such a branch,

---

19 *Amin Rasheed Shipping v Kuwait Insurance Co* [1983] 2 WLR 250.
20 [1901] AC 572.

agency or establishment, the place where the branch, agency or other establishment is located shall be treated as the place of habitual residence.'

**9.28** So, the presumption in the absence of an express or implied choice of law is that the governing law of a contract is the law of the principal place of business of the main performing party, ie, whoever is required to render 'characteristic performance'. This is a concept novel to the common law. It is a presumption which leads not to the place of performance, but to the place of residence or central administration of the person required to render the characteristic performance. This is an approach found in Swiss cantonal law and subsequently adopted in the Netherlands. Its later adoption in the Rome Convention was much criticised because it is difficult to apply and is too narrow for contracts involving mutual obligations but it remains in the Rome 1 Regulation. The concept involves an attempt to distil from a contract the obligation that is unique to that contract or which marks the nature of the contract, and then to link that peculiar obligation to the social and economic environment of which it will form a part. Payment of money however, is expressly disregarded as an example of characteristic performance. The adoption of this doctrine therefore creates difficulties in the context of loan agreements.

**9.29** Article 4(2) adds that 'Where the contract is not covered by paragraph 1 or where the elements of the contract would be covered by more than one (of the preceding points in Art 3(1)), the contract shall be governed by the law of the country where the party required to effect the characteristic performance of the contract has his habitual residence.'

The problem this causes is that in the case of mutual obligations, eg, a derivative contract, it could be argued that each party is equally "required to effect the characteristic performance."

**9.30** In this context how then is a loan agreement to be analysed? It comprises a contract containing mutual obligations, the bank, (or a syndicate of banks), a commitment to lend subject to the satisfaction various conditions precedent, the borrower agrees to repay the amount lent together with interest thereon; and agrees to comply with various covenants intended to protect the lenders and the reinforce the borrower's covenant to repay. Who then is the 'service provider'? Presumably the banks. It would it one sense be curious to identify the obligation to lend on this basis when the reality is that the structure and nature of the contract requires far more in terms of performance from the borrower than from the lender, unless an entirely artificial argument was to be applied, namely that nothing is required from the borrower unless and until the lenders have fulfilled their obligation to fund. Also, if the lenders were to be determined to be the person from whom performance was required, what would be the governing law of a syndicated loan agreement? Although a syndicated loan comprised a series of loans made by banks on the same terms, creating several and joint obligations on the participating banks, chaos would undoubtedly ensue if each of these loans were held to be governed by a different legal jurisdiction, according to the place of incorporation (or 'central administration'). What that would mean in this context of each syndicate bank? Such an approach would also prejudice clauses intended to equalise the position of syndicate banks vis-à-vis each other, eg, the pro rata sharing clause.

**9.31** This results in a potentially different outcome from that in in *Libyan Arab Foreign Bank v Bankers Trust Co,*[21] namely that the law governing a debt is assumed to be the law of the residence of the debtor, which may not be what the syndicate intended either as it would leave them open to the vagaries of the local law of the borrower. A bank account will normally be governed by the law of the place in which the account holding branch is located. This is complicated by the Guiliano Lagarde report stating that obligations of payment alone are not characteristic. However, it is possible to argue that the obligations of a bank as a service provider are characteristic, so the location of the branch concerned would then be crucial. In the case of a syndicated loan the arrangement is going to be most closely connected with the market by reference to which it is syndicated. This will be the state of the arranging bank. This would appear to be the most convincing argument.

**9.32** Some assistance is provided by the wording of Art 4(3) which states:

> 'Where it is clear from all the circumstances of the case that the contract is manifestly more closely connected with a country other than that indicated in paragraphs 1 or 2, the law of that other country will apply.'

It can be suggested that in the case of a syndicated loan, the presumption would not apply because there would be no single party to whose place of business the presumption would point. Thus, the applicable law would be determined on the basis of close connection, usually the financial market by reference to which the loan is made. This too is a problematic solution. What if the loan is multi-currency, or multi-option; which financial market is then applicable?

**9.33** The question of what law will apply in the absence of a choice of law clause was discussed in *PT Pan Indonesia Bank Ltd TBK v Marconi Communications International Ltd.*[22] The case concerned a letter of credit with no choice of law clause and was decided on the basis of the wording of the Rome Convention, which was slightly different on the point from that of the Rome I Regulation. Article 4(1) of the

---

21 [1989] QB 728, [1989] 3 All ER 228.

22 [2005] EWCA Civ 422, [2005] 2 All ER (Comm) 325.

Convention stated that in such a case, in the absence of an express or implied choice, the governing law will be that of the country with which the contract is most closely connected, and the old Article 4(2) operated on the assumption that a contract is most closely connected with the country where performance is characteristic of the contract. The Guiliano Lagarde Report states that '... it is the party who is providing the goods or services whose performance should be regarded as characteristic of the contract, rather than the recipient of them.' The issue in an international banking contract is thus to determine where this is. If this cannot be done Article 4(5) stated that Article 4(2) does not apply if 'the characteristic performance cannot be determined, and ... if it appears from the circumstances ...that the contract is more closely connected with another country.'[23] This seems closely in line with the English common law approach of the closest and most real connection (see below). The Court of Appeal held that in determining which was the appropriate law the matter would not be wholly determined by a desire to see each of a connected series of contracts governed by the same law.[24] In this case it was held that it was the place where the documents were to be presented and checked, and any payment made that was the applicable law.

**9.34** In any event it seems likely that the case would have been decided the same way under the Rome I Regulation. Now it is the 'law of the country where the service provider has his habitual residence' that would apply. The same reasoning as was used in the case would probably follow from this point. The 'closet and most real connection' point is now raised by Article 4(3) which states:

> 'Where it is clear from all the circumstances of the case that the contract is manifestly more closely connected with a country other that that indicated in paragraphs 1 or 2, the law of that other country will apply.'

**9.35** There remains little limit on the capacity of the parties to choose the applicable law. Articles 3(3) and (4) permit the courts to allow another system of law from the one chosen but only where 'all the other elements relevant to the situation at the time of the choice are located in a country other than the country whose law has been chosen' or 'Where all the other elements relevant to the situation at the time of the choice are located in one or more Member States, the parties' choice of applicable law other than that of a Member State shall not prejudice the application of provisions of Community Law; where appropriate as implemented in the Member State of the forum'. However, in both instances it is subject to the caveat 'from which it cannot be derogated by agreement.' Thus, the limitation on choice is

---

[23] For examples of the application of this see *Samcrete Egyptian Engineers and Contractors SAE v Land Rover Exports Ltd* [2001] EWCA Civ 20019 and *Ennstone Building Products Ltd v Stanger Ltd* [2002] EWCA Civ 916.

[24] *Bank of Credit and Commerce Hong Kong Ltd v Sonali Bank* [1995] 1 Lloyd's Rep 227.

just to stop such a choice from debarring the operation of relevant law in the jurisdiction of non-avoidable statute, common law or relevant aspects of a code. There is also the public policy limitation in Article 21.

**9.36** Factors distilled in days before the Rome Convention or Rome I Regulation point to certain factors as connoting a connected choice of law:

(a) choice of forum;

(b) reference to local laws;

(c) peculiar legal terminology;

(d) contract attraction, ie, the loan is covered by English law, so, therefore, a connected guarantee will be as well;

(e) place of performance;

and a number of weaker elements:

(f) currency;

(g) language (as English is the lingua franca); and

(h) location.

## Effect of choice of law under the Rome I Regulation

**9.37** There is a common law principle that a contract, whether lawful under its governing law or not, was in general invalid insofar as its performance was unlawful by the law of the country where the contract was to be performed (*lex loci solutionis*). This is the principle in *Ralli Bros v Compania Naviera Sota y Azharii.*[25] The question that then arises is whether the principle in *Ralli Bros* is a rule of the choice of law or a principle of domestic law relating to supervening illegality. If the latter it will be unaffected by the Rome I Regulation, but it would be limited to contracts governed by English law. If a contract is illegal in the *lex loci solutioni* at the time it is entered into, it will not be enforced on the grounds of English public policy (Art 21). The principle is that English courts will not enforce a contract whose object is to violate the laws of a friendly country.[26] The *Ralli Bros* principle applies rather to cases that are not against English public policy but which nevertheless involve doing something illegal by the *lex loci solutionis*, usually as a consequence of a change in the *lex loci solutionis* after the date on which the contract was entered into. Note that for the principle to apply, performance must involve the commission of an unlawful act under the *lex loci solutionis*, if performance can be rendered in another way the principle will not apply. For example, if exchange

[25] [1920] 1 KB 614, [1920] 2 KB 287.
[26] See, eg, *Foster v Driscoll* [1929] 1 KB 470.

controls are re-implemented in the jurisdiction of the borrower those laws are irrelevant if the loan agreement does not require the borrower to repay the loan in that jurisdiction. The only jurisdictions relevant to the question are the governing law of the contract and the *lex loci solutionis* (see *Libyan Arab Bank* case above).

### Alternative heads of liability

**9.38** The issue of choice of law can arise where the claim involves alternative heads of liability. Claims can be brought on such a basis and if both or all are successful the claimant can then decide which remedy it wishes to pursue.[27] In *Base Metal Trading Ltd v Shamurin*[28] the Court of Appeal considered a claim involving alternative heads of liability on the same facts, the claim covering contract, tort and breach of equitable duties. The court held that it was for the *lex fori* to determine whether concurrent claims could be brought. In this case English law applied and permitted such an approach.

## Rome II Regulation[29] and tortious claims

**9.39** The Rome II Regulation[30] created a set of rules across the EU governing choice of law in non-contractual civil and commercial matters with specific rules for a number of areas including tort and delicit.[31] It does not extend to non-contractual obligations arising under bills of exchange, cheques, promissory notes and other negotiable instruments.[32] Nor does it determine non-contractual obligations arising out of companies and unincorporated bodies including capacity and winding up[33] or the relations between settlers, trustees and beneficiaries of trusts.[34]

**9.40** Essentially the regulation states that the applicable law in non-contractual obligations shall be:

---

27 *Henderson v Merrett Syndicates Ltd* [1995] 2 AC 145 and *Bristol and West Building Society v Mothew* [1998] Ch 1.

28 [2004] EWCA Civ 1316.

29 For useful background reading see: TC Hartley, 'Choice of Law for Non-Contractual Liability: Selected Problems under the Rome II Regulation' (2008) 57(4) ICLQ 899 , J von Hein, 'Something Old and Something Borrowed, but Nothing New? Rome II and the European Choice of Law Revolution.' 82 Tulane Law Review, 1663 (2007–2008) and J R Weintraub, 'The Choice of Law Rules of the European Community Regulation on the Law Applicable to Non-Contractual Obligations: Simple and Predictable, Consequence Based, or Neither?' 43 Texas International Law Journal, 401 (2007–2008).

30 EC Reg No 864/2007.

31 As is the case with the Rome I Regulation, it has not been adopted by Denmark.

32 Rome II Regulation, Art 1(2)(c).

33 *Ibid*, Art 1(2)(d).

34 *Ibid*, Art 1(2)(e).

> 'the law of the country in which the damage occurs irrespective of the country in which the event giving rise to the damage occurred and irrespective of the country or countries in which the indirect consequences of that event occur.'[35]

**9.41** However, this straightforward approach is qualified by two caveats:

> '2 ... where the person claimed to be liable and the person sustaining damage both have their habitual residence in the same country at the time when the damage occurs, the law of that country shall apply.
>
> 3 Where it is clear ... that the tort/delicit is manifestly more closely connected with a country other than that indicated in paragraphs 1 and 2 the law of that other country shall apply. A manifestly closer connection with another country might be based in particular on a pre-existing relationship between the parties, such as a contract, that is closely connected with the tort/delicit in question.'

Crucially, Article 14 maintains freedom of choice and provides that the parties may agree to submit non-contractual obligations to the law of their choice either before or after the event giving rise to the damage concerned. In practice it will normally be covered by the choice of law clause in the contract as it is standard practice in banking contracts today to include a choice of law clause covering both contractual and non-contractual obligations.

**9.42** Article 14 raises a potentially serious problem as it states that the parties' choice of law will only be effective if it has been 'freely negotiated', a term which the Regulation does not define. Standard form contracts are found quite often in international banking transactions. The ISDA Master Agreement is an obvious case in point, and in some instances loan agreements closely following an LMA standard could be argued as coming within this category. However, the aim of this is to protect those who have standard term contracts foisted onto them and in the case of international banking the parties tend to be large, can afford expert legal advice and have the capacity to argue for changes should they wish. For example, the ISDA Master Agreement has a Schedule to facilitate amendments to the contractual terms. It would be surprising if the courts saw Art 14 as a vehicle for overturning a contract entered into on between such parties.

## The common law approach

**9.43** The traditional common law approach is still applied in those instances where the Rome I Regulation does not apply as set out at **9.9**

---

35 *Ibid*, Art 4(1).

above. For that reason a brief summary of the common law is considered. Perhaps the first key case was *P & O Steam Navigation Co v Shand*[36] where the Privy Council abandoned the previously preferred law of the place of contracting. Later that same year, in *Lloyd v Guibert,*[11] Willes J stressed:

> '...it is necessary to consider by what general law the parties intended that the transaction should be governed, or rather to what general law it is just to presume that they have submitted themselves in the matter.'

**9.44** Generally speaking, this approach was followed in subsequent cases and there have been no reported cases where an English court has refused to give effect to an express choice of law made by the parties. However, although prima facie one cannot deny that under English law parties are free to stipulate the system of law which is to apply in their contract, closer examination of the relevant case law reveals some interesting limitations which have been placed on this supposed freedom. The leading case on party autonomy under English common law was *Vita Food Products Inc v Unus Shipping Co,*[37] in which Lord Wright, giving the leading opinion of the Privy Council said:

> '...where there is an express statement by the parties of their intention to select the law of the contract, it is difficult to see what qualifications are possible provided the intention expressed is bona fide and legal and provided there is no reason for avoiding the choice on the ground of public policy.'

**9.45** The decision of the Privy Council in this case has been the subject of considerable criticism,[38] much of which has centred on the qualifications expressed by Lord Wright. Lord Wright's first limitation, that the choice must be bona fide and legal, has been particularly difficult to clarify. A choice will undoubtedly be mala fide if it is made with a morally impeachable or anomalous and unreasonable intention. This would presumably cover a choice which is made deliberately to avoid some mandatory rule of law which would have applied to the contract if the 'objectively connected' proper law had been chosen.[39] However, other cases may be less clear. For example, would an 'eccentric' or 'capricious' choice be struck down? Would an attempt to evade any mandatory provision of the foreign law be enough, or must the provision in question be a fundamental one? The answers to such questions are far from settled, due to the fact that the term 'bona fide' has been given a variety of meanings depending on the subject matter

---

36 (1865) 3 Moo PCNS 272.

37 [1939] AC 277; [1939] 1 All ER 513.

38 See *Morris and Cheshire* (1949) 56 LQR 320; *Morris* (1950) 31 LQ 60.

39 See, eg, *Golden Acres Ltd v Queensland Estates Pty Ltd* [1969] QdLR 378 where the Court struck down a contact in Queensland for the sale of land which was expressed to be subject to Hong Kong law. The only reason for this clause was to evade a Queensland law governing the level of commission that could be charged.

at issue. However, in the context of international banking law they are somewhat academic.

**9.46** Turning to the second limb of Lord Wright's limitation, namely that the choice must be legal, the position is again confusing. Lord Wright failed to indicate by what law the legality of the express choice was to be determined. North presumes that, as with the general problems of creation of contractual obligations, this is to be decided by the proper law 'objectively ascertained' but one can suggest a number of credible alternatives.[40] At least one commentator suggests that it cannot fall to be determined by the proper law since 'the question is whether the selection of the proper law itself is in fact legal.'[41]

**9.47** A further consideration is whether the chosen law must be connected in some way with the contract. In the *Vita Food* case Lord Wright addressed this question and concluded: '[C]onnection with English law is not matter of principle essential.'[42] Nevertheless, he still found it necessary to identify connections with English law, albeit rather tenuous ones, because 'the underwriters are likely to be English' and 'parties may reasonably desire that the familiar principles of English commercial law should apply.' An alternative view was taken by Upjohn J in *Re Helbert Wagg & Co Ltd* [43] when he remarked that the court:

> '...will not necessarily regard "the parties' express choice of law" as being the governing consideration where a system of law is chosen which has no real or substantial connection with the contract looked at as a whole.'[44]

**9.48**

> Lord Reid took much the same line in *Miller and Partners Ltd v Whitworth Street Estates Ltd* [45] where he remarked:
>
> 'Parties are entitled to agree what is to be the proper law of their contract. [...] there have been from time to time suggestions that parties ought not to be so entitled, but in my view there is no doubt that they are entitled to make such an agreement, and I see no good reason why, subject it may be to some limitations, that they should not be so entitled.'

**9.49** Where the lack of connection is evidence of evasive intent, there is little doubt that such a choice would be struck down by an

---

40 Cheshire, North and Fawcett, *Private International Law*, 15th edn (Oxford University Press, 2017).

41 Gabriel, *Legal Aspects of Syndicated Loans* (Butterworths, 1986), p 11.

42 [1939] AC 277; 1 All ER 513.

43 [1956] Ch 323. See also T*he Fehmarn* [1958] 1 WLR 159.

44 See also *Boissevain v Weil* [1949] 1 KB 482 and *Tzortzis v Monark Line AB* [1968] 1 WLR 406 where, at p 411, Lord Denning MR stated that an express choice of law clause would be 'conclusive in the absence of some public policy to the contrary.'

45 [1970] AC 583 at p 603.

English court, but in almost every other case it is submitted that lack of connection would not be fatal. As seen above the Rome I Regulation[46] means that for contracts covered by that Regulation the courts do not have the power to override choice of law on the grounds of bad faith or lack of nexus with the contract.

## Alternative choice of law clauses

**9.50** In some situations the parties will be unable to reach agreement on the choice of governing law. This frequently arises when one party, as a matter of policy or because of some provision under its own mandatory law, is constitutionally prohibited from submitting to an external governing law clause. This is a particular problem in the case of those South American countries use the Calvo doctrine (see **Chapter 11**). Various solutions, other than expressing no choice of law in the agreement, have been attempted to deal with this problem, but all would seem to be of dubious validity. The two most common are the alternative choice of law clause and the frozen choice of law clause.

**9.51** A typical alternative choice of law clause would read as follows:

> 'This Agreement shall be governed by English law, provided that in any suit, claim or proceeding with respect to this agreement brought by any party to the contract in the courts of the Republic of ......... this Agreement shall be governed in accordance with the law of the Republic of ......'

The proponents of this type of clause argue that such a clause circumvents the difficulties outlined above yet still enables the parties to apply English law should proceedings be brought in any country other than the one to which the prohibition applies. It is submitted, however, that such clauses adopting the Calvo doctrine, (see **Chapter 11**) would not be effective under English rules of private international law since a contract must have a proper law from the outset and cannot be determined retrospectively ' ... by reference to an event (ie, the bringing of proceedings) which was uncertain in the future at the time when obligations under the contract had already been undertaken.'[47] The contract cannot float in the absence of law until the proper law is determined by one of the parties taking an appropriate course of action.

**9.52** On a more practical note, it is difficult to imagine a clause which would bring greater uncertainty to the contract, since there would always be a possibility of proceedings being brought in at least two jurisdictions, one where the prohibition applies and another where it does not. In such a case, since different laws could be applied to the

---

[46] Article 3(1).

[47] Per Megaw LJ in *Armar Shipping Co Ltd v Caisse Algerienne D'Assurance Ei De Reassurance* [1980] 2 Lloyd's Rep 450 at p 455.

same question, it is quite likely that different conclusions could be reached by the respective courts. That said, the standard ISDA Master Agreement[48] contain a choice of law and jurisdiction clause of England and the State of New York. In the context of derivatives (see *Chapter 6*) this is necessary as each counterparty may wish to enforce in their own jurisdiction. However, once proceedings have started it is normally very difficult to get a court in another state to permit a second action to begin on the same facts.

### Freezing the proper law

**9.53** Where the parties are unable to agree on the incorporation of an external governing law the bank (for it is normally the borrower who is impeded by the prohibitions described above) could try to achieve the goals of predictability and stability by 'freezing' the borrower's local law at the date of the contract, viz:

> 'This agreement shall be governed by the laws of the Republic of ...... as in effect on the date hereof.'

Such a clause would need to be reinforced by an event of default in the contract whereby any change in the relevant law enables the bank to terminate the contract and accelerate the outstanding facility.[49]

**9.54** The difficulty with such a clause is that even if it is a valid choice of the proper law any subsequent change in the chosen law will unquestionably bind the parties, since it is well settled that the proper law is a living law and must be applied when the contract is to be performed, not when the contract was made. Such a clause may, however, be deemed not a choice of law but rather an incorporation of law, in which case the contract will be without an express choice of governing law, and subsequent changes in local law, whilst not affecting the incorporation of law clause, may nevertheless negate the effect of any acceleration provisions. In either case the use of such freezing clauses places the bank in a position of uncertainty.

## Applicable law where no express choice is made

**9.55** The importance of incorporating, whenever possible, an express governing law clause, cannot be over emphasised, and it must be said that in practice few international banking transactions fail to provide for an express proper law. As we have seen, however, it may be impossible for the parties to agree on such a clause such as in *Apple*

48 Both the 1992 and 2002 versions.
49 Events of default are considered in the context of term loans in **Ch 4** and of derivative contracts in **Ch 7**.

*Corps Ltd v Apple Computers Inc*,[50] or their choice may be held invalid in subsequent proceedings. It is therefore appropriate to consider how the English courts would ascertain the proper law in the absence of a valid express choice.

## Is there an implied choice?

**9.56** If there is no express choice, then the English courts endeavour to find an implied choice which can be inferred from the terms and nature of the contract and from the general circumstances of the case.[51]

**9.57** An obvious difficulty with this test is that it begs the question: 'How, and in what circumstances, can an intention be inferred?' The court will only have regard to the terms and nature of the contract, not to extraneous circumstances. Furthermore, 'the only certain guide is to be found in applying sound ideas of business, convenience, and sense to the language of the contract itself, with a view to discovering from it the true intention of the parties.'[52]

**9.58** Unfortunately, experience has shown that 'sound ideas of business etc' may be difficult to apply in practice. In *Tzortzis v Monark Line AB*[53] a contract was both made and was to be performed in Sweden. The subject matter of the contract concerned the sale of a ship by Swedish sellers to Greek buyers with no connection whatsoever with England apart from a single clause in the contract providing for arbitration in London. There was no express governing law clause within the terms of the contract. Notwithstanding the absence of any significant connection with England, the Court of Appeal held that English law was the applicable law of the contract. Salmon LJ felt that the arbitration clause 'raises an irresistible inference which overrides all other factors.'[54] It seems probable however, that this is overstating the significance of an arbitration clause, and more recent decisions appear to indicate that such a clause is simply one of many factors which the court will take into account. In so far as international banking contracts are concerned it will be particularly difficult to find an implied choice, since many of the factors, such as

---

50 [2004] EWHC 768 (Ch). In the words of Mann J: 'The evidence before me showed that each of the parties was overtly adamant that it did not wish to accept the other's jurisdiction or governing law, and could reach no agreement on any other jurisdiction or governing law. As a result, [the relevant agreement] contains no governing law clause and no jurisdiction clause. In addition, neither party wanted to give the other an advantage in terms of where the agreement was finalised. If their intention in doing so was to create obscurity and difficulty for lawyers to debate in future years, they have succeeded handsomely.'

51 See *Compagnie d'Armenent Maritime SA v Compagnie tunisienne de navigation SA* [1971] AC 572 at p 595.

52 *Jacobs v Credit Lyonnais (*1884) 12 QBD 589 per Bowen LJ at p 601.

53 [1968] 1 WLR 406.

54 *Ibid* at p 413. See also *Kwik Too Hong Handel Maatschappij NV v James Finlay & Co Ltd* [1927] AC 604.

language, terminology and currency, which might otherwise indicate an implied choice, are commonly used to comply with standard market practices which have developed over many years, and not because of any preference by the parties.

## The closest and most real connection

**9.59** Where the parties have not made an express choice and the court is unable to infer an implied choice, the contract will be governed by the system of law with which the transaction has its closest and most real connection.

**9.60** There are many connecting factors which the court will consider in determining which system of law has the closest and most real connection, including: the place where the contract is to be performed;[55] the choice of forum; the language and terminology used in the contract,[56] though this may not be so compelling where the language used is standard market practice;[57] the currency in which payment is to be made,[58] although again this would not be a dominant factor if the currency in question is frequently used in the market such as dollars, euros, sterling or yen. Other factors may be perceived as important and obviously much will depend on the circumstances of each case. Typical ones in banking transactions would be the place of entering into the contract, the situation of the lending office, the place of business of the borrower and the situation of the lending market, depending on the nature of the transaction. Having identified the factors which are connected to the transaction, the court then weighs them, qualitatively rather than quantitatively, the aim being to ascertain 'how a just and reasonable person would have regarded the problem.'[59]

**9.61** It is obviously difficult to draw a clear distinction between the second test, that of implied intention, and the closest and most reasonably related test. The factors which the court might consider appear to be very similar for both tests. This does not mean, however, that the tests themselves are identical. There is a fundamental difference in approach for, as one commentator points out, referring to the implied intention test:

> '... in the latter case, the court would not have before it the systems of law but the contract document and the conduct of the parties and even customs and usage. All these only go to throw

---

55 *The Assunzione* [1954] P 150.

56 *The Industrie* [1894] P 58; *James Miller and Partners Ltd v Whitworth Street Estates (Manchester) Ltd* [1970] AC 583; *The Adriatic* [1931] P 241; *The Njegos* [1936] P 90.

57 *Re Helbert Wagg & Co Ltd* [1956] Ch 323, where English language being used was not held to be decisive.

58 See *The Industrie (*above n 57); *R v International Trustee for the Protection of Bondholders AG* [1937] AC 500 and *Sayers v International Drilling Co NV* [1971] 1 WLR 1176.

59 *The Assunzione* [1954] P 150, Singleton LJ at p 176.

> further light on the contractual document so as to make clear the implied intention: it is thus derived from the contract document and only from within it. This is the actual difference between the two tests.'[60]

Whilst it could be argued that this is a technical difference, not one of substance, the distinction has, nevertheless, been approved in more recent cases, all of which have endorsed the three tier approach.[61]

### Conclusion

**9.62** The importance of an express choice of law clause in international banking transactions cannot be over emphasised. However, where the agreement fails to incorporate such a clause, a party seeking to bring predictability to the contract would be well advised to localise the agreement, as far as possible, in the country of the desired law. This in itself will not be as effective as an express choice, and much will depend on how the courts interpret the contacts in issue. Nevertheless, it may bring some degree of predictability to a contract which otherwise would have none.

## What does the applicable law govern?

**9.63** Having identified the importance of controlling, whenever possible, the determination of the applicable law, it next falls to consider what the applicable law actually governs. This is an extremely complex question for, as we shall find, although the applicable law governs the substantive aspects of the transaction, there will always be some important aspects which are not so governed and which, therefore, cannot be changed by agreement of the parties. An extensive treatise examining this question is beyond the scope of this book, and it must be emphasised that an international banking transaction, and its documentation, will potentially function under more than one legal system. It will be crucial, therefore, for the parties to the transaction to obtain advice from local lawyers situated in jurisdictions whose legal system has an impact upon the transaction. Local lawyers will give valuable assistance in structuring the transaction so as to effect binding legal obligations in the jurisdiction in question, and their involvement is essential in many international banking contracts. This is discussed further in **Chapter 13**.

---

60 Gabriel, above n 41, p 22.

61 See *James Miller and Partners Ltd v Whitworth Street Estates (Manchester) Ltd* above n 57, *Compagnie d'Armement Maritime SA v Compagnie Tunisienne de navigation SA* above n 52 and *Coast Lines v Hudig and Veder Chartering NV* [1972] 2 QB 34, [1972] 2 WLR 280.

## Those matters governed by the applicable law

### *Essential validity*

**9.64** The essential validity of the contract or of any particular term used in the contract is governed by the applicable law.[62] Validity in this sense refers to matters in the contract itself and not preliminary issues such as power and authority of the parties to enter into legally binding obligations. Similarly, the construction and interpretation of contractual terms will be governed by the applicable law: that is to say, the meaning of the words used in the contract.[63] Once the meaning of the words has been deduced it falls to be determined what the legal effect of such words will be. Again, this question is governed by the applicable law. The parties are free, therefore, to select the system of law which will interpret the often technical expressions used in an international banking contract. This is most important, since although it will basically be a question of fact in each case, a question of law will also arise if the parties use technical expressions which have different meanings in different legal systems. Many of the expressions used in international banking transactions fall into this category, and it is imperative that they be interpreted in a manner consistent with the parties' intentions.

### *Discharge*

**9.65** As a general rule the question of whether a contract has been discharged also falls to be determined by the applicable law,[64] and therefore, a purported discharge which is not effective under such law, but is perhaps under an alternative system of law, will not be a valid discharge. Thus, the question of whether there has been an effective discharge either by performance, frustration, insolvency or subsequent legislation will be determined by the applicable law. The practical consequence of such legislation appears to be that, although it may not be an effective discharge under the applicable law, it may in effect operate in precisely the same way, since the obligations become impossible to enforce in the local jurisdiction which imposed the moratorium legislation.

### *Illegality*

**9.66** The question of whether the contract or a contractual term is illegal is another matter which is not governed by the applicable law. The following principles can be extracted from case law:

---

62 *P & O Steam Navigation Co v Shand* (1865) 3 Moo PCNS 272, *Sayers v International Drilling Co* [1971] 1 WLR 1176.

63 *Chatenay v Brazilian Submarine Telegraph Co* [1891] 1 QB 79.

64 *Ralli v Dennisform* (1851) 6 Exch 483; *Perry v Equitable Life Assurance Co* (1929) 45 TLR 468; *R v International Trustee for the Protection of Bondholders AG* above n 59; *Kahler v Midland Bank* [1950] 2 All ER 621 and *Re Helbert Wagg & Co Ltd* above n 44.

- A contract which is illegal by its applicable law cannot be enforced in England.[65]
- A contract which is contrary to English public policy cannot be enforced in England.
- A contract which is contrary to an English statute which is intended to apply to the transaction will also be illegal.
- A contract which is illegal in the place of performance (the *lex loci solutionis*) cannot be enforced in England if English law is the applicable law.[66]

**9.67** A distinction must be made, however, between contracts which are illegal from the outset and those where the illegality arises at a later stage. The effect of any subsequent illegality will fall to be determined by the applicable law, whereas initial illegality will, under the applicable law, normally render the contract void unless the relevant legal provision provides otherwise.

### Those matters not governed by the applicable law

**9.68** The applicable law, although governing many important matters, is not of universal application. Procedural questions are governed by the law of the place where proceedings are brought (the *lex fori*). This will include such matters as: whether the courts have jurisdiction to hear the dispute; laws of evidence, including questions as to the admissibility of evidence;[67] and the procedures to be followed during the hearing. The evidential provisions of the *lex fori* may be particularly important with regard to documents subject to a stamp duty or other tax. If England were the lex fori certain documents would not be admissible in evidence if the tax or duty had not been paid. Certain other jurisdictions have similar requirements.

**9.69** The availability of pre-judgment attachment orders, such as the Mareva injunction for example, would also be determined by the *lex fori* as would the availability of legal remedies to enforce any claim,[68] and the execution thereof. The question of whether either party enjoys immunity will also fall to be determined by the *lex fori*. This is obviously an issue of considerable importance in some contracts and local legal advice should once again be sought in appropriate cases.

---

65 *Kahler v Midland Bank* above n 65; *Zivnostenska Banka National Corporation v Frankman* [1950] AC 57.

66 *Ralli Brothers v Compania Naviera Sota y Aznar* [1920] 2 KB 287; *R v International Trustee for the Protection of Bondholders AG* above n 59.

67 *Yates v Thompson* (1835)3 C & F 544; *Bain v Whitehaven and Furness Ry* (1850) 3 HL Cas 1.

68 *Phrantzes v Argenti* [1960] 2 QB 19.

### *Status and capacity*

**9.70** The various types of institutions that might contract under an international banking transaction are myriad. Corporations, partnerships, states, trusts and supra-national organisations all have recognised status and powers under English law. As a general rule, these questions are determined by the law of the institution's domicile (the *lex domicili*) and by the institution's constitutional documents.

### *The currency of international damages*

**9.71** Damages for breach of an international banking contract will fall to be determined under the applicable law of the contract. Where the applicable law is English law the principles applicable are those laid down by Lord Wilberforce in *The Folias* [69] which require that prima facie any judgment in respect of a breach of contract should be given in the currency designated in the contract either expressly or impliedly to be the money of account. In many cases this will be the same as the money of payment, but where they are different it is the money of account that should be selected.[70] Where the parties' intention cannot be deduced from the contract, which in the case of an international banking contract would be an extremely unlikely event, damages should be given in the currency in which the loss was suffered by the plaintiff, or more accurately, the currency which the defendant knew or could reasonably have contemplated, at the time of the contract, would be the currency in which the plaintiff would suffer his loss.[71]

**9.72** In most cases the calculation of damages will be determined by the content of the contract under dispute. In banking contracts, where the subject matter of the agreement is not in the host state's currency the key concern of the lender will be to obtain payment of any judgment in the currency of the facility. In *Miliangos v George Frank Ltd* [72] it was determined that creditors under a contract can obtain judgment in a foreign currency and that the rate of payment would be the date of conversion of the currency at the date of enforcement of the judgment. In an age where the exchange rates of most developed countries float against each other this approach seems perfectly sensible. It will be more attractive to UK lenders of course where sterling has depreciated

---

69 *Sub nom The Despiria R* [1979] AC 685.

70 *George Veflings Rederi AS v President of India* [1978] 1 WLR 982.

71 *The Folias, sub nom The Despiria R* [1979] AC 685. This was followed in *Barings Plc (in Liquidation) and Another, Barings Futures (Singapore) Ltd (in Liquidation) v Coopers and Lybrand (A Firm) and Others, Mattar and 36 Others* [2003] EWHC 2371 Ch, where a company was incorporated in Singapore and carried out its internal finances and was required to submit its accounts in Singapore dollars. However, the court held that the currency that best expressed the loss over which they were litigating were Japanese yen and therefore damages would be awarded in that currency.

72 [1976] AC 443.

against the currency which is the subject of the loan agreement since the date of the breach.

## Public international law

**9.73** As an alternative to choosing a domestic system of law as the governing law of the contract, the parties may consider the selection of international or 'transnational' law. This proposal begs the question, however, as to whether there is an international law of contract which can be used to determine the rights and obligations of parties contracting under an international banking agreement. The orthodox answer is no, because international law is concerned only with legal relations between states, and not between states and private persons. Indeed, generally speaking, individuals, including banks and corporate bodies, have no standing in international law to bring claims against states and must rely on their governments to bring such a claim on their behalf. Experience has shown that the governments of lender countries have been reluctant to bring these claims, principally for political reasons, and they cannot be relied upon to enforce rights under international loan agreements or other banking contracts.

**9.74** Since individuals have no standing in international law, it would obviously be totally inappropriate to select international law as the governing law in a contract where neither party was a state. Even in cases where one of the contracting parties is a state, it is submitted that international law is presently incapable of satisfying the paramount requirement which the parties perceive as being a pre-requisite of any governing law, namely, predictability of result. This view is reinforced by one of the most significance cases, the *Serbian Loans* case[73] (see below) on international loan agreements which came before the Permanent Court of International Justice, and which held that a loan from a private lender to a foreign sovereign necessarily had to have the municipal law of some country as its proper law.

**9.75** The general view is that international law has undergone significant changes since the *Serbian Loans* case and, notwithstanding significant practical and theoretical problems, there is now no reason why international law cannot be selected to govern certain international loan agreements. It is submitted that such a position has not been reached. Few, if any, lenders would agree that international law is sufficiently developed to confer predictability upon international banking contracts, and it is debatable whether any court or tribunal possesses the necessary degree of sophistication to apply 'recognised principles of international law' to a dispute arising under such contracts. These fears have been echoed by a number of commentators who recognise the familiar concern that international law is, 'too

---

73 The PCIJ Ser A 15–24 No 14 (1929).

rudimentary to supply all the answers to complex financial schemes,' and would adversely affect the marketability of international banking instruments. Of perhaps more significance is the fact that lenders have a natural disinclination to deviate in any way from established patterns of business.

**9.76** There can be little doubt that familiarity with the present status quo regarding governing law will continue to prejudice the internationalisation of banking contracts in relation to the adoption of international law. It is unlikely that this status quo will change in the foreseeable future unless a majority of states determine that they will abide by and enforce recognised principles of international law. A decision of the Court of Appeal[74] suggests that the attitude in England might be moving in favour of accepting principles of public international law to govern contractual relations. The case also clarifies the principle that contracts governed by public international law can be enforced by the English courts without offending public policy. Perhaps the position is not quite as pessimistic as previously suggested.

## Sharia law

**9.77** An increasing number of transactions are governed by Sharia law. However, in *Beximco Pharmaceuticals Ltd v Shamil Bank of Bahrain EC*[75] the question arose as to whether Sharia law could be chosen as the proper law of a contract. The choice of law clause itself read:

> 'Subject to the principles of the Glorious Sharia'a, this Agreement shall be governed by and construed in accordance with the laws of England.'

**9.78** The bank sued to recover a debt and was met with the defence that the agreement was invalid under Sharia law as they bore interest even though this element of the contract was disguised. It was held by Potter LJ that the Rome Convention (still currently in force at the time) determined that the choice of law had to be that of a country and not a non-national system of which Sharia law was a type. Article 1(1) of the Rome Convention stated:

> 'the rules of this Convention shall apply to contractual obligations in any situation involving a choice between the laws of different countries'.

**9.79** It is possible to incorporate elements from the laws of one state into a contract and this is commonly done in shipping contracts with

---

[74] *Deutsche Schachthau und Tiefhohrgesellschaft GmbH v Government of the State of R'As all-Khaimah and Another* [1987] The Times 27 April.

[75] [2004] EWCA Civ 19, [2004] 1 WLR 1784.

the Hague-Visby rules. However, there must be a certain set of rules to be adopted, and in the case of Sharia law there are a number of variations to be found in different parts of the world. The adoption of Sharia law thus did not provide the court with a definite set of rules which they could apply. Nor was it clear which aspects of Sharia law were being applied from the wording used. The agreement was thus held to be determined by the laws of England alone and the contract was enforceable. This surely remains the position following the adoption of the Rome 1 Regulation, which does state at Preamble (13) 'The Regulation does not preclude parties from incorporating by reference into their contract a non-state body of law or an international convention.' However, as seen, in this case there was uncertainty as to exactly what body of law the parties were seeking to incorporate. In such a situation the parties should specify the law of a mutually agreed Islamic state as the choice of law.

# Chapter 10 Jurisdiction

## Introduction

**10.1** It is important to appreciate that choice of law (see **Chapter 9**) and jurisdiction are entirely separate issues. Whether or not the courts of a particular legal system have jurisdiction is a matter for the law of the forum to decide in accordance with its own rules of private international law. Notwithstanding the parties' choice of an express governing law, it does not necessarily follow that the courts of the chosen governing law shall have jurisdiction or shall have exclusive jurisdiction to hear any dispute which may arise between the parties or to enforce the terms of any judgment. The question of which courts have jurisdiction for the adjudication of disputes and enforcement of judgments is as important as the choice of law issue. Therefore, it is common for international banking agreements to contain an express forum selection clause which invariably encompasses the courts of the country whose law has been chosen to govern the agreement.

### Factors influencing the choice of forum

**10.2** In selecting a particular forum the parties, particularly a lending bank, will be influenced by factors similar to those which favour the choice of a particular governing law. The parties will obviously want to ensure that any suit will be heard by an unbiased experienced judiciary capable of dealing with complex commercial disputes. The relationship between the chosen forum and the governing law will also be most important, since many of the objectives behind the express choice of law will fail if the only courts empowered to hear a dispute either refuse to recognise the choice of law or only recognise it insofar as it is consistent with local law. As we have already seen, the ability to insulate the agreement against adverse changes of law in the borrower's country is of paramount importance to lending banks.

**10.3** Practical financial considerations will also be influential. The lending bank will wish to ensure, so far as possible, that any judgment eventually obtained could be effectively enforced. Of particular interest, therefore, would be the location of the borrower's assets, how easily a judgment obtained in the chosen jurisdiction could be enforced against those assets, and the availability of a summary procedure whereby the borrower's assets can be secured against removal to another jurisdiction. The advance of modern technology has greatly eased the burden of moving assets cross-border, and the availability of remedies akin to pre-trial attachment is now crucially important. In England the freezing[1] injunction provides such a remedy, although it is discretionary and only granted on the balance of convenience. The purpose of the freezing injunction is to prevent a defendant rendering a judgment against him ineffective by removing or dissipating his assets abroad. It does not, however, improve the position of the claimant as against other creditors of the defendant.

**10.4** Aside from purely financial considerations, the respective parties will also be interested in choosing a forum which is geographically convenient, and where evidence can be fully deployed without unnecessary inconvenience and expense. Language can also be an important factor, particularly if claims are ultimately brought in one language and the often voluminous documentation evidencing the agreement between the parties is in another. In such a situation the cost and delay of obtaining a translation may be significant, and there is always a risk that the translation may not accurately reflect the complex legal concepts encapsulated in the original language. Matching jurisdiction with the governing law is also sensible as it saves money.

**10.5** It is usual for the parties and their advisors to give active consideration to these and other factors before entering into any binding agreement. The bargaining position of the parties will obviously be crucial in determining the ultimate choice of forum, and the importance of such choice, providing it is effective, cannot be over emphasised.

**10.6** On the UK's departure from the EU the Recast Brussels Regulation[2] ceased to apply in the UK. It was anticipated that the UK would sign up to the similar Lugano Convention, but the European Parliament blocked this in 2023. It may be the case that at some point this position will reverse itself. The UK considers that the Hague Convention[3] has continued in force uninterrupted since 1 October 2015, when the EU became a signatory. The European Commission however has indicated that it considers the Hague Convention entered into force in the UK only on 1 January 2021 when the UK joined in its own right following departure from the EU. Either way, the relevant law in the UK is therefore primarily governed by the Hague Convention. In 2025 the UK also joined the Hague Judgments Convention.

**10.7** The relevant laws are therefore:

1 Also known as a Mareva injunction.
2 Council Regulation (EC) No 1215/2012 of 12 December 2012 on jurisdiction and the recognition and enforcement of judgments in civil and commercial matters.
3 It applies to the UK, the EU, Mexico, Montenegro and Singapore. States which have signed it but not yet put it into force are the People's Republic of China, Israel, North Macedonia, the Ukraine and the United States.

- the Hague Convention on Choice of Court Agreements 2005 and the Hague Enforcement Convention 2025;
- the Foreign Judgments (Reciprocal Enforcement) Act 1933; and
- English common law.

For cases where the jurisdiction is in an EU state the recast Brussels 1 Regulation applies.

## The Hague Convention

**10.8** Article 1 of the Convention permits the parties to choose the jurisdiction applicable to an international contract. In the case of a federal country this may be a court of a constituent state.[4] Non-exclusive choice of jurisdiction clauses such as those seen In the ISDA Master Agreement (see **Chapter 6**) are also recognised provided the state concerned has specifically accepted this.[5] Any such choice must be in writing.[6] However, now that the UK has joined the Hague Judgments Convention 2025 non-exclusive jurisdiction clauses are covered anyway.

**10.9** Fortunately, matters are straightforward:

- The chosen court must hear the dispute.[7]
- Parallel proceedings are not permitted so any other court that has permitted proceedings to start must suspend or dismiss them.[8] However, there are exceptions here: where the contract would be null and void under the laws of the chosen court, if the party lacked the capacity to act in that jurisdiction, if it would lead to manifest injustice or be contrary to public policy, and if the agreement could not reasonably be performed due to causes beyond the control of the parties or the chosen court has decided not to hear the case. Any of these are likely to be an extremely rare occurrence.
- Judgments given by the chosen court must be enforced in other signatory states.[9] There are limited exceptions to this, namely: where the agreement was null and void under the law of the state of the chosen court, a party lacked capacity to act under the law of the chosen state, or the document instituting proceedings was not served on the other party in sufficient time to prepare a defence or in a manner inconsistent with the fundamental principles of

4 Article 25 of the Hague Convention on Choice of Court Agreements 2005.
5 Article 22, *ibid.*
6 Article 3(c)(i) and (ii), *ibid.*
7 Article 5, *ibid.*
8 Article 6, *ibid.*
9 Article 8, *ibid.*

the law of the chosen court concerning the service of documents. Likewise, where the original judgment was obtained by fraud in connection with a matter of procedure, where enforcement would be contrary to public policy and procedural fairness, the judgment concerned contradicts another judgment or an earlier judgment in the same cause of action in the chosen jurisdiction between the same two parties which would be enforceable in the second state. Recognition of a judgment can be refused if it involved exemplary or punitive damages beyond what is compensatory.[10] There is a further significant exclusion where enforcement can be refused if the parties are resident in the state of the enforcing court and all other elements of the case other than the chosen court are connected with that state.[11]

**10.10** Certain types of contract are excluded and English common law will therefore apply. These areas are not generally relevant to international banking contracts apart from insolvency and related matters, anti-competition issues and rights in rem in immovable property, the last of which may be relevant where security over real property is taken.[12] The other key exclusion is arbitration proceedings but these are rarely used in cases involving banks as the banks prefer the certainty of being able to enforce any outstanding debt.

**10.11** Contracts where a party is a sovereign state, a government agency or someone acting on their behalf are also covered by the Hague Convention. This is relevant where loans are made to sovereign states or they engage in other financial contracts (see **Chapter 11**).

**10.12** The procedure for enforcement is straightforward, with a certified copy of the original judgment being sent to the enforcing court together with any documents showing that the judgment has taken effect.[13] In England and Wales, the process under the Hague Convention is that the judgment creditor applies (without notice) for 'registration' of the judgment in the High Court. Provided that the court receives the required documents and evidence,[14] it will usually grant the registration. Once registered, the judgment takes effect as if issued by the English court, although the other party could seek to contest this if there was insufficient notice, fraud, that it contradicts public policy, the judgment conflicts with another judgment or an there is an argument that the original court lacked jurisdiction.

---

[10] Article 11(1), *ibid.*
[11] Article 14, *ibid.*
[12] A full list of the exclusions can be found in Art 2(2).
[13] Article 13, *ibid.*
[14] See also CPR, Part 74.

## Where judgment is obtained in an overseas jurisdiction and the Hague Judgments Convention 2025

### Enforcement of foreign judgments

**10.13** It will obviously be of little practical advantage for a plaintiff to obtain a judgment or award in any court or tribunal if such judgment or award remains ultimately unsatisfied. It may transpire, for example, that a judgment obtained in an overseas state cannot be satisfied since all the defendant's assets are to be found in England. In such a situation if the judgment is enforceable in that state it is enforceable in the UK if both are signatories to the Hague Judgments Convention 2025.[15,16] This was recently entered into and applies to all judgments including asymmetric and non-exclusive jurisdiction agreements.

**10.14** The rules applicable to the enforcement of a non-Hague Convention jurisdiction are the private international law rules of the jurisdiction whose courts are being asked to enforce the judgment, not those of the jurisdiction which granted the judgment. These rules obviously vary from jurisdiction to jurisdiction, and an extensive treatise is neither desirable nor realistically possible. Discussion will, therefore, concentrate first upon the English rules of private international law, secondly the position under English common law and finally, the comprehensive system of enforcement within the EU.

### Distinction between recognition and enforcement

**10.15** Before considering the English rules it is necessary first to distinguish recognition from enforcement. A judgment may be recognised by a court without being enforced, but if a court enforces a foreign judgment it must have first recognised that judgment. Recognition on its own is a defensive process which acts as a shield to block fresh proceedings being commenced in a foreign jurisdiction when judgment has already been obtained elsewhere. Providing the foreign judgment is recognised, the court hearing the fresh proceedings may well dispose of them as *res judicata*. By contrast, where a court is asked to enforce a foreign judgment the requirement is a much more positive one since if enforcement is granted the court will apply all the legal sanctions within its power in order to ensure that the foreign judgment is given effect. Enforcement will not be permitted if, amongst other things, the judgment is impeachable for fraud[17] or

---

15 The signatories are the UK, the EU Member States (apart from Denmark), Albania, Andorra, Ukraine and Uruguay. Other states which have signed but not yet ratified include Costa Rica, Israel, Montenegro, Kosovo, North Macedonia, Russia and the United States.

16 Article 38.

17 *Commercial Innovation Bank Alfa Bank v Vitcor Kozeny* [2002] UKPC 66.

breach of natural justice or in the case of bankruptcy proceedings has not been recognised.[18]

## New proceedings or enforcement of the foreign judgment

**10.16** A judgment creditor with a judgment from outside the UK from a state which is not a signatory to the Hague Convention or Hague Judgments Convention cannot enforce the foreign judgment directly in England but must first bring an action in England on the foreign judgment unless they are enforcing under the Administration of Justice Act 1920 or the Foreign Judgments (Reciprocal Enforcements) Act 1933 (see below). Rather than do this they may prefer to bring fresh proceedings in England, in which case the action will be heard again on its merits, a course of action which runs the risk of the court reaching a different conclusion. A new action cannot be commenced, however, if the judgment creditor lost the original action or if the foreign judgment has already been satisfied.

### *Enforcement at common law*

**10.17** The common law doctrine follows the basic principle that a foreign judgment cannot be enforced in England without the institution of fresh proceedings. The plaintiff can, however, apply for summary judgment in such proceedings under Pt 24 of the Civil Procedure Rules on the basis that the defendant has no real prospect of successfully defending the claim. This procedure, if successful, will bring a speedy conclusion to enforcement proceedings.

### *Enforcement under statute*

**10.18** The common law doctrine is subject to a number of important statutory exceptions arising under the Administration of Justice Act 1920, the Foreign Judgments (Reciprocal Enforcements) Act 1933 and the State Immunity Act 1978. Of these the first two are the most important and the last of these is discussed in **Chapter 11**.

**10.19** The Administration of Justice Act and the Foreign Judgments (Reciprocal Enforcements) Act 1933 provide for direct enforcement in England by means of registration of the foreign judgment for those situated in states which also recognise UK judgments. The Administration of Justice Act 1920 provides for the reciprocal enforcement by registration of judgments obtained from the courts of certain Commonwealth countries. Registration of such judgments is, however, not a right, and the court in exercising its discretion will consider all the circumstances of the case and determine whether

18 *Servis-Terminal LLC v Drelle* [2025] EWCA Civ 62.

it is just and convenient that the judgment be enforced in England. Registration will not be allowed if the original court lacked jurisdiction to hear the case or if the defendant did not appear in the original proceedings, was not served with process or if it is shown that the judgment was obtained by fraud and the original cause of action would have been contrary to English public policy and, therefore, could not have been brought in England. A judgment which is effectively registered under the Act will be treated as if it had been obtained in the country in which it is registered.

**10.20** The Foreign Judgments (Reciprocal Enforcement) Act 1933 facilitates the direct enforcement by registration of foreign judgments obtained in signatory countries.[19] The Act provides that registration is available as of right, subject only to the following requirements:

- that the foreign court acted with jurisdiction;
- that the defendant received notice of the foreign proceedings;
- that the judgment was not obtained by fraud;
- that the judgment is not contrary to public policy in England; and
- that the subject matter of the judgment has not previously been the subject of a final and conclusive judgment by another court having jurisdiction over the matter.

The effect of registration is that the foreign judgment has the same force and effect as if it had been given by the court in which it has been registered.

## Requirements for recognition and enforcement

**10.21** There are a number of important requirements which must be satisfied before an English court will recognise or enforce a foreign judgment, whether at common law or under the two statutes mentioned above. Some of the requirements, like jurisdiction, have been briefly touched upon, but for the sake of completeness the most important requirements will now be considered.

### *Jurisdiction of the foreign court*

**10.22** The most fundamental requirement is that the foreign court which gave the original judgment must have been a court of competent jurisdiction according to English legal principles of law. In the case

[19] Australia, Canada (except Nunavut and Quebec), Guernsey, India, the Isle of Man, Israel, Jersey and Pakistan. It also applies to some European countries: Austria, Belgium, France, Germany, Italy, the Netherlands and Norway, which all have bilateral arrangements with the UK distinct from their EU membership. It can be extended to other states by statutory instrument.

of a corporation, the relevant test is whether the corporation carries on business in the foreign country at some definite and more or less permanent place. The presence of a representative in the foreign jurisdiction will not be enough, even if that person is a director who contracts on behalf of the corporation. The Foreign Judgments (Reciprocal Enforcement) Act 1933 is even more restrictive and requires the corporation to have its place of business, and carry on business, in the foreign country. The safest course of action will obviously be to include an effective clause within the documentation evidencing the original contract whereby the defendant submits to the jurisdiction of the foreign court. This would clearly be sufficient in England, and most other jurisdictions. Alternatively, the requirement will be satisfied if the defendant appeared in the foreign proceedings to contest the case or to launch a counterclaim against the claimant.

**10.23** As a general rule the foreign court must have possessed original jurisdiction and the requirement will not be satisfied if jurisdiction was based on 'long-arm' or extended rules such as nationality, location of assets within the jurisdiction, or those arising under provisions similar to those found in the Civil Procedure Rules at rule 6.30 et seq.

### *Fraud*

**10.24** The foreign judgment will not be recognised if it was obtained by fraud, and this defence has been confirmed in both the Administration of Justice Act 1920 and the Foreign Judgments (Reciprocal Enforcements) Act 1933. Fraud, however, will usually be difficult to prove, and in most cases it will be necessary to reopen the whole case in order to establish that the foreign court has been deceived.

### *Public policy*

**10.25** The judgment will not be recognised in England if its recognition would be contrary to English principles of public policy. This common law defence was confirmed in both the Administration of Justice Act 1920 and the Foreign Judgments (Reciprocal Enforcements) Act 1933. The English courts have, however, limited the scope of public policy as a defence by taking a very narrow view of its application. As a consequence, there are very few reported cases in which such a plea has been successful and of these the majority have related to matrimonial rather than commercial matters.

### *Contrary to natural justice*

**10.26** A foreign judgment which has been obtained in contravention of the rules of natural justice cannot be enforced in England and this 'notion of fair trial' appears to be a pre-requisite for enforcement in most jurisdictions. We have already seen that fraud will generally be a bar to enforcement, but in cases falling short of fraud it is extremely difficult to define the scope of this defence. The merits of the case will obviously be irrelevant, even though the foreign judgment may be manifestly wrong. It would seem that the defence is based upon the principle that the defendant must be given an opportunity to present his side of the case. Therefore, this defence may well be satisfied in cases where the defendant has not been given sufficient notice of the hearing to prepare his case, or where the foreign court has refused him the right to plead, but even in such apparently obvious cases the court may still refuse the defence.

#### *Foreign tax laws*

**10.27** It is generally recognised that the courts of one country will not recognise or enforce the revenue laws of another country. This principle is followed by the English courts which scrutinise every case in order to ascertain whether the claim is being brought to collect the debts of a foreign country. They will reject both direct and indirect enforcement of such taxes. It has even been suggested that proceedings in England by a foreign government for direct enforcement of that government's currency control regulations would be contrary to the principle of non-enforcement of foreign revenue laws.

#### *Enforcement must relate to a money judgment*

**10.28** As a general rule, enforcement will only be available in respect of money judgments and not, for example, in respect of an injunction to prevent the defendant from breaching a covenant in an international loan agreement.

## Jurisdiction of the English courts in respect of actions in personam

**10.29** This will only be relevant when the Hague Convention does not apply. As mentioned above, these will be cases relating to insolvency and related matters, anti-competition issues and rights in rem in immovable property, the last of which may be relevant where security over real property has been taken.[20]

**10.30** A claim in personam is simply a claim between parties designed to settle rights and obligations as between them. Such an action will cover almost every claim which can be brought in an international

[20] A full list of the exclusions can be found in the Hague Convention 2019, Art 2(2).

banking dispute, including claims for breach of contract or for tort, claims for specific performance of contractual obligations, or for an injunction preventing a possible breach of contract.

## The traditional bases of jurisdiction

**10.31** The traditional bases of jurisdiction will be considered under the following headings:

- submission;
- presence; and
- extended/discretionary jurisdiction.

### *Express submission*

**10.32** The English courts will have jurisdiction over a contractual dispute if the defendant voluntarily submits to the jurisdiction of the English courts. However, it must also be possible to serve process on the defendant within the jurisdiction. Leave of the court may be required[21] to serve process abroad. Submission will not be deemed voluntary however, if the defendant appears before the court solely to contest the jurisdiction of the court. Submission may be effected in a variety of ways, but in international banking agreements it is common to provide for express submission within the terms of the contract. A typical example of a non-exclusive jurisdiction clause would read as follows:

> 'The borrower hereby irrevocably submits to the non-exclusive jurisdiction of the English Courts in relation to any claim or dispute arising hereunder and hereby (but without prejudice to any other effective method of service) appoints and designates ............ of ........... as its authorised agent for service of proceedings.'

### *Appointing an agent for service*

**10.33** It has already been stressed that a submission to English jurisdiction clause will only be effective if it is possible to serve process on the defendant. Unless process can be served within the jurisdiction, leave of the court may be required, and, therefore, in order to avoid the unpredictability of an application for service out of the jurisdiction, it is common to appoint an agent for service within the English jurisdiction, providing of course English courts are selected as the forum. If such an agent is present in England, service may be effected upon the agent as of right. If the agent himself is also abroad at the appropriate

[21] It should not be in most cases. See CPR, rr 6.32 and 6.33.

time, then leave of the court may have to be obtained for service out of the jurisdiction. It is most important, therefore, to select carefully an agent who will be present within the jurisdiction. Various bodies specialise in this type of appointment and it is common to insist within the submission to jurisdiction clause that the agent be maintained by the borrower.

### *Presence*

**10.34** It is the service of process within the jurisdiction which effectively provides the basis of jurisdiction. This extends to a company having a branch in the jurisdiction.[22] Insofar as individuals are concerned, any physical presence in England is enough, although recent litigation suggests that a degree of permanence is necessary and that historic or administrative ties are insufficient where insolvency litigation is concerned.[23] In other cases transient presence may be enough. Presence is also accepted as a basis of jurisdiction in most common law countries.

**10.35** In the case of a partnership, process can be served on any individual member of the partnership who is present in England at the time of service. Alternatively, process may be served at the partnership's principal place of business in England upon the person in control of the partnership business. Similarly, with regard to corporations the crucial factor is presence in England, but this begs the question; when is a corporation present in England? A company registered in England under the Companies Act 2006 is regarded as present in England and process can be served on the registered office of the company or on a senior person such as a director, company secretary, etc. If the company is registered abroad, the position is less straightforward, although such a company, if it establishes a place of business in England can file with the registrar of companies the name(s) and address(es) of the person(s) resident in England[24] and authorised to accept process on its behalf. Service upon such a person will be sufficient, even though at the relevant time the company no longer carries on business in England.[25] Whilst this will suffice for the purposes of the Companies Act 2006 in the context of English common law matters are less flexible under the Brussels I Regulation. The

---

22 *Durbeck GmbH v Den Norske Bank SA* [2003] EWCA Civ 147, [2003] QB 1160. See also *Lloyd's Register of Shipping v Society Campenon Bernard* (C-439/93) [1995] ECR I-961.

23 *Mobile Telecommunications Co KSCP v HRH Prince Hassam Bin Saud Bin Abdulaziz Al Saud* [2025] EWHC 85 (Ch). Enforcement of overseas bankruptcy litigation is also dependent on the overseas judgment having been recognised: *Servis-Terminal LLC v Drelle* [2025] EWCA Civ 62.

24 Companies Act 2006, s 1046.

25 Companies Act 2006, s 1139(2).

position here[26] is that a company or other legal person or association is domiciled in the place where it has its statutory seat, or central administration or principal place of business. In the context of the United Kingdom, 'statutory seat' means the registered office.[27]

**10.36** Traditionally a corporation was seen as being 'present' in England if it does business within the English jurisdiction. A non-resident corporation will only be 'doing business' however, if it has appointed an agent in England with authority to enter into transactions binding upon the company. If, on the other hand, the agent merely acts as a conduit transmitting offers abroad for acceptance, then the company will not be 'doing business' in England. Furthermore, the agent must carry on business at some fixed place in England for a definite period of time; although this requirement is not an onerous one. The presence of assets within the jurisdiction is deemed sufficient by some countries' substantive rules of private international law, but this would not be sufficient to ground *in personam* jurisdiction in England. Nor would presence of a local subsidiary be sufficient unless it could be argued that the subsidiary was doing business on behalf of its parent in England, as the parent's agent.

**10.37** In the case of a trust, the action should be brought in the state where the trust is domiciled, or if the trust deed has a choice of jurisdiction clause to that effect. Likewise, where a breach of the trust has taken place here. The same principle should apply in the case of Swiss-style foundations. If a breach of a fiduciary duty were to take place in the jurisdiction, then a court would also determine the case should also be heard there.[28]

**10.38** There would also be a potential presumption of English jurisdiction where the contract was entered into in England.[29]

**10.39** However, under the Civil Procedure Rules,[30] bringing proceedings overseas is easier and these technical elements are not normally too much of an issue.

### *Extended/discretionary jurisdiction of the English courts*

**10.40** In circumstances where the defendant is not present in England and does not submit to the jurisdiction, the court may exercise its discretionary power under the Civil Procedure Rules (CPR) at 6.30 onwards and allow service out of the jurisdiction.

---

26 See Brussels I Regulation, Art 60.
27 In the case of a trust the domicile has to be resolved by reference to the rules of private international law (Brussels I Regulation, Art 60).
28 For a more detailed list see CPR, r 6.36 and Practice Direction 6B, paras 3.1(12)–(16)
29 D McClean, *Morris: The Conflict of Laws*, 11th edn (Sweet & Maxwell, 2025).
30 See CPR, r 6.

*Is England an appropriate forum and forum non conveniens?*

**10.41** The test here is *Spiliada Maritime Corp v Cansulex Ltd,*[31] a House of Lords decision which determined that an overseas jurisdiction will only be determined to be more appropriate if:

- it is more suitable for the administration of justice or the needs of the parties;
- the burden of proof rests on the party seeking to convince the court that the overseas jurisdiction is more appropriate. Once they have done so the burden moves to the other party to show that there are special reasons why the case should still take place here;
- the party with the burden resting on them must show not only that England is not a reasonable forum but that the other state is clearly or distinctly more appropriate;
- the court must then consider what factors point in the direction of the other forum, such as the presence of witnesses, the law and the location and place of business of the parties;
- if the court is not convinced that another forum is more appropriate they will not grant a stay;[32] and
- if the court is convinced the other forum is more appropriate they will grant a stay.[33]

The purpose of this approach is to determine the 'natural forum' for the case, which is 'that which the action has the most real and substantial connection.'[34]

**10.42** However, more recent developments in cases such as *Vedanta Resources Plc v Lungowe*[35] are of less relevance in the context of international banking as they effectively widened the cases where England would be a suitable forum on the basis that those bringing the action would be unable to sue in their own jurisdiction due to poverty and the lack of relevant specialised lawyers in their own jurisdiction. The latter argument might have some relevance in the context of bond issues engaged in a legal dispute with the issuer in the same circumstances.

31 [1987] AC 460. Followed by *VTB Capital Plc v Nutriek International Corp* [2013] UKSC 5; [2013] 2 AC 337. See also *Nilon Ltd v Royal Westminster Investments SA* [2015] UKPC 2, [2015] 3 All ER 372.
32 *Magomedov and others v TPG Group Holdings (SPS) LP and others* [2025] EWHC 59 (Comm).
33 Per Lord Goff, *ibid.*
34 Per Lord Keith in *The Abidin Daver* [1984] AC 398 at 415.
35 [2019] UKSC 20, [2020] AC 1045.

### *Lis alibi pendens*[36]

**10.43** The court in this jurisdiction can be asked to stay an action here or enjoin an action in another state where the same claimant has tried to sue in both jurisdictions at once or where one claimant has claimed in one jurisdiction and vice versa. Such a court order is to the party not to the overseas court.[37] The grounds on which such an order will be made are as follows:[38]

- it is in the interests of justice to do so;
- the party seeking an injunction against the case being heard overseas can show that it would be 'vexatious or oppressive'. This is interpreted to mean that England is a more appropriate forum and justice requires that the claimant in the foreign court should be restrained from bringing the action there;
- the fact that England is the natural forum does not automatically mean that the case must take place here;
- the stronger the connection between the foreign court and the parties together with the subject matter of the dispute, the less likely it is that an English judge will intervene. The mere fact that a foreign judge will possibly come to a different conclusion than an English one does not automatically mean that the case must be heard here due to the principle of comity;
- parallel proceedings taking place at the same time in different states should be avoided where possible;
- in the event that there is an exclusive jurisdiction clause the court will normally enforce it but can decline to do so where foreign litigation is the only way of resolving multi-party disputes;[39]
- in the event of a non-exclusive jurisdiction clause neither party can claim that the chosen jurisdiction is unsuitable unless the factors relied on were unforeseeable at the time of the agreement;
- weakness in any foreign claim is a factor to be considered where England is the natural forum subject to the caveat that English courts are not always in a position to judge the strength of a foreign claim; and
- the decision is a discretionary one.

---

36 The relationship between *lis alibi pendens* and *forum non conveniens* is that the former has a much longer history in English law. The latter originally developed in the Scottish courts in the 18th century and was developed by the US courts who faced regular disputes in this area due to the federal structure of the country. The English courts later followed them and in practice l*is alibi pendens* has become a sub-set of *forum non conveniens*.

37 *Love v Baker* (1665) 1 Ch Cas 67 and more recently *AES Ust-Kamenogorsk Hydropower Plant JSC* [2013] UKSC 35; [2013] 1 WLR 1889.

38 *Deutsche Bank AG v Highland Crusader Offshore Partners LP* [2009] EWCA Civ 725; [2010] 1 WLR 1023.

39 *Donohoe v Armco Inc* [2001] UKHL 64; [2002] 1 All ER 749.

## Position where the chosen court is in an EU State or the parties are resident there

**10.44** The position in the European Union (EU) is governed by two documents:

(1) the recast Brussels I Regulation[40] which has largely replaced the earlier documents in EU Member States.[41] The key purpose of the Regulation was to tidy up problems that existed under the earlier Brussels Convention.[42] Some of these measures relate to consumer contracts and are not relevant to international banking. However, the balance is relevant to commercial contracts and can have an impact on commercial disputes.

(2) the new Lugano Convention[43] in force between the EU, Norway, Switzerland and Iceland.

This chapter focuses on the Brussels I Regulation in the form in which it was recast and came into operation from 10 January 2015, and to a lesser extent the second Lugano Convention, which closely replicates it, as these are now the sources that will be at issue when drafting current legal contracts in the EU.

**10.45** The Brussels I Regulation covers civil and commercial matters but does not apply to revenue, customs, administrative affairs[44] or insolvency.[45] Its starting point is that:

> '... persons domiciled in a Member State shall, whatever their nationality, be sued in the courts of that Member State.' (Art 4(1))

and

> 'Persons who are not nationals of the Member State in which they are domiciled shall be governed by the rules of jurisdiction applicable to nationals of that State.' (Art 4(2))

There is an additional provision in Art 5 which states that:

> 'Persons domiciled in a Member State may be sued in the courts of another Member State only by virtue of the rules set out in Sections 2 to 7 of this Chapter.'

However, crucially Art 25 (examined below) permits a choice of jurisdiction by the parties.

---

40 Council Regulation (EC) No 1215/2012 of 12 December 2012 on jurisdiction and the recognition and enforcement of judgments in civil and commercial matters.

41 Although not a signatory to the original Regulation, Denmark has now signed up to it by special agreement.

42 Some commentators are not convinced that this has been done in a satisfactory way. For example, see Harris. 'The Brussels Regulation.' (2001) 20 CJQ 218.

43 The Convention of 2009 on jurisdiction and the enforcement of judgments in civil and commercial matters.

44 Brussels I Regulation, Art 1(1).

45 *Ibid*, Art 1(2).

**10.46** The standard of proof in this context is that the court must be satisfied that there is a good arguable case[46] that the court concerned has jurisdiction. If a party is contesting the jurisdiction then the key issue is which party has the better side of the argument.[47]

## Bases of jurisdiction under the Brussels I Regulation and Lugano Conventions where no jurisdiction clause is included in the agreement

**10.47** Whenever possible, an international banking agreement should contain an express jurisdiction clause which affords the greatest degree of predictability to the question of jurisdiction. In the unlikely event that such a clause is not incorporated within the terms of the agreement, the Regulation and Conventions provide a general basis of jurisdiction, which confers jurisdiction on the court of the contracting state of the defendant's domicile and also 'special' bases of jurisdiction which can confirm jurisdiction on the courts of states other than the defendant's domicile. These bases of jurisdiction will now be considered, before express jurisdiction clauses under the Regulation are examined.

### General jurisdiction

**10.48** The general rules for jurisdiction are to be found in Brussels I Regulation, Arts 2–4, which provide that individuals or corporations domiciled in a contracting state should, whatever their nationality, be sued in the courts of that state. The intention of Art 2 is to prevent the claimant from engaging in forum shopping among contracting states. This general intention is reinforced by Art 3 which prohibits contracting states from using certain 'exorbitant' bases of jurisdiction against persons domiciled in a contracting state.

### Special jurisdiction

**10.49** The special rules for jurisdiction are to be found in Brussels I Regulation, Arts 7 and 8 and will only apply in circumstances where the defendant is being sued in a contracting state in which he is not domiciled. If an action is being brought in a contracting state in which one of the parties is domiciled, the courts in that state will not require special jurisdiction since jurisdiction will be derived by virtue of his domicile there under Brussels I Regulation, Art 4. The Brussels

---

46 *Bols Distilleries BV v Superior Yacht Services Ltd* [2006] UKPC 45, [2007] 1 WLR 12.

47 In addition to the *Bols* case (above) see also *Konkola Copper Mines plc v Coromin Ltd* [2006] EWCA Civ5, [2006] 1 Lloyd's Rep 410. In the event of the matter being finely balanced the legal position remains unclear.

I Regulation or the Lugano Conventions will have no application if the defendant is not domiciled in a contracting state and in such circumstances jurisdiction will depend on the traditional bases of jurisdiction. The special bases of jurisdiction which are relevant to international banking transactions include the following.

### *Contract*

**10.50** In matters relating to a contract, the courts of the place of performance of the obligation in question may have jurisdiction.[48] In determining the place of performance the court will apply its own rules of private international law. However, if the parties agree on the place of performance such place will be recognised, provided it is not a sham. Many international banking contracts entail several obligations and in such cases it will be the place of performance of the specific obligation upon which the action is founded which determines jurisdiction under the Regulation.

### *Tort*

**10.51** In matters relating to tort, delict or quasi-delict,[49] the courts for the place where the harmful event occurred or the place of the event giving rise to the damage that has occurred, where this is a different jurisdiction,[50] may have jurisdiction – Brussels I Regulation, Art 7(2). This basis of jurisdiction may be particularly important where misrepresentation is alleged by the claimant and would vest jurisdiction in the courts of either the place where the misrepresentation was uttered or where the damage was suffered providing, of course, that this was in a contracting state.

**10.52** In the context of international banking it is probable that the commonest basis for tortious dispute is under the law of negligent misrepresentation and the position here is that the tort is committed in the place where the misrepresentation was received. See *Alfred Dunhill Ltd v Diffusion Internationale de Maroquinerie de Prestige SARL* for a case on the point.[51]

---

48 Brussels 1 Regulation, Art 5(1)(b). Cases determining where Art 5 may not take effect because the contract was not effectively created include *Boss Group Ltd v Boss Finance SA* [1997] 1 WLR 351; *Agnew v Länsförsäkringsbolagens* AB [2001] 1 AC 223; *Effer SpA v Kantner* (38/81) [1982] ECR 825; *Jacob Handte & Co GmbH v Soc Traitments Mécano-Chemiques des Surfaces* (C-26/91) [1992] ECR 1–3967 at para 18; and *Benatti v WPP Holdings Italy SRL* [2007] EWCA Civ 263, [2007] 1 WLR 2316 at [53] to [55].

49 This seems to be widely defined as any case where the defendant's liability does not relate to a contract.

50 *Hadelswekerif GJ Bier BV v Mines de potasse d'Alsace* (21/76) [1976] ECR 1735, [1978] QB 708 at paras 19 and 25.

51 [2002] 1 All ER (Comm) 950.

### *Branches and agencies*

**10.53** As regards a dispute arising out of the operation of a branch, agency or other establishment, the courts for the place in which the branch, agency or other establishment is situated may have jurisdiction.[52] The control exercised by the parent body will be taken into account in determining whether the establishment vests jurisdiction in the local courts, as will a period of location within the jurisdiction which implies some degree of permanence. It is crucial that they can legally act on behalf of the defendant.[53]

## Exclusive jurisdiction

**10.54** There are certain circumstances in which the courts of a particular contracting state will have exclusive jurisdiction regardless of domicile. The cases in which exclusive jurisdiction will be vested in a court are to be found in Brussels I Regulation, Art 16.

### *Immovable property*

**10.55** In proceedings relating to rights in rem in immovable property, the courts of the contracting state in which the property is situated have exclusive jurisdiction.

### *Corporations*

**10.56** In proceedings relating to the validity of a corporate constitution, the nullity or dissolution of companies or associations, the courts of the contracting state in which the company or association has its seat will have exclusive jurisdiction. This will not, however, include proceedings relating to the winding up of insolvent companies since such proceedings are outside the scope of the Convention.

# Jurisdiction clauses under the Brussels I Regulation

**10.57** Article 25 of the Brussels I Regulation sets out the circumstances in which a contractual agreement on jurisdiction will be effective to confer either exclusive or non-exclusive jurisdiction on the courts of a contracting state, and provides as follows: [54]

---

[52] Art 5(5).

[53] *De Bloo Sprl v Bouyer SA* (14/76) [1976] ECR 1497 and *SAR Schotte GmbH v Parfums Rothschild Sârl* (218/86) [1987] ECR 4905.

[54] The essential differences between this and the previous form of the Regulation is that the domicile requirement has now been dropped. A clause will fall under Brussels I Regulation, Art 25 even where none of the parties are domiciled in a Member State.

'1. If the parties, regardless of their domicile, have agreed that a court or the courts of a Member State are to have jurisdiction to settle any disputes which have arisen or which may arise in connection with a particular legal relationship, that court or those courts shall have jurisdiction, unless the agreement is null and void as to its substantive validity under the law of that Member State.[55] Such jurisdiction shall be exclusive unless the parties have agreed otherwise. The agreement conferring jurisdiction shall be either:

(a) in writing or evidenced in writing;

(b) in a form which accords with practices which the parties have established between themselves; or

(c) in international trade or commerce, in a form which accords with a usage of which the parties are or ought to have been aware and which in such trade or commerce is widely known to, and regularly observed by, parties to contracts of the type involved in the particular trade or commerce concerned.

2. Any communication by electronic means which provides a durable record of the agreement shall be equivalent to "writing".

3. The court or courts of a Member State on which a trust instrument has conferred jurisdiction shall have exclusive jurisdiction in any proceedings brought against a settlor, trustee or beneficiary, if relations between those persons or their rights or obligations under the trust are involved.

4. Agreements or provisions of a trust instrument conferring jurisdiction shall have no legal force if they are contrary to Articles 15, 19 or 23, or if the courts whose jurisdiction they purport to exclude have exclusive jurisdiction by virtue of Article 24.

5. An agreement conferring jurisdiction which forms part of a contract shall be treated as an agreement independent of the other terms of the contract.'[56]

The validity of the agreement conferring jurisdiction cannot be contested solely on the ground that the contract is not valid.

**10.58** Article 25 of the Brussels I Regulation will only be relevant, therefore, if the parties can agree upon the court or courts of a

---

55 Guidance is not given regarding how this rule will be applied by Member States where there is a dual exclusivity clause.

56 This is a useful addition to the earlier form of the Brussels Regulation as it means the issue of Jurisdiction will still be determined by the clause choosing it even if a party is claiming that the rest of the contract is invalid.

contracting state which are to be vested with exclusive or non-exclusive jurisdiction. If one or more of the parties to an international banking agreement is domiciled in a contracting state, an express jurisdiction clause should, whenever possible, be included within the terms of the agreement for reasons which have already been discussed. Before considering the precise wording which such a clause may take, there are a number of issues arising out of Art 25 which are worthy of mention.

**10.59** Although Brussels I Regulation, Art 25 speaks of a court or courts of a contracting state having exclusive jurisdiction, it also applies if the courts of more than one contracting state are contemplated within the terms of the parties' contract. In other words, 'exclusive jurisdiction' under Art 25 does not mean 'sole jurisdiction.' Where a jurisdiction clause is effective under Art 25, the choice of a particular court or courts cannot be overridden by other courts in a contracting state. Furthermore, even when the relevant agreement is concluded by parties none of whom is domiciled in a contracting state, courts in another contracting state shall have no jurisdiction unless the chosen court has declined jurisdiction. Without more one may assume, therefore, that the question of domicile is not important. This is not in fact the case and the subtle difference relates to the obligation placed on the chosen court(s). Where the parties are all domiciled outside the contracting states, the chosen court is not obliged to take jurisdiction and will determine such matter in accordance with its own law. It is, therefore, national law and not the Regulation which deprives all other courts from taking jurisdiction. The Regulation only covers cases where the chosen court is a court of a contracting state. However, it would appear that where the parties choose a court in a non-contracting state, the Regulation does not prevent a court in a contracting state from declining jurisdiction, although this will again be a matter for national law.

**10.60** The issue of asymmetric jurisdiction clauses was discussed in this context in *Mauritius Commercial Bank Ltd v Hestia Holdings Ltd & Sujana Universal Industries.*[57] Here Mauritius Commercial Bank had acted as lender to Hestia, also in Mauritius on a loan guaranteed by Sujana, an Indian company. The loan agreement stated that choice of law and jurisdiction were both that of Mauritius. This was followed by an amended agreement which stated: 'Jurisdiction (a) The courts of England have exclusive jurisdiction to settle any dispute……This clause….is for the benefit of the Lender only. As a result, the Lender shall not be prevented from taking proceedings related to a Dispute in any other courts in any other jurisdiction.'

**10.61** After a series of repayment defaults by Hestia the Mauritius Bank started proceedings in England. The issue arose as to whether

57 [2013] EWHC 1328 (Comm).

proceedings could be brought in England. Popplewell J determined that the clause was valid and that proceedings could be brought in England. He added that the governing law of a jurisdiction clause is to be determined by the choice of the parties if they make an express choice. There was no legal objection to this being amended by a later agreement between the parties provided that there were no overwhelming policy objections. He pointed out that there might be commercial reasons for this, or a change of control of one of the parties, or they may have discovered that some aspect of the governing law was unattractive.[58] This decision was reached in applying Art 23 of the earlier Brussels I Regulation but an analysis of the decision suggests it would be the same under the new Art 25. Since the UK's departure from the EU this case would no longer be applicable under UK law, but the principle will still be relevant in the EU. He specifically declined to say whether this could be done retrospectively.

## The wording of the clause

**10.62** Since the Regulation only applies to contracting states, it is likely that jurisdiction clauses in international banking agreements, where at least one of the parties is domiciled in a Regulation country, will be drafted in such a way so as to select the courts of a contracting state (thereby impliedly excluding the courts of other contracting states) and will, additionally, select the courts of a non-contracting state. This is not universal, for example the ISDA Master Agreement used in most derivative contracts (see **Chapter 6**) often use New York State jurisdiction, regardless of where the parties are based. The jurisdiction of the courts of the non-contracting state will undoubtedly be non-exclusive, thereby permitting the lender to bring proceedings in a number of different jurisdictions, should this prove necessary. The other possibility is to opt for dual exclusive jurisdiction. An example of such a clause may be drafted as follows:

'(i) For the benefit of the Agent Bank, each Manager and each Bank, all the parties irrevocably agree that the courts of England are to have jurisdiction to settle any disputes which may arise out of or in connection with this Agreement and that accordingly any suit, claim or proceedings arising out of or in connection with this Agreement may be brought in such courts.

(ii) Without prejudice to sub-clause (i), The Borrower further irrevocably agrees that any suit, claim or proceedings arising out of or in connection with this Agreement may be brought

---

58 This takes a different line from the much criticised decision by the Court de Cassation in *Banque Privee Edmond de Rothschild Europe v X*, 26 September 2012, Cass Civ (1 ère).

in the courts of the State of New York or of the United States for the Southern District of New York or in the courts of [the jurisdiction of the Borrower if such jurisdiction is not a Contracting State] and submits to the non-exclusive jurisdiction of each such court (this would be amended if one of the other alternatives were used).

(iii) The Borrower irrevocably waives any objection which it may have now or hereafter to the laying of any suit, claim or proceedings in any such court as is referred to in this Clause and any claim that any suit, action or proceedings have been brought in an inconvenient forum and further irrevocably agrees that a judgment in any suit, claim or proceedings brought in any court as is referred to in this Clause shall be conclusive and binding upon the Borrower and may be enforced in the courts of any other jurisdiction.

(iv) Nothing contained in this Clause shall limit the right of any Bank to take suit, claim or proceedings against the Borrower in any court of competent jurisdiction, nor shall the taking of any suit, claim or proceedings in one or more jurisdictions preclude the taking of any suit, claim or proceedings in any other jurisdiction whether concurrently or not.'

**10.63** As this example indicates, a clause incorporated into an agreement which, it is hoped, will take advantage of the Regulation, will have to be drafted very widely, and clearly,[59] in order to cover the lending bank(s) against every eventuality. It will not be necessary, however, to stipulate that the court of the relevant EU State, referred to in sub-clause (1), have either exclusive or non-exclusive jurisdiction because in relation to contracting states they expressly or impliedly have exclusive jurisdiction. In addition to those clauses outlined in the example, an effective provision for appointment of an agent for service should also be included. Conferral of a non-exclusive jurisdiction clause is:

> '... simply another way of saying that the parties confer general jurisdiction on [the selected courts] in addition to the jurisdiction which would have existed.'[60]

**10.64** It is permissible, where the exclusive jurisdiction clause has been incorporated for the benefit of one of the parties, for that party to waive the benefit of the clause by bringing proceedings in another court which, but for the exclusive jurisdiction clause, would have jurisdiction under the Regulation.

---

[59] *Partereedereims Tilly Russ and Ernest Russ v N V Haven & Vervoerboeriff Nova and N V Geominne Huut* (71/83) [1984] ECR 2417.

[60] Lord Hoffman in *Kurz v Stella Musical Veronstaltungs GmbH* [1992] Ch 196.

**10.65** Contracting states cannot require additional formalities to those required under Brussels I Regulation, Art 25 and national laws which attempt to impose additional formalities have no effect.

## Submission before the courts of a contracting state

**10.66** Article 26(1) of the Brussels I Regulation provides that, in addition to jurisdiction derived from other provisions of the Regulation a court of a contracting state shall have jurisdiction if the defendant appears before the court, but as seen above there is no submission where the appearance is solely to contest the jurisdiction. Thus, a clause incorporated into an agreement which, it is hoped, will take advantage of the Regulation, will have to be drafted very widely in order to cover the lending bank(s) against every eventuality. Indeed, even this may not be enough, and we are faced with a situation where a regulation designed to stop forum shopping may have the effect of stimulating it. Indeed, in *J P Morgan Europe Ltd v Primacom Management GmbH & others*[61] there is evidence of this happening. The facts were that a large lending arrangement had been put in place by a syndicate of banks (the 'senior facility') headed by J P Morgan as agent to enable the Primacom group to refinance its existing indebtedness and the engage in future capital expenditure. In addition, the borrowers entered into a short term bridging loan until a bond issue took place. The bond issue did not occur and Primacom then replaced the bridging loan with a second secured facility part of which was used to repay part of the senior facility. Certain other amendments were also made to the lending arrangements. In due course various proceedings were brought by the borrowers in Germany[62] in connection with the second facility. The German proceedings were started in breach of the exclusive jurisdiction clause in the contract, which stated that English law and courts should have jurisdiction over the matter. The borrowers sought to proceed in Germany to seek the benefit of certain rules of German law to try and escape some of the payments.

**10.67** Later proceedings were brought in England by the lenders seeking a declaration that the interest provisions which, inter alia, the German proceedings had been brought to try and nullify, were valid and that a breach of them by the borrowers would amount to an event of default. The defendants successfully sought a stay of proceedings under Art 27 of the old Regulation[63] (now Art 29, which states that where proceedings are brought in two states the second shall stay proceedings in favour of the court first seized) on the basis of the *Erich Gasser* case[64] on the basis that as the German courts were already

---

[61] [2005] EWHC 2426 (Comm).
[62] In both Mainz and Frankfurt.
[63] Though their claim under Art 28 failed.
[64] *Erich Gasser GmbH v MISAT Srl* [2005] 1 QB 1.

seized of the same causes of action and that those proceedings should be determined.

**10.68** Further proceedings were brought in England by the lenders in the senior facility on the basis that the German proceedings potentially threatened their right to enforce the debt. The court noted that under the principle in *Wallersteiner v Noir*[65] a court should only provide declaratory relief without a trial where a failure to do so would impose injustice on the claimant. In this instance the underlying facts of the claim were unchallenged and it seemed to the court to be unjust not to grant it as otherwise the lenders would remain at risk of tactical proceedings by the borrower. The lenders therefore succeeded.

## Legal restrictions on jurisdiction

**10.69** There are several grounds upon which an EU court's supposed jurisdiction may be called into question and situations where proceedings in such courts may be stayed or struck out. Similarly, they may, in certain circumstances, restrain by injunction the institution or continuation of proceedings in a foreign court. This inherent jurisdiction is, however, discretionary and has been sparingly used. It will only be exercised when it is necessary to prevent an injustice.

### Lis alibi pendens (dispute pending elsewhere)

**10.70** One of the most common situations in which a local court may be called upon to exercise its discretion is where simultaneous actions are pending in its own state and in a foreign jurisdiction between the same parties and involving the same or similar issues *(lis alibi pendens)*. For this purpose, actions are deemed to be related when they are so closely connected that it is expedient to hear them together to avoid the risk of irreconcilable judgments. As we have seen, the typical non-exclusive jurisdiction clause included in most international banking agreements is liberally drafted and will make it possible for proceedings to be commenced contemporaneously in two or more different jurisdictions. In an EU context however any discretion has now disappeared and the Brussels I Regulation must be followed. This is discussed below.

**10.71** Under the recast Brussels I Regulation a court can agree to permit an action to begin even though an action has already been started elsewhere. The reason for this is that a habit had developed whereby those fearing litigation was about to be started against them started court actions in either Italy or Greece where proceedings tend to be very slow.[66] This could then be used as an argument for debarring

65 [1974] 1 WLR 991.
66 Often referred to as the 'Italian torpedo' approach.

any action brought elsewhere. Thus, Recital 22 of the Regulation refers to the need to avoid 'abusive litigation tactics' and Art 29 states that:

> '1. Without prejudice to Article 31 (2), where proceedings involving the same cause of action and between the same parties are brought in the courts of different Member States, any court other than the court first seised shall on its own motion stay its proceedings until such time as the jurisdiction of the court first seised is established.'

**10.72** What then does Brussels I Regulation, Art 31(2) say?

> 'Without prejudice to Article 26, where a court of a Member State on which an agreement as referred to in Article 25 confers exclusive jurisdiction is seised, any court of another Member State shall stay the proceedings until such time as the court is seised on the basis of the agreement declares that it has no jurisdiction under the agreement.'

This suggests that the second court can continue to hear a case without waiting for the first court to stay its proceedings. Unfortunately, however there is no guidance as to how the second court should determine whether or not to hear the proceedings.

**10.73** An issue which remains unclear is whether this can be relied on by parties where there is an asymmetric jurisdiction clause because there is no definite legal ruling as to whether they are 'exclusive' for this purpose. This is something of a problem as asymmetric clauses are very common in international banking and the capital markets.

### Exclusive jurisdiction clauses

**10.74** Banks obviously prefer non-exclusive jurisdiction clauses which only allow the borrower to sue in one jurisdiction but which allow the lender to sue wherever they wish, since such a clause enables them to select the most appropriate forum in which to bring proceedings. Borrowers, on the other hand, recognise that unless the forum is exclusive they may be exposed to a multiplicity of suits in various jurisdictions, any one of which may be hostile to the interests of the borrower.

**10.75** As we have already seen, local courts may stay proceedings locally or restrain by injunction the institution or continuation of proceedings abroad depending upon the circumstances of the case. Insofar as exclusive jurisdiction clauses are concerned, a distinction must be made between those clauses to which Art 24 of the Regulation applies which have already been discussed, and those which are not affected by the Regulation, which will now be considered.

**10.76** Generally speaking, where a contract provides for a foreign court to have exclusive jurisdiction, a local court will stay proceedings brought locally in breach of such a clause. However, the claimant will be allowed to proceed if he can prove that it is just and proper for the local proceedings to continue. The onus is on the claimant, not the defendant, as in *lis alibi pendens*, and the claimant's case must be a strong one, showing more than a balance of convenience. In exercising its discretion, the court will take into account all the circumstances of the particular case including the issues traditionally relied on in England in such cases:

'(a) In what country the evidence on the issues of fact is situated, or more readily available, and the effect of that on the relative convenience and expense of trial as between the local and foreign courts.

(b) Whether the law of the foreign court applies and, if so, whether it differs from local law in any material respects.

(c) With what country either party is connected, and how closely.

(d) Whether the defendants genuinely desire trial in the foreign country or are only seeking procedural advantages.

(e) Whether the plaintiffs would be prejudiced by having to sue in the foreign court because they would:

(i) be deprived of security for their claim;

(ii) be unable to enforce any judgment obtained;

(iii) be faced with a time-bar not applicable locally; or

(iv) for political, racial, religious or other reasons be unlikely to get a fair trial.'[67]

**10.77** If the plaintiff seeks leave to serve process outside the jurisdiction in disregard of an exclusive foreign jurisdiction clause, the burden placed upon him will be even greater. A local court will be very reluctant to permit service in such circumstances. Whether the clause effectively provides for 'exclusive' jurisdiction will be determined by the proper law of the contract of which the clause forms part.

### Floating jurisdiction clauses

**10.78** Floating jurisdiction clauses, which permit one of the parties to select the country whose courts will have exclusive jurisdiction, are common in international contracts. Such clauses may find more favour with borrowers since the choice ultimately made (by the lender) is commonly selected from one of a number of jurisdictions specified in the clause from the outset and once selected such courts will have

[67] *The Elftheria* [1970] at 100.

exclusive jurisdiction. The clause may be expressed in the following terms:

> 'The Borrower irrevocably agrees that any suit, action or proceedings arising out of or in connection with this Agreement shall, at the option of the Lender to be declared by him, be brought ...
>
> (1) before the court of the state of ......... such courts possessing exclusive jurisdiction; or
>
> (2) before the courts of the State of New York such courts possessing exclusive jurisdiction; or
>
> (3) before the courts of ........... (the borrower's jurisdiction), such courts possessing exclusive jurisdiction.'

**10.79** Providing the borrower is able to influence the choice of alternative jurisdictions which are included in the clause, he should feel reasonably at ease that proceedings will not be instituted in a hostile country. Furthermore, because the courts ultimately chosen will possess exclusive jurisdiction he will not be exposed to a multiplicity of suits in different jurisdictions. The validity of floating choice of forum clauses will be determined by the proper law of the contract and if local law in an EU State is the proper law, such a choice of forum clause should be deemed valid and may be given effect.

**10.80** Floating choice of forum clauses do however pose significant problems with regard to predictability of result, since they are often accompanied by floating choice of law clauses which may be struck down as invalid, thereby leaving the parties with a totally inappropriate legal document.

### The new international lis alibi pendens rule and forum non conveniens

**10.81** The doctrine of forum non conveniens cannot be applied by an EU court from a State which has signed the Brussels Regulation or the Lugano Convention in favour of another contracting State because the Regulation or Convention itself sets out the procedure for allocating jurisdiction and conflicts thereof.[68]

**10.82** In addition, the case of *Owusu v Jackson*[69] seems to have greatly reduced the scope for the EU courts applying forum non conveniens at all. This case concerned a defendant who sought the stay of proceedings in England (at a time when the UK was part of the EU) to have a case heard in Jamaica where the cause of action in contract and tort had arisen. The case concerned Art 2 of the Brussels

---

68 See *Spiliada Maritime Corp v Cansulex Ltd (The Spiliada)* [1987] AC 460; *Connelly v RTZ Corp* [1988] AC 854 and *Lubbe v Cape plc* [2000] 1 WLR 1545.

69 *Owusu v Jackson* (C-281/02) [2005] QB 801.

Convention (now the Art 4(1) recast Brussels I Regulation and Lugano Convention) which states that 'persons who are domiciled in a Member State shall, whatever their nationality, be sued in the courts of that Member State.' The ECJ ruled that this was mandatory and that the Convention precludes the court of a contracting state from deferring to the jurisdiction conferred on it by Art 4 on the ground that a court of a non-contracting state would be a more appropriate forum, even if the jurisdiction of no other contracting state is at issue or the proceedings have no connecting factors to any other contracting state. The rationale behind this decision is questionable. The ECJ based its decision on the necessity of the defendant to an action having certainty concerning the jurisdiction in a court case. However, statistically it tends to be defendants who have pleaded *forum non conveniens* in the past.

**10.83** The case is also unsatisfactory in that the ECJ do not seem to have thought through the consequences of the decision. It may mean that a court in the EU will be unable to stay proceedings in their own state if the defendant is domiciled there even though proceedings are also taking place before a foreign court in the same matter. This occurred in *Konkola Copper Mines Plc v Coromin*[70] where the defendant, who was domiciled in England sought a stay of proceedings in England in favour of foreign proceedings brought under an exclusive jurisdiction clause in the contract. The external court was in a state not a signatory to the Regulation or Conventions discussed above. It was determined that the principle in *Owusu v Jackson* did not extend to such cases where the English court was prepared to stay its own proceedings. The same legal position applies when an English court in a matter where there was an exclusive English jurisdiction clause, where the court is requested to issue an injunction against the proceedings continuing in a foreign court and this is likely to be the case throughout the EU.[71] Factors that will be relevant to a court in making such a decision are:

(a) where the evidence is situated and the effect of that on the cost of the trial;

(b) whether the foreign state's law will apply and how that differs from local law on the matter in hand;

(c) how closely the parties are connected to the states concerned;

(d) whether there is a genuine desire to use another court or just an attempt to take advantage of procedural approaches there; and

(e) whether the party who wishes the case to proceed locally would be disadvantaged because they would lose security, face enforceability problems, face limitation issues or not be able to get a fair hearing.

---

70 [2004] EWCA Civ 1598; [2005] 1 Lloyd's Rep 67.

71 *Donohoe v Armco Inc* [2002] 1 Lloyd's Rep 425.

**10.84** However, the new Regulation has added Art 33 and 34 which develop this area.[72] Article 33 states that where proceedings are pending before the court of a third state where the jurisdiction is based on either Arts 4, 7, 8 or 9 and a court of a Member State is seised of an action between the same parties, then the court of the member state can stay proceedings. However, they can only do this if it is expected that the court of the third state will give a judgment capable of recognition by and enforcement by a Member State and the court believes that 'it is satisfied that a stay is necessary for the proper administration of justice.' What precisely this means unfortunately has not yet been clarified by the courts.

## Arbitration

**10.85** Arbitration, as opposed to litigation, is often preferred in international trade transactions but it was traditionally seldom considered appropriate for disputes arising out of international loan agreements. One major exception to this general rule can be made, however, in relation to contracts, including loan agreements, with a sovereign state or state entity. Some sovereign governments cannot, because of constitutional prohibitions, or will not, submit to the jurisdiction of a foreign court. In such cases the lending bank may prefer to submit disputes to arbitration rather than risk bringing proceedings in the sovereign government's local courts, a course of action which may not meet with any success. Sovereign governments often prefer arbitration, since it is considered that such proceedings do not compromise sovereign dignity in the same way that litigation most certainly would. Furthermore, arbitration permits the parties to select a truly neutral international body, which will, if so requested, keep all proceedings confidential. However, notwithstanding the obvious appeal of arbitration in the cases already mentioned, it is not without its disadvantages, and it is debatable whether it has any place in the majority of international banking transactions.

**10.86** The advantages of arbitration are enforceability, privacy, expert adjudication, flexibility, speed, cost, the potential for compromise and limitations on the right of appeal. Banks will very occasionally consider arbitration clauses, especially when doing business with emerging markets. This is because of the issue of enforceability and the fact that it is often easier to enforce under the New York Convention to which 172 states are now signatories, rather than a local court judgment. Optional arbitration clauses are also growing in popularity.

---

[72] In the course of drafting the recast Brussels I Regulation, the possibility of extending the regime to all third state matters was considered, but dropped.

## Where judgment is obtained from a court within a Member State under the recast Brussels I Regulation or a contracting state under the Lugano Convention

**10.87** The jurisdictional provisions of the Brussels I Regulation were discussed earlier in this chapter and here our attention will focus on those provisions relating to recognition and enforcement of judgments. These provisions are remarkably liberal and are designed to allow judgments given in one Member State to run freely throughout the EU. The provisions are not limited to money judgments but extend to any form of judgment or order, including injunctions and orders for specific performance which fall within the scope of the Regulation.

**10.88** The court in which enforcement is sought has no power to investigate the jurisdiction of the foreign court which originally gave judgment, nor, subject to what is said below, review the merits of the judgment. It will be for the original court to determine whether or not it has jurisdiction and once determined its decision cannot be called into question.

### The defendant need not be domiciled in the EU

**10.89** An important principle to bear in mind is that the enforcement provisions of the Regulation apply to all judgments falling within its scope, whether or not such judgments are against persons domiciled or ordinarily resident in a Member State. As we have already seen most of the jurisdictional bases under the Regulation relate only to persons 'domiciled' in a Member State. This restriction does not apply to the enforcement of judgments and, therefore, if an exorbitant or extended basis of jurisdiction is utilised by the courts of a contracting state against a defendant domiciled outside the EU a judgment against such a defendant will be enforced throughout the EU.

### Recognition

**10.90** The fundamental provision relating to recognition can be found in Art 36(1) of the Regulation which provides:

> 'A judgment given in a Member State shall be recognised in the other Member States without any special procedure being required.'

A request for recognition or enforcement must be supported by an authenticated copy of the judgment and in cases where the judgment has been given in default it must be established that the party in default was served with process.[73] Likewise, a party applying for

---

[73] Brussels I Regulation, Art 37(1) (a). The court can require a translation to be made – Brussels I Regulation, Art 37(2).

enforcement must establish, according to the law of the state in which judgment was given, that the judgment is enforceable and has been effectively served upon the defendant.

### Enforcement by registration

**10.91** Enforcement is governed by the Brussels I Regulation, Arts 39 to 44 and because the application for registration can be made *ex parte* the defendant will not then be informed of the proceedings and will have no right to be heard. This latter requirement enables the claimant to preserve the element of surprise and, hopefully, prevents the defendant's assets from being spirited out of the jurisdiction before an attachment order can be made. However, once enforcement has been authorised the defendant is promptly notified and may apply to the local court to set aside the registration.

### Grounds for refusal

**10.92** The grounds on which recognition or enforcement may be refused are set out in Brussels I Regulation, Art 45 which provides that a judgment shall not be recognised:

(1) if such recognition is contrary to public policy in the State in which recognition is sought;

(2) where it was given in default of appearance, if the defendant was not served with the document which instituted the proceedings or with an equivalent document in sufficient time to enable him to arrange for his defence unless the defendant failed to commence proceedings to challenge the judgment when it was possible for him to do so;

(3) the judgment is irreconcilable with a judgment given in a dispute between the same parties in the Member State in which recognition is sought;

(4) if the judgment conflicts with Sections 3, 4, 5 or 6 of Chapter II of the Regulation.

**10.93** There is no specific provision in the Brussels I Regulation for refusal based upon the ground that the original judgment was obtained by fraud. Under civil law systems this ground is subsumed within the head of public policy.

## Conclusion

**10.94** Insofar as international banking transactions are concerned, lenders will obviously be well advised to investigate the position relating to recognition and enforcement in the borrower's own jurisdiction that of any guarantor and in those jurisdictions where the borrower's assets are located. These questions should be addressed before any agreement is executed, and the advice of local lawyers will normally be required to confirm the position. As we have seen, the rules can be very complex, but providing appropriate precautions are taken it should be possible for a lending bank to take advantage of the relevant provisions relating to recognition and enforcement of foreign judgments.

# Chapter 11 Sovereign Risk

## Sovereign risk

**11.1** One issue arising in relation to determining jurisdiction is what view the courts of that state will take if one of the parties to the action is a sovereign state or a state entity. This brings in the doctrine of sovereign risk. This is one aspect of country risk, which refers to the assessment of the risk of default by a borrower in a particular country which has regard to a large number of risk factors.

**11.2** The concern in this context is with the legal aspects of sovereign risk, and it must be appreciated that these affect not only sovereign borrowers (which includes state controlled entities), but also private borrowers who may be affected by sovereign actions such as expropriation of property, or the imposition of exchange controls. Thus, this chapter uses the term 'state' to include both the state and entities inseparable from the state, such as departments of the central government. With this in mind this chapter takes the issues in the following order:

- has the state been recognised;
- sovereign immunity; and
- changes in the law of the state in question.

## Recognition of states

### General UK position

**11.3** Normally this is not an issue as it will be the case that there is clearly a legally recognised government in power in an overseas state with which the UK has diplomatic relations. It is worth briefly considering the issue however as problems normally arise from *coups d'etat,* where by unconstitutional means a government can be overthrown. In some cases, for a time, which may possibly be prolonged, there may be two rival governments. A change in government without a change of the Head of State calls for no new recognition. One need consider only those cases in which the whole regime, including its Head of State, is overthrown.

**11.4** It is essential to appreciate that, unlike questions of immunity, recognition is not a legal matter for judges, but a political matter for the government of the United Kingdom to decide. The UK government recognises only states, because it is sometimes an embarrassing political matter to be called upon to recognise, or not to recognise, a government the UK government has extracted itself from the difficulty by refusing to do so. The courts must infer the political question of recognition from the UK government's dealings with the new regime. The means by which this is to be done remains obscure, in part because the number of cases where the matter arises remain so few, but presumably the most relevant feature is whether or not the UK government meets with, deals with, or enters contracts with the new regime. It is uncertain whether the UK courts should consider the matters traditionally considered by the UK Foreign Office such as occupation of territory, size of the population controlled, whether that control is effective and whether the ability exists to conduct international relations. These seem to be factors relevant to the making of a political decision, whereas the question the UK courts must ask themselves is the factual question of whether, on the basis of such considerations, the UK government has made a political decision on recognition, but also others, such as, say, hostility to the policies of the foreign regime. The question for the courts is not 'do the facts justify recognition' but 'has the UK government recognised?' Presumably, however, the UK government would not recognise a state without standard criteria such as territory, population and control, so that these facts may remain relevant for consideration by the courts, while being insufficient in themselves.

**11.5** The guidelines were set out in *Republic of Somalia v Woodhouse, Drake & Carey (Suisse) SA (The Mary)*[1] later applied in *Sierra Leone Telecommunications Co Ltd v Barclays Bank Plc*[2] and are:

- is the foreign body the constitutional government of the state;
- what is the degree, nature and suitability of the administrative control that it exercises over the territory of the state concerned;
- whether Her Majesty's government has had any dealings with it and if so their nature; and
- in marginal cases, the extent of international recognition that it has as the government of the state.

It should be noted that once a government is recognised, this confers retroactive legitimacy on its previous acts and legislation, etc. However,

---

1 [1993] QB 54. See also *Serbia v Imageset International NV* [2009] EWHC 2853; *R (on application of Kibris Turk Hava Tallari) v Secretary of State for Transport* [2009] EWHC 1918; *AY Bank (in liquidation) v Bosnia and Herzegovnia* [2006] EWHC 830 Ch, [2006] All ER Comm 463. There is some useful material in A Grossman, 'Nationality and the Unrecognised State' (2001) 50(4) ICLQ 849–876 and J Hopkins, 'Government of Foreign State – Proof of Existence', (1998) 57(3) CLJ 436–438.

2 [1998] 2 All ER 820.

recognition of a de facto government as de jure does not invalidate previous acts of the previous de jure government[3].

**11.6** Applying this principle was the case of *Bouhadi v Breish.*[4] Here proceedings took place to determine which of competing appointees should be able to Chair Libya's Sovereign Wealth Fund. The parties concerned represented competing regime factions who were seeking to be the government of that state. As the British government were supporting attempts to agree on a government of national accord it was deemed premature to rule on the matter.

### Liability of one regime for debts of another: state continuity

**11.7** A change of government, including change of Head of State, does not affect the continuance of the state, which remains bound by its obligations. This principle treats a government rather like an agent who contracts debts for his principal, the state, and is very widely accepted, throughout the world. The former communist states, for example, have tended to agree to honour bonds issued by the previous state. In large measure this is a pragmatic state of affairs to maintain access to world financial markets.

## Sovereign immunity

**11.8** In the days when sovereigns were mainly individual persons, they were seen as being above ordinary trade, and were widely exempted from ordinary trade laws.[5] Today, with personal monarchy having ceased to be a significant part of world affairs, and the considerable growth in the extent to which governments are involved in trade, the immunity given to sovereigns is greatly reduced. The modern idea of immunity is generally thought of as restrictive, and a distinction is drawn between governmental acts *(acta imperil)* and commercial acts *(acta gestionis).* Generally, in most commercial jurisdictions, the state has immunity in relation to governmental acts, and not in relation to commercial acts. However, there are numerous differences of approach. Some jurisdictions differentiate 'commercial' from 'governmental' by reference to the purpose of a transaction, eg, a loan agreement for arms purchases may be governmental, while others look to the nature of the transaction. For example, a loan agreement is by definition commercial. Some jurisdictions allow declaratory judgments, but not legal remedies if the state fails to comply. Some allow seizure

---

3 See also *Hashi v Sec of State for the Home Department* [2016] EWCA Civ 1136.

4 [2016] EWHC 602 (Comm).

5 This area of law has a long history and started with Pope Gelasius 1 (492–496) creating it to protect the Catholic Church and its property. For a modern English precedent on the point see *Compania Naviera Vascongado v Steamship Cristina* [1938] AC 485.

of commercial but not governmental assets. Some restrict pre-trial remedies, such as injunctions. Some extend the range of actions and remedies if the state consents, and others will not.

**11.9** On public policy grounds English courts will not enforce the claim of a foreign state based on its own sovereign authority. In *The Government of India v Taylor*[6] it was held that the tax laws of one state could not be enforced in another.[7] In *Mbasogo v Logo Ltd*[8] it was determined that the Government of Equitorial Guinea could not sue in the English courts for costs against those engaged in a coup attempt against it. However, claims by states are admissible if it is to enforce a private right, ie, one that could be brought by a private person.[9] State immunity cannot however be invoked in a wider area and it is limited to a state's property, its servants and agents.[10]

**11.10** The law here is primarily regulated by the State Immunity Act 1978. Nevertheless, it is necessary to first consider the common law where the Act does not apply to the transaction.

## The common law

**11.11** A state has general immunity from suit, but not when it engages in commercial transactions. The key case is *I Congresso del Partido*[11] in which Cuban State enterprises contracted to deliver sugar to a Chilean company, delivery to be aboard Cuban ships owned by Cuban State controlled companies. After the violent fall of the Chilean government, Cuba broke off diplomatic relations with Chile, decided to end commercial dealings and accordingly sold the sugar elsewhere. Following arbitration in the UK, the matter went to the House of Lords, which applied the restrictive theory already referred to. Considering the nature of the transaction rather than its purpose, this was a commercial sale of sugar. The Cuban government, therefore, had no immunity from suit. Clearly, the only connection in this case with the UK was the arbitration clause which brought the parties to London. The issue of a necessary connection was not raised. Lord Denning MR has said that a UK court should adjudicate on the liability of a state only if the commercial transaction has a close connection, either by the presence of the parties or by the nature of the dispute.

---

6 [1955] AC 491. However, this principle is not applied to the enforcement of foreign financial services proceedings. See *United States Securities and Exchange Commission v Manterfield* [2009] EWCA Civ 27, [2010] 1 WLR 172.

7 See also *Att Gen (New Zealand) v Oritz* [1984] AC 1, *Re Norway's Application (Nos 1 and 2)* [1990] 1 AC 723 and *United States v Inkley* [1989] QB 255.

8 [2006] EWCA Civ 1370.

9 *Emperor of Austria v Day and Kossuth* [1861] 3 De GF & J 217.

10 *Belhaj v Straw; Rahmatullah v Ministry of Defence* [2014] EWCA Civ 1394; [2015] 2 WLR 1105; [2016] 1 All ER 121.

11 [1983] AC 244.

**11.12** The common law of immunity did not apply to entities separate from the state. These will be considered in due course.

## State Immunity Act 1978

**11.13** The Act is the result of a European (not EU) Convention on State Immunity, and it has effect for affected transactions. This governs court actions in the UK against other sovereign states, not actions against the UK itself.[12] It will be seen that it is necessary to distinguish between the state itself, constituent territories of a federal state, separate entities which are not part of the government of its executive organs, and central banks. It is also necessary to distinguish between jurisdiction and enforcement. The Act does not affect any diplomatic immunities given by the Diplomatic Privileges Act 1964[13] or the Consular Relations Act 1968,[14] by which, for example, diplomatic premises are given immunity[15].

### *States*

**11.14** 'State' is defined by s 14(1) of the State Immunity Act 1978 as the state itself, its sovereign or head of state, the government of the state, and any government department. The Secretary of State may certify whether a territory is a state, or a person its head.

### *Immunity from jurisdiction*

**11.15** The general rule, stated in the State Immunity Act 1978, s 1, is that the state is immune from the jurisdiction of the UK courts, except as provided in the Act. 'State' covers officials and employees when acting in an official capacity. This has been interpreted by the courts in an extremely wide manner in that it has been taken to cover acting in a malicious manner or involving criminal behaviour if done in their pursuance of their official capacity.[16] This has also been taken to cover behaviour amounting to libel,[17] contempt of court,[18] negligence and corruption.[19] The immunity is automatic and need not be claimed. The exceptions are all important, but it should be noted that the mere fact that immunity is removed does not mean that an English court

---

12 These are covered by the Crown Proceedings Act 1947.
13 Putting into effect the Vienna Convention on Diplomatic Relations.
14 Putting into effect the Vienna Convention on Consular Relations.
15 See *Re P (Diplomatic Immunity: Jurisdiction)* [1988] 1 FLR 1026 CA Civ Div. For an analysis see Barker CJ 'State Immunity, Diplomatic Immunity and Act of State: a triple protection against legal action.' (1998) 47(4) ICLQ 950.
16 *Jones v Minister of the Interior* [2006] UKHL 26 [2007] 1 AC 270.
17 *Holland v Lampen-Wolfe* [2000] 1 WLR 1573.
18 *Propend Finance Pty Land Ltd v Sing* (1997) The Times, 2 May.
19 *Zoernsch v Waldock* [1964] 1 WLR 675.

has jurisdiction where the case is unconnected with the UK. There are two steps:

(1) Is the state immune? If the answer is yes, no action may proceed. If the answer is no, the second question which must be asked is;

(2) has the UK court got jurisdiction?[20] This depends on matters examined elsewhere, and depends on such matters as submission, presence, or the effect of Civil Procedure Rules, Pt 11. In the case of submission, this would simultaneously remove immunity and give the court jurisdiction. This being said, the exceptions, where the state is not immune, are as follows:

- Submission to jurisdiction.[21] Submission may occur at the time of the action or in a prior contract. Merely agreeing to English governing law is insufficient.[22] Submission can be given by the state's ambassador in the UK. Submission both removes immunity, and under ordinary principles applicable to any defendant, gives the UK court jurisdiction.

- Commercial transactions.[23] A state is not immune as regards proceedings relating to a 'commercial transaction into by the State.'

**11.16** It will, however, be immune even for commercial transactions if the other party is also a state, or if the parties have agreed otherwise in writing. Here the contract might exclude the Act entirely, in which case the common law would apply, and the state may not be immune. Or it might expressly say in writing that the state is immune, in which case neither the Act, nor the common law would apply. It is thought that an agreement that other courts have jurisdiction would amount to a contrary agreement.

### *Common law issue estoppel*

**11.17** In the recent case of *Hulley Enterprises Ltd and others v The Russian Federation*[24] it was held that sovereign immunity has no special status beyond that set out in the State Immunity Act 1978 and thus has no precedence over issues of public policy. Thus, the principle of issue estoppel was relevant which determines that a case already determined by a foreign court with competent jurisdiction cannot be re-litigated in the English courts.

---

20 CPR, Pt 11, Disputing the Court's Jurisdiction.
21 State Immunity Act 1978, s 2(1).
22 *Ibid*, s 2(2).
23 *Ibid*, s 3.
24 [2025] EWCA Civ 108.

*Investment treaties*

**11.18** Bilateral investment treaties do not waive sovereign immunity unless they specifically say so and this position does not change if a state ratifies the New York Convention.[25] In the recent case of *The Republic of India v CC Devas (Mauritius) Ltd and others*[26] it was determined that India's ratification of the New York Convention did not of itself amount to submission to the jurisdiction of the English courts. Here, two arbitration awards made under the India-Mauritius Bilateral Investment Treaty against the Government of India could not be enforced against them in the English courts. Sovereign immunity is one of the fundamental rules of the international legal order and will only be over-ridden by the terms of the State Immunity Act 1978. There was no evidence that the New York Convention was intended to override sovereign immunity, and any such waiver would require statement to that effect which was clear and express.

**11.19** However, the converse applies where the ICISD Convention applies.[27] In *Republic of Zimbabwe v Border Timbers and another,*[28] the Privy Council held that Article 54 of the ICISD Convention did waive sovereign immunity and thus the awards could be enforced. Likewise, when in an arbitration the phrase 'final, binding and wholly enforceable' was used, it amounted to written consent for the purposes of the State Immunity Act 1978, s 13(3) for both submission and execution.[29] Banking contracts do not normally contain arbitration clauses, but the case is useful as the wording would have the same effect if included in a banking contract.

**11.20** Service against a state is normally via the Foreign and Commonwealth Office who will forward it to the foreign ministry of the relevant state.[30] An alternative arises where a state has publicly announced that it can be served in a particular manner.[31]

**11.21** 'Commercial transaction' means (a) a contract for the supply of goods or services, (b) a loan, financial transaction or guarantee

25 The Convention on the Recognition and Enforcement of Foreign Arbitral Awards ('New York Convention') 1958 which applies to the recognition and enforcement of arbitral awards and the referral by a court to arbitration.

26 [2025] EWHC 964 (Comm). The same conclusion was reached in Australia in the case of *India v CCDM Holdings LLC* [2025] FCAFC 2 although the reasoning there was that the arbitration ruling did not relate to a commercial matter.

27 The Convention on the Settlement of Investment Disputes between States and Nationals of Other States 1966.

28 [2026] UKSC 9 .See also the linked case of *Infrastructure Services Luxembourg SARL and another v Kingdom of Spain* [2026] UKSC 9..

29 *General Dynamics United Kingdom Ltd v The State of Libya* [2025] EWCA Civ 134.

30 State Immunity Act 1978, s 12.

31 *ABCI v Banque Franco-Tunisienne* [2002] 1 Lloyd's Rep 511 at [177]–[185]; [2003] 2 Lloyd's Rep 146, at [29]-[34].

or indemnity in respect of these,[32] and (c) any other transaction not involving the exercise of sovereign authority. It follows from the definition that except for the third of these it is, as at common law, the nature, not the purpose of a transaction which counts, and that the reason for breach of financial expediency, or state policy is immaterial.

**11.22** Further an obligation of a State which is to be performed wholly or partly in the UK is not immune whether it is a commercial transaction or not.[33] In this context a loan is regarded as a commercial arrangement regardless of the transaction it relates to.[34]

**11.23** Other exceptions, which are of less importance to bankers in view of the commercial transaction exception, concern written agreements for arbitration in the UK, ships used for commercial purposes,[35] contracts of employment relating to non-governmental functions,[36] death or personal injury or damage to or loss of tangible propertycaused by an act or omission in the UK (although the exception does not extend to computer hacking from abroad as the act concerned takes place in the UK),[37] any interest of the state in, or its possession or use of, immoveable property in the UK or any obligation of the state arising out of its interest in, or possession or use of such property,[38] intellectual property[39] and the membership of a state (in certain circumstances) of a corporation, unincorporated body, or partnership.[40]

**11.24** If any of the exceptions above apply, the state is not immune from jurisdiction. Enforcement is another matter.

### *Immunity from enforcement*

**11.25** The de-immunisation in relation to jurisdiction is very clear for a commercial transaction. However, having obtained judgment, ie, a declaration of liability, or judgment for damages or a sum of money, it may not be possible for the claimant to avail himself of all the ordinary legal remedies against a state or others. The Act proceeds by first excluding all the available remedies, injunctions, specific performance, orders for the recovery of land and other property, all proceedings

---

32 In *Svenska Petroleum Exploration AB v Government of the Republic of Lithuania* [2006] EWCA Civ 1529, [2007] QB 886. The Court of Appeal said that this mirrored the distinction in the UN Convention on Jurisdictional Immunities of States and Their Property (Resolution 59/38 of 16 December 2004) and that found in English common law.

33 State Immunity Act 1978, s 3.

34 *Ibid*, s 3(3)(b).

35 *Ibid*, s 10.

36 *Ibid*, s 4. *Royal Embassy of Saudi Arabia (Cultural Bureau) v Costantine* [2025] UKSC 9 and *Kingdom of Spain v Lorenzo* [2024] EWCA Civ 1602.

37 State Immunity Act 1978, s 5. *Shehabi and another v Kingdom of Bahrain* [2024] EWCA Civ 1158.

38 State Immunity Act 1978, s 6.

39 *Ibid*, s 7.

40 *Ibid*, s 8.

against the state property to enforce judgments or arbitration awards, and any actions in rem or orders for the arrest, detention or sale of the property, and then goes on to provide for exceptions from immunity.[41] The exceptions are as follows:

- If the state gives written consent at the time, or in the contract, or by treaty. Such consent may be partial, eg, exempting military assets. A complicating factor here is that the State Immunity Act 1978, s 13(5) states that 'the head of a State's diplomatic mission in the UK, or the person for the time being performing his functions, shall be deemed to have authority to give on behalf of the State any such consent as is mentioned in s.13(3).' This is different from the wording in the State Immunity Act 1978, s 2(7) which states that a person who has authority to contract on behalf of a state shall be deemed to have authority to give consent with regard to proceedings arising out of it. It would be wise therefore to err on the side of caution and make sure that in a contract providing a waiver permitting enforcement is signed by someone who satisfies the definition in the State Immunity Act 1978, s 13(5) or s 13(3). Section 13(3) states that enforcement can be permitted if consent has been given to that effect but that consent to jurisdiction alone is insufficient. It is, therefore, important to bear this in mind when a contract is signed with a state. Does the signatory have the legal capacity to bind the state where a waiver of immunity against enforcement clause is included?

- Process such as orders against property, rather than personal orders such as injunctions or specific performance, may be issued if property is used or intended to be used for commercial purposes.[42] One could obtain a distress warrant, or a garnishee order, or an order charging land, etc. 'Property' is widely defined and covers all real and personal property and any legal or equitable interest in it held by a state.[43] It makes no difference whether the property is held legally or beneficially. This includes the balance on a bank account.[44]

However, personal orders, such as injunctions and specific performance are never available[45] because the penalty for non-compliance is punishment for contempt of court, involving arrest, and fine and imprisonment of the offender.[46]

---

41 *Ibid,* s 13.

42 *Ibid,* s 13(4).

43 See *Aikens J in AIG Capital Partners Inc v Republic of Kazakhstan* [2005] EWHC 2239, [2006] 1 All ER 284 at [45].

44 *Alcom Ltd v Republic of Colombia* [1984] AC 580.

45 Though see *Saba Shipyard (Pakistan) v Islamic Republic of Pakistan* [2002] EWCA Civ 1643 which is discussed later in the chapter.

46 However, a freezing order in relation to property in relation to which immunity against enforcement has been given is permissible. *A Co Ltd v Republic of X* [1990] 2 Lloyd's Rep 520.

**11.26** The difficulty with seizing property under the second exception above is that the most likely target will be funds in a bank account, and it may be difficult to prove the purpose of funds. Apart from that, State Immunity Act 1978, s 13(5) allows the ambassador to certify that the property is not for commercial purposes, and this is prima facie proof of the matter unless the contrary is proved. Furthermore, in the notorious case of *Alcom Ltd v Republic of Columbia*[47] the House of Lords held that it was insufficient for a creditor to show that some of the funds in an account were for commercial purposes. If any was used for immunised purposes the whole fund was immunised, and the creditor must show that the entire fund is intended for commercial purposes. The case involved an embassy bank account, however, and the judgment leaves it uncertain whether this principle applies only to embassy accounts, or to any fund. If the latter, the creditor's task is practically impossible. The case was applied in *SerVaas Incorporated v Rafidain Bank & Republic of Iraq and Ors*[48] where SerVaas tried to obtain a third party debt order against Rafidain, an Iraqi state owned bank, on the basis that because the funds had arisen from commercial transactions they were for commercial purposes and therefore covered the exception to state immunity in State Immunity Act 1978, s 13(2). The Supreme Court held that the claim wrongly conflated the origin of a debt with its current or intended use. It is only not immune if earmarked solely for commercial liabilities. The assessment of the use of the bank account is taken as at the date of enforcement being taken[49] and the onus of proof rests on the claimant.[50]

**11.27** Furthermore, if the state is a contracting state under the European Convention on State Immunity, enforcement is impossible except in the case of an arbitration agreement or where the state has de-immunised itself under the Convention. However, all Convention states have agreed to give effect to judgments against them in any other Convention state.

**11.28** A useful case where enforcement of an injunction against a State was allowed despite the normal rule being that they will not be provided was *Sabah Shipyard (Pakistan) Ltd v Islamic Republic of Pakistan.*[51] Here the government of Pakistan had provided a guarantee containing an English jurisdiction clause. Sabah, the beneficiary of the guarantee had commenced proceedings in the English courts to enforce the guarantee. The government of Pakistan had commenced proceedings in Pakistan to restrain Sabah's proceedings and to obtain a declaration that the guarantee and any demand pursuant to it was invalid. Sabah sought an injunction from the English courts debarring the Pakistan government's action. The Court of Appeal held that

---

47 [1984] AC 580.
48 [2012] UKSC 40.
49 *AIC Ltd v The Federal Republic of Nigeria* [2003] EWHC 1357 (Comm).
50 *Alcom v Republic of Columbia* [1984] AC 580.
51 [2002] EWCA Civ 1643.

normal rules of construction applied even though one party was a state[52] and that the government of Pakistan had consented to English jurisdiction. The clause contained a waiver of immunity, and whilst it granted non-exclusive jurisdiction it did permit either party to commence proceedings in England. A party could choose to commence proceedings elsewhere but could not do so to block English proceedings. The Court therefore granted an injunction against the government of Pakistan.[53]

### *State entities*

**11.29** Not all state owned or controlled entities can be treated as part of the state. State immunity is granted to sovereigns, governments and any department of that government.[54] However, there are also separate entities which are distinct from the executive organs of the government of the State and these are capable of suing or being sued. It is vital to analyse this definition, because the immunity given to entities which are separate from the state is less significant, both as to jurisdiction and as to enforcement, than that given to a state. In essence immunity is lost where the state entity is distinct from the separate organs of government but it is retained where that entity is carrying out a function for which the state would be immune were it doing so. A separate entity cannot claim immunity just because it is owned by the state because it still might be carrying on commercial activities. However, it would be immune if it were carrying out sovereign orders on a matter that would have been covered by immunity had it been carried out by the state.[55] The question of capacity would fall to be determined by the law of the state in question. What must be shown, apart from that, is that it is not a department of state, but is distinct from the government's executive organs. For example, in *Grovit v De Nederlandische Bank*[56] it was held that a central bank was entitled to claim sovereign immunity. In this instance the immunity was held to cover communications containing libellous material.

### *Immunity from jurisdiction – state entities*

**11.30** Generally, and certainly for commercial contracts, the separate entity is not immune from jurisdiction. It is immune only if the state itself would have been immune because it is a non-commercial

[52] Applying *A Company v Republic of X* [1990] 2 Lloyd's Rep 520 and *Alcom v Republic of Colombia* [1984] AC 580.
[53] Applying *Turner v Grovitt* [2002] 1 WLR 10; *Donohoe v Armco Ltd* [2002] 1 Lloyd's Rep 425 and *Glencore International v Exeter Shipping* [2002] 2 All ER (Comm) 1.
[54] State Immunity Act 1978, s 14(1).
[55] *Kuwait Airways Corp v Iraqi Airways Co* [1995] 1 WLR 1147.
[56] [2005] EWHC 2944, [2006] 1 Lloyd's Rep 636.

transaction, and the entity is exercising sovereign authority. In the words of s 14(2) of the Act, the entity is immune if, and only if:

'(a) the proceedings relate to anything done by it in the exercising of sovereign authority; and

(b) the circumstances are such that a state … would have been so immune.'

Since the state would not be immune from jurisdiction given a commercial transaction unless the contract so stated; then for present purposes concerning commercial transactions a separate entity will never be immune. Even if it were immune, it can submit to jurisdiction, just as a state can.

*Immunity from enforcement – state entities*

**11.31** Although it is not stated in the Act, the rule as to enforcement provides no immunity, and that if, as will normally be case, the entity is not immune from jurisdiction, it is subject to normal enforcement, including injunctions and specific performance, and remedies to recover land, etc. It is stated that if the entity is not subject to jurisdiction, but submits to it, enforcement is on the same basis as for states, in which case, for example, injunctions would not normally be available.

*Central banks*

**11.32** Central banks are ordinarily entities separate from the state. Problems with them may arise particularly where the bank is requested to give a guarantee of some kind in respect of the debts or liabilities of the state, or of a separate entity. It is essential that when it gives the guarantee, the central bank should be de-immunised by the insertion of an appropriate clause in the guarantee. Such clauses are considered shortly. Without the insertion of such de-immunising clauses, it is necessary to rely upon the extent to which the central bank and its home state consider it important to maintain the reputation of the central bank, for even if one may obtain judgment against the bank, the remedies may be illusory, and to that extent, the guarantee is legally worthless.

*Constituent territories of federal states*

**11.33** Many states are federations, such as the US, Canada, Australia, and India. The constituent territories are treated as separate entities, and have lesser immunity, though an Order in Council may be made treating given territories as states.[57] In *Petroleum Co Ltd v Kurdistan*

[57] State Immunity Act 1978, s 14(3) and (4).

*Regional Government of Iraq,*[58] a contract for oil and gas exploration was entered into by the regional Iraqi government of Kurdistan. Although the nature of the contract would have attracted immunity had it been entered into by the central government, the regional government was a separate entity and was not entitled to immunity.

### *Forms of clause waiving immunity*

**11.34** It will be appreciated that in drafting an appropriate clause, the lender's aim is threefold:

1 to secure 'ordinary jurisdiction';

2 to secure waiver of immunity from jurisdiction; and

3 to secure the widest possible range of remedies, with a state or central bank, which has some immunity from enforcement.

The securing of 'ordinary jurisdiction' which one needs to secure in order to sue any debtor, whether sovereign or not is dealt with earlier in this chapter, and all that needs adding is that it may be achieved by a submission to the jurisdiction of the English courts. In order to avoid the need to serve writs outside the country, the practice is to appoint an agent inside the country or countries concerned to receive service.

**11.35** The securing of a waiver of immunity overlaps with the securing of ordinary jurisdiction, in as much as sovereign immunity to enforcement or to jurisdiction may be removed by submission to the jurisdiction. Thus, at the same time a state submits to jurisdiction, it waives its immunity. A waiver of immunity, as we have observed, is effective in the UK in relation to both immunity from jurisdiction and enforcement provided appropriate wording to that effect is used. A typical agreement requires the borrower to agree that if a legal claim or proceedings is brought:

- against it or its assets;
- in relation to the loan agreement and matters arising from it;
- the borrower shall not claim for itself and irrevocably waives over its assets any immunity which it has, thus consenting to jurisdiction and enforcement; and
- so as to make the matter of enforcement abundantly clear, consents generally to the giving of any relief or the sum of any process, including the making, enforcement or execution against any property whatsoever or any order or judgment which the court may make. This last provision allows 'relief,' including interlocutory actions, such as freezing injunctions, and also allows 'process' such as claims against property.

58 [2015] EWHC 3361 (Comm).

## Changes to the law of the state in question

**11.36** Whether the borrower is a state or private borrower, the loan contract may be affected by changes in the law of the borrower's state. Those changes may be introduced either by a state borrower to protect itself, or by the state to protect private borrowers (such as moratoria, reductions of interest rates, cancellation of maintenance of value clauses), or by the state to afflict private borrowers or lenders (such as withholding taxes, confiscation and expropriation). In earlier parts of this work, the rules governing the proper law applicable to the contract have been analysed, and it has been seen that the proper law governs most aspects of the contract, and in particular, matters relating to performance, breach, and discharge. If, therefore, a state attempts to change its laws so as to excuse itself from breach, or to change the terms of its obligations, or to discharge its obligations entirely, then whether this is effective is a matter for the proper law of the contract. If the proper law of the contract is the law of the state in question, then a change in the law is effective. These propositions are illustrated by *R v International Trustee*[59] where a change in the proper law (New York) was held to be effective to abrogate certain 'gold clauses' in a British bond issue. Similarly, in *Re Helbert Wagg & Co Ltd*[60] where the agreement was governed by German law, a change in that proper law requiring repayment to be made in German currency to a German custodian was effective to override the contractual provisions for repayment in sterling in London. This was a change in the law made as part of the economic crisis that beset Germany in the mid-1930s and the changes in repayment provisions were seen by the court in this context and were thus allowed, even though the English creditor ended up losing a considerable amount of money as a result. It is for this reason that lenders should attempt to insulate themselves from changes in the law of the borrower's state by expressly choosing some other law.

**11.37** If, however, the proper law is not that of the state in question, ie, the defaulting state, whether the state itself, or a resident or national is the borrower, then the general rule is that changes in its law have no legal effect on the loan agreement, though different problems concerning legal immunity from an action, or the practicalities of enforcement, may then arise. This proposition is illustrated by the two *Bank of Greece* cases[61] (discussed later in this chapter) where the Greek government failed to remove the liability of certain bank debtors whose agreements were governed by English law.

---

59 [1937] AC 500.

60 [1956] Ch 323; [1956] 2 WLR 183; [1956] 1 All ER 129; (1956) 100 SJ 53; also known as *Re Prudential Assurance Co Ltd*.

61 *National Bank of Greece v Metlis* [1958] AC 509, *Adams v National Bank of Greece SA* [1961] AC 255.

**11.38** There are, however, exceptions to the general rule that the proper law determines the effect of changes in the law of the borrower or lender's state. The most important of these exceptions are as follows:

(a) Regardless of the proper law, an English court will enforce a mandatory domestic law of the UK.

(b) If English law is the proper law, an English court will recognise and defer to laws imposed in the place of performance. If English law is not the proper law, the proper law would normally be applied.

(c) If there is a knowing and conspiratorial attempt to evade the laws of a foreign and friendly country, public policy may prevent the recognition of the agreement. This would not apply to laws subsequent to the agreement, or to inadvertent contraventions.

(d) Where property is concerned, English proper law defers to the law of the state in which the property is situated and may recognise an expropriation of property. There may be a departure from this exception, in as much as certain penal, tax gathering, or morally repugnant actions or laws may not be recognised.

(e) Certain procedural remedies, involving the cooperation of foreign courts, may be refused by an English court.

(f) If a state effectively abolishes a legal entity or takes measures which otherwise affect its capacity to be sued, this may be effective, these being matters for the law of the domicile or place of incorporation of the borrower.

(g) Statutes of limitation may have some effect imposing time limits after which debts may not be enforced.

(h) Exchange Controls may be recognised by an English court.

The first three of these are considered elsewhere, and in this chapter the next four of these are dealt with in turn, leaving Exchange Controls to be dealt with in **Chapter 12**.

## Expropriations

**11.39** If the expropriation is of the loan agreement itself, as where a moratorium is declared, the question of whether the change is effective will be determined by the proper law. If the moratorium is of property, the question generally depends on where the property is situated. Most nations recognise the futility of attempting to insist upon legal rights over property which is within the territory of another state, when that state denies the existence of those rights. One can distinguish between property inside the state at the time of expropriation, property outside the state at the time of expropriation, and property originally inside the state at the time of expropriation which is afterwards removed. The first and last of these are subject to the same principles.

*Property inside the state, whether or not subsequently removed*

**11.40** The general rule is that English law recognises an expropriation of property within the territory of a state at the time of the expropriation. In *Luther v Sagor*[62] the court recognised the nationalisation by the Russian government of timber situated in Russia. In *Princess Paley Olga v Weis*[63] the expropriation of personal property was recognised. In both of these cases the action involved a person claiming to have acquired title subsequent to the expropriation, who had afterwards taken the property out of the state in question. A more recent decision is *Williams & Humbert Ltd v W & H Trade Marks (Jersey) Ltd* [64] (the '*Rumasa* case') where a Spanish company controlled shares in other companies, including (i) an English company (W & H) which held licenses from a Jersey company, and (ii) a Dutch company. The Spanish government expropriated shares in the Spanish company, thus obtaining control over the companies which it controlled. The Jersey company then terminated the licenses which it had given to company W & H, claiming to be entitled to do so by its contract. In this action, the question arose whether the plaintiff company (W & H) could sue and also whether the Dutch company was now owned by the Spanish government as owner of the shares in the parent Spanish company. The defendants, the Jersey company and others, argued that the English court should not recognise the expropriations of the shares in the Spanish company, as this was an attempt to enforce in England an expropriatory law. The House of Lords upheld the decisions of the lower courts, confirming the effectiveness of the expropriations, and the ownership by the Spanish government of the shares in the Spanish company. It made no difference that ownership of Spanish property, being shares, produced effects outside of Spain. These effects being: ownership of the Dutch company and the right to sue for breach of contract as owner of W & H, the English company. Compulsory acquisition, held the court, was universally recognised and practised, and an English court would recognise the foreign acquisition law in respect of title to property under the control of that state, and it would also recognise the consequences of that change of title. It would not consider the merits of compulsory acquisition.

**11.41** The same principle was evident in *JSC BTA Bank v Ablyazov.*[65] Here an insolvent Kazak bank was held to be not abusing the legal process by pursuing legal proceedings to recover misappropriated assets. It made no difference that the President of that state may have persuaded the bank to do this to destroy a political opponent. There was an undeniable legitimate purpose in recovering the funds for the benefit of the bank and its creditors.

---

62 [1921] 1 KB 456.
63 [1929] 1 KB 718.
64 [1986] AC 368.
65 [2011] EWHC 1136 (Comm); [2011] 1 WLR 2996.

### *Expropriation of property not in the same jurisdiction of the expropriating state*

**11.42** The general rule here is that the expropriation is ineffective. In *Banco de Vizcaya v Don Alfonso de Borbon y Austria*[66] a London bank held bonds and other securities which had been deposited by the King of Spain, to the order of the bank's Madrid branch. The King ordered the London branch to hold to the order of the Bank of Vizcaya. He was then declared a traitor by the new Spanish government, and his property was expropriated, and Spanish banks were ordered to deliver up property to the Spanish government. The Bank of Vizcaya then requested the London branch to surrender the property, and this action arose. The court held that the King was entitled to the property, as, being outside Spain, it was not subject to Spanish jurisdiction. The expropriatory laws of Spain were local to Spain, affecting only property situated there. Similarly, in *Bank voor Handel en Sheepvart NV v Slatford* [67] a requisition by the Dutch government of gold held in London was not recognised.

**11.43** A particular problem arises with ambulatory property, such as ships and aircraft. While this is subject to some doubt, the rule may be that such property, eg, a ship, cannot be expropriated if at the time it is in an English port, but that an expropriation occurring while the ship is on the high seas and where its port of registry is in the expropriating country, will be recognised. This distinction seems unsatisfactory, especially given that many ships are registered in places with which their owners have no real connection, and the better rule may be that expropriations should not be recognised except for property within the control of the expropriating state. A further problem arises in those cases where a state attempts to expropriate a debt or chose in action. In the *Rumasa* case, the property expropriated was a chose in action, ie, the rights attaching to shares in a Spanish registered company. It seems undoubtedly correct that such a chose should be held to be situated in Spain. The question arises, however, as to the location of debts not so clearly situated. The English view seems to be that the debt is 'situated' in the place where it is required to be paid. That place may be specified, but otherwise it would be where the debtor is resident. In *Ralli Bros v Compania Naviera Sola y Aznar*[68] a contract was governed by English law but provided for payment in Spain. A change in Spanish law affected the amount payable, and the English court would enforce only the amount so limited, as that was the amount now legally owing in the place of performance. English law thus defers to the law of the place of payment of a debt. Similarly, in *International Corporation Ltd v Besser Manufacturing Co Ltd*[69] the place of payment

---

66 [1935] 1 KB 140.
67 [1953] 1 QB 248.
68 [1920] 2 KB 287.
69 [1950] 1 KB 488.

of a commission was England, and when non-payment occurred, it was held that the place of breach was in the place where payment should have been made. That being so, an English court had the discretionary jurisdiction available.

**11.44** Generally, however, where loans are concerned they are made payable in a particular place and usually in the currency of that place by the contractual documentation, so that in the context of term loans, and other contractual agreements of that nature, the problem rarely arises in practice.

**11.45** It is thought that there are different problems involved, which require to be more clearly differentiated. Since debts are treated as property, then when an expropriation is in question, as with other property one must determine the situs of the property in order to determine the effect of an expropriation. But it may be that a different solution applies to a freezing order if there is a branch of the defendant debtor bank in the UK. A freezing order does not involve a change of owner but is merely a bar upon payment.

**11.46** First, it may be that one country attempts to freeze a debt owed to a lender, payable in that country in its own currency. In that case, if the law of the contract is that of the same country, the order is effective. If the law of the contract is English law, England not being the country concerned, then the order is effective, in the sense that the *Ralli Bros* case indicates that under a contract governed by English law, an English court will not require a person to do an act which is illegal in the place where that act is to be performed. Conversely, no English attachment or freezing order would be given by the courts in these circumstances, since the order would have extraterritorial effect.

**11.47** Secondly, it may be that the country concerned attempts to freeze a debt owed to a lender, and payable in the country in the currency of another state. If the governing law of the contract is that of the original country, the order is effective. If the contract is governed by English law then it would seem that the order is still effective, in the sense that an English court would not in the face of the freezing order, require the bank in the other country, where the account is credited, to arrange any transfer or form of payment for the account holder, even if that bank had an English branch which could be the subject of an order. The English court would not order the performance in the other country if the act concerned would be illegal in that country.

**11.48** Thirdly, it may be that the original country attempts to freeze a debt owed to a lender and payable in another country in the currency of the second country. In this case, the order will be ignored by an English court unless the contract is governed by the law of the original country.

**11.49** Fourthly, it may be that the original country attempts to freeze a debt owed to a lender and payable in another country in the currency of the first country. Again, if the contract is governed by the law of the second country, this is effective. But if it is not so governed, the question for an English court, under the *Ralli Bros* principle, must simply be 'are any acts to be performed in the country concerned by any person which under the law of that country are illegal?' If so, the English court will not require those acts to be done. That is to say, the 'situs' of the debt is irrelevant, as is the question of 'place of payment.' The only question which is relevant is whether acts are illegal in the country concerned. Whether those acts amount to 'payment' or 'performance' is irrelevant.

**11.50** Crucial is the case of *Libyan Arab Bank v Bankers Trust Co*[70] where the plaintiffs, a Libyan Bank had accounts with the defendants in both London and New York. Funds were transferred each day between the accounts to retain an agreed sum left as a balance in New York each night. Two sums of US$165.2 million and US$161.4 million were available for transfer in the usual way from New York to London, the first of these on 2 July and the second on 8 July, two hours before a Presidential Order was made freezing all Libyan assets in the US. The Libyan bank demanded payment in London of these amounts, but Bankers Trust refused citing the Presidential Order. It was held by the court that payment could only be avoided if it was unlawful in the place of performance. The jurisdiction covering a bank account is that of the law of the place where the account is kept, in this case England. Although the New York account was covered by the Presidential Order and this suspended the contractual obligations between the parties it did not discharge future performance and therefore the contract was not frustrated. The Libyan Bank were therefore entitled to demand payment of the two sums in London in cash.[71]

**11.51** Finally, it may be remarked that an English court certainly could freeze an account held in England but denominated in a foreign currency. The order would require the bank not to pay except as directed by the court. It may be that an order directing the bank to pay some third party, may involve complications if a contrary order, affecting a branch of that bank in the country of the currency concerned, was to be made in that country.

## Summary

**11.52** So far as one can say with any certainty, the position would seem to be as follows:

---

[70] [1989] QB 728, [1989] 3 WLR 314. For a US take on this case see CR Rutzke 'The Libyan Asset Freeze and Its Application to Foreign Government Deposits in Overseas Branches of United States Banks: Libyan Foreign Bank v Bankers Trust Co.' American University International Law Review. (1988) Vol 3, Issue 1, Art 6.

[71] See also *Toprak Mahsulleri Ofsi v Finagrain Compagnie Commerciale Agricole et Financiere* [1979] 2 Lloyd's Rep 98. For useful reading see C McLachlan, 'Splitting the Proper Law in Private International Law.' (1990) 61 British Year Book of International Law 311–337 and C McLachlan, 'Foreign Exchange Claims against banks in Dispute' (1989) 4(5) BJIB & FL 204–206.

- Expropriations of tangible property situated in a state are subject to the laws of the state, while property situated outside the state is unaffected by changes in the law of that state.
- Expropriations of debts are governed by the law of the place where the debt is situated, and if payment is in the currency of the place of payment, the situs of the debt is the place of payment,
- If a temporary freezing order is made, or there is an alteration in the amount of the debt, or a change in the currency of payment, this may be a matter of breach, which is primarily a matter for the proper law. If this is English law, it still defers to the place of performance, and where the currency of payment is the same as that of the place of final performance, English law defers to that.

### *Exceptions to the general rule*

**11.53** There are exceptions to the general rule that expropriations of property are recognised where the property is within the control of the expropriating state. These exceptions exist where the provision in question is morally repugnant, or where an attempt is made in England to enforce a foreign revenue or penal provision. An example of a morally repugnant provision occurred in *Frankfurter v WL Exner Ltd* [72] where a Nazi decree expelled the Jewish plaintiff from the operation of a business in Austria. The English court considered both the purpose of the decree and its terms and refused to recognise it. The courts in the *Rumasa* case agreed that such legislation, affecting human rights, would not be given effect here.

**11.54** As seen above the English courts will not enforce foreign revenue provisions and this was taken further in the case of *Peter Buchanan Ltd & Macharg v McVey*,[73] where McVey removed himself and all assets from the jurisdiction so as to avoid tax. The tax being unpaid, the Revenue attempted to have the company wound up, and the liquidator sued McVey in the jurisdiction in which he was now resident in order to recover the money owing. The court refused to permit the action on the ground that the only creditor was the Revenue, and that this was a disguised attempt by the Revenue to enforce revenue debts even though the company under its new controller, the liquidator, otherwise had a perfectly valid cause of action against McVey. The decision may be distinguished from the *Rumasa* case, where the new controller of the company, the Spanish government, merely wished to enforce a broken contract, and was not enforcing revenue or penal provisions. The *Rumasa* case recognised the principle in question, but the House of Lords pointed out that the proceedings were not an attempt to enforce Spanish law, but to enforce the English law of contract. It was not an

---

72 [1947] Ch 429.
73 [1956] AC 516.

attempt indirectly to enforce here penal Spanish expropriatory laws, because first it was doubtful that those laws were penal, and secondly, the argument ignored the separate legal personality of the company and its shareholders, and thirdly, as previously discussed, English courts generally recognised expropriations by states of property within their jurisdictions. The defendants attacked the motives of the Spanish legislation, and alleged oppression, questioning good faith. No English judge could properly entertain such an attack on a friendly state[74].

### Availability of procedural remedies

**11.55** In *Settebello Ltd v Banco Totta & Acores*[75] a Portuguese company had a contract with a customer outside Portugal. The Portuguese government issued a decree which enabled companies to suspend for two years any right which their customers had to cancel any contracts exceeding one billion escudos in value. The claimants claimed that this decree should not be enforced because it was discriminatory, like the morally repugnant cases already referred to. In order to show this, they required evidence from Portugal, and they applied to an English court for a procedural order, namely Letters of Request, which would ask the Portuguese judicial authorities to help the claimants acquire such evidence. It is hardly strange that the English Court of Appeal declined to ask the Portuguese judiciary to assist in producing evidence designed to show that the laws of Portugal were discriminatory, unjust and should not be enforced in England. No such procedural remedy would be given, and in this sense the court gave effect to the act of a friendly state. The court indicated that it might have done otherwise had the Portuguese decree failed to reach civilised standards or was abhorrent on its nature. If, of course, the contract had been governed by English law, then the contract having merely been broken by the Portuguese company, the claimants could have sued in England, since the Portuguese decree would have given no defence. The contracts being governed by Portuguese law, the change in the law was effective, unless morally repugnant as already described.

### Changes made to the capacity of an organisation to be sued

**11.56** A familiar example of the problem occurs in the United Kingdom when a liquidator or administrator, takes control of an insolvent company, sets up a new company, transfers the assets of the old company to the new in return for shares in the new, and then sells the new, debt free, company at a reasonable price. Since we accept this type of activity domestically, it should not be remarkable that it or

---

[74] The principle was applied in *re State of Norway's application (Nos 1 and 2)* (HL) [1990] 1 AC 723.

[75] [1985] 1 WLR 1050.

something like it is also effective internationally to divest a borrower of either his assets or his liabilities.

**11.57** If, therefore, a state wishes to rid its domestic borrower of onerous debts, it may transfer all of the assets of the borrower to another company, such an expropriation being recognised by UK courts, and then either wind up the borrower or allow its creditors to proceed against it in fruitless insolvency proceedings. Merely instructing the borrower not to pay will be insufficient, for non-payment is a breach, governed by the proper law. Alternatively, the state can cause the merger of the original borrower with another company, causing the legal existence of the original borrower to cease. Unless the obligations of the original borrower are transferred to the new entity, there would remain no one to be sued.

**11.58** Inept examples of a state's attempt to achieve something along these lines occurred in the *Bank of Greece* cases. In *National Bank of Greece v Metlis Bank*[76] one bank issued sterling bearer bonds, interest to be paid half yearly in London, guaranteed by a second bank. Both banks were Greek banks. In 1949 the Greek government imposed a moratorium suspending payments under the bonds and also relieving the guarantors of liability to pay. In 1953 the government made a decree (a) dissolving the second bank, (b) amalgamating it with another bank to form the National Bank, and (c) providing that the National Bank succeeded to that bank's rights and liabilities. In this action, bondholders sued the National Bank on the guarantee. It is well established that the capacity of a corporation is governed by the law of the place of incorporation, and the House of Lords so held. Looking at Greek law, therefore, the result was that the National Bank could be sued, because the decree provided that it succeeded to the liabilities of the dissolved bank. As to whether that bank was liable, in view of the 1949 moratorium, the House of Lords held, of course, that this matter went to the discharge of obligations, and the discharge of obligations depended on the proper law of the contract, which was English. Under English law, the dissolved bank remained liable, and under Greek law the National Bank succeeded to its liabilities.

**11.59** The Greek government then issued another decree, retrospectively relieving the National Bank from its obligations under the guarantee. This came before the House of Lords in *Adams v National Bank of Greece*[77] and again the House decided that this amounted to a discharge of an existing obligation, was governed by English law, and that the change in Greek law was ineffective. If the decree of 1953 had not transferred the bank's liabilities to the National Bank, the latter could not have been liable. The Greek government could have transferred all of that bank's liabilities except for the

---

[76] [1958] AC 509.
[77] [1961] AC 255.

liability under the guarantee, and that also would have been effective. But having transferred the liability, its removal was a question of discharge, which was governed by English law.

**11.60** In many cases, the old company, the original borrower, will be wound up or will have no assets. If, however, it has assets and remains in existence, the question arises as to how an English court would regard a decree or law simply saying that 'X no longer has the capacity to be sued.' This might be regarded by English law as a valid change in X's capacity, and if that is the case English law holds that questions of capacity to sue, or to be sued, etc are governed by the law of the place of incorporation of a company. If so regarded, the foreign decree would effectively prevent the company from being sued. Alternatively, an English court might regard such a decree not as affecting capacity, but as an attempt to discharge X's liability. If that is the case, the question of discharge would be governed by the proper law and would be ineffective if the law of the foreign state is not the proper law. Which approach, therefore, is to be adopted? It would seem from dicta in the *Metliss* case that there is a difference between cases where all of X's liabilities are transferred, the question then being regarded as one of capacity, with the result then depending on the law of incorporation, and cases where particular liabilities are transferred, the question being regarded as one of discharge, with the result depending on the proper law. In *Re United Railways of Havana and Regla Warehouses*[78] the transfer by the state of Cuba of particular liabilities of a company for hire payments was held to be a question of discharge, governed by the proper law, which happened to be that of Pennsylvania. If, therefore, the original borrower is left with any capacity to remain liable for old debts or to incur new debts, it would seem to be a question of discharge, governed by the proper law. If all capacity is removed, it is a question of capacity, governed by the law of the state of incorporation.

## Statutes of limitation

**11.61** A state may also pass a law providing that debts remain actionable only for a certain period: for example, in England, on a simple debt, debts are actionable for six years unless acknowledged in writing thereafter. English courts regard limitations of this sort as procedural matters: and procedural matters, as we have already seen, are governed under English Conflicts rules by the *lex fori*. If, therefore, the action is brought in England, the six year period would be applicable,[79] notwithstanding contrary provisions under the foreign law. Having established the six year period in this way, however, English courts distinguish within that period between foreign rules which bar the debt entirely, and those which merely remove the

---

[78] [1961] AC 1007.
[79] Limitation Act 1980, s 5.

remedy. This depends on the phrasing of the foreign law: thus, 'no debt shall be actionable' removes the remedy, while 'no debt shall exist' removes the debt. Having made the distinction the result is that if the debt is barred, this is a question of discharge, governed by the proper law, and if the remedy is removed, it is a question for the *lex fori*. If state X imposes a limitation on actions, by barring the debt, then if the law of X is the proper law, but not otherwise, it is effective. If state X's limitation bars the remedy, then regardless of whether the law of X is the proper law, an English court would allow six years.

## Exchange controls

**11.62** Exchange controls are a fact of life in certain parts of the world, in as much as a borrower may be affected by controls imposed by his state, so that regardless of foreign legal rules or judgments, he simply cannot pay the money. One cannot sue him in his own country, and if he has no assets elsewhere, actions elsewhere may be pointless. The legal problem raised, however, is whether the imposition of exchange controls is any defence to an English action. Regarding the matter simply as a change in the laws of the state, the answer prima facie is that if the law of that state is the proper law of the contract, the exchange controls are effective. Otherwise, they are not. We have observed a number of exceptions to this general rule, so that if there is a knowing attempt to evade a foreign rule, it may not be recognised on the ground of public policy. If the foreign exchange law is the law of the place of performance, and if English law is the proper law, then the principle of the *Ralli Bros* case may cause English law to defer to the place of performance.

**11.63** It is clear that exchange controls are of considerable significance in international loan agreements in certain parts of the world. The most obvious protection is that the loan agreement provides for payment not in the borrower's country, but in the currency loaned where that country is unlikely to impose exchange controls, eg, dollars in New York or sterling in the United Kingdom. Under the English restrictive approach to fund agreements, it will be seen that regulations of the borrower's country affecting such an agreement would not be enforced by English courts assuming a proper law choice. Even so, the reality is that foreign legal remedies may prove fruitless if a borrower's state prohibits repayment. Loan documentation therefore deals with the problem in a variety of clauses as discussed in **Chapter 1**. Obviously one factor in making the loan will, therefore, be that a country is judged likely to impose exchange controls. This is one of the numerous factors involved in the difficult task of assessing country risk. Exchange controls are discussed in more detail in **Chapter 12.**

# Chapter 12 Exchange Controls

**12.1** When making a loan, one factor that will concern the lender is whether or not the state in which the borrower is located has exchange controls.[1] This is far less widespread than in the past but in many less developed nations exchange controls are still found.[2] In the instance where the borrower is located in such a state it will be necessary for the borrower to be able to provide central bank consent for the loan to be repaid in the place and currency that the lender requires, otherwise the loan should not be made. Likewise, if a guarantor is in another jurisdiction or a loan is secured and the assets are in another jurisdiction, checks must be made regarding whether there are exchange controls there. Secondly, there is the risk of exchange controls being reintroduced in the course of a loan being repaid. In times of financial crises states can be forced to reintroduce exchange controls as an emergency measure,[3] even if only on a temporary basis. The financial situation in 2026 with excessive state borrowing in many countries significantly raises the risk of this. Finally, the borrower's state may share a currency, such as the Eurozone members. It is possible at a time of financial crisis that some Member States with weaker economies could be forced out by market forces, or even that a state may leave for political reasons, so even here the currency risk factor is an element that a lending bank must consider. These categories are not always mutually exclusive, for example in March 2013 Cyprus, which is a member of the Eurozone briefly imposed exchange controls.

**12.2** The reason that this is so important is that when exchange controls are introduced it is, by definition, going to be at a time of financial crisis for that state. Exchange controls, once introduced mean that the borrower will not normally be able to repay the lender in the lender's state or in the currency of the loan. This tends to mean that the borrower will have to pay the loan back in their own currency and within their own state. This was discussed in **Chapter 9** in the context of governing law in cases such as *Re Helbert Wagg*.[4] Once the financial crisis has ended, the exchange controls will at some point be lifted.

---

1 Exchange controls can exist in a number of forms but in essence they all consist of measures to restrict the exchange of the host currency for others. The aim is to reduce the risk of capital flight from the host state.

2 They were abolished in the UK by the Finance Act 1987, s 72(7) having been suspended earlier in 1979 under the powers granted by Finance Act 1947, s 37.

3 Eg, the Asian Financial crisis of 1997 saw Malaysia and Thailand introduce exchange controls for a year.

4 [1956] Ch 323 (see **Ch 1**). See also *Bank of Athens v Mettliss* [1958] AC 509.

However, the lender's problems do not stop at the delay they will have faced in recovering the loan. Such a period of financial crisis will almost certainly have involved a significant devaluation of the borrower's currency resulting in a loss of the percentage of the devaluation to the lender. Clauses can be inserted into the arrangement (see **Chapter 1** 'Term Loans' and **Chapter 8** 'Derivatives') requiring an international borrower or counterparty to repay a loan in such circumstances in the currency of the loan in a jurisdiction nominated by the lender. This may be enforceable against an international company that has offices in more than one state[5] but its efficacy will be dependent on the exact situation the borrower, or in the case of a derivative contract, the counterparty is in. For this reason, the lender needs to include exchange control risk as one of the elements in determining whether to make the loan and if so on what terms. The same principles apply to a party entering into a derivative contract on a cross-border basis. A useful guideline here will be the sovereign risk rating given to the borrower's state by the main rating agencies.

**12.3** This is one of the numerous factors involved in the difficult judgment of country risk. Exchange controls may be relevant first by reason of the governing law rules which are applied in English law when it considers the effect of a change in the laws of a foreign State. As has been seen earlier in the book the answer depends on whether or not the contract is governed by the law of the State which imposes the exchange controls. But even if not governed by the law of that State such controls must be regarded as a fact of life, in as much as a borrower may be affected by controls imposed by his state, so that, regardless of foreign legal rules or judgments, he simply cannot pay the money. There would be no point suing him in his own country as this would not change the position, and if he has no assets elsewhere, actions elsewhere may be pointless. The legal problem raised, however, is whether the imposition of exchange controls is any defence to an English action, when the contract is not governed by the law of the foreign State but is governed by English law. Even where English law was the proper law there have been a number of exceptions to the rule that the proper law determines the question. The major exception, however, is that the proper law will not govern the case if there is a 'Fund Agreement'. In considering this it is essential to bear in mind that there is no need to be concerned with a 'Fund Agreement' if the proper law is the law of the State applying the exchange contract, or if the other exceptions apply.

**12.4** References to a 'Fund Agreement' are references to the Articles of Agreement of the International Monetary Fund, signed in 1944, at Bretton Woods. This agreement has been incorporated into the municipal law of the UK and of many other countries. In the UK it is now governed by the International Monetary Fund Act 1979.

---

5 See, eg, cl 10(a) of the ISDA 2002 Multicurrency Master Agreement.

**12.5** Under the IMF Articles of Agreement,[6] Article VIII (2) (a) states that:

> 'No member of the Fund shall without the approval of the Fund, impose restrictions on the making of payments and transfers for current international transactions.'

However, there is a facility for Members imposing exchange controls provided they act in line with Article VIII 2(b), which provides as follows:

> 'Exchange contracts which involve the currency of any member and which are contrary to the exchange control regulations of that member maintained or imposed consistently with this Agreement shall be unenforceable in the territories of any member.'[7]

Practically every phrase of this Article contains legal issues. Therefore, this text considers the meaning of: 'exchange contracts'; 'contracts ... shall be unenforceable'; 'involve the currency'; 'exchange control regulations'; and 'consistently'. The concern is primarily with the approach to the construction of the treaty taken by English courts, though the attitudes of other courts will be considered where appropriate. In construing treaties, an English court will have regard to the underlying policy of the treaty[8] and will not apply technical rules applicable to Acts of Parliament. If at all possible they will attempt to harmonise their interpretations with those of foreign courts, particularly if there is already a consistent corpus of foreign law on the subject. But where there are differing decisions, they will interpret the text in a normal, non-technical, fashion, having regard to the policy of the treaty.

## 'Exchange contracts'

**12.6** English courts take a fairly restrictive view of this phrase, interpreting it to mean a contract to exchange the currency of one country into the currency of another. A foreign currency loan in which there is no term to repay in a given currency would not be an exchange contract, because there is no 'contract to exchange.' Any agreement with a currency conversion clause is affected. In *Wilson, Smithett &*

---

6 According to Art XX(1) of the IMF Articles of Agreement, each Member State is required to deposit an instrument stating that it has taken all necessary steps to comply with the Agreement, and thus, by implication they have amended their domestic law accordingly.

7 www.imf.org/external/pubs/ft/aa/aa08.htm [Accessed 4 March 2026].

8 The interpretation published by the Executive Directors of the IMF in 1949 states that contracts that breach Art VIII(2)(b) 'will be treated as unenforceable notwithstanding that under the private international law of the forum, the law under which the foreign exchange controls are maintained or imposed is not the law which governs the exchange contract or its performance' and...parties to such contracts 'will not receive the assistance of the judicial or administrative authorities of other members in obtaining performance of such contracts.'

*Cope Ltd v Terruzzi* [9] an Italian resident dealt in contracts on the London Metal Exchange and had an obligation to pay sterling to English metal dealers. Italian exchange controls which existed at the time affected his ability to pay, and the question arose whether his obligation to pay in sterling made the contract an exchange contract. The court held that it did not: there was no obligation to convert Italian currency into English currency.

**12.7** But the courts are prepared to look beyond the appearance of a transaction, and in particular are prepared to consider other related agreements to determine whether, taken together, there is an exchange contract. In *United City Merchants (Investments) Ltd v Royal Bank of Canada*[10] an English exporter agreed with the Peruvian importer to artificially increase the price of goods sold on terms that the amount of the increase would be paid by the English bank to a Miami dollar account in the name of the Peruvian company. The purpose of this was to enable the Peruvian importer to take money abroad. Payment to the English exporter was first to be made by a bank in England acting as confirming bank under a letter of credit[11] issued by a Peruvian bank. The House of Lords held that this was an exchange contract, because the contract between the exporter and importer imposed an obligation to swap money paid under the letter of credit. Peruvian currency was to be swapped for US dollars. The defendant bank, therefore, was not bound to pay under the credit, even though on the face of it the credit provided for payment against documents, and itself contained no contract to exchange currencies. This was despite the well-established principle that credits are transactions quite separate and autonomous from the underlying contract. Taking the contract and the credit together, it was a disguised exchange contract. Similarly, in *Mansouri v Singh*[12] a person desiring to take money out of Iran bought airline tickets there, and brought them to England, where, relying on a term in the contract to refund them in sterling, he asked for a sterling refund. Because of the term, this was held to be an exchange contract, and the seller could raise Iranian exchange controls as a defence.[13]

**12.8** The restrictive view taken by English courts is shared by the US courts[14] and has been applied in Belgium.[15] It may be contrasted

9 [1976] QB 683

10 [1983] 1 AC 168, [1982] 2 All ER 720.

11 This was a commercial letter of credit. **Chapter 7** of this book deals with standby letters of credit and commercial letters involve the use of such arrangements in the international trade of goods.

12 [1986] NLJ Rep 260 (CA).

13 For a useful analysis of this area see 'Bretton Woods Agreement 1948 Article 8(2)(d) – exchange control' (1986) 57 British Yearbook of International Law, 421–423 and *Dicey, Morris and Collins on The Conflict of Laws,* 16th edn (Sweet & Maxwell, 2025), Ch 36, s 3.

14 *Banco do Brasil v AC Israel Commodity Co* (1993) 12 NY 2d 371 (especially 375–6); 190 NE 2d 235, (1964) cert denied 376 US 906.

15 *Emek v Bossers & Mouthaan* (1955) 22 ILR 725.

with a much less restrictive view taken in Germany,[16] Luxembourg,[17] and France.[18] In those jurisdictions, the phrase 'exchange contract' is interpreted to include any agreement which would affect, even if only indirectly, exchange resources of the State in question: that is, not a 'contract to exchange currencies' but a 'contract which affects the exchange resources of a country.' This wide view obviously encompasses most agreements, including all term loans or bond agreements (except Germany in the case of the latter).[19] If the borrower is required to repay in foreign currency he will have to sell domestic currency to pay for the foreign currency. Even if he is allowed to repay in his own currency it may be subject to a legal action abroad, eg, if he defaults, and this might affect exchange resources. The extent of the proposition is shown by a French case[20] in which a contract occurring in France for a sale of shares in a French company for the then French currency of francs, between a Dutch resident seller and a German resident buyer, was held to be an unenforceable exchange contract because of Dutch exchange control regulations (the Netherlands had an interest in the repatriation of foreign currency obtained from the sale of the shares). Given a choice, the lender should obviously bring his action in countries like the UK, where the restrictive view holds sway.

## 'Involve the currency of any Member'

**12.9** It will be recalled that an exchange contract is a 'contract to exchange' currency. Accordingly, it would seem that in the UK this phrase means to 'involve an exchange of the actual currency of the member whose exchange controls are considered.' But where the wider view of 'exchange contract' is taken, and 'exchange contract' means 'contract affecting the currency of any member', the phrase means 'involves an exchange or affects in any direct or indirect way the currency or exchange resources of the member …'.[21] Suppose that a bank in country A makes a loan to a borrower in country B in the currency of country C and this is prohibited by regulations of country B. It would seem that on the restrictive view in the UK this is not covered by the Article, but on the wider view (as in France) it would be, because it affects the exchange resources of B, even though not directly a contract to exchange B's actual currency.

---

16 *Lessinger v Mirau* (1955) 22 ILR 725.

17 *Société Filature et Tissage X Jourdain v Epous Heymen-Bintner* (1955) 22 ILR 727.

18 *De Boer, Widow Moojen v von Reichert* 89 J Droit Int'l 718, (Cour d'appel, Paris, 1962).

19 14 March 2003, JZ 2003, 1010. Likewise, the German courts regard bills of exchange as capital payments – German Federal Supreme Court, 22 February 1994, NJW 1994, 1868 or IPRspr, 1994 No 129.

20 *De Boer* case, above n 18.

21 *De Boer* case *ibid.*

## 'Contracts shall be unenforceable'

**12.10** In *United City Merchants (Investments) Ltd v Royal Bank of Canada*[22] it was explained that the significance of the word 'unenforceable' is that the contract is neither illegal in any criminal sense nor void. It exists but cannot be enforced by legal action. No legal remedies are available. Continental courts have in contrast held that the contract is entirely void and a nullity. Since in the UK the contract exists, then if at any subsequent time exchange controls were removed, the contract could be enforced normally. Additionally, non-judicial remedies such as the right to combine accounts may be available. Even a contractual set off clause may be enforceable by the lender, since where he exercises his right to set off, he needs no assistance from the court, and if sued for the deposit in question, he can rely on the contractual set off clause as a defence and does not need to ask the court's aid in assisting him towards a remedy.

**12.11** The Article refers only to 'contracts', and actions based on property rights may be unaffected, provided that the property right is not created by the contract rendered unenforceable. It may be that an action to enforce a judgment is unaffected, so that a lender who is able to sue in one jurisdiction which takes a restrictive approach to the Article can enforce his judgment in another jurisdiction where the wider approach is taken. The Article does not seem to extend to tort, though one unfortunate German case indicates the contrary.[23] Nor can it be a basis for actions in rem, restitution, unjust enrichment or the enforcement of foreign judgments.

**12.12** A most important question is whether the lender can recover sums already paid by claiming in quasi-contract. Overseas decisions have held not, and it is thought that the same would apply in the UK. A quasi-contract depends on an implied contract and is designed to prevent unjust enrichment. It would seem likely that the lender could rescind, on the ground of failure of the condition implied in nearly all contracts that the other party must be ready, willing and able to perform. But, having rescinded, it is unlikely that an English court would imply a promise to repay, for this implied contract would be to do something prohibited by the exchange control regulations in question. Similarly, the remedy of tracing would be unavailable, that requiring a fiduciary relationship not ordinarily existing between lender and borrower.

**12.13** If the term which is affected by the Article is a minor part of the contract, and can be severed from the rest, leaving a comprehensible and workable contract, severance is possible. But this would not assist with a contract on a loan or bond where the repayment obligation is the major part of the contract or a derivative contract where the payment obligation falls into the same category.

---

[22] See above n 10.

[23] District Court of Hamburg, 24 February 1978, IPRsps 1978.

**12.14** The Article does not allow direct enforcement by one state in another state. If, say, property is transferred contrary to the regulations, it cannot be recovered. Contracts are merely made unenforceable.

## 'Exchange control regulations'

**12.15** The Article presumably covers both regulations controlling capital transfers of a current nature, the capital of loans for example, and current transactions such as interest on loans. It does not cover capital transactions generally.[24] Countries may impose a wide range of restrictions, including, for example tariffs, trade restrictions, price controls, trading with the enemy regulations, legal tender regulations, and so on. Which, if any of these, are 'exchange control regulations'? The test must be whether the regulation is aimed at preserving a country's exchange resources, in which case none of the above would be within the Article. In *Loeffler-Bekrens v Beermann*[25] Brazilian legal tender regulations were held, by a German court acting on advice from the IMF, to be excluded. The Brazilian law prohibited contracts from being performed in Brazil by stipulating that payment had to be in a currency other than Brazilian. Even a law requiring the acceptance of payment in Brazilian currency would not be an exchange control law, since in itself it does not prevent the person paid from exchanging the currency received.

**12.16** Wood argued[26] that to be an exchange control regulation it must be: (i) a direct control; on (ii) the financial aspects of a transaction; (iii) controlling the movement of currency, property or services; so as (iv) to protect the exchange resources of a country.

## 'Consistently with this agreement'

**12.17** Under Article VIII 2(a) restrictions on current transactions are not allowed unless there is a scarcity of a member's currency, or the Fund approves, which it might do tacitly or subsequently. If a restriction is otherwise imposed, it is inconsistent with the agreement, and a foreign court could ignore it. The IMF will provide advice where there is doubt. 'Current transactions' include payments due in connection with foreign trade and interest on loans. Under Article VI.3 members are free to make restrictions on capital transfers, so that the problem of whether such restrictions are 'consistent' with the Agreement does not arise.

---

24 See German Federal Supreme Court, 8 November 1993, NJW 1994, 390 or IPRspr 1993, No 127. The IMF discussed extending the rule to this area in 1997. See Carreau and Juillard, *Droit international éonomique,* 6th edn (Dalloz, 2017).

25 1964–5 IPRspr No 194.

26 P Wood, *Law and Practice of International Finance* (Sweet & Maxwell, 1980), p 139. (The later version of this work, currently extended to nine volumes no longer deals with this in any detail).

## Overriding public policy?

**12.18** In a Dutch case, a court has held that it might ignore regulations which affront Dutch public policy.[27] But that approach is not available directly to an English court, for the Article is, by virtue of the International Monetary Fund Act 1979, part of English domestic law, and the Article states that the agreement is unenforceable. Similarly, US courts have rejected this argument.[28] However, as to current account controls, it may be possible that regulations which are discriminatory or oppressive are not aimed at protecting scarce resources and are not 'consistent' with the Fund Agreement may be held invalid.

## Imposition of exchange controls

**12.19** The abolition of UK exchange controls in 1987 referred to above makes it difficult to re-impose them because the need for legislative action would inevitably lead to an immediate and probably very dramatic flight of capital from the country. Like many other countries, the UK has accepted the provisions of Article VIII, ss 2, 3 and 4 of the International Monetary Fund (IMF) Agreement. Section 2 of that Article involves an undertaking by members not to impose restrictions on the making of payment or transfers for current international transactions without the approval of the IMF. In particular, under s 2(b), members undertake not to enforce contracts which involve the currency of any member and which are contrary to the exchange control regulations of that member, if they are not imposed consistently with the Fund Agreement. Under s 3, members agree not to indulge in discriminatory currency practices. Under s 4, they undertake to buy back balances of their currencies held by another member if these have been acquired recently as a result of current transactions, or if their conversion is required in order to make payments for current transactions. If a member has accepted all of these obligations, the currency of that member is said to be 'convertible.'

## Types of exchange controls

**12.20** Many different types of controls may be imposed to protect the currency of a state. Some controls are 'direct investment controls' that is, controls on direct investments, ie, 'inward' investments by non-residents. For example, foreign investments may have to be registered, or the remittance of profits and dividends to non-residents may be

---

[27] *Indonesian Corporation PT Escomptobank v NV Assurantie Maatschappij de Netherlanden Van 1945*, (1964) 40 ILR 7.

[28] *Perutz v Bohemian Discount Bank in Liquidation* 279 App. Div 386, 110 NYS 2d 446 (1952), revised 304 NY 533, 110 NE 2d 6 (1953).

restricted, absolutely, partially, or in relation to currencies, or there may be restrictions on the payment of royalty and service payments to non-residents, or there may be restrictions on the repatriation of capital invested by non-residents in the state. The failure to register, where this is required, may itself prevent remittance of profits, or capital repatriation, etc. Some failures may be remediable in some states, possibly within a limited time, but in other cases it may be irremediable, in which case the investor would, if appropriate saving provisions were not in the agreement, be locked into the transaction where the borrower is restricted in his ability to repay.

**12.21** A second type of exchange control may be described as 'borrowing regulations,' which concern the effect of those regulations concerning a resident borrower and non-resident lender. One may also distinguish 'lending regulations,' which concern the effect of those regulations concerning a resident lender and non-resident borrower. In relation to borrowing, some countries may control not only foreign borrowings, but also domestic borrowings if the borrower has non-resident shareholders. In some cases, if a resident subsidiary borrows from a non-resident parent the transaction may be treated as a direct investment, subject to controls already mentioned, or to special rules. In the case of lending regulations, some rules may treat domestic loans to non-resident unrelated companies as an outward investment. In the UK there are no borrowing or lending regulations of this type.

**12.22** A third type of exchange control relevant to this discussion are controls upon currency. For example, some regulations may prevent persons from entering into arrangements to provide forward exchange cover. Another type of currency regulation may control the holding of a state's currency or of foreign currency, by either residents or non-residents. In the UK, there are no restrictions on currency nor are gold bullion and gold coin subject to exchange control.

## Loan documentation and exchange controls

**12.23** It is obvious from the foregoing that exchange controls are of considerable significance in international loan agreements, though the restrictive approach taken by UK courts to the meaning of 'Fund Agreements' limits their scope where the law of the state imposing the controls does not govern the contract.

## Specifying place and currency of payment

**12.24** The most obvious protection that a lender may take is that the loan agreement provides for payment in currency A in the country of currency A where that country is unlikely to impose exchange controls, eg, dollars, in New York. Under the restrictive approach, regulations affecting this are not observed by English courts, assuming a proper law choice, etc. Even so, the reality is that foreign legal remedies may prove fruitless if a borrower's state prohibits repayment. Loan documentation deals with the problem in a variety of clauses.[29]

## Consents and conditions precedent

**12.25** In many cases, exchange controls may be lifted or waived if a resident authority, such as a Central Bank or Treasury consents. Some countries may give consents in advance and some only after the executed loan agreement is filed with the relevant authority, or maybe only after a drawdown. Some countries will not authorise anything but scheduled payments or principal and interest, or perhaps also commitment commissions. They may not give advance approval to accelerated amounts in a case of prepayment, or perhaps on default. Generally speaking, any international loan agreement will make provision for whatever consents may be obtained. First, it will be a condition precedent of a loan agreement that consent has been obtained, for borrowing, repayment, commission, additional payments, etc bonds will advertise the exchange control position. Where consents cannot be obtained in advance, the borrower or lender may approach the relevant authority for an indication of the likely result of an application, and some comfort may be obtained from this. But in this case, or in cases where, for example, advance approval for accelerated amounts is required, the lender must essentially make a judgment of the commercial risks involved, having regard to the economic and political situation in the borrower's country.

## Currency transfer agreements

**12.26** If consent can be given by a central body, such as a Central Bank, that body may be required to give a 'currency transfer agreement', whereby it undertakes to sell the borrower sufficient currency to repay to ensure that it is made available, and to allow him to remit it abroad. Such an agreement is a contract, rendering the Central Bank liable for default.

**12.27** In the case of a transaction with a sovereign, or with a public entity, it is also usual to attempt to acquire a currency transfer agreement from the Central Bank of the State, in place of the exchange control consents which apply in case of a private borrower. The Central Bank agrees to: (a) obtain; and (b) to sell sufficient foreign currency to the borrower to enable it to meet its obligations; and also agrees (c) to allow the borrower to remit this abroad. The agreement should be governed by the same law as the main loan agreement, and should contain similar terms as to jurisdiction, etc if negotiable. The Central

---

[29] See **Ch 1**.

Bank, under UK law, will tend to be immune from jurisdiction[30] even though it is a separate entity, unless it is engaged in commercial activity. Its assets thus have special immunity, unless it consents to execution against those assets. While it is subject to declaratory actions therefore, stating its liability in damages for breach of any such agreement, it may, without consent to execution, be impossible to enforce. An additional problem is that such a currency transfer agreement seems within Article VIII 2(b) of the Fund Agreement, to be 'a contract involving the currency of a member' and therefore to be subject, even under a contract governed otherwise by UK law, to exchange controls imposed by the state. The Central Bank, therefore, could be relieved of any liability under its agreement by a change in the law of the state.

## Warranties, covenants and events of default

**12.28** All loan agreements but not bond issues will additionally contain an express warranty that all necessary exchange controls have been obtained, or will be obtained as they become necessary, and it should be an event of default if any exchange control consent is or becomes necessary and is unobtainable for any cause, or is revoked, or refused, or materially varied. In other words, the warranties are made evergreen and if at any time consents are varied or revoked, it will entitle the lender to accelerate though he still may not be repaid, if the exchange controls prevent the borrower from doing so. In most loan agreements representations concern powers and authority, legal validity, that there is no conflict with laws relating to the borrower, consents, and other matters. All of these clauses might relate to exchange controls, and the consent clause certainly would where consent is obtainable in advance. In the case of a private borrower, exchange controls might be specifically mentioned.

**12.29** The illegality clause, to which reference has already been made in **Chapter 1**, will also give some protection by allowing the lender to call for a prepayment if the law of his own country, including exchange controls, affects his ability to continue with the agreement. However, the speed with which exchange controls are brought in will normally preclude the lender having sufficient warning to do this.

**12.30** Legal opinions should be obtained,[31] and these will state whether exchange controls are imposed and whether consents are needed, etc. The obtaining of a satisfactory legal opinion will be included as a condition precedent in a term loan agreement.

**12.31** Currency indemnity clauses, considered already, dealing with local rules permitting payment to be made, or judgments to be

30 *Grovit v De Nederlandische Bank* [2005] EWHC 2944, [2006] 1 Lloyd's Rep 636.
31 See **Ch 13**.

given in the borrower's currency, may have some effect. These require the borrower to indemnify the lender for any conversion losses. The borrower's obligation under such clauses, however, may also be affected by exchange control regulations.[32]

## The euro

**12.32** It is worth concluding by briefly considering the legal issues arising for lenders if a state withdraws from the euro. The history of shared currencies is that states tend to leave either for political reasons, eg, the ex-Soviet states leaving the rouble or the ex-states of Yugoslavia leaving the dinar when Member States declared independence. Alternately it can happen due to economic pressures. This has tended to occur both with arrangements such as the Latin Franc[33] and pegged currency systems. The UK's withdrawal from the European Monetary System is a case in point. There is a further element in that Montenegro uses the euro but is not a member of the EU. Its withdrawal would involve fewer political complications.

**12.33** Either situation could lead a state to leave the euro at some point in the future. The issue that then arises is what would the legal position be for banks that had loaned money to a borrower in that state in euros where the contract was governed by English law?

**12.34** On departure from the euro[34] the state concerned would presumably issue its own currency. Where economic forces have been the primary reason why the state left in the first place it is highly probable that a significant devaluation of the new currency against the euro would be part of the arrangement. For a lender in euros to a borrower in that state this would be a major concern. The issue could arise in international banking in a number of ways:

(1) as mentioned, a loan could be made in euros to a borrower in a state which later ceases to use that currency;

(2) a loan could be made in euros which later has to be enforced against a guarantor where the original debt is in the state which has ceased to use it as a currency; and

(3) a bond issue could be made by a borrower in such a state; or

---

32 Re *Helbert Wagg* above n 4.

33 This was created in 1865 between France, Belgium, Italy and Switzerland with Greece joining later. If effectively collapsed with the outbreak of the First World War in 1914 and was formally abolished in 1927.

34 In theory entry to the euro is irreversible – Art 123(4) of the EC Treaty and Protocol 24 on the Transition to the Third Stage of Monetary Union. However, there are inconsistencies; for example, the ECB has indicated that it would involve itself in the process if someone withdrew: see para 18 of the ECB's Opinion at CON/2003/20. In any event it is a situation where political reality is likely to overwhelm any legal objections.

(4) a derivative contract could be entered into which is denominated in euros where the counterparty is situated in the state which ceases to use the euro.

The issue that arises in each set of circumstances is that the borrower or counterparty may wish to repay in the new currency. In an extreme case where the issuance of the new currency is combined with exchange controls being put in place the situation is as set out in the main part of this chapter.[35] If not however, matters become more complicated.

**12.35** If the new currency is set up and the euro still exists, and the contractual arrangements are covered by English law, the debt repayment or contractual payment would still need to be made in euros. If on the other hand a new currency has been set up and the highly unlikely situation arose of the euro having ceased to exist, presumably because European Monetary Union has collapsed, matters become yet more complicated.[36] In the case of (1) and (2) above the probability is that repayment would be in the euro unless it had ceased to exist, in which case the debt would be repaid in the new host currency at whatever rate of exchange rate applied on its creation. In the case of (2), a guarantee could give rise to problems where the guarantor is in another state and that state's law were to apply. To simplify matters it is vital that the guarantee is drafted to be subject to English law and jurisdiction, though it is not always possible to be certain that the law of the guarantor's home state may not become an issue. In the case of bond issues and derivatives no real problem arises as long as the euro exists. It is not a condition of either arrangement that the currency involved is that of the home state of the bond issuer, or of either party in the case of derivative contracts. If the euro ceased to exist then the situation would be as just described for 1 and 2.

**12.36** Matters may be different if a state unilaterally withdraws from the euro without the agreement of the other states. In the immediate aftermath of this an English court would probably recognise the choice of law and jurisdiction clause in the contract. If English law were chosen it is probable that enforcement of the payment in euros would be ordered by the courts if that was what had been contracted. It has been suggested that this would need to be done on public policy grounds.[37] In due course and given the economic realities of the situation the EU would end up facing a *fait accompli* by the breakaway state and the

---

[35] This would breach Art 56 of the EU Treaty (as amended) and so is most likely to happen because a state leaves the EU.

[36] Mann discusses the possibility that this could result in the contract's validity being challenged on the basis either of mistake on the grounds that the parties had assumed the euro would continue to exist when they made the contract or that the Law Reform (Frustrated Contracts) Act 1943 might apply. The conclusion reached is that if the English courts are prepared to give judgment in the new currency then an objection on either basis will fail. C Proctor, *Mann and Proctor on the Law of Money*, 8th Edn (Oxford University Press, 2023).

[37] Rome I Regulation, Art 21.

new situation would end up being recognised. At this point the public policy issue would disappear. It may be that the public policy issues should not be overstated. There are precedents, for example *Duke of Brunswick v King of Hanover*[38] to the effect that an English court will not adjudge a foreign government's activities in its own state. Nor can they judge the obligations of an overseas state under treaties to which that state is a signatory.[39]

---

38 (1848) 2 HLC 1.

39 *Republic of Italy v Hambros Bank Ltd* [1950] 1 All ER 480 and *J H Rayner (Mincing Lane) Ltd v Department of Trade and Industry* [1990] 2 AC 418. See also *Westland Helicopter Ltd v Arab Organisation for Industrialisation* [1995] QB 282.

# Chapter 13 Legal Opinions

## Introduction

**13.1** It is common practice in international banking transactions for the lenders to require formal legal opinions confirming the legal validity of the documentation which evidences their agreement with the borrower. The opinions are usually given by the lawyers who have been involved in the transaction, and they are addressed to the banks and underwriters who are involved in providing, or arranging the provision of, the finance. The practice of obtaining legal opinions originated in the US, where they were originally produced to satisfy the banks' auditors that the necessary legal procedures had been followed and that the loans could be enforced against borrowers. After that the practice of obtaining legal opinions became widespread in international transactions and they are obtained in the course of good banking practice and not only to satisfy the banks' auditor's requirements. Over more recent years the ABA and the TriBar Association in the US have produced guidelines for US attorneys producing such documents.

**13.2** It has been pointed out in an earlier chapter of this work that a number of legal systems may impinge on an international banking transaction and it is the function of the legal opinions to address the legal issues that arise under the laws of the various legal systems concerned, and to give the lenders some assurance that the issues have been met and do not cause any impediment to proceeding with the transaction. Alternatively, where there are difficulties, the lenders will be able to assess the risks which arise from the issues raised in the legal opinions. It is also useful to distinguish legal opinions[1] from other sources of advice such as advice on specific legal issues, due diligence reports, title reports and legal opinions necessitated by regulatory requirements.

**13.3** Occasionally legal opinions may be required for other purposes such as regulators, who may require it either as part of the regulatory process in granting a license or because they wish to have confirmation of the effect of a particular transaction on the firm. This last occasion may occur in relation to capital adequacy requirements. They may also be relied on by rating agencies.

---

1 P R Wood, *International Loans, Bonds, Guarantees and Legal Opinions*, 3rd Edn (Sweet & Maxwell, London, 2019).

**13.4** Although legal opinions are important, their limitations should not be overlooked. A legal opinion is not an assurance that a good credit decision has been made in respect of a particular borrower, nor is it a guarantee that the borrower will be financially sound or able to repay the loan. The legal opinion speaks only of the transaction as documented and negotiated with the borrower. Accordingly, a legal opinion does not constitute an undertaking that the documents contain the devices necessary to browbeat a borrower in the possible situations that may arise. Nor does a legal opinion state that the document contains every possible provision which might apply in the future to any conceivable set of facts or circumstances. A legal opinion relates to the documents as entered into by the parties and states the validity and enforceability of the documents in the state in which they were executed.

**13.5** As one commentator said:

> 'If you cannot get a clean legal opinion you should not lend; if you get a clean legal opinion you still have to make the lending decision. And that is an entirely separate matter.'[2]

**13.6** A legal opinion should state that it addresses the law concerning a transaction as at the date on which it is given. A legal opinion cannot look into the future and predict what effect a change of law will have upon a given transaction after it has been entered into. The law to which the legal opinion speaks is the domestic law of the jurisdiction of the lawyer who is giving the legal opinion. Any comfort which the opinion gives is, therefore, local, not universal. A lawyer should not be asked to express a view on the law of another jurisdiction in which he is not admitted to practise. A lawyer can only be held out as an expert in the laws of his own jurisdiction and it would be unrealistic for a party to insist upon a lawyer giving an opinion on the law of another jurisdiction. Indeed a lawyer would refuse to provide one. The main difference here is that a large international law firm could arrange for an overseas branch to provide an opinion relating to their own jurisdiction. Smaller law firms sometime have relationships with overseas firms that can facilitate a similar arrangement.[3]

**13.7** The type of legal opinion which will be addressed in this chapter is one which covers the transaction generally. The differing circumstances can result in quite different styles of opinion and for this reason there are three appendices to this chapter showing how opinions differ in three disparate circumstances. On some occasions a particularly difficult point of law might arise concerning a specific aspect of the transaction and in that case a lawyer might be asked to

---

2 Youard, 'And if You Want my Opinion', Euromoney (September 1982), p 251.

3 Not only would they not have the expertise but very probably would not have sufficient insurance cover for risks related to the opinion.

deal specifically with that aspect of law, most usually in a separate form of opinion.

## Conditions precedent

**13.8** As indicated earlier in this work,[4] legal opinions are commonly required as a condition precedent to drawdown under the financing documents. The forms of opinions which are required to satisfy the condition precedent are often set out in schedules which are annexed to the loan documentation and these should be given careful consideration during the process of negotiating the loan documentation. If the forms of the proposed opinions are agreed at an early stage, before the form of the transaction has been settled, they will help to raise any legal issues which might cause difficulty. The negotiation and settlement of the forms of legal opinions should not be confused with or be traded as part of the negotiations of the terms of the loan transaction itself. The lawyer who gives a legal opinion does so as an expert and is giving his opinion in relation to the law as it affects the provisions in the documentation. What is said in the legal opinion should not affect the commercial terms or negotiations between the parties as to the transaction. That said, it is often the case that a party to a transaction might be asked to warrant or covenant as to a particular set of facts which the lawyer is unable to cover in his opinion.

## Opinions should cover matters of law only, not matters of fact

**13.9** As far as possible, legal opinions should be confined to matters of law and a lawyer should not be asked to give a warranty as to a state of facts, especially where the facts are not matters within his control or as to which he cannot be certain by investigation.[5] This applies particularly in the case of independent lawyers, although it might be modified in the case of in-house counsel employed by the borrower, who might be expected to have access to more information concerning the borrower, especially in relation to outstanding litigation, prior encumbrances and internal borrowing limitations. A borrower's independent legal advisers will not usually have access to such information and, if asked to give an opinion on such matters, will either qualify their opinion or refuse to express an opinion at all. On the other hand the in-house lawyer is unlikely to have the same depth of insurance cover and this might influence the extent to which they would be prepared to comment.

---

4 **Ch 1**.

5 Indeed lawyers will normally refuse to go outside a purely legal interpretation as they will cease to have professional indemnity once they do so.

**13.10** A legal opinion will often state that certain facts have been assumed and the lenders will need to bear that in mind when reading the opinion because the onus is then upon them to check the assumed facts or to take the risk that the assumptions are not correct.

## The jurisdictions in relation to which opinions should be obtained

**13.11** There is usually more than one jurisdiction in relation to which it may be desirable to obtain a legal opinion. The relevant jurisdictions may include:

(a) The place where the borrower is incorporated or, in the case where the borrower is a sovereign state or state entity, the jurisdiction of the sovereign. Of particular concern in this regard will be legal matters concerning the existence, powers and capacity of the borrower and any necessary authorities that may be needed for the borrower to enter into the transactions contemplated and to perform its obligations. In addition, the legal opinion should cover the ability of the borrower to make the necessary repayments and other payments under the documentation, the question of taxation on interest and other payments by the borrower, such as withholding tax and interest payments, and the ability to sue the borrower and obtain and enforce judgment against the borrower in that jurisdiction.

If the borrower is an international organisation then there may be some difficulty in determining what the relevant law will be governing these issues and regard will have to be had to the principles of international law on these matters requiring advice.

(b) If the funds are being disbursed to the borrower or payments are to be made or other matters are to be performed in jurisdictions other than the jurisdiction of the borrower's incorporation or place of domicile, as for instance is often the case in capital market transactions or project financing, then legal opinions may need to be obtained from lawyers in the jurisdictions where those matters are to take place.

(c) The jurisdiction of the proper law of the loan agreement. This opinion covers matters pertaining to the validity and enforceability of the documentation under the proper law of the documents and the ability to obtain a judgment in the courts of that jurisdiction. This opinion is usually in a briefer form than the opinions referred to in (a) and (b) above and makes several assumptions on the matters covered by those other opinions.

(d) In specific cases it might also be relevant to obtain legal opinions from other relevant jurisdictions if, for instance, security is being given over assets in another jurisdiction or, in the case of ship financings, in the jurisdiction of the flag of the vessel concerned. For example, such an opinion would cover the ability, under the *lex situs*, to take security over the assets concerned and any steps that may be necessary to perfect the taking of the security, such as registration procedures.

## From whom should the opinions be obtained?

**13.12** The lenders will need to consider from whom the various legal opinions covering the transaction should be obtained. In some cases there will be a duplication of opinions in that the lawyers retained by the borrower and the lawyers retained by the lenders will be asked to give separate opinions. To save on the costs of the transaction, the borrower may suggest to the lenders that its own lawyers should furnish the legal opinion in its jurisdiction concerning the matters referred to in (a) above. Alternatively, the lenders may insist that an independent lawyer should give the opinion or may indeed ask for both the borrower's own lawyers and an independent lawyer to give opinions. There is no hard and fast rule of practice on this but it is not unusual for one opinion in that jurisdiction to be given by the borrower's lawyers alone. If the borrower has its own in-house counsel then the borrower may suggest that that person should give the opinion. In the case of an international organisation established by treaty, it will often be the case that only the in-house counsel will be able or willing to give the opinion.

**13.13** It is the usual practice for the lawyers appointed by the lenders to give the opinion referred to in (c) above.

## Liabilities of the lawyer

**13.14** In giving an opinion, lawyers are expected to assume responsibility for the views expressed in the opinion. Primarily, that responsibility will be to the persons to whom the opinion is addressed which, in most cases, will be the financial institutions providing or arranging for the provision of finance and also, perhaps, such a person as the trustee of any security that might be taken. The lawyers will need to consider who else might seek to hold them responsible on the opinion and, commonly, the lawyers will attempt to restrict their responsibility to the named addressees of the opinion.

**13.15** It is a good idea for the opinion to state that it is for the benefit of the addressee only, normally the lender and no one else may rely on it. In the case of an opinion being sought by the agent bank for a syndicate it should be stated to be for the benefit of the original banking syndicate. This matters because lawyers are expected to assume responsibility for the views expressed in their opinions. Normally that responsibility is limited to the party to whom it is addressed with a statement making it clear that it is only those persons to whom the opinion is addressed who may rely upon it.[6] It is possible, however, to add that the opinion may be passed to named third parties but that they may not rely on its contents. The main candidates for receipt on such terms would be (according to the nature of the transaction):

- rating agencies;
- counterparties;
- the trustee for bond or note holders, the lead manager and any underwriters in the case of a bond issue; and
- a security trustee.

**13.16** The opinion sometimes states, specifically, that the opinion may not be relied upon by assignees of the lenders or any other person who might have or acquire an interest derived through the lenders, such as a sub-participant.[7] Notwithstanding such an express limitation and disclaimer, a lawyer may find that some other person may seek to hold him responsible for the views that have been expressed or, more generally, for the way in which the transaction has been structured.

**13.17** It is, therefore, necessary to consider the grounds upon which a lawyer will assume responsibility for the views that he has expressed in his opinion or, more generally, for his involvement in the transaction. To a large extent, this will depend upon the jurisdiction in which the lawyer has been working, but he may also find himself exposed to the laws of the jurisdictions in which his opinion was received or in which his advice was acted upon. What follows is limited to a brief and very general view of English law on these questions.

**13.18** The lawyer instructed by or on behalf of the lenders will have a responsibility to the lenders for the accuracy of his opinion. Where he has been retained directly by a lender then the responsibility will be a contractual responsibility arising from the retainer. In the case of a syndicated facility the lawyer will usually be retained by the arranging bank and will not be retained separately by each of the lenders. In that case, the lawyer would have a contract with the arranging bank but not with the lenders, unless it could be shown that each of the lenders expressly authorised the arranger to retain the lawyer on behalf of the lenders. That may be difficult, especially if the documentation contains the usual provision by which the lenders acknowledge that they have not relied upon the arranging bank for legal advice. To overcome any theoretical problems that this may give rise to concerning the reliance that the lenders in the syndicate may place upon the legal opinion, it will usually be addressed to the arranger and to each of the lenders. In

---

6 Of particular concern here will be banks coming to a syndicate as a secondary party (see **Ch 3**) and purchasers of bonds (see **Ch 4**) not being able to seek to rely on the opinion.

7 See **Ch 3**.

that situation, the responsibility of the lawyer would be governed by the law of tort which, at the end of the day, would be much the same as in the law of contract, namely, not to be negligent in giving the opinion.

**13.19** In the absence of a legal opinion, a lawyer who knows that the lenders are relying upon his advice would have a general responsibility to advise correctly and not to give negligent advice. The duty would probably extend to pointing out any pitfalls in the documents and there would be a general responsibility to ensure that the lawyers were appraised of any legal risks to which they might be exposed by the transaction. In rendering his legal opinion, the lawyer will formally set out his advice and, in the qualifications and assumptions contained in the opinion, he will cover or limit most of the matters which he would otherwise, need to advise upon generally, including the pitfalls. It is perhaps ironic that the rendering of a legal opinion has the practical effect of limiting the various matters which the lawyer would otherwise need to explain to the lenders in quite some detail.

**13.20** If the legal opinion has been given by the borrower's lawyer as, for instance, with respect to the laws of the borrower's domicile, then that lawyer will have a responsibility in the law in tort to the lenders. That responsibility would be that he should not be negligent in giving his opinion and, again, the assumptions and qualifications stated in the opinion will limit the scope of his responsibility. He will not have a responsibility in contract as he was not instructed by the lenders.

**13.21** Insofar as third parties are concerned, the persons who might seek to establish some form of liability against a lawyer involved in a transaction would be investors or assignees of the original lenders who have suffered a loss on the transaction and who have derived their interest in the transaction at some later time, usually through one of the original parties. This might, for instance, include a bond holder. They would not have a claim in contract and so they would seek to establish a claim in tort based upon a failure to take reasonable care in the legal work done by the lawyer, but it is difficult to imagine how such a claim could be successfully mounted, except in the most unusual of circumstances, *Caparo Industries v Dickman*[8]. Such an investor would need to establish that he relied upon the lawyer in circumstances where it was reasonable to do so, that the lawyer ought to have known that a person such as the investor concerned would so rely on the lawyer and that such reliance played a significant part in the decision to invest. It is suggested that merely knowing the names of the lawyers who were involved would be insufficient.

---

[8] [1990] UKHL 2, followed by *Essenden Finance Corp Ltd v Peat Marwick Hungerfords (Reg)* [1997] 188 CLR 241. Essentially the position is that to liability to arise in this context in negligence harm must be reasonably forseeable as a result of the conduct, the parties must be in a position of proximity and it must be fair, just and reasonable to impose liability. The current legal position is thus that the courts will not hold the author of a legal opinion liable to those beyond whom it was prepared for except in very limited circumstances.

**13.22** The relevance of the distinction between a liability in contract and in tort will relate primarily to the time limits for instituting a suit against the lawyer if his advice or opinion has proved to be incorrect. Generally speaking, those time limits are calculated from the date from which the law deems the cause of action to have accrued.[9] The damages which could be recovered against the lawyer would be limited, basically, to the loss that the lawyer should reasonably have expected at the time, that he gave his advice, to have resulted from his negligence.[10] The lawyer would not be responsible for any other loss such as, for instance, resulting from a bad commercial decision which was not based upon the lawyer's advice.

## Structure of a legal opinion

**13.23** Legal opinions are usually structured in four parts and are set forth in letter form on the headed notepaper of the lawyers concerned. The first part briefly describes the transaction and the documents to which the opinion relates. The second part sets forth the assumptions which the lawyers have made on matters of fact concerning the transaction. The third part of the opinion contains the actual matters upon which the lawyers are giving an opinion. The fourth part of the opinion sets forth the qualifications and exceptions as to the matters of law on which the opinion has been given. Each of those aspects will now be dealt with separately.

### Addresses and description of transaction

**13.24** The opinion should commence by setting out the parties to whom it is addressed. In the case of a syndicated loan, the opinion should be addressed to the arranging bank and to each of the lenders. Where the lawyers giving the opinion have been retained specifically for the transaction and do not act generally for the lenders or the borrower, as the case may be, they may describe themselves as being specially retained in relation to the particular transaction, so as to negate any suggestion that they have any general knowledge of the party concerned or its affairs.

**13.25** The opinion will then proceed to describe the transaction and the documents to which it relates. If there is time, the principal documents to be addressed will have been executed and the opinion will state this and be based on them. Sometimes, if time pressures do not permit the inspection of executed documents, the opinion will refer to drafts of the documents and there will then be a specific assumption

---

9 Limitation Act 1980 and Latent Damage Act 1986.

10 *Donoghue v Stevenson* [1932] AC 562; *Hedley Byrne & Co Ltd v Heller and Partners Ltd* [1964] AC 465.

set forth that the lawyers have assumed that the documents as executed were in the same form as in the draft documents that they have reviewed for the purposes of giving their opinion. Obviously, it is best if the lawyers are able to review the documents as executed so as to avoid any possibility of confusion, but it is often the case that time does not permit this to happen. The lawyers should then state that in giving their opinion they have examined the listed documents and that they have had regard to the laws of their jurisdiction as at the date of the opinion, but not the laws of any other jurisdiction, and 'such other matters as they have considered relevant' in giving their opinion. The purpose of this additional statement, from the point of view of the addressees of the opinion, is to make it clear that the lawyers have not deliberately shut their eyes to any matter that they should reasonably have considered. The opinion should also state on whose behalf the lawyers have received instructions and sometimes they will also state that they have participated in discussions with the lender or agent for the lenders. In reviewing an opinion, the addressees should bear this in mind because the lawyers may have raised points on matters which are not strictly addressed in the opinion, for instance, the desirability of inserting certain provisions which have not appeared in the documentation in its final form.

## Assumptions

**13.26** The next matter that will be referred to in the opinion is the assumptions that the lawyers have made in giving their opinion. The assumptions often relate to matters which are essential facts relating to the documentation and the transaction. The assumptions deal with such matters as the genuineness of signatures, conformity of copies of documents with the originals of those documents, the due execution of the documents by the parties, including the due authorisation of the persons who signed the documents on behalf of their principals, and the accuracy of the certificates that have been furnished, for instance, certificates concerning board resolutions. It would not, however, usually be proper for a lawyer giving an opinion with reference to a specific party to make all of those assumptions so far as they concern that party. For instance, if a lawyer acting for the borrower is giving an opinion relating to the borrower and its participation in the transaction, then the lawyer should not state as an assumption that the borrower has duly authorised the execution of the documents. Sometimes, lawyers prefer to state matters as assumptions rather than to insert them as qualifications at the end of their opinion, but this is really a matter of style.

## Matters on which an opinion is given

**13.27** Having stated the assumptions upon which the opinion is given, the opinion will then proceed to set out specific matters on which an opinion is being given. Set out below are paragraphs commonly found in this section of legal opinions. The contents of this section will vary depending upon who is giving the legal opinion. Usually, it is the legal opinion furnished by the borrower's lawyers which is the most extensive, as it has a number of different matters to deal with concerning the borrower. For convenience of description, 'Arcadia' will be the country in which the borrower is incorporated and England will be the country of the agreed proper law of the loan agreement.

(1) *'The Borrower is a company duly incorporated for an unlimited duration and is validly existing under the laws of Arcadia, with power and authority to own its assets and conduct its business as presently being conducted and no liquidator, administrator, receiver or trustee of the borrower, its business or assets, has been appointed'*

These are matters principally concerning the jurisdiction of the domicile of the borrower and are usually opined upon in the opinion furnished by the borrower's lawyers. There are several different elements to this paragraph, as follows:

*'Duly incorporated for an unlimited duration'*

This refers to the setting up of the borrower as a corporation and will involve checking the relevant certificates of incorporation and other matters to ensure that the borrower was properly established. In some jurisdictions, corporations are established only for a limited period of time and if that is the case for a particular borrower then it would be relevant for this to be expressly covered. The language of this paragraph will be different if the borrower is not a corporation but instead a state instrumentality or an international organisation. In either case, the paragraph would need to refer to the basis upon which the borrower was established and continues to exist, such as the treaty under which the international organisation was established.

*'Validly existing'*

This refers to the continuing existence of the borrower as opposed to its original incorporation. It effectively means that the borrower has not been wound up or dissolved. Most opinions do not deal with the situation where the borrower is about to dissolve, merge, or consolidate or where steps are being taken to such an end. If a lawyer is aware of such facts, he should disclose them in his opinion.

*'In good standing'*

This phrase originated in the US and refers to the fact that the corporation has paid all of its taxes, non-payment of which might threaten its continuing existence. 'Good standing' opinions are often supported by certificates from the relevant state authority which do not certify that the borrower is in good standing but certify its existence and the absence of unpaid taxes. In jurisdictions where the concept has no relevance, it is best if this phrase were not used.

'*Power and authority to own its assets and conduct its business as presently conducted'*

This phrase is needed because without such authorisation the borrower would not be able to generate the funds necessary to service the loan. In certain cases, the lenders might request a wider statement to cover authority to carry on business in jurisdictions other than the jurisdiction of the lawyers giving the opinion. This should be resisted. If the lenders are particularly concerned about any particular jurisdictions then they should seek legal opinions from the lawyers in those relevant jurisdictions.

*'No liquidator, administrator, receiver or trustee of the borrower, its business or assets has been appointed'*

This wording is intended partly to cover the situation where the borrower has sought protection from its creditors as, for instance by the appointment of a liquidator or administrator under the Insolvency Act 1986 or of a similar official under Chapter 11 of the US bankruptcy legislation. It also refers to certain, non-voluntary, appointments, for example, the appointment of a liquidator, receiver or a trustee. These situations would not always necessarily be covered by the phrase 'validly existing.'

(2) *'The Borrower has power to enter into and perform the Loan Agreement and to borrow hereunder'*

This establishes that the borrower is authorised by its certificate of incorporation or by local statute and by its constitutive documents, to enter into a particular agreement and, essentially, that the borrower will not be acting ultra vires. Again, this is a matter to be covered in the legal opinion of the borrower's lawyers, being a matter relating to the borrower's domicile. Generally speaking, these will be matters concerning the borrower's Articles of Association (in some jurisdictions known as the statutes or byelaws) and general principles of law concerning the corporate capacity of corporations under the relevant law. In the case of statutory bodies or international organisations, the relevant authorities will usually be found in the statutes, treaties or charters establishing the borrower.

Where security over assets is being given or a guarantee is being taken, then the legal opinion will need to address not only the power of the borrower to borrow, but also the powers and capacity of the guarantor to give the guarantee and the powers and capacity of the relevant corporation to create the security over the assets concerned.[11] In addition, where security is being given over assets in a jurisdiction other than the corporation's domicile, the laws of the lex situs will be relevant to determine whether the assets concerned are of a type over which the relevant security can be given. This may require a separate legal opinion from the lawyers of that jurisdiction.

(3) *'All necessary action to authorise the borrowing on the terms and conditions of the Loan Agreement and to authorise the execution, delivery and performance of the Loan Agreement in accordance with its terms has been taken'*

This refers to the procedural matters which are required with respect to the particular borrowing concerned. It will go to such matters as the authority of the directors or shareholders of the borrower to authorise the transaction and would also cover any particular limits on their powers, such as a limit on the power of the directors to commit the borrower to borrowing at any time in excess of a stated limit. It will also cover, in the case of state instrumentalities, any limits on the authority of that instrumentality to enter into the transaction and any ratification or additional authorities that may be required to commit the borrower, such as legislative, cabinet or other executive authorisations.

On the face of it, the lawyer giving the legal opinion will need to be satisfied that the necessary formalities were met when the decision was made to commit the borrower to the transaction. This means, for instance, the lawyers being satisfied that the meeting of the directors of the borrower who authorised the transaction was duly convened, that quorum requirements were met and that any requirements as to conflicts of interest and the like were satisfied. Some of these points, however, will come within the assumptions stated by the lawyers and it may be difficult to determine if they satisfied themselves that all of the procedural requirements for the borrower to act have been met. For instance, if they have assumed the correctness and validity of the certificates that have been given, then they will have assumed that the proper procedures were observed in convening and holding a board meeting and, indeed, that the board meeting was held and the necessary resolutions passed as set forth in the certified copy of the board minutes furnished to him. It is not usually practical to expect lawyers to go any further than this and it must, therefore, be a risk for the lenders to rely upon the correctness and accuracy of the certificates upon which the lawyers have relied.

---

11 Corporate capacity is much less of an issue since the changes across much of the world in largely abolishing the *ultra vires* doctrine. This is discussed in **Ch 1**.

(4) *'The Loan Agreement has been duly executed and delivered on behalf of the Borrower'*

This refers to the authority of the individuals who purported to sign the documents on behalf of the borrower. The lawyers giving the legal opinion will need to be satisfied that the individuals were properly authorised under, for instance, the board resolutions of the directors of the borrower or under any relevant legislation. Sometimes, the relevant documents will be signed on behalf of a borrower under a power of attorney and if this is the case then the lawyers will need to check whether the borrower is entitled to give such a power of attorney and, if so, whether all the necessary formalities have been satisfied. The terms of the power of attorney will also need to be examined to ensure that in its scope they have permitted the attorney to act. Sometimes, a power of attorney will only authorise the attorney to execute a document in the form attached. In other instances, the power of attorney will be phrased more widely and will give the attorney power to negotiate some or all of the provisions of the documents or to agree amendments to those provisions. The lenders will need to be satisfied that under the law of the domicile of the borrower and under the law of the place where the power of attorney was executed, the attorney had been validly appointed to do what is described in the power of attorney.

(5) *'The Loan Agreement, as executed and delivered, constitutes a legal, valid and binding obligation of the Borrower enforceable in accordance with its terms'*

This statement should usually be contained in the opinion given by the lawyers in the jurisdiction of the proper law of the loan agreement. It would also be given, in a slightly varied form, in the opinion given by the lawyers in the jurisdiction of the domicile of the borrower. The latter opinion would add that the statement is made on the assumption that it would be legally valid, binding and enforceable in accordance with its terms under the proper law of the contract. There are several different elements to this paragraph, as follows:

*'Legal, valid'*

To a large extent these words overlap with other each other. What they mean is that there is nothing illegal or void in the document.

*'Binding obligation enforceable in accordance with its terms'*

The word 'enforceable' should be distinguished from the words 'in accordance with its terms.' The word 'enforceable' should not be taken as meaning specifically enforceable in the sense of being able to obtain an order for specific performance or some other equitable remedy requiring each obligation to be performed in the precise form set forth. Instead, what the word 'enforceable' should mean is that proceedings could be taken before the courts for breach of the Agreement and that the courts would award some remedy. Usually, the remedy would be damages. However, the lawyers will not normally be able to predict what the quantum of damages will be for any particular breach.

There are many reasons why equitable remedies, such as an order for specific performance, would not be awarded to enforce positive action as required by the literal terms of the documents. For that reason and because the lawyers cannot predict the quantum of damages for all possible breaches, lawyers giving an opinion should avoid using the words 'in accordance with its terms.'

(6) *'The authorisations, approvals, consents, licences, exemptions, filings, registrations, notarisations and other requirements under the laws of Arcadia with respect to the Loan Agreement and the performance by the Borrower of its provisions, have been obtained and are in full force and effect.'*

This will cover such matters as exchange control requirements and other licences and authorities imposed by the state authorities having jurisdiction over the borrower. It should be noted that in certain jurisdictions exchange control consents for the remittance of payments by the borrower may not be given on a blanket basis but might only be given with respect to payments due in the ordinary event. If the lenders sought to accelerate the loan due to default, the exchange control consents which were originally obtained may not permit the accelerated payment to be made. The lawyers should also check that the relevant exchange control consents cover not only principal and interest but other amounts such as fees and the like which might be payable.

(7) *'Under the laws of Arcadia, no deduction or withholding will be required to be made from any payment due by the Borrower under the Loan Agreement'*

If it is the case that withholding taxes might apply then that should be specifically addressed in the opinion. It would not be good practice for the lenders to rely on a grossing up clause in a loan agreement and not require an investigation as to the liability to pay withholding taxes and the like or the rate at which those taxes are payable. The effect of a grossing up obligation is to make the loan more expensive for a borrower and to increase the amounts which the borrower may have to repatriate from its resources. The lenders may need to take this into account in making their credit assessment of the borrower.

(8) *No stamp or registration or similar taxes or charges are payable under the laws of Arcadia in respect of the Loan Agreement'*

This provision is necessary as, under the laws of a number of jurisdictions, if stamp duty is not paid then the documents may not be enforceable before the courts of the relevant country until the duty has been assessed and paid. The other point to bear in mind about stamp duties is that there is often a penalty duty payable if the stamp duty is not paid within the applicable period for payment and, practically speaking, it would be the lenders in the first instance who would need to pay the penalty if they sought to enforce the documents. Care should also be taken that there is no stamp duty on security documents such as a mortgage. If stamp duty is payable then the amount of the duty which is payable should be stated.

(9) *'It is not necessary under the laws of Arcadia in order to ensure the legality, validity or enforceability of the Loan Agreement that it should be filed, registered or recorded in any Public Office or elsewhere in Arcadia'*

In some senses this provision overlaps with the provisions as to licences and consents. A similar provision may also be of relevance to security documents where security is being given over assets within the jurisdiction. In that case it might be advisable for this provision to be expanded to deal with what action needs to be taken and the effect on priorities, vis-à-vis other creditors, of taking such action.

(10) *'The execution and delivery by the Borrower of the Loan Agreement, the borrowing thereunder and the performance by the Borrower of the terms of the Loan Agreement will not conflict with or infringe the provisions of: (1) the laws of Arcadia; (2) the Memorandum and Articles of the Borrower; (3) any order of any judicial or other authority of Arcadia; or (4) any mortgage, contract or other undertaking which is binding upon the Borrower or its assets'*

This provision is very wide in its scope and to some extent overlaps with the other provisions of the opinion. Lawyers should resist including in this opinion the fourth limb of this paragraph as it requires them effectively to undertake an audit review of the borrower's affairs and all of the transactions in which the borrower might have been involved or which may have involved its assets, whether such transactions were public or private. That wording might, for instance, cover negative pledges that might have been agreed in a transaction of which the lawyers may not be aware.

The fourth limb is usually covered, instead, in representations and warranties given by the borrower in the Loan Agreement itself.

(11) *'There is no actual, pending or threatened litigation, arbitration or administrative proceedings concerning the Borrower or its*

*assets before the Courts of or any other judicial or administrative tribunal in Arcadia'*

Again, this is a provision that lawyers should resist including in their legal opinion because it would require the lawyer to undertake a legal audit of all possible matters in which the borrower might be involved and indeed, of which the borrower itself may not be fully aware, especially so far as threatened litigation is concerned. Lawyers should also refuse to compromise by agreeing to insert in their opinion an additional statement relating to the materiality of such litigation because that would require the lawyers to form a value judgment as to the outcome of the litigation. Once again, this is a matter that should more appropriately be dealt with in the representations and warranties given by the borrower in the Loan Agreement.

(12) *'Under the laws of Arcadia the obligations of the Borrower under the Loan Agreement will rank pari passu with all its other unsecured indebtedness'*

This paragraph will be subject to the qualification as to insolvency, as to which see below. It should be noted that this paragraph does not purport to state what the position will be as regards any security that the borrower may have given either at the time of execution of the loan agreement or subsequently, as it would not be reasonable to expect the lawyers to know of all the possible security that might have been given or may arise, whether in documentary form or as a matter of law, for instance, liens.

(13) *'The choice of English law to govern the Loan Agreement would be recognised and given effect to by the courts of Arcadia and accordingly if proceedings were brought against the Borrower before those courts, those courts would apply the laws of England as the proper law of the Loan Agreement'*

This is an important provision from the lender's point of view because the lenders may wish to commence proceedings against the borrower in the courts of the borrower's jurisdiction and the lenders will need to know that those courts would apply the agreed proper law of the loan agreement in interpreting the obligations of the borrower. Foreign lawyers will usually state as a qualification to their opinion that they have assumed that the English courts would apply English law as the proper law of the loan agreement.

(14) *'A judgment of the Courts of England would be recognised and enforced in Arcadia by the Courts of Arcadia'*

The purpose behind this provision is to ascertain whether a judgment obtained in the courts nominated as having express jurisdiction in the loan agreement, would be enforced in the local courts of the jurisdiction in which the borrower is situated. It is not normally the case that a court will automatically and without any qualification recognise and enforce the judgment of the courts of another jurisdiction and it would not be unusual for lawyers giving their opinion to qualify this paragraph. What the paragraph seeks to ascertain is that it will not be necessary to have a complete retrial of the merits of the case by the local courts. Sometimes this matter is governed by a treaty between the two countries concerned dealing with the recognition and enforcement of the judgments of their respective courts, but it is not always the case that such a treaty will exist. In so far as the mutual recognition and enforcement of judgments between parties within the EU is concerned, reference should be made to the recast Brussels I Regulation. In the case of the UK reference should be made to the Hague Convention on Choice of Court Agreements 2005 and the Hague Enforcement Convention 2025 (see **Chapter 10**).

The qualifications which are often found in an opinion dealing with this subject are that a foreign judgment will only be recognised if the following types of matter have been satisfied:

(a) that the procedural rules of the court giving the judgment had been observed;

(b) that the foreign court had jurisdiction to determine the matter;

(c) that the foreign court's judgment was final and conclusive;

(d) that the decision of the foreign court was for a fixed sum;

(e) that the decision of the foreign court had not been obtained by fraud or a trick;

(f) that enforcement of the decision of the foreign court would not be contrary in the local jurisdiction to public policy or constitute the enforcement of a judgment of a penal or revenue nature; and

(f) that the decision of the foreign court was not contrary to natural justice.

(15) *'Under the laws of Arcadia neither the Borrower nor its assets is entitled to immunity from suit or enforcement of judgment with respect to any action or proceeding that might be brought in the courts of Arcadia arising out of or relating to the Loan Agreement'*

This paragraph addresses the question of sovereign immunity and is particularly important in a situation where the borrower is a state instrumentality. In that case, the statement may well need to be qualified at least insofar as it concerns execution of judgment against the assets of the borrower. It is also normal to qualify this statement by saying that diplomatic assets will be immune from enforcement proceedings.

(16) *'A judgment in the courts of Arcadia may be expressed in (the relevant currency of the Loan Agreement').*

English courts permit a judgment to be awarded in a foreign currency other than sterling both in situations where the proper law of the obligation to make the payment is a foreign law and where the proper law is English law. It may not be the case, however, that all of the other common law jurisdictions will be prepared to follow this line of reasoning of the English courts and so it is common to find qualifications inserted in opinions to the effect that the courts of the relevant jurisdiction may not be prepared to award a judgment denominated in a foreign currency. Sometimes, this is further qualified by an express provision as to the effect of insolvency.

(17) *'It is not necessary under the laws of Arcadia in order to enable the Lenders to enforce their rights under the Loan Agreement that they should be licensed, qualified, or otherwise entitled to carry on business in Arcadia'*

The purpose of this paragraph is to provide an assurance to the lenders that they will be able to enforce the loan agreement against the borrower in its jurisdiction without the necessity of having to establish for themselves a place of business, etc in that jurisdiction.

(18) *'By reason only of the execution, delivery and performance of the Loan Agreement by the Lenders, they will not be deemed to be resident, domiciled or carrying on business in Arcadia or subject to taxation under the laws of Arcadia'*

This paragraph is of importance to the lenders in that it establishes whether they are likely to be deemed to be carrying on business and accordingly subject to taxation in a foreign jurisdiction only by reason of the loan agreement and their connection with it. Of course, they might already be so affected or the transaction might be taken in conjunction with other activities and that is a risk the lenders will have to bear.

## Qualifications

**13.28** Having set forth the matters which are expressly given as part of their opinion, the lawyers will then set forth the qualifications to which their opinion is subject. The qualifications will vary from one jurisdiction to another. Some of those matters have already been referred to above, but the following are qualifications that are commonly found in legal opinions:

(1) *'The Loan Agreement provides for default interest to be paid on overdue amounts. Such interest may amount to a penalty under the laws of Arcadia and may therefore not be recoverable'*

It was indicated in an earlier chapter of this work that some loan agreements provide for default interest to be paid on overdue amounts. Whenever default interest might be categorised as a penalty and thus not enforceable by the courts[12] a qualification to this effect should be included within the opinion. However, in England and Wales it is normally going to be the case that increased rates of interest upon sums payable in an event of default should not be regarded as a penalty unless excessive.[13]

(2) *'No opinion is expressed as to whether the Courts of Arcadia would give effect to the currency indemnity contained in the Loan Agreement'*

Currency indemnity clauses are commonly found in loan agreements but to date English lawyers have not been prepared to give opinions as to whether such a clause would be enforceable. A lawyer in the relevant jurisdiction may be prepared to do so. In any event, such a provision would not be likely to survive an insolvency.

(3) *'The Courts of Arcadia may stay proceedings if concurrent proceedings are being brought elsewhere'*

This qualification might apply, at least so far as the English courts are concerned, if they were presented with a claim at the same time as a similar claim is being heard in another jurisdiction or after it has been heard.

(4) *'The Courts of Arcadia might not treat as conclusive those certificates and determinations which the Loan Agreement states are to be so treated'*

This qualification is aimed at provisions in a loan agreement which provide that a certificate by a lender, as to an amount due or as to an interest calculation, is to be binding upon the borrower, save for manifest error and the like. Notwithstanding such a provision, the courts may require evidence to be given as to the facts upon which the certificate is based.

(5) *'Equitable remedies, such as an order for specific performance or the issue of an injunction, are available only at the discretion of the court and nothing in this opinion is to be taken as indicating that such a remedy would be available in respect of the obligations of the Borrower under the Loan Agreement'*

---

12 *Cavendish Square Holding BV v Tala (El Makdessi); Parking Eye v Beavis* [2015] UKSC 67.

13 *Lordsvale Finance plc v Bank of Zambia* [1996] 3 WLR 688.

This qualification relates to the provisions in the opinion which go to the validity and binding effect of the loan agreement upon the borrower and should be taken in conjunction with the comments made above on those provisions.

(6) *'The obligations of the Borrower may be limited by bankruptcy, insolvency, liquidation, administration, reorganisation and other laws of general application relating to or affecting the rights of creditors'*

Under the laws of many jurisdictions, including most common law jurisdictions, insolvency and the like proceedings affecting the borrower may have a drastic effect upon its stated obligations under a loan agreement. For instance, an obligation to pay interest may cease upon insolvency and a right to accelerate a loan agreement may be modified or otherwise affected. The claims of the lenders under a loan agreement may be converted into a right to prove as a creditor in the insolvency, but that may mean that only a dividend will be received and that damages for repayment of the whole amount advanced may not be available or enforceable. Insolvency may also mean that certain claims against the borrower may be paid in advance of those of the lenders for instance, preferential claims for unpaid taxes.

(7) *'Claims may become barred under the Statute of Limitations or may be or become subject to defences of set off or counterclaim'*

The first limb of this qualification is to the effect that the rights of a lender to bring an action against the borrower will be subject to the applicable limitation period of the jurisdiction in which the claim may be made. A claim will need to be brought within that period, otherwise it will be statute barred. The second limb relates to the right of the defendant in proceedings to set up a counterclaim or right of set off to the action. The contractual provisions in a loan agreement, which purport to negate the borrower's right to do this, may not be given effect in certain jurisdictions.

(8) *'Where obligations are to be performed in a jurisdiction outside Arcadia they may not be enforceable in Arcadia to the extent that performance would be illegal or contrary to public policy under the laws of that jurisdiction'*

This qualification states that the courts of one jurisdiction may not be willing to enforce an obligation of the borrower which has to be performed outside that jurisdiction, if to do so would be illegal or contrary to the laws of the jurisdiction in which the obligation is to be performed.

(9) *'No opinion is expressed with respect to the laws of any jurisdiction other than Arcadia'*

This qualification reflects what was said above to the effect that the lawyers who give a legal opinion can only be expected to opine upon the laws of their own jurisdiction.

(10) *'The effectiveness of terms exculpating a party from a liability or duty otherwise owed are limited by law'*

This qualification means that a lender may not be able to bring a claim against the borrower if the lender is itself in breach or, alternatively, that a breach committed by the lender may be taken into account, for instance, by way of set off or counterclaim, in reducing a claim taken against the borrower.

(11) *'Where a person is vested with a discretion to determine a matter in his opinion then the Courts of Arcadia may require that such discretion is exercised objectively and reasonably or that such opinion is based upon reasonable and objective grounds'*

In other words, the courts may refuse to give effect to an arbitrary decision of a lender which it purports to impose upon the borrower.

(12) *'The enforceability of the Loan Agreement may be limited by the provisions of Arcadian law applicable to contracts held to have been frustrated by events happening after their execution'*

In some jurisdictions this qualification may be amended to refer to the civil law doctrine of force majeure.[14]

(13) *'An Arcadian Court may refuse to give effect to a purported contractual obligation to pay costs imposed upon another party in respect of the costs of any unsuccessful litigation brought against that party and such a court may not award by way of costs all of the expenditure incurred by a successful litigant in proceedings brought before that court'*

This qualification relates to clauses sometimes found in a loan agreement which purport to impose upon a borrower all of the costs incurred by the lenders in enforcing or attempting to enforce what they believe to be the obligations of the borrower. If in fact judgment is awarded in favour of the borrower then it is likely that the courts would refuse to impose upon the borrower the obligation to pay the unsuccessful lender's costs of bringing the proceedings. Even in a situation where the lenders were successful, the courts may not oblige the borrower to pay all of the lenders' cost but only a proportion thereof and the ascertainment of that proportion will usually be subject to assessment by the courts.

(14) *'Provisions as to severability in the Loan Agreement may not be binding and the question of whether or not provisions relating to invalidity may be severed from other provisions in order to save such other provisions would be determined by the Arcadian Courts at their discretion'*

---

[14] See **Ch 1.**

This qualification relates to the clause often found in a loan agreement providing for severability of unenforceable or void provisions of the loan agreement. Effectively, the qualification states that the courts may take a different view and refuse to sever the tainted provisions so as to keep the other provisions intact.

**13.29** Where security is being given then further qualifications may be inserted relating to the effectiveness of the security and as to matters concerning the priority of the security over other competing interests.

**13.30** At least, insofar as English law and the other common law jurisdictions which follow English law are concerned, it is necessary in giving a legal opinion on security to consider in depth the matters relating to any guarantees and any security and the effectiveness of that security.

# Chapter 13 – Appendix 1

## Sample Legal Opinions: (A) Loan Agreement

To: [Agent Bank]

Dear Sirs,

**RE: [BORROWER] – $ FACILITY AGREEMENT**

### Introduction

1 We have acted as legal advisers as to English law to [Agent Bank] (the 'Agent'), in its capacity as agent in respect of a US$ guaranteed and secured term loan facility (the 'Facility') to [Borrower], a company incorporated under the laws of Arcadia (the 'Borrower'). We have been requested by our client to deliver this opinion as a condition precedent to drawdown of the Facility. This opinion is being delivered to the Agent only on behalf of the Lenders. We have taken our instruction in relation to the opinion solely from the Agent.

2 For the purposes of this opinion, we have reviewed:

(a) a [faxed] executed original of the facility agreement dated ......... (the 'Facility Agreement') among:

(1) the Borrower,

(2) [name Lenders], and

(3) the Agent; and

(b) a [faxed] original of the guarantee dated ......... given by [Guarantor] (the 'Guarantor') in favour of the Agent for the benefit of the Secured Parties, as defined in the Facility Agreement (the 'Guarantee').

We have not examined or reviewed any other document relating to the arrangements referred to in the Facility Agreement or the Guarantee.

3 Terms defined in the Facility Agreement have the same meanings in this opinion unless the contrary is indicated. Headings and sub-headings in this opinion are for ease of reference only, and do not affect its interpretation.

## English law

4 This opinion is limited to English law as applied by the English courts at the date hereof and is given on the basis that it will be governed by and construed in accordance with English law as at the date hereof. We express no opinion as to the laws of any jurisdiction other than England and Wales or European Union law as it affects any jurisdiction other than England. We express no opinion on any documents or agreements other than the Facility Agreement and the Guarantee; in particular, but without prejudice to the generality of the foregoing statement, we express no opinion on any Transaction Document, other than the Facility Agreement and the Guarantee. Insofar as laws of Arcadia may be relevant to our opinion, we refer you to the opinion of [Arcadian counsel] dated .........; we have made no investigation of such laws. This opinion addresses issues of English law only and we express no opinion nor make any comment on the content, adequacy or sufficiency of the commercial terms negotiated by the parties to the Transaction Documents or any of them.

## Assumptions

5 In considering the Facility Agreement and the Guarantee and rendering this opinion we have, with your consent and without further enquiry, assumed:

### Veracity and bona fides

(a) [the conformity to the original of the emailed copies of the Facility Agreement and the Guarantee received by us;]

(b) that each of the Facility Agreement and the Guarantee represents and contains the entirety of the agreements of the parties thereto in or in connection with the transactions contemplated thereby;

(c) the lack of bad faith and absence of fraud, coercion, duress or undue influence on the part of any party to the Facility Agreement, their respective directors, employees, agents and advisers;

(d) that the Guarantor entered into the Guarantee freely and without coercion or duress; that no undue influence was brought to bear on the Guarantor in relation to his entering into the Guarantee; that full and proper consideration has been given to the Guarantor for his assumption of obligations under the Guarantee; that the Guarantor received proper and independent advice in relation to the giving of the Guarantee and the implications for him of any default by the Borrower under the Facility Agreement; and that the Agent, its directors, employees, agents and advisers acted in good faith and without fraud in obtaining the Guarantee;

(e) that the representations and warranties given by any party to any other party pursuant to the Facility Agreement or the Guarantee (other than any representations and warranties in relation to any of the matters of English law expressly opined on in this opinion) are and will be when made or repeated or when deemed made or repeated, as the case may be, true and accurate in all respects, and that such representations and warranties will at all relevant times be true and accurate;

(f) that any representation or warranty given by any of the parties to the Facility Agreement or the Guarantee that it is not aware of or has no notice of any act, matter, thing or circumstance means that the same does not exist or has not occurred;

**Capacity**

(g) that each party to the Facility Agreement is duly incorporated, validly existing and (where relevant) in good standing under the laws of its respective jurisdiction of incorporation and has full corporate power and authority to enter into, execute and deliver the Facility Agreement and perform its obligations thereunder;

(h) that the Guarantor has the legal capacity to enter into and perform his obligations under the Guarantee, and that such capacity is not removed or limited by age, mental infirmity or bankruptcy;

(i) that the Facility Agreement was duly executed and delivered by each party thereto in accordance with the requirements of all applicable laws, other than English law;

(j) that the Guarantee was duly signed by the Guarantor in accordance with the requirements of all applicable laws, other than English law;

**Solvency**

(k) that none of the parties to the Facility Agreement is bankrupt or insolvent (in each case, within the meaning of any applicable legislation), or subject to any bankruptcy, insolvency, corporate reorganisation or analogous proceedings in any relevant jurisdiction; and that none of the parties to the Facility Agreement would be or become bankrupt or insolvent (within the meaning of any applicable legislation) by reason of its entering into or performing any of its obligations under the Facility Agreement or any other Transaction Document to which it is a party;

## Approvals, consents and registrations

(l) that all relevant corporate, shareholder and other approvals, consents, authorisations or resolutions required to be obtained or passed by or in respect of any party to the Facility Agreement in connection therewith or the transactions contemplated thereby, were duly obtained or passed prior to the execution of the Facility Agreement, have not been revoked or varied since the date or dates on which they were obtained or passed, and that they remain in full force and effect as at the date of this opinion;

(m) that any consent, licence, approval or authorisation of any person which is required in relation the execution and delivery of the Facility Agreement or the signing of the Guarantee and the performance and observance of the terms thereof by the parties thereto had been obtained at the date of execution of the Facility Agreement and the Guarantee;

(n) that each of the parties to each of the Facility Agreement will, prior to entering into any transaction contemplated by the Facility Agreement which would require the obtaining of any consent, approval (including credit approvals), authorisation or permission in relation thereto, have obtained all such consents, approvals, authorisations or permissions and will thereafter maintain and comply with all such consents, approvals, authorisations or permissions;

(o) that the Guarantor will, prior to entering into the Guarantee, have obtained any consent, approval, authorisation or permission required in connection with his giving of the Guarantee, and that he will thereafter maintain and comply with all such consents, approvals, authorisations or permissions;

## Performance by the parties

(p) that the terms of each of the Facility Agreement and the Guarantee and the procedures set out therein are and will continue to be observed and performed by each of the parties thereto (although any failure to effect such observance may only affect the validity of this opinion to the extent that it related to the subject matter of the failure); and

### Foreign law

(q) that there are no provisions of the laws of any jurisdiction outside England which would be contravened by the execution or delivery of the Transaction Documents or the performance by the parties thereto of their obligations thereunder, and that none of the opinions expressed below will be affected by the laws (including the public policy) of any jurisdiction outside England.

## Opinion

6 On the basis of the foregoing assumptions, and subject to the qualifications set out below, we are of the following opinions.

### Facility Agreement

(a) The Facility Agreement constitutes the legal, valid, binding and enforceable obligations of the Borrower, enforceable against it in accordance with its terms.

### Guarantee

(b) The Guarantee constitutes the legal, valid and binding and enforceable obligations of the Guarantor, enforceable against the Guarantor in accordance with its terms.

### Approvals and consents, filing, taxes

(c) There is no authorisation, approval or consent of, or registration or filing with, any Governmental Authority of or within England in relation to the Facility Agreement or the Guarantee that is required:

(i) to enable the Borrower lawfully to enter into, exercise its rights under and perform the obligations expressed to be assumed by it in the Facility Agreement;

(ii) to ensure that the obligations expressed to be assumed by the Borrower in the Facility Agreement are legal, valid and binding on it in accordance with the terms thereof;

(iii) to enable the Guarantor lawfully to enter into, exercise its rights under and perform the obligations expressed to be assumed by it in the Guarantee; or

(iv) to ensure that the obligations expressed to be assumed by the Guarantor under the Guarantee are legal, valid and binding on the Guarantor in accordance with the terms thereof.

(d) It is not necessary, in order to ensure the validity, enforceability or admissibility in evidence in proceedings taken in the English courts, that the Facility Agreement or the Guarantee be filed, recorded or enrolled with any court or other authority in England or that any stamp, registration or similar documentary tax be paid on or in relation to the Facility Agreement or the Guarantee in England.

(e) It is not necessary under the laws of England, in order to enable the Agent or the Lenders to enforce its or their rights under the Facility Agreement, that either of them should be licensed, qualified or otherwise entitled to carry on business in England. It is not necessary under the laws of England, in order to enable the Agent to enforce its rights under the Guarantee, that it should be licensed, qualified or otherwise entitled to carry on business in England.

### Governing law and jurisdiction

(f) The choice of English law to govern the Facility Agreement and the Guarantee will be recognised and upheld by the English courts.

(g) The submissions to the non exclusive jurisdiction of the courts of England contained in the Facility Agreement and the Guarantee are legal, valid and binding on the Borrower and the Guarantor, respectively. The appointment by the Borrower of an agent to accept service of process out of the English courts under the Facility Agreement is legal, valid and binding on the Borrower.

## Qualifications

7 The opinions expressed above are subject to the qualifications listed below.

(a) A determination, designation, calculation or certificate by any party to the Facility Agreement or the Guarantee as to any matter provided for therein might, in certain circumstances, be held by an English court not to be final, conclusive and binding (if, for example, it could be shown to have been made arbitrarily or in bad faith) notwithstanding the provisions of the relevant document.

(b) Any provision of the Facility Agreement or the Guarantee providing for the payment of additional moneys consequent on the breach of any provision thereof by any person expressed to be a party thereto, whether expressed by way of penalty, additional interest, liquidated damages or otherwise, would be unenforceable if such provision were held to constitute a penalty and not a genuine and reasonable pre-estimate of the loss likely to be suffered as a result of the breach in question. We express no opinion as to whether any such provision in the Facility Agreement or the Guarantee does in fact constitute a genuine and reasonable pre-estimate of loss. However, we note the case of, *Lordsvale Finance plc v Bank of Zambia* [1996] 3 W.L.R. 688 a decision of the court of first instance, whereby the rate of interest payable in a loan agreement was increased by 1% per annum from the date of default was held not to be a penalty on the basis that this was a modest increase in the contractual rate of interest which could be explained as commercially justifiable, that its dominant purpose was not to deter the paying party from breach, and that the increase in the interest rate did not take effect retrospectively. The recent relaxing of the definition of 'penalty clause' in *Cavendish Square Holding BV v Tala (El Makdessi), Parking Eye v Beavis [2015] UKSC 67* means that the risk of this clause being struck down as a penalty is negligible.

(c) To the extent that any fees or expenses are expressed to be in amounts to be agreed, or any other matter is expressed to be determined by agreement between the respective parties, the relevant provision may be unenforceable for uncertainty in default of such agreement.

(d) In some circumstances, an English court will not give effect to any provision of a document which provides that, in the event of any invalidity, illegality or unenforceability of any provision of such document, the remaining provisions thereof shall not be affected or impaired, particularly if to do so would not accord with public policy or would require that the court make a new contract for the parties.

(e) An English court may refuse to give effect to any provision of the Facility Agreement or the Guarantee:

   (i) for the payment of expenses in respect of the costs of enforcement (actual or contemplated) or of unsuccessful litigation brought before an English court or where the court has itself made an order for costs; or

   (ii) which would involve the enforcement of foreign revenue or penal laws.

(f) This opinion is not to be taken to imply that any obligation would necessarily be capable of enforcement in all circumstances in accordance with its terms. The term 'enforceable', as used in this opinion, means that the obligations assumed by the parties to the Facility Agreement or the Guarantee are of the type which an English court enforces. In particular:

(i) an English court will not necessarily grant any remedy the availability of which is subject to equitable considerations or which is otherwise in the discretion of the court. In particular, orders for specific performance and injunctions are, in general, discretionary remedies under English law and specific performance is not available where damages are considered by the court to be an adequate alternative remedy;

(ii) claims may become barred under the Limitation Act 1980 or the Foreign Limitation Periods Act 1984 or may be or become subject to the defence of set off or to counterclaim;

(iii) where obligations are to be performed in a jurisdiction outside England, they may not be enforceable in England to the extent that performance would be illegal under the laws, or contrary to the exchange control regulations, of the other jurisdiction;

(iv) the enforcement of the obligations of the parties to each of the Facility Agreement and the Guarantee may be limited by the provisions of English law applicable to agreements held to have been frustrated by events happening after their execution;

(v) enforcement of obligations may be invalidated by reason of fraud; and

(vi) certain provisions of the Guarantee may be held to be 'unfair' under the provision of Unfair Terms in the Consumer Rights Act 2015, particularly if the terms of the Guarantee were imposed on the Guarantor without affording the Guarantor any opportunity to negotiate the terms of the Guarantee. Any provision so deemed 'unfair' will be void, and thus unenforceable. Furthermore, the Guarantee will be unenforceable against the Guarantor if the Guarantor entered into it as a result of duress or undue influence being brought to bear on him by the Borrower, the Agent, the Lender or any other shareholder in the Borrower.

(g) This opinion is subject to all applicable laws relating to insolvency, bankruptcy, administration, reorganisation, liquidation or analogous circumstances.

(h) An English court may refuse to give effect to any provision of the Facility Agreement or the Guarantee which would be inconsistent with English public policy. In particular, any undertakings or indemnities in relation to stamp duties payable in the United Kingdom given by any party to the Facility Agreement or the Guarantee are likely to be void under the provisions of section 117 of the Stamp Act 1891.

(i) Notwithstanding the submission to the jurisdiction of the English courts, an English court could decline jurisdiction or stay proceedings on the ground that proceedings involving the same or a related issue are pending in a foreign jurisdiction. Furthermore, an English court has power to stay an action where it is shown that there is some other forum having competent jurisdiction which is more appropriate for the trial of the action. In relation to the Guarantee, the English courts may decline to accept jurisdiction if the Guarantor is not physically present in England and Wales at the time at which proceedings are brought against him, or if there are valid concerns that the Guarantor will not be able to obtain proper representation before the English courts.

(j) The effectiveness of terms exculpating a party from liability or a duty otherwise owed are limited by law.

(k) If any party to the Facility Agreement for the Guarantee fails to maintain an agent for service of process in England, it may be necessary to initiate any legal proceedings in England against such party by serving a claim form outside the jurisdiction, and for this purpose the leave of the court (as to which the court has a discretion) may have to be obtained. We note, in this regard, that the Guarantor has not appointed, under the terms of the Guarantee, an agent for service of process out of the English courts.

(l) There is some possibility that an English court would hold that a judgment on the Facility Agreement or the Guarantee, whether given in an English court or elsewhere, would supersede the terms of the Facility Agreement or the Guarantee, as applicable, to all intents and purposes so that the obligations set forth in the Facility Agreement or the Guarantee, as applicable, would not be held to survive such a judgment.

This opinion is given for the sole benefit of the Agent and the Lenders as at the date of this opinion. It may not be disclosed to or relied upon by any other person nor quoted or referred to in any public document nor filed with any governmental agency without our consent.

Yours faithfully,

# Chapter 13 – Appendix 2

## Sample Legal Opinions: (B) Credit DefaultSwap

To: [Addressee]

[Date]

Dear Sirs

**CREDIT DEFAULT SWAP**

1 We have acted as legal advisers as to English law to [.........] ('Party A') in connection with the entry into by Party A of a single transaction credit default swap transaction with [..........] ('Party B'), as evidenced by:

(a) ISDA Master Agreement (2002 Cross-Border) dated as of .......... (the 'Swap Agreement') and the Schedule thereto among as Party A and Party B (the 'Schedule'); and

(b) Single Transaction Confirmation dated ......... from Party A to Party B (the 'Confirmation' and, together with the Swap Agreement and the Schedule, the 'Opinion Documents').

2 Although this letter is addressed to the persons listed in the Schedule to this letter (the 'Addressees'), we have received instructions only from our client, Party A. We have not advised Party B on the content of the Opinion Documents, or on any other of the agreements and documents referred to in the Confirmation or assisted Party B in relation to the negotiation of the Opinion Documents or any of the documents referred to therein or connected with the transaction referred to in the Confirmation. The provision of this letter and the opinions contained herein to Addressees other than our client is not to be taken as implying that we owe any duty of care to anyone other than our client in relation to the content of the Opinion Documents or the commercial and financial implications thereof. Notwithstanding the provision of this letter to Party B, we expressly reserve the right to represent our client (if it so requests) in relation to any matters affecting the Opinion Documents or any other document relating to the transactions described therein at any time in the future.

3 For the purposes of giving the opinions stated in paragraph 7 of this letter, we have examined originals or copies, certified or

otherwise, identified to our satisfaction, of the Opinion Documents and such other documents as we have deemed necessary or appropriate in order to give this opinion. Our opinion is limited to the Opinion Documents, and we express no opinion on any other agreements entered into in connection with the transaction described in the Confirmation.

4 Headings and sub headings in this letter are for ease of reference only, and do not affect its interpretation.

## English Law

5 The opinions stated in this letter are limited to English law as applied by the English courts at the date hereof and are given on the basis that this letter will be governed by and construed in accordance with English law as at the date hereof. We express no opinion as to the laws of any jurisdiction other than England and Wales as it affects a jurisdiction other than England.

## Assumptions

6 In considering the Opinion Documents and in rendering the opinions set out in paragraph 7 of this letter we have, with your consent and without further enquiry, assumed:

### Veracity and bona fides

(a) the genuineness of all signatures on, and the authenticity and completeness of, all documents submitted to us, whether as originals or copies;

(b) the conformity to originals of all documents supplied to us as photocopies or facsimile copies;

(c) that the Opinion Documents represent and contain the entirety of the agreements of Party A and Party B in connection with the transactions which are the subject of the Opinion Documents;

(d) the lack of bad faith and absence of fraud, coercion, duress or undue influence on the part of any party to the Opinion Documents, their respective directors, employees, agents and;

(e) that the representations and warranties given by any party to any other party contained in Opinion Documents (other than any representations and warranties made in the Opinion Documents in relation to any of the matters the subject of any of the opinions given in this letter) are and will be when made or repeated or when deemed made or repeated, as the case may be, true and accurate in all respects, and that such representations and warranties were at all relevant times true and accurate;

(f) that any representation or warranty given by any of the parties to the Opinion that it is not aware of or has no notice of any act, matter, thing or circumstance means that the same does not exist or has not occurred;

**Capacity**

(g) that each of the Party A and Party B is duly incorporated or organised, validly existing and (where relevant) in good standing under the laws of its respective jurisdiction of incorporation or organisation and has full corporate power and authority to enter into the Opinion Documents;

(h) that each of the Opinion Documents has been duly executed and delivered by each party thereto in accordance with all applicable laws, other than English law;

**Solvency**

(i) that each party to the Opinion Documents was, at the time of entering into the Opinion Documents, not in receivership, bankrupt or insolvent (in each case within the meaning of any applicable legislation) or subject to bankruptcy, insolvency, corporate reorganisation or analogous proceedings in any relevant jurisdiction; and that none of the parties to the Opinion Documents would be or become bankrupt or insolvent by reason of its entering into and performing the transaction contemplated by the Opinion Documents;

**Approvals, consents and registrations**

(j) that all relevant corporate, shareholder and other approvals, consents, authorisations or resolutions required to be obtained or passed by or in respect of each of Party A and Party B in connection with the Opinion Documents or the transactions contemplated thereby, have been duly obtained or passed, have not been revoked or varied since the date or dates on which they were obtained or passed, and that they remain in full force and effect as at the date of this opinion;

(k) that any consent, licence, approval or authorisation of any person which is required in relation the execution and delivery of the Opinion Documents and the performance and observance of the terms thereof by the parties thereto has been obtained at the date of this opinion;

(l) that each of the parties to the Opinion Documents will, prior to entering into any transaction contemplated by the Opinion Documents which would require the obtaining of any consent, approval (including credit approvals), authorisation or permission in relation thereto, including, without prejudice to our opinion in paragraph 7(b) of this letter, any approvals required for the purposes of the Financial Services and Markets Act 2000, as amended (the 'FSMA'), have obtained all such consents, approvals, authorisations or permissions and will thereafter comply with all applicable provisions of any such consents, approvals, authorisations or permissions (including under the FSMA and all applicable regulations and rules from time to time in effect thereunder or in connection therewith);

### Parties' intention

(m) that the Opinion Documents correctly reflect the intentions of the parties thereto and that the procedures contemplated for settlement of the transaction specified in the Confirmation will be capable of performance in the manner contemplated by the Confirmation at the time such performance is required;

### Foreign Law

(n) that there are no provisions of the laws of any jurisdiction outside England which would be contravened by the execution or delivery of the Opinion Documents and that none of the opinions expressed below will be affected by the laws (including the public policy) of any jurisdiction outside England.

## Opinion

7 On the basis of these assumptions, and subject to the qualifications set out below, we are of the following opinions.

### Documents

(a) Those provisions of the Opinion Documents that are expressly stated to be governed by English law constitute the legal, valid and binding obligations of Party A, enforceable against it in accordance with their terms. Please note, however, the qualification in paragraph 8(i) below.

### Approvals and Consents

(b) No consents, licences, approvals or authorisations of, or registrations or filings with, any governmental or other authority or agency of or in the United Kingdom are required by law or regulation in relation to the execution and delivery of the Opinion Documents by Party A.

### Governing Law

(c) The choice of English law to govern the Opinion Documents will be recognised and upheld by the English courts.

### Submission to Jurisdiction

(d) The submission by Party A to the jurisdiction of the English courts in connection with any disputes or proceedings under any such document or agreement, is valid and binding on each such party.

### Public Policy

(e) As at the date of this opinion, we are not aware of any circumstances concerning the transactions contemplated by the Opinion Documents that would give rise to an English court holding that such transaction violates English public policy.

## Qualifications

8 The opinions stated in paragraph 7 above are subject to the following qualifications:

(a) Without prejudice to our opinion in paragraph 7(c), the choice of English law to govern the Opinion Documents would not be recognised or upheld if there were reasons for avoiding the choice of law on the grounds that its application would be contrary to English public policy.

(b) A determination, designation, calculation or certificate by any party to the Opinion Documents as to any matter provided for therein might, in certain circumstances, be held by an English court not to be final, conclusive and binding (if, for example, it could be shown to have been made arbitrarily or in bad faith) notwithstanding the provisions of the relevant document.

(c) In some circumstances, an English court will not give effect to any provision of a document which provides that, in the event of any invalidity, illegality or unenforceability of any provision of such document, the remaining provisions thereof shall not be affected or impaired, particularly if to do so would not accord with public policy or would require that the court make a new contract for the parties.

(d) An English court may refuse to give effect to any provision of the Opinion Documents:

   (i) for the payment of expenses in respect of the costs of enforcement (actual or contemplated) or of unsuccessful litigation brought before an English court or where the court has itself made an order for costs; or

   (ii) which would involve the enforcement of foreign revenue or penal laws.

(e) An English court may refuse to give effect to any provision of the Opinion Documents which would be inconsistent with English public policy. Such provisions may include any indemnity for the payment of stamp duties or like documentary taxes. We also express no opinion on any provision in the Opinion Documents that purports to prohibit or limit the ability of any party thereto to exercise mutual rights of set off upon the occurrence of an insolvency of any other party.

(f) English Courts can give judgments in currencies other than sterling if, subject to the terms of the relevant contract, it is the currency which most fairly reflects the claimant's loss, but such a judgment may be required to be converted into sterling for enforcement purposes.

(g) Any action brought against a party to the Opinion Document in the English courts would be subject to the rules and procedures of the English courts, including the power of an English court, at its discretion, to order a claimant in an action, if such claimant is not ordinarily resident in some part of the United Kingdom, to provide security for costs.

(h) If Party A fails to maintain an agent for service of process in England and Wales, it may be necessary to initiate any legal proceedings in England and Wales against such party by serving a writ or claim form outside the jurisdiction, and for this purpose the leave of the court (as to which the court has a discretion) may have to be obtained.

(i) This opinion is not to be taken to imply that any obligation would necessarily be capable of enforcement against the parties to the Opinion Documents in all circumstances in accordance with its terms. The term 'enforceable', as used in this opinion, means that the obligations assumed by the parties to the Opinion Documents are of the type which an English court customarily enforces. In particular:

(i) an English court will not necessarily grant any remedy the availability of which is subject to equitable considerations or which is otherwise in the discretion of the court. In particular, orders for specific performance and injunctions are, in general, discretionary remedies under English law and specific performance is not available where damages are considered by the court to be an adequate alternative remedy;

(ii) claims may become barred under the Limitation Act 1980 or the Foreign Limitation Periods Act 1984 or may be or become subject to set off or to counterclaim;

(iii) where obligations are to be performed in a jurisdiction outside England, they may not be enforceable in England to the extent that performance would be illegal under the laws, or contrary to the exchange control regulations, of the other jurisdiction;

(iv) the enforcement of the obligations of the parties to the Opinion Documents may be limited by the provisions of English law applicable to agreements held to have been frustrated by events happening after their execution; and

(v) enforcement of obligations may be invalidated by reason of fraud;

(j) The opinions given in this letter are subject to all applicable laws relating to insolvency, bankruptcy, administration, reorganisation, liquidation or analogous circumstances.

(k) An English court has power to stay an action where it is shown that there is some other forum having competent jurisdiction which is more appropriate for the trial of the action, in which the case can be tried more suitably for the interests of all the parties and the ends of justice, and where the staying of the action is not inconsistent with the Hague Judgments Convention.

(l) The effectiveness of terms exculpating a party from liability or a duty otherwise owed is limited by law.

(m) We express no view on any provision requiring written amendments or waivers insofar as such provision suggests that oral or other modifications, amendments or waivers could not effectively agreed upon or granted by or between the parties or implied by the course of conduct of the parties.

(n) Any provision of the Opinion Document providing for the payment of additional moneys by any party consequent on the breach of any provision thereof by any party, whether expressed by way of penalty, additional interest, liquidated damaged or otherwise, would be unenforceable if such provision were held to constitute a penalty and not a genuine and reasonable pre-estimate of the loss likely to be suffered as a result of the breach in question.

(o) The effect of contractual netting provisions such as those contained in the Swap Agreement will be determined, in the event of an insolvency of Party A or Party B, in accordance with the laws governing such insolvency and not merely English law as the law chosen to govern this provision of the Swap Agreement. Neither of the parties to the Swap Agreement is incorporated under the laws of England.

(p) No opinion is expressed on stamp duty, withholding tax or any other taxes that may be payable on, or arise by reason of, the Swap Agreement.

The opinions stated in this letter are given for the sole benefit of the Addressees. This letter may not be disclosed to nor relied upon by any other person nor quoted or referred to in any public document nor filed with any governmental agency, without, in any such case, our consent.

Yours faithfully,

# Chapter 13 – Appendix 3

# Sample Legal Opinions: (C) Securitisation Opinion

To: [Lead Manager]

[Trustee]

[Closing Date]

Dear Sirs

**[Issuer]**

## 1. Introduction

(a) We have acted as legal advisers as to English law to the Lead Manager in connection with the issue of £• Class A • Mortgage Backed Floating Rate Notes due 2027, £• Class B • Mortgage Backed Floating Rate Notes due 2027, £• Class C • Mortgage Backed Floating Rate Notes due 2027 and £• Class D • Mortgage Backed Floating Rate Notes due 2027 (collectively, the 'Notes') by the Issuer and the other transactions effected by the documents (the 'Transaction Documents') listed in Schedule 1 to this Opinion. We have taken our instructions solely from the Lead Manager.

(b) We have been asked by the Lead Manager to deliver this opinion, pursuant to Clause X of the Subscription Agreement dated [Signing Date] relating to the issue of the Notes. This opinion is also being delivered to the Trustee at the request of our client, the Lead Manager, and based upon instructions received from our client alone. The provision of this opinion to the Trustee is not to be taken as implying that we owe any duty of care to anyone other than our client in relation to the drafting and negotiation of the Transaction Documents or the commercial and financial implications thereof. Notwithstanding the provision of this opinion to the Trustee, we expressly reserve the right to represent our client (if it so requests) in relation to any matters affecting the Transaction Documents at any time in the future.

(c) For the purpose of giving this Opinion we have examined originals or copies, certified or otherwise, identified to our satisfaction, of the Transaction Documents listed in Schedule 1 to this Opinion and the documents listed in Schedule 2 to this Opinion. We have not, for the purposes of giving this Opinion, examined any other contracts, instruments or other documents or any corporate records of the Issuer or any other person. We express no opinion on, and make no comment in respect of, the commercial terms negotiated in the documents opined on in this Opinion, or the nature and effect, otherwise than under English law, of the transactions effected pursuant to those documents.

(d) We understand that the Notes will be [admitted to the Official List/admitted to trading on] of the [.........] Stock Exchange today.

(e) Terms defined in the Master Definitions Agreement listed in Schedule 1 to this Opinion have the same meanings in this Opinion unless the contrary is indicated. Headings and sub-headings in this Opinion are for ease of reference only, and do not affect its interpretation. In this Opinion, the expression 'Notes' includes Global Notes, unless the contrary is indicated.

(f) This Opinion is limited to English law as applied by the English courts at the date hereof and is given on the basis that it will be governed by and construed in accordance with English law as at the date hereof. In particular, we express no opinion as to the laws of any jurisdiction other than England and Wales as it affects a jurisdiction other than England. To the extent that the laws of the State of New York and the federal laws of the United States of America may be relevant to the issuance of the Notes or the transactions contemplated by the Transaction Documents, we refer you to the opinion of [.........], dated the date of this opinion. We express no view on the validity or otherwise of the matters set forth in the foregoing opinion. In respect of matters relating to UK taxation, we refer you to our tax opinion dated the date of this opinion.

(g) We have made no independent investigation of the adequacy or enforceability of the Loans made by [Originator of securitised loans] to the Borrowers, or the existence or capacity of any Borrower or the validity or enforceability of the security interests securing such Loans, or of the title of the Borrowers to the Properties the subject of such security. We note from Warranty 10(a) of the Loan Sale Agreement and the disclosure in the Offering Circular that a report on title (each a 'Report on Title') will have been prepared in respect of each Property by solicitors acting for or approved by [the Originator]. We have not reviewed any Reports on Title, any title deeds, leases or occupational leases of or in respect of the Properties and we have not carried out any independent searches or enquiries or inspected the Properties. We express no view on the adequacy or validity of the Reports on Title.

## 2. Assumptions

In considering the Transaction Documents and in rendering this Opinion, we have with your consent and without further enquiry assumed:

**Veracity and bona fides**

(a) the genuineness of all signatures on, and the authenticity and completeness of, all documents submitted to us, whether as originals or copies;

(b) the conformity to originals of all documents supplied to us as electronic copies or photocopies;

(c) that, where a document has been examined by us in draft or specimen form, it will be or has been executed in the form of that draft or specimen;

(d) the lack of bad faith and absence of fraud, coercion, duress or undue influence on the part of any party to the Transaction Documents, or any Borrower or Mortgagor, or their respective directors, employees, agents and advisers;

(e) the truth, accuracy and completeness at all relevant times of each statement contained in all board minutes and directors' certificates submitted to us and referred to in Schedule 2 to this Opinion, whether as originals or copies;

(f) that the representations and warranties given by any party (including, without limitation, the Warranties given by [the Originator] under the Loan Sale Agreement) to any other party contained in the Transaction Documents (other than any representations and warranties as to certain matters of English law expressly opined upon in this Opinion) are and will be when made or repeated or when deemed made or repeated, as the case may be, true and accurate in all respects, and that such representations and warranties were at all relevant times true and accurate;

(g) that any representation or warranty, including, without limitation, the Warranties contained in the Loan Sale Agreement, given by any of the parties to the Transaction Documents that it is not aware of or has no notice of any act, matter, thing or circumstance, means that the same does not exist or has not occurred;

**Corporate power, authorisation and execution**

(h) that each of the parties to the Transaction Documents, other than the Issuer and [Originator], is duly incorporated, validly existing and (where relevant) in good standing under the laws of its jurisdiction of incorporation; and that each of the parties to the Transaction Documents (other than the Issuer and [Originator]) is able lawfully to enter into the transactions described in the Transaction Documents and to which it is a party and to execute, deliver and perform its obligations thereunder;

(i) that the execution and delivery of the Transaction Documents have been duly authorised by each of the parties thereto (other than, in the case of all Transaction Documents other than the Loan Sale Agreement and the Assignments referred to therein, the Issuer and [Originator]), and that such Transaction Documents have been duly executed and delivered by such parties (other than, in the case of all Transaction Documents other than the Loan Sale Agreement and the Assignments referred to therein, the Issuer;

(j) that the directors of each of the Issuer and [Originator], in authorising the execution and delivery of each of the Transaction Documents to which such company is a party and the performance of such company's obligations thereunder, have exercised their powers and duties in accordance with all applicable laws;

(k) that the Memorandum and Articles of Association of each of the Issuer and [Originator] filed at Companies Registration Office are true, complete and up-to-date, and that no amendments have been made thereto since such filing;

(l) that (based on the representation and warranty given by [Originator] in Clause X of the Subscription Agreement) the execution and delivery of each Transaction Document to which [Originator] is a party and the performance by it of all the obligations assumed by it thereunder will not violate any mortgage, agreement or other undertaking or instrument to which [Originator] is a party or which is binding upon it or upon any of its assets;

(m) that each of the parties to the Subscription Agreement and the Agency Agreement and that each of the parties to the Transaction Documents who is carrying on, or purporting to carry on, regulated activities in the United Kingdom is an authorised person or an exempted person under the Financial Services and Markets Act 2000, as amended (the 'FSMA');

(n) that the issue of the Notes and the consummation of the transactions contemplated by the Transaction Documents will not cause the Issuer to breach the provisions of any other agreement, deed or document to which it is a party or by which it is bound;

(o) that the Transaction Documents have been entered into for *bona fide* commercial purposes and on arm's length terms and each of the persons party thereto had reasonable grounds for believing that the same would benefit such party; in this regard, we refer you to the Issuer's board minutes referred to in Schedule 2;

**Solvency**

(p) that none of the parties to the Transaction Documents other than the Issuer was, at the time of entering into the Transaction

Documents to which it is a party, in receivership or bankrupt or insolvent (in each case, within the meaning of any applicable legislation), or subject to any bankruptcy, insolvency, corporate reorganisation or analogous proceedings in any relevant jurisdiction; and that none of the parties to a Transaction Document other than the Issuer would be or become bankrupt or insolvent (within the meaning of any applicable legislation) by reason of its entering into or performing any of its obligations under that Transaction Document;

(q) that, at the time of entering into the Deed of Charge and Assignment:

(i) the Issuer is not unable to pay its debts within the meaning of section 123 of the Insolvency Act 1986; and

(ii) the Issuer would not become, as a consequence of entering into the Deed of Charge and Assignment, unable to pay its debts within the meaning of that Section;

**Deed of charge and assignment**

(r) that, based on Warranty 9(e), [Originator] was, immediately prior to the sale of the Loans to the Issuer, the absolute legal and beneficial owner of the Loans, free and clear of all encumbrances, claims and equities;

(s) that (based on Warranty 6(a)) in relation to each Mortgage and Loan in respect of a Property located in England and Wales, the relevant Mortgagor had as at the date of the relevant Mortgage and has, as at the date of this opinion, a good and marketable title to that Property;

(t) that (based on Warranties 9(d), 9(e) and 12) [Originator] is the legal and beneficial owner of each of the English Mortgages immediately prior to the completion of the sale and purchase of the English Mortgages and the Loans to the Issuer, free and clear of all Encumbrances, overriding interests (other than those to which the relevant Properties are subject) and equities (including, without limitation, rights of set off or counterclaim), and there were, at the date of any relevant Loan, no adverse entries of Encumbrances or applications for adverse entries of Encumbrances against any title at H.M. Land Registry to any relevant Property which entries would rank prior to the interests of [Originator] in such Mortgages;

(u) that (based on Warranties 9(a) and 9(b)) each English Mortgage and each Loan is a valid and binding obligation of and enforceable against the relevant Borrower subject only, in the case of English Mortgages required to be registered at H.M. Land Registry, to such registration;

(v) that there is and, up and until such time as registration of its interest is effected at H.M. Land Registry, there will continue to be, no adverse entries of Encumbrances against any relevant title at H.M. Land Registry in the case of those English Mortgages over land, title to which is registered at H.M. Land Registry ('**registered land**') which entry would rank prior to the interests of the Security Trustee in such Mortgages;

(w) that (based on Warranty 6(e)) in relation to each Mortgage of a Property comprising unregistered land in England, title to which is required to be registered at H.M. Land Registry in order to transfer a legal estate in land, an application for registration of the relevant Borrower's title to the Property and [Originator's] legal title to the Mortgage has been or will be delivered to H.M. Land Registry within the period of two months from the date of dealing giving rise to first registration;

(x) that (based on Warranties 6(b) and 9(b)) in relation to each Mortgage of a Property comprising registered land in England, all things necessary to complete [Originator's] legal title to that Mortgage have been duly done at the appropriate time or are in the process of being done with all due diligence and within the relevant priority period conferred by an official search against the relevant title at H.M. Land Registry;

(y) (based on Warranties 6(b) and 9(c)) that, in relation to each English Mortgage, such Mortgage was completed or will be duly completed within the priority period conferred by an official search against the relevant title at H.M. Land Registry (in the case of registered land);

(z) that (based on Warranty 25) subject to completion of any registration which may be pending at H.M. Land Registry, the Mortgage Deeds and the Loan Files are in the possession or held to the order of [Originator];

(aa) that (based on Warranty 43) where an Encumbrance (which would have otherwise ranked ahead of, or *pari passu* with, any Debenture or Mortgage) is postponed to and ranks in priority behind that Debenture or Mortgage by virtue of a deed of priorities or postponement, the right, title and interest of [Originator] in each relevant deed of priorities or postponement may be assigned absolutely to the Issuer or a third party;

(bb) that, if any Borrower were to be adjudged insolvent at a 'relevant time' (as defined in section 240 of the Insolvency Act 1986), no Mortgage and no advances secured by that Mortgage would be deemed to be a transaction at an undervalue or a preference with respect to such Borrower for the purposes of Section 238 and 239 of the Insolvency Act 1986;

(cc) based on the foregoing assumptions, that immediately before the execution of the Deed of Charge and Assignment, the Issuer was the absolute legal and/or beneficial owner of the property, rights and assets expressed to be mortgaged, assigned or charged by it pursuant to the Deed of Charge and Assignment, free and clear of any Encumbrance in favour of any third party;

## Issue of the Notes

(dd) that the Subscription Agreement and the Agency Agreement are not agreements to which section 26(1) or 27(1) of the FSMA applies and that neither the Subscription Agreement, the Agency Agreement nor any transactions, agreements or documents contemplated thereby (including, but without limitation, the issue of the Notes) have been entered into in the course of, or in consequence of , or in consequence of a communication in breach of Section 21 of the FSMA, *provided that* if this assumption is incorrect, this will not prejudice or impair the rights of the Noteholders;

(ee) that the Offering Circular and any other document in respect of the Notes constituting an investment advertisement within the meaning of the FSA or a communication within the meaning of the FSMA has only been made or caused to be made and will only be made or caused to be made in circumstances in which Section 21(1) of the FSMA does not apply, *provided* that if this assumption is incorrect, this will not prejudice or impair the rights of the Noteholders;

(ff) that all opinions and intentions expressed in the Offering Circular are honestly held and all statements contained therein were true and accurate when made and remain true and accurate (as to which we refer to Clauses 6.1(a), 6.2(a) and 6.3(a) of the Subscription Agreement);

(gg) that the net proceeds of the issue of the Notes are accounted for and have been paid in full by the Issuer to [Originator];

(hh) that the authorised issued and paid up share capital of the Issuer is as set out in the Capitalisation and Indebtedness Statement of the Issuer in the Offering Circular;

(ii) that any act done or any course of conduct engaged in for the purpose of stabilising the price of the Notes has been, done or engaged in conformity with the rules made under Section 118 and 144 of the FSMA, *provided that* if this assumption is incorrect, this will not prejudice or impair the rights of the Noteholders;

## Searches of Public Registries

(jj) that the information disclosed by the search carried out on our behalf by RM Information Consultants Limited on [Closing Date] at Companies Registration Office and our enquiry of the Central Registry of Winding-Up Petitions on [Closing Date] in relation to the Issuer and [Originator], was then accurate and has not since been altered, and that such searches did not fail to disclose any information which had been delivered for registration but did not appear from the information available at the time of our search, and that such oral enquiry did not fail to elicit any material information;

**General Matters**

(kk) that the Issuer does not own any assets which are not described in the Offering Circular;

(ll) that within 21 days of the Closing Date, the Deed of Charge and Assignment will be presented to the Registrar of Companies in England and Wales for registration;

(mm) that no exchange of the whole or part of the Global Notes for Definitive Notes shall take place other than in accordance with the Relevant Documents;

(nn) that the terms of the Transaction Documents are being and will be observed and performed by the parties thereto (without prejudice to our opinion as to the effectiveness and enforceability of the Deed of Charge and Assignment in the event that a Note Enforcement Notice is validly and effectively served);

(oo) that insofar as any obligation falls to be performed in any jurisdiction outside England, its performance will not be illegal or ineffective by virtue of the laws of that jurisdiction;

(pp) that where amounts payable under the Notes are expressed to be payable by reference to a calculation effected by reference to a formula or index or procedure, the formula or index or procedure relating to such Notes, reflects correctly the intention of the Issuer;

(qq) that the Reg S Notes and the Rule 144A Notes will be delivered in the form of the Reg S Global Notes and the Rule 144A Global Notes, as applicable, set out in the Trust Deed;

(rr) that there are no provisions of the laws of any jurisdiction outside England which would be contravened by the execution or delivery of the Transaction Documents and that none of the opinions expressed below will be affected by the laws (including the public policy) of any jurisdiction outside England.

We have also assumed, with your consent, that the Issuer is an insolvency-remote entity and will not be subject to insolvency proceedings in England and Wales or elsewhere. Accordingly, except as expressly opined in this opinion, we express no opinion on the validity or effectiveness of the Deed of Charge and Assignment in the event of any liquidation of or other insolvency proceedings relating to the Issuer.

## 3. Opinion

The following opinions are given on the basis of the assumptions set out above, the qualifications set out below, any matter not disclosed to us or as to which we have no ability to be aware.

### Enforceability Opinion

(a) The obligations of the Issuer and [Originator] under the Transaction Documents (other than the Loan Sale Agreement and those Transaction Documents referred to in paragraph 3(b) below) to which each is a party constitute the legal, valid, binding and enforceable obligations of the Issuer and [Originator] thereunder.

(b) Each of the Rule 144A Global Notes and the Reg S Global Notes constitutes, and each of the Notes in definitive form (when they have been executed with the facsimile signature of any director of the Issuer, authenticated and delivered as provided in the Trust Deed) will constitute, the legally valid, binding and enforceable obligations of the Issuer.

(c) Each Transaction Document (other than the Loan Sale Agreement) to which the Issuer and [Originator] is, respectively, a party has been duly authorised, executed and delivered by each of the Issuer, as applicable.[1]

(d) The Depository Agreement and the Exchange Rate Agency Agreement have been duly authorised, executed and delivered by the Issuer.[2]

(e) A search made on our behalf by RM Information Consultants Limited against the Issuer and [Originator] on [Closing Date] at Companies Registration Office, and enquiries made to the Central Registry of Winding-Up Petitions on [Closing Date], revealed no petition, order or resolution for the winding up of the Issuer and [Originator] and no petition for, and no notice of, appointment of a receiver or administrator in respect of the Issuer and [Originator] and that no security interests have been registered against the Issuer.

---

1 A separate opinion, including a true sale opinion, would be delivered in relation to the Loan Sale Agreement.

2 These are documents required by DTC (US bond clearing system) for 144A Notes.

## The Deed of Charge and Assignment

(f) The following security interests have been validly created, as a matter of English law, by the Issuer in favour of the Trustee under the terms of the Deed of Charge and Assignment:

(i) an assignment by way of first fixed security of the Issuer's rights under the Loans and the Credit Agreements;

(ii) an assignment by way of first fixed security of the Issuer's rights in, to and under:

(a) the Issuer's beneficial interests in the Security Trusts created over the Related Security;

(b) the Related Security to the extent not otherwise assigned by way of security as described above;

(c) any Eligible Investments of the Issuer;

(d) the Relevant Documents (to the extent not effectively assigned as described in paragraph (iii));

(e) its goodwill, its uncalled capital (if any) and the benefit of all licences, consents and authorisations (statutory or otherwise) held or to be held by it in connection with its business or the use of any Charged Property;

(iii) an assignment by way of first fixed security of the Issuer's rights, title and interest in and to the Loan Sale Agreement (including, without limitation, the Assignment), the Servicing Agreement, the Liquidity Facility Agreement, the Swap Agreement and the Swap Transactions, the Swap Guarantee, the Cash Management Agreement, the Corporate Services Agreement, the Declaration of Trust, the Agency Agreement, the Exchange Rate Agency Agreement, the Depository Agreement and the Master Definitions Agreement;

(iv) an assignment by way of first fixed security over the Issuer's rights to all monies standing to the credit of the Transaction Account, the Swap Collateral Cash Account (if and when opened) and the Swap Collateral Custody Account (if and when opened); and

(v) a first floating charge over all the Issuer's undertaking, property and assets (both present and future) whatsoever situated in England and Wales except for any such property or assets otherwise effectively charged or assigned by way of fixed security under the Deed of Charge and Assignment.

Provided that notice of the assignment by the Issuer to the Trustee is given to the Borrowers under the Credit Agreements and the other parties to the Related Security, the assignments so effected will take effect as legal assignments. The assignment by the Issuer of its rights in, to and under the Security Trusts is an assignment of equitable interests and, therefore, will take effect in equity only.

We comment in paragraphs 4(n), (o) and (p) below on the nature and effect of the assignment of the Issuer's rights in, to and under the Transaction Account, the Swap Collateral Cash Account and the Swap Collateral Custody Account.

(g) The security interests created by the Issuer under the Deed of Charge and Assignment are binding on the creditors of the Issuer and neither the liquidator, the administrator nor any creditor of the Issuer (including, without limitation, [Originator]) has or will have (save as a result of a preferential claim or lien or priority rights arising by operation of law) any right or claim against the Issuer which ranks in priority to or *pari passu* with the rights and claims of the Trustee secured by the Deed of Charge and Assignment. In a liquidation or administration of the Issuer, neither the Issuer nor any of the creditors of the Issuer nor a liquidator or administrator of the Issuer would be able to contest successfully or avoid or have set aside:

(i) the validity of the security created by the Issuer pursuant to the Deed of Charge and Assignment;

(ii) the right on the part of the Trustee conferred by the power of attorney contained in clause X of the Deed of Charge and Assignment to exercise the powers thereby conferred;

(iii) the appointment by the Trustee of a receiver in accordance with clause X of the Deed of Charge and Assignment; or

(iv) the application by the Trustee under clause X of the Deed of Charge and Assignment of monies received or recovered by it or by a receiver appointed by it after the Deed of Charge and Assignment becomes enforceable in the order of priority contained in that clause.

The Trustee's interest may, however, be or become subject to prior third party rights, claims or interests, as noted in the Qualifications to this Opinion set out below.

**Interest rate calculation**

(h) The Assignments of the Loans are effective to give the Issuer the right to calculate the rate or rates of interest payable under the Loans. Clause ... of the Servicing Agreement is effective to grant to the Servicer the right to calculate such rate in accordance with the terms of each Loan and to the extent permitted thereby.

(i) Additionally, by execution of the [Originator] Power of Attorney, the Trustee is appointed attorney of [Originator] and may, upon service of a Note Enforcement Notice, *inter alia*, calculate the 'Interest Rate' (as defined in the Loans).

## Investment advertisements; stabilisation

(j) Section 21 of the FSMA, as amended by section 20 of the FSMA 2023, contains a prohibition by a person other than an authorised person under the FSMA who has been given specific permission to approve financial promotions, of making or causing to be made a communication of an invitation or inducement to engage in investment activities (within the meaning of section 21), subject to certain exceptions, and contravention of such prohibition in connection with the issue of the Notes could involve, inter alia, certain agreements relating to the issue being unenforceable. No document issued by the Issuer relating to the Notes, including the Offering Circular, will be subject to such prohibition if the only person to whom the document was issued or passed on to in the United Kingdom were persons whom the Issuer reasonably believes to be persons of the kind and the communication is made or caused to be made in circumstance in which Section 21(1) of the FSMA does not apply. In any event, breach of this prohibition will not prejudice the rights of the Noteholders under the Notes.

(k) Any transactions effected to stabilise or maintain the market price of any Notes at levels other than those which might otherwise prevail in the open market as contemplated in the Subscription Agreement will not contravene section 118 and section 397(2) of the FSMA 2000 or the provisions of Part V of the Criminal Justice Act 1993 provided that such transactions are effected only in compliance with the relevant rules relating to price stabilisation. In any event, breach of this prohibition will not prejudice the rights of Noteholders under the Notes;

## Authorisations and consents

(l) Save:

(i) for the delivery to the Registrar of Companies in England and Wales for registration of the Deed of Charge and Assignment (which it is intended will be effected within 21 days of the Closing Date);

(ii) as may be required by any authorised person under any rules or regulations under the FSA and/or the FSMA 2000 which were or are applicable to it;

(iii) that, as an informational matter, the Inland Revenue may require a paying agent in the United Kingdom to give to it certain particulars of the issue of the Notes in connection with the provisions of regulations made under the Income and Corporation Taxes Act 1988 (as amended by the Finance Act 1996); and

(iv) that the Bank of England will require to be notified of the main details of the issue of the Notes both before and at the time each is made (which we understand has been done by the Lead Manager),

it is not necessary, either to ensure the validity of the Notes or the Transaction Documents or to perfect the security created thereby or to ensure compliance by the Managers referred to in the Subscription Agreement or the Trustee with mandatory provisions of English law, to obtain any authorisation, approval, consent, order or permission of, or to file, record or register any document with, any public authority or governmental agency in respect of:

(i) the execution and delivery of the Transaction Documents and the performance by the Issuer of its obligations thereunder;

(ii) the execution, issue and delivery of the Notes;

(iii) the initial offering or sale of the Notes or the distribution of the Offering Circular in preliminary or final form in or from Great Britain; or

(iv) the creation of the security referred to in paragraph 3(f) above.

## Governing law

(m) The choice of English law to govern those Transaction Documents, or those provisions of the Transaction Documents, expressly stated to be governed by English law, will be recognised and upheld by the English Courts.

## Public policy

(n) As of the date of this opinion and subject to other statements made in this opinion, we are not aware of any circumstances concerning the transactions contemplated by the Transaction Documents that would give rise to an English court holding that such transaction violate English public policy.

## Subordination

(o) Amounts payable to the Noteholders under the Trust Deed and the Conditions will not be recoverable by them (whether in a winding-up, administration or receivership of the Issuer or otherwise) otherwise than in accordance with the order of priorities set out in the Conditions and the Deed of Sub-Charge and Assignment. See also the Qualification in paragraphs 4(z) and (aa) below.

## 4. Qualifications

Our opinions set out above are subject to the qualifications set out below.

### Winding-Up and Related Searches

(a) The searches at the Company Registration Office referred to in paragraph 3(e) above are not conclusively capable of revealing whether or not:

   (i) a winding up order has been made in respect of a company or a resolution passed for the winding up of a company;

   (ii) an administration order has been made in respect of a company; or

   (iii) a receiver, administrative receiver, administrator or liquidator has been appointed in respect of a company,

   as notice of these matters might not be filed with the Registrar of Companies immediately and, when filed, might not be entered on the public record of the relevant company immediately. In addition, that search is not capable of revealing, prior to the making of the relevant order, whether or not a winding up petition or a petition for an administration order has been presented.

(b) The enquiry at the Central Registry of Winding up Petitions referred to in paragraph 3(e) above related only to a compulsory winding up and is not capable to revealing conclusively whether or not a winding up petition in respect of a compulsory winding up has been presented since details of the petition may not have been entered on the records of the Central Registry of Winding up Petitions immediately or, in the case of a petition presented to a County Court, may not have been notified to the Central Registry and entered on such records at all, and the response to an enquiry only relates to the period of six months prior to the date when the enquiry was made.

(c) The search at the Companies Registry referred to in paragraph 3(e) above is not conclusive that no security interest exists because (i) a period of 21 days is allowed within which to effect registration of a charge pursuant to section 859 of the Companies Act 2006, so that a registrable charge created within 21 days prior to the date of such search could have been delivered to the Registrar of Companies together with the prescribed particulars and yet not appear on the file and/or could still be delivered to the Registrar of Companies after the date of such search, but within such 21 day period, in either case without affecting the validity and priority of that earlier charge and (ii) not all security interests created by a company require to be registered at the Companies Registry.

**General matters**

(d) The choice of English law to govern the Transaction Documents, or those provisions of the Transaction Documents expressly stated to be governed by English law, and the interpretation of those defined terms in the Master Definitions Agreement would not be recognised or upheld if there were reasons for avoiding the choice of law on the grounds that its application would be contrary to English public policy.

(e) A determination, designation, calculation or certificate by any party to the Transaction Documents as to any matter provided for therein might, in certain circumstances, be held by an English Court not to be final, conclusive and binding (if, for example, it could be shown to have been an unreasonable or arbitrary basis or not to have been reached in good faith) notwithstanding the provisions of the relevant Transaction Documents. Where any party to a Transaction Document is vested with a discretion or may determine a matter in its opinion, English law may require that such discretion is exercised reasonably or that such opinion is based on reasonable grounds.

(f) In some circumstances an English court would not give effect to any provision of any of the Transaction Documents which provide that in the event of any invalidity, illegality, or unenforceability of any provision of any such document the remaining provisions thereof shall not be affected or impaired, in particular if to do so would not accord with public policy or would involve the court in making a new contract for the parties.

(g) An English court may refuse to give effect to any provision of the Transaction Documents:

   (i) order for the payment of expenses in respect of the costs of enforcement (actual or contemplated) or of unsuccessful litigation brought before an English court where the court has itself made an for costs; or

   (ii) which would involve the enforcement of foreign revenue or penal laws; or

   (iii) would be inconsistent with English public policy.

## Enforceability

(h) This opinion is not be taken to imply that any obligation would necessarily be capable of enforcement in all circumstances in accordance with its terms. Also, the term 'enforceable' as used in this opinion means that the obligations assumed by any party to the Transaction Documents where such obligations arise under or are otherwise governed by English law are of the type which an English court enforces. In particular:

(i) enforcement of obligations of a party to be performed after the date hereof may be limited by bankruptcy, insolvency, liquidation, reorganisation and other laws of general application relating to or affecting the rights of creditors as such law may be applied in the event of the bankruptcy, insolvency, liquidation, reorganisation or other similar proceedings with respect to such parties. This paragraph is not intended to qualify our opinions in paragraphs 3(g) and 3(o) above;

(ii) an English court will not necessarily grant any remedy, the availability of which is subject to equitable considerations or which is otherwise in the discretion of the court. In particular, orders for specific performance and injunctions are, in general, discretionary remedies under English law and specific performance is not available where damages are considered by the court to be an adequate remedy;

(iii) claims may become barred under the Limitation Act 1980 or the Foreign Limitation Periods Act 1984 or may be or become subject to the defence of set off or to counterclaim;

(iv) where obligations are to be performed in a jurisdiction outside England, they may not be enforceable in England to the extent that performance would be illegal under the laws, or contrary to the exchange control regulations, of the other jurisdictions;

(v) the enforcement of the obligations to the parties to the Transaction Documents may be limited by the provisions of English law applicable to agreements held to have been frustrated by events happening after their execution; and

(vi) enforcement of obligations may be invalidated by reason of fraud.

## Registration of charges

By the provisions of Chapter I of Part 25 of the Companies Act 2006, a company registered under the Companies Act 2006 (or its predecessor legislation) must, in order to ensure that certain classes of security over its assets are not rendered void against a liquidator, an administrator or any creditor of the company and that the money secured by such security does not immediately become payable, deliver the instrument creating or evidencing the security, together with prescribed particulars thereof in the manner required by Chapter I of Part 25 of the Companies Act , to the Registrar of Companies for registration within 21 days after the creation of such security. These classes include a charge for the purpose of securing an issue of debentures, a charge on land or an interest therein, a charge on book debts and a floating charge on the company's undertaking or property. We understand that [.........] have agreed to deliver the Deed of Charge and Assignment and the required particulars within 21 days from the date of its creation.

## Matters Relating to the Insolvency Act

(i) Under section 8 of the Insolvency Act 1986 (the 'Insolvency Act'), a court may make an administration order in relation to a company in certain circumstances, the effect of which would be that, during the period for which the order is in force, the affairs, business and property of the company will be managed by a person (the administrator) appointed for this purpose by the court. During the period beginning with the presentation of a petition for an administration order and ending with the making of the order (the petition period), and while the administration order is in force, no steps may be taken to enforce any security over the company's property except, where an administrator has been appointed, with the consent of the administrator, or with the leave of the court and subject to such terms as the court may impose.

## Transactions at an undervalue

(j) If the Issuer went into liquidation or administration, the court could, on the application of the liquidator or administrator under section 238 of the Insolvency Act, set aside a transaction entered into by the Issuer within two years prior to the onset of insolvency which is a transaction at an undervalue. A transaction is at an undervalue if the transaction constitutes a gift or if the value of the consideration, in money or money's worth, obtained by the company is significantly less than the value of the consideration, in money or money's worth, which it provides. Case law and, in particular, the decision of Millet J in *In re M C Bacon Ltd* [1990] BCC 78, indicates that, for the purposes of section 238(4) of the Insolvency Act, a comparison must be made between the value obtained by the company for the transaction and the value provided by the company in the transaction. Both values must be capable of being measurable in money or money's worth and both must be considered from the company's point of view. Finally, Millet J held in *In re M C Bacon Ltd.* that for a transaction to constitute an undervalue, it must result in a depletion of the relevant company's assets.

Even if a particular transaction is determined by a court, applying the foregoing principles, to have constituted a transaction at an undervalue, no order would be made under section 238 (to release or discharge the company from the relevant transaction) if the court is satisfied, pursuant to section 238(5), that (i) the company entered into the transaction in good faith and for the purpose of carrying on its business and there were reasonable grounds for believing that the transaction would benefit the company (referred to below as the good faith test), and (ii) the company was able, at the time of the transaction, to pay its debts as they fell due, within the meaning of section 123 of the Insolvency Act, and did not become unable to do so in consequence of the transaction (referred to below as the solvency test). In considering whether a transaction which forms part of a larger transaction is a transaction at an undervalue, we believe that it is appropriate on the facts presented in the case of the security granted by the Issuer, to look at the transactions as a whole, as disclosed in the Transaction Documents. The possibility of a court having regard only to the particular transaction complained of and ignoring the wider context cannot, however, be ruled out. In the case of the grant of security by Issuer under the Deed of Charge and Assignment (even assuming that, contrary to the decision in *M C Bacon*, a grant of security can constitute an undervalue for the purposes of section 238 – see below), the security is clearly granted for the benefit of a number of stated beneficiaries, with the express intention that it should stand as security for certain specified, linked liabilities. This intention is also borne out in the Board Minutes of the meeting of the Board of Directors of the Issuer on [Closing Date] and the Issuer's Solvency Certificate.

We have considered whether the security created by the Deed of Charge and Assignment might, in principle, constitute a transaction at an undervalue. Millet J, in the case of *In re M C Bacon Ltd*, indicated that the mere giving of security for obligations already incurred may not, in principle, be capable of constituting a transaction at an undervalue, on the basis that the mere creation of security over a company's assets does not deplete or diminish those assets, it merely appropriates them to the satisfaction or discharge of certain specified debt obligations. Notwithstanding this, there may be some circumstances in which the grant of security by a company may constitute a transaction at an undervalue, and accordingly we consider whether the Deed of Charge and Assignment might do so.

The Solvency Certificate of the Issuer dated [Closing Date] contains a statement that, in the opinion of the directors of the Issuer giving the certificate, the creation of the security pursuant to the Deed of Charge and Assignment in favour of the Trustee (upon trust) would not be a transaction at an undervalue and that the solvency test is satisfied. Furthermore, the Board Minutes of the Issuer in respect of the meeting held by its Board of Directors on [Closing Date] contain a statement to the effect that the requirements of the good faith test are satisfied in relation to the creation of the security pursuant to the Deed of Charge and Assignment, through the consideration of and approval given by the directors of the Issuer to the form of the Solvency Certificate produced to that meeting. On the assumption that such statements were true and accurate at the time made, in our opinion a court would not make an order under section 238 avoiding, releasing or discharging the security constituted by the Deed of Charge and Assignment.

**Preferences**

(k) If the Issuer went into liquidation or administration, the court could, on the application of the liquidator or administrator under section 239 of the Insolvency Act, set aside a transaction which amounts to a preference given to a creditor, surety or guarantor within six months (or two years, if given to a connected person) prior to the onset of insolvency. A preference is given if a company does or suffers anything to be done in relation to an existing creditor, surety or guarantor which has the effect of putting that creditor, surety or guarantor into a position which, in the event of the company's insolvent liquidation or administration, would be better than would have been the case without such action and, in so acting, the company was influenced by a desire to produce that result. There is a rebuttable presumption of such influence if the person to whom the preference was given was a person 'connected' with the company at that time, within the meaning of section 249 of the Insolvency Act. If a preference is found to have been committed, the court may make such order as it thinks fit, including an order for the release of security. An order would not be made under section 239, however, if the court was satisfied that the company was, at the time of giving the preference, able to pay its debts as they fell due (within the meaning of section 123 of the Insolvency Act) and did not become unable to do so in consequence of giving the preference (referred to below as the 'solvency test').

We have considered whether the grant of the security created by the Deed of Charge and Assignment might, in principle, constitute a preference in favour of the Trustee or any of the beneficiaries of the security granted under the Deed of Charge and Assignment. We have been advised that neither the Trustee nor the beneficiaries were creditors of the Issuer immediately prior to the execution and delivery of the Deed of Charge and Assignment.

The execution and delivery of the Deed of Charge and Assignment and the creation of the fixed and floating security granted thereby are conditions precedent to the subscription for the Notes, the provision of the facility granted under the Liquidity Facility Agreement and the entry in the Swap Agreement. On this basis, the creation of the Deed of Charge and Assignment will not put the Trustee or the beneficiaries under the Deed of Charge and Assignment in a better position than that which each of them would have been in the event of the insolvent liquidation of the Issuer because, in the absence of the existing grant of security or the accession mechanism provided by the Deed of Charge and Assignment, the various lending and funding arrangements that are or may in the future be extended to the Issuer would not have been, or will not be, extended, and the Trustee and the beneficiaries of the security would not, therefore, be creditors in the winding up or administration of the Issuer. section 239 will not, therefore, be relevant to the status of the Deed of Charge and Assignment. In any event, if the court is satisfied that the solvency test is satisfied, no order would be made under section 239. On the basis, therefore, that the Solvency Certificate of the Issuer is true and accurate, and that the statements made therein are sufficient to rebut the presumption that the Issuer was influenced by a desire to prefer the Trustee or the beneficiaries of the security (as to which we express no opinion), the creation of the security in favour of the Trustee (upon trust for the beneficiaries) pursuant to the Deed of Charge and Assignment would not, in our opinion, be set aside as amounting to a preference.

## Avoidance of floating charges

(1) If the Issuer went into liquidation or administration, a floating charge created by it in favour of a person in the period of one year (two years in the case of a connected person) ending with the onset of the Issuer's insolvency, in the circumstances set out in section 245 of the Insolvency Act, could be invalid except to the extent of money paid, or services supplied to it, in consideration for the charge at the same time as, or after, the creation of the floating charge. A floating charge means, for these purposes, any charge which was originally created as a floating charge, even if the floating charge is subsequently fixed.

A floating charge granted in favour of a person who is *not* connected with the grantor of the charge will only be capable of avoidance if, at the time the floating charge was created, the grantor was unable to pay its debts within the meaning of section 123 of the Insolvency Act or becomes unable to pay its debts within the meaning of that section in consequence of the transaction under which the charge was created. By contrast, a floating charge granted in favour of a person who *is* connected with the grantor may be avoided under section 245 even if the grantor was *not* unable to pay its debts at the time, within the meaning of section 123. We are advised that none of the Trustee or any of the beneficiaries under the Deed of Charge and Assignment is 'connected' to the Issuer for these purposes.

In our opinion, the effect of section 245 on the granting of the floating charge by the Issuer pursuant to the Deed of Charge and Assignment is that, provided that the financial accommodation to be provided by the beneficiaries is advanced to the Issuer at the same time as or after the Deed of Charge and Assignment has been entered into, such security will stand as security, and will not be capable of avoidance under section 245 of the Insolvency Act, to the extent of any monies advanced, or services supplied, by a beneficiary or the Trustee to the Issuer at the same time as or after the creation of the Deed of Charge and Assignment.

**Recharacterisation of fixed security interests**

(m) The Encumbrances created pursuant to the Deed of Charge and Assignment over the Issuer's Accounts or the Standby Account or any other bank account in respect of which the Issuer has an interest will take effect as a fixed rather than a floating charge. The case of *National Westminster Bank v Spectrum Plus Ltd* [2005] UKHL 41 made clear that a fixed charge could only be created over assets when there was a full denial to the chargor to those assets.

(n) A charge giving the chargor actual or *de facto* control of revolving assets or cash until enforcement is a floating charge. It is inconsistent with the existence of a fixed charge that the assets subject to it can be released from the security at the will of the chargor without the consent of the chargee, there must be some real, and not merely illusory consent and control provision and arrangement for the use of proceeds by the chargor.

(o) If any of the charges were held to take effect as floating charges rather than, as expressed, fixed charges, the claims of the Trustee for itself or the Noteholders under the charges created under the Deed of Charge and Assignment will be subject to the claims which are given priority over a floating charge by law, including prior charges, the expenses of any winding-up and the claims of preferential creditors.

**Preferential debts**

(p) Under section 175 of the Insolvency Act, in a winding-up of a company, preferential debts are required to be paid in priority to all other debts other than those secured by a fixed charge.

Preferential debts therefore have priority over debts secured by a floating charge. If the other assets of the company are insufficient to pay the preferential debts, they are required to be paid out of the property subject to the floating charge.

(q) Under section 40 of the Insolvency Act, where a receiver in respect of a company is appointed on behalf of a debenture holder secured by a charge which, as created, was a floating charge and such company is not in the course of being wound up, its preferential debts shall be paid out of the assets coming into the hands of the receiver in priority to any claims for principal or interest in respect of the debentures.

(r) Under section 176(a) of the Insolvency Act 1986 the holder of a floating charge who takes possession of property subject to the floating charge when the company is not in the course of being wound up is required to pay the prescribed part of that sum to the ordinary creditors in priority to principal and interest secured by the floating charge.

(s) The 'preferential debts' as referred to in such sections are defined in section 386 of and Schedule 6 to the Insolvency Act and comprise, amongst other things pension scheme contributions, remuneration of employees and the expenses of liquidation (should it occur) of a company. 'Prescribed parts' of the money covered by a floating charge must be paid to the unsecured creditors on insolvency. In addition to the foregoing, preferential debts, where a company goes into liquidation prior to the appointment of a receiver, or prior to crystallisation of the floating charge, expenses of the liquidation will rank ahead of preferential creditors and the holder of the floating charge (see *re Barleycorn Enterprises Limited* [1970] 2 All ER 155 and *re Christonette International Limited* [1982] 3 All ER 225). Furthermore, where a company goes into liquidation post-receivership or post-crystallisation of a floating charge, there is authority for the proposition that expenses of a winding-up rank ahead of any preferential creditors and holders of a floating charge (see *Re Portbase Clothing Limited* [1993] Ch 388, subsequently applied by the Court of Appeal in *Mond v Hammond Suddards, sub nom Re RS&M Engineering Company Limited* [1999] 3 WLR 697).

(t) Also, a receiver's expenses will rank ahead of other secured parties both by virtue of the relevant provisions of the Deed of Charge and Assignment and also by reason of section 45 of the Insolvency Act.

(u) The priority of preferential debts applies to the charges contained in the Deed of Charge and Assignment which are described as floating charges and to any of those charges which are described as fixed charges but which, for the reasons set out above, were held by a court to take effect as floating charges.

### Disclaimer

(v) A liquidator of any company may, by the giving of the prescribed notice, disclaim any onerous property pursuant to section 178 of the Insolvency Act. The disclaimer determines the rights, interests and liabilities of the company in the relevant property but does not affect the rights or liabilities of any other person, except so far as is necessary to release the company from any liability. A notice of disclaimer may not be given if a person interested in the property has written to the liquidator requiring him to decide whether or not to disclaim and no disclaimer has been made within 28 days (or such longer period as the Court may allow). A person sustaining loss or damage as a result of the disclaimer is deemed to be a creditor of the company to the extent of the loss or damage and may prove for the loss or damage in the winding-up.

(w) Onerous property is any unprofitable contract and any other property of the company which is unsaleable or not readily saleable or is such that it may give rise to a liability to pay money or perform any other onerous act. In our opinion, the Notes and the security constituted by the Deed of Charge and Assignment are not capable of constituting onerous property as defined in section 178 and, therefore, may not be disclaimed by the Issuer.

### Rescission order

(x) Pursuant to section 186 of the Insolvency Act, the Court may, on the application of a person who is, as against the liquidator, entitled to the benefit or subject to the burden of a contract made with the company, make an order rescinding the contract on such terms as to payment by or to either party of damages for the non-performance of the contract, or otherwise as the Court thinks fit.

### Subordination

(y) Section 107 of the Insolvency Act and Rule 4.181 of the Insolvency Rules 1986 provide generally that, subject to the provisions of the Insolvency Act as to preferential payments, a company's property in a winding-up shall, upon that winding-up, be applied in satisfaction of the company's liabilities pari passu. In light of such provisions the critical issue on any subordination (for example the subordination of the rights of certain classes of Noteholders) is whether a company can contract out of the statutory provisions by providing in one or more contract that, upon its winding-up, one or more categories of debt will rank ahead of another. The case of *Re Maxwell Communications Corporation plc (No 3)* [1993] BCC 369 is authority for the proposition that a contract providing for a debt due to a creditor to be subordinated on the insolvent winding-up of a company to another unsecured debt is not rendered void by the insolvency legislation. In *Re Maxwell Communications Corporation plc (No 2)* [1994] 1 All ER 737, Vinelott J found contractual subordination to be effective. Vinelott J distinguished the 1975 House of Lords decision (*British Eagle v Air France* [1975] 2 All ER 390), in which a multi-partite netting arrangement involving an English company which went into insolvent liquidation was held to be invalid insofar as it purported to net a debt owing to the company by A against a debt owing by the company to B, since this was not 'mutual' (so as to bring it within the statutory set-off provisions) and would otherwise, in breach of public policy, have prevented the liquidator from realising one of the company's assets (the debt owing by A) for the benefit of the creditors generally.

(z) Prior to the decision in *Maxwell Communications*, there had also been concern that the House of Lords decision in *National Westminster Bank Limited v Halesowen Presswork & Assemblies Limited* [1972] AC 785 would invalidate contractual subordination. As in the *British Eagle* case, the debtor in the *Halesowen* case had attempted to contract out of his statutory right of set-off and the court held that he was not able to do so. The *Maxwell Communications* decision draws a distinction between an arrangement where a creditor is preferred above other creditors (eg by purporting to contract out of the insolvency set-off provisions as the parties had attempted to do in the *British Eagle* and *Halesowen* cases) and the situation where a creditor agrees to subordinate its claim (thereby waiving the benefit of the pari passu rule). In the latter situation, the court held that the *pari passu* rule was not mandatory and that such an arrangement would be effective in the event of the debtor's liquidation. We note, however, that *Maxwell Communications* is a decision of a court of first instance.

### Third party rights

(aa) The Contracts (Rights of Third Parties) Act 1999 (the 'Third Party Rights Act') was enacted on 11 November 1999. Pursuant to subsection 1(1) of the Third Party Rights Act, a person who is not a party to a contract (a 'third party') may, subject to the provisions of the Act, in his own right enforce the term of a contract if either the contract expressly provides that he may or, subject to subsection 1(2), the term purports to confer a benefit on him. Subsection (2) of section 1 to the Third Party Rights Act provides that subsection 1 of that section does not apply if, on a proper construction of the contract, it appears that the parties did not intend the term to be enforceable by the third party.

Subsection (3) of section 1 provides that the third party must be expressly identified in the contract by name, as a member of a class, or as answering a particular description, but need not be in existence when the contract is entered into. Section 2 of the Third Party Rights Act provides that, subject to the provisions of that section, where a third party has a right under section 1 of the Act to enforce a term of a contract, the parties to the contract may not, by agreement, rescind the contract or vary it in such a way as to extinguish or alter his entitlement under that right without his consent if (a) the third party has communicated his consent to the term to the promisor, or (b) the promisor is aware that the third party has relied on the term, or (c) the promisor can reasonably be expected to have foreseen that the third party would rely on the term and the third party has in fact relied upon it.

(bb) Each of the Transaction Documents and the Terms and Conditions of the Notes expressly exclude the application of the Third Party Rights Act. Accordingly, third parties which might otherwise accrue rights under the Transaction Documents or the Notes, including unsecured creditors of the Issuer referred to in the order of priority of payments contained in Clause 8.3 of the Deed of Charge and Assignment, will not acquire any rights under the Transaction Documents or the Notes against the Issuer, the Trustee or any other party thereto under or by virtue of the Third Party Rights Act.

**Powers of attorney**

(cc) A power of attorney may, in limited circumstances, be revoked by the winding-up or dissolution of the donor company. However, under section 4 of the Powers of Attorney Act 1971, a power of attorney will not be revoked by the winding-up or dissolution of the donor (except with the consent of the donee) if it is expressed to be irrevocable and is given to secure either a proprietary interest of the donee or the performance of an obligation owed to that donee, so long as the donee has that interest or the obligation remains undischarged (see *Sowman v David Samuel Trust Limited* [1978] 1WLR 22). The power of attorney given by the Issuer to the Trustee under clause X of the Deed of Charge and Assignment is expressed to be irrevocable and granted by way of security. Provided that the Trustee has a subsisting proprietary interest in the Charged Property, or that an obligation owed by the Issuer to the Trustee under the Deed of Charge and Assignment or the Trust Deed remains undischarged, and provided that the Trustee has not consented to a revocation of the power of attorney contained in clause X of the Deed of Charge and Assignment, we are of the opinion that a winding-up or dissolution of the Issuer would not revoke this power of attorney.

### Judgment currencies

(dd) English courts can give judgments in currencies other than sterling if, subject to the terms of the contract, it is the currency which most fairly reflects the plaintiff's loss but such a judgment may be required to be converted into sterling for enforcement purposes.

### Default interest

(ee) Any provision of the Transaction Documents providing for the payment of additional moneys by any party consequent on the breach of any provision thereof by any party, whether expressed by way of penalty, additional interest, liquidated damages or otherwise, would be unenforceable if such provision were held to constitute a penalty and not a genuine and reasonable pre-estimate of the loss likely to be suffered as a result of the breach in question.

(ff) In *Lordsdale Finance plc v Bank of Zambia* [1996] QB 752, Coleman J held that there was no justification for striking down as a penalty a default interest provision which provided for only a modest increase in the rate of interest, and of which the dominant purpose was not to deter the other party from breach. The increased rate of interest merely reflected the greater credit risk represented by a borrower in default. No view was expressed as to whether a default interest provision with a substantial increase in the rate of interest following a default would amount to a penalty. A default interest provision which imposed a higher rate of interest retrospectively would be likely to be designated as a penalty. While none of the default interest provisions in the Transaction Documents may be intended as a penalty, it nonetheless would be open to a court to find that the dominant purpose of one or more of the provisions was to deter a breach and that the rise in the rate of interest was heavily disproportionate to the increased credit risk. Since the case of *Cavendish Square Holding BV v Tala (El Makdessi); Parking Eye v Beavis* [2015] UKSC 67 the risk of this is very low.

### Severability

(gg) In some circumstances an English court will not give effect to any provision of any of the Transaction Documents which provides that in the event of any inability, illegality or enforceability of any provision of any such document the remaining provisions thereof shall not be affected impaired, in particular if to do so would not accord with public policy or would involve the Court in making a new contract for the parties.

**Equities**

(hh) The Trustee's rights under the Deed of Charge and Assignment will be subject to equities and other third party rights. Such equities and rights include:

(i) rights of set-off which exist at the date the relevant party possessing a right of set-off against the Issuer is notified of the security created by the Issuer Deed of Charge and Assignment;

(ii) rights of set-off existing under the Loans and the Loan Documentation against [Originator] at the time of the sale of the Loans to the Issuer and prior to the notice of transfer of the Loans to the Issuer; and

(iii) the rights of any person having a legal interest or an overriding interest in the land secured by the Mortgages or a prior ranking equitable interest in any security trust under which a Mortgage is held, which interest ranks ahead of the estate or interest of the Security Trustee or the Issuer, as applicable. We understand that the existence or otherwise of these rights is addressed in the Warranties.

(ii) Any undertaking or indemnity given in any Transaction Document in relation to UK stamp duty may be void under section 117 of the Stamp Act 1891.

## 5. Observations

It should be understood that we have not been responsible for investigating or verifying the accuracy of facts, or the reasonableness of any statements of opinion or intention, contained in the Offering Circular. Furthermore, we have taken no steps to investigate or verify, and express no opinion on, the accuracy of the statements made in the documents referred to in Schedule 2; and we express no view on any provision requiring written amendments or waivers insofar as such provision suggests that oral or other modifications, amendments or waivers could not effectively agreed upon or granted by or between the parties or implied by the course of conduct of the parties.

## 6. Benefit Of Opinion

This Opinion is addressed to the Addressees solely for their benefit in relation to the issue of the Notes and, except with our prior written consent, is not to be transmitted or disclosed to or used or relied upon by any other person or for any other purpose except that copies may be released to [rating agencies] and their respective advisers for the purposes of information only, on the understanding that each of them wished to know that an opinion has been given and to be made aware of its terms and on the strict understanding that we assume no responsibility whatsoever to them as a result or otherwise.

Yours faithfully,

## Schedule 1: The Transaction Documents

(1) An original of the Subscription Agreement dated [Signing Date];

(2) An original of the Agency Agreement dated [Signing Date];

(3) An original of the Master Definitions Agreement dated [Closing Date];

(4) An original of the Servicing Agreement dated [Closing Date];

(5) An original of the Loan Sale Agreement dated [Closing Date];

(6) An original of the Trust Deed dated [Closing Date];

(7) An original of the Deed of Charge and Assignment dated [Closing Date];

(8) An original of the Liquidity Facility Agreement dated [Closing Date];

(9) An original of the Swap Agreement and the Schedule thereto dated as of [Closing Date];

(10) An original of the Cash Management Agreement dated [Closing Date]; and

(11) The forms of the Notes set out in the First Schedule to the Trust Deed.

## Schedule 2

(1) A copy of the Offering Circular relating to the Notes dated [Signing Date];

(2) Certified copies of the minutes of the meetings of the board of directors of the Issuer held on [Signing Date and Closing Date];

(3) Secretary's certificates of the Issuer dated [Signing and Closing Date];

(4) Solvency Certificate of the Issuer dated [Closing Date];

(5) Form of Notice of Assignment to Borrowers;

(6) Legal Opinion of ………, legal advisers to the Issuer and Originator in England dated [Closing Date]; and

(7) Legal Opinion of in-house Counsel of the Swap Counterparty and Swap Guarantor dated [Closing Date].

# Appendix Loan Markets Association Multicurrency Term And Revolving Facilities Agreement



The page numbers listed in the Contents page of this document refer to the original pagination of the Agreement, not the pagination of this book.

*MULTICURRENCY TERM AND REVOLVING FACILITIES AGREEMENT*

[*amount in numbers*]

FACILITY AGREEMENT

dated [____________]

for

[*NAME OF PRINCIPAL COMPANY*]

arranged by
[*NAME OF ARRANGERS*]

with

[*NAME OF AGENT*]
acting as Agent

[***NAME OF LAW FIRM***]

**JOINT STATEMENT**

The recommended form of syndicated facility agreements (the "**Primary Documents**") were developed by a working party consisting of representatives of the Loan Market Association, The Association of Corporate Treasurers and major City law firms. It is hoped that the existence of the Primary Documents will facilitate more efficient negotiation of loan documentation to the benefit of the primary and secondary loan markets.

Through the involvement of the associations in the working party, together with the law firms represented, the objective was to balance the interests of borrowers and lenders. In the Primary Documents, financial covenants and related definitions have been deliberately left blank.

When considering use of the Primary Documents it is recommended that borrowers and lenders should:

- consider the option of continuing to use existing documentation
- carefully consider changes to the Primary Documents that may be required
- always have the benefit of independent legal advice

The associations believe that the Primary Documents will provide a valuable aid to the development and efficiency of the syndicated loan market.

**CONTENTS**

**Clause** **Page**

**THIS AGREEMENT** is dated [______________] and made between:

(1) [__________] (the "**Company**");

(2) **THE SUBSIDIARIES** of the Company listed in Part I of Schedule 1 as original borrowers ([together with the Company] the "**Original Borrowers**");

(3) **THE SUBSIDIARIES** of the Company listed in Part I of Schedule 1 as original guarantors ([together with the Company] the "**Original Guarantors**");

(4) [_______] [and [_______]] as mandated lead arranger[s] ([whether acting individually or together] the "**Arranger**");

(5) **THE FINANCIAL INSTITUTIONS** listed in Part II and Part III of Schedule 1 as lenders (the "**Original Lenders**"); and

(6) [_______] as agent of the other Finance Parties (the "**Agent**").

**IT IS AGREED** as follows:

## SECTION 1
## INTERPRETATION

### 1. DEFINITIONS AND INTERPRETATION

#### 1.1 Definitions

In this Agreement:

"**Accession Letter**" means a document substantially in the form set out in Schedule 7 (*Form of Accession Letter*).

"**Additional Borrower**" means a company which becomes an Additional Borrower in accordance with Clause 25 (*Changes to the Obligors*).

"**Additional Guarantor**" means a company which becomes an Additional Guarantor in accordance with Clause 25 (*Changes to the Obligors*).

"**Additional Obligor**" means an Additional Borrower or an Additional Guarantor.

"**Affiliate**" means, in relation to any person, a Subsidiary of that person or a Holding Company of that person or any other Subsidiary of that Holding Company.

"**Agent's Spot Rate of Exchange**" means:

(a) the Agent's spot rate of exchange; or

(b) (if the Agent does not have an available spot rate of exchange) any other publicly available spot rate of exchange selected by the Agent (acting reasonably),

for the purchase of the relevant currency with the Base Currency in the London foreign exchange market at or about 11:00 a.m. on a particular day.

"**Assignment Agreement**" means an agreement substantially in the form set out in Schedule 6 (*Form of Assignment Agreement*) or any other form agreed between the relevant assignor and assignee.

"**Authorisation**" means an authorisation, consent, approval, resolution, licence, exemption, filing, notarisation or registration.

"**Availability Period**" means:

(a) in relation to Facility A, the period from and including the date of this Agreement to and including [__________]; and

(b) in relation to Facility B, the period from and including the date of this Agreement to and including [__________].

"**Available Commitment**" means, in relation to a Facility, a Lender's Commitment under that Facility minus:

(a) the Base Currency Amount of its participation in any outstanding Loans under that Facility; and

(b) in relation to any proposed Utilisation, the Base Currency Amount of its participation in any Loans that are due to be made under that Facility on or before the proposed Utilisation Date,

other than, in relation to any proposed Utilisation under Facility B only, that Lender's participation in any Facility B Loans that are due to be repaid or prepaid on or before the proposed Utilisation Date.

"**Available Facility**" means, in relation to a Facility, the aggregate for the time being of each Lender's Available Commitment in respect of that Facility.

"**Base Currency**" means [____________].

"**Base Currency Amount**" means, in relation to a Loan, the amount specified in the Utilisation Request delivered by a Borrower for that Loan (or, if the amount requested is not denominated in the Base Currency, that amount converted into the Base Currency at the Agent's Spot Rate of Exchange on the date which is three Business Days before the Utilisation Date or, if later, on the date the Agent receives the Utilisation Request) as adjusted to reflect any repayment (other than, in relation to Facility A, a repayment arising from a change of currency), prepayment, consolidation or division of a Loan.

["**Benchmark Rate**" means, in relation to any Loan in a Non-LIBOR Currency:

(a) the applicable Screen Rate as of the Specified Time for the currency of that Loan and for a period equal in length to the Interest Period of that Loan; or

(b) as otherwise determined pursuant to Clause 11.1 (*Unavailability of Screen Rate*)[,

and if, in either case, that rate is less than zero, the Benchmark Rate shall be deemed to be zero].]

"**Borrower**" means an Original Borrower or an Additional Borrower unless it has ceased to be a Borrower in accordance with Clause 25 (*Changes to the Obligors*).

"**Break Costs**" means the amount (if any) by which:

(a) the interest which a Lender should have received for the period from the date of receipt of all or any part of its participation in a Loan or Unpaid Sum to the last day of the current Interest Period in respect of that Loan or Unpaid Sum, had the principal amount or Unpaid Sum received been paid on the last day of that Interest Period;

exceeds:

(b) the amount which that Lender would be able to obtain by placing an amount equal to the principal amount or Unpaid Sum received by it on deposit with a leading bank for a period starting on the Business Day following receipt or recovery and ending on the last day of the current Interest Period.

"**Business Day**" means a day (other than a Saturday or Sunday) on which banks are open for general business in London [, ______] and:

(a) (in relation to any date for payment or purchase of a currency other than euro [or a Non-LIBOR Currency]) the principal financial centre of the country of that currency; [or]

(b) (in relation to any date for payment or purchase of euro) any TARGET Day[; or

(c) (in relation to any date for payment or purchase of (or the fixing of an interest rate in relation to) a Non-LIBOR Currency) any day specified as such in respect of that currency in Schedule 14 (*Other Benchmarks*)].

"**Code**" means the US Internal Revenue Code of 1986.

"**Commitment**" means a Facility A Commitment or Facility B Commitment.

["**Compliance Certificate**" means a certificate [substantially in the form set out in Schedule 9 (*Form of Compliance Certificate*)]/[in form and substance satisfactory to the Agent].]

"**Confidential Information**" means all information relating to the Company, any Obligor, the Group, the Finance Documents or a Facility of which a Finance Party becomes aware in its capacity as, or for the purpose of becoming, a Finance Party or which is received by a Finance Party in relation to, or for the purpose of becoming a Finance Party under, the Finance Documents or a Facility from either:

(a) any member of the Group or any of its advisers; or

(b) another Finance Party, if the information was obtained by that Finance Party directly or indirectly from any member of the Group or any of its advisers, in whatever form, and includes information given orally and any document, electronic file or any other way of representing or recording information which contains or is derived or copied from such information but excludes:

(i) information that:

(A) is or becomes public information other than as a direct or indirect result of any breach by that Finance Party of Clause 36 (*Confidential Information*); or

(B) is identified in writing at the time of delivery as non-confidential by any member of the Group or any of its advisers; or

(C) is known by that Finance Party before the date the information is disclosed to it in accordance with paragraphs (a) or (b) above or is lawfully obtained by that Finance Party after that date, from a source which is, as far as that Finance Party is aware, unconnected with the Group and which, in either case, as far as that Finance Party is aware, has not been obtained in breach of, and is not otherwise subject to, any obligation of confidentiality; and

(ii) any Funding Rate [or Reference Bank Quotation].

"**Confidentiality Undertaking**" means a confidentiality undertaking substantially in a recommended form of the LMA as set out in Schedule 11 (*LMA Form of Confidentiality Undertaking*) or in any other form agreed between the Company and the Agent.

"**CTA**" means the Corporation Tax Act 2009.

"**Default**" means an Event of Default or any event or circumstance specified in Clause 23 (*Events of Default*) which would (with the expiry of a grace period, the giving of notice, the making of any determination under the Finance Documents or any combination of any of the foregoing) be an Event of Default.

"**Disruption Event**" means either or both of:

(a) a material disruption to those payment or communications systems or to those financial markets which are, in each case, required to operate in order for payments to be made in connection with the Facilities (or otherwise in order for the transactions contemplated by the Finance Documents to be carried out) which disruption is not caused by, and is beyond the control of, any of the Parties; or

(b) the occurrence of any other event which results in a disruption (of a technical or systems-related nature) to the treasury or payments operations of a Party preventing that, or any other Party:

(i) from performing its payment obligations under the Finance Documents; or

(ii) from communicating with other Parties in accordance with the terms of the Finance Documents, and which (in either such case) is not caused by, and is beyond the control of, the Party whose operations are disrupted.

"**Eligible Institution**" means any Lender or other bank, financial institution, trust, fund or other entity selected by the Company [and which, in each case, is not a member of the Group][1].

["**EURIBOR**" means, in relation to any Loan in euro:

(a) the applicable Screen Rate as of the Specified Time for euro and for a period equal in length to the Interest Period of that Loan; or

(b) as otherwise determined pursuant to Clause 11.1 (*Unavailability of Screen Rate*)[,

and if, in either case, that rate is less than zero, EURIBOR shall be deemed to be zero].]

"**Event of Default**" means any event or circumstance specified as such in Clause 23 (*Events of Default*).

"**Facility**" means Facility A or Facility B.

"**Facility A**" means the term loan facility made available under this Agreement as described in Clause 2 (*The Facilities*).

"**Facility A Commitment**" means:

(a) in relation to an Original Lender, the amount in the Base Currency set opposite its name under the heading "Facility A Commitment" in Part II or Part III of Schedule 1 (*The Original Parties*) and the amount of any other Facility A Commitment transferred to it under this Agreement or assumed by it in accordance with Clause 2.2 (*Increase*); and

(b) in relation to any other Lender, the amount in the Base Currency of any Facility A Commitment transferred to it under this Agreement or assumed by it in accordance with Clause 2.2 (*Increase*),

to the extent not cancelled, reduced or transferred by it under this Agreement.

"**Facility A Loan**" means a loan made or to be made under Facility A or the principal amount outstanding for the time being of that loan.

"**Facility A Repayment Date**" means [____________].

"**Facility B**" means the revolving loan facility made available under this Agreement as described in Clause 2 (*The Facilities*).

[1] If the Company is not listed consideration may need to be given to adding any holding companies of the Company as non-Eligible Institutions.

"**Facility B Commitment**" means:

(a) in relation to an Original Lender, the amount in the Base Currency set opposite its name under the heading "Facility B Commitment" in Part II or Part III of Schedule 1 (*The Original Parties*) and the amount of any other Facility B Commitment transferred to it under this Agreement or assumed by it in accordance with Clause 2.2 (*Increase*); and

(b) in relation to any other Lender, the amount in the Base Currency of any Facility B Commitment transferred to it under this Agreement or assumed by it in accordance with Clause 2.2 (*Increase*),

to the extent not cancelled, reduced or transferred by it under this Agreement.

"**Facility B Loan**" means a loan made or to be made under Facility B or the principal amount outstanding for the time being of that loan.

"**Facility Office**" means the office or offices notified by a Lender to the Agent in writing on or before the date it becomes a Lender (or, following that date, by not less than five Business Days' written notice) as the office or offices through which it will perform its obligations under this Agreement.

["**Fallback Interest Period**" means [ ][2] [or, if the Loan is in a Non-LIBOR Currency, the period specified as such in respect of that currency in Schedule 14 (*Other Benchmarks*)].]

"**FATCA**" means:

(a) sections 1471 to 1474 of the Code or any associated regulations;

(b) any treaty, law or regulation of any other jurisdiction, or relating to an intergovernmental agreement between the US and any other jurisdiction, which (in either case) facilitates the implementation of any law or regulation referred to in paragraph (a) above; or

(c) any agreement pursuant to the implementation of any treaty, law or regulation referred to in paragraphs (a) or (b) above with the US Internal Revenue Service, the US government or any governmental or taxation authority in any other jurisdiction.

"**FATCA Application Date**" means:

(a) in relation to a "withholdable payment" described in section 1473(1)(A)(i) of the Code (which relates to payments of interest and certain other payments from sources within the US), 1 July 2014;

[2] If using Historic Screen Rates as a fallback option users should consider the length of this period in the context of (a) the maturities for which the applicable Screen Rates are quoted and (b) the period of time for which the use of a Historic Screen Rate is considered appropriate.

(b) in relation to a "withholdable payment" described in section 1473(1)(A)(ii) of the Code (which relates to "gross proceeds" from the disposition of property of a type that can produce interest from sources within the US), 1 January 2019; or

(c) in relation to a "passthru payment" described in section 1471(d)(7) of the Code not falling within paragraphs (a) or (b) above, 1 January 2019,

or, in each case, such other date from which such payment may become subject to a deduction or withholding required by FATCA as a result of any change in FATCA after the date of this Agreement.

"**FATCA Deduction**" means a deduction or withholding from a payment under a Finance Document required by FATCA.

"**FATCA Exempt Party**" means a Party that is entitled to receive payments free from any FATCA Deduction.

"**Fee Letter**" means any letter or letters dated on or about the date of this Agreement between the Arranger and the Company (or the Agent and the Company) setting out any of the fees referred to in Clause 12 (*Fees*).

"**Finance Document**" means this Agreement, any Fee Letter, any Accession Letter, any Resignation Letter and any other document designated as such by the Agent and the Company.

"**Finance Party**" means the Agent, the Arranger or a Lender.

"**Financial Indebtedness**" means any indebtedness for or in respect of:

(a) moneys borrowed;

(b) any amount raised by acceptance under any acceptance credit facility or dematerialised equivalent;

(c) any amount raised pursuant to any note purchase facility or the issue of bonds, notes, debentures, loan stock or any similar instrument;

(d) the amount of any liability in respect of any lease or hire purchase contract which would, in accordance with GAAP, be treated as a balance sheet liability [(other than any liability in respect of a lease or hire purchase contract which would, in accordance with GAAP in force [prior to 1 January 2019] / [prior to [ ]] / [ ][3], have been treated as an operating lease)][4];

[3] Insert the appropriate reference point for the applicable GAAP (see footnote 3 below).

[4] IFRS 16 will require most leases to appear as balance sheet liabilities in relation to accounting periods from 1 January 2019. Similar changes are expected to be made in other accounting regimes. Insert this exclusion if the commercial agreement is to exclude the effect of old "operating leases" appearing as balance sheet liabilities and insert the appropriate reference point for the applicable GAAP. For example, the reference point of 1 January 2019 is **only** suitable if the applicable GAAP is IFRS. If the Agreement is entered into before the accounting change under the applicable GAAP takes effect, a reference to GAAP in force "*as at the date of this Agreement*" may be an appropriate reference point.

(e) receivables sold or discounted (other than any receivables to the extent they are sold on a non-recourse basis);

(f) any amount raised under any other transaction (including any forward sale or purchase agreement) of a type not referred to in any other paragraph of this definition having the commercial effect of a borrowing;

(g) any derivative transaction entered into in connection with protection against or benefit from fluctuation in any rate or price (and, when calculating the value of any derivative transaction, only the marked to market value (or, if any actual amount is due as a result of the termination or close-out of that derivative transaction, that amount) shall be taken into account);

(h) any counter-indemnity obligation in respect of a guarantee, indemnity, bond, standby or documentary letter of credit or any other instrument issued by a bank or financial institution; and

(i) the amount of any liability in respect of any guarantee or indemnity for any of the items referred to in paragraphs (a) to (h) above.

"**Funding Rate**" means any individual rate notified by a Lender to the Agent pursuant to paragraph (a)(ii) of Clause 11.4 (*Cost of funds*).

"**GAAP**" means generally accepted accounting principles in [          ][, including IFRS].

"**Group**" means the Company and its Subsidiaries for the time being.

"**Guarantor**" means an Original Guarantor or an Additional Guarantor, unless it has ceased to be a Guarantor in accordance with Clause 25 (*Changes to the Obligors*).

["**Historic Screen Rate**" means, in relation to any Loan, the most recent applicable Screen Rate for the currency of that Loan and for a period equal in length to the Interest Period of that Loan and which is as of a day which is no more than [   ] days before the Quotation Day.]

"**Holding Company**" means, in relation to a person, any other person in respect of which it is a Subsidiary.

["**IFRS**" means international accounting standards within the meaning of the IAS Regulation 1606/2002 to the extent applicable to the relevant financial statements.]

"**Increase Confirmation**" means a confirmation substantially in the form set out in Schedule 13 (*Form of Increase Confirmation*).

"**Increase Lender**" has the meaning given to that term in Clause 2.2 (*Increase*).

["**Information Memorandum**" means the document in the form approved by the Company concerning the Group which, at the Company's request and on its behalf, was prepared in relation to this transaction and distributed by the Arranger to selected financial institutions [during [          ]]/[before the date of this Agreement].]

"**Interest Period**" means, in relation to a Loan, each period determined in accordance with Clause 10 (*Interest Periods*) and, in relation to an Unpaid Sum, each period determined in accordance with Clause 9.3 (*Default interest*).

["**Interpolated Historic Screen Rate**" means, in relation to any Loan, the rate [(rounded [to the same number of decimal places as the two relevant Screen Rates])] which results from interpolating on a linear basis between:

(a) the most recent applicable Screen Rate for the longest period (for which that Screen Rate is available) which is less than the Interest Period of that Loan; and

(b) the most recent applicable Screen Rate for the shortest period (for which that Screen Rate is available) which exceeds the Interest Period of that Loan,

each for the currency of that Loan and each of which is as of a day which is no more than [ ] days before the Quotation Day.]

"**Interpolated Screen Rate**" means, in relation to any Loan, the rate [(rounded [to the same number of decimal places as the two relevant Screen Rates])][5] which results from interpolating on a linear basis between:

(a) the applicable Screen Rate for the longest period (for which that Screen Rate is available) which is less than the Interest Period of that Loan; and

(b) the applicable Screen Rate for the shortest period (for which that Screen Rate is available) which exceeds the Interest Period of that Loan,

each as of the Specified Time for the currency of that Loan.

"**ITA**" means the Income Tax Act 2007.

"**Lender**" means:

(a) any Original Lender; and

(b) any bank, financial institution, trust, fund or other entity which has become a Party as a "Lender" in accordance with Clause 2.2 (*Increase*) or Clause 24 (*Changes to the Lenders*),

which in each case has not ceased to be a Party as such in accordance with the terms of this Agreement.

"**LIBOR**" means, in relation to any Loan:

(a) the applicable Screen Rate as of the Specified Time for the currency of that Loan and for a period equal in length to the Interest Period of that Loan;[6] or

[5] If specifying the rounding convention users may wish to consider altering this suggested convention to that used in any corresponding hedging product.

[6] Users should note that ICE LIBOR (formerly known as BBA LIBOR) is produced for a limited range of tenors and currencies. See the Intercontinental Exchange Group website for more information.

(b) as otherwise determined pursuant to Clause 11.1 (*Unavailability of Screen Rate*)[,

and if, in either case, that rate is less than zero, LIBOR shall be deemed to be zero].

"**LMA**" means the Loan Market Association.

"**Loan**" means a Facility A Loan or a Facility B Loan.

"**Majority Lenders**" means a Lender or Lenders whose Commitments aggregate more than [$66^2/_3$]% of the Total Commitments (or, if the Total Commitments have been reduced to zero, aggregated more than [$66^2/_3$]% of the Total Commitments immediately prior to the reduction).

["**Mandatory Cost**" means the percentage rate per annum calculated by the Agent in accordance with Schedule 4 (*Mandatory Cost formulae*).]

"**Margin**" means [______________] per cent. per annum.

"**Material Adverse Effect**" means [______________].

"**Month**" means a period starting on one day in a calendar month and ending on the numerically corresponding day in the next calendar month, except that:

(a) [other than where paragraph (b) below applies:]

(i) (subject to paragraph (iii) below) if the numerically corresponding day is not a Business Day, that period shall end on the next Business Day in that calendar month in which that period is to end if there is one, or if there is not, on the immediately preceding Business Day;

(ii) if there is no numerically corresponding day in the calendar month in which that period is to end, that period shall end on the last Business Day in that calendar month; and

(iii) if an Interest Period begins on the last Business Day of a calendar month, that Interest Period shall end on the last Business Day in the calendar month in which that Interest Period is to end[; and

(b) in relation to an Interest Period for any Loan (or any other period for the accrual of commission or fees) in a Non-LIBOR Currency for which there are rules specified as Business Day Conventions in respect of that currency in Schedule 14 (*Other Benchmarks*), those rules shall apply].

The [above] rules [in paragraph (a) above] will only apply to the last Month of any period.

"**New Lender**" has the meaning given to that term in Clause 24 (*Changes to the Lenders*).

["**Non-LIBOR Currency**" means [ ].][7]

"**Obligor**" means a Borrower or a Guarantor.

"**Optional Currency**" means a currency (other than the Base Currency) which complies with the conditions set out in Clause 4.3 (*Conditions relating to Optional Currencies*).

"**Original Financial Statements**" means:

(a) in relation to the Company, the audited consolidated financial statements of the Group for the financial year ended [__________]; and

(b) in relation to each Original Obligor other than the Company, its audited financial statements for its financial year ended [__________].

"**Original Obligor**" means an Original Borrower or an Original Guarantor.

"**Participating Member State**" means any member state of the European Union that has the euro as its lawful currency in accordance with legislation of the European Union relating to Economic and Monetary Union.

"**Party**" means a party to this Agreement.

"**Qualifying Lender**" has the meaning given to it in Clause 13 (*Tax gross-up and indemnities*).

"**Quotation Day**" means, in relation to any period for which an interest rate is to be determined:

(a)

(i) (if the currency is sterling) the first day of that period;

(ii) [(if the currency is euro) two TARGET Days before the first day of that period;][8] or

(iii) (for any other currency [(other than a Non-LIBOR Currency)]), two Business Days before the first day of that period,

(unless market practice differs in the Relevant Market for that currency, in which case the Quotation Day for that currency will be determined by the Agent in accordance with market practice in the Relevant Market (and if quotations would normally be given on more than one day, the Quotation Day will be the last of those days))[; or

(b) (if the currency is a Non-LIBOR Currency) the day specified as such in respect of that currency in Schedule 14 (*Other Benchmarks*)].

["**Reduction Date**" means [__________].]

[7] Insert details of any currency that is, or may be, available under the Agreement for which the interest rate is not intended to be determined by reference to LIBOR or EURIBOR. The details in Schedule 14 (*Other Benchmarks*) must be completed for each Non-LIBOR Currency.

[8] Insert if the interest rate for Loans in euro is to be determined by reference to EURIBOR.

["**Reduction Instalment**" means [            ].]

["**Reference Bank Quotation**" means any quotation supplied to the Agent by a Reference Bank.]

["**Reference Bank Rate**" means:

(a) the arithmetic mean of the rates (rounded upwards to four decimal places) as supplied to the Agent at its request by the Reference Banks:

(i) in relation to LIBOR as either:

(A) if:

(1) the Reference Bank is a contributor to the applicable Screen Rate; and

(2) it consists of a single figure,

the rate (applied to the relevant Reference Bank and the relevant currency and period) which contributors to the applicable Screen Rate are asked to submit to the relevant administrator; or

(B) in any other case, the rate at which the relevant Reference Bank could fund itself in the relevant currency for the relevant period with reference to the unsecured wholesale funding market[; or

(ii) in relation to EURIBOR:

(A) (other than where paragraph (B) below applies) as the rate at which the relevant Reference Bank believes one prime bank is quoting to another prime bank for interbank term deposits in euro within the Participating Member States for the relevant period; or

(B) if different, as the rate (if any and applied to the relevant Reference Bank and the relevant period) which contributors to the applicable Screen Rate are asked to submit to the relevant administrator][; or

(b) in relation to a Benchmark Rate for a Loan in a Non-LIBOR Currency, the rate specified as such in respect of that currency in Schedule 14 (*Other Benchmarks*)].]

["**Reference Banks**" means, in relation to LIBOR, the principal London offices of [ ], [ ] and [ ] [and, in relation to EURIBOR, the principal office in [ ] of [ ],[ ] and [ ]] [and, in relation to the Benchmark Rate for a Loan in a Non-LIBOR Currency, the entities specified as such in respect of that currency in Schedule 14 (*Other Benchmarks*)] or[, in each case,] such other entities as may be appointed by the Agent in consultation with the Company.]

"**Related Fund**" in relation to a fund (the "**first fund**"), means a fund which is managed or advised by the same investment manager or investment adviser as the first fund or, if it is managed by a different investment manager or investment adviser, a fund whose investment manager or investment adviser is an Affiliate of the investment manager or investment adviser of the first fund.

"**Relevant Market**" means [, in relation to euro, the European interbank market] [, in relation to a Non-LIBOR Currency, the market specified as such in respect of that currency in Schedule 14 (*Other Benchmarks*)] [and, in relation to any other currency,] the London interbank market.

["**Repayment Instalment**" means [            ].]

"**Repeating Representations**" means each of the representations set out in Clauses 19.[__], 19.[__] and 19.[__].

"**Representative**" means any delegate, agent, manager, administrator, nominee, attorney, trustee or custodian.

"**Resignation Letter**" means a letter substantially in the form set out in Schedule 8 (*Form of Resignation Letter*).

"**Rollover Loan**" means one or more Facility B Loans:

(a) made or to be made on the same day that a maturing Facility B Loan is due to be repaid;

(b) the aggregate amount of which is equal to or less than the amount of the maturing Facility B Loan;

(c) in the same currency as the maturing Facility B Loan (unless it arose as a result of the operation of Clause 6.2 (*Unavailability of a currency*)); and

(d) made or to be made to the same Borrower for the purpose of refinancing that maturing Facility B Loan.

"**Screen Rate**" means[9]:

(a) in relation to LIBOR, the London interbank offered rate administered by ICE Benchmark Administration Limited (or any other person which takes over the administration of that rate) for the relevant currency and period displayed [(before any correction, recalculation or republication by the administrator)] on pages LIBOR01 or LIBOR02 of the Thomson Reuters screen (or any replacement Thomson Reuters page which displays that rate)[; and

(b) in relation to EURIBOR, the euro interbank offered rate administered by the European Money Markets Institute (or any other person which takes over the administration of that rate) for the relevant period displayed [(before any

[9] The potential for subsequent intra-day correction, recalculation or republication of an originally published Screen Rate can raise difficult issues that should be considered carefully to ensure that the parties achieve the desired commercial outcome. Users should carefully consider the extent to which excluding the effects of any such correction, recalculation or republication is suitable for the transaction in question. See the LMA note entitled "*ICE LIBOR and EURIBOR refixing policies and LMA facility documentation*" (available through the LMA website).

correction, recalculation or republication by the administrator)] on page EURIBOR01 of the Thomson Reuters screen (or any replacement Thomson Reuters page which displays that rate)],

or[, in each case,] on the appropriate page of such other information service which publishes that rate from time to time in place of Thomson Reuters. If such page or service ceases to be available, the Agent may specify another page or service displaying the relevant rate after consultation with the Company[10][; and

(c) in relation to a Benchmark Rate, the rate specified as such in respect of the relevant currency in Schedule 14 (*Other Benchmarks*)].

"**Security**" means a mortgage, charge, pledge, lien or other security interest securing any obligation of any person or any other agreement or arrangement having a similar effect.

"**Selection Notice**" means a notice substantially in the form set out in Part II of Schedule 3 (*Requests*) given in accordance with Clause 10 (*Interest Periods*) in relation to Facility A.

"**Specified Time**" means a day or time determined in accordance with Schedule 12 (*Timetables*).

"**Subsidiary**" means [a subsidiary undertaking within the meaning of section 1162 of the Companies Act 2006]/[a subsidiary within the meaning of section 1159 of the Companies Act 2006]/[__________].

"**TARGET2**" means the Trans-European Automated Real-time Gross Settlement Express Transfer payment system which utilises a single shared platform and which was launched on 19 November 2007.

"**TARGET Day**" means any day on which TARGET2 is open for the settlement of payments in euro.

"**Tax**" means any tax, levy, impost, duty or other charge or withholding of a similar nature (including any penalty or interest payable in connection with any failure to pay or any delay in paying any of the same).

"**Termination Date**" means:

(a) in relation to Facility A [________]; and

(b) in relation to Facility B [________].

"**Total Commitments**" means the aggregate of the Total Facility A Commitments and the Total Facility B Commitments, being [________] at the date of this Agreement.

10 This definition is intended to have the effect of referencing (i) the LIBOR rate which is currently known as ICE LIBOR and (ii) the euro interbank offered rate which is currently known as Euribor, irrespective of any change of administrator or publisher occurring after the date of the Agreement. It may not be suitable if this effect does not represent the commercial agreement. Users should note that changes to this definition may have implications under associated interest rate hedging arrangements.

"**Total Facility A Commitments**" means the aggregate of the Facility A Commitments, being [_____] at the date of this Agreement.

"**Total Facility B Commitments**" means the aggregate of the Facility B Commitments, being [____] at the date of this Agreement.

"**Transfer Certificate**" means a certificate substantially in the form set out in Schedule 5 (*Form of Transfer Certificate*) or any other form agreed between the Agent and the Company.

"**Transfer Date**" means, in relation to an assignment or a transfer, the later of:

(a) the proposed Transfer Date specified in the relevant Assignment Agreement or Transfer Certificate; and

(b) the date on which the Agent executes the relevant Assignment Agreement or Transfer Certificate.

"**Unpaid Sum**" means any sum due and payable but unpaid by an Obligor under the Finance Documents.

"**US**" means the United States of America.

"**US Tax Obligor**" means:

(a) a Borrower which is resident for tax purposes in the US; or

(b) an Obligor some or all of whose payments under the Finance Documents are from sources within the US for US federal income tax purposes.

"**Utilisation**" means a utilisation of a Facility.

"**Utilisation Date**" means the date of a Utilisation, being the date on which the relevant Loan is to be made.

"**Utilisation Request**" means a notice substantially in the form set out in Part I of Schedule 3 (*Requests*).

"**VAT**" means:

(a) any tax imposed in compliance with the Council Directive of 28 November 2006 on the common system of value added tax (EC Directive 2006/112); and

(b) any other tax of a similar nature, whether imposed in a member state of the European Union in substitution for, or levied in addition to, such tax referred to in paragraph (a) above, or imposed elsewhere.

1.2 **Construction**

(a) Unless a contrary indication appears, any reference in this Agreement to:

(i) the "**Agent**", the "**Arranger**", any "**Finance Party**", any "**Lender**", any "**Obligor**" or any "**Party**" shall be construed so as to include its successors in title, permitted assigns and permitted transferees to, or of, its rights and/or obligations under the Finance Documents;

(ii) "**assets**" includes present and future properties, revenues and rights of every description;

(iii) a "**Finance Document**" or any other agreement or instrument is a reference to that Finance Document or other agreement or instrument as amended, novated, supplemented, extended or restated;

(iv) a "**group of Lenders**" includes all the Lenders;

(v) "**indebtedness**" includes any obligation (whether incurred as principal or as surety) for the payment or repayment of money, whether present or future, actual or contingent;

(vi) a "**person**" includes any individual, firm, company, corporation, government, state or agency of a state or any association, trust, joint venture, consortium, partnership or other entity (whether or not having separate legal personality);

(vii) a "**regulation**" includes any regulation, rule, official directive, request or guideline (whether or not having the force of law) of any governmental, intergovernmental or supranational body, agency, department or of any regulatory, self-regulatory or other authority or organisation;

(viii) a provision of law is a reference to that provision as amended or re-enacted; and

(ix) a time of day is a reference to London time.

(b) The determination of the extent to which a rate is "**for a period equal in length**" to an Interest Period shall disregard any inconsistency arising from the last day of that Interest Period being determined pursuant to the terms of this Agreement.

(c) Section, Clause and Schedule headings are for ease of reference only.

(d) Unless a contrary indication appears, a term used in any other Finance Document or in any notice given under or in connection with any Finance Document has the same meaning in that Finance Document or notice as in this Agreement.

(e) A Default (other than an Event of Default) is "**continuing**" if it has not been remedied or waived and an Event of Default is "**continuing**" if it has not been [remedied or waived]/[waived].

1.3 **Currency symbols and definitions**

["**$**", "**USD**" and "**dollars**" denote the lawful currency of the United States of America]/["**£**", "**GBP**" and "**sterling**" denote the lawful currency of the United

Kingdom]/["**€**", "**EUR**" and "**euro**" denote the single currency of the Participating Member States]/[    ][11].

1.4 **Third party rights**

[A person who is not a Party has no right under the Contracts (Rights of Third Parties) Act 1999 to enforce or to enjoy the benefit of any term of this Agreement.] /

(a) [Unless expressly provided to the contrary in a Finance Document a person who is not a Party has no right under the Contracts (Rights of Third Parties) Act 1999 (the "**Third Parties Act**") to enforce or to enjoy the benefit of any term of this Agreement.

(b) [Subject to Clause 35.3 (*Other exceptions*) but otherwise] notwithstanding any term of any Finance Document, the consent of any person who is not a Party is not required to rescind or vary this Agreement at any time.]

[11] ~~Users should consider carefully the~~ appropriate currency definition(s) in the context of the transaction and should consider defining any other currency referred to in the Agreement.

## SECTION 2
## THE FACILITIES

2. **THE FACILITIES**

2.1 **The Facilities**

Subject to the terms of this Agreement, the Lenders make available to the Borrowers:

(a) a multicurrency term loan facility in an aggregate amount equal to the Total Facility A Commitments; and

(b) a multicurrency revolving loan facility in an aggregate amount equal to the Total Facility B Commitments.

2.2 **Increase**

(a) The Company may by giving prior notice to the Agent [by no later than the date falling [__][12]] after the effective date of a cancellation of the Commitments of a Lender in accordance with:

(i) Clause 8.1 (*Illegality*); or

(ii) paragraph (a) of Clause 8.6 (*Right of replacement or repayment and cancellation in relation to a single Lender*),

request that the Commitments relating to any Facility be increased (and the Commitments relating to that Facility shall be so increased) in an aggregate amount in the Base Currency of up to the amount of the Commitments relating to that Facility so cancelled as follows:

(iii) the increased Commitments will be assumed by one or more Eligible Institutions (each an "**Increase Lender**") each of which confirms in writing (whether in the relevant Increase Confirmation or otherwise) its willingness to assume and does assume all the obligations of a Lender corresponding to that part of the increased Commitments which it is to assume, as if it had been an Original Lender in respect of those Commitments;

(iv) each of the Obligors and any Increase Lender shall assume obligations towards one another and/or acquire rights against one another as the Obligors and the Increase Lender would have assumed and/or acquired had the Increase Lender been an Original Lender in respect of that part of the increased Commitments which it is to assume;[13]

[12] Insert agreed time period.

[13] Any guarantees provided under this Agreement may not in all jurisdictions continue to guarantee the increased Commitment or be for the benefit of the Increase Lender. It is the responsibility of the Increase Lender to ascertain whether any other documents or other formalities are required to confirm the guarantees in any jurisdiction and/or for it to benefit from such guarantees and, if so, to arrange for execution of those documents and completion of those formalities.

(v) each Increase Lender shall become a Party as a "Lender" and any Increase Lender and each of the other Finance Parties shall assume obligations towards one another and acquire rights against one another as that Increase Lender and those Finance Parties would have assumed and/or acquired had the Increase Lender been an Original Lender in respect of that part of the increased Commitments which it is to assume;

(vi) the Commitments of the other Lenders shall continue in full force and effect; and

(vii) any increase in the Commitments relating to a Facility shall take effect on the date specified by the Company in the notice referred to above or any later date on which the Agent executes an otherwise duly completed Increase Confirmation delivered to it by the relevant Increase Lender.

(b) The Agent shall, subject to paragraph (c) below, as soon as reasonably practicable after receipt by it of a duly completed Increase Confirmation appearing on its face to comply with the terms of this Agreement and delivered in accordance with the terms of this Agreement, execute that Increase Confirmation.

(c) The Agent shall only be obliged to execute an Increase Confirmation delivered to it by an Increase Lender once it is satisfied it has complied with all necessary "know your customer" or other similar checks under all applicable laws and regulations in relation to the assumption of the increased Commitments by that Increase Lender.

(d) Each Increase Lender, by executing the Increase Confirmation, confirms (for the avoidance of doubt) that the Agent has authority to execute on its behalf any amendment or waiver that has been approved by or on behalf of the requisite Lender or Lenders in accordance with this Agreement on or prior to the date on which the increase becomes effective in accordance with this Agreement and that it is bound by that decision to the same extent as it would have been had it been an Original Lender.

(e) [The Company shall promptly on demand pay the Agent the amount of all costs and expenses (including legal fees) reasonably incurred by it in connection with any increase in Commitments under this Clause 2.2.]

(f) [The Increase Lender shall, on the date upon which the increase takes effect, pay to the Agent (for its own account) a fee in an amount equal to the fee which would be payable under Clause 24.4 (*Assignment or transfer fee*) if the increase was a transfer pursuant to Clause 24.6 (*Procedure for transfer*) and if the Increase Lender was a New Lender.]

(g) [The Company may pay to the Increase Lender a fee in the amount and at the times agreed between the Company and the Increase Lender in a letter between the Company and the Increase Lender setting out that fee. A reference in this

Agreement to a Fee Letter shall include any letter referred to in this paragraph (g).]

(h) Neither the Agent nor any Lender shall have any obligation to find an Increase Lender and in no event shall any Lender whose Commitment is replaced by an Increase Lender be required to pay or surrender any of the fees received by such Lender pursuant to the Finance Documents.

(i) Clause 24.5 (*Limitation of responsibility of Existing Lenders*) shall apply *mutatis mutandis* in this Clause 2.2 in relation to an Increase Lender as if references in that Clause to:

(i) an "**Existing Lender**" were references to all the Lenders immediately prior to the relevant increase;

(ii) the "**New Lender**" were references to that "**Increase Lender**"; and

(iii) a "**re-transfer**" and "**re-assignment**" were references to respectively a "**transfer**" and "**assignment**".

2.3 **Finance Parties' rights and obligations**

(a) The obligations of each Finance Party under the Finance Documents are several. Failure by a Finance Party to perform its obligations under the Finance Documents does not affect the obligations of any other Party under the Finance Documents. No Finance Party is responsible for the obligations of any other Finance Party under the Finance Documents.

(b) The rights of each Finance Party under or in connection with the Finance Documents are separate and independent rights and any debt arising under the Finance Documents to a Finance Party from an Obligor is a separate and independent debt in respect of which a Finance Party shall be entitled to enforce its rights in accordance with paragraph (c) below. The rights of each Finance Party include any debt owing to that Finance Party under the Finance Documents and, for the avoidance of doubt, any part of a Loan or any other amount owed by an Obligor which relates to a Finance Party's participation in a Facility or its role under a Finance Document (including any such amount payable to the Agent on its behalf) is a debt owing to that Finance Party by that Obligor.

(c) A Finance Party may, except as specifically provided in the Finance Documents, separately enforce its rights under or in connection with the Finance Documents.

3. **PURPOSE**

3.1 **Purpose**

(a) Each Borrower shall apply all amounts borrowed by it under Facility A towards [____].

(b) Each Borrower shall apply all amounts borrowed by it under Facility B towards [____].

3.2 **Monitoring**

No Finance Party is bound to monitor or verify the application of any amount borrowed pursuant to this Agreement.

4. **CONDITIONS OF UTILISATION**

4.1 **Initial conditions precedent**

(a) No Borrower may deliver a Utilisation Request unless the Agent has received all of the documents and other evidence listed in Part I of Schedule 2 (*Conditions precedent*) in form and substance satisfactory to the Agent. The Agent shall notify the Company and the Lenders promptly upon being so satisfied.

(b) Other than to the extent that the Majority Lenders notify the Agent in writing to the contrary before the Agent gives the notification described in paragraph (a) above, the Lenders authorise (but do not require) the Agent to give that notification. The Agent shall not be liable for any damages, costs or losses whatsoever as a result of giving any such notification.

4.2 **Further conditions precedent**

(a) The Lenders will only be obliged to comply with Clause 5.4 (*Lenders' participation*) if on the date of the Utilisation Request and on the proposed Utilisation Date:

(i) in the case of a Rollover Loan, no Event of Default is continuing or would result from the proposed Loan and, in the case of any other Loan, no Default is continuing or would result from the proposed Loan; and

(ii) the Repeating Representations to be made by each Obligor are true in all material respects.

(b) The Lenders will only be obliged to comply with Clause 6.3 (*Change of currency*) if, on the first day of an Interest Period, no Default is continuing or would result from the change of currency and the Repeating Representations to be made by each Obligor are true in all material respects.

4.3 **Conditions relating to Optional Currencies**

(a) A currency will constitute an Optional Currency in relation to a Loan if:

(i) it is readily available in the amount required and freely convertible into the Base Currency in the wholesale market for that currency on the Quotation Day and the Utilisation Date for that Loan; and

(ii) it [is [ ] or] has been approved by the Agent (acting on the instructions of all the Lenders) on or prior to receipt by the Agent of the relevant Utilisation Request or Selection Notice for that Loan.[14]

[14] When specifying a pre-approved Optional Currency users should consider the extent to which that currency ~~should be listed as a Non-LIBOR C~~urrency and the agreed Screen Rate (and related terms) included in Schedule 14 (*Other Benchmarks*).

(b) If the Agent has received a written request from the Company for a currency to be approved under paragraph (a)(ii) above, the Agent will confirm to the Company by the Specified Time:

(i) whether or not the Lenders have granted their approval; and

(ii) if approval has been granted, the minimum amount (and, if required, integral multiples) for any subsequent Utilisation in that currency.

4.4 **Maximum number of Loans**

(a) A Borrower may not deliver a Utilisation Request if as a result of the proposed Utilisation:

(i) [__] or more Facility A Loans would be outstanding; or

(ii) [__] or more Facility B Loans would be outstanding.

(b) A Borrower may not request that a Facility A Loan be divided if, as a result of the proposed division, [__] or more Facility A Loans would be outstanding.

(c) Any Loan made by a single Lender under Clause 6.2 (*Unavailability of a currency*) shall not be taken into account in this Clause 4.4.

If the Clause is amended to allow for subsequent approval of Optional Currencies with less than all Lender consent, users should consider providing for a mechanic to agree a suitable Screen Rate (and related terms) at the same time.

## SECTION 3
## UTILISATION

5. **UTILISATION**

5.1 **Delivery of a Utilisation Request**

A Borrower may utilise a Facility by delivery to the Agent of a duly completed Utilisation Request not later than the Specified Time.

5.2 **Completion of a Utilisation Request**

(a) Each Utilisation Request is irrevocable and will not be regarded as having been duly completed unless:

(i) it identifies the Facility to be utilised;

(ii) the proposed Utilisation Date is a Business Day within the Availability Period applicable to that Facility;

(iii) the currency and amount of the Utilisation comply with Clause 5.3 (*Currency and amount*); and

(iv) the proposed Interest Period complies with Clause 10 (*Interest Periods*).

(b) Only one Loan may be requested in each Utilisation Request.

5.3 **Currency and amount**

(a) The currency specified in a Utilisation Request must be the Base Currency or an Optional Currency.

(b) The amount of the proposed Loan must be:

(i) if the currency selected is the Base Currency, a minimum of [______] for Facility A and [______] for Facility B or in either case, if less, the Available Facility; or

(ii) [if the currency selected is [    ], a minimum of [    ] for Facility A and [    ] for Facility B or in either case, if less, the Available Facility; or]

(iii) if the currency selected is an Optional Currency [other than [______]], the minimum amount (and, if required, integral multiple) specified by the Agent pursuant to paragraph (b)(ii) of Clause 4.3 (*Conditions relating to Optional Currencies*) or, if less, the Available Facility; and

(iv) in any event such that its Base Currency Amount is less than or equal to the Available Facility.

5.4 **Lenders' participation**

(a) If the conditions set out in this Agreement have been met, [and subject to Clause 7.2 (*Repayment of Facility B Loans*),][15] each Lender shall make its

[15] Include this wording if the optional cashless rollover language is included in Clause 7.2 (*Repayment of Facility B Loans*).

participation in each Loan available by the Utilisation Date through its Facility Office.

(b) The amount of each Lender's participation in each Loan will be equal to the proportion borne by its Available Commitment to the Available Facility immediately prior to making the Loan.

(c) The Agent shall determine the Base Currency Amount of each Loan which is to be made in an Optional Currency and shall notify each Lender of the amount, currency and the Base Currency Amount of each Loan, the amount of its participation in that Loan [and, in the case of a Facility B Loan and if different, the amount of that participation to be made available in accordance with Clause 29.1 (*Payments to the Agent*)],[16] in each case by the Specified Time.

**5.5 Cancellation of Commitment**

(a) The Facility A Commitments which, at that time, are unutilised shall be immediately cancelled at the end of the Availability Period for Facility A.

(b) The Facility B Commitments which, at that time, are unutilised shall be immediately cancelled at the end of the Availability Period for Facility B.

**6. OPTIONAL CURRENCIES**

**6.1 Selection of currency**

(a) A Borrower (or the Company on behalf of a Borrower) shall select the currency of a Loan:

(i) (in the case of an initial Utilisation) in a Utilisation Request; and

(ii) (afterwards in relation to a Facility A Loan made to it) in a Selection Notice.

(b) If a Borrower (or the Company on behalf of a Borrower) fails to issue a Selection Notice in relation to a Facility A Loan, the Loan will remain denominated for its next Interest Period in the same currency as that in which it is denominated, pursuant to paragraph (a) above, for its current Interest Period.

(c) If a Borrower (or the Company on behalf of a Borrower) issues a Selection Notice requesting a change of currency and the first day of the requested Interest Period is not a Business Day for the new currency, the Agent shall promptly notify the Borrower and the Lenders and the Loan will remain in the existing currency (with Interest Periods running from one Business Day until the next Business Day) until the next day which is a Business Day for both currencies, on which day the requested Interest Period will begin.

[16] Include this wording if the optional cashless rollover language is included in Clause 7.2 (*Repayment of Facility B Loans*).

6.2 **Unavailability of a currency**

If before the Specified Time on any Quotation Day:

(a) a Lender notifies the Agent that the Optional Currency requested is not readily available to it in the amount required; or

(b) a Lender notifies the Agent that compliance with its obligation to participate in a Loan in the proposed Optional Currency would contravene a law or regulation applicable to it,

the Agent will give notice to the relevant Borrower to that effect by the Specified Time on that day. In this event, any Lender that gives notice pursuant to this Clause 6.2 will be required to participate in the Loan in the Base Currency (in an amount equal to that Lender's proportion of the Base Currency Amount or, in respect of a Rollover Loan, an amount equal to that Lender's proportion of the Base Currency Amount of the Rollover Loan that is due to be made) and its participation will be treated as a separate Loan denominated in the Base Currency during that Interest Period.

6.3 **Change of currency**

(a) If a Facility A Loan is to be denominated in different currencies during two successive Interest Periods:

(i) if the currency for the second Interest Period is an Optional Currency, the amount of the Loan in that Optional Currency will be calculated by the Agent as the amount of that Optional Currency equal to the Base Currency Amount of the Loan at the Agent's Spot Rate of Exchange at the Specified Time;

(ii) if the currency for the second Interest Period is the Base Currency, the amount of the Loan will be equal to the Base Currency Amount;

(iii) (unless the Agent and the Borrower agree otherwise in accordance with paragraph (b) below) the Borrower that has borrowed the Loan shall repay it on the last day of the first Interest Period in the currency in which it was denominated, pursuant to this Clause 6, for that Interest Period; and

(iv) (subject to Clause 4.2 (*Further conditions precedent*)) the Lenders shall re-advance the Loan in the new currency in accordance with Clause 6.5 (*Agent's calculations*).

(b) If the Agent and the Borrower that has borrowed the Facility A Loan agree, the Agent shall:

(i) apply the amount paid to it by the Lenders pursuant to paragraph (a)(iv) above (or so much of that amount as is necessary) in or towards purchase of an amount in the currency in which the Facility A Loan is denominated, pursuant to this Clause 6, for the first Interest Period; and

(ii) use the amount it purchases in or towards satisfaction of the relevant Borrower's obligations under paragraph (a)(iii) above.

(c) If the amount purchased by the Agent pursuant to paragraph (b)(i) above is less than the amount required to be repaid by the relevant Borrower, the Agent shall promptly notify that Borrower and that Borrower shall, on the last day of the first Interest Period, pay an amount to the Agent (in the currency of the outstanding Facility A Loan for the first Interest Period) equal to the difference.

(d) If paragraph (b) above applies and any part of the amount paid to the Agent by the Lenders pursuant to paragraph (a)(iv) above is not needed to purchase the amount required to be repaid by the relevant Borrower, the Agent shall promptly notify that Borrower and pay that Borrower, on the last day of the first Interest Period that part of that amount (in the new currency).

**6.4 Same Optional Currency during successive Interest Periods**

(a) If a Facility A Loan is to be denominated, pursuant to this Clause 6, in the same Optional Currency during two successive Interest Periods, the Agent shall calculate the amount of the Facility A Loan in the Optional Currency for the second of those Interest Periods (by calculating the amount of Optional Currency equal to the Base Currency Amount of that Facility A Loan at the Agent's Spot Rate of Exchange at the Specified Time[17]) and (subject to paragraph (b) below):

(i) if the amount calculated is less than the existing amount of that Facility A Loan in the Optional Currency during the first Interest Period, promptly notify the Borrower that has borrowed that Facility A Loan and that Borrower shall pay, on the last day of the first Interest Period, an amount equal to the difference; or

(ii) if the amount calculated is more than the existing amount of that Facility A Loan in the Optional Currency during the first Interest Period, promptly notify each Lender and, if no [Default/Event of Default] is continuing, each Lender shall, on the last day of the first Interest Period, pay its participation in an amount equal to the difference.

(b) If the calculation made by the Agent pursuant to paragraph (a) above shows that the amount of the Facility A Loan in the Optional Currency for the second of those Interest Periods converted into the Base Currency at the Agent's Spot Rate of Exchange at the Specified Time[18] has increased or decreased by less than [_____] per cent. compared to its Base Currency Amount (taking into account any payments made pursuant to paragraph (a) above), no notification shall be made by the Agent and no payment shall be required under paragraph (a) above.

[17] The Specified Time to be inserted in Schedule 12 (*Timetables*) for the purposes of this paragraph (a) is the ~~Quotation Day for the second Interest~~ Period.

[18] The Specified Time to be inserted in Schedule 12 (*Timetables*) for the purposes of this paragraph (b) is the Business Day on which the Agent originally calculated the Base Currency Amount.

6.5 **Agent's calculations**

(a) All calculations made by the Agent pursuant to this Clause 6 will take into account any repayment, prepayment, consolidation or division of Facility A Loans to be made on the last day of the first Interest Period.

(b) Each Lender's participation in a Loan will, subject to paragraph (a) above, be determined in accordance with paragraph (b) of Clause 5.4 (*Lenders' participation*).

## SECTION 4
## REPAYMENT, PREPAYMENT AND CANCELLATION

### 7. REPAYMENT

**7.1 Repayment of Facility A Loans**

(a) [________________].

(b) No Borrower may reborrow any part of Facility A which is repaid.

**7.2 Repayment of Facility B Loans**

(a) Each Borrower which has drawn a Facility B Loan shall repay that Loan on the last day of its Interest Period.

(b) [Without prejudice to each Borrower's obligation under paragraph (a) above, if:

(i) one or more Facility B Loans are to be made available to a Borrower:

(A) on the same day that a maturing Facility B Loan is due to be repaid by that Borrower;

(B) in the same currency as the maturing Facility B Loan (unless it arose as a result of the operation of Clause 6.2 (*Unavailability of a currency*)); and

(C) in whole or in part for the purpose of refinancing the maturing Facility B Loan; and

(ii) the proportion borne by each Lender's participation in the maturing Facility B Loan to the amount of that maturing Facility B Loan is the same as the proportion borne by that Lender's participation in the new Facility B Loans to the aggregate amount of those new Facility B Loans,

the aggregate amount of the new Facility B Loans shall, unless the Company notifies the Agent to the contrary in the relevant Utilisation Request, be treated as if applied in or towards repayment of the maturing Facility B Loan so that:

(D) if the amount of the maturing Facility B Loan exceeds the aggregate amount of the new Facility B Loans:

(1) the relevant Borrower will only be required to make a payment under Clause 29.1 (*Payments to the Agent*) in an amount in the relevant currency equal to that excess; and

(2) each Lender's participation in the new Facility B Loans shall be treated as having been made available and applied by the Borrower in or towards repayment of that Lender's participation in the maturing Facility B Loan and that Lender will not be required to make a payment under Clause 29.1 (*Payments to the Agent*) in respect of its participation in the new Facility B Loans; and

(E) if the amount of the maturing Facility B Loan is equal to or less than the aggregate amount of the new Facility B Loans:

(1) the relevant Borrower will not be required to make a payment under Clause 29.1 (*Payments to the Agent*); and

(2) each Lender will be required to make a payment under Clause 29.1 (*Payments to the Agent*) in respect of its participation in the new Facility B Loans only to the extent that its participation in the new Facility B Loans exceeds that Lender's participation in the maturing Facility B Loan and the remainder of that Lender's participation in the new Facility B Loans shall be treated as having been made available and applied by the Borrower in or towards repayment of that Lender's participation in the maturing Facility B Loan.]

7.3 **Reduction of Facility B**

[________________].

8. **PREPAYMENT AND CANCELLATION**

8.1 **Illegality**

If, in any applicable jurisdiction, it becomes unlawful for any Lender to perform any of its obligations as contemplated by this Agreement or to fund or maintain its participation in any Loan [or it becomes unlawful for any Affiliate of a Lender for that Lender to do so]:

(a) that Lender shall promptly notify the Agent upon becoming aware of that event;

(b) upon the Agent notifying the Company, each Available Commitment of that Lender will be immediately cancelled; and

(c) to the extent that the Lender's participation has not been transferred pursuant to paragraph (d) of Clause 8.6 (*Right of replacement or repayment and cancellation in relation to a single Lender*), each Borrower shall repay that Lender's participation in the Loans made to that Borrower on the last day of the Interest Period for each Loan occurring after the Agent has notified the Company or, if earlier, the date specified by the Lender in the notice delivered to the Agent (being no earlier than the last day of any applicable grace period permitted by law) and that Lender's corresponding Commitment(s) shall be cancelled in the amount of the participations repaid.

8.2 **Change of control**

(a) If [[     ] ceases to control the Company]/[any person or group of persons acting in concert gains control of the Company]:

(i) the Company shall promptly notify the Agent upon becoming aware of that event;

(ii) [a Lender shall not be obliged to fund a Utilisation (except for a Rollover Loan);]

(iii) if [the Majority Lenders so require]/[a Lender so requires and notifies the Agent within [ ] days of the Company notifying the Agent of the event], the Agent shall, by not less than [__] days notice to the Company, cancel the [Total Commitments]/[Commitment of that Lender] and declare [the participation of that Lender in] all outstanding Loans, together with accrued interest, and all other amounts accrued under the Finance Documents immediately due and payable, whereupon the [Total Commitments]/[Commitment of that Lender] will be cancelled and all such outstanding Loans and amounts will become immediately due and payable.

(b) For the purpose of paragraph (a) above "**control**" means [_____].

(c) [For the purpose of paragraph (a) above "**acting in concert**" means [ ].]

**8.3 Voluntary cancellation**

The Company may, if it gives the Agent not less than [__] Business Days' (or such shorter period as the Majority Lenders may agree) prior notice, cancel the whole or any part (being a minimum amount of [_____]) of an Available Facility. Any cancellation under this Clause 8.3 shall reduce the Commitments of the Lenders rateably under that Facility.

**8.4 Voluntary prepayment of Facility A Loans**

(a) A Borrower to which a Facility A Loan has been made may, if it gives the Agent not less than [___] Business Days' (or such shorter period as the Majority Lenders may agree) prior notice, prepay the whole or any part of any Facility A Loan (but, if in part, being an amount that reduces the Base Currency Amount of the Facility A Loan by a minimum amount of [_____]).

(b) A Facility A Loan may only be prepaid after the last day of the Availability Period for Facility A (or, if earlier, the day on which the applicable Available Facility is zero).

(c) [Any prepayment under this Clause 8.4 shall satisfy the obligations under Clause 7.1 (*Repayment of Facility A Loans*) in [ ] order.]

**8.5 Voluntary prepayment of Facility B Loans**

The Borrower to which a Facility B Loan has been made may, if it gives the Agent not less than [_____] Business Days' (or such shorter period as the Majority Lenders may agree) prior notice, prepay the whole or any part of a Facility B Loan (but if in part, being an amount that reduces the Base Currency Amount of the Facility B Loan by a minimum amount of [_____]).

**8.6 Right of replacement or repayment and cancellation in relation to a single Lender**

(a) If:

(i) any sum payable to any Lender by an Obligor is required to be increased under paragraph (c) of Clause 13.2 (*Tax gross-up*); or

(ii) any Lender claims indemnification from the Company under Clause 13.3 (*Tax indemnity*) or Clause 14.1 (*Increased costs*),

the Company may, whilst the circumstance giving rise to the requirement for that increase or indemnification continues, give the Agent notice of cancellation of the Commitment(s) of that Lender and its intention to procure the repayment of that Lender's participation in the Loans or give the Agent notice of its intention to replace that Lender in accordance with paragraph (d) below.

(b) On receipt of a notice of cancellation referred to in paragraph (a) above, the Commitment(s) of that Lender shall immediately be reduced to zero.

(c) On the last day of each Interest Period which ends after the Company has given notice of cancellation under paragraph (a) above (or, if earlier, the date specified by the Company in that notice), each Borrower to which a Loan is outstanding shall repay that Lender's participation in that Loan.

(d) If:

(i) any of the circumstances set out in paragraph (a) above apply to a Lender; or

(ii) an Obligor becomes obliged to pay any amount in accordance with Clause 8.1 (*Illegality*) to any Lender,

the Company may, on [ ] Business Days' prior notice to the Agent and that Lender, replace that Lender by requiring that Lender to (and, to the extent permitted by law, that Lender shall) transfer pursuant to Clause 24 (*Changes to the Lenders*) all (and not part only) of its rights and obligations under this Agreement to an Eligible Institution which confirms its willingness to assume and does assume all the obligations of the transferring Lender in accordance with Clause 24 (*Changes to the Lenders*) for a purchase price in cash payable at the time of the transfer in an amount equal to the outstanding principal amount of such Lender's participation in the outstanding Loans and all accrued interest [(to the extent that the Agent has not given a notification under Clause 24.10 (*Pro rata interest settlement*))], Break Costs and other amounts payable in relation thereto under the Finance Documents.

(e) The replacement of a Lender pursuant to paragraph (d) above shall be subject to the following conditions:

(i) the Company shall have no right to replace the Agent;

(ii) neither the Agent nor any Lender shall have any obligation to find a replacement Lender;

(iii) in no event shall the Lender replaced under paragraph (d) above be required to pay or surrender any of the fees received by such Lender pursuant to the Finance Documents; and

(iv) the Lender shall only be obliged to transfer its rights and obligations pursuant to paragraph (d) above once it is satisfied that it has complied with all necessary "know your customer" or other similar checks under all applicable laws and regulations in relation to that transfer.

(f) A Lender shall perform the checks described in paragraph (e)(iv) above as soon as reasonably practicable following delivery of a notice referred to in paragraph (d) above and shall notify the Agent and the Company when it is satisfied that it has complied with those checks.

8.7 **Restrictions**

(a) Any notice of cancellation or prepayment given by any Party under this Clause 8 shall be irrevocable and, unless a contrary indication appears in this Agreement, shall specify the date or dates upon which the relevant cancellation or prepayment is to be made and the amount of that cancellation or prepayment.

(b) Any prepayment under this Agreement shall be made together with accrued interest on the amount prepaid and, subject to any Break Costs, without premium or penalty.

(c) No Borrower may reborrow any part of Facility A which is prepaid.

(d) Unless a contrary indication appears in this Agreement, any part of Facility B which is prepaid or repaid may be reborrowed in accordance with the terms of this Agreement.

(e) The Borrowers shall not repay or prepay all or any part of the Loans or cancel all or any part of the Commitments except at the times and in the manner expressly provided for in this Agreement.

(f) Subject to Clause 2.2 (*Increase*), no amount of the Total Commitments cancelled under this Agreement may be subsequently reinstated.

(g) If the Agent receives a notice under this Clause 8 it shall promptly forward a copy of that notice to either the Company or the affected Lender, as appropriate.

(h) If all or part of any Lender's participation in a Loan under a Facility is repaid or prepaid and is not available for redrawing (other than by operation of Clause 4.2 (*Further conditions precedent*)), an amount of that Lender's Commitment (equal to the Base Currency Amount of the amount of the participation which is repaid or prepaid) in respect of that Facility will be deemed to be cancelled on the date of repayment or prepayment.

8.8 **Application of prepayments**

Any prepayment of a Loan pursuant to [Clause 8.2 (*Change of control*),][19] Clause 8.4 (*Voluntary prepayment of Facility A Loans*) or Clause 8.5 (*Voluntary prepayment of Facility B Loans*) shall be applied *pro rata* to each Lender's participation in that Loan.

[19] Insert if Clause 8.2 (*Change of control*) provides for mandatory prepayment of all Loans and the cancellation of the Total Commitments.

## SECTION 5
## COSTS OF UTILISATION

### 9. INTEREST

#### 9.1 Calculation of interest

The rate of interest on each Loan for each Interest Period is the percentage rate per annum which is the aggregate of the applicable:

(a) Margin; [and]

(b) LIBOR [or, in relation to any Loan in euro, EURIBOR] [or, in relation to any Loan in a Non-LIBOR Currency, the Benchmark Rate for that currency][; and

(c) Mandatory Cost, if any].

#### 9.2 Payment of interest

The Borrower to which a Loan has been made shall pay accrued interest on that Loan on the last day of each Interest Period (and, if the Interest Period is longer than six Months, on the dates falling at six-monthly intervals after the first day of the Interest Period).

#### 9.3 Default interest

(a) If an Obligor fails to pay any amount payable by it under a Finance Document on its due date, interest shall accrue on the overdue amount from the due date up to the date of actual payment (both before and after judgment) at a rate which, subject to paragraph (b) below, is [__] per cent. per annum higher than the rate which would have been payable if the overdue amount had, during the period of non-payment, constituted a Loan in the currency of the overdue amount for successive Interest Periods, each of a duration selected by the Agent (acting reasonably). Any interest accruing under this Clause 9.3 shall be immediately payable by the Obligor on demand by the Agent.

(b) If any overdue amount consists of all or part of a Loan which became due on a day which was not the last day of an Interest Period relating to that Loan:

(i) the first Interest Period for that overdue amount shall have a duration equal to the unexpired portion of the current Interest Period relating to that Loan; and

(ii) the rate of interest applying to the overdue amount during that first Interest Period shall be [__] per cent. per annum higher than the rate which would have applied if the overdue amount had not become due.

(c) Default interest (if unpaid) arising on an overdue amount will be compounded with the overdue amount at the end of each Interest Period applicable to that overdue amount but will remain immediately due and payable.

#### 9.4 Notification of rates of interest

(a) The Agent shall promptly notify the relevant Lenders and the relevant Borrower of the determination of a rate of interest under this Agreement.

(b) The Agent shall promptly notify the relevant Borrower of each Funding Rate relating to a Loan.

## 10. INTEREST PERIODS

### 10.1 Selection of Interest Periods

(a) A Borrower (or the Company on behalf of a Borrower) may select an Interest Period for a Loan in the Utilisation Request for that Loan or (if the Loan has already been borrowed) in a Selection Notice.

(b) Each Selection Notice for a Facility A Loan is irrevocable and must be delivered to the Agent by the Borrower (or the Company on behalf of a Borrower) to which that Facility A Loan was made not later than the Specified Time.

(c) If a Borrower (or the Company) fails to deliver a Selection Notice to the Agent in accordance with paragraph (b) above, the relevant Interest Period will, subject to Clause 10.2 (*Changes to Interest Periods*), be [one] Month [or, if the Loan is in a Non-LIBOR Currency, the period specified in respect of that currency in Schedule 14 (*Other Benchmarks*)].

(d) Subject to this Clause 10, a Borrower (or the Company) may select an Interest Period of [[ ] or [ ]] Months [if the Loan is not in a Non-LIBOR Currency or, if the Loan is in a Non-LIBOR Currency, of any period specified in respect of that currency in Schedule 14 (*Other Benchmarks*)][20] or[, in either case,] of any other period agreed between the Company, the Agent and all the Lenders in relation to the relevant Loan. [In addition a Borrower (or the Company on its behalf) may select an Interest Period of:

(i) (in relation to Facility A) a period of less than [one] Month, if necessary to ensure that there are sufficient Facility A Loans (with an aggregate Base Currency Amount equal to or greater than the Repayment Instalment) which have an Interest Period ending on a Facility A Repayment Date for the Borrowers to make the Repayment Instalment due on that date; or

(ii) (in relation to Facility B) a period of less than [one] Month, if necessary to ensure that (when aggregated with the Available Facility for Facility B) there are sufficient Facility B Loans (with an aggregate Base Currency Amount equal to or greater than the Reduction Instalment) which have an Interest Period ending on a Reduction Date for the scheduled reduction to occur.]

(e) An Interest Period for a Loan shall not extend beyond the Termination Date applicable to its Facility.

[20] This Agreement envisages the use of one Screen Rate only per currency. Users should consider the extent to which available Interest Periods should be restricted to tenors for which Screen Rates are available or can be interpolated from those Screen Rates.

(f) Each Interest Period for a Facility A Loan shall start on the Utilisation Date or (if already made) on the last day of its preceding Interest Period.

(g) A Facility B Loan has one Interest Period only.

### 10.2 Changes to Interest Periods

(a) [Prior to determining the interest rate for a Facility A Loan, the Agent may shorten an Interest Period for any Facility A Loan to ensure there are sufficient Facility A Loans (with an aggregate Base Currency Amount equal to or greater than the Repayment Instalment) which have an Interest Period ending on a Facility A Repayment Date for the Borrowers to make the Repayment Instalment due on that date.]

(b) [Prior to determining the interest rate for a Facility B Loan, the Agent may shorten the Interest Period for any Facility B Loan to ensure that, when aggregated with the Available Facility for Facility B, there are sufficient Facility B Loans (with an aggregate Base Currency Amount equal to or greater than the Reduction Instalment) which have an Interest Period ending on a Reduction Date for the scheduled reduction to occur.]

(c) If the Agent makes any of the changes to an Interest Period referred to in this Clause 10.2, it shall promptly notify the Company and the Lenders.

### 10.3 Non-Business Days

(a) [Other than where paragraph (b) below applies, if]/[If] an Interest Period would otherwise end on a day which is not a Business Day, that Interest Period will instead end on the next Business Day in that calendar month (if there is one) or the preceding Business Day (if there is not).

(b) [If the Loan is in a Non-LIBOR Currency and there are rules specified as "Business Day Conventions" for that currency in Schedule 14 (*Other Benchmarks*), those rules shall apply to each Interest Period for that Loan.]

### 10.4 Consolidation and division of Facility A Loans

(a) Subject to paragraph (b) below, if two or more Interest Periods:

(i) relate to Facility A Loans in the same currency made to the same Borrower; and

(ii) end on the same date,

those Facility A Loans will, unless that Borrower (or the Company on its behalf) specifies to the contrary in the Selection Notice for the next Interest Period, be consolidated into, and treated as, a single Facility A Loan on the last day of the Interest Period.

(b) Subject to Clause 4.4 (*Maximum number of Loans*) and Clause 5.3 (*Currency and amount*), if a Borrower (or the Company on its behalf) requests in a Selection Notice that a Facility A Loan be divided into two or more Facility A Loans, that Facility A Loan will, on the last day of its Interest Period, be so divided with Base Currency Amounts specified in that Selection Notice, being an aggregate Base Currency Amount equal to the Base Currency Amount of the Facility A Loan immediately before its division.

## 11. CHANGES TO THE CALCULATION OF INTEREST

### 11.1 [Unavailability of Screen Rate[21]

(a) *Interpolated Screen Rate*: If no Screen Rate is available for LIBOR [or, if applicable, EURIBOR] [or, if applicable, the Benchmark Rate] for the Interest Period of a Loan, the applicable LIBOR [or EURIBOR] [or Benchmark Rate] shall be the Interpolated Screen Rate for a period equal in length to the Interest Period of that Loan.

(b) *Shortened Interest Period*: If no Screen Rate is available for LIBOR [or, if applicable, EURIBOR] [or, if applicable, the Benchmark Rate] for:

(i) the currency of a Loan; or

(ii) the Interest Period of a Loan and it is not possible to calculate the Interpolated Screen Rate,

the Interest Period of that Loan shall (if it is longer than the applicable Fallback Interest Period) be shortened to the applicable Fallback Interest Period and the applicable LIBOR [or EURIBOR] [or Benchmark Rate] for that shortened Interest Period shall be determined pursuant to [the definition of "**LIBOR**"] / [the relevant definition].

(c) *Shortened Interest Period and Historic Screen Rate*: If the Interest Period of a Loan is, after giving effect to paragraph (b) above, either the applicable Fallback Interest Period or shorter than the applicable Fallback Interest Period and, in either case, no Screen Rate is available for LIBOR [or, if applicable EURIBOR] [or, if applicable, the Benchmark Rate] for:

(i) the currency of that Loan; or

(ii) the Interest Period of that Loan and it is not possible to calculate the Interpolated Screen Rate,

the applicable LIBOR [or EURIBOR] [or Benchmark Rate] shall be the Historic Screen Rate for that Loan.

(d) *Shortened Interest Period and Interpolated Historic Screen Rate*: If paragraph (c) above applies but no Historic Screen Rate is available for the Interest Period of the Loan, the applicable LIBOR [or EURIBOR] [or Benchmark Rate] shall be the Interpolated Historic Screen Rate for a period equal in length to the Interest Period of that Loan.

[21] Clause 11.1 (*Unavailability of Screen Rate*) provides for a waterfall of fallbacks if a Screen Rate is unavailable. Two (alternative) forms of Clause 11.1 (*Unavailability of Screen Rate*) are provided. The first form should be used if the commercial agreement is that Historic Screen Rates are to be used as an intermediate fallback before the use of Reference Banks or cost of funds. The second form should be used if the commercial agreement is that Historic Screen Rates are not to be used as such an intermediate fallback.

(e) [*Reference Bank Rate*:] / [*Cost of funds*:] If paragraph (d) above applies but it is not possible to calculate the Interpolated Historic Screen Rate, the Interest Period of that Loan shall, if it has been shortened pursuant to paragraph (b) above, revert to its previous length and [the applicable LIBOR [or EURIBOR] [or Benchmark Rate] shall be the Reference Bank Rate as of the Specified Time for the currency of that Loan and for a period equal in length to the Interest Period of that Loan] / [there shall be no LIBOR [or EURIBOR] [or Benchmark Rate] for that Loan and Clause 11.4 (*Cost of funds*) shall apply to that Loan for that Interest Period].

(f) [*Cost of funds*: If paragraph (e) above applies but no Reference Bank Rate is available for the relevant currency or Interest Period there shall be no LIBOR [or EURIBOR] [or Benchmark Rate] for that Loan and Clause 11.4 (*Cost of funds*) shall apply to that Loan for that Interest Period.]] /

**OR**

11.1 **[Unavailability of Screen Rate**

(a) *Interpolated Screen Rate*: If no Screen Rate is available for LIBOR [or, if applicable, EURIBOR] [or, if applicable, the Benchmark Rate] for the Interest Period of a Loan, the applicable LIBOR [or EURIBOR] [or Benchmark Rate] shall be the Interpolated Screen Rate for a period equal in length to the Interest Period of that Loan.

(b) [*Reference Bank Rate*:] / [*Cost of funds*:] If no Screen Rate is available for LIBOR [or, if applicable, EURIBOR] [or, if applicable, the Benchmark Rate] for:

(i) the currency of a Loan; or

(ii) the Interest Period of a Loan and it is not possible to calculate the Interpolated Screen Rate,

[the applicable LIBOR [or EURIBOR] [or Benchmark Rate] shall be the Reference Bank Rate as of the Specified Time for the currency of that Loan and for a period equal in length to the Interest Period of that Loan] / [there shall be no LIBOR [or EURIBOR] [or Benchmark Rate] for that Loan and Clause 11.4 (*Cost of funds*) shall apply to that Loan for that Interest Period].

(c) [*Cost of funds*: If paragraph (b) above applies but no Reference Bank Rate is available for the relevant currency or Interest Period there shall be no LIBOR [or EURIBOR] [or Benchmark Rate] for that Loan and Clause 11.4 (*Cost of funds*) shall apply to that Loan for that Interest Period.]]

11.2 **[Calculation of Reference Bank Rate**[22]

(a) Subject to paragraph (b) below, if LIBOR [or EURIBOR] [or a Benchmark Rate] is to be determined on the basis of a Reference Bank Rate but a Reference

[22] The timings in this Clause are suggestions only and may need adjustment to accord with the Agent's and Reference Banks' operational requirements.

Bank does not supply a quotation by the Specified Time, the Reference Bank Rate shall be calculated on the basis of the quotations of the remaining Reference Banks.

(b) If at or about:

(i) [noon] on the Quotation Day[; or

(ii) in the case of a Benchmark Rate, the time specified in respect of the relevant currency in Schedule 14 (*Other Benchmarks*),]

none or only one of the Reference Banks supplies a quotation, there shall be no Reference Bank Rate for the relevant Interest Period.]

11.3 **Market disruption**

If before:

(a) close of business in London on the Quotation Day for the relevant Interest Period[; or

(b) in the case of a Loan in a Non-LIBOR Currency, the time specified in respect of that currency in Schedule 14 (*Other Benchmarks*),]

the Agent receives notifications from a Lender or Lenders (whose participations in a Loan exceed [_______] per cent. of that Loan) that the cost to it of funding its participation in that Loan [from whatever source it may reasonably select]/[from the wholesale market for the relevant currency] would be in excess of LIBOR [or, if applicable, EURIBOR] [or, if applicable, the Benchmark Rate] then Clause 11.4 (*Cost of funds*) shall apply to that Loan for the relevant Interest Period.[23]

11.4 **Cost of funds**[24]

(a) If this Clause 11.4 applies, the rate of interest on [each Lender's share of][25] the relevant Loan for the relevant Interest Period shall be the percentage rate per annum which is the sum of:

(i) the Margin;[and]

(ii) [the rate notified to the Agent by that Lender] / [the weighted average of the rates notified to the Agent by each Lender] as soon as practicable and in any event [within [ ] Business Days of the first day of that Interest Period] / [by close of business on the date falling [ ] Business Days after the Quotation Day] (or, if earlier, on the date falling [ ] Business Days before the date on which interest is due to be paid in respect of that Interest Period), to be that which expresses as a percentage rate per annum

[23] Users should consider whether the Company's rights under Clause 8.6 (*Right of replacement or repayment and cancellation in relation to a single Lender*) should be extended to apply to a Lender making a notification to the Agent under Clause 11.3 (*Market disruption*).

[24] Users should consider whether Clause 11.4 (*Costs of funds*) should be amended to allow the relevant Borrower to revoke the Utilisation Request relating to a Loan which falls to be priced on a cost of funds basis.

[25] Include if cost of funds is not calculated on a weighted average basis.

the cost to the relevant Lender of funding its participation in that Loan from whatever source it may reasonably select[; and

(iii) the Mandatory Cost, if any[, applicable to that Lender's participation in the Loan][26]].

(b) If this Clause 11.4 applies and the Agent or the Company so requires, the Agent and the Company shall enter into negotiations (for a period of not more than thirty days) with a view to agreeing a substitute basis for determining the rate of interest.

(c) Any alternative basis agreed pursuant to paragraph (b) above shall, with the prior consent of all the Lenders and the Company, be binding on all Parties.

(d) [If this Clause 11.4 applies pursuant to Clause 11.3 (*Market disruption*) and:

(i) a Lender's Funding Rate is less than LIBOR [or, in relation to any Loan in euro, EURIBOR] [or, in relation to any Loan in a Non-LIBOR Currency, the Benchmark Rate]; or

(ii) a Lender does not supply a quotation by the time specified in paragraph (a)(ii) above,

the cost to that Lender of funding its participation in that Loan for that Interest Period shall be deemed, for the purposes of paragraph (a) above, to be LIBOR [or, in relation to a Loan in euro, EURIBOR] [or, in relation to a Loan in a Non-LIBOR Currency, the Benchmark Rate].]

(e) [If this Clause 11.4 applies [pursuant to Clause 11.1 (*Unavailability of Screen Rate*)][27] but any Lender does not supply a quotation by the time specified in paragraph (a)(ii) above the rate of interest shall be calculated on the basis of the quotations of the remaining Lenders.][28]

11.5 **Notification to Company**

If Clause 11.4 (*Cost of funds*) applies the Agent shall, as soon as is practicable, notify the Company.

11.6 **Break Costs**

(a) Each Borrower shall, within three Business Days of demand by a Finance Party, pay to that Finance Party its Break Costs attributable to all or any part of a Loan or Unpaid Sum being paid by that Borrower on a day other than the last day of an Interest Period for that Loan or Unpaid Sum.

(b) Each Lender shall, as soon as reasonably practicable after a demand by the Agent, provide a certificate confirming the amount of its Break Costs for any Interest Period in which they accrue.

[26] Include if cost of funds is not calculated on a weighted average basis.

[27] Include if paragraph (d) of Clause 11.4 (*Cost of funds*) is included.

[28] Include if cost of funds is calculated on a weighted average basis.

12. **FEES**

12.1 **Commitment fee**

(a) The Company shall pay to the Agent (for the account of each Lender) a fee [in the Base Currency] computed at the rate of:

(i) [______] per cent. per annum on that Lender's Available Commitment under Facility A for the Availability Period applicable to Facility A; and

(ii) [______] per cent. per annum on that Lender's Available Commitment under Facility B for the Availability Period applicable to Facility B.

(b) The accrued commitment fee is payable on the last day of each successive period of three Months which ends during the relevant Availability Period, on the last day of the Availability Period and, if cancelled in full, on the cancelled amount of the relevant Lender's Commitment at the time the cancellation is effective.

12.2 **Arrangement fee**

The Company shall pay to the Arranger an arrangement fee in the amount and at the times agreed in a Fee Letter.

12.3 **Agency fee**

The Company shall pay to the Agent (for its own account) an agency fee in the amount and at the times agreed in a Fee Letter.

**SECTION 6**
**ADDITIONAL PAYMENT OBLIGATIONS**

13. **TAX GROSS UP[29] AND INDEMNITIES**

13.1 **Definitions**

(a) In this Agreement:

"**Borrower DTTP Filing**" means an HM Revenue & Customs' Form DTTP2 duly completed and filed by the relevant Borrower, which:

(i) where it relates to a Treaty Lender that is an Original Lender, contains the scheme reference number and jurisdiction of tax residence stated opposite that Lender's name in Part II of Schedule 1 (*The Original Parties*), and

(A) where the Borrower is an Original Borrower, is filed with HM Revenue & Customs within 30 days of the date of this Agreement; or

(B) where the Borrower is an Additional Borrower, is filed with HM Revenue & Customs within 30 days of the date on which that Borrower becomes an Additional Borrower; or

(ii) where it relates to a Treaty Lender that is not an Original Lender, contains the scheme reference number and jurisdiction of tax residence stated in respect of that Lender in the documentation which it executes on becoming a Party as a Lender; and

(A) where the Borrower is a Borrower as at the date on which that Treaty Lender becomes a Party as a Lender, is filed with HM Revenue & Customs within 30 days of that date; or

(B) where the Borrower is not a Borrower as at the date on which that Treaty Lender becomes a Party as a Lender, is filed with HM Revenue & Customs within 30 days of the date on which that Borrower becomes an Additional Borrower.

"**Protected Party**" means a Finance Party which is or will be subject to any liability, or required to make any payment, for or on account of Tax in relation to a sum received or receivable (or any sum deemed for the purposes of Tax to be received or receivable) under a Finance Document.

[29] This clause is drafted on the assumption that payments made by the Obligor(s) may be subject to withholding tax (if any) under United Kingdom law and not under the law of any other jurisdiction. If this is not the case and the Obligor(s) is/are to gross-up payments, this Clause will need to be modified, in particular, paragraphs (d), (g), (h), (i), (j), (k) and (l) of Clause 13.2 (*Tax gross up*) and the related definitions. If the "Treaty Lender" concept is used, always check the wording of relevant Treaties.
**This clause, and in particular the definition of "Qualifying Lender", should always be considered on a case-by-case basis. Consideration should also be given as to whether the representation in Clause 19.7 (*Deduction of Tax*) requires amendment.**

"**Qualifying Lender**" means:

(i) a Lender which is beneficially entitled to interest payable to that Lender in respect of an advance under a Finance Document and is:

(A) a Lender:

(1) which is a bank (as defined for the purpose of section 879 of the ITA) making an advance under a Finance Document and is within the charge to United Kingdom corporation tax as respects any payments of interest made in respect of that advance or would be within such charge as respects such payments apart from section 18A of the CTA; or

(2) in respect of an advance made under a Finance Document by a person that was a bank (as defined for the purpose of section 879 of the ITA) at the time that that advance was made and within the charge to United Kingdom corporation tax as respects any payments of interest made in respect of that advance; or

(B) [a Lender which is:

(1) a company resident in the United Kingdom for United Kingdom tax purposes;

(2) a partnership each member of which is:

(a) a company so resident in the United Kingdom; or

(b) a company not so resident in the United Kingdom which carries on a trade in the United Kingdom through a permanent establishment and which brings into account in computing its chargeable profits (within the meaning of section 19 of the CTA) the whole of any share of interest payable in respect of that advance that falls to it by reason of Part 17 of the CTA;

(3) a company not so resident in the United Kingdom which carries on a trade in the United Kingdom through a permanent establishment and which brings into account interest payable in respect of that advance in computing the chargeable profits (within the meaning of section 19 of the CTA) of that company; or]

(C) a Treaty Lender[; or

(ii) a Lender which is a building society (as defined for the purpose of section 880 of the ITA) making an advance under a Finance Document].

["**Tax Confirmation**" means a confirmation by a Lender that the person beneficially entitled to interest payable to that Lender in respect of an advance under a Finance Document is either:

(i) a company resident in the United Kingdom for United Kingdom tax purposes;

(ii) a partnership each member of which is:

(A) a company so resident in the United Kingdom; or

(B) a company not so resident in the United Kingdom which carries on a trade in the United Kingdom through a permanent establishment and which brings into account in computing its chargeable profits (within the meaning of section 19 of the CTA) the whole of any share of interest payable in respect of that advance that falls to it by reason of Part 17 of the CTA; or

(iii) a company not so resident in the United Kingdom which carries on a trade in the United Kingdom through a permanent establishment and which brings into account interest payable in respect of that advance in computing the chargeable profits (within the meaning of section 19 of the CTA) of that company.]

"**Tax Credit**" means a credit against, relief or remission for, or repayment of any Tax.

"**Tax Deduction**" means a deduction or withholding for or on account of Tax from a payment under a Finance Document, other than a FATCA Deduction.[30]

"**Tax Payment**" means either the increase in a payment made by an Obligor to a Finance Party under Clause 13.2 (*Tax gross-up*) or a payment under Clause 13.3 (*Tax indemnity*).

"**Treaty Lender**" means a Lender which:

(i) is treated as a resident of a Treaty State for the purposes of the Treaty;

(ii) does not carry on a business in the United Kingdom through a permanent establishment with which that Lender's participation in the Loan is effectively connected [; and

(iii) ________][31].

"**Treaty State**" means a jurisdiction having a double taxation agreement (a "**Treaty**") with the United Kingdom which makes provision for full exemption from tax imposed by the United Kingdom on interest.

[30] This may not be appropriate for all circumstances (for instance for some emerging market financings). For further information see the LMA 2014 *Summary Note on FATCA* (available through the LMA website).

["**UK Non-Bank Lender**" means:

(i) an Original Lender listed in Part III of Schedule 1 (*The Original Parties*); and[32]

(ii) a Lender which is not an Original Lender and which gives a Tax Confirmation in the documentation which it executes on becoming a Party as a Lender.]

(b) Unless a contrary indication appears, in this Clause 13 a reference to "determines" or "determined" means a determination made in the absolute discretion of the person making the determination.

13.2 **Tax gross-up**

(a) Each Obligor shall make all payments to be made by it without any Tax Deduction, unless a Tax Deduction is required by law.

(b) The Company shall promptly upon becoming aware that an Obligor must make a Tax Deduction (or that there is any change in the rate or the basis of a Tax Deduction) notify the Agent accordingly. Similarly, a Lender shall notify the Agent on becoming so aware in respect of a payment payable to that Lender. If the Agent receives such notification from a Lender it shall notify the Company and that Obligor.

(c) If a Tax Deduction is required by law to be made by an Obligor, the amount of the payment due from that Obligor shall be increased to an amount which (after making any Tax Deduction) leaves an amount equal to the payment which would have been due if no Tax Deduction had been required.

(d) A payment shall not be increased under paragraph (c) above by reason of a Tax Deduction on account of Tax imposed by the United Kingdom, if on the date on which the payment falls due:

(i) the payment could have been made to the relevant Lender without a Tax Deduction if the Lender had been a Qualifying Lender, but on that date that Lender is not or has ceased to be a Qualifying Lender other than as a result of any change after the date it became a Lender under this Agreement in (or in the interpretation, administration, or application of)

[31] This is a complex area and in each case relevant treaties should be reviewed and, if appropriate, additional wording inserted to apportion risk as agreed by the Parties.

[32] If UK Non-Bank Lenders are to be envisaged and this definition is, therefore, included but no Original Lender is a UK Non-Bank Lender:

- delete this paragraph (i);
- delete Part III of Schedule 1 (*The Original Parties*); and
- delete the words "other than UK Non-Bank Lenders" from the heading of Part II of Schedule 1 (*The Original Parties*).

**Do not**, however, delete this definition, as a UK Non-Bank Lender may become a Lender after the date of this Agreement.

any law or Treaty or any published practice or published concession of any relevant taxing authority[; or

(ii) the relevant Lender is a Qualifying Lender solely by virtue of paragraph (i)(B) of the definition of Qualifying Lender and:

(A) an officer of H.M. Revenue & Customs has given (and not revoked) a direction (a "**Direction**") under section 931 of the ITA which relates to the payment and that Lender has received from the Obligor making the payment or from the Company a certified copy of that Direction; and

(B) the payment could have been made to the Lender without any Tax Deduction if that Direction had not been made; or

(iii) the relevant Lender is a Qualifying Lender solely by virtue of paragraph (i)(B) of the definition of Qualifying Lender and:

(A) the relevant Lender has not given a Tax Confirmation to the Company; and

(B) the payment could have been made to the Lender without any Tax Deduction if the Lender had given a Tax Confirmation to the Company, on the basis that the Tax Confirmation would have enabled the Company to have formed a reasonable belief that the payment was an "excepted payment" for the purpose of section 930 of the ITA]; or

(iv) the relevant Lender is a Treaty Lender and the Obligor making the payment is able to demonstrate that the payment could have been made to the Lender without the Tax Deduction had that Lender complied with its obligations under paragraph (g) or (h) (as applicable) below.

(e) If an Obligor is required to make a Tax Deduction, that Obligor shall make that Tax Deduction and any payment required in connection with that Tax Deduction within the time allowed and in the minimum amount required by law.

(f) Within thirty days of making either a Tax Deduction or any payment required in connection with that Tax Deduction, the Obligor making that Tax Deduction shall deliver to the Agent for the Finance Party entitled to the payment a statement under section 975 of the ITA or other evidence reasonably satisfactory to that Finance Party that the Tax Deduction has been made or (as applicable) any appropriate payment paid to the relevant taxing authority.

(g)

(i) Subject to paragraph (ii) below, a Treaty Lender and each Obligor which makes a payment to which that Treaty Lender is entitled shall co-operate in completing any procedural formalities necessary for that Obligor to obtain authorisation to make that payment without a Tax Deduction.

(ii)

(A) A Treaty Lender which is an Original Lender and that holds a passport under the HMRC DT Treaty Passport scheme, and which wishes that scheme to apply to this Agreement, shall confirm its scheme reference number and its jurisdiction of tax residence opposite its name in Part II of Schedule 1 (*The Original Parties*); and

(B) a Treaty Lender which is not an Original Lender and that holds a passport under the HMRC DT Treaty Passport scheme, and which wishes that scheme to apply to this Agreement, shall confirm its scheme reference number and its jurisdiction of tax residence in the documentation which it executes on becoming a Party as a Lender,

and, having done so, that Lender shall be under no obligation pursuant to paragraph (i) above.

(h) If a Lender has confirmed its scheme reference number and its jurisdiction of tax residence in accordance with paragraph (g)(ii) above and:

(i) a Borrower making a payment to that Lender has not made a Borrower DTTP Filing in respect of that Lender; or

(ii) a Borrower making a payment to that Lender has made a Borrower DTTP Filing in respect of that Lender but:

(A) that Borrower DTTP Filing has been rejected by HM Revenue & Customs; or

(B) HM Revenue & Customs has not given the Borrower authority to make payments to that Lender without a Tax Deduction within [60] days of the date of the Borrower DTTP Filing,

and in each case, the Borrower has notified that Lender in writing, that Lender and the Borrower shall co-operate in completing any additional procedural formalities necessary for that Borrower to obtain authorisation to make that payment without a Tax Deduction.

(i) If a Lender has not confirmed its scheme reference number and jurisdiction of tax residence in accordance with paragraph (g)(ii) above, no Obligor shall make a Borrower DTTP Filing or file any other form relating to the HMRC DT Treaty Passport scheme in respect of that Lender's Commitment(s) or its participation in any Loan unless the Lender otherwise agrees.

(j) A Borrower shall, promptly on making a Borrower DTTP Filing, deliver a copy of that Borrower DTTP Filing to the Agent for delivery to the relevant Lender.

(k) [A UK Non-Bank Lender which is an Original Lender gives a Tax Confirmation to the Company by entering into this Agreement.

(l) A UK Non-Bank Lender shall promptly notify the Company and the Agent if there is any change in the position from that set out in the Tax Confirmation.]

13.3 **Tax indemnity**

(a) The Company shall (within three Business Days of demand by the Agent) pay to a Protected Party an amount equal to the loss, liability or cost which that Protected Party determines will be or has been (directly or indirectly) suffered for or on account of Tax by that Protected Party in respect of a Finance Document.

(b) Paragraph (a) above shall not apply:

(i) with respect to any Tax assessed on a Finance Party:

(A) under the law of the jurisdiction in which that Finance Party is incorporated or, if different, the jurisdiction (or jurisdictions) in which that Finance Party is treated as resident for tax purposes; or

(B) under the law of the jurisdiction in which that Finance Party's Facility Office is located in respect of amounts received or receivable in that jurisdiction,

if that Tax is imposed on or calculated by reference to the net income received or receivable (but not any sum deemed to be received or receivable) by that Finance Party; or

(ii) to the extent a loss, liability or cost:

(A) is compensated for by an increased payment under Clause 13.2 (*Tax gross-up*);

(B) would have been compensated for by an increased payment under Clause 13.2 (*Tax gross-up*) but was not so compensated solely because one of the exclusions in paragraph (d) of Clause 13.2 (*Tax gross-up*) applied; or

(C) relates to a FATCA Deduction required to be made by a Party.[33]

(c) A Protected Party making, or intending to make, a claim under paragraph (a) above shall promptly notify the Agent of the event which will give, or has given, rise to the claim, following which the Agent shall notify the Company.

(d) A Protected Party shall, on receiving a payment from an Obligor under this Clause 13.3, notify the Agent.

[33] This may not be appropriate for all circumstances (for instance for some emerging market financings). For further information see the LMA *2014 Summary Note on FATCA* (available through the LMA website).

13.4 **Tax Credit**

If an Obligor makes a Tax Payment and the relevant Finance Party determines that:

(a) a Tax Credit is attributable to an increased payment of which that Tax Payment forms part, to that Tax Payment or to a Tax Deduction in consequence of which that Tax Payment was required; and

(b) that Finance Party has obtained and utilised that Tax Credit,

the Finance Party shall pay an amount to the Obligor which that Finance Party determines will leave it (after that payment) in the same after-Tax position as it would have been in had the Tax Payment not been required to be made by the Obligor.

13.5 **Lender status confirmation**

Each Lender which is not an Original Lender shall indicate, in the documentation which it executes on becoming a Party as a Lender, and for the benefit of the Agent and without liability to any Obligor, which of the following categories it falls in:

(a) not a Qualifying Lender;

(b) a Qualifying Lender (other than a Treaty Lender); or

(c) a Treaty Lender.

If such a Lender fails to indicate its status in accordance with this Clause 13.5 then that Lender shall be treated for the purposes of this Agreement (including by each Obligor) as if it is not a Qualifying Lender until such time as it notifies the Agent which category applies (and the Agent, upon receipt of such notification, shall inform the Company). For the avoidance of doubt, the documentation which a Lender executes on becoming a Party as a Lender shall not be invalidated by any failure of a Lender to comply with this Clause 13.5.

13.6 **Stamp taxes**

The Company shall pay and, within three Business Days of demand, indemnify each Finance Party against any cost, loss or liability that Finance Party incurs in relation to all stamp duty, registration and other similar Taxes payable in respect of any Finance Document.

13.7 **VAT**

(a) All amounts expressed to be payable under a Finance Document by any Party to a Finance Party which (in whole or in part) constitute the consideration for any supply for VAT purposes are deemed to be exclusive of any VAT which is chargeable on that supply, and accordingly, subject to paragraph (b) below, if VAT is or becomes chargeable on any supply made by any Finance Party to any Party under a Finance Document and such Finance Party is required to account to the relevant tax authority for the VAT, that Party must pay to such Finance Party (in addition to and at the same time as paying any other consideration for such supply) an amount equal to the amount of the VAT (and such Finance Party must promptly provide an appropriate VAT invoice to that Party).

(b) If VAT is or becomes chargeable on any supply made by any Finance Party (the "**Supplier**") to any other Finance Party (the "**Recipient**") under a Finance Document, and any Party other than the Recipient (the "**Relevant Party**") is required by the terms of any Finance Document to pay an amount equal to the consideration for that supply to the Supplier (rather than being required to reimburse or indemnify the Recipient in respect of that consideration):

(i) (where the Supplier is the person required to account to the relevant tax authority for the VAT) the Relevant Party must also pay to the Supplier (at the same time as paying that amount) an additional amount equal to the amount of the VAT. The Recipient must (where this paragraph (i) applies) promptly pay to the Relevant Party an amount equal to any credit or repayment the Recipient receives from the relevant tax authority which the Recipient reasonably determines relates to the VAT chargeable on that supply; and

(ii) (where the Recipient is the person required to account to the relevant tax authority for the VAT) the Relevant Party must promptly, following demand from the Recipient, pay to the Recipient an amount equal to the VAT chargeable on that supply but only to the extent that the Recipient reasonably determines that it is not entitled to credit or repayment from the relevant tax authority in respect of that VAT.

(c) Where a Finance Document requires any Party to reimburse or indemnify a Finance Party for any cost or expense, that Party shall reimburse or indemnify (as the case may be) such Finance Party for the full amount of such cost or expense, including such part thereof as represents VAT, save to the extent that such Finance Party reasonably determines that it is entitled to credit or repayment in respect of such VAT from the relevant tax authority.

(d) Any reference in this Clause 13.7 to any Party shall, at any time when such Party is treated as a member of a group for VAT purposes, include (where appropriate and unless the context otherwise requires) a reference to the representative member of such group at such time (the term "representative member" to have the same meaning as in the Value Added Tax Act 1994)[34].

(e) In relation to any supply made by a Finance Party to any Party under a Finance Document, if reasonably requested by such Finance Party, that Party must promptly provide such Finance Party with details of that Party's VAT registration and such other information as is reasonably requested in connection with such Finance Party's VAT reporting requirements in relation to such supply [35].

[34] This provision does not operate in an international context, so where there is an international context, this wording should be reviewed and updated accordingly.

[35] This provision does not operate for the benefit of non-Finance Parties and whether this is correct should be considered on a case by case basis.

13.8 **FATCA information**

(a) Subject to paragraph (c) below, each Party shall, within [ten] Business Days of a reasonable request by another Party:

(i) confirm to that other Party whether it is:

(A) a FATCA Exempt Party; or

(B) not a FATCA Exempt Party;

(ii) supply to that other Party such forms, documentation and other information relating to its status under FATCA as that other Party reasonably requests for the purposes of that other Party's compliance with FATCA; and

(iii) supply to that other Party such forms, documentation and other information relating to its status as that other Party reasonably requests for the purposes of that other Party's compliance with any other law, regulation, or exchange of information regime.

(b) If a Party confirms to another Party pursuant to paragraph (a)(i) above that it is a FATCA Exempt Party and it subsequently becomes aware that it is not or has ceased to be a FATCA Exempt Party, that Party shall notify that other Party reasonably promptly.

(c) Paragraph (a) above shall not oblige any Finance Party to do anything, and paragraph (a)(iii) above shall not oblige any other Party to do anything, which would or might in its reasonable opinion constitute a breach of:

(i) any law or regulation;

(ii) any fiduciary duty; or

(iii) any duty of confidentiality.

(d) If a Party fails to confirm whether or not it is a FATCA Exempt Party or to supply forms, documentation or other information requested in accordance with paragraph (a)(i) or (a)(ii) above (including, for the avoidance of doubt, where paragraph (c) above applies), then such Party shall be treated for the purposes of the Finance Documents (and payments under them) as if it is not a FATCA Exempt Party until such time as the Party in question provides the requested confirmation, forms, documentation or other information.

(e) [If a Borrower is a US Tax Obligor or the Agent reasonably believes that its obligations under FATCA or any other applicable law or regulation require it, each Lender shall, within [ten] Business Days of:

(i) where an Original Borrower is a US Tax Obligor and the relevant Lender is an Original Lender, the date of this Agreement;

(ii) where a Borrower is a US Tax Obligor on a date on which any other Lender becomes a Party as a Lender, that date;

(iii) the date a new US Tax Obligor accedes as a Borrower; or

(iv) where a Borrower is not a US Tax Obligor, the date of a request from the Agent,

supply to the Agent:

(A) a withholding certificate on Form W-8, Form W-9 or any other relevant form; or

(B) any withholding statement or other document, authorisation or waiver as the Agent may require to certify or establish the status of such Lender under FATCA or that other law or regulation.

(f) The Agent shall provide any withholding certificate, withholding statement, document, authorisation or waiver it receives from a Lender pursuant to paragraph (e) above to the relevant Borrower.

(g) If any withholding certificate, withholding statement, document, authorisation or waiver provided to the Agent by a Lender pursuant to paragraph (e) above is or becomes materially inaccurate or incomplete, that Lender shall promptly update it and provide such updated withholding certificate, withholding statement, document, authorisation or waiver to the Agent unless it is unlawful for the Lender to do so (in which case the Lender shall promptly notify the Agent). The Agent shall provide any such updated withholding certificate, withholding statement, document, authorisation or waiver to the relevant Borrower.

(h) The Agent may rely on any withholding certificate, withholding statement, document, authorisation or waiver it receives from a Lender pursuant to paragraph (e) or (g) above without further verification. The Agent shall not be liable for any action taken by it under or in connection with paragraphs (e), (f) or (g) above.][36]

13.9 **FATCA Deduction**[37]

(a) Each Party may make any FATCA Deduction it is required to make by FATCA, and any payment required in connection with that FATCA Deduction, and no Party shall be required to increase any payment in respect of which it makes such a FATCA Deduction or otherwise compensate the recipient of the payment for that FATCA Deduction.

(b) Each Party shall promptly, upon becoming aware that it must make a FATCA Deduction (or that there is any change in the rate or the basis of such FATCA

[36] Paragraphs (e), (f), (g) and (h) of Clause 13.8 (*FATCA information*) may be used for loans entered into with US borrowers (or loans where a US borrower may become an Additional Borrower).

[37] This Clause may not be appropriate for all circumstances (for instance for some emerging market financings). For further information see the LMA *2014 Summary Note on FATCA* (available through the LMA website).

Deduction), notify the Party to whom it is making the payment and, in addition, shall notify the Company and the Agent and the Agent shall notify the other Finance Parties.

14. **INCREASED COSTS**

14.1 **Increased costs**[38]

(a) Subject to Clause 14.3 (*Exceptions*) the Company shall, within three Business Days of a demand by the Agent, pay for the account of a Finance Party the amount of any Increased Costs incurred by that Finance Party or any of its Affiliates as a result of (i) the introduction of or any change in (or in the interpretation, administration or application of) any law or regulation or (ii) compliance with any law or regulation made after the date of this Agreement.

(b) In this Agreement "**Increased Costs**" means:

(i) a reduction in the rate of return from a Facility or on a Finance Party's (or its Affiliate's) overall capital;

(ii) an additional or increased cost; or

(iii) a reduction of any amount due and payable under any Finance Document,

which is incurred or suffered by a Finance Party or any of its Affiliates to the extent that it is attributable to that Finance Party having entered into its Commitment or funding or performing its obligations under any Finance Document.

14.2 **Increased cost claims**

(a) A Finance Party intending to make a claim pursuant to Clause 14.1 (*Increased costs*) shall notify the Agent of the event giving rise to the claim, following which the Agent shall promptly notify the Company.

(b) Each Finance Party shall, as soon as practicable after a demand by the Agent, provide a certificate confirming the amount of its Increased Costs.

[38] The form of increased costs clause in this Agreement is drafted in deliberately wide terms in an attempt to cover all circumstances which could increase a Lender's costs as a result of a change in law or regulation. The European legislation (often referred to as "**CRD IV**") which implements the Basel Committee on Banking Supervision's proposed new standards for bank capital and liquidity requirements (labelled "**Basel III**") has come into force and potentially involves greater costs than those envisaged by Basel III. Users may wish to consider whether to supplement the clause to address expressly the extent to which both Basel III costs and CRD IV costs are intended to be within, or outside, the scope of the clause.

14.3 **Exceptions**[39]

(a) Clause 14.1 (*Increased costs*) does not apply to the extent any Increased Cost is:

(i) attributable to a Tax Deduction required by law to be made by an Obligor;

(ii) attributable to a FATCA Deduction required to be made by a Party;[40]

(iii) compensated for by Clause 13.3 (*Tax indemnity*) (or would have been compensated for under Clause 13.3 (*Tax indemnity*) but was not so compensated solely because any of the exclusions in paragraph (b) of Clause 13.3 (*Tax indemnity*) applied);

(iv) [compensated for by the payment of the Mandatory Cost;] or

(v) attributable to the wilful breach by the relevant Finance Party or its Affiliates of any law or regulation.

(b) In this Clause 14.3, a reference to a "**Tax Deduction**" has the same meaning given to that term in Clause 13.1 (*Definitions*).

[39] Basel II was finalised in 2004 and implemented in Europe during 2007 and so it may not be necessary to include a Basel II carve out from the increased costs clause where the syndicate consists of European Lenders. If it is agreed by the parties to exclude Basel II from the increased costs clause, and for example this may be relevant where there are US Lenders in the syndicate as Basel II has not been fully implemented in the US, then users should note that elements of the Basel III papers amend the Basel II paper and so care needs to be taken with the drafting of the carve out. The following provision may be inserted at the end of this paragraph (a) of Clause 14.3 (*Exceptions*) to address this point:

"(vi) attributable to the implementation or application of or compliance with the "International Convergence of Capital Measurement and Capital Standards, a Revised Framework" published by the Basel Committee on Banking Supervision in June 2004 in the form existing on the date of this Agreement (but excluding any amendment arising out of Basel III) ("**Basel II**") or any other law or regulation which implements Basel II (whether such implementation, application or compliance is by a government, regulator, Finance Party or any of its Affiliates)."

The following definition should be added to paragraph (b) of Clause 14.1 (*Increased costs*):

""**Basel III**" means:

(A) the agreements on capital requirements, a leverage ratio and liquidity standards contained in "Basel III: A global regulatory framework for more resilient banks and banking systems", "Basel III: International framework for liquidity risk measurement, standards and monitoring" and "Guidance for national authorities operating the countercyclical capital buffer" published by the Basel Committee on Banking Supervision in December 2010, each as amended, supplemented or restated;

(B) the rules for global systemically important banks contained in "Global systemically important banks: assessment methodology and the additional loss absorbency requirement – Rules text" published by the Basel Committee on Banking Supervision in November 2011, as amended, supplemented or restated; and

(C) any further guidance or standards published by the Basel Committee on Banking Supervision relating to "Basel III"."

Users should note that this definition of Basel III is deliberately wide and includes future Basel III publications. It is, therefore, unlikely to be suitable to describe Basel III in the context of **excluding** Basel III costs from the scope of the increased costs clause generally.

[40] This may not be appropriate for all circumstances (for instance for some emerging market financings). For further information see the LMA *2014 Summary Note on FATCA* (available through the LMA website).

## 15. OTHER INDEMNITIES

### 15.1 Currency indemnity

(a) If any sum due from an Obligor under the Finance Documents (a "**Sum**"), or any order, judgment or award given or made in relation to a Sum, has to be converted from the currency (the "**First Currency**") in which that Sum is payable into another currency (the "**Second Currency**") for the purpose of:

(i) making or filing a claim or proof against that Obligor;

(ii) obtaining or enforcing an order, judgment or award in relation to any litigation or arbitration proceedings,

that Obligor shall as an independent obligation, within three Business Days of demand, indemnify each Finance Party to whom that Sum is due against any cost, loss or liability arising out of or as a result of the conversion including any discrepancy between (A) the rate of exchange used to convert that Sum from the First Currency into the Second Currency and (B) the rate or rates of exchange available to that person at the time of its receipt of that Sum.

(b) Each Obligor waives any right it may have in any jurisdiction to pay any amount under the Finance Documents in a currency or currency unit other than that in which it is expressed to be payable.

### 15.2 Other indemnities

The Company shall (or shall procure that an Obligor will), within three Business Days of demand, indemnify each Finance Party against any cost, loss or liability incurred by that Finance Party as a result of:

(a) the occurrence of any Event of Default;

(b) a failure by an Obligor to pay any amount due under a Finance Document on its due date, including without limitation, any cost, loss or liability arising as a result of Clause 28 (*Sharing among the Finance Parties*);

(c) funding, or making arrangements to fund, its participation in a Loan requested by a Borrower in a Utilisation Request but not made by reason of the operation of any one or more of the provisions of this Agreement (other than by reason of default or negligence by that Finance Party alone); or

(d) a Loan (or part of a Loan) not being prepaid in accordance with a notice of prepayment given by a Borrower or the Company.

### 15.3 Indemnity to the Agent

The Company shall promptly indemnify the Agent against any cost, loss or liability incurred by the Agent (acting reasonably) as a result of:

(a) investigating any event which it reasonably believes is a Default;

(b) entering into or performing any foreign exchange contract for the purposes of paragraph (b) of Clause 6.3 (*Change of currency*);

(c) acting or relying on any notice, request or instruction which it reasonably believes to be genuine, correct and appropriately authorised; or

(d) instructing lawyers, accountants, tax advisers, surveyors or other professional advisers or experts as permitted under this Agreement.

## 16. MITIGATION BY THE LENDERS

### 16.1 Mitigation

(a) Each Finance Party shall, in consultation with the Company, take all reasonable steps to mitigate any circumstances which arise and which would result in any amount becoming payable under or pursuant to, or cancelled pursuant to, any of Clause 8.1 (*Illegality*), Clause 13 (*Tax gross-up and indemnities*) or Clause 14 (*Increased costs*) including (but not limited to) transferring its rights and obligations under the Finance Documents to another Affiliate or Facility Office.

(b) Paragraph (a) above does not in any way limit the obligations of any Obligor under the Finance Documents.

### 16.2 Limitation of liability

(a) The Company shall promptly indemnify each Finance Party for all costs and expenses reasonably incurred by that Finance Party as a result of steps taken by it under Clause 16.1 (*Mitigation*).

(b) A Finance Party is not obliged to take any steps under Clause 16.1 (*Mitigation*) if, in the opinion of that Finance Party (acting reasonably), to do so might be prejudicial to it.

## 17. COSTS AND EXPENSES

### 17.1 Transaction expenses

The Company shall promptly on demand pay the Agent and the Arranger the amount of all costs and expenses (including legal fees) reasonably incurred by any of them in connection with the negotiation, preparation, printing, execution and syndication of:

(a) this Agreement and any other documents referred to in this Agreement; and

(b) any other Finance Documents executed after the date of this Agreement.

### 17.2 Amendment costs

If:

(a) an Obligor requests an amendment, waiver or consent; or

(b) an amendment is required pursuant to Clause 29.9 (*Change of currency*),

the Company shall, within three Business Days of demand, reimburse the Agent for the amount of all costs and expenses (including legal fees) reasonably incurred by the Agent in responding to, evaluating, negotiating or complying with that request or requirement.

17.3 **Enforcement costs**

The Company shall, within three Business Days of demand, pay to each Finance Party the amount of all costs and expenses (including legal fees) incurred by that Finance Party in connection with the enforcement of, or the preservation of any rights under, any Finance Document.

**SECTION 7**
**GUARANTEE**

## 18. GUARANTEE AND INDEMNITY

### 18.1 Guarantee and indemnity

Each Guarantor irrevocably and unconditionally jointly and severally:

(a) guarantees to each Finance Party punctual performance by each Borrower of all that Borrower's obligations under the Finance Documents;

(b) undertakes with each Finance Party that whenever a Borrower does not pay any amount when due under or in connection with any Finance Document, that Guarantor shall immediately on demand pay that amount as if it was the principal obligor; and

(c) agrees with each Finance Party that if any obligation guaranteed by it is or becomes unenforceable, invalid or illegal, it will, as an independent and primary obligation, indemnify that Finance Party immediately on demand against any cost, loss or liability it incurs as a result of a Borrower not paying any amount which would, but for such unenforceability, invalidity or illegality, have been payable by it under any Finance Document on the date when it would have been due. The amount payable by a Guarantor under this indemnity will not exceed the amount it would have had to pay under this Clause 18 if the amount claimed had been recoverable on the basis of a guarantee.

### 18.2 Continuing guarantee

This guarantee is a continuing guarantee and will extend to the ultimate balance of sums payable by any Obligor under the Finance Documents, regardless of any intermediate payment or discharge in whole or in part.

### 18.3 Reinstatement

If any discharge, release or arrangement (whether in respect of the obligations of any Obligor or any security for those obligations or otherwise) is made by a Finance Party in whole or in part on the basis of any payment, security or other disposition which is avoided or must be restored in insolvency, liquidation, administration or otherwise, without limitation, then the liability of each Guarantor under this Clause 18 will continue or be reinstated as if the discharge, release or arrangement had not occurred.

### 18.4 Waiver of defences

The obligations of each Guarantor under this Clause 18 will not be affected by an act, omission, matter or thing which, but for this Clause, would reduce, release or prejudice any of its obligations under this Clause 18 (without limitation and whether or not known to it or any Finance Party) including:

(a) any time, waiver or consent granted to, or composition with, any Obligor or other person;

(b) the release of any other Obligor or any other person under the terms of any composition or arrangement with any creditor of any member of the Group;

(c) the taking, variation, compromise, exchange, renewal or release of, or refusal or neglect to perfect, take up or enforce, any rights against, or security over assets of, any Obligor or other person or any non-presentation or non-observance of any formality or other requirement in respect of any instrument or any failure to realise the full value of any security;

(d) any incapacity or lack of power, authority or legal personality of or dissolution or change in the members or status of an Obligor or any other person;

(e) any amendment, novation, supplement, extension, restatement (however fundamental and whether or not more onerous) or replacement of any Finance Document or any other document or security including without limitation any change in the purpose of, any extension of or any increase in any facility or the addition of any new facility under any Finance Document or other document or security;

(f) any unenforceability, illegality or invalidity of any obligation of any person under any Finance Document or any other document or security; or

(g) any insolvency or similar proceedings.

18.5 **Immediate recourse**

Each Guarantor waives any right it may have of first requiring any Finance Party (or any trustee or agent on its behalf) to proceed against or enforce any other rights or security or claim payment from any person before claiming from that Guarantor under this Clause 18. This waiver applies irrespective of any law or any provision of a Finance Document to the contrary.

18.6 **Appropriations**

Until all amounts which may be or become payable by the Obligors under or in connection with the Finance Documents have been irrevocably paid in full, each Finance Party (or any trustee or agent on its behalf) may:

(a) refrain from applying or enforcing any other moneys, security or rights held or received by that Finance Party (or any trustee or agent on its behalf) in respect of those amounts, or apply and enforce the same in such manner and order as it sees fit (whether against those amounts or otherwise) and no Guarantor shall be entitled to the benefit of the same; and

(b) hold in an interest-bearing suspense account any moneys received from any Guarantor or on account of any Guarantor's liability under this Clause 18.

18.7 **Deferral of Guarantors' rights**

Until all amounts which may be or become payable by the Obligors under or in connection with the Finance Documents have been irrevocably paid in full and unless the Agent otherwise directs, no Guarantor will exercise any rights which it may have by reason of performance by it of its obligations under the Finance Documents or by reason of any amount being payable, or liability arising, under this Clause 18:

(a) to be indemnified by an Obligor;

(b) to claim any contribution from any other guarantor of any Obligor's obligations under the Finance Documents;

(c) to take the benefit (in whole or in part and whether by way of subrogation or otherwise) of any rights of the Finance Parties under the Finance Documents or of any other guarantee or security taken pursuant to, or in connection with, the Finance Documents by any Finance Party;

(d) to bring legal or other proceedings for an order requiring any Obligor to make any payment, or perform any obligation, in respect of which any Guarantor has given a guarantee, undertaking or indemnity under Clause 18.1 (*Guarantee and indemnity*);

(e) to exercise any right of set-off against any Obligor; and/or

(f) to claim or prove as a creditor of any Obligor in competition with any Finance Party.

If a Guarantor receives any benefit, payment or distribution in relation to such rights it shall hold that benefit, payment or distribution to the extent necessary to enable all amounts which may be or become payable to the Finance Parties by the Obligors under or in connection with the Finance Documents to be repaid in full on trust for the Finance Parties and shall promptly pay or transfer the same to the Agent or as the Agent may direct for application in accordance with Clause 29 (*Payment mechanics*).

18.8 **Release of Guarantors' right of contribution**

If any Guarantor (a "**Retiring Guarantor**") ceases to be a Guarantor in accordance with the terms of the Finance Documents for the purpose of any sale or other disposal of that Retiring Guarantor then on the date such Retiring Guarantor ceases to be a Guarantor:

(a) that Retiring Guarantor is released by each other Guarantor from any liability (whether past, present or future and whether actual or contingent) to make a contribution to any other Guarantor arising by reason of the performance by any other Guarantor of its obligations under the Finance Documents; and

(b) each other Guarantor waives any rights it may have by reason of the performance of its obligations under the Finance Documents to take the benefit (in whole or in part and whether by way of subrogation or otherwise) of any rights of the Finance Parties under any Finance Document or of any other security taken pursuant to, or in connection with, any Finance Document where such rights or security are granted by or in relation to the assets of the Retiring Guarantor.

18.9 **Additional security**

This guarantee is in addition to and is not in any way prejudiced by any other guarantee or security now or subsequently held by any Finance Party.

## SECTION 8
## REPRESENTATIONS, UNDERTAKINGS AND EVENTS OF DEFAULT

### 19. REPRESENTATIONS[41]

Each Obligor makes the representations and warranties set out in this Clause 19 to each Finance Party on the date of this Agreement.

#### 19.1 Status

(a) It is a corporation, duly incorporated and validly existing under the law of its jurisdiction of incorporation.

(b) It and each of its Subsidiaries has the power to own its assets and carry on its business as it is being conducted.

#### 19.2 Binding obligations

The obligations expressed to be assumed by it in each Finance Document are, subject to any general principles of law limiting its obligations which are specifically referred to in any legal opinion delivered pursuant to Clause 4 (*Conditions of Utilisation*) or Clause 25 (*Changes to the Obligors*), legal, valid, binding and enforceable obligations.

#### 19.3 Non-conflict with other obligations

The entry into and performance by it of, and the transactions contemplated by, the Finance Documents do not and will not conflict with:

(a) any law or regulation applicable to it;

(b) its or any of its Subsidiaries' constitutional documents; or

(c) any agreement or instrument binding upon it or any of its Subsidiaries or any of its or any of its Subsidiaries' assets.

#### 19.4 Power and authority

It has the power to enter into, perform and deliver, and has taken all necessary action to authorise its entry into, performance and delivery of, the Finance Documents to which it is a party and the transactions contemplated by those Finance Documents.

[41] Lenders may wish to consider amendments, as appropriate, to reflect sanctions laws and regulations that may affect them depending on their jurisdiction of incorporation or business, for example US and EU sanctions (which may prohibit lenders from advancing funds to be made available to targets of any relevant sanctions authority, as well as other restrictions). In addition, lenders in some jurisdictions should take advice in relation to possible conflict of laws that may impact on their ability to include clauses of this nature. For further information see LMA Guidance Note: United States and European Union Sanctions (available through the LMA website).

If any clauses of this nature are included, users should note that some Lenders may have particular sensitivities to the amendment or waiver of any such clause. Users should consider the extent to which Clause 35.2 (*All Lender matters*) should be supplemented to require all Lender consent for such amendment or waiver.

19.5 **Validity and admissibility in evidence**
All Authorisations required or desirable:

(a) to enable it lawfully to enter into, exercise its rights and comply with its obligations in the Finance Documents to which it is a party; and

(b) to make the Finance Documents to which it is a party admissible in evidence in its jurisdiction of incorporation,

have been obtained or effected and are in full force and effect.

19.6 **Governing law and enforcement**

(a) The choice of English law as the governing law of the Finance Documents will be recognised and enforced in its jurisdiction of incorporation.

(b) Any judgment obtained in England in relation to a Finance Document will be recognised and enforced in its jurisdiction of incorporation.

19.7 **Deduction of Tax**[42]
It is not required to make any Tax Deduction (as defined in Clause 13.1 (*Definitions*)) from any payment it may make under any Finance Document to a Lender which is:

(a) a Qualifying Lender:

(i) falling within paragraph (i)(A) of the definition of "Qualifying Lender"; [or]

(ii) [except where a Direction has been given under section 931 of the ITA in relation to the payment concerned, falling within paragraph (i)(B) of the definition of "Qualifying Lender"][43]; or

(iii) [falling within paragraph (ii) of the definition of "Qualifying Lender" or;][44]

(b) a Treaty Lender and the payment is one specified in a direction given by the Commissioners of Revenue & Customs under Regulation 2 of the Double Taxation Relief (Taxes on Income) (General) Regulations 1970 (SI 1970/488).

19.8 **No filing or stamp taxes**
Under the law of its jurisdiction of incorporation it is not necessary that the Finance Documents be filed, recorded or enrolled with any court or other authority in that jurisdiction or that any stamp, registration or similar tax be paid on or in relation to the Finance Documents or the transactions contemplated by the Finance Documents.

[42] This representation should be considered on a case-by-case basis and modified, or deleted, as appropriate. If tax other than UK tax may be relevant, this should be taken into account.

[43] Include if paragraph (i)(B) of the definition of Qualifying Lender is included in Clause 13.1 (*Definitions*).

[44] Include if paragraph (ii) of the definition of Qualifying Lender is included in Clause 13.1 (*Definitions*).

19.9 **No default**

(a) No Event of Default is continuing or might reasonably be expected to result from the making of any Utilisation.

(b) No other event or circumstance is outstanding which constitutes a default under any other agreement or instrument which is binding on it or any of its Subsidiaries or to which its (or any of its Subsidiaries') assets are subject which might have a Material Adverse Effect.

19.10 **No misleading information**

(a) Any factual information provided by any member of the Group for the purposes of the Information Memorandum was true and accurate in all material respects as at the date it was provided or as at the date (if any) at which it is stated.

(b) The financial projections contained in the Information Memorandum have been prepared on the basis of recent historical information and on the basis of reasonable assumptions.

(c) Nothing has occurred or been omitted from the Information Memorandum and no information has been given or withheld that results in the information contained in the Information Memorandum being untrue or misleading in any material respect.

19.11 **Financial statements**

(a) Its Original Financial Statements were prepared in accordance with GAAP consistently applied [unless expressly disclosed to the Agent in writing to the contrary before the date of this Agreement].

(b) Its Original Financial Statements fairly present its financial condition as at the end of the relevant financial year and its results of operations during the relevant financial year (consolidated in the case of the Company) [unless expressly disclosed to the Agent in writing to the contrary before the date of this Agreement].

(c) There has been no material adverse change in its business or financial condition (or the business or consolidated financial condition of the Group, in the case of the Company) since [________________].

19.12 **Pari passu ranking**

Its payment obligations under the Finance Documents rank at least pari passu with the claims of all its other unsecured and unsubordinated creditors, except for obligations mandatorily preferred by law applying to companies generally.

19.13 **No proceedings**

(a) No litigation, arbitration or administrative proceedings of or before any court, arbitral body or agency which, if adversely determined, might reasonably be expected to have a Material Adverse Effect has or have (to the best of its knowledge and belief) been started or threatened against it or any of its Subsidiaries.

(b) No judgment or order of a court, arbitral body or agency which might reasonably be expected to have a Material Adverse Effect has (to the best of its knowledge and belief) been made against it or any of its Subsidiaries.

19.14 **Repetition**

The Repeating Representations are deemed to be made by each Obligor by reference to the facts and circumstances then existing on:

(a) the date of each Utilisation Request and the first day of each Interest Period; and

(b) in the case of an Additional Obligor, the day on which the company becomes (or it is proposed that the company becomes) an Additional Obligor.

20. **INFORMATION UNDERTAKINGS**

The undertakings in this Clause 20 remain in force from the date of this Agreement for so long as any amount is outstanding under the Finance Documents or any Commitment is in force.

20.1 **Financial statements**

The Company shall supply to the Agent in sufficient copies for all the Lenders:

(a) as soon as the same become available, but in any event within [______] days after the end of each of its financial years:

(i) its audited consolidated financial statements for that financial year; and

(ii) the audited financial statements of each Obligor for that financial year; and

(b) as soon as the same become available, but in any event within [______] days after the end of each half of each of its financial years:

(i) its consolidated financial statements for that financial half year[; and

(ii) the financial statements of each Obligor for that financial half year].

20.2 **Compliance Certificate**

(a) [The Company shall supply to the Agent, with each set of financial statements delivered pursuant to paragraph (a)(i) or (b)(i) of Clause 20.1 (*Financial statements*), a Compliance Certificate setting out (in reasonable detail) computations as to compliance with Clause 21 (*Financial Covenants*) as at the date as at which those financial statements were drawn up.

(b) Each Compliance Certificate shall be signed by two directors of the Company [and, if required to be delivered with the financial statements delivered pursuant to paragraph (a)(i) of Clause 20.1 (*Financial statements*), [shall be reported on by the Company's auditors in the form agreed by the Company and all the Lenders before the date of this Agreement]/[by the Company's auditors]].]

20.3 **Requirements as to financial statements**

(a) Each set of financial statements delivered by the Company pursuant to Clause 20.1 (*Financial statements*) shall be certified by a director of the relevant company as fairly presenting its financial condition as at the date as at which those financial statements were drawn up.

(b) [The Company shall procure that each set of financial statements delivered pursuant to Clause 20.1 (*Financial statements*) is prepared using GAAP.]

(c) [The Company shall procure that each set of financial statements of an Obligor delivered pursuant to Clause 20.1 (*Financial statements*) is prepared using GAAP, accounting practices and financial reference periods consistent with those applied in the preparation of the Original Financial Statements for that Obligor unless, in relation to any set of financial statements, it notifies the Agent that there has been a change in GAAP, the accounting practices or reference periods and its auditors (or, if appropriate, the auditors of the Obligor) deliver to the Agent:

(i) a description of any change necessary for those financial statements to reflect the GAAP, accounting practices and reference periods upon which that Obligor's Original Financial Statements were prepared; and

(ii) sufficient information, in form and substance as may be reasonably required by the Agent, to enable the Lenders to determine whether Clause 21 (*Financial covenants*) has been complied with and make an accurate comparison between the financial position indicated in those financial statements and that Obligor's Original Financial Statements.

Any reference in this Agreement to those financial statements shall be construed as a reference to those financial statements as adjusted to reflect the basis upon which the Original Financial Statements were prepared.]

20.4 **Information: miscellaneous**

The Company shall supply to the Agent (in sufficient copies for all the Lenders, if the Agent so requests):

(a) all documents dispatched by the Company to its shareholders (or any class of them) or its creditors generally at the same time as they are dispatched;

(b) promptly upon becoming aware of them, the details of any litigation, arbitration or administrative proceedings which are current, threatened or pending against any member of the Group, and which might, if adversely determined, have a Material Adverse Effect;

(c) promptly upon becoming aware of them, the details of any judgment or order of a court, arbitral body or agency which is made against any member of the Group, and which might have a Material Adverse Effect; and

(d) promptly, such further information regarding the financial condition, business and operations of any member of the Group as any Finance Party (through the Agent) may reasonably request.

20.5 **Notification of default**

(a) Each Obligor shall notify the Agent of any Default (and the steps, if any, being taken to remedy it) promptly upon becoming aware of its occurrence (unless that Obligor is aware that a notification has already been provided by another Obligor).

(b) Promptly upon a request by the Agent, the Company shall supply to the Agent a certificate signed by two of its directors or senior officers on its behalf certifying that no Default is continuing (or if a Default is continuing, specifying the Default and the steps, if any, being taken to remedy it).

20.6 **Use of websites**

(a) The Company may satisfy its obligation under this Agreement to deliver any information in relation to those Lenders (the "**Website Lenders**") who accept this method of communication by posting this information onto an electronic website designated by the Company and the Agent (the "**Designated Website**") if:

(i) the Agent expressly agrees (after consultation with each of the Lenders) that it will accept communication of the information by this method;

(ii) both the Company and the Agent are aware of the address of and any relevant password specifications for the Designated Website; and

(iii) the information is in a format previously agreed between the Company and the Agent.

If any Lender (a "**Paper Form Lender**") does not agree to the delivery of information electronically then the Agent shall notify the Company accordingly and the Company shall supply the information to the Agent (in sufficient copies for each Paper Form Lender) in paper form. In any event the Company shall supply the Agent with at least one copy in paper form of any information required to be provided by it.

(b) The Agent shall supply each Website Lender with the address of and any relevant password specifications for the Designated Website following designation of that website by the Company and the Agent.

(c) The Company shall promptly upon becoming aware of its occurrence notify the Agent if:

(i) the Designated Website cannot be accessed due to technical failure;

(ii) the password specifications for the Designated Website change;

(iii) any new information which is required to be provided under this Agreement is posted onto the Designated Website;

(iv) any existing information which has been provided under this Agreement and posted onto the Designated Website is amended; or

(v) the Company becomes aware that the Designated Website or any information posted onto the Designated Website is or has been infected by any electronic virus or similar software.

If the Company notifies the Agent under paragraph (c)(i) or paragraph (c)(v) above, all information to be provided by the Company under this Agreement after the date of that notice shall be supplied in paper form [unless and until the Agent and each Website Lender is satisfied that the circumstances giving rise to the notification are no longer continuing].

(d) Any Website Lender may request, through the Agent, one paper copy of any information required to be provided under this Agreement which is posted onto the Designated Website. The Company shall comply with any such request within ten Business Days.

20.7 **"Know your customer" checks**

(a) If:

(i) the introduction of or any change in (or in the interpretation, administration or application of) any law or regulation made after the date of this Agreement;

(ii) any change in the status of an Obligor (or of a Holding Company of an Obligor) after the date of this Agreement; or[45]

(iii) a proposed assignment or transfer by a Lender of any of its rights and obligations under this Agreement to a party that is not a Lender prior to such assignment or transfer,

obliges the Agent or any Lender (or, in the case of paragraph (iii) above, any prospective new Lender) to comply with "know your customer" or similar identification procedures in circumstances where the necessary information is not already available to it, each Obligor shall promptly upon the request of the Agent or any Lender supply, or procure the supply of, such documentation and other evidence as is reasonably requested by the Agent (for itself or on behalf of any Lender) or any Lender (for itself or, in the case of the event described in paragraph (iii) above, on behalf of any prospective new Lender) in order for the Agent, such Lender or, in the case of the event described in paragraph (iii) above, any prospective new Lender to carry out and be satisfied it has complied with all necessary "know your customer" or other similar checks under all

[45] If the Company is not listed, consideration should be given to the inclusion of changes in the composition of the shareholders of an Obligor (or of a Holding Company of an Obligor) in this provision. If the Company is listed but the Agreement does not give each Lender an individual right to require prepayment on a change of control of the Company, consideration should be given to the inclusion of a change of control of the Company in this provision.

applicable laws and regulations pursuant to the transactions contemplated in the Finance Documents.

(b) Each Lender shall promptly upon the request of the Agent supply, or procure the supply of, such documentation and other evidence as is reasonably requested by the Agent (for itself) in order for the Agent to carry out and be satisfied it has complied with all necessary "know your customer" or other similar checks under all applicable laws and regulations pursuant to the transactions contemplated in the Finance Documents.

(c) The Company shall, by not less than [10] Business Days' prior written notice to the Agent, notify the Agent (which shall promptly notify the Lenders) of its intention to request that one of its Subsidiaries becomes an Additional Obligor pursuant to Clause 25 (*Changes to the Obligors*).

(d) Following the giving of any notice pursuant to paragraph (c) above, if the accession of such Additional Obligor obliges the Agent or any Lender to comply with "know your customer" or similar identification procedures in circumstances where the necessary information is not already available to it, the Company shall promptly upon the request of the Agent or any Lender supply, or procure the supply of, such documentation and other evidence as is reasonably requested by the Agent (for itself or on behalf of any Lender) or any Lender (for itself or on behalf of any prospective new Lender) in order for the Agent or such Lender or any prospective new Lender to carry out and be satisfied it has complied with all necessary "know your customer" or other similar checks under all applicable laws and regulations pursuant to the accession of such Subsidiary to this Agreement as an Additional Obligor.

## 21. FINANCIAL COVENANTS

[•]

## 22. GENERAL UNDERTAKINGS[46]

The undertakings in this Clause 22 remain in force from the date of this Agreement for so long as any amount is outstanding under the Finance Documents or any Commitment is in force.

[46] Lenders may wish to consider amendments, as appropriate, to reflect sanctions laws and regulations that may affect them depending on their jurisdiction of incorporation or business, for example US and EU sanctions (which may prohibit lenders from advancing funds to be made available to targets of any relevant sanctions authority, as well as other restrictions). In addition, lenders in some jurisdictions should take advice in relation to possible conflict of laws that may impact on their ability to include clauses of this nature. For further information see LMA Guidance Note: United States and European Union Sanctions (available through the LMA website).

If any clauses of this nature are included, users should note that some Lenders may have particular sensitivities to the amendment or waiver of any such clause. Users should consider the extent to which Clause 35.2 (*All Lender matters*) should be supplemented to require all Lender consent for such amendment or waiver.

22.1 **Authorisations**

Each Obligor shall promptly:

(a) obtain, comply with and do all that is necessary to maintain in full force and effect; and

(b) supply certified copies to the Agent of,

any Authorisation required under any law or regulation of its jurisdiction of incorporation to enable it to perform its obligations under the Finance Documents and to ensure the legality, validity, enforceability or admissibility in evidence in its jurisdiction of incorporation of any Finance Document.

22.2 **Compliance with laws**

Each Obligor shall comply in all respects with all laws to which it may be subject, if failure so to comply would materially impair its ability to perform its obligations under the Finance Documents.

22.3 **Negative pledge**

In this Clause 22.3, "**Quasi-Security**" means an arrangement or transaction described in paragraph (b) below.

(a) No Obligor shall (and the Company shall ensure that no other member of the Group will) create or permit to subsist any Security over any of its assets.

(b) No Obligor shall (and the Company shall ensure that no other member of the Group will):

(i) sell, transfer or otherwise dispose of any of its assets on terms whereby they are or may be leased to or re-acquired by an Obligor [or any other member of the Group];

(ii) sell, transfer or otherwise dispose of any of its receivables on recourse terms;

(iii) enter into any arrangement under which money or the benefit of a bank or other account may be applied, set-off or made subject to a combination of accounts; or

(iv) enter into any other preferential arrangement having a similar effect,

in circumstances where the arrangement or transaction is entered into primarily as a method of raising Financial Indebtedness or of financing the acquisition of an asset.

(c) Paragraphs (a) and (b) above do not apply to any Security or (as the case may be) Quasi-Security, listed below:

(i) any Security or Quasi-Security listed in Schedule 10 (*Existing Security*) except to the extent the principal amount secured by that Security or Quasi-Security exceeds the amount stated in that Schedule;

(ii) any netting or set-off arrangement entered into by any member of the Group in the ordinary course of its banking arrangements for the purpose of netting debit and credit balances;

(iii) any payment or close out netting or set-off arrangement pursuant to any hedging transaction entered into by a member of the Group for the purpose of:

(A) hedging any risk to which any member of the Group is exposed in its ordinary course of trading; or

(B) its interest rate or currency management operations which are carried out in the ordinary course of business and for non-speculative purposes only,

excluding, in each case, any Security or Quasi-Security under a credit support arrangement in relation to a hedging transaction;

(iv) any lien arising by operation of law and in the ordinary course of trading;

(v) any Security or Quasi-Security over or affecting any asset acquired by a member of the Group after the date of this Agreement if:

(A) the Security or Quasi-Security was not created in contemplation of the acquisition of that asset by a member of the Group;

(B) the principal amount secured has not been increased in contemplation of or since the acquisition of that asset by a member of the Group; and

(C) the Security or Quasi-Security is removed or discharged within [____] months of the date of acquisition of such asset;

(vi) any Security or Quasi-Security over or affecting any asset of any company which becomes a member of the Group after the date of this Agreement, where the Security or Quasi-Security is created prior to the date on which that company becomes a member of the Group, if:

(A) the Security or Quasi-Security was not created in contemplation of the acquisition of that company;

(B) the principal amount secured has not increased in contemplation of or since the acquisition of that company; and

(C) the Security or Quasi-Security is removed or discharged within [____] months of that company becoming a member of the Group;

(vii) any Security or Quasi-Security entered into pursuant to any Finance Document;

(viii) any Security or Quasi-Security arising under any retention of title, hire purchase or conditional sale arrangement or arrangements having similar effect in respect of goods supplied to a member of the Group in the ordinary course of trading and on the supplier's standard or usual terms and not arising as a result of any default or omission by any member of the Group;

(ix) [________________]; or

(x) any Security or Quasi-Security securing indebtedness the principal amount of which (when aggregated with the principal amount of any other indebtedness which has the benefit of Security or Quasi-Security given by any member of the Group other than any permitted under paragraphs (i) to (ix) above) does not exceed [________] (or its equivalent in another currency or currencies).

22.4 **Disposals**

(a) No Obligor shall [(and the Company shall ensure that no other member of the Group will)], enter into a single transaction or a series of transactions (whether related or not) and whether voluntary or involuntary to sell, lease, transfer or otherwise dispose of any asset.

(b) Paragraph (a) above does not apply to any sale, lease, transfer or other disposal:

(i) made in the ordinary course of trading of the disposing entity;

(ii) of assets in exchange for other assets comparable or superior as to type, value and quality (other than an exchange of a non-cash asset for cash);

(iii) [________]; or

(iv) where the higher of the market value or consideration receivable (when aggregated with the higher of the market value or consideration receivable for any other sale, lease, transfer or other disposal, other than any permitted under paragraphs (i) to [(iii)] above) does not exceed [________] (or its equivalent in another currency or currencies) in any financial year.

22.5 **Merger**

(a) No Obligor shall (and the Company shall ensure that no other member of the Group will) enter into any amalgamation, demerger, merger or corporate reconstruction.

(b) Paragraph (a) above does not apply to any sale, lease, transfer or other disposal permitted pursuant to Clause 22.4 (*Disposals*).

22.6 **Change of business**

The Company shall procure that no substantial change is made to the general nature of the business of the Company or the Group from that carried on at the date of this Agreement.

23. **EVENTS OF DEFAULT**

Each of the events or circumstances set out in Clause 23 is an Event of Default (save for Clause 23.13 (*Acceleration*)).

23.1 **Non-payment**

An Obligor does not pay on the due date any amount payable pursuant to a Finance Document at the place and in the currency in which it is expressed to be payable unless:

(a) its failure to pay is caused by:

(i) administrative or technical error; or

(ii) a Disruption Event; and

(b) [payment is made within:

(i) (in the case of paragraph (a)(i) above) [ ] Business Days of its due date; or

(ii) (in the case of paragraph (a)(ii) above) [ ] Business Days of its due date.] / **OR**

[payment is made within [ ] Business Days of its due date.]

23.2 **Financial covenants**

Any requirement of Clause 21 (*Financial covenants*) is not satisfied.

23.3 **Other obligations**

(a) An Obligor does not comply with any provision of the Finance Documents (other than those referred to in Clause 23.1 (*Non-payment*) [and Clause 23.2 (*Financial covenants*)]).

(b) No Event of Default under paragraph (a) above in relation to Clause [_____] will occur if the failure to comply is capable of remedy and is remedied within:

(i) (in relation to [_________]) [____] Business Days; or

(ii) (in relation to [_________]) [____] Business Days,

of the earlier of (A) the Agent giving notice to the Company and (B) the Company becoming aware of the failure to comply.

23.4 **Misrepresentation**

Any representation or statement made or deemed to be made by an Obligor in the Finance Documents or any other document delivered by or on behalf of any Obligor under or in connection with any Finance Document is or proves to have been incorrect or misleading in any material respect when made or deemed to be made.

23.5 **Cross default**

(a) Any Financial Indebtedness of any member of the Group is not paid when due nor within any originally applicable grace period.

(b) Any Financial Indebtedness of any member of the Group is declared to be or otherwise becomes due and payable prior to its specified maturity as a result of an event of default (however described).

(c) Any commitment for any Financial Indebtedness of any member of the Group is cancelled or suspended by a creditor of any member of the Group as a result of an event of default (however described).

(d) Any creditor of any member of the Group becomes entitled to declare any Financial Indebtedness of any member of the Group due and payable prior to its specified maturity as a result of an event of default (however described).

(e) No Event of Default will occur under this Clause 23.5 if the aggregate amount of Financial Indebtedness or commitment for Financial Indebtedness falling within paragraphs (a) to (d) above is less than [__________] (or its equivalent in any other currency or currencies).

23.6 **Insolvency**

(a) A member of the Group:

(i) is unable or admits inability to pay its debts as they fall due;

(ii) suspends making payments on any of its debts; or

(iii) by reason of actual or anticipated financial difficulties, commences negotiations with one or more of its creditors (excluding any Finance Party in its capacity as such) with a view to rescheduling any of its indebtedness.

(b) The value of the assets of any member of the Group is less than its liabilities (taking into account contingent and prospective liabilities).

(c) A moratorium is declared in respect of any indebtedness of any member of the Group.

23.7 **Insolvency proceedings**

Any corporate action, legal proceedings or other procedure or step is taken in relation to:

(a) the suspension of payments, a moratorium of any indebtedness, winding-up, dissolution, administration or reorganisation (by way of voluntary arrangement, scheme of arrangement or otherwise) of any member of the Group other than a solvent liquidation or reorganisation of any member of the Group which is not an Obligor;

(b) a composition, compromise, assignment or arrangement with any creditor of any member of the Group;

(c) the appointment of a liquidator (other than in respect of a solvent liquidation of a member of the Group which is not an Obligor), receiver, administrative receiver, administrator, compulsory manager or other similar officer in respect of any member of the Group or any of its assets; or

(d) enforcement of any Security over any assets of any member of the Group,

or any analogous procedure or step is taken in any jurisdiction.

This Clause 23.7 shall not apply to any winding-up petition which is frivolous or vexatious and is discharged, stayed or dismissed within [ ] days of commencement.

23.8 **Creditors' process**

Any expropriation, attachment, sequestration, distress or execution affects any asset or assets of a member of the Group [having an aggregate value of [ ]] [and is not discharged within [ ] days].

23.9 **Ownership of the Obligors**

An Obligor (other than the Company) is not or ceases to be a Subsidiary of the Company.

23.10 **Unlawfulness**

It is or becomes unlawful for an Obligor to perform any of its obligations under the Finance Documents.

23.11 **Repudiation**

An Obligor repudiates a Finance Document or evidences an intention to repudiate a Finance Document.

23.12 **Material adverse change**

[____________].

23.13 **Acceleration**

On and at any time after the occurrence of an Event of Default [which is continuing] the Agent may, and shall if so directed by the Majority Lenders, by notice to the Company:

(a) cancel the Total Commitments whereupon they shall immediately be cancelled;

(b) declare that all or part of the Loans, together with accrued interest, and all other amounts accrued or outstanding under the Finance Documents be immediately due and payable, whereupon they shall become immediately due and payable; and/or

(c) declare that all or part of the Loans be payable on demand, whereupon they shall immediately become payable on demand by the Agent on the instructions of the Majority Lenders.

## SECTION 9
## CHANGES TO PARTIES

### 24. CHANGES TO THE LENDERS

#### 24.1 Assignments and transfers by the Lenders

Subject to this Clause 24, a Lender (the "**Existing Lender**") may:

(a) assign any of its rights; or

(b) transfer by novation any of its rights and obligations,

to another bank or financial institution or to a trust, fund or other entity which is regularly engaged in or established for the purpose of making, purchasing or investing in loans, securities or other financial assets (the "**New Lender**").[47]

#### 24.2 Company consent

(a) The consent of the Company is required for an assignment or transfer by an Existing Lender, unless the assignment or transfer is:

(i) to another Lender or an Affiliate of any Lender[; or

(ii) made at a time when an Event of Default is continuing].

(b) The consent of the Company to an assignment or transfer must not be unreasonably withheld or delayed. The Company will be deemed to have given its consent five Business Days after the Existing Lender has requested it unless consent is expressly refused by the Company within that time.

(c) [The consent of the Company to an assignment or transfer must not be withheld solely because the assignment or transfer may result in an increase to the Mandatory Cost.]

#### 24.3 Other conditions of assignment or transfer

(a) An assignment will only be effective on:

(i) receipt by the Agent (whether in the Assignment Agreement or otherwise) of written confirmation from the New Lender (in form and substance satisfactory to the Agent) that the New Lender will assume the same obligations to the other Finance Parties as it would have been under if it had been an Original Lender; and

(ii) performance by the Agent of all necessary "know your customer" or other similar checks under all applicable laws and regulations in relation to such assignment to a New Lender, the completion of which the Agent shall promptly notify to the Existing Lender and the New Lender.

[47] Users should consider whether they wish to expressly address the extent to which transfers to members of the Group are permitted or restricted. The LMA Leveraged Facilities Agreement contains wording alternatively regulating or prohibiting transfers to members of the Group and which can be adapted for use in the LMA Primary Documents.

(b) A transfer will only be effective if the procedure set out in Clause 24.6 (*Procedure for transfer*) is complied with.

(c) If:

(i) a Lender assigns or transfers any of its rights or obligations under the Finance Documents or changes its Facility Office; and

(ii) as a result of circumstances existing at the date the assignment, transfer or change occurs, an Obligor would be obliged to make a payment to the New Lender or Lender acting through its new Facility Office under Clause 13 (*Tax gross-up and indemnities*) or Clause 14 (*Increased Costs*),

then the New Lender or Lender acting through its new Facility Office is only entitled to receive payment under those Clauses to the same extent as the Existing Lender or Lender acting through its previous Facility Office would have been if the assignment, transfer or change had not occurred. This paragraph (c) shall not apply:

(iii) in respect of an assignment or transfer made in the ordinary course of the primary syndication of any Facility; or

(iv) in relation to Clause 13.2 (*Tax gross-up*), to a Treaty Lender that has included a confirmation of its scheme reference number and its jurisdiction of tax residence in accordance with paragraph (g)(ii)(B) of Clause 13.2 (*Tax gross-up*) if the Obligor making the payment has not made a Borrower DTTP Filing in respect of that Treaty Lender.

(d) Each New Lender, by executing the relevant Transfer Certificate or Assignment Agreement, confirms, for the avoidance of doubt, that the Agent has authority to execute on its behalf any amendment or waiver that has been approved by or on behalf of the requisite Lender or Lenders in accordance with this Agreement on or prior to the date on which the transfer or assignment becomes effective in accordance with this Agreement and that it is bound by that decision to the same extent as the Existing Lender would have been had it remained a Lender.

**24.4 Assignment or transfer fee**

The New Lender shall, on the date upon which an assignment or transfer takes effect, pay to the Agent (for its own account) a fee of [____].

**24.5 Limitation of responsibility of Existing Lenders**

(a) Unless expressly agreed to the contrary, an Existing Lender makes no representation or warranty and assumes no responsibility to a New Lender for:

(i) the legality, validity, effectiveness, adequacy or enforceability of the Finance Documents or any other documents;

(ii) the financial condition of any Obligor;

(iii) the performance and observance by any Obligor of its obligations under the Finance Documents or any other documents; or

(iv) the accuracy of any statements (whether written or oral) made in or in connection with any Finance Document or any other document,

and any representations or warranties implied by law are excluded.

(b) Each New Lender confirms to the Existing Lender and the other Finance Parties that it:

(i) has made (and shall continue to make) its own independent investigation and assessment of the financial condition and affairs of each Obligor and its related entities in connection with its participation in this Agreement and has not relied exclusively on any information provided to it by the Existing Lender in connection with any Finance Document; and

(ii) will continue to make its own independent appraisal of the creditworthiness of each Obligor and its related entities whilst any amount is or may be outstanding under the Finance Documents or any Commitment is in force.

(c) Nothing in any Finance Document obliges an Existing Lender to:

(i) accept a re-transfer or re-assignment from a New Lender of any of the rights and obligations assigned or transferred under this Clause 24; or

(ii) support any losses directly or indirectly incurred by the New Lender by reason of the non-performance by any Obligor of its obligations under the Finance Documents or otherwise.

**24.6 Procedure for transfer**

(a) Subject to the conditions set out in Clause 24.2 (*Company consent*) and Clause 24.3 (*Other conditions of assignment or transfer*) a transfer is effected in accordance with paragraph (c) below when the Agent executes an otherwise duly completed Transfer Certificate delivered to it by the Existing Lender and the New Lender. The Agent shall, subject to paragraph (b) below, as soon as reasonably practicable after receipt by it of a duly completed Transfer Certificate appearing on its face to comply with the terms of this Agreement and delivered in accordance with the terms of this Agreement, execute that Transfer Certificate.

(b) The Agent shall only be obliged to execute a Transfer Certificate delivered to it by the Existing Lender and the New Lender once it is satisfied it has complied with all necessary "know your customer" or other similar checks under all applicable laws and regulations in relation to the transfer to such New Lender.

(c) [Subject to Clause 24.10 (*Pro rata interest settlement*),] on the Transfer Date:

(i) to the extent that in the Transfer Certificate the Existing Lender seeks to transfer by novation its rights and obligations under the Finance Documents each of the Obligors and the Existing Lender shall be released from further obligations towards one another under the Finance

Documents and their respective rights against one another under the Finance Documents shall be cancelled (being the "**Discharged Rights and Obligations**");

(ii) each of the Obligors and the New Lender shall assume obligations towards one another and/or acquire rights against one another which differ from the Discharged Rights and Obligations only insofar as that Obligor and the New Lender have assumed and/or acquired the same in place of that Obligor and the Existing Lender;

(iii) the Agent, the Arranger, the New Lender and other Lenders shall acquire the same rights and assume the same obligations between themselves as they would have acquired and assumed had the New Lender been an Original Lender with the rights and/or obligations acquired or assumed by it as a result of the transfer and to that extent the Agent, the Arranger and the Existing Lender shall each be released from further obligations to each other under the Finance Documents; and

(iv) the New Lender shall become a Party as a "Lender".

24.7 **Procedure for assignment**

(a) Subject to the conditions set out in Clause 24.2 (*Company consent*) and Clause 24.3 (*Other conditions of assignment or transfer*) an assignment may be effected in accordance with paragraph (c) below when the Agent executes an otherwise duly completed Assignment Agreement delivered to it by the Existing Lender and the New Lender. The Agent shall, subject to paragraph (b) below, as soon as reasonably practicable after receipt by it of a duly completed Assignment Agreement appearing on its face to comply with the terms of this Agreement and delivered in accordance with the terms of this Agreement, execute that Assignment Agreement.

(b) The Agent shall only be obliged to execute an Assignment Agreement delivered to it by the Existing Lender and the New Lender once it is satisfied it has complied with all necessary "know your customer" or other similar checks under all applicable laws and regulations in relation to the assignment to such New Lender.

(c) [Subject to Clause 24.10 (*Pro rata interest settlement*),] on the Transfer Date:

(i) the Existing Lender will assign absolutely to the New Lender the rights under the Finance Documents expressed to be the subject of the assignment in the Assignment Agreement;

(ii) the Existing Lender will be released by each Obligor and the other Finance Parties from the obligations owed by it (the "**Relevant Obligations**") and expressed to be the subject of the release in the Assignment Agreement; and

(iii) the New Lender shall become a Party as a "Lender" and will be bound by obligations equivalent to the Relevant Obligations.[48]

(d) Lenders may utilise procedures other than those set out in this Clause 24.7 to assign their rights under the Finance Documents (but not, without the consent of the relevant Obligor or unless in accordance with Clause 24.6 (*Procedure for transfer*), to obtain a release by that Obligor from the obligations owed to that Obligor by the Lenders nor the assumption of equivalent obligations by a New Lender) **provided that** they comply with the conditions set out in Clause 24.2 (*Company consent*) and Clause 24.3 (*Other conditions of assignment or transfer*).

24.8 **Copy of Transfer Certificate, Assignment Agreement or Increase Confirmation to Company**

The Agent shall, as soon as reasonably practicable after it has executed a Transfer Certificate, an Assignment Agreement or an Increase Confirmation, send to the Company a copy of that Transfer Certificate, Assignment Agreement or Increase Confirmation.

24.9 **[Security over Lenders' rights**

In addition to the other rights provided to Lenders under this Clause 24, each Lender may without consulting with or obtaining consent from any Obligor, at any time charge, assign or otherwise create Security in or over (whether by way of collateral or otherwise) all or any of its rights under any Finance Document to secure obligations of that Lender including, without limitation:

(a) any charge, assignment or other Security to secure obligations to a federal reserve or central bank; and

(b) any charge, assignment or other Security granted to any holders (or trustee or representatives of holders) of obligations owed, or securities issued, by that Lender as security for those obligations or securities,

except that no such charge, assignment or Security shall:

(i) release a Lender from any of its obligations under the Finance Documents or substitute the beneficiary of the relevant charge, assignment or Security for the Lender as a party to any of the Finance Documents; or

(ii) require any payments to be made by an Obligor other than or in excess of, or grant to any person any more extensive rights than, those required to be made or granted to the relevant Lender under the Finance Documents.]

24.10 **[Pro rata interest settlement**

(a) If the Agent has notified the Lenders that it is able to distribute interest payments on a "pro rata basis" to Existing Lenders and New Lenders then (in

[48] If the Assignment Agreement is used in place of a Transfer Certificate in order to avoid a novation of ~~rights/obligations for reasons relev~~ant to a civil jurisdiction, local law advice should be sought to check the suitability of the Assignment Agreement due to the assumption of obligations referred to in paragraph (c)(iii) of Clause 24.7 (*Procedure for assignment*).

respect of any transfer pursuant to Clause 24.6 (*Procedure for transfer*) or any assignment pursuant to Clause 24.7 (*Procedure for assignment*) the Transfer Date of which, in each case, is after the date of such notification and is not on the last day of an Interest Period):

(i) any interest or fees in respect of the relevant participation which are expressed to accrue by reference to the lapse of time shall continue to accrue in favour of the Existing Lender up to but excluding the Transfer Date ("**Accrued Amounts**") and shall become due and payable to the Existing Lender (without further interest accruing on them) on the last day of the current Interest Period (or, if the Interest Period is longer than six Months, on the next of the dates which falls at six Monthly intervals after the first day of that Interest Period); and

(ii) the rights assigned or transferred by the Existing Lender will not include the right to the Accrued Amounts, so that, for the avoidance of doubt:

(A) when the Accrued Amounts become payable, those Accrued Amounts will be payable to the Existing Lender; and

(B) the amount payable to the New Lender on that date will be the amount which would, but for the application of this Clause 24.10, have been payable to it on that date, but after deduction of the Accrued Amounts.

(b) In this Clause 24.10 references to "Interest Period" shall be construed to include a reference to any other period for accrual of fees.

(c) An Existing Lender which retains the right to the Accrued Amounts pursuant to this Clause 24.10 but which does not have a Commitment shall be deemed not to be a Lender for the purposes of ascertaining whether the agreement of any specified group of Lenders has been obtained to approve any request for a consent, waiver, amendment or other vote of Lenders under the Finance Documents.]

## 25. CHANGES TO THE OBLIGORS

### 25.1 Assignments and transfer by Obligors

No Obligor may assign any of its rights or transfer any of its rights or obligations under the Finance Documents.

### 25.2 Additional Borrowers

(a) Subject to compliance with the provisions of paragraphs (c) and (d) of Clause 20.7 (*"Know your customer" checks*), the Company may request that any of its [wholly owned] Subsidiaries becomes an Additional Borrower. That Subsidiary shall become an Additional Borrower if:

(i) [all the Lenders]/[the Majority Lenders] approve the addition of that Subsidiary;

(ii) the Company delivers to the Agent a duly completed and executed Accession Letter;

(iii) the Company confirms that no Default is continuing or would occur as a result of that Subsidiary becoming an Additional Borrower; and

(iv) the Agent has received all of the documents and other evidence listed in Part II of Schedule 2 (*Conditions precedent*) in relation to that Additional Borrower, each in form and substance satisfactory to the Agent.

(b) The Agent shall notify the Company and the Lenders promptly upon being satisfied that it has received (in form and substance satisfactory to it) all the documents and other evidence listed in Part II of Schedule 2 (*Conditions precedent*).

(c) Other than to the extent that the Majority Lenders notify the Agent in writing to the contrary before the Agent gives the notification described in paragraph (b) above, the Lenders authorise (but do not require) the Agent to give that notification. The Agent shall not be liable for any damages, costs or losses whatsoever as a result of giving any such notification.

25.3 **Resignation of a Borrower**

(a) The Company may request that a Borrower (other than the Company) ceases to be a Borrower by delivering to the Agent a Resignation Letter.

(b) The Agent shall accept a Resignation Letter and notify the Company and the Lenders of its acceptance if:

(i) no Default is continuing or would result from the acceptance of the Resignation Letter (and the Company has confirmed this is the case); and

(ii) the Borrower is under no actual or contingent obligations as a Borrower under any Finance Documents,

whereupon that company shall cease to be a Borrower and shall have no further rights or obligations under the Finance Documents.

25.4 **Additional Guarantors**

(a) Subject to compliance with the provisions of paragraphs (c) and (d) of Clause 20.7 (*"Know your customer" checks*), the Company may request that any of its [wholly owned] Subsidiaries become an Additional Guarantor. That Subsidiary shall become an Additional Guarantor if:

(i) the Company delivers to the Agent a duly completed and executed Accession Letter; and

(ii) the Agent has received all of the documents and other evidence listed in Part II of Schedule 2 (*Conditions precedent*) in relation to that Additional Guarantor, each in form and substance satisfactory to the Agent.

(b) The Agent shall notify the Company and the Lenders promptly upon being satisfied that it has received (in form and substance satisfactory to it) all the documents and other evidence listed in Part II of Schedule 2 (*Conditions precedent*).

(c) Other than to the extent that the Majority Lenders notify the Agent in writing to the contrary before the Agent gives the notification described in paragraph (b) above, the Lenders authorise (but do not require) the Agent to give that notification. The Agent shall not be liable for any damages, costs or losses whatsoever as a result of giving any such notification.

25.5 **Repetition of Representations**

Delivery of an Accession Letter constitutes confirmation by the relevant Subsidiary that the Repeating Representations are true and correct in relation to it as at the date of delivery as if made by reference to the facts and circumstances then existing.

25.6 **Resignation of a Guarantor**

(a) The Company may request that a Guarantor (other than the Company [or [*insert details of any other Guarantor which is not permitted to resign*]]) ceases to be a Guarantor by delivering to the Agent a Resignation Letter

(b) The Agent shall accept a Resignation Letter and notify the Company and the Lenders of its acceptance if:

(i) no Default is continuing or would result from the acceptance of the Resignation Letter (and the Company has confirmed this is the case);

(ii) all the Lenders have consented to the Company's request; and

(iii) [______________].

**SECTION 10**
**THE FINANCE PARTIES**

26. **ROLE OF THE AGENT [AND] THE ARRANGER [AND THE REFERENCE BANKS]**

26.1 **Appointment of the Agent**

(a) Each of the Arranger and the Lenders appoints the Agent to act as its agent under and in connection with the Finance Documents.

(b) Each of the Arranger and the Lenders authorises the Agent to perform the duties, obligations and responsibilities and to exercise the rights, powers, authorities and discretions specifically given to the Agent under or in connection with the Finance Documents together with any other incidental rights, powers, authorities and discretions.

26.2 **Instructions**

(a) The Agent shall:

(i) unless a contrary indication appears in a Finance Document, exercise or refrain from exercising any right, power, authority or discretion vested in it as Agent in accordance with any instructions given to it by:

(A) all Lenders if the relevant Finance Document stipulates the matter is an all Lender decision; and

(B) in all other cases, the Majority Lenders; and

(ii) not be liable for any act (or omission) if it acts (or refrains from acting) in accordance with paragraph (i) above.

(b) The Agent shall be entitled to request instructions, or clarification of any instruction, from the Majority Lenders (or, if the relevant Finance Document stipulates the matter is a decision for any other Lender or group of Lenders, from that Lender or group of Lenders) as to whether, and in what manner, it should exercise or refrain from exercising any right, power, authority or discretion. The Agent may refrain from acting unless and until it receives any such instructions or clarification that it has requested.

(c) Save in the case of decisions stipulated to be a matter for any other Lender or group of Lenders under the relevant Finance Document and unless a contrary indication appears in a Finance Document, any instructions given to the Agent by the Majority Lenders shall override any conflicting instructions given by any other Parties and will be binding on all Finance Parties.

(d) The Agent may refrain from acting in accordance with any instructions of any Lender or group of Lenders until it has received any indemnification and/or security that it may in its discretion require (which may be greater in extent than that contained in the Finance Documents and which may include payment in advance) for any cost, loss or liability which it may incur in complying with those instructions.

(e) In the absence of instructions, the Agent may act (or refrain from acting) as it considers to be in the best interest of the Lenders.

(f) The Agent is not authorised to act on behalf of a Lender (without first obtaining that Lender's consent) in any legal or arbitration proceedings relating to any Finance Document.

26.3 **Duties of the Agent**

(a) The Agent's duties under the Finance Documents are solely mechanical and administrative in nature.

(b) Subject to paragraph (c) below, the Agent shall promptly forward to a Party the original or a copy of any document which is delivered to the Agent for that Party by any other Party.

(c) Without prejudice to Clause 24.8 (*Copy of Transfer Certificate, Assignment Agreement or Increase Confirmation to Company*), paragraph (b) above shall not apply to any Transfer Certificate, any Assignment Agreement or any Increase Confirmation.

(d) Except where a Finance Document specifically provides otherwise, the Agent is not obliged to review or check the adequacy, accuracy or completeness of any document it forwards to another Party.

(e) If the Agent receives notice from a Party referring to this Agreement, describing a Default and stating that the circumstance described is a Default, it shall promptly notify the other Finance Parties.

(f) If the Agent is aware of the non-payment of any principal, interest, commitment fee or other fee payable to a Finance Party (other than the Agent or the Arranger) under this Agreement, it shall promptly notify the other Finance Parties.

(g) The Agent shall have only those duties, obligations and responsibilities expressly specified in the Finance Documents to which it is expressed to be a party (and no others shall be implied).

26.4 **Role of the Arranger**

Except as specifically provided in the Finance Documents, the Arranger has no obligations of any kind to any other Party under or in connection with any Finance Document.

26.5 **No fiduciary duties**

(a) Nothing in any Finance Document constitutes the Agent or the Arranger as a trustee or fiduciary of any other person.

(b) Neither the Agent nor the Arranger shall be bound to account to any Lender for any sum or the profit element of any sum received by it for its own account.

**26.6 Business with the Group**

The Agent and the Arranger may accept deposits from, lend money to and generally engage in any kind of banking or other business with any member of the Group.

**26.7 Rights and discretions**

(a) The Agent may:

(i) rely on any representation, communication, notice or document believed by it to be genuine, correct and appropriately authorised;

(ii) assume that:

(A) any instructions received by it from the Majority Lenders, any Lenders or any group of Lenders are duly given in accordance with the terms of the Finance Documents; and

(B) unless it has received notice of revocation, that those instructions have not been revoked; and

(iii) rely on a certificate from any person:

(A) as to any matter of fact or circumstance which might reasonably be expected to be within the knowledge of that person; or

(B) to the effect that such person approves of any particular dealing, transaction, step, action or thing,

as sufficient evidence that that is the case and, in the case of paragraph (A) above, may assume the truth and accuracy of that certificate.

(b) The Agent may assume (unless it has received notice to the contrary in its capacity as agent for the Lenders) that:

(i) no Default has occurred (unless it has actual knowledge of a Default arising under Clause 23.1 (*Non-payment*));

(ii) any right, power, authority or discretion vested in any Party or any group of Lenders has not been exercised; and

(iii) any notice or request made by the Company (other than a Utilisation Request or Selection Notice) is made on behalf of and with the consent and knowledge of all the Obligors.

(c) The Agent may engage and pay for the advice or services of any lawyers, accountants, tax advisers, surveyors or other professional advisers or experts.

(d) Without prejudice to the generality of paragraph (c) above or paragraph (e) below, the Agent may at any time engage and pay for the services of any lawyers to act as independent counsel to the Agent (and so separate from any lawyers instructed by the Lenders) if the Agent in its reasonable opinion deems this to be necessary.

(e) The Agent may rely on the advice or services of any lawyers, accountants, tax advisers, surveyors or other professional advisers or experts (whether obtained by the Agent or by any other Party) and shall not be liable for any damages, costs or losses to any person, any diminution in value or any liability whatsoever arising as a result of its so relying.

(f) The Agent may act in relation to the Finance Documents through its officers, employees and agents.

(g) Unless a Finance Document expressly provides otherwise the Agent may disclose to any other Party any information it reasonably believes it has received as agent under this Agreement.

(h) Notwithstanding any other provision of any Finance Document to the contrary, neither the Agent nor the Arranger is obliged to do or omit to do anything if it would, or might in its reasonable opinion, constitute a breach of any law or regulation or a breach of a fiduciary duty or duty of confidentiality.

(i) Notwithstanding any provision of any Finance Document to the contrary, the Agent is not obliged to expend or risk its own funds or otherwise incur any financial liability in the performance of its duties, obligations or responsibilities or the exercise of any right, power, authority or discretion if it has grounds for believing the repayment of such funds or adequate indemnity against, or security for, such risk or liability is not reasonably assured to it.

26.8 **Responsibility for documentation**

Neither the Agent nor the Arranger is responsible or liable for:

(a) the adequacy, accuracy or completeness of any information (whether oral or written) supplied by the Agent, the Arranger, an Obligor or any other person in or in connection with any Finance Document or the Information Memorandum or the transactions contemplated in the Finance Documents or any other agreement, arrangement or document entered into, made or executed in anticipation of, under or in connection with any Finance Document; [or]

(b) the legality, validity, effectiveness, adequacy or enforceability of any Finance Document or any other agreement, arrangement or document entered into, made or executed in anticipation of, under or in connection with any Finance Document[; or

(c) any determination as to whether any information provided or to be provided to any Finance Party is non-public information the use of which may be regulated or prohibited by applicable law or regulation relating to insider dealing or otherwise].

26.9 **No duty to monitor**

The Agent shall not be bound to enquire:

(a) whether or not any Default has occurred;

(b) as to the performance, default or any breach by any Party of its obligations under any Finance Document; or

(c) whether any other event specified in any Finance Document has occurred.

26.10 **Exclusion of liability**

(a) Without limiting paragraph (b) below (and without prejudice to any other provision of any Finance Document excluding or limiting the liability of the Agent), the Agent will not be liable for:

(i) any damages, costs or losses to any person, any diminution in value, or any liability whatsoever arising as a result of taking or not taking any action under or in connection with any Finance Document, unless directly caused by its gross negligence or wilful misconduct;

(ii) exercising, or not exercising, any right, power, authority or discretion given to it by, or in connection with, any Finance Document or any other agreement, arrangement or document entered into, made or executed in anticipation of, under or in connection with, any Finance Document, other than by reason of its gross negligence or wilful misconduct; or

(iii) without prejudice to the generality of paragraphs (i) and (ii) above, any damages, costs or losses to any person, any diminution in value or any liability whatsoever ([including, without limitation, for negligence or any other category of liability whatsoever][49] but not including any claim based on the fraud of the Agent) arising as a result of:

(A) any act, event or circumstance not reasonably within its control; or

(B) the general risks of investment in, or the holding of assets in, any jurisdiction,

including (in each case and without limitation) such damages, costs, losses, diminution in value or liability arising as a result of: nationalisation, expropriation or other governmental actions; any regulation, currency restriction, devaluation or fluctuation; market conditions affecting the execution or settlement of transactions or the value of assets (including any Disruption Event); breakdown, failure or malfunction of any third party transport, telecommunications, computer services or systems; natural disasters or acts of God; war, terrorism, insurrection or revolution; or strikes or industrial action.

(b) No Party (other than the Agent) may take any proceedings against any officer, employee or agent of the Agent in respect of any claim it might have against the Agent or in respect of any act or omission of any kind by that officer, employee or agent in relation to any Finance Document and any officer, employee or

[49] Only include words in brackets if the optional Clause 29.10 (*Disruption to payment systems etc.*) has been included.

agent of the Agent may rely on this Clause [subject to Clause 1.4 (*Third party rights*) and the provisions of the Third Parties Act].

(c) The Agent will not be liable for any delay (or any related consequences) in crediting an account with an amount required under the Finance Documents to be paid by the Agent if the Agent has taken all necessary steps as soon as reasonably practicable to comply with the regulations or operating procedures of any recognised clearing or settlement system used by the Agent for that purpose.

(d) Nothing in this Agreement shall oblige the Agent or the Arranger to carry out:

(i) any "know your customer" or other checks in relation to any person; or

(ii) any check on the extent to which any transaction contemplated by this Agreement might be unlawful for any Lender [or for any Affiliate of any Lender],

on behalf of any Lender and each Lender confirms to the Agent and the Arranger that it is solely responsible for any such checks it is required to carry out and that it may not rely on any statement in relation to such checks made by the Agent or the Arranger.

(e) Without prejudice to any provision of any Finance Document excluding or limiting the Agent's liability, any liability of the Agent arising under or in connection with any Finance Document shall be limited to the amount of actual loss which has been suffered (as determined by reference to the date of default of the Agent or, if later, the date on which the loss arises as a result of such default) but without reference to any special conditions or circumstances known to the Agent at any time which increase the amount of that loss. In no event shall the Agent be liable for any loss of profits, goodwill, reputation, business opportunity or anticipated saving, or for special, punitive, indirect or consequential damages, whether or not the Agent has been advised of the possibility of such loss or damages.

26.11 **Lenders' indemnity to the Agent**

Each Lender shall (in proportion to its share of the Total Commitments or, if the Total Commitments are then zero, to its share of the Total Commitments immediately prior to their reduction to zero) indemnify the Agent, within three Business Days of demand, against any cost, loss or liability [(including, without limitation, for negligence or any other category of liability whatsoever)][50] incurred by the Agent (otherwise than by reason of the Agent's gross negligence or wilful misconduct) [(or, in the case of any cost, loss or liability pursuant to Clause 29.10 (*Disruption to payment systems etc.*), notwithstanding the Agent's negligence, gross negligence or any other category of liability whatsoever but not including any claim based on the fraud of the Agent)][51] in acting as Agent under the

[50] Users should consider including this wording if the optional Clause 29.10 (*Disruption to payment systems etc.*) ~~has been included.~~

[51] Include words in brackets if the optional Clause 29.10 (*Disruption to payment systems etc.*) has been included.

Finance Documents (unless the Agent has been reimbursed by an Obligor pursuant to a Finance Document).

26.12 **Resignation of the Agent**

(a) The Agent may resign and appoint one of its Affiliates acting through an office [in the United Kingdom] as successor by giving notice to the Lenders and the Company.

(b) Alternatively the Agent may resign by giving 30 days' notice to the Lenders and the Company, in which case the Majority Lenders (after consultation with the Company) may appoint a successor Agent.

(c) If the Majority Lenders have not appointed a successor Agent in accordance with paragraph (b) above within 20 days after notice of resignation was given, the retiring Agent (after consultation with the Company) may appoint a successor Agent [(acting through an office in the United Kingdom)].

(d) [If the Agent wishes to resign because (acting reasonably) it has concluded that it is no longer appropriate for it to remain as agent and the Agent is entitled to appoint a successor Agent under paragraph (c) above, the Agent may (if it concludes (acting reasonably) that it is necessary to do so in order to persuade the proposed successor Agent to become a party to this Agreement as Agent) agree with the proposed successor Agent amendments to this Clause 26 [and any other term of this Agreement dealing with the rights or obligations of the Agent] consistent with then current market practice for the appointment and protection of corporate trustees together with any reasonable amendments to the agency fee payable under this Agreement which are consistent with the successor Agent's normal fee rates and those amendments will bind the Parties.]

(e) The retiring Agent shall[, at its own cost,] make available to the successor Agent such documents and records and provide such assistance as the successor Agent may reasonably request for the purposes of performing its functions as Agent under the Finance Documents. [The Company shall, within three Business Days of demand, reimburse the retiring Agent for the amount of all costs and expenses (including legal fees) properly incurred by it in making available such documents and records and providing such assistance.]

(f) The Agent's resignation notice shall only take effect upon the appointment of a successor.

(g) Upon the appointment of a successor, the retiring Agent shall be discharged from any further obligation in respect of the Finance Documents (other than its obligations under paragraph (e) above) but shall remain entitled to the benefit of Clause 15.3 (*Indemnity to the Agent*) and this Clause 26 (and any agency fees for the account of the retiring Agent shall cease to accrue from (and shall be payable on) that date). Any successor and each of the other Parties shall have the same rights and obligations amongst themselves as they would have had if such successor had been an original Party.

(h) After consultation with the Company, the Majority Lenders may, by notice to the Agent, require it to resign in accordance with paragraph (b) above. In this event, the Agent shall resign in accordance with paragraph (b) above.

(i) The Agent shall resign in accordance with paragraph (b) above (and, to the extent applicable, shall use reasonable endeavours to appoint a successor Agent pursuant to paragraph (c) above) if on or after the date which is [three] months before the earliest FATCA Application Date relating to any payment to the Agent under the Finance Documents, either:

(i) the Agent fails to respond to a request under Clause 13.8 (*FATCA information*) and [the Company or] a Lender reasonably believes that the Agent will not be (or will have ceased to be) a FATCA Exempt Party on or after that FATCA Application Date;

(ii) the information supplied by the Agent pursuant to Clause 13.8 (*FATCA information*) indicates that the Agent will not be (or will have ceased to be) a FATCA Exempt Party on or after that FATCA Application Date; or

(iii) the Agent notifies the Company and the Lenders that the Agent will not be (or will have ceased to be) a FATCA Exempt Party on or after that FATCA Application Date;

and (in each case) [the Company or] a Lender reasonably believes that a Party will be required to make a FATCA Deduction that would not be required if the Agent were a FATCA Exempt Party, and [the Company or] that Lender, by notice to the Agent, requires it to resign.

**26.13 Confidentiality**

(a) In acting as agent for the Finance Parties, the Agent shall be regarded as acting through its agency division which shall be treated as a separate entity from any other of its divisions or departments.

(b) If information is received by another division or department of the Agent, it may be treated as confidential to that division or department and the Agent shall not be deemed to have notice of it.

**26.14 Relationship with the Lenders**

(a) [Subject to Clause 24.10 (*Pro rata interest settlement*), the]/[The] Agent may treat the person shown in its records as Lender at the opening of business (in the place of the Agent's principal office as notified to the Finance Parties from time to time) as the Lender acting through its Facility Office:

(i) [entitled to or liable for any payment due under any Finance Document on that day; and]

(ii) entitled to receive and act upon any notice, request, document or communication or make any decision or determination under any Finance Document made or delivered on that day, unless it has received not less than five Business Days' prior notice from that Lender to the contrary in accordance with the terms of this Agreement.

(b) [Each Lender shall supply the Agent with any information required by the Agent in order to calculate the Mandatory Cost in accordance with Schedule 4 (*Mandatory Cost formulae*).]

(c) Any Lender may by notice to the Agent appoint a person to receive on its behalf all notices, communications, information and documents to be made or despatched to that Lender under the Finance Documents. Such notice shall contain the address, fax number and (where communication by electronic mail or other electronic means is permitted under Clause 31.5 (*Electronic communication*)) electronic mail address and/or any other information required to enable the transmission of information by that means (and, in each case, the department or officer, if any, for whose attention communication is to be made) and be treated as a notification of a substitute address, fax number, electronic mail address (or such other information), department and officer by that Lender for the purposes of Clause 31.2 (*Addresses*) and paragraph (a)(ii) of Clause 31.5 (*Electronic communication*) and the Agent shall be entitled to treat such person as the person entitled to receive all such notices, communications, information and documents as though that person were that Lender.

26.15 **Credit appraisal by the Lenders**

Without affecting the responsibility of any Obligor for information supplied by it or on its behalf in connection with any Finance Document, each Lender confirms to the Agent and the Arranger that it has been, and will continue to be, solely responsible for making its own independent appraisal and investigation of all risks arising under or in connection with any Finance Document including but not limited to:

(a) the financial condition, status and nature of each member of the Group;

(b) the legality, validity, effectiveness, adequacy or enforceability of any Finance Document and any other agreement, arrangement or document entered into, made or executed in anticipation of, under or in connection with any Finance Document;

(c) whether that Lender has recourse, and the nature and extent of that recourse, against any Party or any of its respective assets under or in connection with any Finance Document, the transactions contemplated by the Finance Documents or any other agreement, arrangement or document entered into, made or executed in anticipation of, under or in connection with any Finance Document; and

(d) the adequacy, accuracy or completeness of the Information Memorandum and any other information provided by the Agent, any Party or by any other person under or in connection with any Finance Document, the transactions contemplated by any Finance Document or any other agreement, arrangement or document entered into, made or executed in anticipation of, under or in connection with any Finance Document.

26.16 **[Agent's management time**

Any amount payable to the Agent under Clause 15.3 (*Indemnity to the Agent*), Clause 17 (*Costs and expenses*) and Clause 26.11 (*Lenders' indemnity to the Agent*) shall include the cost of utilising the Agent's management time or other resources and will be calculated on the basis of such reasonable daily or hourly rates as the Agent may notify to the Company and the Lenders, and is in addition to any fee paid or payable to the Agent under Clause 12 (*Fees*).]

26.17 **Deduction from amounts payable by the Agent**

If any Party owes an amount to the Agent under the Finance Documents the Agent may, after giving notice to that Party, deduct an amount not exceeding that amount from any payment to that Party which the Agent would otherwise be obliged to make under the Finance Documents and apply the amount deducted in or towards satisfaction of the amount owed. For the purposes of the Finance Documents that Party shall be regarded as having received any amount so deducted.

26.18 **[Role of Reference Banks**

(a) No Reference Bank is under any obligation to provide a quotation or any other information to the Agent.

(b) [No Reference Bank will be liable for any action taken by it under or in connection with any Finance Document, or for any Reference Bank Quotation, unless directly caused by its gross negligence or wilful misconduct.

(c) No Party (other than the relevant Reference Bank) may take any proceedings against any officer, employee or agent of any Reference Bank in respect of any claim it might have against that Reference Bank or in respect of any act or omission of any kind by that officer, employee or agent in relation to any Finance Document, or to any Reference Bank Quotation, and any officer, employee or agent of each Reference Bank may rely on this Clause 26.18 subject to Clause 1.4 (*Third party rights*) and the provisions of the Third Parties Act.]

26.19 **Third party Reference Banks**

A Reference Bank which is not a Party may rely on Clause 26.18 (*Role of Reference Banks*), Clause 35.3 (*Other exceptions*) and Clause 37 (*Confidentiality of Funding Rates [and Reference Bank Quotations]*) subject to Clause 1.4 (*Third party rights*) and the provisions of the Third Parties Act.][52]

27. **CONDUCT OF BUSINESS BY THE FINANCE PARTIES**

No provision of this Agreement will:

(a) interfere with the right of any Finance Party to arrange its affairs (tax or otherwise) in whatever manner it thinks fit;

(b) oblige any Finance Party to investigate or claim any credit, relief, remission or repayment available to it or the extent, order and manner of any claim; or

[52] If this Clause is included use the second option in Clause 1.4 (*Third party rights*).

(c) oblige any Finance Party to disclose any information relating to its affairs (tax or otherwise) or any computations in respect of Tax.

## 28. SHARING AMONG THE FINANCE PARTIES

### 28.1 Payments to Finance Parties

If a Finance Party (a "**Recovering Finance Party**") receives or recovers any amount from an Obligor other than in accordance with Clause 29 (*Payment mechanics*) (a "**Recovered Amount**") and applies that amount to a payment due under the Finance Documents then:

(a) the Recovering Finance Party shall, within three Business Days, notify details of the receipt or recovery to the Agent;

(b) the Agent shall determine whether the receipt or recovery is in excess of the amount the Recovering Finance Party would have been paid had the receipt or recovery been received or made by the Agent and distributed in accordance with Clause 29 (*Payment mechanics*), without taking account of any Tax which would be imposed on the Agent in relation to the receipt, recovery or distribution; and

(c) the Recovering Finance Party shall, within three Business Days of demand by the Agent, pay to the Agent an amount (the "**Sharing Payment**") equal to such receipt or recovery less any amount which the Agent determines may be retained by the Recovering Finance Party as its share of any payment to be made, in accordance with Clause 29.5 (*Partial payments*).

### 28.2 Redistribution of payments

The Agent shall treat the Sharing Payment as if it had been paid by the relevant Obligor and distribute it between the Finance Parties (other than the Recovering Finance Party) (the "**Sharing Finance Parties**") in accordance with Clause 29.5 (*Partial payments*) towards the obligations of that Obligor to the Sharing Finance Parties.

### 28.3 Recovering Finance Party's rights

On a distribution by the Agent under Clause 28.2 (*Redistribution of payments*) of a payment received by a Recovering Finance Party from an Obligor, as between the relevant Obligor and the Recovering Finance Party, an amount of the Recovered Amount equal to the Sharing Payment will be treated as not having been paid by that Obligor.

### 28.4 Reversal of redistribution

If any part of the Sharing Payment received or recovered by a Recovering Finance Party becomes repayable and is repaid by that Recovering Finance Party, then:

(a) each Sharing Finance Party shall, upon request of the Agent, pay to the Agent for the account of that Recovering Finance Party an amount equal to the appropriate part of its share of the Sharing Payment (together with an amount as is necessary to reimburse that Recovering Finance Party for its proportion of any interest on the Sharing Payment which that Recovering Finance Party is required to pay) (the "**Redistributed Amount**"); and

(b) as between the relevant Obligor and each relevant Sharing Finance Party, an amount equal to the relevant Redistributed Amount will be treated as not having been paid by that Obligor.

28.5 **Exceptions**

(a) This Clause 28 shall not apply to the extent that the Recovering Finance Party would not, after making any payment pursuant to this Clause, have a valid and enforceable claim against the relevant Obligor.

(b) A Recovering Finance Party is not obliged to share with any other Finance Party any amount which the Recovering Finance Party has received or recovered as a result of taking legal or arbitration proceedings, if:

(i) it notified that other Finance Party of the legal or arbitration proceedings; and

(ii) that other Finance Party had an opportunity to participate in those legal or arbitration proceedings but did not do so as soon as reasonably practicable having received notice and did not take separate legal or arbitration proceedings.

## SECTION 11
## ADMINISTRATION

29. **PAYMENT MECHANICS**

29.1 **Payments to the Agent**

(a) On each date on which an Obligor or a Lender is required to make a payment under a Finance Document, that Obligor or Lender shall make the same available to the Agent (unless a contrary indication appears in a Finance Document) for value on the due date at the time and in such funds specified by the Agent as being customary at the time for settlement of transactions in the relevant currency in the place of payment.

(b) Payment shall be made to such account in the principal financial centre of the country of that currency (or, in relation to euro, in a principal financial centre in such Participating Member State or London, as specified by the Agent) and with such bank as the Agent, in each case, specifies.

29.2 **Distributions by the Agent**

Each payment received by the Agent under the Finance Documents for another Party shall, subject to Clause 29.3 (*Distributions to an Obligor*) and Clause 29.4 (*Clawback and pre-funding*) be made available by the Agent as soon as practicable after receipt to the Party entitled to receive payment in accordance with this Agreement (in the case of a Lender, for the account of its Facility Office), to such account as that Party may notify to the Agent by not less than five Business Days' notice with a bank specified by that Party in the principal financial centre of the country of that currency (or, in relation to euro, in the principal financial centre of a Participating Member State or London, as specified by that Party).

29.3 **Distributions to an Obligor**

The Agent may (with the consent of the Obligor or in accordance with Clause 30 (*Set-off*)) apply any amount received by it for that Obligor in or towards payment (on the date and in the currency and funds of receipt) of any amount due from that Obligor under the Finance Documents or in or towards purchase of any amount of any currency to be so applied.

29.4 **Clawback and pre-funding**

(a) Where a sum is to be paid to the Agent under the Finance Documents for another Party, the Agent is not obliged to pay that sum to that other Party (or to enter into or perform any related exchange contract) until it has been able to establish to its satisfaction that it has actually received that sum.

(b) Unless paragraph (c) below applies, if the Agent pays an amount to another Party and it proves to be the case that the Agent had not actually received that amount, then the Party to whom that amount (or the proceeds of any related exchange contract) was paid by the Agent shall on demand refund the same to the Agent together with interest on that amount from the date of payment to the date of receipt by the Agent, calculated by the Agent to reflect its cost of funds.

(c) If the Agent [has notified the Lenders that it] is willing to make available amounts for the account of a Borrower before receiving funds from the Lenders then if and to the extent that the Agent does so but it proves to be the case that it does not then receive funds from a Lender in respect of a sum which it paid to a Borrower:

(i) [the Agent shall notify the Company of that Lender's identity and] the Borrower to whom that sum was made available shall on demand refund it to the Agent; and

(ii) the Lender by whom those funds should have been made available or, if that Lender fails to do so, the Borrower to whom that sum was made available, shall on demand pay to the Agent the amount (as certified by the Agent) which will indemnify the Agent against any funding cost incurred by it as a result of paying out that sum before receiving those funds from that Lender.

29.5 **Partial payments**

(a) If the Agent receives a payment that is insufficient to discharge all the amounts then due and payable by an Obligor under the Finance Documents, the Agent shall apply that payment towards the obligations of that Obligor under the Finance Documents in the following order:

(i) **first**, in or towards payment pro rata of any unpaid amount owing to the Agent under the Finance Documents;

(ii) **secondly**, in or towards payment pro rata of any accrued interest, fee or commission due but unpaid under this Agreement;

(iii) **thirdly**, in or towards payment pro rata of any principal due but unpaid under this Agreement; and

(iv) **fourthly**, in or towards payment pro rata of any other sum due but unpaid under the Finance Documents.

(b) The Agent shall, if so directed by the Majority Lenders, vary the order set out in paragraphs (a)(ii) to (a)(iv) above.

(c) Paragraphs (a) and (b) above will override any appropriation made by an Obligor.

29.6 **No set-off by Obligors**

All payments to be made by an Obligor under the Finance Documents shall be calculated and be made without (and free and clear of any deduction for) set-off or counterclaim.

29.7 **Business Days**

(a) Any payment under the Finance Documents which is due to be made on a day that is not a Business Day shall be made on the next Business Day in the same calendar month (if there is one) or the preceding Business Day (if there is not).

(b) During any extension of the due date for payment of any principal or Unpaid Sum under this Agreement interest is payable on the principal or Unpaid Sum at the rate payable on the original due date.

29.8 **Currency of account**

(a) Subject to paragraphs (b) to (e) below, the Base Currency is the currency of account and payment for any sum due from an Obligor under any Finance Document.

(b) A repayment of a Loan or Unpaid Sum or a part of a Loan or Unpaid Sum shall be made in the currency in which that Loan or Unpaid Sum is denominated, pursuant to this Agreement, on its due date.

(c) Each payment of interest shall be made in the currency in which the sum in respect of which the interest is payable was denominated, pursuant to this Agreement, when that interest accrued.

(d) Each payment in respect of costs, expenses or Taxes shall be made in the currency in which the costs, expenses or Taxes are incurred.

(e) Any amount expressed to be payable in a currency other than the Base Currency shall be paid in that other currency.

29.9 **Change of currency**

(a) Unless otherwise prohibited by law, if more than one currency or currency unit are at the same time recognised by the central bank of any country as the lawful currency of that country, then:

(i) any reference in the Finance Documents to, and any obligations arising under the Finance Documents in, the currency of that country shall be translated into, or paid in, the currency or currency unit of that country designated by the Agent (after consultation with the Company); and

(ii) any translation from one currency or currency unit to another shall be at the official rate of exchange recognised by the central bank for the conversion of that currency or currency unit into the other, rounded up or down by the Agent (acting reasonably).

(b) If a change in any currency of a country occurs, this Agreement will, to the extent the Agent (acting reasonably and after consultation with the Company) specifies to be necessary, be amended to comply with any generally accepted conventions and market practice in the Relevant Market and otherwise to reflect the change in currency.

29.10 **[Disruption to payment systems etc.**

<u>If either the Agent determines (in its discretion) that a Disruption Event has occurred or the Agent is notified by the Company that a Disruption Event has occurred:</u>

(a) <u>the Agent may, and shall if requested to do so by the Company, consult with the Company with a view to agreeing with the Company such changes to the</u>

operation or administration of the Facilities as the Agent may deem necessary in the circumstances;

(b) the Agent shall not be obliged to consult with the Company in relation to any changes mentioned in paragraph (a) above if, in its opinion, it is not practicable to do so in the circumstances and, in any event, shall have no obligation to agree to such changes;

(c) the Agent may consult with the Finance Parties in relation to any changes mentioned in paragraph (a) above but shall not be obliged to do so if, in its opinion, it is not practicable to do so in the circumstances;

(d) any such changes agreed upon by the Agent and the Company shall (whether or not it is finally determined that a Disruption Event has occurred) be binding upon the Parties as an amendment to (or, as the case may be, waiver of) the terms of the Finance Documents notwithstanding the provisions of Clause 35 (*Amendments and Waivers*);

(e) the Agent shall not be liable for any damages, costs or losses to any person, any diminution in value or any liability whatsoever (including, without limitation for negligence, gross negligence or any other category of liability whatsoever but not including any claim based on the fraud of the Agent) arising as a result of its taking, or failing to take, any actions pursuant to or in connection with this Clause 29.10; and

(f) the Agent shall notify the Finance Parties of all changes agreed pursuant to paragraph (d) above.]

## 30. SET-OFF

A Finance Party may set off any matured obligation due from an Obligor under the Finance Documents (to the extent beneficially owned by that Finance Party) against any matured obligation owed by that Finance Party to that Obligor, regardless of the place of payment, booking branch or currency of either obligation. If the obligations are in different currencies, the Finance Party may convert either obligation at a market rate of exchange in its usual course of business for the purpose of the set-off.

## 31. NOTICES

### 31.1 Communications in writing

Any communication to be made under or in connection with the Finance Documents shall be made in writing and, unless otherwise stated, may be made by fax or letter.

### 31.2 Addresses

The address and fax number (and the department or officer, if any, for whose attention the communication is to be made) of each Party for any communication or document to be made or delivered under or in connection with the Finance Documents is:

(a) in the case of the Company, that identified with its name below;

(b) in the case of each Lender or any other Obligor, that notified in writing to the Agent on or prior to the date on which it becomes a Party; and

(c) in the case of the Agent, that identified with its name below,

or any substitute address or fax number or department or officer as the Party may notify to the Agent (or the Agent may notify to the other Parties, if a change is made by the Agent) by not less than five Business Days' notice.

31.3 **Delivery**

(a) Any communication or document made or delivered by one person to another under or in connection with the Finance Documents will only be effective:

(i) if by way of fax, when received in legible form; or

(ii) if by way of letter, when it has been left at the relevant address or [five] Business Days after being deposited in the post postage prepaid in an envelope addressed to it at that address;

and, if a particular department or officer is specified as part of its address details provided under Clause 31.2 (*Addresses*), if addressed to that department or officer.

(b) Any communication or document to be made or delivered to the Agent will be effective only when actually received by the Agent and then only if it is expressly marked for the attention of the department or officer identified with the Agent's signature below (or any substitute department or officer as the Agent shall specify for this purpose).

(c) All notices from or to an Obligor shall be sent through the Agent.

(d) Any communication or document made or delivered to the Company in accordance with this Clause will be deemed to have been made or delivered to each of the Obligors.

(e) Any communication or document which becomes effective, in accordance with paragraphs (a) to (d) above, after 5:00 p.m. in the place of receipt shall be deemed only to become effective on the following day.

31.4 **Notification of address and fax number**

Promptly upon changing its address or fax number, the Agent shall notify the other Parties.

31.5 **Electronic communication**

(a) Any communication to be made between any two Parties under or in connection with the Finance Documents may be made by electronic mail or other electronic means (including, without limitation, by way of posting to a secure website) if those two Parties:

(i) notify each other in writing of their electronic mail address and/or any other information required to enable the transmission of information by that means; and

(ii) notify each other of any change to their address or any other such information supplied by them by not less than five Business Days' notice.

(b) Any such electronic communication as specified in paragraph (a) above to be made between an Obligor and a Finance Party may only be made in that way to the extent that those two Parties agree that, unless and until notified to the contrary, this is to be an accepted form of communication.

(c) Any such electronic communication as specified in paragraph (a) above made between any two Parties will be effective only when actually received (or made available) in readable form and in the case of any electronic communication made by a Party to the Agent only if it is addressed in such a manner as the Agent shall specify for this purpose.

(d) Any electronic communication which becomes effective, in accordance with paragraph (c) above, after 5:00 p.m. in the place in which the Party to whom the relevant communication is sent or made available has its address for the purpose of this Agreement shall be deemed only to become effective on the following day.

(e) Any reference in a Finance Document to a communication being sent or received shall be construed to include that communication being made available in accordance with this Clause 31.5.

31.6 **English language**

(a) Any notice given under or in connection with any Finance Document must be in English.

(b) All other documents provided under or in connection with any Finance Document must be:

(i) in English; or

(ii) if not in English, and if so required by the Agent, accompanied by a certified English translation and, in this case, the English translation will prevail unless the document is a constitutional, statutory or other official document.

## 32. CALCULATIONS AND CERTIFICATES

### 32.1 Accounts

In any litigation or arbitration proceedings arising out of or in connection with a Finance Document, the entries made in the accounts maintained by a Finance Party are *prima facie* evidence of the matters to which they relate.

### 32.2 Certificates and Determinations

Any certification or determination by a Finance Party of a rate or amount under any Finance Document is, in the absence of manifest error, conclusive evidence of the matters to which it relates.

### 32.3 Day count convention

Any interest, commission or fee accruing under a Finance Document will accrue from day to day and is calculated on the basis of the actual number of days elapsed and a year of 360 days or, in any case where the practice in the Relevant Market differs, in accordance with that market practice.

## 33. PARTIAL INVALIDITY

If, at any time, any provision of a Finance Document is or becomes illegal, invalid or unenforceable in any respect under any law of any jurisdiction, neither the legality, validity or enforceability of the remaining provisions nor the legality, validity or enforceability of such provision under the law of any other jurisdiction will in any way be affected or impaired.

## 34. REMEDIES AND WAIVERS

No failure to exercise, nor any delay in exercising, on the part of any Finance Party, any right or remedy under a Finance Document shall operate as a waiver of any such right or remedy or constitute an election to affirm any of the Finance Documents. No election to affirm any Finance Document on the part of any Finance Party shall be effective unless it is in writing. No single or partial exercise of any right or remedy shall prevent any further or other exercise or the exercise of any other right or remedy. The rights and remedies provided in each Finance Document are cumulative and not exclusive of any rights or remedies provided by law.

## 35. AMENDMENTS AND WAIVERS

### 35.1 Required consents

(a) Subject to Clause 35.2 (*All Lender matters*) and Clause 35.3 (*Other exceptions*) any term of the Finance Documents may be amended or waived only with the consent of the Majority Lenders and the Obligors and any such amendment or waiver will be binding on all Parties.

(b) The Agent may effect, on behalf of any Finance Party, any amendment or waiver permitted by this Clause 35.

(c) [Paragraph (c) of Clause 24.10 (*Pro rata interest settlement*) shall apply to this Clause 35.][53]

35.2 **All Lender matters**

[Subject to Clause 35.4 (*Replacement of Screen Rate*) an]/[An] amendment or waiver of any term of any Finance Document that has the effect of changing or which relates to:

(a) the definition of "Majority Lenders" in Clause 1.1 (*Definitions*);

(b) an extension to the date of payment of any amount under the Finance Documents;

(c) a reduction in the Margin or a reduction in the amount of any payment of principal, interest, fees or commission payable;

(d) [a change in currency of payment of any amount under the Finance Documents;]

(e) an increase in any Commitment, an extension of any Availability Period or any requirement that a cancellation of Commitments reduces the Commitments of the Lenders rateably under the relevant Facility;

(f) a change to the Borrowers or Guarantors other than in accordance with Clause 25 (*Changes to the Obligors*);

(g) any provision which expressly requires the consent of all the Lenders;

(h) Clause 2.3 (*Finance Parties' rights and obligations*), [Clause 5.1 (*Delivery of a Utilisation Request*),] Clause 8.1 (*Illegality*), [Clause 8.2 (*Change of control*),][54] [Clause 8.8 (*Application of prepayments*),] Clause 24 (*Changes to the Lenders*), Clause 25 (*Changes to the Obligors*), [Clause 28 (*Sharing among the Finance Parties*),] this Clause 35, Clause 39 (*Governing law*) or Clause 40.1 (*Jurisdiction*);

(i) the nature or scope of the guarantee and indemnity granted under Clause 18 (*Guarantee and indemnity*); or

(j) [________],

shall not be made without the prior consent of all the Lenders.

35.3 **Other exceptions**

An amendment or waiver which relates to the rights or obligations of the Agent or the Arranger [or a Reference Bank] (each in their capacity as such) may not be effected without the consent of the Agent, the Arranger [or that Reference Bank], as the case may be.

53 Include if the optional Clause 24.10 (*Pro rata interest settlement*) is included.

54 If Clause 8.2 (*Change of control*) gives each Lender the unilateral right to require prepayment on a change of control, users should consider the extent to which this right should be protected by making amendments and waivers to that Clause subject to all Lender consent.

35.4 **[Replacement of Screen Rate**

(a) Subject to Clause 35.3 (*Other exceptions*), if any Screen Rate is not available for a currency which can be selected for a Loan, any amendment or waiver which relates to providing for another benchmark rate to apply in relation to that currency in place of that Screen Rate (or which relates to aligning any provision of a Finance Document to the use of that other benchmark rate) may be made with the consent of the Majority Lenders and the Obligors.

(b) [If any Lender fails to respond to a request for an amendment or waiver described in paragraph (a) above within [ ] Business Days (unless the Company and the Agent agree to a longer time period in relation to any request) of that request being made:

(i) its Commitment(s) shall not be included for the purpose of calculating the Total Commitments under the relevant Facility/ies when ascertaining whether any relevant percentage of Total Commitments has been obtained to approve that request; and

(ii) its status as a Lender shall be disregarded for the purpose of ascertaining whether the agreement of any specified group of Lenders has been obtained to approve that request.]]

36. **CONFIDENTIAL INFORMATION**

36.1 **Confidentiality**

Each Finance Party agrees to keep all Confidential Information confidential and not to disclose it to anyone, save to the extent permitted by Clause 36.2 (*Disclosure of Confidential Information*) [and Clause 36.3 (*Disclosure to numbering service providers*)], and to ensure that all Confidential Information is protected with security measures and a degree of care that would apply to its own confidential information.

36.2 **Disclosure of Confidential Information**

Any Finance Party may disclose:

(a) to any of its Affiliates and Related Funds and any of its or their officers, directors, employees, professional advisers, auditors, partners and Representatives such Confidential Information as that Finance Party shall consider appropriate if any person to whom the Confidential Information is to be given pursuant to this paragraph (a) is informed in writing of its confidential nature and that some or all of such Confidential Information may be price-sensitive information except that there shall be no such requirement to so inform if the recipient is subject to professional obligations to maintain the confidentiality of the information or is otherwise bound by requirements of confidentiality in relation to the Confidential Information;

(b) to any person:

(i) to (or through) whom it assigns or transfers (or may potentially assign or transfer) all or any of its rights and/or obligations under one or more Finance Documents or which succeeds (or which may potentially succeed) it as Agent and, in each case, to any of that person's Affiliates, Related Funds, Representatives and professional advisers;

(ii) with (or through) whom it enters into (or may potentially enter into), whether directly or indirectly, any sub-participation in relation to, or any other transaction under which payments are to be made or may be made by reference to, one or more Finance Documents and/or one or more Obligors and to any of that person's Affiliates, Related Funds, Representatives and professional advisers;

(iii) appointed by any Finance Party or by a person to whom paragraph (b)(i) or (ii) above applies to receive communications, notices, information or documents delivered pursuant to the Finance Documents on its behalf (including, without limitation, any person appointed under paragraph (c) of Clause 26.14 (*Relationship with the Lenders*));

(iv) who invests in or otherwise finances (or may potentially invest in or otherwise finance), directly or indirectly, any transaction referred to in paragraph (b)(i) or (b)(ii) above;

(v) to whom information is required or requested to be disclosed by any court of competent jurisdiction or any governmental, banking, taxation or other regulatory authority or similar body, the rules of any relevant stock exchange or pursuant to any applicable law or regulation;

(vi) to whom information is required to be disclosed in connection with, and for the purposes of, any litigation, arbitration, administrative or other investigations, proceedings or disputes;

(vii) [to whom or for whose benefit that Finance Party charges, assigns or otherwise creates Security (or may do so) pursuant to Clause 24.9 (*Security over Lenders' rights*);][55]

(viii) who is a Party; or

(ix) with the consent of the Company;

in each case, such Confidential Information as that Finance Party shall consider appropriate if:

(A) in relation to paragraphs (b)(i), (b)(ii) and b(iii) above, the person to whom the Confidential Information is to be given has entered into a Confidentiality Undertaking except that there shall be no requirement for a Confidentiality Undertaking if the recipient is a professional adviser and is subject to professional obligations to maintain the confidentiality of the Confidential Information;

(B) in relation to paragraph (b)(iv) above, the person to whom the Confidential Information is to be given has entered into a

[55] Include if optional Clause 24.9 (*Security over Lenders' rights*) is included.

Confidentiality Undertaking or is otherwise bound by requirements of confidentiality in relation to the Confidential Information they receive and is informed that some or all of such Confidential Information may be price-sensitive information;

(C) in relation to paragraphs (b)(v), (b)(vi) [and (b)(vii)][56] above, the person to whom the Confidential Information is to be given is informed of its confidential nature and that some or all of such Confidential Information may be price-sensitive information except that there shall be no requirement to so inform if, in the opinion of that Finance Party, it is not practicable so to do in the circumstances; [and]

(c) to any person appointed by that Finance Party or by a person to whom paragraph (b)(i) or (b)(ii) above applies to provide administration or settlement services in respect of one or more of the Finance Documents including without limitation, in relation to the trading of participations in respect of the Finance Documents, such Confidential Information as may be required to be disclosed to enable such service provider to provide any of the services referred to in this paragraph (c) if the service provider to whom the Confidential Information is to be given has entered into a confidentiality agreement substantially in the form of the LMA Master Confidentiality Undertaking for Use With Administration/Settlement Service Providers or such other form of confidentiality undertaking agreed between the Company and the relevant Finance Party[; and

(d) to any rating agency (including its professional advisers) such Confidential Information as may be required to be disclosed to enable such rating agency to carry out its normal rating activities in relation to the Finance Documents and/or the Obligors [if the rating agency to whom the Confidential Information is to be given is informed of its confidential nature and that some or all of such Confidential Information may be price-sensitive information]].

36.3 **[Disclosure to numbering service providers**

(a) Any Finance Party may disclose to any national or international numbering service provider appointed by that Finance Party to provide identification numbering services in respect of this Agreement, the Facilities and/or one or more Obligors the following information:

(i) names of Obligors;

(ii) country of domicile of Obligors;

(iii) place of incorporation of Obligors;

(iv) date of this Agreement;

[56] Include this reference if the optional paragraph (b)(vii) of Clause 36.2 (*Disclosure of Confidential Information*) is included.

(v) Clause 39 (*Governing law*);

(vi) the names of the Agent and the Arranger;

(vii) date of each amendment and restatement of this Agreement;

(viii) amounts of, and names of, the Facilities (and any tranches);

(ix) amount of Total Commitments;

(x) currencies of the Facilities;

(xi) type of Facilities[57];

(xii) ranking of Facilities;

(xiii) Termination Date for Facilities;

(xiv) changes to any of the information previously supplied pursuant to paragraphs (i) to (xiii) above; and

(xv) such other information agreed between such Finance Party and the Company,

to enable such numbering service provider to provide its usual syndicated loan numbering identification services.[58]

(b) The Parties acknowledge and agree that each identification number assigned to this Agreement, the Facilities and/or one or more Obligors by a numbering service provider and the information associated with each such number may be disclosed to users of its services in accordance with the standard terms and conditions of that numbering service provider.

(c) [[The Company]/[Each Obligor] represents that none of the information set out in paragraphs (i) to (xv) of paragraph (a) above is, nor will at any time be, unpublished price-sensitive information.][59]

57 Term/Revolver etc.

58 This wording has been included to ensure that disclosure is made only for the purposes of enabling a numbering service provider to allocate an identification number to a syndicated facility agreement, one or more facilities made available under such facility agreement or any Obligor party to such facility agreement. The purpose of disclosure is not therefore to enable products that are directly or indirectly related to a facility agreement, its facilities or its Obligors to be allocated an identification number.

59 The information listed in paragraph (a) reflects the information that is likely to be required to enable a numbering service provider ("**NSP**") to assign identification numbers/codes to this Agreement, the Facilities and their ranking. Disclosure has been restricted to descriptive information about the Facility Agreement (including changes to that information) for two main reasons. Firstly, because once delivered to the NSP that information will not be subject to any confidentiality obligations on the part of the NSP or subscribers to the NSP. It has been assumed that as the NSP needs to disclose the information to its subscribers they would not be prepared to sign up to a confidentiality undertaking or require their subscribers to do so to protect Borrower confidential information. However, no dialogue has been had with NSP's in this regard.

The second reason for restricting the information that can be disclosed to NSP's is to limit the risk of that information being unpublished price-sensitive or inside-information (meaning, if it were known to the public it

(d) [The Agent shall notify the Company and the other Finance Parties of:

(i) the name of any numbering service provider appointed by the Agent in respect of this Agreement, the Facilities and/or one or more Obligors; and

(ii) the number or, as the case may be, numbers assigned to this Agreement, the Facilities and/or one or more Obligors by such numbering service provider.][60]]

36.4 **Entire agreement**

This Clause 36 constitutes the entire agreement between the Parties in relation to the obligations of the Finance Parties under the Finance Documents regarding Confidential Information and supersedes any previous agreement, whether express or implied, regarding Confidential Information.

36.5 **Inside information**

Each of the Finance Parties acknowledges that some or all of the Confidential Information is or may be price-sensitive information and that the use of such information may be regulated or prohibited by applicable legislation including securities law relating to insider dealing and market abuse and each of the Finance Parties undertakes not to use any Confidential Information for any unlawful purpose.

36.6 **Notification of disclosure**

Each of the Finance Parties agrees (to the extent permitted by law and regulation) to inform the Company:

(a) of the circumstances of any disclosure of Confidential Information made pursuant to paragraph (b)(v) of Clause 36.2 (*Disclosure of Confidential Information*) except where such disclosure is made to any of the persons

would be likely to have an effect on the price of securities issued by the relevant Borrower that are publicly traded). If unpublished price-sensitive or inside information were disclosed to a NSP (with or without the consent of the Borrower) by a Lender in circumstances where that information will be disclosed only to subscribers of the NSP (and not to the public), that Lender and the individuals concerned could be guilty of an offence under the insider dealing/market abuse regime in the UK. Restricting the information that can be disclosed by Lenders to NSP's to relatively anodyne and descriptive information helps to minimise the risk that the information will be unpublished price-sensitive or inside information.

However, because of the potential seriousness of this issue, because it is possible to envisage circumstances where all or part of the information specified in paragraph (a) may be unpublished price-sensitive or inside information and because only the Obligors can know with certainty whether any of that information is unpublished price-sensitive or inside information, the permission also requires the Obligors to represent to the Lenders that none of that information is unpublished price-sensitive information. The representation is contained in paragraph (c) as a means of ensuring reasonable steps have been taken to avoid inside or price-sensitive information being selectively disclosed with no confidentiality restrictions.

In most cases where the relevant Obligor has publicly traded securities, the information that is listed in paragraph (a) would, in any event, need to be disclosed by that Obligor in accordance with the UK disclosure requirements on issuers of listed securities and so the representation should not be onerous for such Obligors.

60 This requirement has been limited to the Agent on the assumption that if the Agent requests an identification number, it will, in any event, require all Parties to use that number in communications etc. If this is not the case, this Clause can be deleted.

referred to in that paragraph during the ordinary course of its supervisory or regulatory function; and

(b) upon becoming aware that Confidential Information has been disclosed in breach of this Clause 36.

36.7 **Continuing obligations**

The obligations in this Clause 36 are continuing and, in particular, shall survive and remain binding on each Finance Party for a period of [twelve] months from the earlier of:

(a) the date on which all amounts payable by the Obligors under or in connection with this Agreement have been paid in full and all Commitments have been cancelled or otherwise cease to be available; and

(b) the date on which such Finance Party otherwise ceases to be a Finance Party.

## 37. CONFIDENTIALITY OF FUNDING RATES [AND REFERENCE BANK QUOTATIONS]

37.1 **Confidentiality and disclosure**

(a) The Agent and each Obligor agree to keep each Funding Rate [(and, in the case of the Agent, each Reference Bank Quotation)] confidential and not to disclose it to anyone, save to the extent permitted by paragraphs (b), (c) [and (d)] below.

(b) The Agent may disclose:

(i) any Funding Rate [(but not, for the avoidance of doubt, any Reference Bank Quotation)] to the relevant Borrower pursuant to Clause 9.4 (*Notification of rates of interest*); and

(ii) any Funding Rate [or any Reference Bank Quotation] to any person appointed by it to provide administration services in respect of one or more of the Finance Documents to the extent necessary to enable such service provider to provide those services if the service provider to whom that information is to be given has entered into a confidentiality agreement substantially in the form of the LMA Master Confidentiality Undertaking for Use With Administration/Settlement Service Providers or such other form of confidentiality undertaking agreed between the Agent and the relevant Lender [or Reference Bank, as the case may be].

(c) The Agent may disclose any Funding Rate [or any Reference Bank Quotation], and each Obligor may disclose any Funding Rate, to:

(i) any of its Affiliates and any of its or their officers, directors, employees, professional advisers, auditors, partners and Representatives if any person to whom that Funding Rate [or Reference Bank Quotation] is to be given pursuant to this paragraph (i) is informed in writing of its confidential nature and that it may be price-sensitive information except that there shall be no such requirement to so inform if the recipient is subject to professional obligations to maintain the confidentiality of that Funding Rate [or Reference Bank Quotation] or is otherwise bound by requirements of confidentiality in relation to it;

(ii) any person to whom information is required or requested to be disclosed by any court of competent jurisdiction or any governmental, banking, taxation or other regulatory authority or similar body, the rules of any relevant stock exchange or pursuant to any applicable law or regulation if the person to whom that Funding Rate [or Reference Bank Quotation] is to be given is informed in writing of its confidential nature and that it may be price-sensitive information except that there shall be no requirement to so inform if, in the opinion of the Agent or the relevant Obligor, as the case may be, it is not practicable to do so in the circumstances;

(iii) any person to whom information is required to be disclosed in connection with, and for the purposes of, any litigation, arbitration, administrative or other investigations, proceedings or disputes if the person to whom that Funding Rate [or Reference Bank Quotation] is to be given is informed in writing of its confidential nature and that it may be price-sensitive information except that there shall be no requirement to so inform if, in the opinion of the Agent or the relevant Obligor, as the case may be, it is not practicable to do so in the circumstances; and

(iv) any person with the consent of the relevant Lender [or Reference Bank, as the case may be].

(d) [The Agent's obligations in this Clause 37 relating to Reference Bank Quotations are without prejudice to its obligations to make notifications under Clause 9.4 (*Notification of rates of interest*) **provided that** (other than pursuant to paragraph (b)(i) above) the Agent shall not include the details of any individual Reference Bank Quotation as part of any such notification.]

**37.2 Related obligations**

(a) The Agent and each Obligor acknowledge that each Funding Rate [(and, in the case of the Agent, each Reference Bank Quotation)] is or may be price-sensitive information and that its use may be regulated or prohibited by applicable legislation including securities law relating to insider dealing and market abuse and the Agent and each Obligor undertake not to use any Funding Rate [or, in the case of the Agent, any Reference Bank Quotation] for any unlawful purpose.

(b) The Agent and each Obligor agree (to the extent permitted by law and regulation) to inform the relevant Lender [or Reference Bank, as the case may be]:

(i) of the circumstances of any disclosure made pursuant to paragraph (c)(ii) of Clause 37.1 (*Confidentiality and disclosure*) except where such disclosure is made to any of the persons referred to in that paragraph during the ordinary course of its supervisory or regulatory function; and

(ii) upon becoming aware that any information has been disclosed in breach of this Clause 37.

37.3 **No Event of Default**

No Event of Default will occur under Clause 23.3 (*Other obligations*) by reason only of an Obligor's failure to comply with this Clause 37.

38. **COUNTERPARTS**

Each Finance Document may be executed in any number of counterparts, and this has the same effect as if the signatures on the counterparts were on a single copy of the Finance Document.

## SECTION 12
## GOVERNING LAW AND ENFORCEMENT

39. **GOVERNING LAW**

This Agreement [and any non-contractual obligations arising out of or in connection with it][61] [is/are] governed by English law.

40. **ENFORCEMENT**

40.1 **Jurisdiction**[62]

(a) The courts of England have exclusive jurisdiction to settle any dispute arising out of or in connection with this Agreement (including a dispute relating to the existence, validity or termination of this Agreement [or any non-contractual obligation arising out of or in connection with this Agreement][63]) (a "**Dispute**").

(b) The Parties agree that the courts of England are the most appropriate and convenient courts to settle Disputes and accordingly no Party will argue to the contrary.

(c) Notwithstanding paragraph (a) above, no Finance Party shall be prevented from taking proceedings relating to a Dispute in any other courts with jurisdiction. To the extent allowed by law, the Finance Parties may take concurrent proceedings in any number of jurisdictions.

40.2 **Service of process**

Without prejudice to any other mode of service allowed under any relevant law, each Obligor (other than an Obligor incorporated in England and Wales):

(a) irrevocably appoints [the Company]/[______] as its agent for service of process in relation to any proceedings before the English courts in connection with any Finance Document; and

(b) agrees that failure by a process agent to notify the relevant Obligor of the process will not invalidate the proceedings concerned.

**This Agreement has been entered into on the date stated at the beginning of this Agreement.**

61 This wording is intended to make non-contractual obligations arising out of or in connection with the agreement subject to English law. However, if the document is used in a cross-border transaction where different transaction documents are governed by different governing laws, consider whether it is appropriate, in the context of that transaction, for English law to apply to non-contractual obligations arising out of or in connection with the transaction documents which are not governed by English law.

62 Users should consider the extent to which this clause may require amendment in light of the decision of the French *Cour de cassation* in *Mme X v Rothschild*. For a discussion of the issues involved, see the LMA note entitled "*Jurisdiction Clauses in LMA facility documentation*" (available through the LMA website).

63 To the extent that the square bracketed wording relating to non-contractual obligations in Clause 39 (*Governing law*) is included, this wording should be included in paragraph (a) of Clause 40.1 (*Jurisdiction*).

## SCHEDULE 1

### THE ORIGINAL PARTIES

### Part I

### The Original Obligors

| Name of Original Borrower | Registration number (or equivalent, if any) |
|---|---|

| Name of Original Guarantor | Registration number (or equivalent, if any) |
|---|---|

**Part II**

**The Original Lenders [- other than UK Non-Bank Lenders]**[64]

| Name of Original Lender | Facility A Commitment | Facility B Commitment | Treaty Passport scheme reference number and jurisdiction of tax residence (if applicable)[65] |
|---|---|---|---|

[64] If no Original Lender is a UK Non-Bank Lender, delete the words in square brackets from the heading of this Part.

[65] Each of these must be included if the Original Lender holds a passport under the HMRC DT Treaty Passport scheme and wishes that scheme to apply to the Agreement.

**Part III**

**[The Original Lenders - UK Non-Bank Lenders]**[66]

| Name of Original Lender | Facility A Commitment | Facility B Commitment |
| --- | --- | --- |

[66] If no Original Lender is a UK Non-Bank Lender, delete this part of the Schedule and all references to it in the body of the Agreement.

## SCHEDULE 2

### CONDITIONS PRECEDENT

### Part I
### Conditions Precedent To Initial Utilisation

1. **Original Obligors**

(a) A copy of the constitutional documents of each Original Obligor.

(b) A copy of a resolution of the board of directors of each Original Obligor:

(i) approving the terms of, and the transactions contemplated by, the Finance Documents to which it is a party and resolving that it execute the Finance Documents to which it is a party;

(ii) authorising a specified person or persons to execute the Finance Documents to which it is a party on its behalf; and

(iii) authorising a specified person or persons, on its behalf, to sign and/or despatch all documents and notices (including, if relevant, any Utilisation Request and Selection Notice) to be signed and/or despatched by it under or in connection with the Finance Documents to which it is a party.

(c) A specimen of the signature of each person authorised by the resolution referred to in paragraph (b) above.

(d) [A copy of a resolution signed by all the holders of the issued shares in each Original Guarantor, approving the terms of, and the transactions contemplated by, the Finance Documents to which the Original Guarantor is a party.]

(e) A certificate of the Company (signed by a director) confirming that borrowing or guaranteeing, as appropriate, the Total Commitments would not cause any borrowing, guaranteeing or similar limit binding on any Original Obligor to be exceeded.

(f) A certificate of an authorised signatory of the relevant Original Obligor certifying that each copy document relating to it specified in this Part I of Schedule 2 is correct, complete and in full force and effect as at a date no earlier than the date of this Agreement.

2. **Legal opinions**

(a) A legal opinion of [__________], legal advisers to the Arranger and the Agent in England, substantially in the form distributed to the Original Lenders prior to signing this Agreement.

(b) If an Original Obligor is incorporated in a jurisdiction other than England and Wales, a legal opinion of the legal advisers to [the Arranger and the Agent] in the relevant jurisdiction, substantially in the form distributed to the Original Lenders prior to signing this Agreement.

3. **Other documents and evidence**

(a) Evidence that any process agent referred to in Clause 40.2 (*Service of process*), if not an Original Obligor, has accepted its appointment.

(b) A copy of any other Authorisation or other document, opinion or assurance which the Agent considers to be necessary or desirable (if it has notified the Company accordingly) in connection with the entry into and performance of the transactions contemplated by any Finance Document or for the validity and enforceability of any Finance Document.

(c) The Original Financial Statements of each Original Obligor.

(d) Evidence that the fees, costs and expenses then due from the Company pursuant to Clause 12 (*Fees*) and Clause 17 (*Costs and expenses*) have been paid or will be paid by the first Utilisation Date.

**Part II**
**Conditions Precedent Required To Be Delivered By An Additional Obligor**

1. An Accession Letter, duly executed by the Additional Obligor and the Company.

2. A copy of the constitutional documents of the Additional Obligor.

3. A copy of a resolution of the board of directors of the Additional Obligor:

   (a) approving the terms of, and the transactions contemplated by, the Accession Letter and the Finance Documents and resolving that it execute the Accession Letter;

   (b) authorising a specified person or persons to execute the Accession Letter on its behalf; and

   (c) authorising a specified person or persons, on its behalf, to sign and/or despatch all other documents and notices (including, in relation to an Additional Borrower, any Utilisation Request or Selection Notice) to be signed and/or despatched by it under or in connection with the Finance Documents.

4. A specimen of the signature of each person authorised by the resolution referred to in paragraph 3 above.

5. [A copy of a resolution signed by all the holders of the issued shares of the Additional Guarantor, approving the terms of, and the transactions contemplated by, the Finance Documents to which the Additional Guarantor is a party.]

6. A certificate of the Additional Obligor (signed by a director) confirming that borrowing or guaranteeing, as appropriate, the Total Commitments would not cause any borrowing, guaranteeing or similar limit binding on it to be exceeded.

7. A certificate of an authorised signatory of the Additional Obligor certifying that each copy document listed in this Part II of Schedule 2 is correct, complete and in full force and effect as at a date no earlier than the date of the Accession Letter.

8. A copy of any other Authorisation or other document, opinion or assurance which the Agent considers to be necessary or desirable in connection with the entry into and performance of the transactions contemplated by the Accession Letter or for the validity and enforceability of any Finance Document.

9. If available, the latest audited financial statements of the Additional Obligor.

10. A legal opinion of [____________], legal advisers to the Arranger and the Agent in England.

11. If the Additional Obligor is incorporated in a jurisdiction other than England and Wales, a legal opinion of the legal advisers to the Arranger and the Agent in the jurisdiction in which the Additional Obligor is incorporated.

12. If the proposed Additional Obligor is incorporated in a jurisdiction other than England and Wales, evidence that the process agent specified in Clause 40.2 (*Service of process*), if not an Obligor, has accepted its appointment in relation to the proposed Additional Obligor.

**SCHEDULE 3**
**REQUESTS**

**Part I**
**Utilisation Request**

From: [*Borrower*]

To: [*Agent*]

Dated:

Dear Sirs

**[Company] – [ ] Facility Agreement dated [ ] (the "Agreement")**

1. We refer to the Agreement. This is a Utilisation Request. Terms defined in the Agreement have the same meaning in this Utilisation Request unless given a different meaning in this Utilisation Request.

2. We wish to borrow a Loan on the following terms:

| | |
|---|---|
| Proposed Utilisation Date: | [ ] (or, if that is not a Business Day, the next Business Day) |
| Facility to be utilised: | [Facility A]/[Facility B]* |
| Currency of Loan: | [ ] |
| Amount: | [ ] or, if less, the Available Facility |
| Interest Period: | [ ] |

3. We confirm that each condition specified in Clause 4.2 (*Further conditions precedent*) of the Agreement is satisfied on the date of this Utilisation Request.

4. [This Loan is to be made in [whole]/[part] for the purpose of refinancing [*identify maturing Facility B Loan*]/[The proceeds of this Loan should be credited to [*account*].][67]/[The proceeds of this Loan should be credited to [*account*].][68]

5. This Utilisation Request is irrevocable.

* Delete as appropriate.

67 Include if the optional paragraph (b) to Clause 7.2 (*Repayment of Facility B Loans*) is included.

68 Include if the optional paragraph (b) to Clause 7.2 (*Repayment of Facility B Loans*) is not included.

Yours faithfully

.......................................
authorised signatory for
[*name of relevant Borrower*]

**PART II**
**Selection Notice**

APPLICABLE TO A FACILITY A LOAN

From: [*Borrower*]

To: [*Agent*]

Dated:

Dear Sirs

**[Company] - [ ] Facility Agreement dated [ ] (the "Agreement")**

1. We refer to the Agreement. This is a Selection Notice. Terms defined in the Agreement have the same meaning in this Selection Notice unless given a different meaning in this Selection Notice.

2. We refer to the following Facility A Loan[s] in [*identify currency*] with an Interest Period ending on [ ].*

3. [We request that the above Facility A Loan[s] be divided into [ ] Facility A Loans with the following Base Currency Amounts and Interest Periods:]**

   *or*

   [We request that the next Interest Period for the above Facility A Loan[s] is [ ]].***

4. We request that the above Facility A Loan[s] [is]/[are] [denominated in the same currency for the next Interest Period]/[denominated in the following currencies: [ ]. As this results in a change of currency we confirm that each condition specified in Clause 4.2 (*Further conditions precedent*) of the Agreement is satisfied on the date of this Selection Notice. The proceeds of any change in currency should be credited to [*account*]].

5. This Selection Notice is irrevocable.

Yours faithfully

....................................
authorised signatory for
[the Company on behalf of]
[*name of relevant Borrower*]

* Insert details of all Facility A Loans in the same currency which have an Interest Period ending on the same date.

** Use this option if division of Loans is requested.

*** Use this option if sub-division is not required.

## SCHEDULE 4
## [MANDATORY COST FORMULAE]

[____________________][69]

[69] The extent to which Mandatory Costs are chargeable to the borrower on any transaction, and the method for calculating any such Mandatory Costs, is a matter for commercial agreement between the parties. Users should refer to the LMA note entitled "*Withdrawal of the Mandatory Costs Schedule*" (available through the LMA website) for a discussion of some of the issues involved in formulating any calculation methodology.

**SCHEDULE 5**

**FORM OF TRANSFER CERTIFICATE**

To: [ ] as Agent

From: [*The Existing Lender*] (the "**Existing Lender**") and [*The New Lender*] (the "**New Lender**")

Dated:

**[Company] – [ ] Facility Agreement dated [ ] (the "Agreement")**

1. We refer to the Agreement. This is a Transfer Certificate. Terms defined in the Agreement have the same meaning in this Transfer Certificate unless given a different meaning in this Transfer Certificate.

2. We refer to Clause 24.6 (*Procedure for transfer*) of the Agreement:

   (a) The Existing Lender and the New Lender agree to the Existing Lender transferring to the New Lender by novation, and in accordance with Clause 24.6 (*Procedure for transfer*) of the Agreement, all of the Existing Lender's rights and obligations under the Agreement and the other Finance Documents which relate to that portion of the Existing Lender's Commitment(s) and participations in Loans under the Agreement as specified in the Schedule.

   (b) The proposed Transfer Date is [ ].

   (c) The Facility Office and address, fax number and attention details for notices of the New Lender for the purposes of Clause 31.2 (*Addresses*) of the Agreement are set out in the Schedule.

3. The New Lender expressly acknowledges the limitations on the Existing Lender's obligations set out in paragraph (c) of Clause 24.5 (*Limitation of responsibility of Existing Lenders*) of the Agreement.

4. The New Lender confirms, for the benefit of the Agent and without liability to any Obligor, that it is:

   (a) [a Qualifying Lender (other than a Treaty Lender);]

   (b) [a Treaty Lender;]

   (c) [not a Qualifying Lender].[70]

5. [The New Lender confirms that the person beneficially entitled to interest payable to that Lender in respect of an advance under a Finance Document is either:

   (a) a company resident in the United Kingdom for United Kingdom tax purposes;

[70] Delete as applicable - each New Lender is required to confirm which of these three categories it falls within.

(b) a partnership each member of which is:

(i) a company so resident in the United Kingdom; or

(ii) a company not so resident in the United Kingdom which carries on a trade in the United Kingdom through a permanent establishment and which brings into account in computing its chargeable profits (within the meaning of section 19 of the CTA) the whole of any share of interest payable in respect of that advance that falls to it by reason of Part 17 of the CTA; or

(c) a company not so resident in the United Kingdom which carries on a trade in the United Kingdom through a permanent establishment and which brings into account interest payable in respect of that advance in computing the chargeable profits (within the meaning of section 19 of the CTA) of that company.][71]

5. [The New Lender confirms that it holds a passport under the HMRC DT Treaty Passport scheme (reference number [ ]) and is tax resident in [ ] [72], so that interest payable to it by borrowers is generally subject to full exemption from UK withholding tax, and requests that the Company notify:

(a) each Borrower which is a Party as a Borrower as at the Transfer Date; and

(b) each Additional Borrower which becomes an Additional Borrower after the Transfer Date,

that it wishes that scheme to apply to the Agreement.][73]

[5/6]. This Transfer Certificate may be executed in any number of counterparts and this has the same effect as if the signatures on the counterparts were on a single copy of this Transfer Certificate.

[6/7]. This Transfer Certificate [and any non-contractual obligations arising out of or in connection with it] [is/are][74] governed by English law.

[7/8]. This Transfer Certificate has been entered into on the date stated at the beginning of this Transfer Certificate.

[71] Include if New Lender comes within paragraph (i)(B) of the definition of Qualifying Lender in Clause 13.1 (*Definitions*)

[72] Insert jurisdiction of tax residence.

[73] Include if New Lender holds a passport under the HMRC DT Treaty Passport scheme and wishes that scheme to apply to the Agreement.

[74] This clause should follow the approach adopted as regards non-contractual obligations in Clause 39 (*Governing law*). This should be done (and this footnote deleted) before the Facility Agreement is signed.

**THE SCHEDULE**

**Commitment/rights and obligations to be transferred**

[*insert relevant details*]

[*Facility Office address, fax number and attention details for notices and account details for payments,*]

[Existing Lender] [New Lender]

By: By:

This Transfer Certificate is accepted by the Agent and the Transfer Date is confirmed as [ ].

[Agent]

By:

## SCHEDULE 6

### FORM OF ASSIGNMENT AGREEMENT

To: [ ] as Agent and [ ] as Company, for and on behalf of each Obligor

From: [the *Existing Lender*] (the "**Existing Lender**") and [the *New Lender*] (the "**New Lender**")

Dated:

**[Company] - [ ] Facility Agreement**
**dated [ ] (the "Agreement")**

1. We refer to the Agreement. This is an Assignment Agreement. Terms defined in the Agreement have the same meaning in this Assignment Agreement unless given a different meaning in this Assignment Agreement.

2. We refer to Clause 24.7 (*Procedure for assignment*) of the Agreement:

   (a) The Existing Lender assigns absolutely to the New Lender all the rights of the Existing Lender under the Agreement and the other Finance Documents which relate to that portion of the Existing Lender's Commitment(s) and participations in Loans under the Agreement as specified in the Schedule.

   (b) The Existing Lender is released from all the obligations of the Existing Lender which correspond to that portion of the Existing Lender's Commitment(s) and participations in Loans under the Agreement specified in the Schedule.

   (c) The New Lender becomes a Party as a Lender and is bound by obligations equivalent to those from which the Existing Lender is released under paragraph (b) above.[75]

3. The proposed Transfer Date is [ ].

4. On the Transfer Date the New Lender becomes Party to the Finance Documents as a Lender.

5. The Facility Office and address, fax number and attention details for notices of the New Lender for the purposes of Clause 31.2 (*Addresses*) of the Agreement are set out in the Schedule.

6. The New Lender expressly acknowledges the limitations on the Existing Lender's obligations set out in paragraph (c) of Clause 24.5 (*Limitation of responsibility of Existing Lenders*) of the Agreement.

[75] If the Assignment Agreement is used in place of a Transfer Certificate in order to avoid a novation of rights/obligations for reasons relevant to a civil jurisdiction, local law advice should be sought to check the suitability of the Assignment Agreement due to the assumption of obligations contained in paragraph 2(c). This issue should be addressed at primary documentation stage.

7. The New Lender confirms, for the benefit of the Agent and without liability to any Obligor, that it is:

   (a) [a Qualifying Lender (other than a Treaty Lender);]

   (b) [a Treaty Lender;]

   (c) [not a Qualifying Lender]. [76]

8. [The New Lender confirms that the person beneficially entitled to interest payable to that Lender in respect of an advance under a Finance Document is either:

   (a) a company resident in the United Kingdom for United Kingdom tax purposes;

   (b) a partnership each member of which is:

      (iii) a company so resident in the United Kingdom; or

      (iv) a company not so resident in the United Kingdom which carries on a trade in the United Kingdom through a permanent establishment and which brings into account in computing its chargeable profits (within the meaning of section 19 of the CTA) the whole of any share of interest payable in respect of that advance that falls to it by reason of Part 17 of the CTA; or

   (c) a company not so resident in the United Kingdom which carries on a trade in the United Kingdom through a permanent establishment and which brings into account interest payable in respect of that advance in computing the chargeable profits (within the meaning of section 19 of the CTA) of that company.][77]

8. [The New Lender confirms that it holds a passport under the HMRC DT Treaty Passport scheme (reference number [ ]) and is tax resident in [ ] [78], so that interest payable to it by borrowers is generally subject to full exemption from UK withholding tax, and requests that the Company notify:

   (a) each Borrower which is a Party as a Borrower as at the Transfer Date; and

   (b) each Additional Borrower which becomes an Additional Borrower after the Transfer Date,

   that it wishes that scheme to apply to the Agreement.][79]

[8/9]. This Assignment Agreement acts as notice to the Agent (on behalf of each Finance Party) and, upon delivery in accordance with Clause 24.8 (*Copy of Transfer Certificate, Assignment Agreement or Increase Confirmation to Company*) of the Agreement, to the

[76] Delete as applicable - each New Lender is required to confirm which of these three categories it falls within.

[77] Include only if New Lender is a UK Non-Bank Lender - i.e. falls within paragraph (i)(B) of the definition of Qualifying Lender in Clause 13.1 (*Definitions*).

[78] Insert jurisdiction of tax residence.

[79] Include if New Lender holds a passport under the HMRC DT Treaty Passport scheme and wishes that scheme to apply to the Agreement.

Company (on behalf of each Obligor) of the assignment referred to in this Assignment Agreement.

[9/10]. This Assignment Agreement may be executed in any number of counterparts and this has the same effect as if the signatures on the counterparts were on a single copy of this Assignment Agreement.

[10/11].This Assignment Agreement [and any non-contractual obligations arising out of or in connection with it] [is/are][80] governed by English law.

[11/12].This Assignment Agreement has been entered into on the date stated at the beginning of this Assignment Agreement.

[80] This clause should follow the approach adopted as regards non-contractual obligations in Clause 39 (*Governing law*). This should be done (and this footnote deleted) before the Facility Agreement is signed.

**THE SCHEDULE**

**Rights to be assigned and obligations to be released and undertaken**

[*insert relevant details*]

[*Facility Office address, fax number and attention details for notices and account details for payments*]

| | |
|---|---|
| [Existing Lender] | [New Lender] |
| By: | By: |

This Assignment Agreement is accepted by the Agent and the Transfer Date is confirmed as [ ].

Signature of this Assignment Agreement by the Agent constitutes confirmation by the Agent of receipt of notice of the assignment referred to herein, which notice the Agent receives on behalf of each Finance Party.

[Agent]

By:

## SCHEDULE 7
### FORM OF ACCESSION LETTER

To: [ ] as Agent

From: [*Subsidiary*] and [*Company*]

Dated:

Dear Sirs

**[Company] – [ ] Facility Agreement dated [ ] (the "Agreement")**

1. We refer to the Agreement. This is an Accession Letter. Terms defined in the Agreement have the same meaning in this Accession Letter unless given a different meaning in this Accession Letter.

2. [*Subsidiary*] agrees to become an Additional [Borrower]/[Guarantor] and to be bound by the terms of the Agreement as an Additional [Borrower]/[Guarantor] pursuant to [Clause 25.2 (*Additional Borrowers*)]/[Clause 25.4 (*Additional Guarantors*)] of the Agreement. [*Subsidiary*] is a company duly incorporated under the laws of [*name of relevant jurisdiction*].

3. [The Company confirms that no Default is continuing or would occur as a result of [*Subsidiary*] becoming an Additional Borrower.][81]

4. [*Subsidiary's*] administrative details are as follows:

   Address:

   Fax No:

   Attention:

5. This Accession Letter <u>[and any non-contractual obligations arising out of or in connection with it]</u> <u>[is/are]</u>[82] governed by English law.

   [This Accession Letter is entered into by deed.]

   [Company] [Subsidiary]

[81] Include in the case of an Additional Borrower.

[82] This clause should follow the approach adopted as regards non-contractual obligations in Clause 39 (*Governing law*). This should be done (and this footnote deleted) before the Facility Agreement is signed.

## SCHEDULE 8
### FORM OF RESIGNATION LETTER

To: [ ] as Agent

From: [*resigning Obligor*] and [*Company*]

Dated:

Dear Sirs

**[Company] – [ ] Facility Agreement**
**dated [ ] (the "Agreement")**

1. We refer to the Agreement. This is a Resignation Letter. Terms defined in the Agreement have the same meaning in this Resignation Letter unless given a different meaning in this Resignation Letter.

2. Pursuant to [Clause 25.3 (*Resignation of a Borrower*)]/[Clause 25.6 (*Resignation of a Guarantor*)] of the Agreement, we request that [*resigning Obligor*] be released from its obligations as a [Borrower]/[Guarantor] under the Agreement.

3. We confirm that:

   (a) no Default is continuing or would result from the acceptance of this request; and

   (b) [ ][*]

4. This Resignation Letter [and any non-contractual obligations arising out of or in connection with it] [is/are][83] governed by English law.

[Company] [Subsidiary]

By: By:

---

[*] Insert any other conditions required by the Facility Agreement.

[83] This clause should follow the approach adopted as regards non-contractual obligations in Clause 39 (*Governing law*). This should be done (and this footnote deleted) before the Facility Agreement is signed.

## SCHEDULE 9

### FORM OF COMPLIANCE CERTIFICATE

To: [ ] as Agent

From: [*Company*]

Dated:

Dear Sirs

**[Company] – [ ] Facility Agreement dated [ ] (the "Agreement")**

1. We refer to the Agreement. This is a Compliance Certificate. Terms defined in the Agreement have the same meaning when used in this Compliance Certificate unless given a different meaning in this Compliance Certificate.

2. We confirm that: [Insert details of covenants to be certified]

3. [We confirm that no Default is continuing.]*

Signed: ………………… …………………
Director Director
of of
[*Company*] [*Company*]

[*insert applicable certification language*]**

…………………
[for and on behalf of
[*name of auditors of the Company*]]***

---

* If this statement cannot be made, the certificate should identify any Default that is continuing and the steps, if any, being taken to remedy it.

** To be agreed with the Company's auditors and the Lenders prior to signing the Agreement.

*** Only applicable if the Compliance Certificate accompanies the audited financial statements and is to be signed by the auditors. To be agreed with the Company's auditors prior to signing the Agreement.

## SCHEDULE 10

### EXISTING SECURITY

| Name of Obligor | Security | Total Principal Amount of Indebtedness Secured |
| --- | --- | --- |

## SCHEDULE 11

## LMA FORM OF CONFIDENTIALITY UNDERTAKING[84]

[84] The current form of LMA Confidentiality Letter (Seller) or Confidentiality Letter (Purchaser) for the secondary trading of loans should be included in this Schedule. In the case where primary syndication takes place after the Facility Agreement is signed, the current LMA Confidentiality and Front Running Letter should also be included to avoid confusion over which form of confidentiality letter is appropriate.

## SCHEDULE 12
### TIMETABLES[85]

| | **Loans in euro** | **Loans in sterling** | **Loans curren** |
|---|---|---|---|
| Agent notifies the Company if a currency is approved as an Optional Currency in accordance with Clause 4.3 (*Conditions relating to Optional Currencies*) | | | |
| Delivery of a duly completed Utilisation Request (Clause 5.1 (*Delivery of a Utilisation Request*)) or a Selection Notice (Clause 10.1 (*Selection of Interest Periods*)) | | | |
| Agent determines (in relation to a Utilisation) the Base Currency Amount of the Loan, if required under Clause 5.4 (*Lenders' participation*) and notifies the Lenders of the Loan in accordance with Clause 5.4 (*Lenders' participation*) | | | |
| Agent receives a notification from a Lender under Clause 6.2 (*Unavailability of a currency*) | | | |
| Agent gives notice in accordance with Clause 6.2 (*Unavailability of a currency*) | | | |
| Agent determines amount of the Facility A Loan in Optional Currency in accordance with Clause 6.3 (*Change of currency*) | | | |

[85] When completing the timetables, not all times/days should be determined by reference to the Utilisation Date. ~~certain cases (i.e. in relation to Cl~~ause 6.2 (*Unavailability of a currency*), Clause 6.3 (*Change of currency*) ar paragraphs (a) and (b) of Clause 6.4 (*Same Optional Currency during successive Interest Periods*)) the tin inserted should be determined by reference to the Quotation Day or the relevant day during the Interest Period.

| | **Loans in euro** | **Loans in sterling** | **Loans in** **currencie** |
|---|---|---|---|
| Agent determines amount of the Facility A Loan in Optional Currency in accordance with paragraph (a) of Clause 6.4 (*Same Optional Currency during Successive Interest Periods*).[86] | | | |
| Agent determines amount of Facility A Loan in Optional Currency converted into Base Currency in accordance with paragraph (b) of Clause 6.4 (*Same Optional Currency during Successive Interest Periods*).[87] | | | |
| LIBOR or EURIBOR is fixed | Quotation Day 11:00 a.m. in respect of LIBOR and 11:00 a.m. (Brussels time) in respect of EURIBOR | Quotation Day 11:00 a.m. | Quotation 11:00 a.m |
| [Benchmark Rate is fixed for a Loan in a Non-LIBOR Currency] | [-] | [-] | [As specif such in res that currer Schedule *(Other Benchmar* |

[86] This should be determined by reference to the Quotation Day for the **second** of the two successive Interest Periods in question.

[87] This should be determined by reference to the Business Day on which the Agent calculated the Base Currency Amount of the Facility A Loan for the purposes of the initial Utilisation of that Facility A Loan.

| | **Loans in euro** | **Loans in sterling** | **Loans in other currencies** |
|---|---|---|---|
| [Reference Bank Rate calculated by reference to available quotations in accordance with Clause 11.2 (*Calculation of Reference Bank Rate*)] | [[Noon] on the Quotation Day in respect of LIBOR [and Quotation Day [11:30 a.m. (Brussels time)] in respect of EURIBOR]] | [[Noon] on the Quotation Day] | [[Noon] on the Quotation Day in respect of LIBOR [and as specified as such in respect of the relevant currency in Schedule 14 (*Other Benchmarks*) in respect of a Benchmark Rate]] |

## SCHEDULE 13

### FORM OF INCREASE CONFIRMATION

To: [ ] as Agent and [ ] as Company, for and on behalf of each Obligor

From: [*the Increase Lender*] (the "**Increase Lender**")

Dated:

**[Company] – [ ] Facility Agreement**
**dated [ ] (the "Agreement")**

1. We refer to the Agreement. This is an Increase Confirmation. Terms defined in the Agreement have the same meaning in this Increase Confirmation unless given a different meaning in this Increase Confirmation.

2. We refer to Clause 2.2 (*Increase*) of the Agreement.

3. The Increase Lender agrees to assume and will assume all of the obligations corresponding to the Commitment(s) specified in the Schedule (the "**Relevant Commitment(s)**") as if it had been an Original Lender under the Agreement in respect of the Relevant Commitment(s).

4. The proposed date on which the increase in relation to the Increase Lender and the Relevant Commitment(s) is to take effect (the "**Increase Date**") is [ ].

5. On the Increase Date, the Increase Lender becomes party to the Finance Documents as a Lender.

6. The Facility Office and address, fax number and attention details for notices to the Increase Lender for the purposes of Clause 31.2 (*Addresses*) of the Agreement are set out in the Schedule.

7. The Increase Lender expressly acknowledges the limitations on the Lenders' obligations referred to in paragraph (i) of Clause 2.2 (*Increase*) of the Agreement.

8. The Increase Lender confirms, for the benefit of the Agent and without liability to any Obligor, that it is:

   (a) [a Qualifying Lender (other than a Treaty Lender);]

   (b) [a Treaty Lender;]

   (c) [not a Qualifying Lender].[88]

9. [The Increase Lender confirms that the person beneficially entitled to interest payable to that Lender in respect of an advance under a Finance Document is either:

   (a) a company resident in the United Kingdom for United Kingdom tax purposes;

[88] Delete as applicable - each Increase Lender is required to confirm which of these three categories it falls within.

(b) a partnership each member of which is:

(i) a company so resident in the United Kingdom; or

(ii) a company not so resident in the United Kingdom which carries on a trade in the United Kingdom through a permanent establishment and which brings into account in computing its chargeable profits (within the meaning of section 19 of the CTA) the whole of any share of interest payable in respect of that advance that falls to it by reason of Part 17 of the CTA; or

(c) a company not so resident in the United Kingdom which carries on a trade in the United Kingdom through a permanent establishment and which brings into account interest payable in respect of that advance in computing the chargeable profits (within the meaning of section 19 of the CTA) of that company.][89]

9. [The Increase Lender confirms that it holds a passport under the HMRC DT Treaty Passport scheme (reference number [ ]) and is tax resident in [ ]*, so that interest payable to it by borrowers is generally subject to full exemption from UK withholding tax and requests that the Company notify:

(a) each Borrower which is a Party as a Borrower as at the Increase Date; and

(b) each Additional Borrower which becomes an Additional Borrower after the Increase Date,

that it wishes the scheme to apply to the Agreement.]**

[9/10]. This Increase Confirmation may be executed in any number of counterparts and this has the same effect as if the signatures on the counterparts were on a single copy of this Increase Confirmation.

[10/11]. This Increase Confirmation [and any non-contractual obligations arising out of or in connection with it] [is/are][90] governed by English law.

[11/12]. This Increase Confirmation has been entered into on the date stated at the beginning of this Increase Confirmation.

[89] Include only if Increase Lender is a UK Non-Bank Lender i.e. falls within paragraph (i)(B) of the definition of Qualifying Lender in Clause 13.1 (*Definitions*).

* Insert jurisdiction of tax residence.

** This confirmation must be included if the Increase Lender holds a passport under the HMRC DT Treaty Passport scheme and wishes that scheme to apply to the Agreement.

[90] This clause should follow the approach adopted as regards non-contractual obligations in Clause 39 (*Governing law*). This should be done (and this footnote deleted) before the Agreement is signed.

**THE SCHEDULE**

**Relevant Commitment(s)/rights and obligations to be assumed by the Increase Lender**

[*insert relevant details*]

[*Facility Office address, fax number and attention details for notices and account details for payments*]

[Increase Lender]

By:

This Increase Confirmation is accepted by the Agent and the Increase Date is confirmed as [ ].

Agent

By:

**SCHEDULE 14**
**[OTHER BENCHMARKS]**

**[Part] [ ]** [91]
**[*Insert Benchmark label*] Currency/ies**

| | |
|---|---|
| **[CURRENCY:** | [ ] |
| ***Definitions*** | |
| **Business Day:** | [ ] |
| **Business Day Conventions (definition of "Month" and Clause 10.3 (*Non-Business Days*)):** | [ ] |
| **[Fallback Interest Period:** | [ ]] |
| **Quotation Day:** | [ ] |
| **[Reference Bank Rate:** | [ ] |
| **Reference Banks:** | [ ]] |
| **Relevant Market:** | [ ] |
| **Screen Rate:** | [ ]. If [such page or service] ceases to be available the Agent may specify another page or service displaying the relevant rate after consultation with the Company. |
| ***Interest Periods*** | |
| **Length of Interest Period in absence of selection (paragraph (c) of Clause 10.1 (*Selection of Interest Periods*)):** | [ ] |
| **Periods capable of selection as Interest Periods (paragraph (d) of Clause 10.1 (*Selection of Interest Periods*)):** | [ ] |
| ***Rate fixing timings*** | |
| **Time at which Benchmark Rate is fixed (Schedule 12 (*Timetables*)):** | [ ] |
| **[Time at which Reference Bank Rate falls to be calculated by reference to available quotations (Schedule 12 (*Timetables*)):** | [ ] |

[91] Complete a separate Part of this Schedule for each Non-LIBOR Currency.

| | |
|---|---|
| **Deadline for quotations to establish a Reference Bank Rate (paragraph (b) of Clause 11.2 (*Calculation of Reference Bank Rate*)):** | [____________]] |
| **Deadline for Lenders to report market disruption (Clause 11.3 (*Market disruption*)):** | [____________]] |

# Index

*[All references are to paragraph number]*